ENCYCLOPEDIA OF COMPUTER SCIENCE AND TECHNOLOGY

VOLUME 20

INTERNATIONAL EDITORIAL ADVISORY BOARD

SHUHEI AIDA, Tokyo, Japan

J. M. BENNETT, Sydney, Australia

DOV CHEVION, Jerusalem, Israel

LUIGI DADDA, Milan, Italy

RUTH M. DAVIS, Washington, D.C.

A. S. DOUGLAS, London, England

LESLIE C. EDIE, New York, New York

S. E. ELMAGHRABY,
  Raleigh, North Carolina

A. P. ERSHOV, Novosibirsk, U.S.S.R.

HAROLD FLEISHER,
  Poughkeepsie, New York

BRUCE GILCHRIST,
  New York, New York

V. M. GLUSHKOV, Kiev, U.S.S.R.

C. C. GOTLIEB, Toronto, Canada

EDWIN L. HARDER,
  Pittsburgh, Pennsylvania

GRACE HOPPER, Washington, D.C.

A. S. HOUSEHOLDER,
  Florida

MANFRED KOCHEN,
  Ann Arbor, Michigan

E. P. MILES, JR., Tallahassee, Florida

JACK MINKER, College Park, Maryland

DON MITTLEMAN, Oberlin, Ohio

W. J. POPPELBAUM, Urbana, Illinois

A. ALAN B. PRITSKER,
  Lafayette, Indiana

P. RABINOWITZ, Rehovot, Israel

JEAN E. SAMMET,
  Cambridge, Massachusetts

SVERRE SEM-SANDBERG,
  Stockholm, Sweden

J. C. SIMON, Paris, France

WILLIAM A. SMITH, JR.,
  Raleigh, North Carolina

T. W. SZE, Pittsburgh, Pennsylvania

RICHARD I. TANAKA,
  Anaheim, California

DANIEL TEICHROEW,
  Ann Arbor, Michigan

ISMAIL B. TURKSEN, Toronto, Canada

MURRAY TUROFF, Newark, New Jersey

MICHAEL S. WATANABE,
  Honolulu, Hawaii

ENCYCLOPEDIA OF COMPUTER SCIENCE AND TECHNOLOGY

EXECUTIVE EDITORS

Allen Kent   *James G. Williams*

UNIVERSITY OF PITTSBURGH
PITTSBURGH, PENNSYLVANIA

ADMINISTRATIVE EDITOR

Rosalind Kent

PITTSBURGH, PENNSYLVANIA

VOLUME 20
SUPPLEMENT 5

MARCEL DEKKER, INC. • NEW YORK and BASEL

COPYRIGHT © 1989 by MARCEL DEKKER INC.
ALL RIGHTS RESERVED

Neither this book nor any part may be reproduced or transmitted in any form or by any means, electronic or mechanical, including photocopying, microfilming, and recording, or by any information storage and retrieval system, without permission in writing from the publisher.

MARCEL DEKKER, INC.
270 Madison Avenue, New York, New York 10016

LIBRARY OF CONGRESS CATALOG CARD NUMBER: 74-29436
ISBN: 0-8247-2270-1

Current printing (last digit):
10 9 8 7 6 5 4 3 2 1

PRINTED IN THE UNITED STATES OF AMERICA

CONTENTS OF VOLUME 20

Contributors to Volume 20	v
Errata	vii
AUTOMATIC PLACEMENT AND FLOORPLANNING FOR VLSI CIRCUITS Bryan T. Preas and Patrick G. Karger	1
BENCHMARKING Kenneth M. Dymond	25
CHINESE CHARACTERS AND ARTIFICIAL INTELLIGENCE Patrick Shen-pei Wang	37
CRYPTOLOGIC RESEARCH IN THE LATE TWENTIETH CENTURY Wyn L. Price	60
DATA STRUCTURES C. Kim and S. A. Westin	81
THE ENTITY–RELATIONSHIP APPROACH Martin E. Modell	111
HARDWARE DESCRIPTION LANGUAGE Masahiro Fujita and Tohru Moto-oka	141
IMAGE ENHANCEMENT Nickolas L. Faust	180
IMAGE PROCESSING Jeffrey L. Star	242
INTEGRATED PROJECT SUPPORT ENVIRONMENTS R. J. Lauber	262
INTERVAL MATHEMATICS H. Ratschek	287
JAPANESE CHARACTERS, COMPUTER INPUT OF Ichiko T. Morita	309
MANAGEMENT OF UNCERTAINTY IN KNOWLEDGE-BASED SYSTEMS Bernadette Bouchon	327

MOTOROLA, INC.
Laura R. Tolpen and Robert A. King   338

OPEN SYSTEMS INTERCONNECTION
Ray Denenberg   345

PARALLEL PROCESSING
Tse-yun Feng and A.R. Hurson   368

CONTRIBUTORS TO VOLUME 20

BERNADETTE BOUCHON, Centre National de la Recherche Scientifique, Université Paris 6, LaForia, Paris, France: *Management of Uncertainty in Knowledge-Based Systems*

RAY DENENBERG, Senior Network Specialist, Library of Congress, Washington, D.C.: *Open Systems Interconnection*

KENNETH M. DYMOND, Institute for Computer Sciences and Technology, National Bureau of Standards, Gaithersburg, Maryland: *Benchmarking*

NICKOLAS L. FAUST, Ph.D., Georgia Tech Research Institute, Georgia Institute of Technology, Atlanta, Georgia: *Image Enhancement*

TSE-YUN FENG, Computer Engineering Program, Department of Electrical Engineering, Pennsylvania State University, University Park, Pennsylvania: *Parallel Processing*

MASAHIRO FUJITA, Fujitsu Laboratories, Ltd., Kawasaki, Japan: *Hardware Description Language*

A. R. HURSON, Computer Engineering Program, Department of Electrical Engineering, Pennsylvania State University, University Park, Pennsylvania: *Parallel Processing*

PATRICK G. KARGER, MSEE, Consultant, Beaverton, Oregon: *Automatic Placement and Floorplanning for VLSI Circuits*

C. KIM, Ph.D., Department of Management Science, University of Rhode Island, Kingston, Rhode Island: *Data Structures*

ROBERT A. KING, Manager of Technical Communications, Motorola, Inc., Austin, Texas: *Motorola, Inc.*

R. J. LAUBER, Director, IRP Institute, University of Stuttgart, West Germany: *Integrated Project Support Environments*

MARTIN E. MODELL, Author, Consultant, Lecturer, Waltham, Massachusetts: *The Entity–Relationship Approach*

ICHIKO T. MORITA, Associate Professor, Library Administration, and Head, Automated Processing Department, University Libraries, The Ohio State University, Columbus, Ohio: *Japanese Characters, Computer Input of*

TOHRU MOTO-OKA, University of Tokyo, Tokyo, Japan: *Hardware Description Language*

BRYAN T. PREAS, Ph.D., Principal Scientist, Xerox PARC, Palo Alto, California: *Automatic Placement and Floorplanning for VLSI Circuits*

WYN L. PRICE, Ph.D., D.Sc., Head, Data Security Group, National Physical Laboratory, Teddington, Middlesex, England: *Cryptologic Research in the Late Twentieth Century*

H. RATSCHEK, Professor, Mathematisches Institut der Universität Düsseldorf, West Germany: *Interval Mathematics*

JEFFREY L. STAR, Ph.D., Geography Department, University of California, Santa Barbara: *Image Processing*

LAURA R. TOLPEN, Business Planner, MPG, Final Test Operations, Motorola, Inc., Austin Texas: *Motorola, Inc.*

PATRICK SHEN-PEI WANG, Professor, College of Computer Science, Northeastern University, Boston, Massachusetts: *Chinese Characters and Artificial Intelligence*

S.A. WESTIN, Ph.D., Department of Management Science, University of Rhode Island, Kingston, Rhode Island: *Data Structures*

ERRATA

Due to an inadvertent error, the first line of text was omitted from the second paragraph of the article by Dineh M. Davis, "Computer-Aided Composition" which appeared on page 69 of Volume 19 of *Encyclopedia of Computer Science and Technology*.

The corrected page is printed below.

COMPUTER-AIDED COMPOSITION

INTRODUCTION

In his comprehensive 1975 article for the *Encyclopedia of Computer Science and Technology*, Arthur Phillips identified eight areas where computers were being used in the composition and presentation of typographic quality text. Such applications ranged from the recording and storage of alphabetic text and numeric data to the intricate manipulation of the format and content of such stored information. In addition, Phillips provided an invaluable history of the printer's font, as well as mechanical and electromechanical typesetting devices. The reader interested in a historical perspective on this subject should refer to Phillips' article.

Changes in technology have expanded the computer's domain in the field of composition in two divergent directions. On the one hand, more sophisticated hardware and software have allowed designers of composition systems to redefine the boundaries of computer-aided composition by producing digitized type fonts. On the other hand, microminiaturization of hardware has made possible the expansion of the field to include the following dramatic departures from the state of the art in the early 1970s:

Heavy Reliance on Microcomputers

Used as stand-alone systems, as smart workstations connected to mainframes, or as a part of a distributed, a wide, or local area network, microcomputers have established their worth and versatility in the composition, printing, and publishing market.

Dependence on a Variety of Visual
Display Terminals

Video display terminals (VDTs) are currently the most common electronic output device for works in progress that require manipulation of text and graphics before typesetting. Current VDT technology is still highly dependent on cathode-ray tubes (CRTs), but the advent of the luggable and portable computers has increased consumer interest in alternative flat-screen technologies.

Increasing Industry Awareness of
End-User Needs

The users' need to concentrate on end-product development rather than to learn to become a computer scientist has, in turn, led to major advances in interface design, with the ultimate aim of making the inner workings of the computer "invisible" to the end user. Current examples of such VDT-based trends include the interface designers' emphasis on WYSIWYG (what you see is what you get) screen output, menu- and icon-based systems, and direct data manipulation techniques.

ENCYCLOPEDIA OF COMPUTER SCIENCE AND TECHNOLOGY

VOLUME 20

AUTOMATIC PLACEMENT AND FLOOR-PLANNING FOR VLSI CIRCUITS

1 INTRODUCTION

This article describes the placement and floorplanning functions within automatic layout systems. Automatic placement and floorplanning are defined and the data abstractions, or models, are discussed. The important algorithms, as well as their applications within layout systems, are described. References are provided to allow the article's use as an introduction to the literature.

Physical design of an electronic circuit consists of transforming a circuit design specification into a physical representation that can be used to manufacture the circuit. The speed with which this transformation takes place is greatly enhanced by the use of *automatic layout* techniques. Automatic layout is a subset of the physical design process that maps a structural representation of the circuit into a physical representation consisting of geometric coordinates for all of the circuit elements and the wiring that interconnects the elements. The structural representation, that is input to the layout process, consists of a list of circuit elements, or *components*, that are to be included in the layout, and a list of signal sets indicating the terminals, or *pins* on the components, that are to be made electrically common by the layout process. The *interconnection nets*, or simply nets, are the connections among the signal sets. Preas and Lorenzetti provide an in-depth discussion of the physical design process [1].

Automatic layout consists of two primary functions: determining positions of components on a layout surface, called *placement* (which includes floorplanning in a broader sense) and interconnecting the components with wiring, called *routing*, according to a set of *design rules*. Although placement and routing are intimately related and interdependent historically, they have been separated because of computational complexity. Automatic placement, the focus of this article, is responsible for determining the locations of the components within the circuit being designed, subject to the constraints imposed by the designer and the design rules. Sometimes the term *placement* is used in a narrow sense to mean the positioning of components of a fixed size and shape on the layout surface (sometimes called *component placement*). The term is also used in a broader sense to refer to any function involved in positioning components on a layout surface; this broader definition includes floorplanning. Although this is somewhat confusing, both usages of the term placement are well established; therefore, both are used here. The context should serve to clarify the usage.

Good placement is a key aspect of automatic layout, but it sometimes receives insufficient attention. A poor placement can leave the router with a difficult or impossible task, whereas a good placement can make a router's job easy. Also, placement directly determines the minimum length of the interconnection wiring, and because wiring delay may be the dominant part of the response time of electrical signals on the wiring, placement often determines the performance of the physical circuit.

The design of very large-scale integrated (VLSI) systems and the associated placement subproblems are typically defined hierarchically. Placement algorithms normally operate on one hierarchical cell at a time: the placement of (sub) components within a single (higher level) component is normally considered as a separate problem with boundary conditions defined by the other components at the same level as the (higher level) component. Because of the confusion of components at different levels of the design hierarchy, the term *placeable objects* is used to refer to the components being placed.

This article defines the placement problem and categorizes and reviews the placement techniques that are available. It concentrates on placement of components in the upper and intermediate levels of the design hierarchy. The components may be small- to medium-scale integration gates, or they may be large functional units such as microprocessors or memories. Specifically excluded from discussion is the generation of the lowest part, or *leaf cells*, of a hierarchical structure. A more complete description of automatic placement is available in Chapter 4 of Ref. 1.

Section 2 describes the placement problem, whereas section 3 describes abstractions used, the components being placed, the interconnection nets, and the layout surface on which the components reside. As a result of a *technology-independent* presentation, the placement concepts are applicable to electronic circuit design for a wide range of circuit manufacturing technologies and design styles, including *hybrid chip carriers* and silicon VLSI circuits such as *gate arrays, standard cell* designs, and *general cell* designs. The basic algorithms (the focus of sections 4–6) must be tailored to the specific applications (design styles, and fabrication technologies) as described in section 7.

Component placement methods fall into two groups: *constructive* and *iterative*. Constructive methods (described in section 4) produce a *complete placement* (all components have assigned positions) based on a *partial placement* (some or all components do not have assigned positions) as input. Iterative methods (discussed in section 5) improve a complete placement by modifying it to produce a better, complete placement. The size and shape of the circuit elements are determined as part of the design process for some VLSI design styles; floor planning (described in section 6) aids this process. Floorplanning occurs before placement in the design process but it is discussed after placement in this article. This order allows floorplanning to be discussed as an extension of placement.

A large number of techniques for placement and floorplanning have been developed. The only hope of describing the seemingly myriad variations is to impose a taxonomy and to explain the basic algorithms. Variations are described as deviations from the basic algorithms.

2 DESCRIPTION OF THE PLACEMENT PROBLEM

2.1 Component Placement

The *placement problem* consists of mapping the components in a structural representation onto *positions* on a layout surface. Pins on the components

define locations at which the circuitry within the component connects to
interconnection routing among the circuitry. External pins designate the
interface area between the circuitry inside and the environment outside of
the component being designed; they are the pins of the component at the
next higher level of hierarchy. The subsets of pins, termed *signal sets*,
which are to be connected by wiring to form electrically common interconnection nets, are part of the structural representation.

The actual goal of placement is to determine non-overlapping positions
for the components that permit completely automatic routing of the interconnection wiring within a small area. It may be necessary to honor any number
of other (possibly conflicting) goals, such as minimizing layout area or
crosstalk among the signals carried by the wiring, equalizing heat dissipation across the layout surface, or maximizing circuit performance. Because
such goals are difficult to cast into objective functions that can be evaluated
by a computer, more restricted objective functions must be substituted.
When a placement operation derives a good placement as measured by a
restricted objective, it is hoped that the placement is also good with respect
to the actual goal. The restricted objective function is used as a metric to
compare alternative placements. Ideally, it should reflect the actual goal
accurately and should be fast to compute. These conflicting goals have led
to a plethora of objective functions; some are discussed in the next section.

Placement problems may contain many thousands of components. This
results in huge placement state spaces. For example, a design with 1,000
components (modest by today's standards) has approximately 10^{2562} different
placements. To put this number in perspective, if a computer that could
evaluate a trial placement in 1 microsecond had begun enumerating those
placements at the beginning of the universe, today it would have evaluated
10^{24} states. To complicate matters further, it has been shown that the
placement problem is nondeterministic polynomial (NP)-complete. Thus, optimum solutions cannot be guaranteed, and methods based on heuristics must
be used for all but the smallest problems.

2.2 Floorplanning

Early in the process of designing VLSI circuits, designers must make far
reaching decisions based on incomplete or tentative information. The external interface of cells (size and shape and the positions of the pins) must
sometimes be determined before the cell has been designed. In addition to
placing the components (instances of the cells), floorplanning must determine constraints on external interfaces for those cells that have flexible
interfaces. Floorplanning is related to placement, and many of the same
techniques are used. However, floorplanning is performed earlier in the
design process where less information and more flexibility exists. This
extra degree of freedom (the flexibility of the cells) makes the problem
significantly more difficult.

3 ABSTRACT MODELS OF PLACEMENT

To apply an algorithm to a real problem, the problem must be transformed
into an abstract model. Abstraction replaces an object with a simplified
model that defines the interaction of the object with its environment: details
of internal organization are deleted. This reduces the amount of data, adds

structure to the problem, and makes the problem easier to solve. After the algorithm is applied in the abstract domain, the abstract results must be transformed back into the real domain. This section describes the abstract models that are important to placement algorithms. The important aspects of electronic circuits that must be modeled are the circuit elements, the interconnections, and the carrier. The models of these aspects, the cell and component, the pin, the interconnection net, the objective function and the layout surface, and their relation to the physical circuit, are discussed.

3.1 Cells and Components

Automatic placement systems typically use an object/instance paradigm to describe the circuit structure. The definition of a circuit element (the object) is called a *cell* and describes how the circuit element is constructed from transistors or other primitives; these elements are placeable objects that may have been obtained from a library or constructed by any of the physical design methods. Figure 1 shows one view of a cell consisting of a D latch; it illustrates the properties of the cell that are important for placement. Many of the details of the cell definition are abstracted away; only those properties that are important to the electrical and physical interface with the rest of the circuit and the layout surface are considered. An important aspect of the cell-based design style is that cells exhibit local autonomy over their internal area and function. Thus, a means for controlling the interaction between the inside and outside of a cell is needed. Pins provide the appropriate abstraction. Pins define the area at which the internal circuitry of a cell connects to the external circuitry.

Although cells carry the information pertaining to the definition of circuit elements, the components carry the information pertaining to their application; thus, a component is an instance of a cell. Because the components are entities that are placed, they must carry the placement information: current location and orientation (rotation and reflection).

3.2 Interconnection Nets

The circuit elements, as represented by their abstractions (cells and components), must be interconnected according to the signal set specifications. It is the responsibility of the placement function to place the components so that the interconnection wiring can be routed effectively. Thus, an important factor within a placer is the modeling of the wiring.

It is important to model the topology of the interconnection nets, because the actual wiring paths will be determined by a router and are unknown during placement. Assume the pins of a signal set to be vertices of an un-

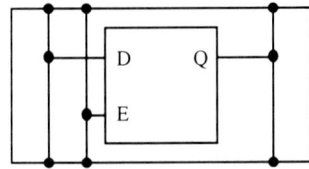

FIGURE 1 This cell definition is a D latch from a standard cell library. Only the information important to placement is retained by the cell abstraction.

directed graph; the connections among them form the arcs of a graph. Automatic layout systems, the circuit elements, routers, and the manufacturing technologies combine to impose restrictions on the form of the connection tree. Figure 2 shows examples of the interconnection forms. Topologies for interconnection nets with only two pins are simple: only one arc is meaningful. Nets with three or more pins are more complex. The most general form, called a Steiner tree, permits vertices of the connection graph to be at pins, as well as at locations other than the pins, and places no restrictions on the *degree* (the number of incident connections) of the vertices. This is typical of connections within integrated circuits. A more restrictive interconnection method is the spanning tree in which the vertices are restricted to the pin locations. Other restrictions may apply; e.g., *wire-wrap* fabrication imposes constraints on the degree of the vertices because the posts that implement the pins have a fixed height and thus can have a limited number of connected wires (typically three). An even more restricted method of interconnection is the chain, where no branching of the interconnection wiring (i.e., degree of vertices $\leq$ 2) is permitted. Some

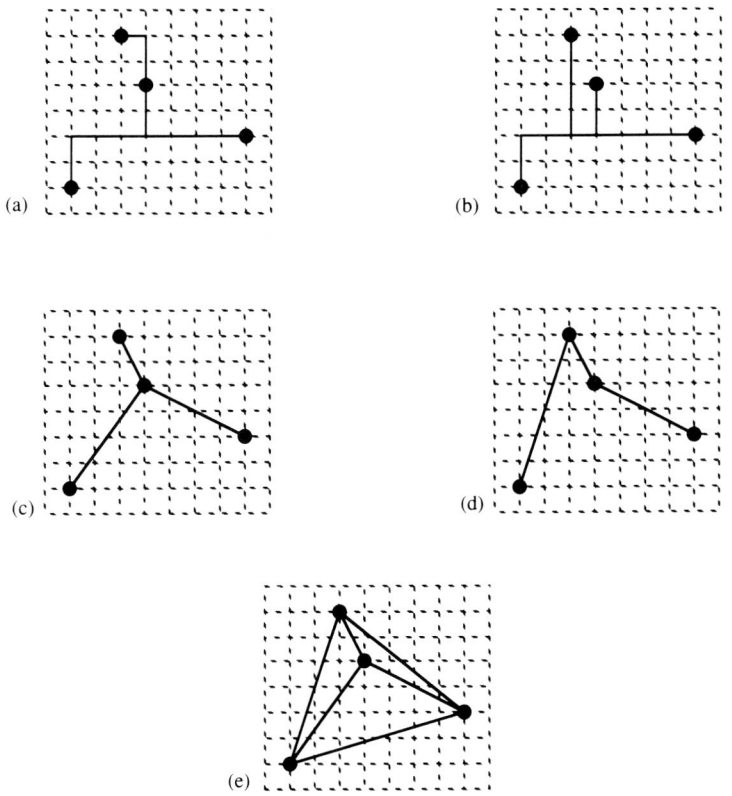

FIGURE 2 These interconnection topologies are important for placement. (a) Steiner tree, rectilinear length = 14; (b) Steiner tree with trunk, rectilinear length = 15; (b) minimum spanning tree, rectilinear length = 16; (c) chain, rectilinear length = 17; (e) complete graph, rectilinear length = 42.

placement algorithms model the interconnection tree as a complete graph for computational simplicity, although the interconnection net will be routed more simply. Placement systems may model these interconnection topologies directly or they may use simpler approximations.

3.3 Objective Functions

The quality of a placement is based on many factors; some examples are routing completion rate, circuit performance characteristics, and layout area. Metrics based on these factors can compare alternative placements and are used by placement algorithms to compute a *score* that measures the quality of a placement. The metrics are divided into two classes: those that assume that the net routings do not interact with other nets, and those that account for this interaction, or *congestion*. Congestion metrics may also consider the interaction of nets with the components or with predefined features on the layout surface.

3.3.1 Net Metrics

The simplest metrics assume that the nets can be routed without interfering with each other or with the components. One widely used metric is *wire length*; this is the sum over all of the nets of the lengths of the interconnection trees. The length of an interconnection tree is the sum of the individual arcs of the tree. This metric is fast to compute, and the algorithm is easy to implement. Another technique to measure placement quality models the connections as springs that exert forces on components. This leads to a force metric where a good placement is one that minimizes the sum of forces on the components.

3.3.2 Congestion Metrics

The net metrics quantify only the amount of wiring; they do not measure where the wiring is located. This can lead to wiring buildup or congestion, as demonstrated by Figure 3. In this example, a smaller wire length leads to incomplete routing because wiring is in the "wrong" place. The second class of interconnection metrics incorporates the interaction among the nets, the components, and the layout surface in the measure of placement quality. Congestion metrics often correlate better with routability than wire length metrics do because congestion metrics include the areas where routing resources are needed.

3.4 Layout Surface

The characteristics of the physical surface, or *carrier*, on which the circuit elements are placed must be modeled. The abstraction of the carrier is called the layout surface. Carrier models divide into two categories: geometric and topological.

3.4.1 The Geometric Model

Geometric models are appropriate for the gate array style; the aspects of placement such as size and shape of the layout surface and external pin positions do not change the layout process. Some geometric models place components on a continuous plane and use geometric interference checking. Other models restrict components to fixed positions called *slots*; this gives

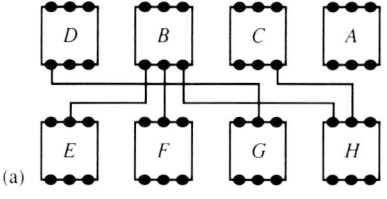

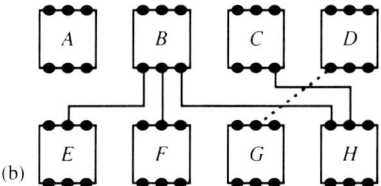

FIGURE 3 Wire length reduction can cause routing failures. Placement that minimizes wire length can be worse than a placement with longer wire length if the wiring is in the wrong place. (a) Two tracks are required. All connections can be routed if two tracks are available. (b) This placement has a shorter wire length than the placement in a, but three tracks are required. A routing failure occurs if only two tracks are available.

rise to a placement approach that assigns components to slots that carry the geometric coordinates. This approach is simple when all components fit uniformly in all slots; matters become much more complicated when components vary in size or can be assigned to only a subset of the slots.

3.4.2 The Topological Model

The second category of layout surface applies to standard-cell and general-cell VLSI design styles; the size, shape, and external pin positions of the cell being laid out as well as the components' positions are determined by the layout system. Furthermore, these positions are interdependent in complex ways and vary during the layout process. For example, routing areas can be made the exact size necessary to accommodate the interconnections. This suggests a *topological model* composed of directed and undirected graphs. Such a model provides an efficient representation of placement, is easy to modify as the placement changes, and allows rapid computation of geometric functions of topology.

A placement composed of rectangular components can be represented explicity as a *rectangular dissection*. It can be represented as an undirected planar graph (called a *channel intersection graph*), where the vertices represent the intersections of the dissection and the edges represent the adjacencies of the intersections [2]. A placement composed of rectangular components can also be represented by a pair of directed graphs (one for the horizontal direction and one for the vertical direction). The vertices of the horizontal graph represent the vertical lines of the dissection, and the edges indicate whether a line is to the right of another line of the dissection. A similar description holds for the vertical graph. These graphs, called *channel position graphs* allow the positions of the components to be computed easily. An extension of the basic (rectangular) model represents the placement of a subset of rectilinear-shaped components (arbitrary rectangles with arbitrary rectangles removed from 0 to 4 of the corners) [3].

4 CONSTRUCTIVE PLACEMENT ALGORITHMS

Component placement techniques are divided into constructive placement (this section) and iterative placement (section 5). Constructive placement algorithms share the characteristic that their input is a partial placement and their output is a complete placement. Although some constructive placement algorithms permit a *seed* placement as an initial condition, the ability to operate on unplaced components differentiates these algorithms from the iterative algorithms. Constructive placement algorithms are used for initial placement, and are normally followed by one or more (iterative) placement improvement algorithms. Constructive placement techniques as a group are discussed and compared with various placement improvement algorithms in Ref. 4. The constructive placement algorithms are divided into the following classes: cluster growth, partitioning-based placement, global techniques, and branch-and-bound techniques, which are discussed below.

4.1 Cluster Growth

Cluster growth constructive placement is a *bottom-up* method (consistently considers the most detailed level of abstraction) that operates by selecting components and adding them to a partial, or incomplete, placement. This method is differentiated from other placement methods in that cluster growth selects and places the components independently.

The generic cluster growth algorithm is shown in Figure 4, and its operation is illustrated in Figure 5. In Figure 5, the dots represent the slots in which rectangular components may be placed. The first step is to determine a seed placement. The components in the seed placement and their positions may be chosen by the user in order to guide the placement process or may be determined algorithmically. Next, unplaced components are selected sequentially and placed in relation to those components already placed. This process continues until all components are placed.

The positions adjacent to previously placed components (the *candidate positions*) are investigated by calculating the score that results when the selected component is placed in the candidate positions. The *SELECT* function of the cluster growth algorithms determines the order in which unplaced components are included in the placement. The order is determined by how

```
    seedComponents := Determine component(s) for seed
    currentPlacement := PLACE[seedComponents,currentPlacement]
    UNTIL all components are placed do
       selectedComponents := SELECT[currentPlacement]
       currentPlacement := PLACE[selectedComponents,currentPlacement]
    endloop
```

FIGURE 4 The cluster growth placement algorithm selects unplaced components and places them in the slots that will result in the best score.

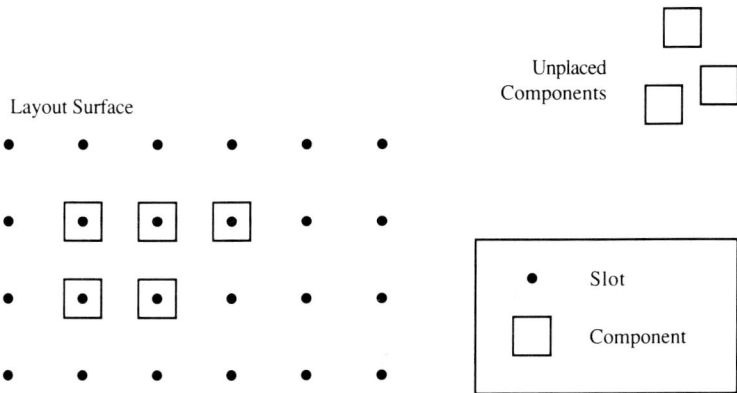

FIGURE 5 This illustrates the operation of the cluster growth placement algorithm given in Fig. 4. Unplaced components are selected and placed in relation to the already placed components.

"strongly" the unplaced components are connected to the placed components. The *PLACE* function determines the best positions for the selected components. The component is placed at the candidate position that results in the best score. By necessity, the score must be based on incomplete information, as unplaced components cannot contribute to the scoring. *Ties* can be resolved by a secondary metric such as finding the candidate position closest to the "center of gravity" of the component connected directly to the candidate component.

The complexity of the cluster growth algorithms is dependent on the number of interconnections and the number of pins per net, but the dominant factor is the number of components, n; the algorithms have a computational complexity of n^2. These algorithms are easy to implement but modern systems favor the partitioning-based placement, or global methods, for initial placement. These methods are described in the following two sections.

4.2 Partitioning-Based Placement

Placement algorithms based on partitioning divide components into two or more partitions or *blocks,* while reserving space for the components during the partitioning process; these algorithms are widely used in modern layout systems. This *top-down* design approach considers higher levels of abstraction before it considers more detailed levels and tends to avoid heavy wiring congestion typically found in the center of the layout surface. These algorithms differ from the cluster growth algorithms in the following way: partitioning based algorithms consider all interconnections in parallel and then move the components in steps by partitioning the components into specific areas of the layout surface.

4.2.1 Partitioning Foundations

Although determining optimal partitioning is NP-complete, several good heuristics have been developed. Kernighan and Lin [5] developed a two-way partitioning scheme based on iterative improvement of an initial (possibly *random*) partitioning. The procedure, based on pairwise exchange, judiciously selects the pairs to exchange and allows multiple exchanges to occur before deciding to accept the sequence of exchanges.

Although this heuristic works quite well for general graph partitioning, it does not take into account a special property of electrical circuits: a group of vertices in a single net do not have to be interconnected pairwise; they need only be connected by a spanning tree. Schweikert and Kernighan [6] modified the Kernighan–Lin algorithm to keep track of the decrease in the number of nets cut if a component moves from one partition to the other. Improvements are judged over a sequence of exchanges so that groups of components that are highly interconnected can move from one partition to the other.

Fiduccia and Mattheyses [7] developed a further modification that allows only a single component to be moved at a time from one partition to the other. The component is chosen because of its effect on both the net-cut score and the balance of the size of the partitions. This results in a linear time heuristic for a single pass through the components. The Fiduccia–Mattheyses technique is not quite as good as the Kernighan–Lin technique, but the execution time is substantially reduced [8].

4.2.2 Placement Based on Partitioning

Using the various partitioning algorithms, many *min-cut placement* techniques have been developed. The algorithms are distinguished by how finely the layout surface is partitioned into blocks (i.e., how many components are in a block) before the components are placed, how and where cut lines are generated, and how connections to external components (not in the block currently being partitioned) are treated.

The bipartitioning algorithms illustrated in Figure 6 divide the components into two sets such that the weighted number of connections between the sets is minimized, and the total component area in each set is approximately equal. This process is repeated recursively until each partition contains only one component [9]. This technique physically partitions the components into blocks on the layout surface; each block has an exact physical location, and when each block contains only one component, the circuit is completely placed. Lauther [10] developed a partitioning-based placement technique where the blocks generated during the partitioning process are represented by polar graphs, which retain information about the relative positions of the blocks.

Most partitioning-based algorithms consider only the connections between components within the block being partitioned. However, connections to other components also influence the result. One min-cut procedure introduces *terminal propagation* [8]. This technique reflects external components' positions onto the boundary of the block being partitioned.

The partitioning-based algorithms make use of the interconnection information at a global level and defer local considerations until late in the placement process. Although these procedures produce good results, they are computationally expensive. These methods also tend to be less effective when components are constrained to fixed positions or when partitions of grossly unequal areas are produced.

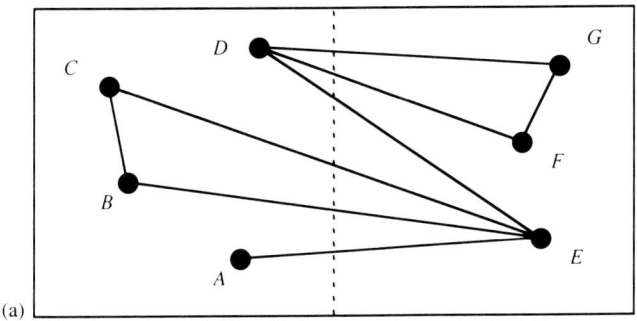

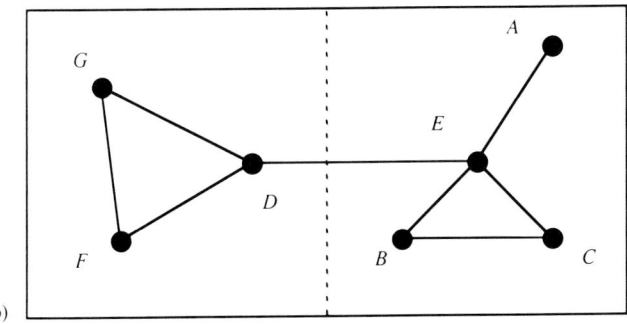

FIGURE 6 Min-cut placement places components on either side of a cut in such a manner as to minimize the number of interconnections crossing the cut. (a) Original placement; (b) improved placement.

4.3 Global Placement

All placement techniques keep global notions of better or worse placements, but global placement techniques are distinguished by the way in which they move components. Global methods move all of the components simultaneously along an n-dimensional gradient. This contrasts with cluster growth methods, which consider each component sequentially, and with partitioning methods, which first divide the components by partitioning and then deal with the components individually. Global placement techniques divide into two categories: *quadratic assignment* and *convex function optimization*. It is possible to find the optimum solution to the quadratic assignment and convex function optimization problems associated with a placement problem. However, an optimum solution to the quadratic assignment or convex function optimization problem does not guarantee an optimum solution to the original placement problem. The global methods use a quadratic objective function that heavily penalizes long nets. As a result, connection lengths tend to cluster tightly around the mean net length. This produces small standard deviations of net lengths compared to linear functions, but the effect on routability is yet to be determined. Both methods also use a complete graph to model the interconnection net topology. Thus, if all nets have the same weight, nets

with more than two pins can have a disproportionately large impact [6].
This may be compensated for by weighting nets according to the number of
pins, p, according to $1/(p - 1)$, $2/p$, or $(2/p)^{3/2}$ [11].

4.3.1 Quadratic Assignment

The quadratic assignment problem is usually formulated as follows: given a cost matrix $C = [c_{ij}]$, where c_{ij} is the strength of the connection (number and weight of connections) between two components i and j, and a distance matrix $D = [d_{kl}]$, where d_{kl} is the distance between positions k and l, minimize

$$\sum_{i,j} c_{ij} d_{P_i P_j}$$

over all permutations, P, of the components' positions. Hanan and Kurtzberg [12] describe the quadratic assignment method and how a placement problem can be transformed into (approximated by) an associated quadratic assignment problem. Although the quadratic assignment method uses a quadratic metric, it does not exploit the convexity of the metric.

4.3.2 Convex Function Optimization

It is possible to formulate the placement problem as an objective to be minimized and to use conventional mathematical optimization techniques to solve the problem. Optimization techniques work best when both the domain and the objective function are convex; in this case, only a single minimum exists. Through appropriate abstractions that produce a convex domain (primarily the absence of slots and absence of components with finite size) and the use of a quadratic metric, it is possible to transform a placement problem into one that may be solved using gradient techniques.

In general, these techniques suffer from an inability to deal with practical constraints such as finite component size and constraints imposed on component positions. These drawbacks are addressed by Blanks [13] through the use of quadratic constraints and a two-step procedure to map the global (ideal) placement onto the layout surface without violating any physical constraints. Sha and Dutton [14] attempt to alleviate the need for the second step by encoding all geometric information into constraints placed on the scoring function. A multidimensional geometric approach couples eigenvector probes and linear assignment to provide a more systematic mapping of the ideal placement onto the carrier [11]. As few comparisons have been performed, it is difficult to evaluate the relative merits of the global methods versus other placement methods; however, good results have been reported [11,13].

4.4 Branch-and-Bound Placement

The branch-and-bound method can be used to find an optimum solution for small placement problems. This is done by systematically searching a decision tree representing all possible placements. The "branch" step divides the solution state space (creates a branch in the decision tree), whereas the "bound" step prunes the decision tree, The "bound" step potentially reduces computational requirements: the more accurately the lower bound in calculated, the sharper the pruning. However, there is a trade-off: it takes longer to calculate a more accurate lower bound. Because it is necessary to either calculate accurate lower bounds or to explore a large number of branches, this technique is quite time-consuming. Heuristics have been suggested to prune the tree [12]; these heuristics have a computational complexity of n^3 or n^4. Although branch-and-bound algorithms do not appear in modern layout systems, the technique is interesting for theoretical studies where optimum solutions are required for small problems.

5 ITERATIVE PLACEMENT

The goal of iterative placement is to manipulate a complete placement to produce an improved, complete placement. This process is iterated until some stopping criterion is met. For example, the stopping criterion might be relative or absolute improvement in the placement metric or perhaps the time expended in the iterative process. Within one iteration loop, components are selected and moved to alternate locations. If the resulting configuration is better than the previous, the new configuration is retained; otherwise, the previous configuration is restored. The improvement process and the more important iterative improvement algorithms are discussed in this section.

5.1 Three Phases of Iterative Placement

Many different iterative placement techniques exist. Even though they differ substantially, they share the same underlying structure and have three main phases: *selection*, *movement*, and *scoring*. The generic form of iterative improvement placement algorithms is shown in Figure 7. These three phases are discussed next.

5.1.1 Selection

The *SELECT* function chooses the components to participate in movement. This mechanism reduces the set of all possible combinations of components to move simultaneously to a computationally feasible subset. The selection process may simply select components to be interchanged in a predefined sequence (such as trying all possible pairs) or may involve intelligence to select those components that are placed poorly. Incorporating intelligence

```
currentScore := SCORE[currentPlacement]
until stopping criterion is satisfied do
   selectedComponents := SELECT[currentPlacement]
   trialPlacement := MOVE[selectedComponents,currentPlacement]
   trialSCORE := SCORE[trialPlacement]
   if trialScore < currentScore then
      currentScore := trialScore
      currentPlacement := trialPlacement
   else currentPlacement := MOVE[selectedComponents,trialPlacement]
endloop{until stopping criterion is satisfied}
```

FIGURE 7 The generic iterative improvement placement algorithm is defined in terms of *SELECT*, *MOVE*, and *SCORE* functions.

into the selection process typically allows placement to converge more quickly but may not improve the quality of the solution. There is also a danger that an overly restrictive selection function may miss productive moves and degrade the quality of the solution.

5.1.2 Movement

Once the components are selected for trial interchange, the *MOVE* function determines the new locations for the selected components. If a pair of components is selected, the components' positions are interchanged. Of course, it must be physically possible for each component to fit at the location of the other. Some iterative placers are limited to moving components among positions that are slots for certain types of components. This restriction eliminates the need to dynamically check for component overlap and thus results in much faster placement techniques at the sacrifice of placement quality.

5.1.3 Scoring

After the selected components have been moved to new positions, the objective function measures the quality of the new arrangement. At this stage, the representation of interconnections should be as accurate as possible, consistent with the time available for iterative improvement; the interconnection graph should correspond to the actual routes that will be generated. The scoring metric may be the same as that used by the initial placer or may incorporate more detail concerning the routing resources. The iterative placement scoring metric should work in concert with any metric used by the initial placer; otherwise any initial placement quality is wasted.

5.2 Iterative Improvement Techniques

Now that the three main functions within the iterative placement loop have been described, the various iterative algorithms will be reviewed in terms of these functions.

5.2.1 Interchange

In *pairwise interchange*, each component is selected in turn to be the *primary* component and is trial interchanged with every other component. If a trial interchange results in an improved placement, the interchange is accepted; otherwise, the components are returned to their previous positions. Any objective function can be used as the basis for acceptance of an exchange. This technique results in $n(n - 1)/2$ trial interchanges, making the computational complexity $O(n^2)$, where n is the number of components. The *neighborhood interchange* technique is similar to pairwise interchange; however, the primary component is interchanged only with components in its vicinity.

5.2.2 Force-Directed Methods

Force-directed interchange uses a force analog to select components to move, as well as to determine the positions to which the components should be moved. However, the position to which the selected component should be moved may already be occupied by another component. Furthermore, the location of the selected component may not be a good position for the component occupying its favored position. Experimental results using force-directed interchange are given in Ref. 4.

Force-directed relaxation is similar to the force-directed interchange method. In this technique, however, the primary component is positioned in the compatible slot nearest to the desired zero force point. The component that was occupying that slot is chosen as the next primary component. The process results in a series of components to be relaxed.

The *force-directed pairwise relaxation* method [4] also uses force vectors to find the zero force target locations for each component. In this method, however, the primary component is not allowed to initiate a series as in force-directed relaxation. Instead, the primary component A is trial interchanged with a component B in the vicinity of the target location only if the target location of B is in the vicinity of component A. The interchange is accepted only if the placement score improves.

Force-directed techniques share the characteristic that the force is a restrictive selection method. Iteration converges quickly, but the process tends to stop even when many productive exchanges still remain.

5.2.3 Unconnected Sets

Steinberg describes a technique [15] that selects components by dividing them into sets of components that have no nets in common, or *unconnected sets* of components. Each component in such a set can be trial placed without considering the other components of the set. The placement of these components can be obtained by solving the resulting linear assignment problem, as the score does not depend on the interaction of the components' locations. After each unconnected set has been processed, the cycle is complete. Experience with this technique indicates limited success because components in highly interconnected groupings (a common occurrence in modern circuits) are not moved with respect to each other, and nets with large numbers of pins (e.g., clocks) limit component movement.

5.2.4 Simulated Annealing

The previous techniques share the characteristic that trials are accepted only if the score does not increase. This limitation can cause the placement to reach a local minima but miss the global optimum. Kirkpatrick et al. describe a technique, *simulated annealing*, that addresses this issue (Ref. 16).

The optimization of a circuit placement with a very large number of components is analogous to the process of annealing, in which a material is melted and cooled slowly so that it will crystallize into a highly ordered state. The energy corresponds to the placement score, and an *annealing schedule* specifies the beginning and ending scores, as well as the rate of change of the score. The method begins with a random initial placement. An altered placement is generated and the resulting change in score, Δs, is calculated. If $\Delta s < 0$ (the system went to a lower energy level), the move is accepted. If $\Delta s \geq 0$, the move is accepted with probability $e^{-\Delta s/t}$. As the simulated temperature t decreases, the probability of accepting an increased score decreases.

The objective function used for scoring may be any of the functions described in Section 3; wire length and net half-perimeter are often used. Simulated annealing has been used extensively as an iterative improvement technique. The generic iterative placement algorithm is rearranged (as shown in Fig. 8) to illustrate the simulated annealing concepts.

```
t := t_0
currentPlacement := randomInitialPlacement
currentScore := SCORE[currentPlacement]
until freezing point reached do
  until freezing point reached do
    selectedComponents := SELECT[atRandom]
    trialPlacement := MOVE[selectedComponents, atRandom]
    trialScore := SCORE[trialPlacement]
      Δs := trialScore − currentScore
    if Δs < 0 then currentScore := trialScore
    else begin
      r := uniformly random number {0 ≤ r ≤ 1}
      if r < e^−Δs/t then currentScore := trialScore
      else currentPlacement := MOVE[selectedComponents, trialPlacement]
    end
  endloop
  t := αt {0 < α < 1}
endloop
```

FIGURE 8 Simulated annealing placement uses random selection, movement, and acceptance to explore the placement state space. This method produces good placements at the expense of long run times.

Simulated annealing can climb out of local minima to find a global optimum if the proper conditions on the annealing schedule are satisfied. However, this implies an infinite number of iterations at each temperature in practical problems. This is clearly impossible, but massive computational resources are required for practical problems. Thus, various approaches have been proposed to speed up the process. The approaches fall into three categories: move set design, cost function manipulation, and cooling schedule improvements.

One move set design is based on range limiting [17]. This discards moves involving components that are more than some specified distance apart; the specified distance decreases as temperature decreases. Cost function manipulation may involve altering the probability of acceptance or approximating the objective function at high temperatures. A *rejectionless method*, in which the probability of selecting a move is based on its probability of being accepted, is described in Ref. 18.

Annealing schedule improvement is the third approach to improving simulated annealing performance. An annealing schedule is composed of a beginning temperature, a temperature decrement, an equilibrium condition at each temperature, and a convergence condition. White proposes the use of an initial temperature that is much greater than the standard deviation of the cost distribution that occurs when all moves are accepted [19]. A widely used temperature decrement is geometric progression, $t := \alpha t$, where typical α is 0.95. Huang [20] derives the temperature decrement, $t := te^{-0.7t}$, based on the condition required to maintain quasiequilibrium. The equilibrium condition at each temperature may be a fixed Markov chain length, a minimum acceptance, or a dynamic Markov chain length. A typical stopping criterion is when the average score is unchanged for a few consecutive temperatures. Even with these speed-up techniques, simulated annealing remains computationally intensive compared to other techniques, but it is robust over a wide range of problem types.

5.3 Summary of Placement Techniques

Although finding the optimum solution to the general placement problem is NP-complete, the placement methods discussed provide heuristic techniques that attempt to provide a "good" placement. These techniques are divided into two categories: constructive placement and iterative placement. Many other heuristics are possible, but the methods discussed represent the most popular placement techniques.

6 FLOORPLANNING

During the early stages in the design of electronic systems, decisions are made that have a dramatic effect on the quality (performance, density, or area) of the resulting circuit design. Choices must be made in partitioning functions into physical cells and in choosing interface characteristics (such as size, shape, and pin positions) of the cells. These choices are difficult because they must be made with relatively little information and because their effects are hard to predict and may not become apparent until much later in the design process.

Floorplanning is closely related to general-cell placement (described in section 7). Both problems are concerned with the placement of (usually rectangular) cells of arbitrary aspect and size such that the total area occupied by the cells and their interconnections is minimized. Thus, many techniques of general cell placement have been adapted to floorplanning. However, floorplanning has an extra degree of freedom: at least some of the cells' interface characteristics must be determined and fixed. The flexibility in the interface of the cells is constrained by the function and layout of the cells and must be modeled by the floorplanner.

6.1 Models of Floorplanning

Because of the similarity to general-cell placement, many floorplanning techniques use the models described in section 3. The most important exception is in the modeling of the cells; floorplanning algorithms must model the cells' interface flexibility and any constraints on that flexibility. Three classes of cells are used in floorplanning:

- Some cells are already laid out and are stored in a library. These fixed cells comprise the class used by placement algorithms; all of their interface characteristics are known and fixed.
- The designs of some cells are known, but their layouts are flexible and can be influenced by the results of floorplanning. For example, the standard cell layout method can produce a wide range of shapes for a given design. Programmable logic arrays can be distorted through folding or layout design. Several versions of a cell with different characteristics may be stored in a library.
- Cells of a third class are flexible because their design (and perhaps even the design methods) are uncertain or not known. In this case, it is difficult for designers or algorithms to specify either nominal interface characteristics or constraints thereon.

An important aspect of cell modeling is estimation of area and shape. Four approaches have been reported: experimental, analytical, procedural, and knowledge-based. Experimental approaches develop area estimates through empirical formulas and are usually tuned to a design style or even to a particular system [21]. Analytical approaches concentrate on wirability analysis and routing area analysis [22]. Procedural cell models have the ability to sense their context (e.g., the neighboring cells and their relation to the subject cell) and optimize their interface characteristics for the current position. Knowledge-based approaches can operate on more uncertain cell designs. A more precise method of area estimation is available if a slicing structure is used and constraints on shapes of all of the children components of a cell are known. Otten describes a method of computing the bounds on shapes that a cell can assume, based on the bounds on shapes of its constituent components [23].

6.2 Approaches to Floorplanning

There are three major thrusts in floorplanning. One accepts that floorplanning is so difficult that a circuit designer must be an integral part of the process; therefore, interactive graphics must be included in addition to algorithmic approaches. The second major thrust uses floorplanning in the initial stages of design synthesis to develop constraints that can be passed to later, separate stages in the design process. The third major thrust relies on the existence of powerful module generators that can generate modules to specifications. This allows the floorplanner to be integrated with layout generators and permits truly automatic layout.

Many approaches have been proposed for solving floorplanning problems, but the methods may be grouped as constructive and iterative. Constructive methods include cluster growth, connectivity clustering, and partitioning/slicing. The placement methods described in Ref. 2 have been adapted to floorplanning by using procedural methods to estimate or define cell shapes during each placement trial. A clustering method based on circuit connectivity is described in Ref. 24. Clusters are mapped onto floorplan templates that have simplified topologies. Complex circuits are planned by applying the same algorithm recursively. Partitioning/slicing placement has also been applied to floorplanning with some degree of success. Constructive floorplanning methods share the characteristic that they construct a floorplan algorithmically.

In contrast to the constructive floorplanning methods, iterative techniques operate on complete floorplans to improve the layout quality. These methods fall into three categories: interchange, relaxation, and knowledge based. The iterative placement algorithms described in section 5 have been adapted to floorplanning. These algorithms have been generalized to handle flexible cell shapes and to define new floorplanning states. Typically, cells are optimized at the time of interchange. In some cases, the channel position and channel intersection graphs of the topological model are manipulated directly [2] to perform pairwise interchange. In other cases, the regularity of slicing structures is exploited to define new floorplanning states. Relaxation is different from interchange techniques in that relaxation implies an obvious or preferred next state. The relaxation method consists of modifying the channel graphs of the layout surface as well as the cell shapes. Knowledge-based floorplanning approaches have also been tried [25].

It is extremely difficult to compare floorplanning approaches because results are highly dependent on the circuit design, the design styles, and the design methodology. Furthermore, because floorplanning occurs early

Automatic Placement and Floor Planning for VLSI Circuits

in the design process, the subsequent layout steps can partially mask the quality of floorplanning. As a result, comparisons are nonexistent.

7 APPLICATIONS OF PLACEMENT AND FLOORPLANNING ALGORITHMS

So far, discussion has been limited to models and technology-independent algorithms for component placement and floorplanning. However, the ways in which the algorithms are applied can vary significantly, depending on problem and design environment attributes. Some of these attributes are explored in this section: large number of components, design styles, and circuit performance criticality.

7.1 Large Number of Components

Most placement algorithms operate on *flat* representations of hierarchial descriptions, i.e., the placement algorithms do not make use of information at higher or lower levels of their design hierarchy. However, because placement algorithms may be $O(n^2)$ or higher, it may be impossible to consider all placeable objects within a containing component simultaneously in a very large circuit. At this point, there are three choices: partitioning, hierarchical placement, and hardware accelerators or multiple processors.

7.1.1 Partitioning

In this approach, flat placement problems are divided into separate but interdependent subproblems that are solved sequentially. The subproblems are not independent because the decisions made in one subproblem affect the others; decisions that improve the placement within one partition might degrade the overall placement. However, subdividing the problem reduces the complexity of the problem. For an algorithm that has complexity of $O(n^\alpha)$ (n is the number of components and $\alpha > 1$), a problem that is subdivided into p parts has a complexity of $O(p[n/p]^\alpha)$ or $O(n^\alpha/p^{\alpha-1})$. Khokhani et al. describe a method that partitions a circuit into "super nodes" and uses constructive initial placement and iterative placement to improve the assignment of the super nodes to "super locations." The super nodes are then decomposed into primitives and placed [26].

7.1.2 Hierarchy

In hierarchical placement, problem complexity is reduced by subdividing the circuit into multiple levels. The top level divides the circuit into first-level components, which are partitioned into lower level components. This subdivision continues recursively until (for purposes of placement) primitive placement components are defined. The hierarchical subdivision may be the same as that defined in the structural representation, or the layout system may provide automatic hierarchical partitioning before invoking placement algorithms separately on the resultant components.

7.1.3 Hardware Accelerators and Multiple Processors

It is possible to reduce the execution times through the use of special-purpose hardware optimized for placement tasks and/or multiple processors that allow parallel processing. An in-depth discussion of the architectures of hardware accelerators is not attempted here: a discussion of special-purpose hardware for design automation is given in Ref. 27. A discussion of a placement hardware accelerator implementation with comparative results is given in Ref. 28.

Hancock and DasGupta [29] discuss multiprocessors applied to design automation problems, as well as the multiprocessor configuration known as the hypercube. Kravitz and Rutenbar [30] give a taxonomy of parallel algorithms, as well as three different implementations of parallel algorithms for simulated annealing on one to four processors. They present the concepts of object and function decomposition; object decomposition is an assignment of entities (such as cells or nets) to processors, whereas function decomposition is an assignment of operations (such as wire length calculation) to processors. They also present the idea of static versus dynamic decomposition; this describes whether the assignment of objects or functions to processors is done once or changes over time.

7.2 Layout Design Styles

The demands placed on, and the design of placement algorithms vary greatly depending on the design style that is addressed. The styles considered here are gate array, standard cell, and general cell. More information on VLSI design styles can be found in Chapter 1 of Ref. 1.

7.2.1 Gate Arrays

Because gate arrays have fixed, legal gate sites, the placement algorithms must have knowledge of these sites and any location restrictions for various cells. For instance, I/O pad sites are around the periphery and I/O drivers are near the periphery. Furthermore, the total routing resources are fixed before the layout process begins, so it is important to use the resources wisely. Thus, it may be necessary to model congestion in the placement objective function. It is sometimes possible to find alternate placements that have longer wire lengths but less congestion.

7.2.2 Standard Cells

In standard-cell designs component and routing area sizes and positions are not fixed. The layout size is defined dynamically by the layout program based on the requirements of the specific circuit. Although the final topology is arranged with rows of standard cells and routing channels between the rows, the number, lengths, and positions of the component rows and the routing channels can be adjusted dynamically. The cells may have varying heights and widths and are retrieved from a library or constructed using module generation techniques. Power is usually distributed through the cells and does not intrude on the routing area. It is necessary to make trade-offs between the number and size of the channels and the number of rows. Row lengths must be kept uniform or space is wasted at the end of short rows. Additionally, it is beneficial to consider routing density uniformity along the cell rows. These issues necessitate capabilities in the placement algorithms and underlying data structures that are significantly different than those used with gate arrays. Metrics such as wire length must be augmented to account for the dynamic nature of the design style. Due to the complexity of dynamically adjusting cell rows and routing channels, the underlying data structure is typically a topological model.

7.2.3 General Cells

General-cell placement extends the topological model further. General cells are not restricted to similar sizes or arrangement in rows. This adds considerable complexity. Careful consideration must be given to the placement of the large cells, as their positions will have a large impact on the resulting topology. Also, the placement model must account for routing resources needed in the vicinity of each component, because the way in which the various components fit together and the way the routing areas align is extremely important.

The basic placement algorithms discussed in sections 4 and 5 have been adapted to general-cell placement. The reader is also directed to section 6 because of the many similarities with floorplanning. However, the general nature of the two-dimensional cell placement problem (the lack of a predefined array of slots for gate arrays, or rows for standard cell design styles) has led to placement techniques that are applicable to general-cell placement. These techniques include cluster growth [2], clustering, merging, and rearranging [31], force-directed approaches [32], global placement [13], and partitioning [10].

7.3 Placement Based on Circuit Performance

Two primary factors influence the propagation delay along a path in the circuit; switching delays of the components along the path and interconnection delays caused primarily by resistance and capacitance of the wiring. Until recently, propagation delays were not considered important during placement because the switching delays dominated the interconnection delays (interconnection delay is the only factor that placement can influence). However, fabrication processes are improving, and switching delays are dropping substantially; thus, it is important to consider performance during the placement process, as placement determines the minimum delays of the nets of a circuit. Consideration of circuit performance during placement is referred to as performance-based or timing-driven placement.

There are many ways to include performance considerations in the placement process. However, because placement can only impact performance characteristics through the interconnections, all of the techniques modify the objective function to influence the length and topology of the wiring paths. One performance-based placement system is able to derive the timing requirements on the nets as a function of the structural representation, the timing parameters of the cells, and the input-to-output delay requirements of the circuit [33]. This system generates all possible paths through the circuit; the criticality of each path is determined automatically. Based on the *timing margin* (the difference between the required and predicted delay), the net priorities are set and placement is performed.

8 CONCLUSION

Automated placement is important because it greatly influences the amount and the location of wiring required to interconnect the components. The placement phase impacts the router's ability to complete the required interconnections, as well as affecting the performance of the circuit. The placement models and algorithms chosen for a particular layout system depend on many factors. When considering speed versus performance trade-offs, it is difficult, if not impossible, to find a single model and algorithm that works best for all circuits encountered.

This article describes the major placement algorithms that are available. A large number of choices is available because electronic circuits have a wide variety of attributes that must be considered. Good placement is critical in order to generate high-quality layouts. Inclusion of superior placement techniques is therefore essential to the success of a design automation system.

REFERENCES

1. B. T. Preas and M. J. Lorenzetti, eds., *Physical Design Automation of VLSI Systems*, Benjamin-Cummings Publishing Company, Menlo Park, California, 1988.
2. B. T. Preas and W. M. vanCleemput, "Placement Algorithms for Arbitrarily Shaped Blocks," in *Proceedings of the Sixteenth Design Automation Conference*, 1979, pp. 474–480.
3. B. T. Preas and C. S. Chow, "Placement and Routing Algorithms for Topological Integrated Circuit Layout," in *Proceedings of the International Symposium on Circuits and Systems*, 1985, pp. 17–20.
4. M. Hanan, P. K. Wolff, Sr., and B. J. Agule, "Some Experimental Results on Placement Techniques," in *Proceedings of the Thirteenth Design Automation Conference*, 1976, pp. 214–224.
5. B. W. Kernighan and S. Lin, "An Efficient Heuristic Procedure for Partitioning Graphs," *Bell Sys. Tech. J.*, 49(2), 291–307 (1970).
6. D. G. Schweikert and B. W. Kernighan, "A Proper Model for the Partitioning of Electrical Circuits," in *Proceedings of the Ninth Design Automation Workshop*, 1972, pp. 57–62.
7. C. M. Fiduccia and R. M. Mattheyses, "A Linear-Time Heuristic for Improving Network Partitions," in *Proceedings of the Nineteenth Design Automation Conference*, 1982, pp. 175–181.
8. A. E. Dunlop and B. W. Kernighan, "A Procedure for Placement of Standard-Cell VLSI Circuits," *IEEE Trans. Comp.-Aided Design of Circuits and Sys.*, CAD-4(1), 92–98 (1985).
9. M. A. Breuer, "A class of min-cut placement algorithms," in *Proceedings of the Fourteenth Design Automation Conference*, 1977, pp. 284–290.
10. U. Lauther, "A Min-Cut Placement Algorithm for General Cell Assemblies Based on a Graph Representation," in *Proceedings of the Sixteenth Design Automation Conference*, 1979, pp. 1–10.
11. J. Frankle and R. M. Karp, "Circuit Placements and Cost Bounds by Eigenvector Decomposition," in *Digest of the International Conference on Computer-Aided Design*, 1986, pp. 414–417.
12. M. Hanan and J. M. Kurtzberg, "Placement Techniques," in *Design Automation of Digital Systems. Volume 1: Theory and Techniques*, (M. A. Breuer, ed.), Prentice-Hall, Englewood Cliffs, New Jersey, 1972, pp. 213–282.
13. J. P. Blanks, *Use of a Quadratic Objective Function for the Placement Problem in VLSI Design*, Doctoral Dissertation, Department of Electrical Engineering, University of Texas at Austin, 1985.
14. L. Sha and R. W. Dutton, "An Analytical Algorithm for Placement of Arbitrarily Sized Rectangular Blocks," in *Proceedings of the Twenty-Second Design Automation Conference*, 1985, pp. 602–608.

15. L. Steinberg, "The Backboard Wiring Problem: A Placement Algorithm," *SIAM Rev.*, 3(1), 37–50 (1961).
16. S. Kirkpartick, C. D. Gelatt, and M. P. Vecchi, "Optimization by Simulated Annealing," *Science,* 220(4598), 671–680 (1983).
17. C. Sechen and A. L. Sangiovanni-Vincentelli, "The Timberwolf Placement and Routing Package," in *Proceedings of the 1984 Custom Integrated Circuit Conference,* 1984.
18. J. W. Greene and K. J. Supowit, "Simulated Annealing without Rejected Moves," in *Proceedings of the International Conference on Computer Design,* 1984, pp. 658–663.
19. S. R. White, "Concepts of Scale in Simulated Annealing," in *Proceedings of the International Conference on Computer Design,* 1984, pp. 646–651.
20. M. D. Huang, F. Romeo, and A. Sangionanni-Vincentelli, "An Efficient General Cooling Schedule for Simulated Annealing," in *Proceedings of the International Conference on Computer-Aided Design,* 1986, pp. 381–384.
21. F. J. Kurdahi and A. C. Parker, "PLEST: A Program for Area Estimation of VLSI Integrated Circuits," in *Proceedings of the Twenty-Third Design Automation Conference,* 1986, pp. 467–473.
22. W. R. Heller, W. F. Mikhail, and W. E. Donath, "Prediction of Wiring Space Requirements for LSI," in *Proceedings of the Fourteenth Design Automation Conference,* 1977, pp. 32–42.
23. R. H. J. M. Otten, "Annealing Applied to Floorplan Design in a Layout Compiler," in *Automation '86 High Technology Computer Conference Proceedings,* 1986, pp. 185–228.
24. W. Dai and E. S. Kuh, "Hierarchical Floorplanning for Building Block Layout," in *Digest of International Conference on Computer-Aided Design,* 1986, pp. 454–457.
25. H. Watanabe and B. Ackland, "Flute—A Floorplanning Agent for Full Custom VLSI Design," in *Proceedings of the Twenty-Third Design Automation Conference,* 1986, pp. 601–607.
26. K. H. Kokhani, A. M. Patel, W. Ferguson, J. Sessa, and D. Hatton, "Placement of Variable Size Circuits on LSI Masterslices," in *Proceedings of the Eigthteenth Design Automation Conference,* 1981, pp. 426–434.
27. T. Blank, "A Survey of Hardware Accelerators Used in Computer-Aided Design," *IEEE Design and Test of Comput.*, 1(3), 21–39 (1984).
28. P. M. Spira and C. Hage, "Hardware Acceleration of Gate Array Layout," in *Proceedings of the Twenty-Second Design Automation Conference,* 1985, pp. 359–366.
29. J. M. Hancock and S. DasGupta, "Tutorial on Parallel Processing for Design Automation Applications," in *Proceedings of the Twenty-Third Design Automation Conference,* 1986, pp. 69–77.
30. S. A. Kravitz and R. A. Rutenbar, "Multiprocessor-Based Placement by Simulated Annealing," in *Proceedings of the Twenty-Third Design Automation Conference,* 1986, pp. 567–573.
31. C. C. Chen and E. S. Kuh, "Automatic Placement for Building Block Layout," in *Digest of International Conference on Computer-Aided Design,* 1984, pp. 90–92.
32. N. R. Quinn and M. A. Breuer, "A Force-Directed Component Placement Procedure for Printed Circuit Boards," *IEEE Trans. Circuits and Sys. CAS-26,* 377–388 (1979).

33. M. Burstein and M. N. Youssef, "Timing-Influenced Layout Designs," in *Proceedings of the Twenty-Second Design Automation Conference,* 1985, pp. 124–130.

BRYAN T. PREAS
PATRICK G. KARGER

BENCHMARKING

Benchmarking is a technique for measuring the performance of a computer system by running a program and noting the time taken to execute it. The program used for such a purpose is called a benchmark. (The word benchmark in reference to computers has the sense of "something that serves as a standard by which others may be measured," only one of the dictionary [1] meanings. In still other computer usage, benchmarking refers to a demonstration of the functions or capabilities of a computer system without regard to performance, i.e., to how fast the functions are performed, but such an activity is more properly termed a functional or capability demonstration [2]. This second sense of benchmarking as a functional demonstration is not discussed further in this article.)

Benchmarking is one technique of computer performance analysis, along with simulation and monitoring by software and hardware. Common uses of benchmarking are for change analysis (judging performance effects of new hardware and software on a system); capacity planning (determining unused capacity and the saturation point of a system); architectural evaluation (comparing performance of alternative system designs); and system acquisition (comparing performance of available systems) [3].

A benchmark serves merely as a workload to exercise a computer system; there is generally no distinguishing property required of a program to be a benchmark. However, programs designed especially for performance measurement are called synthetic benchmarks, whereas those that happen to be used for such measurement and that do useful computations otherwise are natural benchmarks. Collections of either kind are called synthetic or natural workloads, respectively. Within each type, benchmarks are computational, if most of their time is spent executing CPU instructions; I/O intensive, if the largest part of their execution time is consumed by I/O operations; or some mix of the two. An interactive benchmark is most commonly a sequence of commands derived from a scenario containing a functional or system-independent description of a user's interaction with a system. The version actually executed is in the form of a "script," a list of commands to a target system in its own syntax for tasks such as editing documents or compiling and executing programs [4]. Similarly, benchmark workloads for database management systems are often a series of queries or update operations in the form of a command stream that can be interpreted by a special test driver program and passed on to the target system [5].

The technical literature on benchmarking, especially that reporting measurement data, is relatively sparse. (For instance, there seems to have been only one book [6] in English ever devoted to the topic.) One reason for this scarcity may be that the chief use of benchmarking has been in computer procurement (an activity that typically results in few scientific publications). For instance, U.S. government procurement regulations mandate that performance requirements be stated in any request for proposal for computer equipment purchase announced by the federal government [7]. These regulations consider benchmarking as a fairly precise technique for validating such requirements. However, it is the practice under competitive bidding rules not to reveal the performance results of the tendered systems on customer benchmarks. Of course, private sector purchasers may also run benchmarks (or ask vendors to do so) before making large investments in computers. These results too are rarely made public. Though computer manufacturers do a great deal of systematic benchmarking, most of the time the only measurement data made public from vendor sources appear in the form of marketing claims in advertising copy for eye-catching execution rates. It is therefore to be expected that there has existed little published performance data on benchmarks, though this situation is changing.

In devising benchmarks for use in procurement of systems, it is important that the benchmarks be representative of an organization's workload. Some selection must be made from the natural workload (current computing job load), for it is impossible to run a whole year's job load, or a month's, or usually even a week's, at a vendor site in order to measure performance. Typically, the jobs run most frequently or those consuming the most system resources, if different, are chosen. Cluster analysis* is a more complicated technique for analyzing an existing workload to identify representative applications and programs by their resource consumption [8]. But characterizing the future workload because of changes in user needs should also be taken into account. Surveys and interviews with project leaders and other users can help to identify anticipated quantitative and qualitative changes in workload such as increased resource use, as when a larger version of an existing job is to be run because of increased memory, and need for new peripherals (e.g., graphics workstations) [9]. Other constraints on representativeness are privacy of data, which may have to be cleansed of personal information before it can be released to a candidate vendor, and lack of standardization in a customer's computer programs, languages, file access methods, and so on, which may cause the vendor (or the potential customer's performance analysis staff) to incur large costs in time and personnel to convert the benchmark set for running on the offered system. This conversion cost represents the problem of portability between systems.

Few organizations have such large investments in current and planned computer systems that they have permanent staffs devoted to workload analysis and benchmark development. One that does is the U.S. National Laboratory at Los Alamos, New Mexico. Other national laboratories such as those at Argonne, Illinois, Livermore, California, and the NASA Ames Research Center, also in California, have been noteworthy in benchmarking supercomputers. The Computing Division at the Los Alamos National

---

*In cluster analysis, a set of data points is arranged into groups according to similarity of parameters characterizing the points. The data points in computer workload analysis are jobs or other units of work having parameters such as CPU time, memory used, I/O operations performed, etc. The aim of cluster analysis is to reduce a large sample of jobs into a smaller set by clustering into groups, each of which can be represented by a single job whose characteristics are similar, by some measure, to those of the group and less similar to other groups.

Laboratory has a particularly extensive record of research in this area marked by publication of performance data from benchmarks as well as analysis of results [10].

With the comparative luxury of a benchmarking staff, it is possible to create synthetic benchmarks. These are extracts from natural benchmarks or programs specially designed for performance comparisons between machines. The extracts are the portions of the codes that impose most of the processing load; kernels are stand-alone versions of the extracts and are usually parameterized so that the amount of processing they do can be systematically varied. A well-known example of such extracts is the set of kernels from the Lawrence Livermore Laboratory; because they are from a FORTRAN workload, the computations are concentrated in DO loops and are usually called the "Livermore Loops." Where a natural benchmark may contain thousands of lines of code, kernels or loops are much smaller. Their representativeness need not be low in spite of being small: They stand for the type of computation done at an installation, even if they are not the actual workload programs [11]. Whatever representativeness may be traded off for small size is made up by ease of use across many systems—the smaller and simpler the program, the easier to convert to another system. Because they can be implemented cheaply on many systems, kernels provide a means of comparing performance among those systems. Also, they can be used for calibration when measuring a new system, as they provide a rough estimate of comparative performance by which to gauge the results of using natural workload benchmarks.

Early synthetic benchmarks were instruction mixes in which the basic statements available in a given programming language were timed by placing each in a loop, which was then executed many times [12]. But comparing the execution speeds over many machines for the 42 basic statements in a language like ALGOL was considered deficient because statement types did not all occur with the same frequency in user programs. Weights were therefore derived which could be applied to execution rates of the basic statements so as to count more heavily those instructions executed more frequently, as shown by analysis of what were considered typical programs. Only a few such weighting schemes were developed; occasionally, benchmarks related to them are still used, though the workload from which the instruction frequency weights were derived may have long been out of existence.

One famous benchmark derived in this way is the so-called Whetstone, developed by Curnow and Wichmann at the National Physical Laboratory in the United Kingdom [12]. Performance with it is measured in "Whetstone instructions per second," though the Whetstone is not the benchmark but an intermediate code into which ALGOL programs were translated (the intermediate code was executed by an interpreter in a British implementation of ALGOL whose compiler was written at the English Electric Co., Whetstone, Leicester). A software tool was designed to count the static and dynamic frequencies of instructions in the intermediate code. Fixing the frequency parameters and running the Curnow—Wichmann synthetic benchmark gave a certain rate of Whetstone instructions, a figure that, for the unwary user, would have nothing to do with the benchmarked system unless its ALGOL compiler (if any) used the Whetstone intermediate code. Another famous "mix" is the Gibson mix. Though often misconstrued as an executable benchmark, it is rather a set of weights (from a workload from the early days of computing) to be applied to the timing data from an instruction mix [13].

Weights are also applied to the measured execution times of programs in a benchmark set to reflect the true contribution of each to the workload represented by the set. Simple arithmetic averaging (dividing the sum of execution times of n benchmarks by n) would be misleading. Recommended practices are to take the harmonic mean (which weights performance on a benchmark by the fraction of total workload represented by the benchmark), when comparing execution times of various machines directly [14], or the geometric mean when comparing relative machine power (by normalizing benchmark execution times of the group of systems under consideration to one system) [15].

For many, benchmarking has acquired a taint from its association with computer manufacturers' claims in advertising copy of so many MIPS (million instructions per second), MFLOPS (million floating-point operations per second), LIPS (logical inferences per second, for artificial intelligence machines), or TPS (transactions per second) [16], etc. The customer who gets a chance to run a benchmark of his or her own often finds that a machine rated at, say, 200 MFLOPS by the vendor often achieves an order of magnitude less on a workaday FORTRAN code. (It is usually supposed that the claims for MIPS rates in marketing literature are backed up by runs of highly optimized codes.) Aside from engendering a mistrust of sales talk, the computing public sometimes acquires a suspicion of benchmarking, so that the process itself, as well as the data it produces and the very units of measurement (MIPS have been called "misleading instructions per second") are mistrusted.

There are many difficulties in benchmarking, but if measurements are done carefully, results should be reproducible and, therefore, trustworthy. The process of benchmarking is one of measurement in a complex environment with many variables that must be strictly controlled. Also, the investigator must understand the characteristics of the benchmark and of the environment, configuration, and architecture of the system on which it is executed. The performance data observed are a function of many variables, not all of which have yet been systematically investigated.

Benchmark performance can be depicted by a generic expression such as

$$P = f(B_{ij}, E_k) \tag{1}$$

where P is the performance attained with benchmark i in the jth version under the kth set of environment conditions. E_k is itself manifold and defined in the open-ended expression

$$E_k = (C_k, CO_k, M_k, L_k, W_k, R_k, \cdots). \tag{2}$$

Here, C_k indicates the compiler (and version); CO_k, the compiler options used (e.g., whether optimized or not); M_k, the machine and configuration (this itself is manifold and includes word size, memory interleaving, machine cycle time, block sizes of I/O devices used, etc.); L_k, the linker and loader options used and messages encountered; W_k, whether other workload was present (identifying it); R_k, the run-time events and messages (e.g., numeric overflow, scratch file overflows, etc.). The mix of terms in (2) would also vary with the type of benchmark: For an interactive benchmark, there might be no compiler term, but there might be terms representing an editor, data base management system, telecommunications interfaces, etc. There seems to be small consensus (and little research) on which of these variables have most effect on measured performance, but settling this question requires experimentation. For a benchmark in the form of a scientific code executed in the batch mode, the major factors are probably those listed here, and among these, the most important in a benchmark measurement (others being held constant) are the program, the compiler, and the machine. The process of rendering benchmark results trustworthy consists, at least partly, in recording and making known, along with the observed MIPS, MFLOPS, or other measures, values for the list of variables (or applicable subset of them) in E_k.

In much of the published benchmark data, not enough of the E_k factors are reported to make the measurements reproducible, a problem not with benchmarking, but with haphazard technique. What is being measured is a system of dependent and mutually interacting entities, almost never the bare machine (except in the special circumstance of attaining peak rates by hand optimization of assembly language code fragments). A reported number of MFLOPS, for example, should never be accepted in isolation from the set of elements whose interaction constitutes the measurement. A naive approach is to take the MFLOPS number as some absolute metric, whereas it should always be placed in the context of an n-tuple of elements and, for greater objectivity, in a fuller context like that of (2). However, even computer scientists tend to fall into the trap of quoting performance numbers as if they were absolute metrics without context.

The units in which to record performance depend on the type of benchmark and the purpose of the measurement. I/O benchmarks might report performance as a transfer rate, e.g., kilowords per second [17]. Natural benchmarks, especially those containing large codes, are measured in elapsed time units (seconds, minutes, or hours) because an important factor in a purchase decision served by benchmarking is job throughput—how fast the selected workload is processed.

The timing can often be done with a relatively crude (compared with computer execution speeds) instrument like a stopwatch. Synthetic codes may access timers in the operating system by calls from within the program. These timers return values accurate to the hundredth, thousandth, or even, millionth of a second. The accuracy of their resolution may be checked by calibration against kernels (see below). If the number of operations performed by the synthetic benchmark is known—almost always the case with kernels—performance can be reported in so many instructions per second. With the finer resolution (instructions and fractions of a second as opposed to jobs and stopwatches) of kernels and internal timers, it may be easier to analyze the contribution of algorithm and architecture to performance. However, internal timers introduce a measurement artifact into use of synthetic benchmarks. The usual method of countering the problem (that measuring the elapsed time of a program affects its elapsed time) is by placing timer calls before and after a loop of code and then executing the loop (but not the timer calls) for sufficient iterations to swamp the overhead of timer calls. A code fragment exemplifying this technique is

```
          CALL TIMER (T0)
          DO 10 L = 1, L
              CALL SUBRX
10        CONTINUE
          CALL TIMER (T1)
          TOTTIM = T1 - T0
```

where L is a sufficiently large integer.

An illustration of the effect of this technique on measurement is given in Figure 1, which shows how the measured execution rate of FORTRAN CALL instructions (with no parameters, as in the code fragment above) can vary with the number of instructions executed.

The mean rates in kilo-ops (thousands of operations per second) vary by about 10%, depending on whether the loop is executed 10^4 or 10^6 times (probably as a result of the relatively slow timer call used to measure a very fast instruction). The much wider range of measured rates at lower numbers of instructions executed, as shown by error bars in Figure 1, indicates that it is critical to adjust for the timer artifact by executing a sufficient number of instructions. In this example, asymptotic performance is not reached until the loop containing the instruction to be benchmarked is executed about 1.25 million times. The peak performance rate will differ according to the environment—computer, compiler, operating system, and perhaps other factors—in which the benchmark is run.

When their performance data on machines of various architectures and configurations are available, kernel benchmarks can be an aid in "calibrating"[†] a new machine, that is, in estimating its performance range over an installation's workload. Because the kernels are relatively simple and the amount of processing load they impose is, by hypothesis, well-known to the user, their performance on a new machine gives information on whether the timers are accurate and what programming changes might have to be made to run other benchmarks in a new system environment.

[†]This is perhaps an odd use of calibrating; in standard usage, it is the measuring instrument, not the thing measured, that is calibrated against some standard. However, a benchmark is not a static unit of measurement (like a meter stick) or even a measurement instrument (like a voltmeter, which still uses a static unit, the volt). It is only a unit of measurement while executing in a computer and is only static in the public or representational form in which it is transported or published. The form in which it does measurement is different, and that form even differs between systems (in machine language, compiler, I/O channel programs, etc.). A benchmark needs a system in order to do measurement, unlike a meter stick, which denotes the same quantity of length no matter what object it is used to measure. A benchmark is not "stand alone" like a meter stick but does measurement only as a 2-tuple (program, system). For this 2-tuple, calibration is not adjusting the measurement instrument to a static standard but transforming the external form of a benchmark into an internal form required for measurement. The process can be called calibration when the benchmark is a kernel and, therefore, transportable.

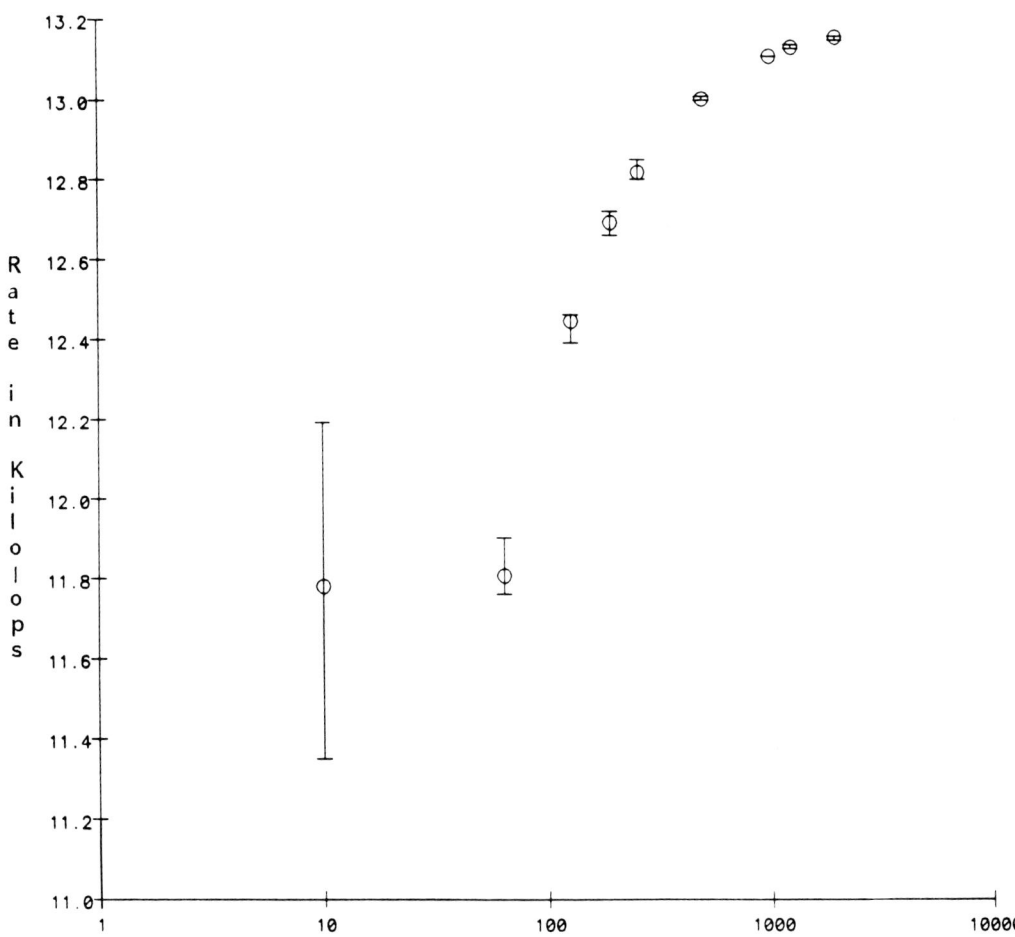

FIGURE 1 An illustration of the timer artifact, as explained in the text. The execution rate of an operation may vary with the number of times the operation is executed, especially when an internal timer is used. The mean execution rate observed is shown by circles, and the range of observations around the mean by error bars. The peak execution rate of about 13,000 operations per second is not reached until approximately 1.25 million instructions in the loop being timed have been executed. The measurement experiment shown here was run on a popular personal computer with widely available operating system and FORTRAN compiler.

Whether benchmarks are to be run by customer or vendor personnel, there should be written rules for the amount of source code and command stream changes to be allowed. A frequent practice is to specify tuning levels at which given numbers of lines may be changed. One synthetic benchmark [18] allows for four tuning levels at which 0, up to 20, up to 50, or more than 50 lines may be changed. These levels provide an idea of the effort required to get a benchmark running at all and to optimize its performance.

The interference from other workload should be eliminated, if possible, by running on a dedicated system and otherwise minimized by running on a system as lightly loaded as practicable. When a natural workload benchmark is to be run, as for a large system procurement, the entire system is usually dedicated to the candidate workload. When the system to be measured is "lent" by a third party, the file system must be copied onto backup storage before the measurement runs because the lender usually cannot risk a possible destruction of files caused by an unknown and, perhaps, capricious, workload. Such protection of the borrowed system entails a large setup cost. When natural workload measurements are to be made at a vendor site, a system is usually reserved for this purpose. The high cost of selecting and weighting the applications for a natural workload benchmark and for obtaining a measurement system make natural benchmarks less convenient than kernels.

The points made above about benchmarks and the uses to which they are put can be summarized in the diagram in Figure 2. Here, benchmarks are arranged in decreasing size, as measured by lines of code. When

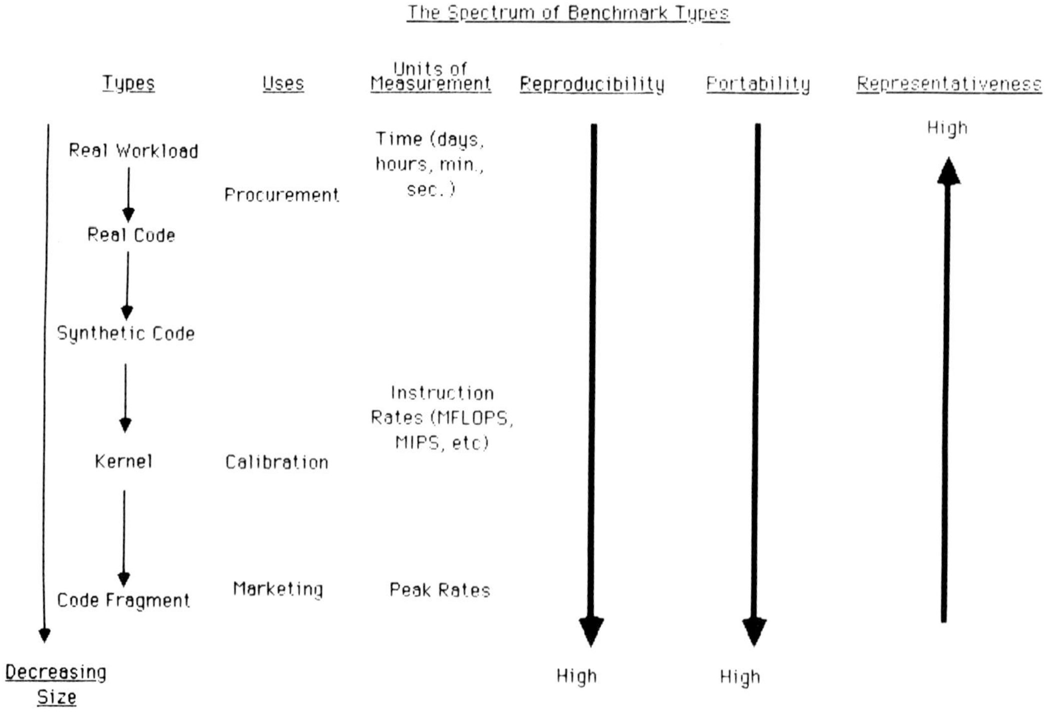

The Spectrum of Benchmark Types

Types	Uses	Units of Measurement	Reproducibility	Portability	Representativeness
Real Workload		Time (days, hours, min., sec.)			High
↓	Procurement				
Real Code					
↓					
Synthetic Code					↑
↓		Instruction Rates (MFLOPS, MIPS, etc)			
Kernel	Calibration				
↓					
Code Fragment	Marketing	Peak Rates	↓	↓	
↓			High	High	

Decreasing Size

FIGURE 2 The spectrum of benchmark types.

ranked in this way, benchmarks can be seen to fall along a spectrum by which their properties, such as purpose and units of measurement, also sort themselves. Moreover, it can be seen that representativeness is traded off against portability and reproducibility of measurement results, because they vary in opposite directions with regard to benchmark size.

The United States federal government provides benchmarking assistance to government agencies and issues guidelines for both government and private sector data-processing organizations. The Federal Computer Performance Evaluation and Simulation Center (FEDSIM), under the General Services Administration, assists agencies in constructing and running benchmarks for procurement. Employing a variety of tools such as resource drivers (which construct an artificial workload to consume specified amounts of system resources) and providing consulting services, FEDSIM support can help an agency's data-processing staff through a difficult performance evaluation. The National Bureau of Standards under the Department of Commerce compiles and publishes guidelines for various aspects of benchmarking [19].

Two trends in computer technology are affecting the way benchmarking is looked upon by the computing community. The spread of supercomputers and the advent of commercially available parallel computers are focusing attention on ways of measuring performance and on the traditional method, benchmarking. Not least, the great cost of supercomputers warrants investment in elaborate benchmarking activities to aid purchase decisions. Despite the promise of parallel systems (containing many computers that can operate separately on parts of a computation but that can communicate when needed), users may need to devote some effort to customize applications for such systems. An important consideration besides execution times or instruction rates will be the amount of effort required by applications programmers to write parallel programs anew or to convert existing serial programs for parallel processing [20]. For some parallel architectures, there may even be a question as to which applications are appropriate. One way of assessing the claim for suitability between application and architecture will be by benchmarking [21].

Another aid to the furthering of objective, as opposed to sales-oriented benchmarking, is the use of "standard" programs for performance measurement. If, at present (1988), there are few, if any, programs for measurement endorsed by standards bodies, there are several benchmarks that are or may become de facto standards, that is, merely by being widely used. Examples are the NAS Kernel Benchmark, the Livermore Loops used since the 1970s, and the Mendez benchmarks [22]. And the Whetstone benchmark, although representative of an old workload, still provides a standard of comparison by being used on many personal computers. Also, the publication by physical scientists of benchmark results on supercomputers [23] allows comparison to vendor-marketing claims. The appearance of measurement data from these other sources is providing an objective, experimental base on which to compare systems.

Leonard Uhr [24] of the University of Wisconsin has argued for cooperation among researchers interested in benchmarking to exchange measurement data, as well as benchmark algorithms and programs in order to achieve a common benchmark set. This set would be added to by the interested scientific community and would come, in time, to cover most application areas and system architectures. No organization, even the largest, could hope to have enough expertise in as many application areas or access to as many machines as the benchmark set would comprise. If the trend of publishing (or otherwise disseminating, as on electronic mail networks) performance measurement data obtained by benchmarking continues, an experimental branch of computer science may arise in this area.

REFERENCES

1. *Webster's Ninth New Collegiate Dictionary*, Merriam-Webster, 1984, p. 143.
2. National Bureau of Standards, Federal Information Processing Standards (FIPS) Publication, "Guidelines for Benchmarking ADP Systems in the Competitive Procurement Environment," FIPS Pub. 42-1, National Technical Information Service, U.S. Dept. of Commerce, Springfield, VA 22161, 1977, p. 5.
3. National Bureau of Standards, "Guidelines on Constructing Benchmarks for ADP System Acquisition," FIPS Pub. 75, National Technical Information Service, U.S. Department of Commerce, Springfield, VA 22161, 1980.
4. Shirley Ward Watkins and Marshall Abrams, *A Survey of Remote Terminal Emulators*, National Bureau of Standards (NBS) Special Pub. 500-4, U.S. Government Printing Office, Washington, D.C., 1977.
5. See Daniel R. Benigni, ed., *Benchmark Analysis of Database Architectures: A Case Study*, National Bureau of Standards Special Pub. 500-132, U.S. Department of Commerce, October, 1985.
6. Nicholas Benwell, ed., *Benchmarking: Computer Evaluation and Measurement*, Hemisphere Pub. Corp., Washington, D.C., 1975. (Proceedings of a conference held at Cambridge University, October 1974.)
7. Nicholas Benwell, ed., *Benchmarking: Computer Evaluation and Measurement*, Hemisphere Pub. Corp., Washington, D.C., 1975, p. viii. See also Federal Information Resources Management Regulations, U.S. General Services Administration, Superintendent of Documents, U.S. Government Printing Office, Washington, D.C. 20402, (various entries for automated data processing equipment procurement and benchmarking).
8. National Bureau of Standards, FIPS Pub. 75. Also see Domenico Ferrari et al., *Measurement and Tuning of Computer Systems*, Prentice-Hall, Englewood Cliffs, NJ, 1983.
9. Ingrid Y. Bucher and Joanne L. Martin, "Methodology for Characterizing a Scientific Workload," in *Proceedings of the Eighteenth Meeting of the Computer Performance Evaluation Users Group (CPEUG)*, NBS Special Pub. 500-95, U.S. Department of Commerce, Washington, D.C., 1982, pp. 121–126.
10. See, for example, Joanne L. Martin, "Los Alamos National Laboratory Computer Benchmarking 1982," Report LA-9698-MS, June, 1983, Los Alamos National Laboratory, Los Alamos, NM 87545 (one of a series of approximately yearly papers giving results of running the Los Alamos Benchmark Set on the laboratory's computer facility, one of the largest in the world). See also the paper on workload characterization by Ingrid Y. Bucher and Joanne L. Martin, "Methodology for Characterizing a Scientific Workload," Los Alamos Report LA-UR-82-1702, 1982.
11. A description of the Livermore loops and code segments can be found in J. P. Riganati and Paul B. Schneck, "Supercomputing," *Computer*, 17(10), 97–113 (October 1984). Somewhat larger kernels and their timing results on various supercomputers are described in David H.

Bailey, "NAS Kernel Benchmark Results," in *Proceedings of the First International Conference on Supercomputing Systems,* St. Petersburg, FL, December 1985, IEEE Computer Society Press, pp. 341–345. Performance comparisons between machines using kernels like Livermore's are also given in U. Schendel, *Introduction to Numerical Methods for Parallel Computers,* Wiley, New York, 1984.

12. H. J. Curnow and Brian A. Wichmann, "A Synthetic Benchmark," *Comput. J.* 19(1), 43–49 (February 1976).
13. Jack C. Gibson, "The Gibson Mix," TR 00.2043, IBM Corp., Systems Development Division, Poughkeepsie, New York, June 18, 1970. The date on this paper, now difficult to obtain, can be misleading as the Gibson mix weights were in use long before 1970. However the paper (even as long ago as 1970) was intended to be a history of the origin of the Gibson mix, which was developed in 1959 for the IBM 704.
14. Jack Worlton, "Understanding Supercomputer Benchmarks," *Datamation,* 121–130 (September 1, 1984).
15. Philip J. Fleming and John J. Wallace, "How Not to Lie with Statistics: The Correct Way to Summarize Benchmark Results," *Commun. ACM,* 29(3), 218–221 (March 1986).
16. The TPS measure is difficult to interpret, as the definition of a transaction can be elusive. See Anon. et al., "A Measure of Transaction Processing Power," *Datamation,* 112–118 (April 1, 1985).
17. If benchmarking itself is under-reported in the literature, articles on I/O benchmarking are even scarcer. One of the rare articles on the subject in the open literature is by Ingrid Y. Bucher and Ann H. Hayes, "I/O Performance Measurement on Cray-1 and CDC 7600 Computers," Los Alamos National Laboratory Report LA-8467-MS, August, 1980. The article gives a good idea of the extreme complexity of designing and carrying out an I/O benchmark measurement and of the many factors that affect performance (such as program size, and operating system buffers).
18. The Numerical Aerodynamic Simulator Kernel Benchmark. See David H. Bailey (Ref. 11).
19. See especially FIPS Pub. 42-1, "Guidelines for Benchmarking ADP Systems in the Competitive Procurement Environment," 1977; FIPS Pub. 75, "Guidelines on Constructing Benchmarks for ADP System Acquisition," 1980; NBS Special Pub. 500-118, "A Guide to Performance Evaluation of Database Systems," 1984; NBS Special Pub. 500-123, "Guide on Workload Forecasting," 1985; NBS Special Pub. 500-113, "Assessment of Techniques for Evaluating Computer Systems for Federal Agency Procurements," 1984.
20. For an experiment involving users converting their own applications to run on parallel machines, see George B. Adams III, Robert L. Brown, and Peter J. Denning, "Report on an Evaluation Study of Data Flow Computation," RIACS Tech. Rep. 85.2, April, 1985, Research Institute for Advanced Computer Science, NASA Ames Research Center, Moffett Field, CA 94035.
21. For an example of benchmarking on a parallel machine, see Harry F. Jordan, "Experience with Pipelined Multiple Instruction Streams," *Proc. IEEE,* 72(1), 113–123 (January 1984).
22. The Livermore loops are frequently cited in the literature on supercomputer, especially vector processing, performance. See Riganati and Schneck (Ref. 11). See also Raul Mendez, "Benchmarks on

Japanese and American Supercomputers—Preliminary Results," *IEEE Trans. Comput.*, *C-33*(4), 374 (April 1984) for an example of natural codes used for benchmarking.
23. See, for example, Reinhart Ahlrichs et al., "Implementation of an Electronic Structure Program System on the CYBER 205," *J. Comput. Chem.*, *6*(3), 200–208 (1985); Harry Partridge and Charles W. Bauschlicher, "Algorithms vs. Architectures for Computational Chemistry," in *Supercomputers: Algorithms, Architectures, and Scientific Computation*, (F. A. Matsen and T. Tajima, eds.), University of Texas Press, Austin, 1986.
24. Leonard Uhr, "On Benchmarks: Dynamically Improving Experimental Comparisons," Tech. Report 571, December, 1984, Univeristy of Wisconsin, Madison. Univeristy of Wisconsin, Computer Sciences Department, 1210 West Dayton, Madison, WI 53706.

KENNETH M. DYMOND

CHINESE CHARACTERS AND ARTIFICIAL INTELLIGENCE

1 INTRODUCTION

At first glance, it seems rather strange to talk about artificial intelligence (AI) and Chinese characters. On one hand, AI is a kind of modern science and technology, whereas on the other, Chinese characters are one of the oldest tools for communication, with thousands of years of history. The question to be answered is what in the world is the relation, if any, between these two seemingly totally unrelated subjects?

In this article, I will point out that there is a very close relation between AI and Chinese characters from the knowledge point of view. A preliminary version of this article was presented in Ref. 1.

It is well known that unlike alphabetic and one-dimensional Western languages such as English, Chinese characters are two-dimensional and non-alphabetic. Each Chinese character is confined in a square area, henceforth called "square word." There is essentially no unique linear way of representing a Chinese character, and some characters are so complicated that they contain more than 30 strokes. Mainly because of this nature, it was widely believed for some time that Chinese characters are rather nonscientific and inappropriate for modern use by mechanical means such as computers. It was even once suggested that Chinese characters should be "alphabetized" (or romanized, latinized). Such an idea, if forcefully put into practice, would have essentially eliminated Chinese characters, thereby, losing all internal knowledge, rich culture, and artistic beauty associated with them.

Fortunately, however, after years of research and experiments, many effective methods have been developed for Chinese character data entry keyboard design, internal/external codes, and output/display techniques. Hundreds of technical papers and reports can be found in the literature, and dozens of different kinds of Chinese computers, typewriters, and word processors are avilable in the markets [2–5]. As a result, Chinese characters not only avoided the fate of being eliminated but people also began to realize that Chinese characters are not that difficult.

The main objective of this article is to point out further that Chinese characters are actually very valuable from the "intelligence" and knowledge points of view.

2 DEFINITIONS, NOTATIONS, AND BACKGROUNDS

According to the "Liu-Shu" 六書 Chinese characters can be basically classified into the following six categories: (a) hsiang-hsing (or pictorial imitative drafts) 象形; (b) chih-shih (or indicative symbols) 指事;

(c) hui-i (or logical aggregates) 會意; (d) hsing-sheng (or phonetic complexes) 形聲; (e) chuan-chu (or derived, adaptive meaning) 轉注; and (f) chia-chieh (or borrowing) 假借. There are more than 40,00 Chinese characters. About one tenth of them are commonly used [3,6-9]. More than 95% of them are in categories b-f and can be logically induced from very simple and basic structural patterns (category a), which bear a great resemblance to Mother Nature; therefore, their semantics meanings, interpretations) are normally immediately known from their imagery syntactic structures (shapes, appearances).

Many modern techniques in computer vision and image processing can be used to interpret the formation and evolution of Chinese characters, especially of category a. For examples, see Figure 1.

1. Thinning or skeletonization:

   ⋯ → 山, 山   (mountain)
   ⋯ → 口   (mouth)
   ⋯ → 火   (fire)
   ⋯ → 竹, 竹   (bamboo)
   ⋯ → 艸, 艹   (grass)
   ⋯ → 氵   (water)
                  [radical]

2. Topological transformation and feature extraction:

   ⋯ → 亻, 人   (man, people)
   ⋯ → 木   (tree)
   ⋯ → 手   (hand)
   ⋯ → 心   (heart)
   ⋯ → 日   (sun)
   ⋯ → 月   (moon)
   ⋯ → 水   (water)
   ⋯ → 田   (farm, field)

FIGURE 1. Some examples of simple Chinese characters and their relations to image processing. (Continued)

3. Rotation (with some variables)

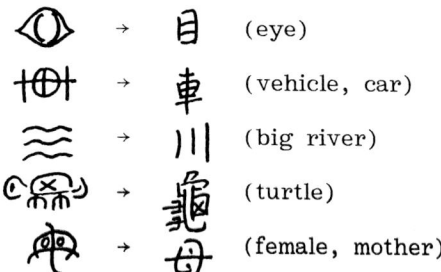

               → 目 (eye)

               → 車 (vehicle, car)

               → 川 (big river)

               → 龜 (turtle)

               → 母 (female, mother)

4. Image compression:

人 (people) → 众 (crowd)

田 (field) 土 (soil) → 墨 (base, castle)

石 (stone) 水 (water) → 泵 (pump)

木 (tree) 木 (tree) → 林 (woods)

木 (tree) 木 (tree) 木 (tree) → 森 (forests)

人 (man) 山 (mountain) → 仙 (fairy)

5. Segmentation: the fact that every character is confined in a square.

FIGURE 1 (Continued)

In this article, one or several combinations of Figure 1 will be called continuous transformation (CT) [5-9]. Through inference rules, CT and category *a* can be used to form (logically infer) more complicated characters (Fig. 2).

Please note that these examples involve image compression and are similar to the ICON concept (such as ⓘ, ⊖ horizontal concatenation, vertical concatenation, inclusion, overlapping, and a combination of some or all of the above [10].

3 SEMANTIC NETWORKS AND CHINESE CHARACTERS

Essentially, every Chinese character, be it a representation of a complicated, tangible, or visible object, or some abstract concept, can be formed from simpler ones. We will illustrate some examples for characterizing Chinese characters using the artificial intelligence concept known as "semantic networks."

A semantic network is a direct graph, in which each node (or vertex) represents some object or a specific concept, and each edge (or link) represents a certain relation (predicate). This node-and-link formalism of semantic networks is one of the most powerful and widely used knowledge representation methods. For instance, it has been developed to represent the meanings of English sentences in terms of objects and relationships among them.

1. Vertical concatenation:

巛 (flood) + 火 (fire) → 災 (disaster)

不 (not) + 正 (straight) → 歪 (tilted)

亡 (absent) + 心 (minded) → 忘 (forget)

亡 (absent) + 目 (eye) → 盲 (blind)

分 (divide) + 貝 (fortune) → 貧 (poor)

日 (sun) above — (horizon) → 旦 (dawn)

2. Horizontal concatenation:

人 (man) + 言 (words) → 信 (letter, trust)

日 (sun) + 月 (moon) → 明 (bright)

魚 (fish) + 羊 (lamb) → 鮮 (fresh, delicious)

3. Combinations of 1 and 2:

車 (car, truck) → 轟 (boom!)

石 (rock) → 磊 (solid, integrity)

4. Inclusion:

人 (man) + 囗 (confined in cell) → 囚 (prisoner)

韋 [phonetics](wei) + 囗 → 圍 (surround)

5. Others:

辶 (walk) + 隹 (bird) → 進 (forward)

止 (stop) + 戈 (spear) → 武 (to arm)

戶 (door) + 方 [phonetics](fong) → 房 (house, room)

宀 (roof) + 玉 (jade) + 缶 (bowl) + 貝 (shell) → 寶 (precious)

FIGURE 2 More complicated characters formed by simpler ones.

Chinese Characters and AI

Furthermore, the neural interconnections of the brain are arranged in a type of network, and the rough similarity between the semantic nets and the natural brain network helped to encourage the development of semantic nets. There are some practical advantages as well. There is an efficiency to be gained by representing each object or concept once and using pointers for cross-referencing, rather than naming an object explicitly every time it is involved in a relation (as in predicate calculus). Thus, not only can we gain an efficiency in space, but also search time may be faster. Therefore, the semantic network approach is clearly valuable for providing a graphic way for the AI researcher or system designer to view knowledge, which frequently suggests a practical and efficient way of implementing knowledge representations. A rather complete survey and further examples of knowledge representation methods and semantic networks can be found in Refs. 4 and 11.

In this section, we will illustrate how Chinese characters are represented by semantic networks. Please notice that in these examples, not only are all primitives (atoms) symbols, but they have meanings associated with them (each of which is naturally reflected from its syntax). Henceforth, they will be called semantic primitives (atoms). Basically, these semantic networks are hierarchial in nature. They can be parsed from the top down for learning purposes and can be hierarchially unfolded from the bottom up for recognition purposes.

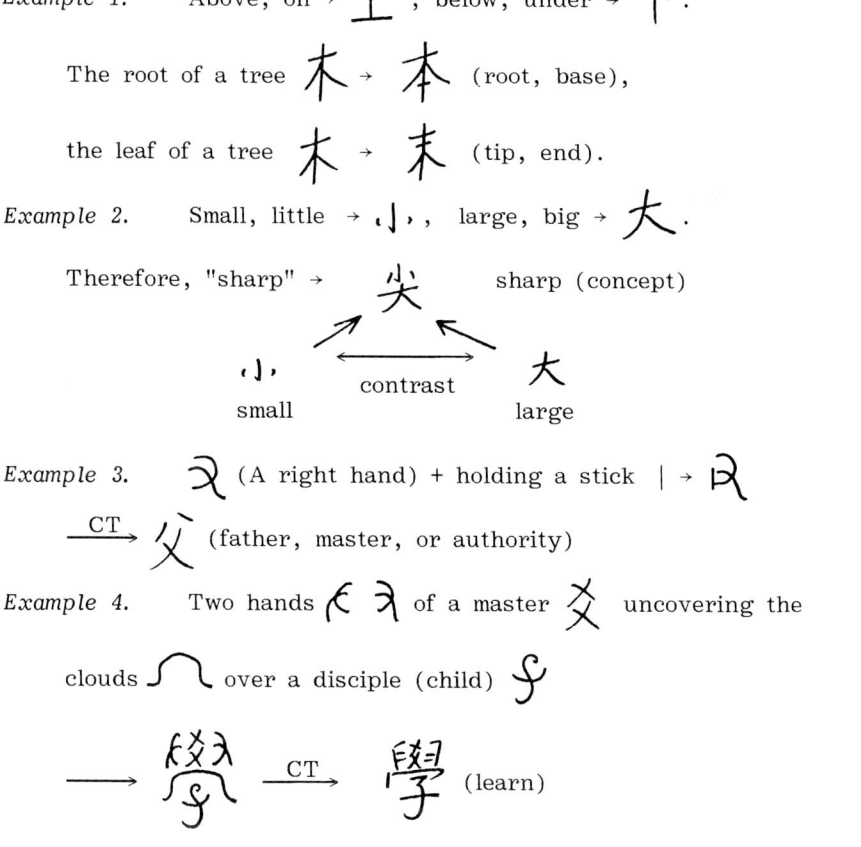

Example 5. Let

A = a giving hand
B = heart
C = a receiving hand

D = willing to sacrifice (to give)
E = something vital
F = the needy; and if A B C, then D E F

Therefore, if 〔giving hand / heart / receiving hand〕, then A B C, and if A B C then D E F.

∴, if 〔giving hand / heart / receiving hand〕 $\xrightarrow{CT}$ 愛 then "willing to give something vital to the needy"

Please note that here we use a well-known AI technique known as forward chaining: $P \supset Q$, $Q \supset R$, $\rightarrow P R$ or to put in PROLOG-like syntax Q:-P and R:-Q implies R:-P [12]. This can also be seen from the following Boolean algebra transformation:

$$P \supset Q = \sim P \vee Q$$
$$Q \supset R = \sim Q \vee r$$
$$\rightarrow \sim P \vee r = P \supset R$$

Example 5 can also be represented by a hierarchial semantic network as shown in Figure 3.

Because of these properties, i.e., hierarchial structures, knowledge inference, and syntax-semantic correlation, Chinese characters are very helpful in terms of understandability, learnability, and recognizability, and they are actually easy to memorize—a fact contrary to most peoples' intuitive impression. A closer look and analysis of 7,000 commonly used words also shows that those properties not only exist at character level but also at multicharacter word, phrase, or expression level. Some examples are the 12 months of the year and the 7 days of the week:

一月 January	五月 May	九月 September
二月 February	六月 June	十月 October
三月 March	七月 July	十一月 November
四月 April	八月 August	十二月 December

| Sunday | Monday | Tuesday | Wednesday | Thursday | Friday | Saturday |
| 星期日 | 星期一 | 星期二 | 星期三 | 星期四 | 星期五 | 星期六 |

Additional examples are 電冰箱 (refrigerator), and 人工智慧, AI. The names of the months and days of the week use numerals; it is easy to understand (and memorize) their sequences (e.g., it is easy to tell which day is before or after another day), and it is comparatively simple to calculate how many days there are between two certain dates. For other examples, please see 6-10.

Predicates: part-of, is-a, to receive, to give
Semantic primitives (atoms):

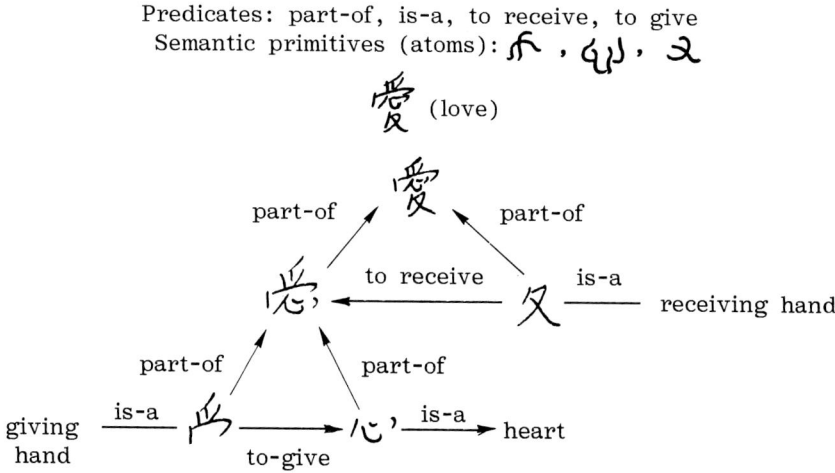

FIGURE 3 A semantic network of "愛".

Example 6. The words 智 and 慧, have the following semantic networks (ignoring all predicates, which are obvious).

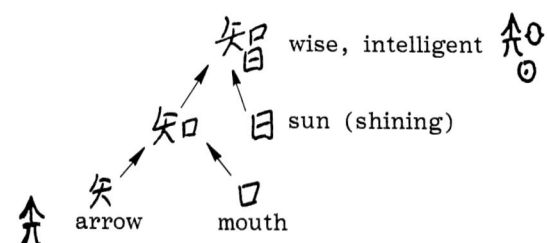

i.e., 智 (wise, intelligent) means quick response (reaction)—as fast and accurate as an arrow and shining like the sun.

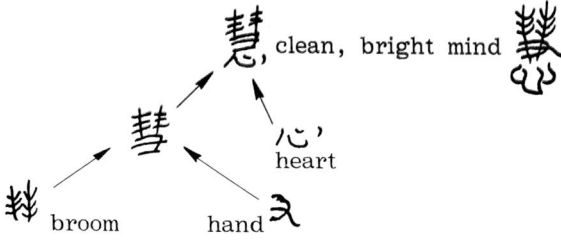

i.e., 慧, means clean and bright mind, as swept by a broom held in a hand

When 智 and 慧, are used together, they become "shining people with quick response (mouth), as accurate and fast as an arrow, whose minds are very clean and bright" → "wisdom."

Please notice that Examples 5 and 6 can also be represented by a propositional representation network (PRN) introduced by Ref. *13*. They are typical examples of category *c*, hui-i (logical aggregates), whereas Example 1 is in category *b*, chih-shih (indicative symbols) of Liu-Shu.

Example 7. For the characters 人工智慧 (AI), e.g., let

A = 人, B = 工, C = 智, D = 慧

Rules: A → man, B → made (elaborate), CD → wisdom = E.

∴ 人工智慧 → ABCD → ABE → man-made wisdom

∴ '人' '工' '智' '慧' → man-made wisdom

On the other hand, comparing this with English,

ARTIFICIAL INTELLIGENCE → ?

It should be noted, however, that many English words can be analyzed in a similar way. Philosophy = love of wisdom, geology = earth knowledge, dictionary = word list, etc. English words also have a rich etymology. The difference is that English words are basically phonetic, whereas Chinese words are rich both in imagery (pictorial, visual) and phonetics.

Example 8. Example 5 can also be demonstrated by the resolution principle [4,11].

Let S = (A → man, B → made, E → wisdom, A, B, E).

We can show that man-made wisdom logically follows from S. Using resolution principle and refutation process, this is equivalent to

S U (~[man-made wisdom]) is unsatisfiable.

A → man = ~A v man
B → made = ~B v made
E → wisdom = ~E v wisdom
~(man-made wisdom) = ~man v ~made v ~wisdom

```
~man v ~made v ~wisdom        ~A v man
       \                      /
   ~A v ~made v ~wisdom      ~B v made
         \                   /
      ~A v ~B v ~wisdom     ~E v wisdom
            \              /
         ~A v ~B v ~E     A
               \         /
             ~B v ~E    B
                 \     /
                  ~E   E
                   \  /
                   nil
```

ヽ, S → man-made wisdom, i.e., '人' '工' '智' '慧' → man-made wisdom.

Example 9. The multicharacter word 電冰箱 (refrigerator) can be analyzed as follows:

$$\begin{matrix} \text{sky} \\ \text{cloud} \\ \text{water drops} \end{matrix} \xrightarrow{\text{vertical concat and superimposition}} 雨 \xrightarrow{CT} 雨 \text{ (rain)}$$

Two hands holding a long stick (stretching from the sky to the ground)

→ 臼㣺| → 申 (stretch or electricity [simplified form])
                CT

雨 + 申 $\xrightarrow{\text{vertical concatenation}}$ 電 (electricity) [lightning induced by thunderstorm]

冫水 stands for "ice, or icy," belonging to the family of "coldness," e.g., 冷 (cold), 冬 (freeze), etc.

箱 stands for "box," belonging to the family of objects made of bamboo or wood (board).

∴ 電 + 冰 + 箱 → 電冰箱 (refrigerator)

meaning "electrical ice box" (to store food and prevent it from perishing. This word contains all essential properties and concise meanings of the object, and these meanings can be directly perceived from their pictorial images. Again, comparing this with English phonetic etymology (from Latin):

   Refrigerator = re (again) + frigerare (make-cold) + tor (that-which)
                = that which makes cold again

4 LOGICAL RELATIONS BETWEEN CHARACTERS

In most cases, objects (or concepts) sharing some common property are also represented by characters sharing the same pattern (also known as "radical" in a dictionary), characterizing the common property of the objects (or concepts) as partially illustrated in Example 9 of Section 3. This is further demonstrated by the following examples.

Example 10. Take the family of water, or liquid (whose radical is 冫) or 水). This is the largest category of more than 400 characters out of about 7,000 commonly used Chinese characters according to Ref. 3. Here is a list of some of them:

液 liquid	淋 shower	浸 soak	洗 to wash
溶 solvent	渴 thirsty	涕 tears	浮 to float
河 river	泡 bubble	清 clean	游 to swim
溪 stream	汪 deep sea	渠 ditch	沈 to sink
海 sea	淫 licentious	港 port	渡 to cross
洋 ocean	湄 shore	湯 soup	淹 to submerge
湖 lake	灘 beach	源 source	灌 to immigrate
油 oil	灣 bay	滾 boiling	澆 to splash
汽 vapor	溝 ditch	洪 flood	沐 to shampoo
決 turbulent	漁 fishery	溢 overflow	注 to pour
潭 deep lake	汁 juice	浪 billow	泣 to wail
泵 pump	泉 spring	汞 mercury	溺 to drown
池 pond	潮 tide	淼 overwhelming	

All of these characters have something in common and share the pattern 氵 or 水, whereas their English counterparts essentially have no relation to each other at all (probably bacause English words come from a variety of sources). Also notice that the pronunciation (phonetics) of most of these characters is characterized by their nonradical parts. For example, 油 is pronounced as 由, and 洋 is pronounced as 羊 etc. These are typical examples of hsing-sheng (phonetic complex) words.

Example 11. The family of 金 (metal), which has more than 200 words out of 7,000—the seventh largest family follows:

金 gold, metal	鉛 lead	鈷 cobalt	鋅 zinc
銀 silver	鈸 cymbals	鎳 nickel	鈴 jingling bell
銅 copper	鏈 chain	鎧 armor	錳 manganese
鐵 iron	鋼 steel	鐮 sickle	鎢 wolfram
錫 tin	鑼 gong	鑛 mineral	鑾 horse bell

銲 to weld　　鋸 to saw　　鈉 sodium
鍍 to gilt　　鎔 to mold　　鉀 potassium
鎖 to lock　　鍊 to refine　　鉑 platinum
鑷 to nip　　鏨 to chisel　　鈾 uranium
鑿 to pierce through　　鑽 to pierce a hole　　鋁 aluminum

These words are characterized by the common pattern 金, which is evolved from the classic form 🝤 representing a mine of ancient age. These are also typical examples of hsing-shen words. Again, the equivalent English words essentially have no logical connections at all, except in the last column. However, interestingly, this also indicates that even Westerners attempted to take advantage of "common patterns" when creating new words.

There are thousands of such examples. The largest 41 families contain more than 4,700 characters, about 68% of 7,000 commonly used Chinese characters. For some larger families, please refer to Example 12.

Example 12.

Family of	Radical	Examples	No. of characters
grass	艹 or 丱	草 (grass) 花 (flower)	350
hand	扌 or 手	打 (hit) 捉 (catch) 拿 (take)	330
plant	木	桿 (stick) 柱 (post)	319
heart	忄 or 心	志 (will) 怕 (fear)	260
mouth	口	吃 (eat) 喝 (drink) 吐 (vomit)	250
speech	言	說 (speak) 誓 (swear)	200
silk	糸	絲 (cotton) 細 (thin)	200
bamboo	竹 or 竹	笛 (flute) 笠 (bamboo hat)	170
worm	虫	蚊 (mosquito) 虱 (louse)	160

Family of	Radical	Examples	No. of characters
flesh	肉 or 月	肚 (stomach) 胖 (fat)	139
walk	辶	退 (return) 進 (forward)	120
man	人 or 亻	信 (letter) 命 (life)	116
illness	疒	病 (sick) 痛 (pain)	112
fire	火 or 灬	燒 (burn) 溫 (hot)	112

There are always some exceptions, i.e., some characters share a common pattern but do not have similar properties, some characters have a similar meaning but do not share a common pattern, and some characters have meanings and shapes that have little relation to each other. Most of these characters belong to the category of chuan-chu (adaptive meaning) or chia-chieh (borrowing) and are only a small portion of all Chinese characters.

5 VISUAL PERCEPTION, LEARNING, AND RECOGNITION

Visual perception plays a very important role in learning. This, perhaps, can be best demonstrated by the following example.

Example 13.

Sign	Meaning
⟶	one way (toward right)
⟵	one way (toward left)
⌐→	right turn only
⟵┐	left turn only
⌐→ (crossed)	no right turn
⟵┐ (crossed)	no left turn
U̸	no U turn
U	U turn allowed
P̸	no parking
?	information
☎	telephone

Chinese Characters and AI 49

Sign	Meaning
![no smoking symbol]	no smoking
![ladies symbol]	ladies' room
![mens symbol]	mens' room

The basic property of these signs is that the meaning (semantics) of each symbol is clearly reflected from its appearance (syntax). A learner can easily perceive these images and needs minimum effort and time to understand, recognize, and memorize them.

Chinese characters basically possess this same advantage as shown in Figure 1 and Example 1. These examples are of categories (a), hsiang-hsing, and (b), chih-shih, of Liu-Shu. Furthermore, existing knowledge accumulated from previous learning processes through visual perception can be very helpful in learning new characters. This is especially true when the new character to be learned has some logical relation with some characters already learned. When the learning process is completed, a certain kind of knowledge structure is formed to be used later to recognize input characters. This "learning recognition" two-phase philosphy for pattern recognition is analogous to the conventional one [6]. The difference here is that a knowledge structure instead of a "data-base dictionary" is used and that during the recognition phase any new input character can be fed back to the knowledge structure as a new addition for later use. This can be summarized in Figure 4. Here, each input Chinese character is viewed as an image, and all preprocessing techniques such as thinning, noise elimination, segmentation, compression, primitive selection, and feature extraction are implied [5, 6, 9].

In many cases, a Chinese character can be viewed as a piece of knowledge, and the character itself is treated as a memory storing the knowledge and subknowledge. One can form a piece of new knowledge from previously accumulated knowledge, and the existing knowledge should help one further to learn new characters. The logical relations between existing pieces of knowledge are essentially reflected from the syntactic structure of the character (refer to Examples 4, 5, 6, 9, and 14–16). Thus, the knowledge

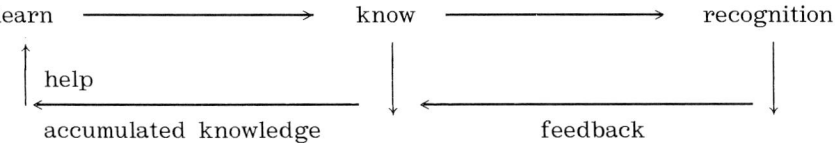

I have learned (understood and memorized); therefore, I know.
I know; therefore, I can recognize.
I now can recognize; therefore, it helps me to understand, memorize, learn, and know more characters.

FIGURE 4   The relation between learning, knowing, and recognizing.

formation, understanding, memorization, and retrieval can be very fast, and the space used to store the knowledge can be very efficient as well. If one can grasp this and take advantage of it, the learning, understanding, recognition, and memorization of Chinese characters could be much easier and faster than one might imagine, e.g., see the following examples.

Example 14.   Putting concepts together.

    A: What is "bright" (明)?

    B: Well, "bright" (明) means shining as, e.g., the sun (日) in the daytime, or the moon (月) in the evening.

The new concept 明 has a very close relation to the old, existing concepts of 日 and 月. Therefore, 日 and 月 can help to learn, understand, memorize, and recognize the new concept bright, denoted by the character 明, because they bear strong logical relations from visual perception. On the other hand, there is no such advantage in learning the English word b r i g h t.

Example 15.   Learning multicharacter Chinese words.

    A. What does "understand" (明　白) mean?

    B. Understand means to know something from darkness to the bright (明), white (白) daylight.

Example 16.   Learning a family of Chinese characters:

The family of "cattle"   牛   (evolved from the classical pictorial form 半, depicting the back view of a cattle)

母牛	cow
公牛	ox
水牛	buffalo
閹牛	bull
小牛	calf
小牛肉	veal
牛肉	beef
牛油	butter
牛排	steak
牛皮	cowhide
牛角	horn

It is well known that "indexing" is a very powerful data structure for organizing, sorting, and retrieving information. Realizing the hierarchial nature of Chinese characters, one could term a "multilevel indexing" system for organizing knowledge of Chinese characters. For instance, characters in Figure 1 and Example 1 are first-level indexing, those in Example 14 are second-level indexing, and those in Example 15 are third-level indexing.

According to Ausubel et al. [14], there are two basic types of learning, namely,

1. Learning by rote: A learning process by which new information is added to have learner's knowledge structure without establishing any relationship to the concepts already existing in the knowledge structure of the learner.
2. Meaningful learning: That learning process by which new information is related to the relevant concepts already existing in the knowledge structure of the learner.

According to Millward [15], "concept formation" is the process of learning appropriate concepts for a given situation, and the learner is guided by some kind of schema. As for learning Chinese characters, as an example, the discussions of Sections 2, 3, and 4 provide a foundation for such a schema. In the past, it was widely believed that Chinese characters were too complicated and too difficult to learn. Actually, such intuitive impression did not come into being because Chinese characters have too many strokes, but because the traditional method for learning Chinese characters is by rote. Learning by rote is a typical example of the inappropriateness of encoding and the inconvenience of retrieval. One simply stores into the memory isolated facts without any connections to other concepts already existing in the knowledge structure of the learner. Such learning generally is slow and gradual, such memorization difficult and partial, and such knowledge organization clumsy for later retrieval and recognition purposes.

On the other hand, meaningful learning takes place through a process of "subsumption," which is an interaction between the new concept (the subsumed) and the more inclusive concepts (subsumer). It results in a modification of both the subsumer and the subsumed concepts. Whereas the subsumer gets enriched by the addition of a new specific instance, the subsumed becomes part of a more general concept. Furthermore, the meaningfully learned material becomes part of the subsuming structure of the learner, which is the most crucial factor in facilitating subsequent learning. (See Fig. 4.) Things learned meaningfully are less likely to be forgotten. Even when forgotten, they leave a trace in the more general structures. Knowledge tends to be organized hierarchically as a result of the subsuming process.

From the discussions above, it is clear that because of their hierarchical structure, syntax-semantics correlation, and logical relations between them—Chinese characters possess a certain kind of rather unique advantage in terms of learning, understanding, memorization, and recognition.

6 ART AND CULTURE ASSOCIATED WITH CHINESE CHARACTERS

It should be pointed out that in many circumstances, language is not only just a tool for communication but also a reflection of culture and social phenomena, and sometimes, is a kind of art itself. It is interesting to see that Chinese characters have some kind of unique advantages in these aspects.

Example 17.   Beauty of balance?

When three trees, 木, are grouped together to form a new word (concept) of "forest," there are many ways of combining them as follows:

, etc.

But only the most beautiful one is adopted: 森. This appearance gives one a feeling of stability and balance, and indeed it looks like many trees growing on a mountain side. There are hundreds of such examples, e.g., 产 (produce), 飞 (fly), etc.

Example 18.   Beauty of symmetry

Numerals: 一, 二, 三, 四, 六, 八, 十, 百, 千, 萬, 兆,
Others: 口, 田, 中, 申, 由, 甲, 日, 車, 東, 亘, 旦, ---

and there are hundreds of other such examples.

Balance and symmetry not only make Chinese characters beautiful but also make them easier to learn and recognize. Mechanically speaking, they can also help save space.

Human relations play a very important role in the evolution of human civilization and culture. As the basic units of Chinese language, Chinese characters are an inherent part of Chinese civilization and culture.

Example 19.   Human relationships.

   A: Who is this gentleman?
   B: He is my uncle.
   A: From your mother's side?
   B: No, from my father's side.
   A: Younger than your father?
   B: No, elder.
   A: Oh, he is your father's elder brother.

The hero of the above dialogue can be represented by a single Chinese character, 伯. There is no such single equivalent word in English. It shows how important Chinese people consider human relationships to be.
In terms of difficulty of pattern recognition, although it is seemingly easier to recognize an English character (letter) than a Chinese character, this is not always the case at the word level. For instance, recognizing the English word "uncle" is not equivalent to recognizing the Chinese character 伯, but recognizing "father's elder brother" is.

Chinese Characters and AI

There are other examples considering the roots or origin of a character related to culture.

Example 20. The word "home" 家 is composed of two parts, a roof 宀 and a pig 豕, which was evolved from pictorial form 豕. From this word, one learns that in ancient times (perhaps still true now in parts of China), almost every family (especially farmers) had some pigs living under the roof as part of the household. It should be pointed out that for thousands of years, much of the Chinese population has been made up of farmers, and pork has always been a major food source.

Example 21. Chinese characters are especially good for literary writing, such as poems. One line from a famous poem by Tu-fu (712-770 A.D.), the Saint of Poetry, reads

感 時 花 濺 淚

(My heart) touched (moved) by the tragic time, (my) tears splash unto the flowers.

The basic spirit and meaning of this paragraph is visibly and vividly reflected from the radicals 心, 日, 艹, 氵, and 氵. It is interesting to see that all of these characters are hsing-sheng words.

7 A COMMENT ON SIMPLIFIED CHINESE CHARACTERS

Even though meaningful learning is a better choice for learning Chinese characters, some Chinese characters contain too many strokes. To ease the difficulty of learning, one would naturally ask, "Should some Chinese characters be simplified? and if yes, how?" This has long been a concern for many people. I think the answer is a cautious yes, but must come with extreme care. A simplified character should essentially maintain (a) syntax-semantics correlation, (b) induced knowledge, (c) culture continuity, and (d) artistic beauty and should (e) avoid ambiguity.

In a way, some existing simplified Chinese characters are reasonable. For instance,

体 body, 礼 rites, 变 change, 台 terrace, etc.

But some simplified characters do not satisfy the above-mentioned five criteria, and they not only cannot help learners but actually might create confusion and frustration. The following illustrates some examples that are especially critical.

Example 22. It is widely believed that "heart" is the most essential part of "love." That is why the symbol ♡ is often used to denote love. It does not need any explanation and is immediately understood even by children. Please see Figure 5.

I ♡   I ♡
M̬y D̬ad   M̬y M̬om
I ♡ NEW YORK   I ♡ MY MOM
I ♡ NEW YORK   I ♡ MY MOM
I ♡ NEW YORK   I ♡ MY MOM
I ♡ NEW YORK   I ♡ MY MOM
I ♡ NEW YORK   I ♡ MY MOM
I ♡ NEW YORK   I ♡ MY MOM
I ♡ NEW YORK   I ♡ MY MOM
I ♡ NEW YORK   I ♡ MY MOM

FIGURE 5   The symbol of love.

If the Chinese character 愛 is too complicated and needs to be simplified, it is the comparatively unimportant part that should be cut, instead of the vital, essential portion. Unfortunately, its simplified version 爱 eliminates the heart. By doing so, the syntax is simplified, but the essential semantics is lost. Furthermore, the simplified version is very similar to another word, 受 (to receive), which has a rather different, if not opposite, meaning, for love normally means to sacrifice or give.

In much of China nowadays, husbands and wives call "lover" to each other. This is easily understood because husbands and wives are supposed to love each other, whole-"heartedly" and from the bottom of one's heart. Yet, everyday and at every corner the word love is heard, seen, and thought of by hundreds of millions of Chinese people; and every time this word is encountered, it is visually perceived as "heartless." To love without heart is just lip service. It is simply not love. The basic spirit and essential meaning of love is lost. The subconscious and psychological impact of this perception could be immeasurable. It is not known how much this has contributed to the rising divorce rate there; but from a knowledge point of view, this simplification is very inappropriate and unfortunate. On the other hand, realizing the knowledge inferred from the syntactic structure of 愛 (please refer to Fig. 3 of Section 3), one will find that it is not difficult and boring but actually very interesting to learn and easy to understand, memorize, and recognize this word.

Example 23. The character 華 means "flowery," or "splendid" and has evolved from the classic pictorial form, 蕐. Although it is a bit complicated and has many strokes, these strokes are just not arbitrary. In fact, from its syntactic structure, one can feel a sense of beauty rising from hundreds of flowers blossoming. This word has long been widely used to denote China—her race, people, land, culture and nation. Unfortunately, however, its simplified version, 华, consists of two parts: 化 (to change, to divide)

and 十 (10). Because of this simplification, it gives one a rather ominous perception. There is a famous saying "United we stand; divided we fall." It is reasonable to say that no nation in this world willingly wants to be divided, not into 2 pieces, let alone 10! Why should China be an exception? Again, the long-term subconscious impact and psychological damage from this visual perception could be beyond measure. This is another example indicating that it is not wise and worthy to save a few strokes by sacrificing the true meaning and spirit of the original character.

Example 24. The word 親 means "dear," or "loving." Therefore, 親人 means "relative," or "beloved ones." Relatives or beloved ones are supposed to see each other often. That is why the character contains 見 (to see), which is evolved from 目 (eye) with two eyebrows, 儿. Yet, the simplified version, 亲, deletes 見, making one perceive 親人不見面 (beloved ones cannot meet each other). This seems a bit unreasonable and inhumane. Even worse, the simplified version is very close to another word, 妾 (concubine). Just imagine the following sentence 我有二亲人 (I have two relatives). It could be misunderstood (misperceived) as 我有二妾 (I have two concubines!) It is easy to see the confusion and frustration that this misperception might cause.

Example 25. The word 躍 means to leap. The basic spirit and meaning of this word are reflected from three parts: 足 (foot), 羽 (wing), and 隹 (bird). The character 進 has the similar spirit reflected by 辶 (move) and 隹 (bird). Yet the simplified versions, 跃 and 进, have lost a major portion of their original spirits and meanings. Even worse, 跃 is close to another word, 妖 (devil), and 进 is similar to 井 (well).

There was once a movement called 大躍進, which later resulted in failure and disaster. It was supposed to mean "great leap forward," but its simplified version, 大跃进, gives one the feeling of "a big devil fell into a well (and is trapped down there)"—entirely opposite the basic spirit and meaning of its original intention. This perception may have contributed to the failure of that movement; nevertheless, this is another example of inappropriate simplification of Chinese characters.

Example 26. I believe that most Chinese people have seen the poster 我愛中華, which means "I(whole heartedly) love China (splendid)."

Original words	Meaning	Simplified words	Could be mistakenly perceived as
我	I	我	I
愛	love	爱	受 accept or tolerate
中	China	中	中 China
華	splendid	化 十	化 十 divide 10

FIGURE 6 An example written vertically.

Everyday, hundreds of millions of people read this poster everywhere. It is a very important piece of work for Chinese people to remember and follow. Yet, its simplified version, 我爱中华, gives one a feeling of "I accept (that) China (be) divided (into) 10 (pieces)" or "I tolerate (that) China (be) divided (into) 10 (pieces)." Because Chinese sentences can also be written vertically, please compare this to the following vertical setting (which should be read vertically) (Fig. 6).

This vertical writing, in particular, can easily be ambiguously misperceived because of the vertical concatenation of 化 and 十. There are many other such examples. For a brief summary, please refer to Figure 7.

8 AMBIGUITY AND THE PRINCIPLES OF NEW CHARACTERS

It is interesting to note that the above findings are consistent with the concept of the degrees of learnability, ambiguity, and recognizability introduced in Ref. 5. In that article, several recognition methods for line-drawing patterns were analyzed and compared with each other. It was concluded that degrees of ambiguity play a very important role in learning, understanding, and recognition of line-drawing patterns such as English. It certainly is also true for Chinese characters. Here the concept of ambiguity is defined as the property of a syntax having two or more different interpretations (semantics) [5,9].

The findings of this article, especially of Sections 5-7, support the following principle of new characters (NC):

In creating or modifying a character, x, if the syntax of character x is very similar to an existing character, y, the semantics of x should also be very similar to that of y.

This principle can be formalized as follows:

Original form	Meaning	Simplified form	Could be mistakenly perceived as (meaning)
愛	love	爱	受 (receive, accept)
賓	honored guest	宾	兵 (soldier, fighter)
親	relative	亲	妾 (concubine)
華	beautiful flowery	华	化十 (divide ten)
躍	leap	跃	妖 (devil)
進	forward	进	井 (well)
聖	saint	圣	怪 (strange)
衛	protect	工	工 (labor)
術	technology	术	求 (beg)
鬥	fight	斗	斗 (Chinese peck, container)
葉	leaf	叶	汁 (juice)
無	none	无	尤 (especially)
鐵	iron	铁	金失 (metaless)
飛	fly, float	飞	[lose semantics and balance]
產	produce	产	[lose semantics and balance]
廠	factory	厂	[lose phonetics and balance]
廣	wide	广	[lose phonetics and balance]
氣	gas	气	[lose phonetics, part of knowledge and balance]

FIGURE 7 A brief summary of some inappropriate simplified Chinese characters. Please notice that 厂 and 丿 are also syntactically too close.

NC Principle 1: Let X = set of all Chinese characters and Sem be a unary predicate, Sem(x) be the semantics of character x ∈ X, Sim be a binary predicate over X, Sim(x,y) + T if x's and y's syntactic structures are similar (i.e., the difference between x and y is within a minimum range), and Simi be a binary predicate over the set of all semantics associated with Chinese characters (i.e., Simi[Sem(x), Sem(y)] = T if Sim(x,y) = T), then

if Sim (x.y) where x, y ∈ X, then Simi(Sem[x],Sem[y])

Since (if A then B) = (if ~B then ~A), it is also true that if the semantics of two words, x and y, are very different, their syntactic structures should also be very different (i.e., see the following).

NC Principle 2:

if ~Simi(Sem[x], Sem[y]) then ~Sim (x,y), where x,y ∈ X

Of course, there are always some exceptions in existing words and they do cause some confusion, e.g., the following English words,

ballot vs. bullet, revolutionary vs. evolutionary, words vs. swords, laboratory vs. lavatory, persecution vs. prosecution, champion vs. champagne vs champaign vs. campaign, etc.

As for Chinese characters, some famous examples are

太 (very, wife) vs. 犬 (dog); 曰 (read) vs. 日 (day), 母 (female) vs. 毋 (not), etc.

There is a famous proverb, 臨難母苟免，臨財母苟得, which means "Don't dodge difficulty and don't take any fortune that does not belong to you." Its syntax and phonetics together could be ambiguously perceived as 臨難母狗免，臨財母狗得, meaning "a female dog can avoid difficulty (disaster) and a female dog can take coming fortune." No wonder there is a joke about someone wanting to be reborn as a female dog.

If we cannot change things from the past, at least, we should correct those inappropriately simplified words and follow the NC principles in the future to avoid further confusion and frustration when simplifying or creating new characters.

9 CONCLUSIONS AND TOPICS FOR FUTURE RESEARCH

In conclusion, Chinese characters are not only semantically meaningful and intelligent sounding but also artistically elegant and culturally rich. It is hoped that this article can stimulate more research in the future such as intelligent learning system for Chinese characters, Chinese language understanding, automatic translation, and semantic pattern recognition of Chinese characters.

1. P. S. P. Wang, "Knowledge Pattern Representation of Chinese Characters," *IJPRAI*, 2(1), 161–179 (1988).
2. Y. H. Chu (ed.), "Chinese/Kanji Text and Data Processing," *IEEE Comput. Special Issue*, 18(1) (1985).
3. Liang Shi-chiu (ed.), *A New Practical Chinese English Dictionary*, Far East Book Co., 1971.
4. S. L. Tanimoto, *The Elements of Artificial Intelligence*, Computer Science Press, 1987.
5. P. S. P. Wang, "A New Character Recognition Scheme with Lower Ambiguity and Higher Recognizability, *Pattern Recognition Lett.*, 3, 431–436 (1985).
6. K. S. Fu, *Syntactic Pattern Recognition and Applications*, Prentice Hall, Englewood Cliffs, NJ, 1982.
7. *Kang-Hsi Dictionary* (new ed.), Chin-Yeh Book Pub. Co., Taipei, 1981.
8. P. S. P. Wang (ed.), "Part 5: Chinese Computing," in *Computer Vision, Image Processing and Communication—Systems and Applications*, World Scientific Pub. Co., Singapore, 1986.
9. P. S. P. Wang, "A More Natural Approach for Recognition of Line-Drawing Pattern," in *Image Pattern Recognition: Algorithm Implementations, Techniques, and Technology*, SPIE, 1987, vol. 755, pp. 141–160.
10. S. K. Chang, "ICON Semantics—A Formal Approach to ICON System Design," *Int. J. Pattern Recognition Artif. Intell. (IJPRAI)*, 1(1), 103–120 (1987).
11. P. Winston, *Artificial Intelligence*, Addison-Wesley, Reading, PA, 1984.
12. L. Sterling and E. Shapiro, *The Art of PROLOG*, MIT Press, Cambridge, MA, 1986.
13. Kai Chu, "Cognitive Aspects in Chinese Character Processing," *IEEE Workshop on Automation Language* (Spain), 1985, pp. 141–163.
14. D. P. Ausubel, J. D. Novak, and H. Hanesian, *Educational Psychology: A Cognitive View*, 2nd ed., Holt, Rinehart, and Winston, New York, 1978.
15. R. B. Millward, "Models of Concept Formation," in *Aptitude, Learning, and Instruction* (R. E. Snow et al., eds.), Lawrence Erlbaum Associates, Hillsdale, NJ, 1980.

PATRICK SHEN-PEI WANG

CRYPTOLOGIC RESEARCH IN THE LATE TWENTIETH CENTURY

INTRODUCTION

Communication has become an increasingly dominant interest of the human race over several millenia. Indeed, we have now come to the point where communication is becoming intrusive; it is thrust upon us whether we like it or not by one of the media. Privacy of communication has also long been another important consideration, being sought first, we are told, by the ancient Egyptians and the Greeks; it is to these early peoples that we owe the invention of the first codes and ciphers. The methods invented 3,000 or 4,000 years ago feature in some of today's systems for ensuring privacy, though the complexity with which these methods are applied has changed out of all recognition; some of the early ciphers, e.g., the Caesar cipher, are trivial in the extreme, though well thought of at the time they were first conceived.

At this point, we must distinguish between codes and ciphers. Codes are based closely on table look-up procedures, with groups of characters being treated together; examples include the commercial codes used mainly for data compression (because the code books for commercial ciphers are published, such codes do not actually provide secrecy of communication). Ciphers, on the other hand, usually take characters one at a time and apply some algorithm to transform them into some other character; ciphers can be divided broadly into transposition ciphers (where characters or bit order is jumbled) and substitution ciphers (where characters are exchanged for other characters); the process is usually, but not always, controlled by a key (a data field). Transposition and substitution are often found in combination in the stronger ciphers known as "product" ciphers. To obtain the original message, a reverse transformation must be applied; usually the same key controls the processes of encipherment and decipherment. Codes and ciphers are sometimes used in combination, but in the discussion that follows we shall be concerned almost exclusively with ciphers and not with codes.

It is well known that governments have always been very much involved in the technology of developing and using codes and ciphers with the object of protecting diplomatic and military communications. In past centuries, the major nations all maintained an organization of the "black chamber" type, with responsibility both for inventing the means of protecting information of national importance and for breaking into the communication systems of rival nations. The science of cryptology could almost have been called a "black art" at this time.

Lay interest in secrecy systems has always been lively. The human race is curious by nature, liking to delve into the unknown or forbidden, and there have been important publications giving an overview of what was known of such systems [1-3]. The most significant study of classical codes and ciphers is of relatively recent date [4]. David Kahn's treatment of the subject can be read in several ways. It is a racy and enthralling account of the personalities involved in cryptology, of the challenges facing them, and of the techniques they developed or demolished. On the other hand, Kahn gives a scholarly analysis and review of the classical systems, pointing out their strengths and weaknesses, right through from the codes and ciphers of the ancient Greeks up to the electromechanical cipher machines that were in use in World War II. As a general introduction to the subject, it is hard to find a better text.

At the time Kahn's book was published, a veil of secrecy still hung over much of the cryptologic technology of the twentieth century. Earlier writers, such as Helen Fouché Gaines [5], had given comprehensive studies of the ciphers in use in the nineteenth century and of their cryptanalysis. However, a study of Gaines' text soon reveals that the cipher systems described therein are not sufficiently strong to withstand cryptanalytic attack using relatively straightforward techniques; such techniques can be implemented very efficiently using today's computing power. Stronger systems were called for and, in due course, they appeared.

Most of the cipher systems of the last century were based on "pencil and paper" methods and were consequently laborious and slow in operation; they were also heavily prone to human error, leading to loss of communication or even misinformation. From the late eighteenth century onward cipher machines began to emerge that were designed to take much of the human factor out of cipher operation. One of the earliest is the Jefferson cylinder, invented by the third president of the United States and reinvented about a century and a quarter later; this is not strictly a mechanical cipher, though its operation required possession of a mechanical device.

Various attempts were made during the nineteenth century to create a machine that would turn plaintext reliably into ciphertext and vice versa; none of these could be said to be really successful, though some of them were quite ingenious, e.g., the disk cipher of Charles Wheatstone; low speed of operation was often a factor discouraging their use. The first practicable cipher machines began to emerge during the years of World War I and in the decade that followed. These were almost all electromechanical, with the exception of one or two pneumatic devices. Their inventors were men like Hagelin, Scherbius, and Hebern. Some devices led to very important developments, whereas others faded out. Perhaps the most important were the series of machines invented by Boris Hagelin, used by many nations, and the series developed from the Scherbius machine, leading to the Enigma, mainly used by the axis powers in World War II.

It is widely held that modern computing techniques have developed from the electromechanical machines that were developed during World War II with the object of cryptanalyzing enemy cipher systems. Since David Kahn wrote his book, much has been written about the "Colossus" series of machines that were built for the U.K. Government Code and Cipher School at Bletchley Park as a means of attacking ciphers of Nazi Germany. The successful work at Bletchley Park is believed to have had an immense influence on the outcome of the war. Of similar significance in the United States was the work of Friedman in breaking Japanese electromechanical cipher systems.

It is fairly obvious that computing techniques not only can be applied to cryptanalysis but also can be used for cryptography, i.e., they can be used to generate ciphers. Since the time of Colossus, we have progressed from electromechanical computers to electronic machines, first with thermionic valves, then with transistors, and now with integrated circuits. This progression has been accompanied by enormous increases in speed of operation and by the availability of vastly greater data stores. It is indeed fortunate for the cryptographer whose task is to protect data against disclosure or alteration that computing techniques can be applied to create stronger ciphers. The fact that computing techniques are also available to the cryptanalyst, the enemy of the cryptographer, is important, but on the whole, modern computing methods have enabled the cryptographer to keep several jumps ahead of the cryptanalyst.

We have already implied that much modern cryptography is subject to secrecy under government control. The methods used to protect diplomatic and military traffic are not made public. They are developed either by special-purpose government establishments or by contractors working for those establishments. The supply of equipment capable of implementing ciphers of this kind is under strict control. Such ciphers cannot therefore be the subject of articles such as this. What, then, is there to write about? There is little room for yet another work on classical ciphers. Indeed, such a work would have largely academic interest, because classical ciphers are believed to be no longer widely in use.

The spread of data communications in the last 25 years has changed the practice of commerce and of industry. It is unthinkable for a modern business corporation of any size to consider not making use of modern computing and communication facilities. Survival of a business may depend on the degree to which the user can trust his computing and communication systems. Trust implies that information processed or transported is not disclosed to unauthorized parties and that it cannot be altered by such parties without detection (often it is not possible to *prevent* alteration; the answer is always to be able to *detect* it). These properties are, respectively, those of privacy and integrity. Encipherment can be used to achieve both of these desiderata. It is for this reason that interest has developed in the technology of cryptology outside the diplomatic and military fields. In this article, an overview is presented of what has been happening in academic circles and in research and development establishments in this field which, for want of a better term, will be called the "civil" field, as distinct from the military and diplomatic. Interest in cryptology in the civil field is now at a very high level, with very many workers active in the field in the United States, Europe, Japan, and elsewhere, and several conferences held each year devoted to the subject. Such is the scale of interest that only broad brush treatment will be given to much of what is going on. An apology is offered in advance to those researchers whose work is not mentioned or is given inadequate coverage.

THE BEGINNING OF CIVIL CRYPTOLOGY

Toward the end of the 1960s, banks were showing an increasing interest in the possibility of giving account holders access to cash through automatic teller machines (ATMs). Clearly, such a service would need protection against fraud; therefore, it was important that the tokens given to customers and the personal identification numbers (PINs) associated with those tokens should be inviolate for practical purposes. ATMs communicating with central processors would need protection. It was realized by system designers that one essential feature of such operations would be the ability to encipher data, either to protect PINs in transit to host computers and the replies from the hosts or to conceal the relationship between PIN and other data on the customer token if PIN validation was to be off-line.

Such a requirement was one of the reasons behind the development of the Lucifer cipher system by IBM. This was a block cipher that handled data in blocks of 128 bits and used a key, also of 128 bits, to control the encipherment process. The design principles included the properties of diffusion and confusion, first defined by Shannon [6] about 20 years earlier; essentially Lucifer was a product cipher. What was different about Lucifer was that IBM found it possible to publish most of the details of its operation in an article [7].

Publication of the way in which a cipher worked was a considerable departure from previous practice. The traditional attitude had always been that part of the security of a system lay in not revealing how the cipher protecting that system worked. With Lucifer, almost all of the security lay in keeping the key secret. It was judged that knowledge of the cipher was not a sufficient advantage for any person trying to attack a system relying on Lucifer for its protection. This policy revealed considerable confidence on the part of IBM in the irreversibility of the Lucifer algorithm.

The next important influence in leading to civil cryptology was the U.S. government. It was judged by the federal government that there was a class of data, below that classified by the military or diplomatic services, which required protection against unauthorized intrusion. The institution charged with providing the means of achieving this protection was the National Bureau of Standards (NBS) of the U.S. Department of Commerce. Under the Brooks Act (Public Law 89-306) the NBS has responsibility for setting federal standards for the effective and efficient use of computer systems. Acting under this remit, the NBS initiated a study program on computer security.

As part of the computer security program, NBS issued a call in May 1973 for submission of cipher algorithms that could form the basis of a Federal Information Processing Standard; the algorithm must be publishable (compare Lucifer, above), it must be easy to implement and to validate, and it must be secure and efficient. Many submissions were made in 1973, but none was found suitable. In August 1974, the call was repeated, and this time it was answered by IBM with an algorithm developed from Lucifer. This algorithm, since called the "Data Encryption Standard," was selected and eventually became a federal standard [8] in 1977. In 1981, it was adopted as an American National Standards Institute (ANSI) standard [9].

The DES is a block cipher, with a block size of 64 bits, and operates under the control of a key of 64 bits, of which 8 are given over to parity; the effective key size is therefore 56 bits. The algorithm contains elements of substitution and transposition, with 16 internal cycles that are controlled by 48-bit "cycle keys" derived from the main 56-bit key. The internal structure of the DES contains a number of bit permutation tables (implementing transposition) and eight substitution tables (the latter are known as S-boxes, accepting 6-bit input fields and producing 4-bit outputs). Since its announcement, there have been many implementations of the DES, ranging from very fast special-purpose hardware to comparatively slow microprocessor implementations.

The relationship between plaintext, ciphertext, and keys for the DES (and for any other symmetric block cipher) is shown in Figure 1.

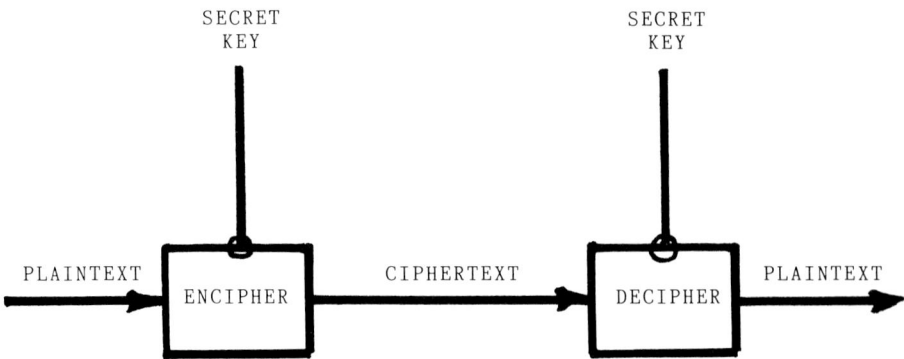

FIGURE 1 Symmetric block cipher.

Perhaps the most comprehensive review of the DES can be found in the book by Meyer and Matyas [10]; their analysis shows that any detectable correlation between plaintext and ciphertext has vanished by the end of the fifth of the 16 internal cycles. Why then should there be any controversy relating to the DES?

There was indeed considerable criticism aimed at the DES within a short time of its publication. One of the chief points of criticism related to the key length adopted. The 56 bits for DES was considerably shorter than the 128 bits for Lucifer from which DES was derived, in part. Much of the criticism at this stage came from M. Hellman, who demonstrated that, given a very powerful cryptanalytic engine specific to the DES, it would be possible to derive a key from a plaintext/ciphertext pair in less than half a day on average. The weakness in this argument lay in the infeasibility of obtaining the necessary cryptanalytic engine, let alone running it successfully.

Another criticism of the DES has been the secrecy surrounding the design criteria for some of its component parts; IBM has been asked not to disclose these criteria for reasons of national security. It has been said that in developing the criteria, IBM rediscovered some design principles that were relevant to other cipher systems not in the public domain.

The volume of academic criticism led NBS to hold two important meetings in 1975 [11] and 1976 [12]. These meetings attempted to place a safe lifetime on the DES, using the best projections of progress in computing technology that might be used in a cryptanalytic attack; in the event these meetings gave the DES a clean bill of health for the applications for which it was intended for at least 5 years. Since that time, the DES has been reviewed at roughly 5-year intervals and is currently undergoing a further review. We shall comment on its possible future later in this article.

ACADEMIC STUDIES OF THE DES

The first important academic study of the DES from the point of view of attempted cryptanalysis was carried out at Stanford University, with the results published in September 1976 [13]; 7 researchers were active, and 10 person-weeks were applied to the work. Bit complementation of plaintext, ciphertext, and key was observed and was claimed to allow a saving of 50%

in cryptanalysis time; this is a fairly obvious property. The effect of altering S-boxes (not an available option in practice) was demonstrated to produce significant weakness; although the S-boxes are not linear, they were seen to be closer to linear than would be expected (the fourth S-box was shown to be 75% redundant). Certain arguments were advanced about the feasibility of building an "exhaustive search" cryptanalytic machine. Apart from these observations, the early work at Stanford did not produce other results of deep significance.

Various other interesting discoveries were made in academic circles concerning the DES early in its lifetime. Apart from the complementation property, another interesting discovery was that there were four keys having the property that a ciphertext produced by one of them, if re-enciphered (note, *not* deciphered) with the same key, would return immediately to the original plaintext. Not so obvious was the property that there were six pairs of keys such that encipherment by one of them, followed by encipherment with the other key of the pair, would also lead back to the original plaintext.

These special keys are known, respectively, as weak and semiweak, and their use is generally discouraged when generating keys for DES systems. The reason for their occurrence is well understood. The difference between encipherment and decipherment with the DES is essentially one of presenting the internal cycle keys in the reverse order; this is a very attractive property, as it facilitates implementation. The internal cycle keys are derived from the 56-bit main key; if the bits of the latter are all one or all zero, there is no difference in any of the internal cycle keys. Hence, if all of the cycle keys are the same, there is no difference between their forward and reverse order; encipherment and decipherment are then exactly the same transformation. The other two weak keys are half-ones and half-zeros. The same kind of reasoning accounts for the semiweak keys.

The semiweak keys were first observed by Donald Davies, who also made the observation that the following of certain "bit paths" around the internal cycle structure of the DES produced certain very regular results with respect to the S-boxes [14]. The S-boxes are customarily numbered 1 through 8, and their 6 input bits can be designated a through g. Taking into account the two permutation operations that occur in the DES main loop, together with the S-box structure, if the paths are followed from one set of inputs to the next and directed arcs are drawn to illustrate what is happening, the directed arcs form Hamiltonian cycles of considerable regularity. It is possible to speculate that this regularity was a design intention, though no explanation has been publicly advanced for the phenomenon.

In 1983 [15], it was suggested that encipherment keys other than the weak and semiweak categories could lead to regular patterns in the internal cycle keys that would lead, in turn, to serious weakness of the DES. The suggestion was made that there were indeed 25 classes of weak keys and that the strongest of these could be cryptanalyzed in 4 hours. At the same time the claim was made that keys in general could be found in 8 hours. No evidence has been advanced in support of these claims and they are generally not accepted.

More recently, closer attention has been paid to the DES and its properties, with the result that several new discoveries have been made and published. These results have come from the University of Louvain in Belgium, MIT, and the Weizmann Institute in Israel. Other groups have also looked at the subject, but with rather less dramatic results; a number of research teams have considered what would be the strength of the algorithm if there were a lesser number of internal cycles. As yet, no insight has been revealed into any weakness of the DES arising from work on a "cut-down" version of the algorithm.

From Louvain, in association with the Belgian company, Philips, a series of papers has been produced giving observations of a number of unexpected properties of the DES algorithm. One of the earliest of these papers appeared in 1983 [16]. Using various equivalent representations of the DES algorithm, the investigators showed that it was possible to specify a totally iterative representation of the DES, that the DES could be properly described with one fewer internal table, and that the algorithm could be related to the mixing transformation of Shannon, to nonlinear shiftback register theory and to permutation networks. The investigators suggest that the main significance of the work is to allow better insight into the design criteria and to permit more efficient implementation. In 1984, members of the Belgian team produced another paper [17] that sought to assess the degree of dependence of output on input of the DES, with particular interest in small avalanche characteristics. In this paper, some new properties of the S-boxes were observed; in particular, the workers investigated the effect of fixing certain S-box input bits and observed the effect on the output bits of varying the other input bits (this parallels the work of Shamir, discussed below). Another test involved complementing certain S-box input bits and observing the effect on the output. A further aspect of the investigation examined the key scheduling, basing the study on a DES with a limited number of internal cycles. Interesting properties connecting the S-box structure with the performance of the algorithm were observed. Readers are encouraged to refer to the original paper for the many observations made. The workers again assert that more light is thrown upon the DES by their results, but no claim is made that cryptanalysis has yet been made any easier.

In 1985, some interesting observations were made of the DES by the MIT team led by Ronald Rivest [18,19]; this team asked the question "Is the Data Encryption Standard a group?" The interest arose from the suggestion that if the set of permutations describing the DES transformation were closed under functional composition, the DES would be vulnerable to a known plaintext attack running in 2^{28} steps, on average. The evidence of this piece of research showed, with a high degree of confidence, that the DES is not a group. However, a surprising result was obtained when, as part of the work, a cycling test was made on the DES for randomly chosen keys and for alternate encipherment with each of a pair of weak keys (all zeros and all ones, respectively). The result from the latter experiment showed that a cycle length of less than 2^{33} was observed, far less than predicted according to a theoretical analysis. The probability of such an occurrence was calculated to be less than 1 in 10^9 if the permutation were chosen at random from the symmetric group on message M. The observation was indeed startling and could have had far-reaching significance. However, the reason for the phenomenon was given by Don Coppersmith [20], who pointed out the previously unsuspected property that, given a weak key, there are 2^{32} fixed points for the DES; in such cases, a plaintext is not altered by the encipherment transformation with the weak key, for each of which there are 2^{32} such plaintexts. A path in message space being traced out by alternate weak key encipherment is immediately reversed when a fixed point is encountered; this results in the short cycle.

The use of weak and semiweak DES keys is discouraged in any case for practical implementations; the discovery of the 2^{32} fixed points makes it more important that tests should be made for any unacceptable keys during the key generation process.

The remaining observation deserving comment was made by Adi Shamir, of the Weizmann Institute. Shamir discovered some remarkable anomalies in the structure of the S-boxes of the DES [21], suggesting that the anomalies were potentially dangerous though not leading as yet to a direct cryptanalytic attack. Stated simply, the phenomenon is based on the bit parity of each of the S-box entries (i.e., a count of the number of 1 bits in each element); the distribution of elements with an even number of ones in each S-box row was observed and a preponderance of rows showed a very biased distribution, either to the left half or the right half of the row. This means that a particular bit (the "b bit," which selects right or left of a row) of the S-box inputs has a very strong influence on the parity of the output from the S-boxes. The phenomenon is most obvious in S-boxes 1, 5, and 8. Shamir suggests that on evidence supplied by Brickell and Coppersmith, the observed properties might be an unintentional consequence of some of the design criteria.

Before leaving the subject of the DES, it is worth noting the way in which use of this algorithm has progressed, even though this is not strictly a matter for cryptologic research. We have remarked how the algorithm was adopted both as a U.S. federal standard and as an ANSI standard; for some time, it appeared that the algorithm would also be adopted as an international standard, but the International Standards Organization (ISO) has recently decided against this, because it was felt that such adoption might result in overdependence on the algorithm by users. ISO has decided to establish a register of encipherment algorithms from which users may choose; this register may contain published and unpublished algorithms, the latter being described only by their external characteristics.

DES is used very widely throughout the world, mainly by banks and financial institutions to secure their transaction systems. The algorithm is used both for obtaining secrecy and for message authentication. A series of "modes of operation" (defined in standard documents) specifies the ways in which a block cipher may safely be used on an extended plaintext. Message authentication employs a chained mode of operation, taking the end result of a sequence of encipherments as a message authentication code (MAC).

In the United States, a Commercial Comsec Endorsement Program (CCEP) has been set up to provide new algorithms that may eventually replace the DES. Under the CCEP, two classes of algorithm will be created, one for U.S. federal use only and the other for U.S. federal and commercial use; devices incorporating either class of algorithm will not be eligible for export from the United States; no CCEP algorithm will be published. After some discussion, the U.S. authorities have agreed to continue beyond 1988 for an undefined period to support new equipment for financial applications incorporating the DES.

None of the research work reported in the foregoing paragraphs in this article leads to the conclusion that the DES is yet unsafe for use in financial systems. One may speculate that the DES will eventually succumb to cryptanalytic attack; it remains to be seen whether such a successful attack is based on an analytic approach or on brute force exhaustive search for a key using an extremely powerful cryptanalytic machine, probably purpose built. It is premature to estimate when such a success will be achieved.

NEW DIRECTIONS IN CRYPTOGRAPHY

Simultaneously with the development and adoption of the DES, new concepts in cryptographic technology were being developed that promised to revolutionize the subject. Various research teams were considering the possibility of totally new cryptographic methods, but the first to publish the ideas were Diffie and Hellman in a very important paper [22] whose title has been borrowed for this section of this article.

After reviewing the state of the art in what may be called "classical" or "conventional" cryptography, Diffie and Hellman proceeded to develop an entirely new concept, that of "public key cryptography." In conventional cryptography (such as that using, e.g., the DES) the sender and receiver of enciphered messages must each possess the same key, used both for encipherment and decipherment; this presents certain problems in key management, in particular the need to transport encipherment keys from the point of generation to the point(s) where they are needed and to achieve the transport without revealing the keys to any unauthorized parties. Quite elaborate key management schemes have been devised by various organizations to achieve this requirement. How much more convenient it would be if instead of the need to transport encipherment keys in secret, it were only necessary to *publish* an encipherment key to be used by all senders of enciphered traffic to a particular destination. The receiver of messages enciphered in this way would possess a corresponding key, kept secret, that would permit decipherment of the messages. Figure 2 indicates the relationship between plaintext, ciphertext, and keys (public and secret).

Prior to the publication of the Diffie and Hellman paper, such a concept had never before been discussed in the literature; the whole idea might be said to have been inconceivable. The investigators did not present a viable system in this paper, only the basis of the idea. However, they did propose a protocol for secure key exchange over an insecure medium, which is itself worthy of mention. This has become known over the years as the "Diffie–Hellman key exchange method" and forms part of some practical security

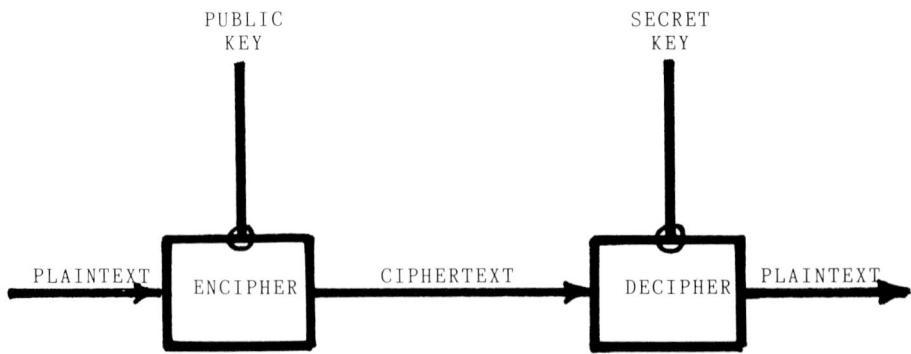

FIGURE 2 Public key cryptosystem.

systems still in use. The idea is based on the ease of obtaining results of finite exponentiation and the corresponding difficulty of obtaining the finite logarithm.

The parties to Diffie-Hellman key exchange need to agree on a prime number p and another number n that is a fixed primitive element in GF(p). Each party then generates at random a number in the range 1 to $p - 1$; call these numbers x and y, respectively for parties A and B. The protocol is exceedingly simple; A generates n^x, mod p, B generates n^y, mod p. A and B now exchange these results over the insecure medium; it does not matter who overhears them. The final step is for each party to take the parameter received from the other and raise that to the power of the locally held value of x (at A) or y (at B). The result at both A and B is then n^{xy}, mod p. Both possess the same calculated value and have achieved this without third parties listening in on the communication channel being able to replicate their result. The value n^{xy}, mod p, can be used as an encipherment key in a conventional encipherment system such as the DES. Note that neither A nor B has any control over the value of the final result that they cooperate to create.

Obtaining x from n^x, mod p is the operation of the finite logarithm, and it is the difficulty of this operation that lends strength to the Diffie-Hellman key exchange method. Clearly, if the finite logarithm were easy, x and y could be derived and the security of the system would be destroyed.

There is one serious drawback to this method of key exchange; this is the possibility that a third party breaks the communication line between them and then conducts a separate key exchange between itself and each of A and B. The latter then believe that they have a secret parameter known only to them, whereas in reality, the intruder knows the two secret parameters created with A and with B, respectively. One answer to this kind of attack is for A and B to check that they possess the same parameter, using some different communication channel. If they possess the same parameter, there has been no intervening intruder.

Because the security of this key exchange scheme depends on the difficulty of calculating the finite logarithm, it is not surprising to find a paper [23] published a couple of years later on an improved method for calculating this function. Prior to this paper, the finite logarithm function required $O(p^{1/2})$ complexity in both time and space; the new algorithm required only $O(\log p)^2$ operations (time), provided that $p - 1$ had only small prime factors. Clearly, then, users of the Diffie-Hellman key exchange method would need to choose primes where $p - 1$ did *not* have small prime factors.

Following publication of the paper on new directions, two independent teams, from MIT and Stanford University, were at work on practicable systems embodying the idea of public key cryptography.

THE RSA PUBLIC KEY CRYPTOSYSTEM

The MIT scheme [24] has become widely known under the initials of the surnames of its inventors, Rivest, Shamir, and Adleman—RSA. The basis of the RSA method is to choose *two* prime numbers and take their product; by convention, these are called p, q, and m, respectively. We then select a number that is itself prime to $p - 1$ and $q - 1$; call this e. Finally, another number is needed d, so that the product of e and d, modulo (lcm p − 1, q − 1), is 1. Then, if we call a plaintext message M and the corresponding ciphertext C, the following relationships hold: $C = M^e$, modulo m and $M = C^d$, modulo m. We have here the essential mechanism for a public key cryptosystem in which the public key is represented by the pair (e, m) and the secret key by d, as m is already public.

In operating a public key cryptosystem service, one of the essentials is to provide users with a reliable source of public keys for those other users to whom they may wish to send secret messages; this could, e.g., be provided by a special server on a communications network. Reliability of the source is vital, because if false keys can be substituted in place of the genuine ones, the confidentiality offered by the system breaks down; users deceived into sending messages enciphered with false keys would have their traffic readable by intruders (responsible for planting the false keys) and unreadable by the intended recipient.

An attractive feature of the RSA public key cryptosystem is the symmetry of its calculation; the algorithm used by sender and receiver is the same; all that is different is the exponent. Therefore, it is possible to transform a plaintext message M with the secret exponent d; the result is a field that can be restored to the original M by transformation with the public exponent e. If the public exponent is unequivocally associated with the owner of this particular key set, then a message subjected to transformation of this kind can be attributed with a useful degree of confidence to the sender. This provides a property of "digital signature," giving proof of origin and a message integrity check as part of the same operation. We can be sure that a message protected in this manner has come without alteration from a particular source. This property is potentially very important for any operator or user of a communication system that carries messages with contractual or value transfer significance. Indeed, the principle is already in use by some banks and financial institutions.

Clearly, the security of the RSA cryptosystem is therefore most important, and considerable attention has been directed at this subject. Because knowledge of the prime factors p and q can allow calculation of the decipherment exponent d from knowledge of the encipherment exponent e, it is very important that p and q cannot be derived easily from the published modulus m. The difficulty of factorizing m is an essential feature of a successful RSA scheme used in practice. The requirements for m to be difficult to factorize are that the factors should be large enough and that they should be chosen according to certain rules designed to frustrate factorization by methods that are efficient in respect to particular types of primes.

Publication of the RSA algorithm and proposals to use it in designing secure communication and processing systems have generated intense interest in the academic world in factorization. Factorization has fascinated mathematicians for at least the last 300 years, but recent progress has been startling, to say the least.

Size of factor is clearly related to difficulty of factorization. In the original RSA paper, the investigators suggested that a modulus of 512 bits, about 154 digits, was sufficiently large. If we accept this advice, then prime numbers of about 77 digits are what we are looking for. However, there are reasons why not all prime numbers of this size are acceptable for RSA primes; we shall consider these reasons later.

It is well beyond the scope of this article to attempt to give a comprehensive account of all modern factorizing methods. We will attempt to give pointers to those that seem most important. A very thorough state-of-the-art review paper on factorization was published in 1984 by Davis et al. [25]. The progression of factoring methods developed in the last 15 years begins with the continued fraction-factoring method of Morrison and Brillhart [26], followed by Pomerance's quadratic sieve [27]; the latter was implemented at the Sandia Laboratories in 1982 on a Cray 1S and yielded the factors of a pair of 51- and 52-digit numbers in less than 2 hours, an improvement in speed of at least an order of magnitude over previous methods. Next, there came another variation of the quadratic sieve [28], the "special q" method, which gave approximately a further order of magnitude improvement in factoring performance. Optimization of the special q method on the Cray gave further improvement in performance by a factor of about 6. Transfer of the work to the faster Cray X-MP has given another small increase in speed to the operation. The largest composite number factored and reported in the 1984 paper was about 73 digits. This was the boundary of success at that time.

Since 1984, further advances in methodology have been made. In 1987, the record for factorization seems to be [29] a composite number of 87 digits factored at Mitre by Silverman using Montgomery's polynomial generators for quadratic residues and a quadratic sieve algorithm implemented on a dozen Sun minicomputers; a month of dedicated running was necessary.

To project forward from this figure toward future performance is to indulge in speculation; a rough guideline may be obtained from Simmons' factor-of-two rule: For three additional digits in the composite number, approximately twice the running time is needed for factorization (this rule was quoted in 1984 as a rule of thumb for composites in the range 40 to 75 digits).

We have indicated that the significance of factorization as a method of attack on the RSA public key cryptosystem has aroused very considerable public interest. Occasionally, the popular media hear of a research result and misinterpret this, leading to sensational and incorrect accounts of "breaking" the RSA algorithm. This has happened recently with respect to the elliptic curve factorization method of Lenstra [30]. This method is particularly effective in factorizing composites where at least one factor is relatively small; it is not as effective as the special q quadratic sieve where the factors are fairly similar in size. It is most important to realize that practical applications of the RSA algorithm should have moduli with factors similar in size.

Clearly, any implementer or user of the RSA public key cryptosystem must choose the prime numbers in such a way as to make factorization difficult. The rules for safe primes have been discussed many times, but we can find them in a convenient summary form in a paper by Gordon [31]. If a prime is represented by p, the following must obtain: $p - 1$ must have a large prime factor r; $r - 1$ must have a large prime factor; and $p + 1$ must have a large prime factor. It is relatively straightforward to build these rules into any mechanism that chooses prime numbers for use in the RSA algorithm.

Other methods of attacking messages enciphered with the RSA algorithm have been proposed. One such was the repeated encipherment attack of Simmons and Norris [32], developed further by Herlestam [33]. The idea here is that a ciphertext is taken and enciphered repeatedly with the public key; eventually the value produced will coincide with the original ciphertext value; when this happens, the previous result represents the original plaintext. Note that this method discovers only one plaintext; it does not give any information regarding the secret key. The answer to this attack is to choose primes according to the rules given above. Doing this ensures that the size of loop traversed in repeated encipherment becomes large enough to defy discovery of the plaintext by this method, i.e., the number of primitive operations becomes excessive.

For practical purposes, the RSA algorithm involving finite exponentiation is very heavy in computational demands, especially so because of the relatively large size of the numbers involved in the computations. Various devices can be used in writing RSA software to reduce the size of the problem; it is quite obvious that full exponentiation followed by the modulus operation is not the way to proceed; it is preferable to tackle the operation piecemeal, with many intermediate modulus operations keeping the intermediate results within reasonable bounds. The exponent can be taken 1 bit at a time, with simple squaring and multiplication operations of the intermediate results. Even with well-designed software, the demands are still considerable, and purpose-built hardware is a much better way of achieving an implementation. Various purpose-built chips have been designed; one of the most advanced is that made by Cylink, of Sunnyvale, California, capable of handling 1024-bit moduli at throughput rates of 6.4Kb per second; the exponentiation time required with 1024-bit modulus is 320 milliseconds, maximum.

KNAPSACK PUBLIC KEY CRYPTOSYSTEMS

The second public key cryptosystem published in 1978 was that of Merkle and Hellman [34]; this was based on the trapdoor knapsack. The classical knapsack problem is one of selecting from a collection of objects a set, which, taken together, will exactly fill a defined space. (Strictly speaking, the knapsack problem is to decide for a given space whether or not any selection from a specified set of objects will fill the space exactly.) Expressed in one-dimensional terms, this is equivalent to selecting rods of different length, which, laid end to end, will equal a specified length exactly. The general knapsack problem is a member of a group of problems called NP-complete, where NP stands for nondeterministic polynomial. At present, only exponential time solutions are known for such problems, which makes them very difficult.

On the other hand, some particular knapsack problems are very easy to solve; e.g., one has a set of superincreasing numbers and the problem is to select a subset from this, which sums to a specified total.

The knapsack problem was used by Merkle and Hellman to develop a public key cryptosystem. Essentially, they took a superincreasing sequence and transformed this into a different (nonsuperincreasing) sequence (NS) using a secret transformation. To encipher a given plaintext bit pattern, the binary elements of the pattern were considered in order; for a zero in the bit pattern, the corresponding knapsack element in NS was ignored; for a one in the bit pattern, the knapsack element was added into a running total. When the full plaintext bit pattern had been scanned, the resulting total was the enciphered form of the plaintext. The key in the encipherment process is the sequence of elements in NS; this key is, of course, public.

Because the total was formed from a NS, the reverse transformation to discover the bits of the plaintext pattern was considered to be extremely difficult, given parameters of adequate size; cryptanalysis, i.e., discovery of the plaintext without knowledge of the decipherment key, was thus thought to be very difficult. The secret decipherment key in this case was a parameter that was used to transform the total to the value that would have been obtained had the hidden superincreasing sequence been used; given a total formed on the basis of the superincreasing sequence, the plaintext bits could be identified easily. This process is best explained in algebraic form.

Let the elements of the superincreasing sequence be represented by the vector v. We then choose a prime number that is greater than the sum of all the elements of v and another number, s, less than p. We transform the individual elements of v by the operation $v'_i = s \cdot v_i$ modulo p. v' is then the NS mentioned above.

If K is the total obtained by the knapsack process using the superincreasing sequence v, and K' is the total obtained by the knapsack process using the NS v', then K and K' are related by the expression $K = t \cdot K'$ modulo p, where $s \cdot t = 1$ modulo p. A numerical example with a few knapsack elements may make things clearer. Consider the following short superincreasing sequence, (23, 57, 91, 179, 353); this is our vector v. If we now select p = 719 and s = 299, we can transform the sequence to v' and obtain (406, 506, 606, 315, 573); the latter sequence is obviously not superincreasing and is the public key in our knapsack encipherment.

If we have a plaintext that reads 10110 in binary form, the following addition is required to represent it in knapsack encipherment: K' = 406 + 0 + 606 + 315 + 0 = 1327. The result, 1327, is the enciphered form of the binary number 10110. To reverse the process and recover the plaintext, we must use the parameters p and s. Using the latter, we derive t (see above). t = 1/299 = 101, modulo 719. We can now use t to transform K' into K. $K = t \cdot K' = 101 \times 1327 = 293$, modulo 719. Taking the appropriate elements of v, we find 23 + 0 + 91 + 179 + 0 = 293, so the plaintext must be 10110.

The knapsack encipherment technique is very attractive because of ease of computation. All that is required in encipherment is a simple addition. Decipherment requires a little more computation, but is still arithmetically trivial. One practical disadvantage of knapsack encipherment is the degree of expansion to which the text is subjected by the encipherment process. Practical knapsack schemes have been suggested where each element in the knapsack vector is 100 bits long and where there are 100 elements. This means that the size of the public key is quite bulky compared even with the substantial key size of the RSA algorithm, which is also disadvantageous. The knapsack does not have the elegance of the RSA method in producing digital signatures; suggested methods of knapsack signatures have been put forward, but these are rather clumsy. Despite these drawbacks, the knapsack encipher system is still distinctly attractive because of the ease of computation.

Why then is the knapsack system not used more widely in practice? The reason is that some knapsacks are not sufficiently secure; indeed demonstrations have been given of breaking knapsacks, so the user public has a feeling of distrust toward them.

The insecurity arises from the fact that the public key vector, although apparently random, is not, in fact, randomly chosen but is derived by a simple transformation from a vector that is superincreasing. Therefore, the solution of the encipherment knapsack cannot be said to be a problem of

NP-complete degree of difficulty, which is the case for the general knapsack problem. In 1982, Shamir published a method [35] for solving the basic Merkle–Hellman knapsack in polynomial time compared with the exponential time required for the general problem.

Because this deficiency of the knapsack encipherment process was recognized early, suggestions have been made for increasing security by multiply iterated knapsacks. Here, a superincreasing knapsack vector is selected and subjected to repeated transformation by different pairs of p and s; the intention is to make the connection between the vector actually used to encipher the plaintext and the original superincreasing vector as remote as possible. This suggestion was made in the original Merkle–Hellman paper.

One of the most dramatic moments in recent conferences on cryptology must have been at the 1982 Crypto meeting at Santa Barbara where Leonard Adleman [36], using a personal computer, broke a single iteration knapsack of Graham and Shamir; this was done by running the machine overnight. Adleman's method was based on the lattice-based reduction algorithm of Lenstra et al. [37]; this method was also very effective against the original Merkle–Hellman knapsack.

A number of papers have been published giving methods of attacking multiple knapsacks. Ernest Brickell published an outline of an attack [38] for breaking iterated knapsacks in polynomial time. The process was demonstrated for 100 element knapsacks and for up to 20 knapsack iterations. The method relies upon the information rate in the ciphertext not being too high; as each iteration of the knapsack lowers the information rate (because of the expansion of the ciphertext), too many iterations make the ciphertext vulnerable to the Brickell attack.

As many knapsack systems have been shown to be vulnerable, there is a tendency not to use them in practical security implementations.

APPLICATIONS OF PUBLIC KEY CRYPTOGRAPHY

In the foregoing remarks on the RSA and knapsack systems, we have touched on their suitability for practical applications. In particular we have indicated that the RSA algorithm has important qualities that make it suitable for use in some transaction processing systems; the digital signature property is particularly important.

Before leaving the subject of public key cryptography we should point out some theoretical studies that have been triggered by the public key concept.

Perhaps the best known of these studies is the "mental poker" concept, which was published by Shamir et al. [39] in 1979. The idea is that a poker deal is to be conducted by players who are remotely located and who do not trust each other. How can a trustworthy deal be accomplished?

Let us take the case of two players, A and B; they agree on a common prime number p; A then chooses a secret number x and its inverse $\bar{x}$, modulo p; B likewise chooses a secret number y and its inverse $\bar{y}$, modulo p. A takes the descriptors of the 52 cards in a random order, raises each descriptor separately to the power of x, modulo p, and sends the set of transformed descriptors to B. B chooses five of the transformed card descriptors and sends them to A, who can retrieve the plaintext card descriptors using the inverse number $\bar{x}$; these five cards constitute A's hand. At the same time, B chooses five other card descriptors as transformed by A, raises them to the power of y, modulo p, and sends the five results to A. A applies his x̄ to them and sends the results back to B, who finally takes his own value ȳ and transforms the result back to the plaintext card descriptors; the latter five card descriptors constitute B's hand. Assuming the infeasibility of the discrete logarithm, the two players now each hold five cards in such a way that neither knows the other's hand and cannot cheat.

The basic principle of the security of the mental poker protocol has not been seriously challenged. Various precautions have to be taken in choosing the prime (see, e.g., Coppersmith [40]). The concept of mental poker has spawned a great deal of work on "secure protocols," where parties need to communicate in such a way that they cannot cheat on the exchange of messages and are also protected against external interference (see, e.g., Even et al. [41]). Another interesting aspect of secure protocols is addressed by Chaum [42], who has applied public key cryptosystems to a number of problems related to making payments anonymously but in a way that can be trusted.

THE APPLICATION OF SHIFT REGISTER THEORY

One of the most important developments in the history of cryptology is the discovery by Vernam [43] that a stream cipher can be created very effectively by adding a random character (or bit) stream to the plaintext; restoration of the plaintext from the ciphertext is achieved by a matching operation carried out by the receiver. In its simplest form, the process consists of the addition of a key bit stream to the plaintext bit stream using addition without carries; in this case, decipherment involves exactly the same operation—noncarry addition (the exclusive-OR function) of the key stream to the ciphertext stream. Sender and receiver of such ciphertext must have access to the same bit stream. The latter must clearly be nonpredictable; otherwise, an intruder could easily carry out decipherment. It is also important that a key bit stream should not be reused on a different text.

An obvious way of deriving a suitable key bit stream would be to use a reliable noise source. The problem is then to make this available at both ends of the communication; if the stream is generated at the sender, some means must be found of providing it securely at the receiver. This method is used in practice where it is possible by secure courier to deliver copies of the stream, recorded, e.g., on tape, to the points where it is needed. This may not always be possible, and other means must then be sought.

Assuming that sender and receiver are able to set up a pseudorandom number generator and that they agree on a suitable seed to start the generator, it may be possible to provide the required key stream at remote locations simultaneously. Many cipher systems of this type are constructed in practice around the shift register principle. A shift register may be regarded as a series of single-bit stores connected in sequence. A bit stream input to the sequence at one end will eventually emerge at the other, each bit passing in the process from bit store to bit store. If there is no feedback path, data will exit at the end of the register. The application of such a device to the generation of a pseudorandom bit stream is derived by providing a feedback path and making the value of the bit fed back from

from end to start not only depend on the value of the bit emerging at the end of the register but also on some of the values of the intermediate bits part way down the register. The diagram in Figure 3 may help understanding; a number of exclusive-OR elements is included in the feedback path; R_n is a single bit store. By closing a different selection of the switches indicated in the diagram, one can cause different bits in the stream to influence the progress of the process. The pseudorandom stream can be tapped off at the input of the register; tapping at the output would mean that the first few bits of the output sequence would consist of the initial state of the register. Input to the system is no longer by a continuous bit stream entering at the input point but by setting up the register to an initial state (the seed) and then letting it run; there is no further external input to the process. The "key" is provided by nominating the selection of switches to be closed between the register elements and the X-OR gates in the feedback path.

Clearly, such a device will not produce an indefinitely long bit stream that does not repeat; once the elements of the register are again in the state at which they started, the bit stream will repeat. In any practical cipher system built on this principle, it is important to ensure that the length of the bit stream before repetition is sufficiently long, because reuse of a key stream is known to lead to insecurity. It is also important that if an intruder learns a short section of a bit stream, he shall not be able to predict the following or preceding parts of the stream with any useful degree of certainty.

The analysis of linear feedback shift registers is a complex matter, and we shall not attempt to provide a treatment of the subject here. A very good introduction to the subject can be found in Beker and Piper [44]. They quote Golomb's randomness postulates for a binary sequence of period p:

1. If p is even, the cycle of length p shall contain an equal number of zeros and ones. If p is odd, the number of zeros shall be one more or less than the number of ones.
2. In a cycle of length p, half the runs have length 1, a quarter have length 2, an eighth have length 3 and, in general, for each i for which there are at least 2^{i+1} runs, $1/2^i$ of the runs have length i. Moreover, for each of these lengths, there are equally many gaps and blocks.
3. The out-of-phase autocorrelation is a constant.

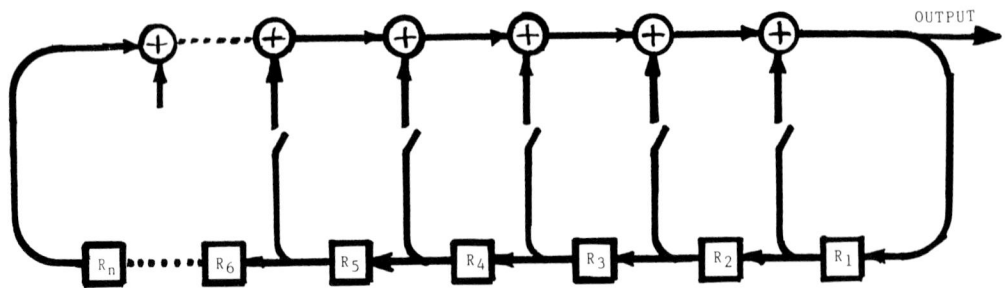

FIGURE 3 Linear feedback shift register.

They then identify essential properties for an output sequence from a finite state machine, such as a feedback shift register, used to provide a cipher according to the Vernam principle:

1. The output sequence must have a guaranteed minimum length for its period.
2. The ciphertext must appear to be random.

One of the conclusions drawn by Beker and Piper is that linear feedback shift registers do not provide bit streams whose characteristics are sufficiently good for use in practical cipher systems of even modest security levels.

The answer to this problem is to introduce a degree of nonlinearity into the process. There are many ways of achieving this, but one of the simplest is to introduce substitution tables that can convert bit patterns into other arbitrary bit patterns (compare the S-boxes in the DES). It is believed that nonlinear feedback shift registers form a basic design element of many of today's proprietary encipherment algorithms.

The importance of the subject can be gauged from the fact that out of 32 papers presented at the Eurocrypt '85 meeting at Linz [45], 8 were on shift register theory or were closely related to that subject. These eight papers present something of a state-of-the-art review of shift register studies in 1985. The fact that only one of these papers originated in the United States is an indication that there is more academic interest in this work outside of the United States than in.

THE FUTURE

This article has tried to give a flavor of a very new subject, cryptologic research, one that is, in the main, less than 15 years old. Developments in this period have been very substantial, with some major discoveries being made. Throughout the world, many research groups are concentrating on the subject, and the number of individual researchers in the field must run into many hundreds.

Looking into the future of the subject is highly speculative; 15 years ago hardly anyone would have dared predict we would stand where we are now. It seems unlikely at present that yet another totally new public key cryptosystem will emerge. Perhaps today's climate of opinion may even discourage efforts in that direction. There will still be intense interest in factorization in attempts to "break" the RSA system. Progress in factorization may force users to adopt larger moduli. No successor to the DES is likely to receive the same publicity and the widespread open scrutiny to which the DES has been subjected. Considerable academic credit will attach to the first successful attack on the DES, especially if the attack is based on formal cryptanalysis and not on brute force.

Application of cipher systems is bound to develop in the civil field, especially in the protection of transaction processing systems. Here, we may expect that greater efficiency of implementation will be the goal.

Whether the next 15 years of civil cryptologic research will be as fascinating as the first 15 years remains to be seen.

REFERENCES

1. A. Kerckhoffs, "La Cryptographie Militaire," *J. Sci. Militaries* (1883).
2. E. Bazeries, *Les Chiffres Sécrètes Dévoilées*, Charpentier et Fasquelle, Paris, 1901.
3. M. Givierge, *Cours de Cryptographie*, Bergére-Levrault, Paris, 1925.
4. D. Kahn, *The Codebreakers*, Macmillan, New York, 1967.
5. H. F. Gaines, *Cryptanalysis*, Dover, New York, 1956.
6. C. E. Shannon, "Communication Theory of Secrecy Systems," *Bell Syst. Tech. J.*, 28, 656−715 (1949).
7. H. Feistel, "Cryptography and Computer Privacy," *Sci. Am.*, 228(5), 15−23 (1973).
8. National Bureau of Standards, *Data Encryption Standard, Federal Information Processing Standard 46*, Washington, D.C., January 1977.
9. American National Standards Institute, *Data Encryption Algorithm, American National Standard X3.92-1981*, Washington, D.C., 1981.
10. C. H. Meyer and S. M. Matyas, *Cryptography: A New Dimension in Computer Data Security*, Wiley, New York, 1982.
11. P. Meissner, "Report of the Workshop on Estimation of Significant Advances in Computer Technology," National Bureau of Standards, Report NBSIR 76-1189, Washington, D.C., December 1976.
12. D. Branstad, J. Gait, and S. Katzke, "Report of the Wrokshop on Cryptography in Support of Computer Security," National Bureau of Standards, Report NBSIR 77-1291, Washington, D.C., September 1977.
13. M. Hellman, R. Merkle, R. Schroeppel, L. Washington, W. Diffie, S. Pohlig, and P. Schweitzer, "Results of an initial attempt to cryptanalyze the NBS Data Encryption Standard," Stanford University, Center for Systems Research, Report SEL 76-042, Stanford, CA, November 1976.
14. D. W. Davies and W. L. Price, *Security for Computer Networks*, Wiley, Chichester, 1984.
15. G. B. Kolata, "Flaws Found in Popular Code," *Science*, 219, 369−370 (January 28, 1983).
16. M. Davio, Y. Desmedt, M. Fosseprez, R. Govaerts, J. Hulsbosch, P. Neutjens, P. Piret, J-J. Quisquater, J. Vandewalle, and P. Wouters, "Analytical Characteristics of the DES," in, *Proceedings of Crypto '83*, Plenum, New York, 1984, pp. 171−202.
17. Y. Desmedt, J-J. Quisquater, and M. Davio, "Dependence of Output on Input in DES: Small Avalanche Characteristics," in *Proceedings of Crypto '84*, Springer, Berlin, 1985, pp. 359−376.
18. B. S. Kaliski, R. L. Rivest, and A. T. Sherman, "Is the Data Encryption Standard a Group?" in *Proceedings of Eurocrypt '85*, Springer, Berlin, 1985, pp. 81−95.
19. B. S. Kaliski, R. L. Rivest, and A. T. Sherman, "Is DES a Pure Cipher? (results of more cycling experiments on DES)," in *Proceedings of Crypto '85*, Springer, Berlin, 1985, pp. 212−226.
20. D. Coppersmith, "The Real Reason for Rivest's Phenomenon," in *Proceedings of Crypto '85*, Springer, Berlin, 1985, pp. 535−536.
21. A. Shamir, "On the Security of DES," in *Proceedings of Crypto '85*, Springer, Berlin, 1985, pp. 280−281.
22. W. Diffie and M. E. Hellman, "New Directions in Cryptography," *IEEE Trans. Inf. Theory*, IT-22, 644−654 (November 1976).

23. S. C. Pohlig and M. E. Hellman, "An Improved Algorithm for Computing Logarithms over GF(p) and Its Cryptographic Significance," *IEEE Trans. Inf. Theory, IT-24,* 106–110 (January 1978).
24. R. L. Rivest, A. Shamir, and L. Adleman, "A Method of Obtaining Digital Signatures and Public Key Cryptosystems," *Comm. ACM, 21,* 120–126 (February 1978).
25. J. A. Davis, D. B. Holdridge, and G. J. Simmons, "Status Report on Factoring (at the Sandia National Laboratories)," in *Proceedings of Eurocrypt '84,* Springer, Berlin, 1985, pp. 183–215.
26. M. A. Morrison and J. Brillhart, "A Method of Factoring and the Factorization of F_7," *Math. Comp., 29,* 183–205 (1975).
27. C. Pomerance, "Analysis and Comparison of Some Integer Factoring Algorithms. Number Theory and Computers," *Math. Centrum Tracts, 154,* 89–139 (1982).
28. J. A. Davies and D. B. Holdridge, "Factorization Using the Quadratic Sieve Algorithm," in *Sandia National Laboratories, Tech. Report SAND83-1346,* Albuquerque, NM, December 1983.
29. G. J. Simmons, Private communication, February 1987.
30. H. W. Lenstra, "Factoring Integers with Elliptic Curves," in Mathematical Sciences Research Institute preprint, Berkeley, CA, 1986.
31. J. Gordon, "Strong RSA Keys," *Electron. Lett., 20,* 514–516 (June 1984).
32. G. J. Simmons and M. J. Norris, "Preliminary Comments on the MIT Public-Key Cryptosystem," *Cryptologia, 1,* 406–414 (October 1977).
33. T. Herlestam, "Critical Remarks on Some Public-Key Cryptosystems," *BIT, 18,* 493–496 (1978).
34. R. C. Merkle and M. E. Hellman, "Hiding Information and Signatures in Trap-Door Knapsacks," *IEEE Trans. Inf. Throry, IT-24,* 525–530 (September 1978).
35. A. Shamir, "A Polynomial Time Algorithm for Breaking the Merkle–Hellman Cryptosystem," in *Proceedings of the Twenty-Third IEEE Symposium on Foundations of Computer Science,* 1982, pp. 145–152.
36. L. Adleman, "On Breaking the Iterated Merkle-Hellman Public-Key System," in *Proceedings of Crypto '82,* Plenum, New York, 1983, pp. 303–308.
37. A. K. Lenstra, H. W. Lenstra, and L. Lovasz, "Factoring Polynomials with Rational Coefficients," *Math. Ann., 261,* 515–534 (1982).
38. E. F. Brickell, "Breaking Iterated Knapsacks," in *Proceedings of Crypto '84,* Springer, Berlin, 1985, pp. 342–358.
39. A. Shamir, R. L. Rivest, and L. Adleman, "Mental Poker," in MIT Laboratory for Computer Science, Report TM-125, Cambridge, MA, November 1978.
40. D. Coppersmith, "Cheating at Mental Poker," in *Proceedings of Crypto '85,* Springer, Berlin, 1986, pp. 104–107.
41. S. Even, O. Goldreich, and A. Shamir, "On the Security of Ping-Pong Protocols When Implemented Using the RSA," in *Proceedings of Crypto '85,* Springer, Berlin, 1986, pp. 58–72.
42. D. Chaum, "Security without Identification: Transaction Systems to Make Big Brother Obsolete," *Comm. ACM, 28,* 1030–1044 (October 1985).
43. G. Vernam, "Cipher Printing Telegraphy Systems for Secret Wire and Radio Telegraphic Communications," *J. AIEE, 45,* 109–115 (February 1926).

44. H. Beker and F. Piper, *Cipher Systems: The Protection of Communications*, Northwood Books, London, 1982.
45. F. Pichler, ed., *Advances in Cryptology—Eurocrypt '85, Lecture Notes in Computer Science*, 219, Springer, Berlin, 1985.

WYN L. PRICE

DATA STRUCTURES

INTRODUCTION

Definitions

Data Objects and Data Elements

A datum is a symbolic representation of an entity or a concept. As such, it is codified and is storable within the computer storage subsystem. Data by themselves are meaningless unless the relationships between them and the context from which they are derived are known. The data element 785 means nothing if the user, say, a manager of a firm, does not know that this is the net profit, in thousands, of the Customer Services Division. Further, the profit of $785,000 means very little if the manager does not also know that all other divisions had profits of $1,000,000 or more.

Unless both the data elements and their relationships are processed, the results of data processing are out of context and are therefore meaningless. When a collection of data elements and their relationships is organized and stored for a certain data processing application, the collection becomes an object of data processing: a data object.

The concepts of data objects and data elements are relative. The instances or the atoms of a data object can be thought of as data elements. For example, the names of the month (JANUARY, FEBRUARY, MARCH, ... DECEMBER) as a data object has 12 data elements. On the other hand, JANUARY by itself can be a data object, with 31 data elements, (1, 2, 3, ... 31), each representing a day of the month. Hence, depending on the data processing objectives, a data object could be a collection of stored characters, fields, records, files, or even data bases in a distributed computer system environment. For a given data processing application, we can have one or several data elements or data objects.

For this reason, we will use data element and data object interchangeably. Generically, they will mean the data that are organized and stored in the computer storage subsystem for the purpose of certain processing.

Data Structures

According to Webster, the term structure means "the manner of building" or "something made up of interdependent parts in a definite pattern of organization." For our purpose, structure will denote the manner in which interdependent data elements are organized, building a definite pattern. By "data structures," we will refer to the various formats that can be used to organize a set of data elements and the relationships among them.

Background

A Conceptual Framework

Fundamental concepts and techniques of data structure design include data organization format, the mechanism for implementation, and tools for configuration. In other words, the process of selecting and implementing a data structure is best understood on three levels of activities: (a) activities of the conceptual level; (b) activities of the algorithmic level; and (c) activities of the storage level (see Fig. 1).

The activities of the conceptual level relate to the initial phase of data processing. Typically, given certain information needs, the user begins by identifying the type and the size of the data elements that are relevant. Once the data elements are identified to be relevant, the format in which they are to be organized and stored, namely, the data structure, is selected.

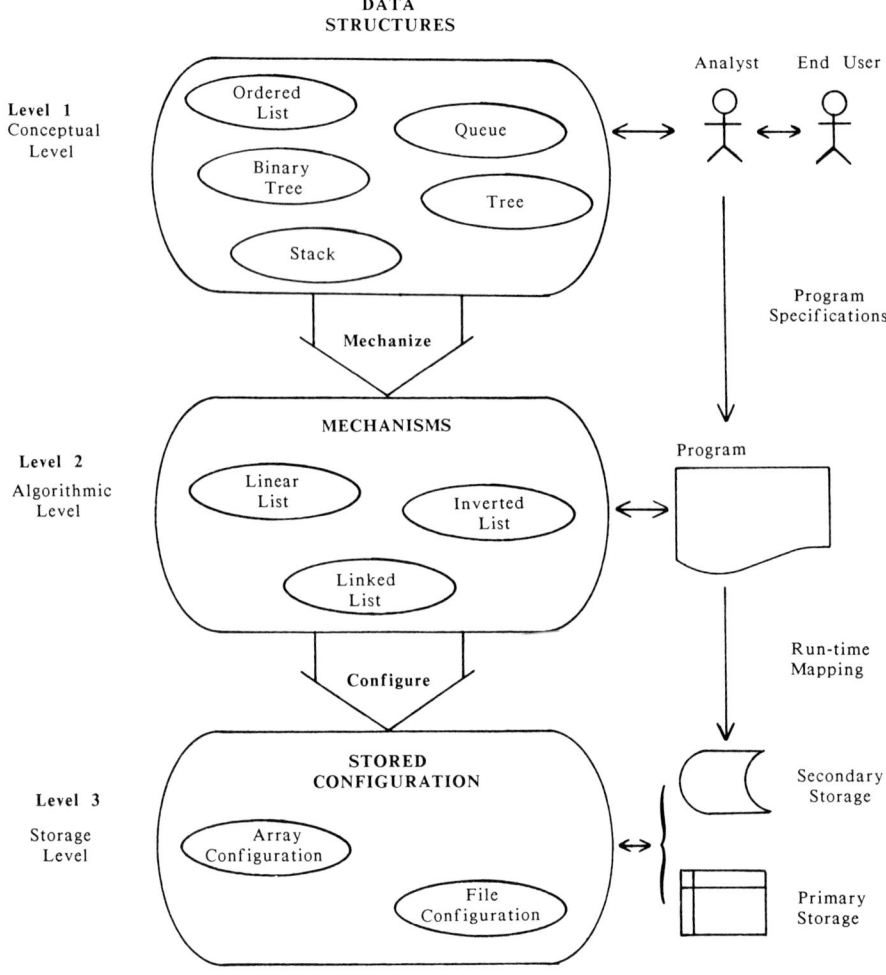

FIGURE 1.

The selected data structure at this level represents merely the user's view of the data and their organization. It exists only conceptually, as its mechanization and implementation are to follow at later stages. Therefore, the data structure merely represents an organizing concept. It is an intellectual abstraction and should not be confused with mechanisms, such as a linked list, which is used to organize the data elements. Furthermore, it should not be confused with devices, such as an array, which is used to configure or represent the data structures in the memory. The types of data structures to be discussed in this article include ordered list, stacks, queues, and trees.

The activities of the algorithmic level represent the initial steps of implementing the selected data structure. They have to do with specifying the required functions of the selected data structure. The operations that are to be facilitated by the chosen data structure need to be specified. Such specifications are coded in a program in a given procedure-oriented programming language.

The concern at this level is *logical* rather than *physical* because it represents the implementation of a data structure in a program not in the memory. The mechanisms utilized in the program to implement various data structures include linear list, inverted list, linked list, and so on. For our purposes, they are not the names of data structures per se. Rather, they are the names of the mechanisms that are adopted by the programmers to implement the data structures of their choice.

The activities of the storage level have to do with the physical representation of the data objects organized in the format of the selected data structure. Therefore, the concern here is on the methods of actually mapping the data elements internally in the memory.

For this reason, the concern at this level is referred to in the literature as the "internal," or "physical," aspect of a data structure. However called, the activities of the algorithmic level and those of the storage level must be clearly distinguished. The former refers to the activities of logically specifying the functions of the selected data structure in the computer program. The latter refers to the activities of physically configuring the data objects, that is, the internal linkage, in the computer storage subsystem.

Arrays and files are tools used to configure or build such mechanisms as linear list and linked list in the memory. Therefore, they too are not the names of data structures as such, but the tools or configurations that hold the data objects in question.

In summary, the notions surrounding data structures must be clearly understood. The design of a data structure involves three distinctly different levels of activities. The activities of the conceptual level have to do with the selection of a format for organizing data elements, the activities of the algorithmic level are the program implementations and, the activities of the storage level have to do with the physical representation of a data structure in the memory. A data structure as a concept for organizing data elements is an abstraction, an intellectual tool, which allows us to think about the organization of data elements apart from particular operations that it facilitates. It represents the structural considerations that are addressed prior to considering the algorithmic details and on the internal linkage in the memory.

Much of the information on the details of implementing a data structure, both on the algorithmic and storage levels, is "hidden" from the end users. In other words, the details of implementing the data structure in the program and in the memory do not concern the end users, as long as their information requirements are satisfied.

The Data Relationship Primitives

Recall our definition of data structures: various formats for organizing data elements and the relationships among them. Several types of data structures exist, and numerous mechanisms are also available for implementing the data structures. All of the data structures identified for our purposes are based on one or more of three basic data relationship constructs: simple sequence relationship, hierarchical relationship, and sibling relationship. These constructs are so basic to the organization of data and their relationships that they are called the "data relationship primitives" in this discussion.

Simple Sequence Relationship: The simple sequence relationship is the primitive most frequently used. It is used to arrange the data objects in such a way that they can be listed in some desired sequence. For example, JANUARY, FEBRUARY, MARCH, ... DECEMBER is a list based on the simple sequence relationship.

The relationship between the data elements in this kind of a list is one of adjacency. With the exception of the first and the last element, each element in the list has an element preceding it and succeeding it, that is, it is related to its predecessor and to its successor. The decision as to which element is to be adjacent to which other elements depends on the purpose of data processing. For example, the list ADAMS, BROWN, CARLSON, DUNN, ... could be an alphabetized list of employees. On the other hand, the list BROWN, DUNN, ADAMS, CARLSON, ... could represent employees in the order of seniority. In any event, the relationship between the data elements, such as the one between BROWN and DUNN in our second example, is a simple sequence relationship.

The use of the simple sequence relationship in organizing the data elements always results in the formation of a data structure called an ordered list. This structure is very frequently utilized in various data processing activities.

Hierarchical relationship: The hierarchical relationship between data elements is analogous to the genealogical relationship between a FATHER and a SON or SONS. Analogously, the relationship between a DEPARTMENT and its STAFF MEMBERS or between YEAR and MONTHS could be termed hierarchical. On a conceptual level, the same kind of relationship can be said to exist between, say, SOCIAL SCIENCE and SOCIOLOGY, between RELIGION and CHRISTIANITY, or between FURNITURE and CHAIRS. The relationship between the two data elements in a hierarchical relationship is therefore one of super and subordinates. The term FURNITURE represents a set whose subordinates include such objects as CHAIRS, TABLES, DESKS, and so forth.

We frequently use the hierarchical relationship between data elements to to eliminate data redundancies and/or to increase the data processing efficiency. As was the case in using the simple sequence relationship, a hierarchical relationship also can be imposed on data elements to formulate a data structure. As will be discussed in the following section, we use the hierarchical relationship, along with the sibling relationship, to construct the data structure called "tree."

Sibling Relationship: Given the hierarchical relationship between a FATHER and his SONS, the relationship among the SONS is called the sibling relationship. This relationship is characterized by the fact that the data objects in consideration have at least one common attribute among them. The SONS in our example have the common FATHER. Likewise, given the task of categorizing the names of academic disciplines, the relationship between SOCIOLOGY and POLITICAL SCIENCE will be identified as a sibling relationship as both disciplines are likely to be categorized together under SOCIAL SCIENCE.

In this way, the sibling relationship and the hierarchical relationship are mutually dependent. The sibling relationship without an associated hierarchical relationship would not be different from the simple sequence relationship. For example, the list of subordinates, without an identified superordinate, FATHER, is the same as a sequenced list of SONS based on any chosen order. Therefore, the data elements in the sibling relationships must individually share a hierarchical relationship with a common superordinate. Likewise, a hierarchical relationship without an associated sibling relationship (i.e., only one subordinate) reverts to a simple sequence relationship.

The sibling relationship, like the hierarchical relationship, is imposed upon the data elements by the designer to formulate a data structure. It is always used in conjunction with a hierarchical relationship. Again, the combined use of the two relationships results in the data structure called "tree."

In summary, all the data structures identified for our purposes are based on one or more of the three relationship primitives. The use of these primitives results in two essentially different data structures: an ordered list and a tree. The former is based on a simple sequence relationship; the latter is based on the hierarchical/sibling relationship. These data structures are implemented by different mechanisms. These, in turn, are constructed differently as various languages provide different facilities for implementation.

IMPLEMENTATION

Implementing the Simple Sequence Relationship: Ordered Lists

As stated above, when the simple sequence relationship is imposed upon a set of data elements, the resulting structure is an ordered list. For our purposes, a list will be defined as a one-dimensional series of elements in which the number of elements is not fixed. Each element of a list, with the exception of the first and the last, is directly related to two other elements: its immediate predecessor and its immediate successor. Each of the two extreme elements of the list is related to one other element.

As is the case with all data structures, the relationships that exist among the elements of an ordered list are an integral part of the structure. Therefore, as its name implies, the sequence in which the items of an ordered list appear is significant.

Data structures are structural frameworks. Within the realm of data processing, we use programs to construct mechanisms that implement these frameworks. In considering mechanisms that can be used to implement an ordered list, we realize that they must deal with two facets of the data structure: (a) the data elements, and (b) the relationships that exist among the data elements. The order that is held by the items in a list can be represented in a variety of ways. Choice as to how to represent this order can have a significant impact on the behavior of the mechanism that is employed for processing them.

The first step in categorizing implementation techniques is to divide the approaches into two general categories: those that represent element sequence (relationships) through element contiguity and those that do not. Mechanisms that fall into the first category are called linear lists. The second category comprises a number of pointer-based techniques.

Before we describe these mechanisms, it should be reiterated that elements organized to form a data structure are often complex objects. An element of an ordered list, for instance, most often comprises a collection of fields rather than a single field. As an example, consider the case of a simple mailing list. It is not sufficient to maintain a person's name only nor is it enough to simply maintain the person's address. If the ordered list is to be of any use, an element must include both attributes of the person: the name and the address.

In most data processing applications, more than two attributes are involved. Consider, for example, a personnel application where we must manage data about an employee's name, salary, social security number, department, tax status, and so on. In considering such situations of multiple attributes, it quickly becomes obvious that a single data object, for example, the employee record mentioned above, can be an element of a number of data structures. Such records can be organized in the form of an ordered list according to name while simultaneously being organized in a different ordered list according to social security number, as well as salary, depending on the data processing requirement. In the descriptions and examples that follow, we ignore this complexity whenever possible to make the material easier to understand.

Linear Lists

Using a linear list (level 2, Fig. 1) is probably the simplest and most obvious method of mechanizing an ordered list. In a linear list, all information describing the relationships that exist among the items is represented through the contiguity of items; the ith item in the list resides between item $i-1$ and item $i+1$ in the representation of the list. The relationships among the items are thus represented implicitly rather than explicitly.

One-dimensional arrays (level 3, Fig. 1) furnish a simple and direct means of constructing linear lists within primary storage. Each list item is simply stored in the respective position of the array. A minor complexity arises when we consider that an array contains a fixed number of elements, whereas the number of items in a list is, by definition, not fixed. Consequently, when using an array to configure a linear list, we must allocate an array that is at least as large as the largest list that will be processed. In BASIC, for example, the statement DIM LIST$(100) allocates an array, LIST$, which can be used to configure a linear list of 100 or fewer alphanumeric items.

Data Structures

When dealing with secondary storage, the simple sequential file (level 3, Fig. 1) is the obvious choice for a vehicle to configure a linear list. The ith item in the list is represented by logical record number i in the file.

As described above, the linear list, whether configured as an array in primary storage or as a sequential file in secondary storage, is a parsimonious means of mechanizing a simple sequence. Creation of the linear list is a simple process when the elements of the list are added to the structure in list order. Similarly, retrieving the elements in list order is a simple task: Iteratively access the next array element or read another record.

It should be restated that although the linear list represents both the data items and the relationships that exist between them, only the data items themselves utilize storage resources—the relationships are represented implicitly through the contiguity of items.

An item can be added to or deleted from the end of the linear list without causing any side effects. Deletion of terminal element n causes the simultaneous deletion of the relationship that existed between this element and the new terminal element $n-1$. The disadvantages of the linear list technique become obvious during some standard list processing operations: adding elements to the linear list and deleting elements from the linear list.

Consider, for example, the implications that surround the addition of a nonterminal element of the list. This operation, which is called inserting, disrupts all elements that follow the new element in the list. Assume, for example, that a list contains 10 elements and that a new item is to be inserted into the fifth position of the list, thus causing a total of 11 elements. To allow for insertion of the new element in position 5, the present fifth element must be moved to position 6. To allow for this movement, the present sixth element must be moved to position 7, and so on, until all successive elements have been repositioned.

A similar type of disruption occurs in the instance of deleting a nonterminal element of a linear list. In this case, assume that item 5 of a 10-element list will be removed, resulting in a new list containing 9 elements. Here, the elements that were originally numbered 4 and 6 in the list should be bound in a new sequence relationship. Because the relationship is to be represented through element contiguity, element 6 must be moved to linear list position 5. This, in turn, gives rise to the need to move element 7 to position 6, and so on, until the remaining elements have been repositioned.

The effects of additions and deletions of this type obviously depend on which element of the list is added or removed. As the element that is the focus of the change moves closer to the end of the list, the side effects that accompany the change decrease. If the end of the list is the target of the change, the side effects are nil—the element is simply added or removed. On average, half of the list must be repositioned as the result of an insertion or a deletion.

This shuffling of elements of a linear list results in the use of a valuable system resource: processing time. Consequently, if insertions and deletions are frequent, as in the so-called volatile list, the costs that accompany these operations may be prohibitive when using the linear list technique. Under such circumstances, an alternative technique to mechanize the simple sequence relationship should be employed. What is needed is a mechanism that is less sensitive to additions and deletions of data elements. The linked list is one such device.

Linked Lists

The disadvantages of the linear list technique come about because elements that are related sequentially must reside contiguously in the configuration of the linear list. When employing a linked list mechanism (level 2, Fig. 1), we are freed from this requirement and, consequently, the need to continually reshuffle data elements disappears. This results in a saving in terms of processing time. Unfortunately, in choosing the linked list over the linear list, the savings in terms of processing time is accompanied by an increase in costs of another kind. Specifically, the linked list requires more storage space than does the linear list. This issue, which is called the time-space trade-off, will be discussed further after the mechanics of the linked list technique have been described.

Recall that the linear list technique represents the relationship (sequence) that exists between two data elements implicitly; contiguity implies sequence. The linked list structure, on the other hand, represents the relationship explicitly. The information as to which elements are related is actually stored within the configuration. This accounts for the additional storage overhead which accompanies the use of the technique.

In a linked list, each element contains two distinct parts: a data part and a link part. The data part stores the value of the data item being represented by the list element, whereas the link part describes the sequence relationship that the element holds with another element in the list. In essence, the link part "points" to the next element in the sequence of the list. For this reason, the link part is often called a pointer.

Because each linked list element directs us to the next item in the sequence of the list, we can access the elements in list order by simply following the series of pointers. This concept is illustrated in Figure 2, which shows a linked list that comprises seven names. Items in the list are ordered alphabetically so the first item of the list is the name AL, which comes first in alphabetic order; the second item of the list is the name BILL, which comes second in alphabetic order and so forth.

Pointers are denoted in the diagram by arrows that flow from one element to another. The object marked HEADER, which is not part of the list itself, contains a single pointer that directs us to the first element. This provides a starting point for processing the list.

Exactly one element of the list, specifically the terminal element, has no arrow flowing from it. This is because the element has nothing to point to—there is no "next" item in the sequence of the list. In this instance the arrow is replaced by an asterisk (*), which denotes END OF LIST.

Note that elements adjacent in the sequence of the ordered list need not reside contiguously in the linked list mechanism. In considering a given element of the list, the next element may reside anywhere, either ahead of it or behind it, in the total configuration of linked list elements.

Before we can understand the mechanics of performing operations on linked lists, we should consider how they can be constructed in the memory. Obviously, arrows do not actually flow from element to element. How, then, can an item direct us to its successor? The answer is based in the concept of "addresses."

Data Structures

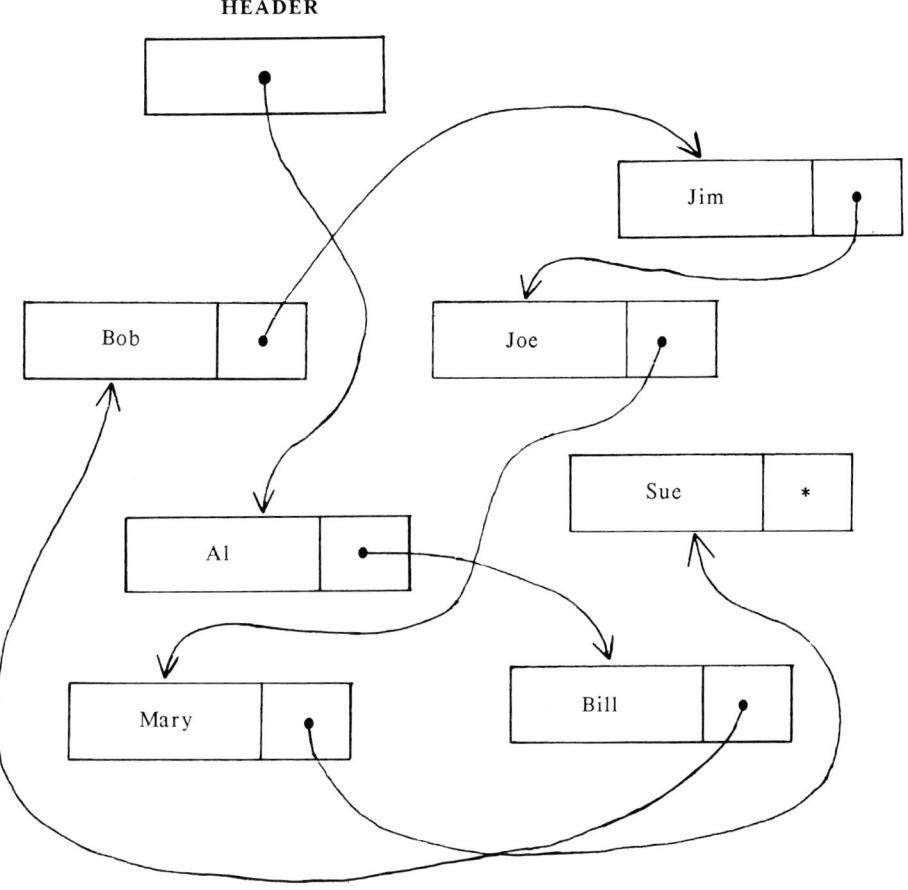

FIGURE 2.

We will use the term address to mean some value that uniquely identifies the location in which an element resides. Assume that the object can be accessed given the address of a data object. In working within the realm of primary storage, consider the subscript value that accompanies an array element as an address. In fact, it is a relative address; its value is generated relative to the beginning of the array. When dealing with secondary storage, the record key value in a direct access file serves as an address. In both of these situations, the data element (array element or record) can be located through use of its address.

If each data element of a linked list has an address, then a pointer mechanism can be implemented by simply storing the address of the successor element in the link part of the list element. Because possession of the address of an item provides the ability to access the item, when one item of a linked list is accessed, the ability to access the next item in the list is automatically obtained through possession of its pointer. In accessing this next item, we obtain the ability to access its successor, and so on, until the terminal element is reached.

The first element of the linked list, like all other elements, can reside in any physical position within the configuration. Some mechanism is therefore needed to locate the start, or head of the list, so that this repetitive process can begin. The HEADER, whose single value is the address of the first element, satisfies this need.

As mentioned previously, the number of items in a list is not fixed. As a consequence, some means of knowing when the terminal element has been reached must be provided. This element has no need for a pointer, so the link part of the element is available for use as an indication of this fact. It is common practice to indicate the end of the list by storing an address value that is undefined in the particular implementation of the data structure. For example, a negative value could be used if all addresses are positive. This END-OF-LIST flag value, which is implementation dependent, is depicted as * in Figure 2.

Like their linear counterparts, lists of the linked variety can be constructed in primary storage through the use of arrays. A linked list element comprises two distinct parts, so its configuration requires the use of two array elements: one for the data part and one for the link part. This is commonly carried out by utilizing parallel arrays, that is, using two one-dimensional arrays that contain the same number of elements. These arrays are usually configured side by side when presented diagrammatically; hence, the name parallel arrays.

As would be expected, one of the arrays, for example, DATA$, is used to store the data parts of the linked list, whereas the other array, say POINTER, is used to store the pointers. The arrays are used in an aligned fashion so that the pointer stored in any POINTER(i) is part of the same linked list element whose data part is stored in DATA$(i). In the case of arrays, a pointer is coded as the value of the subscript of the array element that depicts the next list item. In other words, it is the relative address of the successor item.

Parallel arrays are employed rather than using a single two-dimensional array because the latter option is often restrictive in terms of the type of data that can be stored. In most general-purpose programming languages, two-dimensional arrays must contain data values of a common type (e.g., character, integer, real). When using arrays to implement a linked list, the pointers will generally be in the form of positive integers, whereas the data may be of any type. Two-demensional arrays would therefore be unsuitable for many list applications.

Figure 3 depicts the seven-item linked list of Figure 2 as it would be constructed using parallel arrays. The two one-demensional arrays, DATA$ and POINTER, have 10 elements apiece. Unused array elements are represented by a dash (—).

In the diagram, the simple variable HEADER serves as the list header. The value of HEADER represents the address (2) of the first item in the list. The value of this data item (AL) is found in the second element of DATA$ (i.e., DATA$[2]). The link part of this list item, the value stored at POINTER(2), directs us to the second list item (BILL), which happens to reside at relative address 6 of the array structure. The link part of this item directs us to the third item, and so on, until the terminal item is reached. An undefined address value, specifically a value of -1, is used to signal the end of the list in this implementation.

Data Structures

	DATA $	POINTER	HEADER
1	Bob	8	2
2	Al	6	
3	—	—	
4	Joe	7	
5	—	—	
6	Bill	1	
7	Mary	10	
8	Jim	4	
9	—	—	
10	Sue	-1	

FIGURE 3.

It should be noted that the unused elements of the array are scattered throughout the structure. In other words, the array is not densely packed. The reader should also note that the order in which items appear in the array does not follow the sequence of the ordered list. Although it makes little sense to create the initial linked list in this manner, the lists tend to take on such a scattered appearance after undergoing a number of operations.

Before linked list operations are studied, we will briefly discuss the way in which linked lists can be constructed in secondary storage devices. In describing the concept of addresses, reference was made to the fact that the key value of a record in a direct access file can be considered as an address under our definition. Given the address (key value) of the object (record), the object can be accessed. Because a record can be accessed through possession of its address, a linked list can be formed quite easily using this file type. For each record in the file, we must simply embed the address of its successor record. This is accomplished by adding an extra field to the record format to account for the link part of the linked list item. Again, the terminal element can be flagged by storing an address that is undefined in the particular implementation, for example, a key value that is outside the range of key values for the application.

The behavior of the linked list under processing is essentially the same whether it is constructed in primary storage or in secondary storage. We will focus our discussion of processing and list operations on primary storage because array notation lends itself to simple presentation.

The list operations that raised such havoc in the linear list implementation of an ordered list were insertion and deletion of nonterminal elements. These two operations necessitated the repositioning of all subsequent elements, often resulting in excessive expenditure of processing resources. When a linked list is employed, no such repositioning is required. Instead, only a few pointers need to be changed.

The case of element insertion will be considered first. Let us assume that a new name, ALICE, is to be inserted into the linked list of Figure 2. The data structure that is implemented by the linked list, that is, the initial ordered list, is arranged alphabetically. Consequently, ALICE should be inserted between AL and BILL in the sequence of names.

The ease with which this operation can be performed is best understood if we focus on the relationships that are affected by the change. To insert the new element and maintain proper list sequence, the following actions must take place: (a) The present relationship between AL and BILL must be dissolved; (b) a new relationship between AL and ALICE must be formed; and (c) new relationship between ALICE and BILL must be formed. Although this sounds like the plot of an afternoon soap opera, the actions involved are hardly as complex.

Relationships are represented explicitly using pointers, so a restructuring of the relationships involves a modification of the pointers. By changing the pointer part of the first element (AL) so that it points to ALICE rather than to BILL, the first two required actions are accomplished. By having the pointer part of the new element (ALICE) directed toward BILL, the final requisite action is completed. Thus, by writing or rewriting two pointers, the desired sequence is maintained in the linked list mechanism.

Of course, a discussion of the insertion of an element also raises the question as to where the new element resides in the stored configuration. The answer to this question is anywhere. The new element, as all other elements of the linked list, can take any position in the total configuration of elements. The issue as to how this position is located will be discussed later.

Figure 4(a) shows how insertion of the new name is mechanized in the linked list. Figure 4(b) shows how this change is accomplished within the stored array configuration. The new name is stored in array element DATA$(5) which, you will remember, was an unused "slot." The pointer part of the predecessor element (POINTER[2]) is changed from 6 (address of BILL) to 5 (address of ALICE). The value 6 (address of BILL) is stored in the pointer part of the new element (POINTER [5]) to indicate that BILL is the successor of ALICE.

Note that there is no need to rearrange the positions of the stored elements, as was the case with the linear list mechanism. Insertions in a linked list are always as simple as in the situation described above. However, two special cases deserve quick mention. In the case of inserting a new element at the front of the list, the list header rather than the predecessor is changed to point to the new element. In the case of inserting an element at the end of the list (i.e., adding), the pointer part of the new element is changed to the END-OF-LIST symbol rather than to the address of a successor.

Data Structures

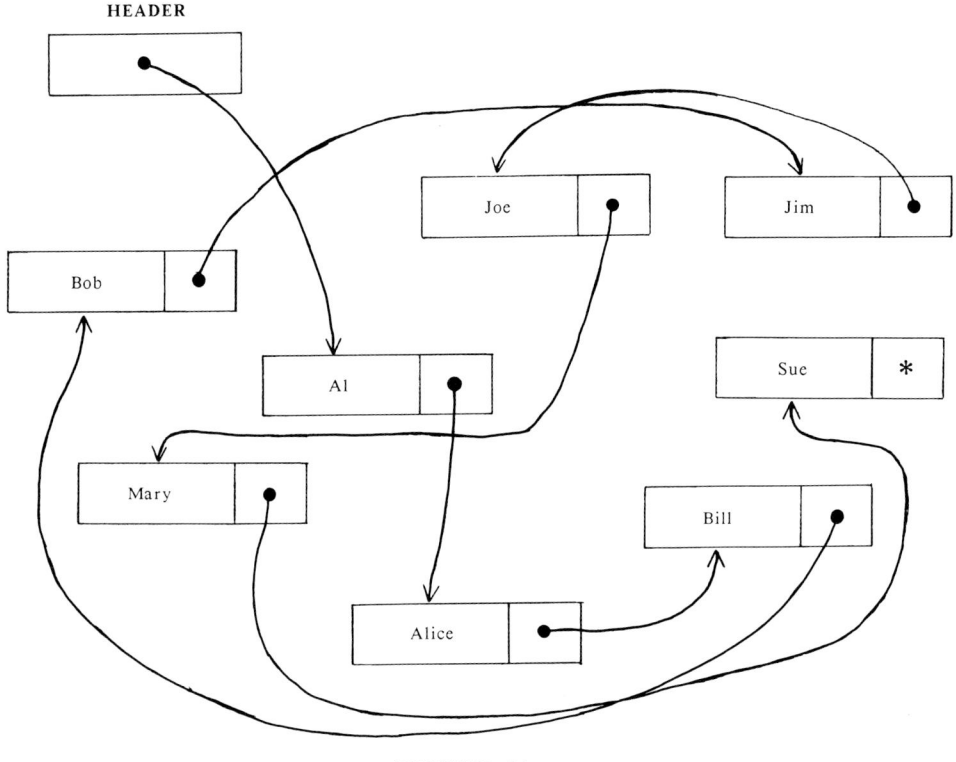

FIGURE 4A.

Deletion of an element in a linked list is as simple as insertion. Again, the change in the structure of the relationships is handled by merely modifying a few pointers. Let us assume that the name JIM is to be deleted from the list. By simply changing the pointer part of the BOB element to point to JOE, JIM is, for all practical purposes, removed from the list. As illustrated in Figure 5, we merely bypass the element.

An obvious question concerning element deletion remains unanswered, specifically, What happens to the deleted element? The actual space utilized by the element should, of course, be available for use later, that is, to hold a new element. When the need to use this space arises, there must be some mechanism at hand to locate the newly available space within the total configuration. A second linked list, designed to operate in harmony with the original linked list, can provide such a mechanism.

Imagine that all available space for the name linked list, that is, all unused array elements, are chained together to form a separate linked list. Let us call this list the storage pool. When an element is deleted from the name list, the newly available slot can be inserted at the head of the storage pool list (see insertion description above). On the other hand, when an element is to be inserted into the name linked list, the required space can be taken (deleted) from the head of the storage pool list. Note that the two mechanisms work in a complementary fashion so that when a slot is added to one list, it is taken away from the other. In this way, the name list can continue to grow and shrink with the users needs. The only limitation is that the size of the mechanism may not exceed the space that is allocated for its stored configuration (e.g., the bounds of the arrays).

DATA $		POINTER	HEADER
1	Bob	8	2
2	Al	5	
3	———	———	
4	Joe	7	
5	Alice	6	
6	Bill	1	
7	Mary	10	
8	Jim	4	
9	———	———	
10	Sue	-1	

FIGURE 4B.

Multilists and Inverted Lists

In many data processing situations, the attribute involved in a data structure is categorical in nature, meaning that there are a limited number of values that may be taken on, and more than one entity can have the same value on the attribute. In the case of employee data, for example, the attribute DEPARTMENT NUMBER is categorical. Similarly, if the data relate to college students, the attribute CLASS STATUS, having values FRESHMAN, SOPHOMORE, JUNIOR, and SENIOR, is categorical. In situations such as these, it makes sense to create a separate linked list for each value of the attribute. In the case of the college student data, we would form a linked list of all freshmen, a second linked list of all sophomores, and so on. The resulting mechanism, which is called a "multilist," is illustrated in Figure 6.

Note that the header in this case is a complex data object rather than a single pointer value. In fact, the header itself is a sequential list in which each data element of the list is a data value pair. The student data, organized in this way, would allow the retrieval, for example, of the names of all sophomore students.

Data Structures 95

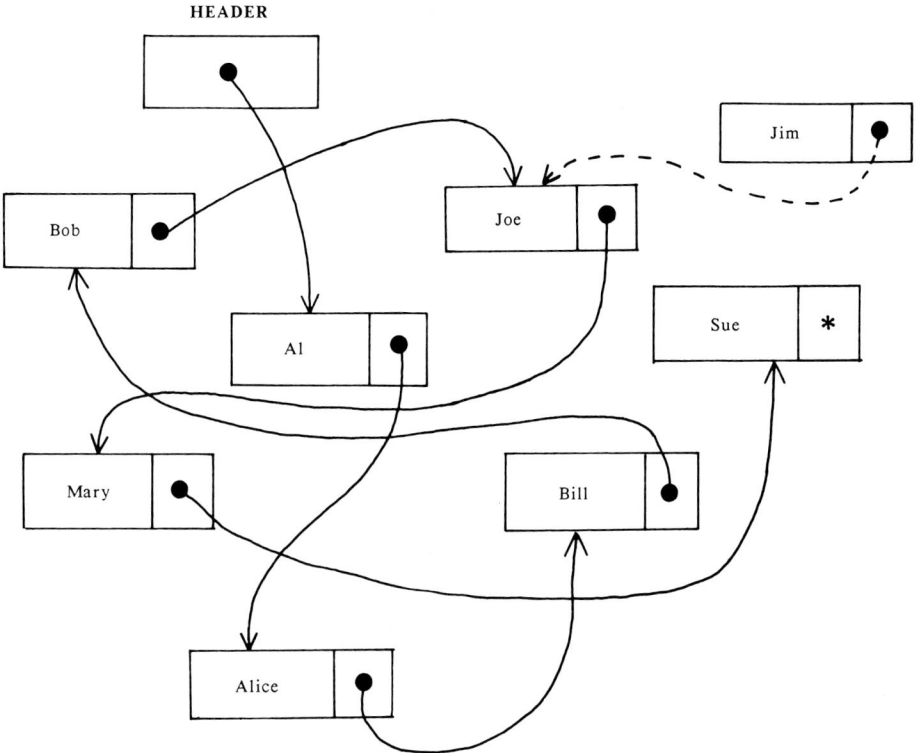

FIGURE 5.

HEADER				NAME	CLASS STATUS	POINTER
Freshman	2		1	Adams, B.	Sophmore	7
Sophomore	1		2	Cook, M.	Freshman	3
Junior	4		3	Kelly, W.	Freshman	9
Senior	5		4	Lewis, D.	Junior	6
			5	Morse, B.	Senior	*
			6	Patton, J.	Junior	8
			7	Powers, M.	Sophmore	*
			8	Reed, S.	Junior	*
			9	Smith, J.	Freshman	10
			10	Ward, G.	Freshman	*

FIGURE 6.

It should be noted that the header, in the case of the multilist mechanism, serves as an "index" to the front of each linked list for the attribute in question. Once the head of a linked list is found, the index can be ignored. This is because the location of each "next" element is stored adjacent to the data for the element. By storing this information as to list sequence in the index rather than with the data, still another mechanism is created.

The process of moving the pointers from their position within the linked list elements to the index is called inverting the attribute. The resulting mechanism is called an "inverted list." The inverted list that relates to our student data are illustrated in Figure 7. In using this mechanism, it is the index rather than the previous list element that directs us to each item. The storage requirement of the technique is the same as that of the linked approach because the same number of pointers is involved.

Double Linked Lists

In some situations, the needs of the application require that an ordered list be processed in both directions. In other words, we may wish to deal with the items in list sequence as well as in reverse list sequence. The concept of reverse list sequence does not "go against the grain" of the data structure because a list element holds a sequence relationship with a predecessor as well as with a successor.

HEADER			NAME	CLASS STATUS
Freshman	2,3,9,10	1	Adams, B.	Sophmore
Sophomore	1,7	2	Cook, M.	Freshman
Junior	4,6,8	3	Kelly, W.	Freshman
Senior	5	4	Lewis, D.	Junior
		5	Morse, B.	Senior
		6	Patton, J.	Junior
		7	Powers, M.	Sophmore
		8	Reed, S.	Junior
		9	Smith, J.	Freshman
		10	Ward, G.	Freshman

FIGURE 7.

Data Structures

In a similar vein, a linear list used to mechanize the data structure lends itself to this type of processing—an element's predecessor resides contiguously as does its successor. The simple linked list described above does not support reverse list processing, however. Of the two relationships held by an element, only the relationship with the successor is represented. If the output requirements demand that the items be processed in both directions, the linked list mechanism must then be modified to support this processing.

The modifications that are required are obvious. The predecessor relationship must be represented as is the successor relationship. Because we cannot rely on element contiguity to imply these relationships, we must represent them explicitly, that is, a second set of pointers is required.

The resulting mechanism is called a double linked list. Each element of a double linked list has two pointers: a forward pointer and a backward pointer. The incremental costs that accompany the use of this technique are obvious—we must incur the additional cost of storing and maintaining the second set of pointers. Because the mechanism is more expensive than the simple linked list, it is only employed in the situation where the output requirements demand reverse list processing.

Figure 8 illustrates the double linked list mechanism. The object labeled TRAILER provides access to the final element when reverse processing is required. The implications that double linking has on the operations and on the stored configuration of the mechanism are straightforward.

Special Cases

It often does not make sense to perform some operations on an ordered list. Consider, for example, the situation where the elements of an ordered list represent a "waiting line" (first come first served) of entities to be processed. Any element that is added to the list must take position "behind" the existing elements. In other words, additions are made at the rear end of the list only. When an item is needed for processing, it is taken from the front of the list. Thus, deletions are only made from the opposite end of the list. The general insertion operation is not applicable in a waiting line setting.

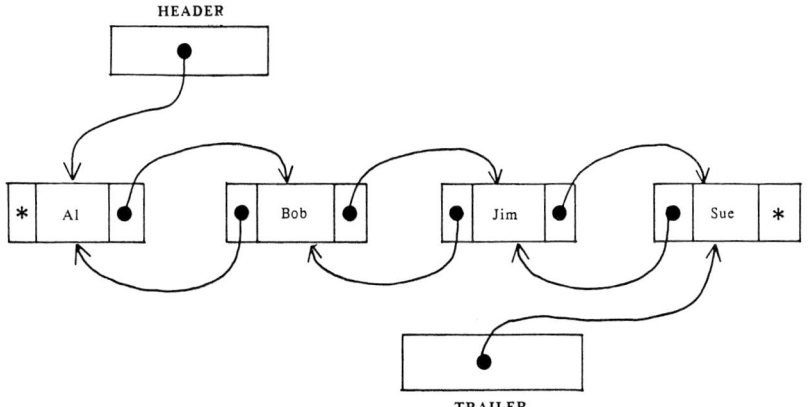

FIGURE 8.

When these restrictions are placed on the operations that can be made on an ordered list, we have a data structure that is called a queue, or a FIFO (first-in-first-out) list. The queue is a commonly used data structure because waiting lines are common occurrences in our world. Because queues are so common in data processing, their mechanization and configuration deserve special attention.

The queue, like the more generic ordered list, can be configured in a sequential fashion. The mechanization is more complex, however, because a queue grows at one end and shrinks at the other end. If the basic linear list technique were used, we would find that the allotted space was quickly overrun even though the length of the queue was relatively short. As each item in the queue was processed (deleted), its space would be deemed useless for further processing.

This problem is solved by using a special addressing technique to reference the storage area in which the data structure is implemented. This technique generates a pattern of addresses that makes a linear sequence of storage locations appear as if they form a circular structure. By the term circular we mean that the storage structure appears to have no beginning or end. Rather, the technique provides an infinite number of "next" storage elements.

As an example, assume that a sequential storage structure, say an array called Q, contains n elements. In the circular design, the elements of the array are referenced, in order of sequence, $Q(0)$, $Q(1)$, $Q(2)$,... $Q(n-1)$, $Q(0)$, $Q(1)$, and so one. Thus, the element with the lowest address, $Q(0)$ in this case, is made to "follow" the element with the highest address, $Q(n-1)$, in the configuration. This repeating pattern of addresses is easily achieved through use of the standard remainder function "mod." In this article the term m mod n is used to denote the remainder when the quotient m/n is calculated. By using this remainder function to calculate storage addresses, we are able to configure the queue in a storage structure that appears to be circular.

Assume that a pointer called REAR directs us to the current rear of the queue, that is, the element after which an item will be added. A pointer called FRONT directs us to the position just ahead of the front of the list. Therefore, when an item is to be deleted, said item resides in the position that follows Q(FRONT) in the circular design.

If REAR = FRONT, the queue is empty. This condition represents a meaningful state in most applications. If the element that follows REAR points to the same element as does front, the mechanism is full, that is, all allotted space is being utilized. An attempt to add an item in this situation results in an "overflow condition" in which the mechanism fails to work properly. The concept of overflow is totally an artifact of the mechanization of a queue; it does not hold any meaning when considering the data structure itself. Note that the technique requires one more element of storage than there are items in the queue.

The circular design is pictured in Figure 9. Shaded elements represent the items in the queue. Unshaded elements are presently unused. Throughout the life of the implementation, the shaded portion inches its way along in a clockwise motion.

Data Structures 99

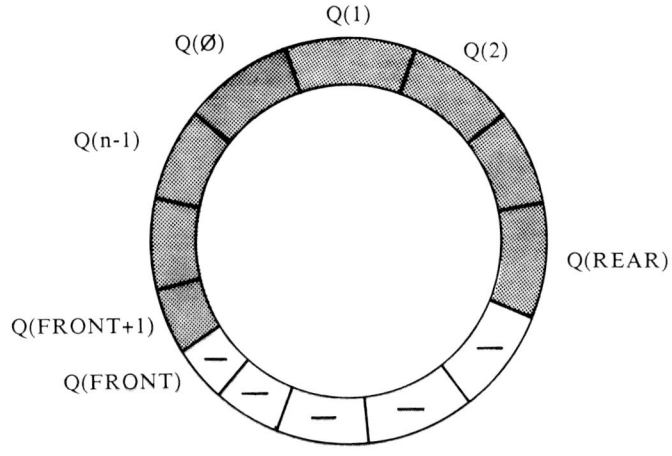

FIGURE 9.

To add an item to the queue, we must first adjust the rear pointer, REAR, to point to the "next" position in the circular structure. This is achieved by means of REAR = (REAR+1 mod n). The item is then stored in array element Q(REAR). Note that a mechanism-full condition should be tested before this is done in order to avoid overflow.

When an item is to be deleted from the queue, we must direct the front pointer, FRONT, toward the first item in line. This is done via FRONT = (FRONT+1 mod n). The item in question resides in array element Q(FRONT). Of course, this action should be taken only after the queue-empty condition has been tested.

It should come as no surprise that a queue can be mechanized in the form of a linked list. Because queue operations are focused on the ends of the structure, the mechanism includes two pointers, FRONT and REAR, which are directed toward the front and the rear of the list, respectively. The mechanism is pictured in Figure 10. The element labeled DUMMY contains no meaningful data, yet it is a requisite of the technique if the queue-empty condition is to be handled. When there are no items in the queue, both FRONT and REAR point to the dummy element. When an item is added to the structure, both REAR and the link part of the previous rear element are directed toward the new element (the dummy element allows this procedure to work in the case of an empty queue). The link part of the new rear is obviously set to *.

In the situation of element deletion, the queue-empty condition must be tested before processing takes place—it must be determined whether or not there exists an item waiting to be processed. If the queue is empty, then we should find * in the element to which FRONT points (DUMMY is the end of the list). If such is not the case, then the link part of DUMMY directs us to the item in question. This element must now take its turn as DUMMY; FRONT is revised to point to it.

Another commonly used data structure is called the stack. Like the queue, the stack is a special case of the ordered list in which only additions and deletions are performed on the structure. The stack differs from the queue in that both of these operations are performed on the same end of

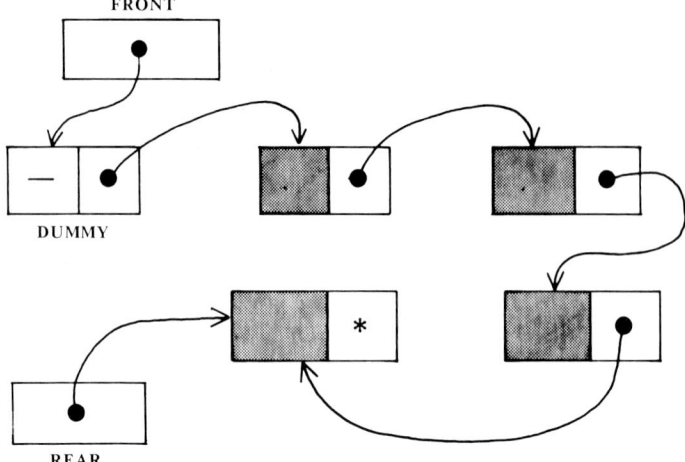

FIGURE 10.

the list. Because much of the complexity that surrounds the mechanization of a queue relates to the fact that we must focus on both ends of the structure, we will see that the implementation of stack is simpler.

In a stack, the item next in line for deletion is the item that was most recently added to the structure. The stack is therefore called a LIFO (last-in-first-out) list. A LIFO list is commonly pictured as a vertical pile of items, so rather than a front and a rear, the structure has a top and a bottom. As is the case with a stack of plates in a cafeteria, when a new item (plate) is added to the arrangement, it is placed on the existing top of the stack. When an item is removed, it is taken from the top. Note that the bottommost items in the stack remain untouched for the life of the structure unless the inventory of items is substantially depleted.

Stacks have a variety of applications in the computer sciences. The LIFO pattern provides an excellent bookkeeping device when a nested structure is involved (e.g., nested subroutine calls or nested loops). The structure also provides a simple method for managing an inventory of computer resources that do not need to be rotated in their allocation (e.g., buffer space).

The mechanization of a stack, like that of a queue, should include checks for two conditions: empty and full. Here again, the concept of "empty" relates to a situation that is meaningful in the world of the application, whereas the concept of "full" is an artifact of the implementation; it relates to the amount of space available to configure the mechanism.

The stack, when implemented in a sequential fashion, is perhaps the simplest mechanism employed in the field of data structures. An array, STACK, of n elements can be used to represent a stack containing up to n items. The bottommost item is stored in STACK(1), the next-to-bottommost item is stored in STACK(2), an so on. Because all activity takes place at the top of the stack, only one pointer is required: TOP, which holds the address of the topmost item. When TOP = 0, STACK is empty, in which case no items may be removed. TOP = N denotes a full condition, that is, the mechanism has reached the limit of its capacity and will fail to function if additional items are added.

Assuming that the stack is not empty, the next item to be removed is found at STACK(TOP). The removal of this item is represented in the mechanism by decrementing the value of TOP by one (i.e., TOP = TOP-1). If the mechanism is not full, the addition of an item is as simple: Increment the value of TOP, and store the new item at STACK(TOP).

Implementing stacks with a linked approach is elementary. The mechanism employed is patterned after the basic linked list, with the HEADER serving as the top-of-stack locating device. Note that in this case of a stack, the mechanism is only required to handle additions and deletions from the head (top) of the list (stack). As discussed previously, these two operations are quite easily accomplished. The insertion operation is unheard of in the stack situation.

Implementing the Hierarchical and Sibling Relationships: Trees

Tree structures are often used as a means of organizing and classifying entities. Common examples are library classification systems, decision trees, and organization charts. Because of their ubiquity as an organizing tool, the tree data structure is found in many data processing situations.

Searching is an activity that is frequently performed in a computer science or data processing environment. It happens that tree-shaped structures lend themselves to situations where searching is involved; consequently, a number of tree-shaped searching mechanisms have been developed and studied in detail. Examples of these mechanisms are the AVL-tree, the B-tree, and the B*-tree. Although widely used and of great importance, these mechanisms are not data structure mechanisms as we use the term. They are searching tools that happen to be tree shaped and, therefore, will not be detailed in this article.

It should be noted, however, that many of the principles discussed below can be applied to these searching trees. This comes from the fact that the searching tools noted above and the data structure concepts described below are based on the same shape—that of the tree.

As described earlier, the tree data structure imposes two primitive relationships upon its elements, specifically, (a) the hierarchical relationship that exists between a parent element and a child (of the parent) element and (b) the sibling relationship that exists among the children of a common parent.

In the general case of the data structure, an element may have any number of children. There is a special case of the data structure called the "binary tree" in which this is not true. In a binary tree, the degree of every element, that is, the number of children of the element, can be no more than two. An important property of trees is that any general tree can be transformed into a binary tree.

Some applications in the real world lend themselves to a binary scheme. Decision trees, for example, are often binary trees. A binary tree is usually simpler to mechanize and to configure than a general tree, as will be discussed later. Consequently, the tree data structure is often transformed into a binary tree, which prepares the data structure for easier implementation. It is important to realize that the binary tree, when used in this way, is an artifact of mechanization of the general tree data structure.

A variety of approaches to mechanizing trees is available. Although the majority of approaches rely on the use of pointers to represent the relationships among data elements, a few do not. We will see, however, that the pointerless techniques are seldom satisfactory.

Implementations of trees tend to be more complex than those of ordered lists. Some of this added complexity arises from the fact that the quantity of relationships is not a part of the definition of the data structure. For any given element, the number of child elements or the number of sibling elements is not fixed. Also, we must deal with the fact that a tree data structure involves so many different kinds of relationships (parent-child, child-parent, sibling-sibling). However, if certain critical relationships are represented explicitly the remaining ones are implied automatically. Most tree mechanisms are based on this concept.

Consider a mechanism in which only the (hierarchical) relationship between a child and its parent is explicitly represented. The number of relationships of this type are easily calculated. Each element, with the exception of the root (topmost element), has exactly one parent. Therefore, if there are n elements in a tree, there are exactly $n-1$ child-parent relationships. Now, assuming that these $n-1$ relationships are known, the remaining ones can be derived mechanically. For example, a sibling relationship exists between any two elements that hold a child-parent relationship with a common parent.

One simple means of implementing a tree does not involve pointers; nevertheless, it engages quite a bit of storage overhead. Assume that the tree pictured in Figure 11 is to be represented within computer storage. The tree has nine elements, so eight hierarchical relationships are involved. Two parallel arrays, each having nine or more elements, can be used to represent this tree. The configuration is presented in Figure 12.

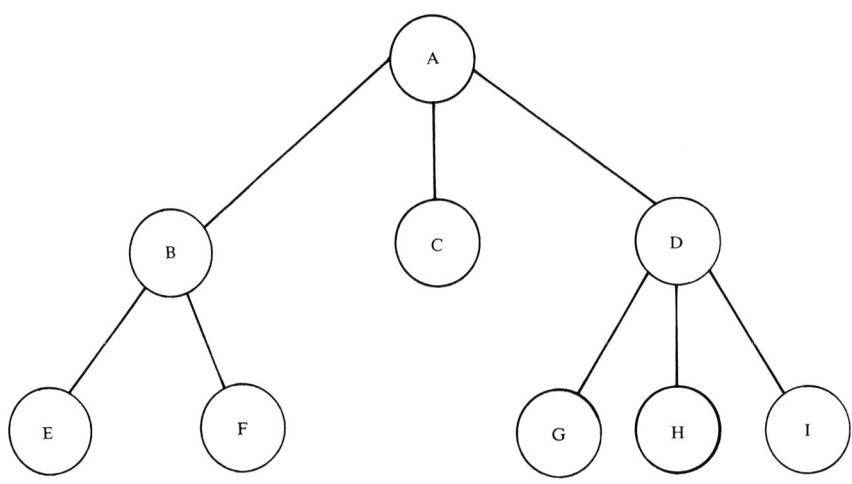

FIGURE 11.

Data Structures

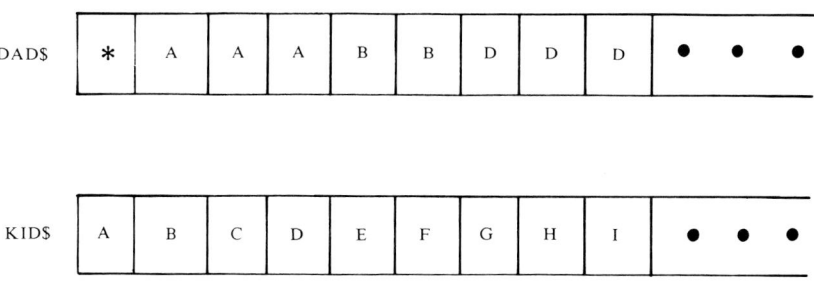

FIGURE 12.

The array KID$ holds the nine elements of the tree. For any position in KID$, the respective position in DAD$ holds that element's single parent. The one occurrence of * in DAD$ is used because the root of the tree has no parent.

The reader should be assured that the original tree structure can be reproduced from this simple stored configuration. Mechanisms on which this configuration is based are quite cumbersome in all but one circumstance. Specifically, the approach is only well suited when the information needs demand that we work our way up rather than down the structure. It should be noted in passing that the storage overhead requirements of the technique would likely be reduced if DAD$ held pointers rather than the parent items themselves.

When the tree being implemented is of the binary variety, it can be configured sequentially using a single array. The utility of this approach increases when we recall that any tree can be transformed into a binary tree. In this approach, the relationships in the structure are represented implicitly through the position of elements, as was the case in the linear list. However, the mapping function involved in deriving the relationships is more complex.

To understand this method, we must first realize that a binary tree having m levels contains at most $n=(2**m)-1$ elements. This fact is easily verified by constructing a few simple examples. The mapping function that is used relies on a specific numbering scheme for tree elements. This scheme, in turn, is based on the structure of a "full" binary tree; that is, if the binary tree has m levels, it has exactly $n=(2**m)-1$ elements.

Figure 13 describes the pattern of the numbering scheme. If the binary tree under consideration is not full, the numbers corresponding to the missing elements are ignored in the implementation.

Assuming that an array called TREE, having at least n elements, is available to configure the tree, the position in which a tree item is stored is defined by the template of Figure 13. Figure 14(a) presents a sample binary tree. Figure 14(b) shows how this tree would be configured in the array. Wasted space depicted by a dash (—), is observed because the sample tree is not full.

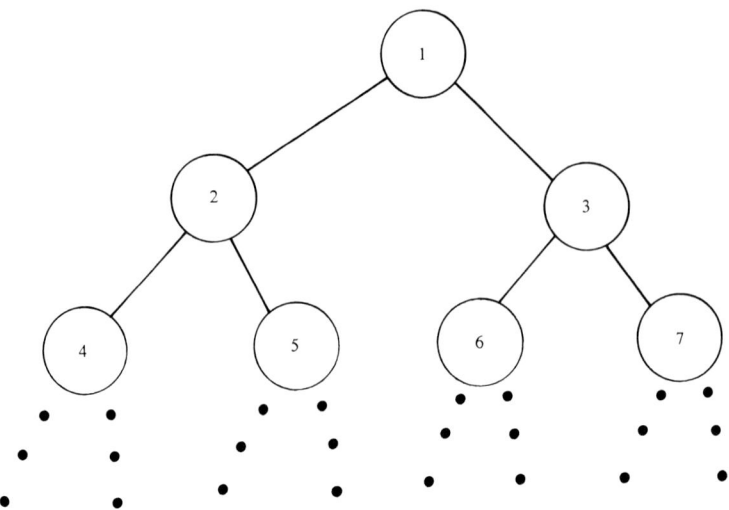

FIGURE 13.

The mechanism that employs the stored configuration can make use of the following rules to determine the relationships of the structure:

1. If $i <> 1$, then the parent of element i resides at position FLOOR($i/2$); otherwise ($i = 1$), there is no parent.
2. If $2i <= n$, then the left child of element i resides at position $2i$ and the right child resides at position $2i+1$; otherwise ($2i>n$), element i has no children.
3. If $i <> 1$, then the sibling of element i resides at position $i+1$ if i is even and at position $i-1$ if i is odd; otherwise ($i=1$), the element has no sibling.

The approach described here works quite well in the situation where the binary tree being implemented is full or nearly full. When such is not the case, the wasted storage that is incurred usually prohibits its use because more space-efficient, pointer-based techniques are available. As a final note, the implementation approach is extendable to any situation in which the maximum degree of tree elements is fixed. For example, a trinary tree could be implemented in a similar way. In the case of a unary tree (maximum degree = 1), the mechanism reverts to the basic linear list technique.

As stated earlier, tree data structures are most often mechanized by means of a linked approach. In looking at the diagrammatic representation of a tree, link-driven mechanisms immediately come to mind. It is obvious that a single parent pointer embedded in each child element facilitates simple movement up the structure.

Data Structures 105

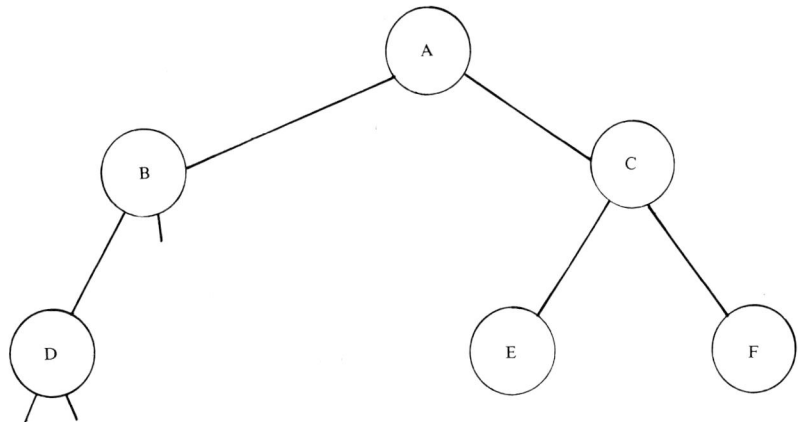

FIGURE 14A.

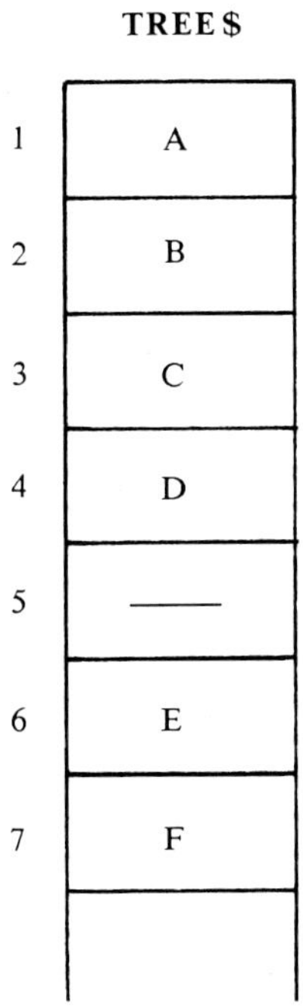

TREE$

1	A
2	B
3	C
4	D
5	—
6	E
7	F

FIGURE 14B.

Unfortunately, most data processing situations require that we work in the other direction (i.e., starting at the root) when dealing with trees. Child pointers are not as easily implemented as parent pointers because, at least in the case of a general tree, any number of pointers may be required to represent the relationships between a parent and its children. If we choose to simply embed child pointers with each parent, major problems can arise during the life of the implementation. When we configure the mechanism, a choice must be made as to how many pointers are to be allocated. If this number is excessive for most elements, a great deal of space is wasted. If this number is too small for even one element, the mechanism fails. This problem leads us to investigate other linked approaches.

One approach uses explicit representation of the sibling relationship and capitalizes on the fact that siblings have a common parent. Consider an implementation of a general tree data structure in which each tree element has four distinct parts. In addition to the data part, each element has two pointers and a logical (true/false) flag. The first pointer, call it L-SON, is directed toward the left-most (first) son of an element. DAD-BRO, the second pointer, links the right brother if one exists; otherwise, it points to the element's father. The logical flag NO-BRO is set to TRUE in the event that there is no right brother; it is FALSE otherwise. Note that the value of NO-BRO indicates the destination of DAD-BRO.

Figure 15(a) reproduces the tree of Figure 11. Figure 15(b) illustrates the workings of the stored configuration. L-SON is depicted as a solid line—, whereas DAD-BRO is a dashed line if it points to a sibling (NO-BRO would be FALSE) and a dotted line if it points to the parent (NO-BRO = TRUE). The value of * would be used and interpreted appropriately in the mechanism.

The approach described above supports movement throughout the tree in a number of directions. In some situations a related element cannot be found directly but must be found through the use of other elements instead. For example, if we wished to reach the parent of C, we must first follow the linked list of siblings. If, on the other hand, we desired the left sibling of C, we would be required to continue past its parent until we found the element B, whose DAD-BRO link points to C.

Obviously, if more flexibility in traversing the tree is desired, we must pay the price of increased storage overhead due to more stored pointers. One approach that has been suggested uses four links: a parent link, a right sibling link, a left sibling link, and a left child link. Other variations are, of course, possible.

The three-pointer design is particularly handy if we periodically have the need to visit every element of the tree only once. This operation, called full traversal, is not an uncommon requirement of tree-based applications. The three-pointer scheme, with the aid of appropriate algorithms, allows us to cycle through the various families of siblings and return to the point from which we started each time.

As noted earlier, the use of a full set of child pointers is unwieldy in the general case because the number of children of a tree item is not fixed. There are special situations where this is not the case. For example, the aforementioned decision tree is very often restricted to the binary variety.

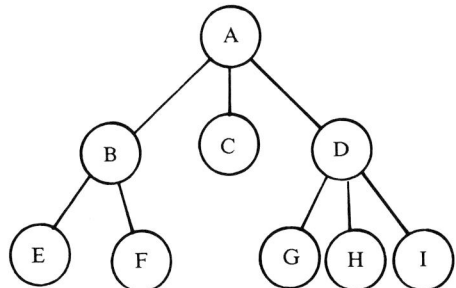

FIGURE 15A.

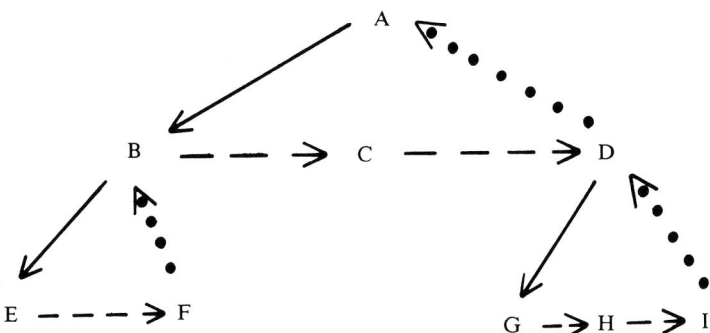

FIGURE 15B.

Trinary trees and others are also possible in certain applications. Also, it should be remembered that any general tree can be transformed into a binary tree. In situations such as these, child pointers are a viable design solution to the mechanization of the data structure. Our description will focus on the binary case, but it will become obvious that the approach is directly extendable to the other cases.

For the binary situation, each element of the mechanism is tripartite; it contains a data part, a left child pointer part, and a right child pointer part. When an item has no child, the particular pointer is set to *. The binary tree of Figure 14(a) is diagramed in Figure 16 as it would be implemented in this way.

One feature of tree structures is that there tends to be a large number of terminal elements in relation to the total number of elements in the structure. In a full binary tree, for example, more than half of the ele-

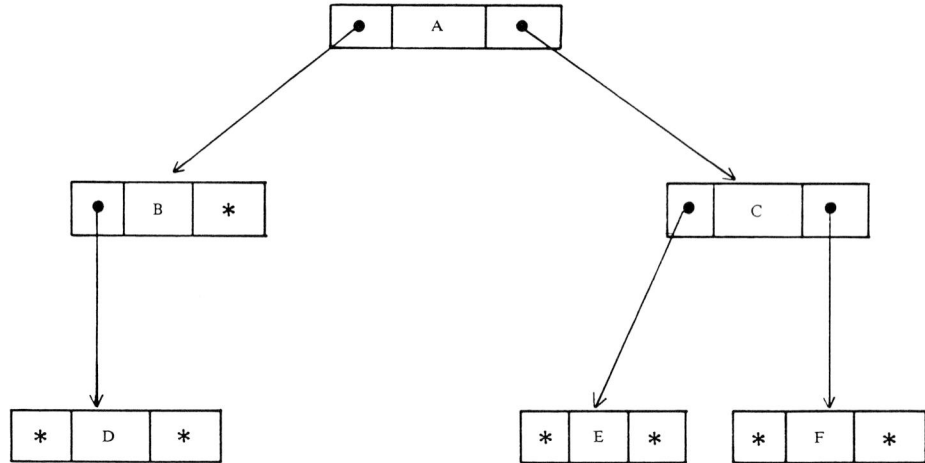

FIGURE 16.

ments are terminal. Consequently, if the mechanism involved in implementing the tree uses child pointers, a great number of these pointers will be unused (i.e., *). Threading is a technique that makes use of these otherwise unproductive bits of storage. Rather than containing *, the child pointer parts of the terminal elements direct processing to another element. The target is chosen so as to aid in the traversal of the structure. These revised pointers, called threads, could point to the parent, to the root, or to any other element that makes sense in the processing situation. Threads are particularly useful in facilitating the full traversal operation.

Finally, the data structure of trees is seldom static, as is the case with ordered lists. Hierarchical and sibling relationships are continually being formed and broken in the world of our application. Consequently, our stored configuration of the data structure must also change. In most cases, tree-based operations such as insert, delete, and add must be built into the mechanism that implements the data structure. The details as to how these operations are carried out will not be presented here because they are highly dependent on the specifics of the chosen design; however, some general comments can be made. First of all, volatile trees are easier to handle when the configuration is link based rather than sequential because a linked representation does not require that elements be reshuffled when a change is made. Second, these operations are usually easier to accomplish when the implementation uses fewer rather than more pointers because fewer pointers require adjustment when the structure is modified.

EVALUATION FACTORS

The Hardware Efficiency

As stated earlier, there are only two fundamentally different data structures: the ordered list and the tree. The others discussed, such as stack,

Data Structures

queue, binary tree, and so on, are variations or special cases of the ordered list or the tree. In theory, one of the fundamental justifications for selecting a particular mechanism for implementing a structure (e.g., selecting linear list instead of linked list) is to achieve hardware efficiency. By hardware efficiency, we refer to the traditional measures of storage space and processing time. However, we do not mean to imply that the optimum trade-offs between these two factors always dictate the selection of the ideal data structure mechanism.

The ever-improving technology has made the traditional measurements of hardware efficiency a very clouded issue. For example, microelectronics, especially very high-speed integraded circuit (VHSIC) technology, and magnetic storage technology have been continuing to dramatically improve the operating speed, memory capacity, and cost of processing.

Each year, the size of chips has been shrinking while achieving incredibly greater CPU speed. It is projected that by 1990, we will see VHSIC chips that operate 100 times faster than most of today's home computers.

The RAM capacity has been improving by leaps and bounds. The secondary storage devices have shown an even more impressive rate of progress in magnetic recording. The storage density of magnetic disk devices, for instance, has been doubling about every $2\frac{1}{2}$ years for the last 30 years. Very high-density magnetic tape storage has also been made available. What all this means to computer users is that they can now have their data processing requirements satisfied much quicker and at a lower cost.

In light of these technological advances, the question as to which data structure mechanism is the most appropriate in terms of saving space and reducing processing time for a given data processing requirement is becoming increasingly academic. In practice, it may not even be a proper question. Therefore, other factors that are actually considered include familiarity with techniques, ease of implementation, ease of maintenance, and so on.

Evaluation Factors Revisited

If hardware efficiency is becoming less and less critical in the evaluation, then what *should* the major trade-off factors be and why? Increasingly, what concerns the systems designers the most are the problems of designing and maintaining software effectively. To them, the considerations on the ease of implementing a data structure mechanism and the subsequent economy of maintenance seem to be more of a critical issue than economizing the resources of computer hardware.

Despite the new tools and techniques of software engineering that have been introduced within the last decade, software maintenance cost continues to be extremely high. Typically, it represents more than 60% of the total software life-cycle cost.

New technological developments such as optical disk storage will almost certainly lower the computing cost even further. As a result, the traditional evaluation factors will become even less significant, thus shifting the evaluation factors further toward the software side in the future.

BIBLIOGRAPHY

Aho, Alfred V., et al., *Data Structures and Algorithms*, Addison-Wesley, Reading, MA, 1983.

Baron, Robert J., and Linda G. Shapiro, *Data Structures and Their Implementation*, von Nostrand, New York, 1980.

Berztiss, A. T., *Data Structures: Theory and Practice*, 2nd ed., Academic Press, New York, 1975.

Chaturvedi, Atindra, "Tree Structures: A Tutorial on Using Tree Structures for Random Data Storage and Retrieval," *PC Tech J*, February 1985, pp. 78–87.

Ellzey, Roy S., *Data Structures: For Computer Information Systems*, Science Research Associates, Chicago, IL, 1982.

Elson, Mark, *Data Structures*, Science Research Associates, Chicago, IL, 1975.

Flores, Ivan, *Data Structures and Management*, Prentice-Hall, Englewood Cliffs, NJ, 1970.

Gotlieb, C. C., and L. R. Gotlieb, *Data Types and Structure*, Prentice-Hall, Englewood Cliffs, NJ, 1979.

Horowitz, Ellis, and Sartaj Sahni, *Fundamentals of Data Structures*, Computer Science Press, Potomac, MD, 1976.

Knuth, D. E., *The Art of Computer Programming 1*, 2nd ed., Addison-Wesley, Reading, MA, 1973.

Kruse, Robert L., *Data Structures and Program Design*, Prentice-Hall, Englewood Cliffs, NJ, 1984.

Langsam, Yedidyah, et al., *Data Structures for Personal Computers*, Prentice-Hall, Englewood Cliffs, NJ, 1985.

Martin, James, *Computer Data-Base Organization*, 2nd ed., Prentice-Hall, Englewood Cliffs, 1975.

Overmars, Mark H., *The Design of Dynamic Data Structures,* Springer-Verlag, New York, 1983.

Page, E. S., and L. B. Wilson, *Information Representation and Manipulation using Pascal*, Cambridge University Press, New York, 1983.

Reingold, Edward M., and Wilfred J. Hansen, *Data Structures*, Little, Brown and Co., Boston, MA, 1983.

Standish, T. A., *Data Structures Techniques*, Addison-Wesley, Reading, MA, 1980.

Singh, Bhagat, and Thomas L. Naps, *Introduction to Data Structures*, West Publishing Co., St. Paul, MN, 1985.

Tsichritzis, Dionysios C., and Frederick H. Lochovsky, *Data Models*, Prentice-Hall, Englewood Cliffs, NJ, 1982.

Wirth, Niklaus, *Algorithms + Data Structures = Programs*, Prentice-Hall, Englewood Cliffs, NJ, 1976.

C. KIM and S. A. WESTIN

THE ENTITY — RELATIONSHIP APPROACH

BACKGROUND AND ORIGINS

The entity—relationship (ER) approach, which consists of an analytical method and a modeling technique, was first described by Dr. Peter Chen in 1976. Since that time, it has evolved into one of the most important tools in the data analysis tool kit.

Most popular analytic approaches, or methodologies, focus either on the processes being performed or on data elements presumed to be needed by the user. Some concentrate on trying to fit lists of data elements into one of the data structure models that can be implemented by a database management system (DBMS), others on designing from reports, screens and files, and still others on following trails of transactions through their various processing stages. From these processes, flows, data elements, and/or outputs, they attempt to recreate the real world. Many attempt to recreate the processes from the desired results.

As data processors, they assume that the world is made up of data, which must be processed. Each method approaches the data problem differently, and many times their results reflect those of the blind men who examined the elephant: to the one examining the tail it felt like a rope, to the one examining the sides it felt like a wall, to the one examining the legs it felt like a tree, and to the one examining the trunk, it felt like a snake. In a sense, they were all right, and none was right.

In the business environment, examining only transactions, processes, outputs, data flows, or even a combination of all four produces a picture that is correct as far as it goes but does not reflect a true or complete picture of the environment. Business environments are populated by people using things, and both people and things are located in places. Any business description must not only include these people, places, and things, but it must also start with them. These people, places, and things are called entities.

These people, either individually or in groups, work with things, or provide services, for other people. Because both the people and the things are real (they physically exist), they can be described, and they must be located somewhere (in some place). Additionally, relationships that exist between people and things, people and places, things and places, and between different types of things, different types of places, and different types of people themselves must be described.

Processes are the actions that people entities (or their mechanical or electromechanical surrogates) perform with other people entities and with other thing entities in place entities. Transactions and reports are mechanisms for recording those processes or for communicating between entities, and data flows are the paths that these transactions, reports etc., take between and among the people entities and the location entities where such reports are stored.

These entities may be well defined in that the firm may know a great number of things about them, or they may be vaguely defined in that the firm may know very little about them. In some cases, such as with either prospective customers or employees, the firm may only know or suspect that they exist but not who they are or where they are.

These entities may exist in large homogeneous groups where all members are capable of being described in the same manner, or they may be fragmented into many different subtypes, each with descriptions that are either slightly different or, in some cases, radically different from the other members of the same group.

The relationships that exist between these entities are real. And as with the entities, these relationships themselves may be well defined in that the firm may know a great number of things about them, or vaguely defined in that the firm may know very little about them, again as little as knowledge or suspicion of their existence.

The power of the ER approach lies in its ability to focus on describing these entities of the real world of the business and the relationships between them. By describing these real-world entities, through the identification, definition, and assignment of attributes to them, and their relationships, the analyst is describing how and why the business operates.

Although the business itself may change, sometimes dramatically, these types of changes occur much less frequently than changes in the routine processes and activities. Regardless of the business changes, the entities of the business rarely change. What may change, however, is the firm's perception of which attributes of those entities are currently of interest. Some relationships between these business entities may also change, but even these relationship changes occur infrequently. Thus, by understanding and properly describing these entities and the relationships between them, the analyst can form a very stable foundation for understanding and analyzing the business itself and for properly recording the results of, or changes caused by, the processes of the business.

CONSTRAINTS ON THE ER APPROACH

As with any analytical method, the effectiveness of the ER approach is limited, or constrained, by three factors, all of which have to do with the analyst's understanding of the business environment. These closely related factors are (a) entity identification and definition, (b) entity description, and (c) business context.

Entity identification and definition consist of recognizing the various entities, determining why they are of interest to the firm, and naming them. The identification and definition process must specify the entity at the exact level of precision, which ensures that it is not so general as to be meaningless and yet not so specific that it fragments into too many subsets. For example, people as an entity would be too general because it includes both customers and employees, among others. On the other hand, full-time employees and part-time employees would be too specific because both are employees, and "full-time" and "part-time" are attributes of employee, and a person may alternate between the two states and still be the same employee.

Entity description consists of identifying which attributes of the identified entities are needed by the firm and why those attributes are of interest. For example, is the firm interested in the attribute "hobbies" or

The Entity—Relationship Approach

"clothing sizes" for the employees? If the firm is a sporting goods firm, the answer to the former might be yes. On the other hand, if the firm provides uniforms for its employees, the answer to the latter might be yes.

Business context involves identifying and defining the relationships that exist between the identified and defined entities and their relative importance to the firm as a whole and to each specific part of the firm. Business context also involves identifying and defining the use or role of each of the entities within the firm. An entity's appearance, role, or use in one firm may be entirely different in another firm, and yet the entity itself is the same.

Just as an entity may have different roles or uses between firms, each part of the firm may also have a different perspective on the business, and each part of the firm may have a different perspective on the entities of the firm. This perspective does not change the fact of the entity's existence—only the attributes and relationships of those entities that are of interest to that portion of the firm and their role or use in that firm.

The specific description of these entities and their relationships with other entities within the firm is relevant only within the context of that firm and is totally dependent on the attributes of the entities that are of interest to the firm. An entity within one firm may be only an attribute of an entity within another firm, and vice versa.

ENTITIES, RELATIONSHIPS, AND ATTRIBUTES

The importance of identification and definition, description, and context can be seen when one looks at the formal definitions of the three key elements that form the heart of the ER approach. These definitions form the basis for both the data analysis method and the data modeling technique of the ER approach.

1. An *entity* is defined as a person, place, or thing that is (a) of interest to the corporation, (b) capable of being described in real terms, and (c) relevant within the context of the specific environment of the firm.
2. An *attribute* is any aspect, quality, characteristic, or descriptor of either an entity or a relationship. An attribute must also be (a) of interest to the corporation, (b) capable of being described in real terms, and (c) relevant within the context of the specific environment of the firm. An attribute must be capable of being defined in terms of words or numbers, i.e., the attribute must have one or more data elements associated with it. An attribute may be the name of the entity or relationship. It may describe what the entity looks like, where it is located, how old it is, how much it weighs, etc. An attribute may describe why a relationship exists, how long it has existed, how long it will exist, or under what conditions it exists.
3. A *relationship* is any association, linkage, or connection between the entities of interest to the corporation. These relationships must also be (a) of interest to the corporation, (b) capable of being described in real terms, and (c) relevant within the context of the specific environment of the firm. It is important to note at this

point that relationships exist only between entities, not between attributes of entities.

To illustrate, the entity "person" could be anyone. When the attributes *name, age,* and *sex* are added, we can identify man from women, adults from children, and one person from another. When the relationships *married to, parent of, child of, member of,* and *works for* are added, we know whether we are talking about a group of unrelated people, a family, or a corporation.

To describe the entity, we must describe it in terms of its attributes and its relationships with other entities. An entity description consists of a series of statements that complete a phrase such as "the entity is...," "the entity has...," "the entity contains...," or "the entity does..." Each attribute relates to the entity in hierarchic terms, i.e., all attributes of the entity are fully dependent on the entity itself because they are the entity individually and together.

However, the question can still be asked "How can we begin to identify these entities"? For example, is the entity identified as "customer" (representing all customers), is it a specific type of customer (such as mail order or retail), or is it a single customer? The answer is that it can be all of these, none of these, or more than these.

The specific identification and definition of the entity has meaning only within the context of that firm. However, most businesses can be described using a fairly restricted set of generic entity types such as customer, product, machine, employee, location, organizational unit, etc.

An entity is whatever the business defines it to be, and that definition must make sense within the context of the firm. Thus, an entity in one firm may be a subset of entities included in the entity definition of another firm or may be the global definition of the entity used within another firm.

These differences in identification and definition can be illustrated by the following example:

A town planning board, with responsibility for community planning and zoning, would describe that community in terms of each of its buildings and further subdefine those buildings into residential, office, stores, warehouses, and factories.

It might be interested in which people or which firms occupy or own those buildings, but for their purposes, that information would be an attribute of the building, just as the size of the building, the number of floors, the number of windows and doors, and the cost of the building are attributes.

On the other hand, the local Chamber of Commerce doing a census, or community directory, would be interested in the people and the firms who live, work, or are located in the community. In that case, they would be interested in the names of the people, their incomes, length of residence, amount of taxes paid, and where they live or are located within the community (the buildings). Here, the buildings become attributes of the people.

Neither the buildings nor the people have changed. Both still exist, physically unchanged. The perspective, however, has changed and the things that are of interest about those buildings and people have changed.

The perspective of the town council would need to know all the information about both the people and the buildings, along with information about roads, utilities, etc. In this case, both the buildings and the people become entities in their own right, along with the relationships between them (who lives or works where, who owns what, etc.).

This need for both attributes and relationships is consistent with the accepted dictionary definition of an entity that defines it as "the fact of existence; being...the existence of something considered apart from its properties." Thus, although the entity exists, its true form and role is only apparent after its attributes are added.

Without attributes, all we know about the entity is that it exists. The distinction between the entity and its attributes and the relationship between the entity and its attributes is so important that the ER diagram distinguishes between the entity and its attributes by using different symbols for each.

The attributes of an entity could be contained in a single record, or it may take a large collection of records, where each contains the data elements of a single attribute. Either way, an entity should not be equated to a record, a logical data record, or a table. Records and logical data records are the means for storing related items of data in the data processing environment.

ER MODELS VERSUS DATA STRUCTURE MODELS

Records hold individual data elements or groups of data elements. Logical data records are representations as to how selected groups of record types are logically and physically connected. Table rows may also be viewed as records from a data processing viewpoint.

Logical data records, also called logical data models, fall into three main formats: hierarchic, network, and relational. These traditional data models represent implementations, specifically DBMS implementations, of logical data records.

Each one models a different view of the structure of data, and in that light, they are more properly *data structure models.* The data structure models are creatures of data processing. When it considers data, the real world does not look at data structures but, rather, it looks at things (usually paper things) that contain data.

The ER model represents a conceptual view of the world, which incorporates all three data models, is independent of any DBMS or data processing considerations, and is a representation of the business environment. The ER model contains the major aspects of all three structural models.

Although we speak of entities as if they were singular, in reality an entity is a set of persons, places, or things, all of which have a common name, a common definition, and a common set of descriptors (properties or attributes). This conforms to the relational model and is equivalent to placing all attributes in the third form of the normalization process (3NF).

Although it may represent a single instance, the entity representation in the model usually represents numerous people, places, or things, all of whom have a common name and common descriptors and thus can be treated as a set, again in conformance with the relational model.

These entities interact (relate) with other entities. The interactions form a complex set of names and discrete relationships, as in the network model.

Although it exists physically, an entity only has physical substance when it is described in terms of what it looks like, where it is, what it does, and how it related to other entities. Each component of that description is a property or an attribute of the entity. The sum of the properties is the entity. This association of attributes to entities, if diagramed hierarchically, would appear as a flat (two-level) structure, with the root being no more than an anchor that names and types or subtypes the entity. In a network diagram, it would appear as a key-only owner record, with multiple set relationships. In relational form, the entity would be the name of the primary relation, and the attributes might be subsumed in that relation or might be separate secondary relations.

Because the ER model incorporates all three data structure models, it can view data in a more complete and realistic manner. Although it can be translated quickly and easily into any or all of the data structure models, the ER model is not a data structure model but, instead, seeks to identify and describe things and how they relate, rather than just data (used to describe those things) and how it can be stored.

The meld of the three data structure models within the ER model reflects the fact that each of these models represents a portion of the way in which those real-world things actually occur.

These entities are physically real, and their real properties can be described; these people perform actions, using and transforming both things and information (which is contained on things as data). The common characteristic between all entities is that they can all be described, and the media we use for that description are words and numbers. These words and numbers are data collectively and data elements individually.

The fact that entities, especially in the data processing environment, are described by data, does not make them data objects, nor is every collection of data elements an entity.

Some writers have suggested that data entities are built from collections of data elements in the same manner that a car is built from a collection of parts. In fact, an ER model can be complete and meaningful with no traditional data elements at all. The parts of a car were specifically chosen because each contributes something to the overall design of the vehicle. Any number of different sets of parts could be assembled and would result in a car, but a specific car can only be built from a specific set of parts.

A car is a thing; it is a subtype of the larger group of things called vehicles and part of another subtype called self-powered vehicles for transporting people and things. Just as there are many different types of vehicles not all of which are cars (some may be boats, planes, or trains), there are also many different types of entities.

A final type of attribute needs to be discussed; one that does not describe the thing itself, but what it does, how it is used, or why it is used. Things that an entity does are called activities, and collectively they are called processes. The attributes that describe these activities are called *processing-related attributes*.

The processes, or activities, of the business are in reality the actions that people take with respect to things, places, or other people. These actions usually result in some change in the physical appearance, state, or condition of one or more other entities, or sometimes in the creation of a new entity itself.

We can use the entity called "car" as an example:

The Entity—Relationship Approach

The physical characteristics of the car—its size, weight, year, make, model, color, and parts list—represent the car itself. Whatever happens to it, as long as it remains a car, these characteristics (except possibly color) will never change. Whether or not it is owned by anyone, is new or used, is in good repair or falling apart, or is driven 1 mile or 100,000 miles does not change these facts of its existence.

However, the fact that the car exists is meaningless unless we put it in context, which tells us why the firm is interested in it.

If we were a new and used car dealer, or a company fleet manager, we might want to know other things about the car, such as ownership, use and usage, options and accessories, etc. We might also want to know how many miles it was driven, how much gas it uses, how many times it was maintained, what was done to it at each maintenance, how many times it was in an accident, how many different people have driven it, what it cost new, its present cost, how much it costs to maintain, etc. These latter attributes are really process attributes. They are part of the description of the car and, in some cases, even part of the physical description; but these attributes tell us about what was done to or with the car, not about the car as a thing.

If we were an auto parts dealer, we might be interested in the parts of the car themselves, both new and used, in which case the year, make, model, and color of the car become attributes of the part, along with its usage characteristics (if it is not a new part), its cost, size, shape, weight, how many are used in a specific year, make, model, etc.

A specific part could be elemental, such as a bolt, tire rim, windshield, etc., or it could be a complex subassembly, such as a transmission, radio, motor, etc. It could fit one year, make, and model of car or any car. By combining several of these parts into a subassembly, we have in effect created a new "part."

All entities and most relationships have these types of process attributes associated with them. In many cases, these attributes tell us why the firm is interested in this entity. In other cases, they help to define how the firm distinguishes between different classes of the entity or why the firm is interested in some instances of the entity and not in others. These attributes also assist in determining when the firm first becomes interested in an entity or ceases to be interested in the entity.

These process attributes are variable in that their values change frequently, and these changes usually involve the participation of some other entity. Thus, because they relate what one entity did to another or where or how many of one entity are contained in another entity, they are normally descriptive of the relationship between the two, rather than descriptive of one entity or the other, although obviously they could be.

The processes of identification and definition, description, and contextual placement of the entities are vital to any understanding of the business and to any effort directed at either application development or file design. Processes like data normalization (a much discussed concept) cannot be meaningful unless we know what those entities are, what the difference is between an entity and an attribute of an entity, and further what relationships exist between those entities.

ER ANALYSIS

ER analysis (and the ER diagrams that result from it) is a multilevel process, where each level produces a clearer and more well-defined view of the environment. The complete results of this analysis are a series of leveled environmental descriptions, along with a diagrammatic representation of each level. These diagrammatic representations, the ER models, are descriptions of the entities, or real components, of the business environment and how they relate to each other.

These ER models are not data structure models. And, although they contain and identify data elements at their most detailed level, they are not data processing models. They are business models, and as such, they model business environments and depict business components.

What is a model? In formal terms, a *model* is a representation, either graphic, narrative, or a combination of both, of a physical or conceptual environment. It must identify the major components of the environment, describe those components in terms of their major attributes, and depict the relationships between the components and the conditions under which the components exist and interact with each other. A model can be composed of several independent or interdependent submodels.

ER diagrams (also referred to as ER models) consist of representations of the various levels and parts of the organization from the strategic to the operational levels. Each of these leveled models represents the entities and relationships from the perspective of that level, and within a level the ER models represent the perspective of one or more particular users at that level.

Although there are numerous variations of the ER approach model notation, the three basic notational components of the model consist of symbols representing an entity, a relationship between two entities, and the attributes, or descriptors, of either entities or relationships.

These symbols are

1. Rectangles—Each unique entity type or entity subtype is represented by a rectangle, which contains the name of that unique entity type or entity subtype.
2. Diamonds—Each relationship that exists between any two different entities or between two occurrences of the same entity is represented by a diamond, which contains the name of that relationship.
3. Circles—Each unique attribute of either an entity or a relationship is represented by a circle, which contains the name of that attribute.

LEVELED ANALYSIS AND MODELS

ER models have been applied to individual business units and even to individual business functions. The full ER approach model addresses the whole organization and each of its parts in a top-down manner. Only by using this top-down leveled approach can a complete and accurate business perspective be attained. The approach develops the models in pyramid fashion, beginning with the senior management level and proceeding downward.
This corresponds most closely to the manner in which most firms view themselves.

The Entity—Relationship Approach

We will present the models in the sequence in which they are most easily developed, a sequence that corresponds to the three levels of the organization: strategic, managerial, and operational.

The ER approach produces a different type of diagram, or set of diagrams, for each of these three basic organizational levels: the enterprise level, the ER level, and the ER attribute level.

Because they are based on a top-down approach, the models at each successively lower level represent a decomposition, or expansion of detail, of the level immediately preceding. The number of diagrams at each level is dependent on the number of entities and relationships involved and on the complexity of those entities and relationships. There is no requirement to maintain the diagrams on a single chart or to break them down into many smaller charts.

Aside from the enterprise level model, which should be a single chart and, by definition, a firm-wide chart, the lower level charts may be developed against any perspective. These perspectives may be firm wide, functional, by business unit, or by product line. Because they are designed to be an aid for analysis and understanding of the environment of the business, the diagrams at each level can be combined or split in any manner that aids comprehension, but above all they should be drawn so that they are easy to follow and meaningful to the analyst, developer, and user.

ENTERPRISE LEVEL ANALYSIS

The analysis at the first, or enterprise, level consists of identifying the major entities of the firm. Although an entity is usually represented as a single instance at this and all succeeding levels, each entity, in fact, represents a set of people, places, or things.

A *set* is a group of things of the same kind that belong together and are so used, or a group of persons sharing a common interest, performing a common function, or who are described in a highly similar, if not identical, manner.

At the enterprise level, the definition of the entity is very general and represents all people, places, or things that relate *to the firm* in the same general manner or that are viewed by the firm in the same manner.

The definition of the entity is as general as is possible, so as to include all current and potential members of the set, but specific enough to retain its meaning within the firm. For instance, a customer may be defined as "any person, or organization, that buys, rents, leases, or otherwise acquires product or service from the company." Product might be "any physical thing or service that the company provides to its customers in the course of conducting its business (not necessarily for a price)."

Enterprise analysis consists of the identification and definition of the major entities of the firm and an indication as to whether or not a relationship exists between them. At this level, there is no differentiation between the various subtypes of any given entity, nor the number or types of relationships between any two entities. The definition of each entity, however, should include the names of all known subtypes, or role variations, for the entity (i.e., salesperson, executive, part-time, full-time, etc.).

Every firm, large or small, deals with multiple types of entities in the course of conducting its business. Although the names of the various entities vary from firm to firm, at the most general level they can be grouped into four major categories: people, places, physical things (such as a document, a product, a machine, etc.), and logical or legal things (such as a corporation or a business unit). Using these four major categories, we can identify some of the most commonly occurring entities, regardless of the type of business a company does.

People entities fall into three major classes: people who make up the firm's workforce, people who are its customers or clients, and/or people who supply it with raw materials, products, parts, and financial or other services.

Place entities also fall into three major classes: places where its services are offered, or its products are made, stored, and/or sold, places where its work force is located, and places where its customers reside or are otherwise located.

Physical thing entities include the actual products of the firm, its physical assets (buildings, land, furniture, machinery or other equipment, inventory, supplies, etc.), its financial assets (money, securities, leases, contracts, bank accounts, loans, notes, credit lines, etc.), and the documents, memoranda, accounts, contracts, orders, invoices, statements, checks, vouchers, reports, and files that record its business transactions and activities.

Logical or legal thing entities include the services offered by the firm, the firms who are its customers or clients, the firms or people who supply it with raw materials, products, parts, and financial or other services, the markets within which the firm operates, the governmental and regulatory units under whose jurisdiction the firm operates, and the organizational units into which the firm's work force is grouped for business, functional, and reporting purposes.

Within any given firm, it can be expected that most, if not all, of the above entities will be represented. What they are called, how they are defined and described, how they are subtyped and, more importantly, what the firm needs to know about them, depends on the specific business of the firm, its culture, and the business rules, policies, mission statements, charters, and procedures that govern what it does and how it operates.

It should be remembered, however, that the business entities being identified and defined at the enterprise level relate to the firm as a whole. As such, these entities and relationships may be numerous, complex, and may lack the precision of definition that lower level models require.

Enterprise analysis depicts entities at the set level. At this level, the entities have the widest possible definition and scope while still maintaining the general physical and role characteristics of the individual entities that comprise them. These entity sets are treated as if there were no variations in type and as if each of their component entities were defined in a similar manner and behaved in a similar manner.

At the enterprise level,

- Entities are identified and named.
- Relationships are defined as either existing or not existing between any given pair of entities.
- All entities and relationships are viewed from a single perspective.
- Business rules are stated at a strategic or policy level and apply firm wide.
- Business activities are functionally stated.

The Entity—Relationship Approach

- Business entities are portrayed at a class or universal level. There is no differentiation between the various subtypes of a given entity, unless those differences have meaning at a firm wide and a functional level.

ENTERPRISE LEVEL MODEL

The enterprise level model, is created in two steps. In step 1, the entity is selected, named, identified, and defined. It is helpful, although not mandatory, to select a primary, or core entity, to begin the model. In most cases, this core entity will be either the customer, product, order, employee, or all four, because normally these are the most important entities to the firm. Each entity is represented as a rectangle with a name in it. The symbols for the selected entity (entities) are placed in the center of the page. All entities directly related to the core entity (entities) are placed, one at a time, in a ring around those at the core. These entities will be called secondary entities only for purposes of describing the model creation process. Each entity symbol should have the entity name within it. This is the entity's primary name (the name of all entities in the set) or its role name (the name of the entities in the subset being depicted).

In step 2, each pair of related entities is connected by a single line. Each pair of entities may be related in multiple distinct ways or in only one way. The line between each related pair does not distinguish between the various types of relationships and thus contains no name or other information. A specific entity may be related to multiple other entities; however, each entity must be related to at least one other entity within the model. Any two entities that have at least one distinct, identifiable relationship between them are connected by a single line. No entity should appear on the model that is unrelated to at least one other entity. There is no differentiation between the number or types of relationships between any two entities. Like the entities themselves, a relationship is a binary condition; it exists or it does not.

An enterprise level model will usually contain from 10 to 30 entities and should fit on a single sheet of paper. The number of entities that appear will depend on the complexity of the corporation and the type of business and the degree to which differentiation between various subtypes is important to the senior management (or strategic) levels of the firm.

Another determinant of the number of entities is the way in which the entities have been defined. A model that contains the general entity "employee" will be less complex than one that contains more specific entities such as "sales," "production," and "back office employee." Again, a model that defines the general entity "organizational unit" will be less complex than one that defines "sectors," "groups," "divisions," or "subsidiaries."

There are no rules governing how the entities are defined at this or any other level, except to say that the definitions should be consistent with respect to their level of abstraction (i.e., do not define one entity as "all employees," and differentiate between all different types of products or customers at the same level).

These definitions should also make sense within the context of the firm, and they should be as specific or as general as necessary to make the diagram clear and readable.

ER LEVEL ANALYSIS

The analysis at the second, or ER, level is an expansion of the work performed at the enterprise level. At the ER level, the entities that were identified previously only at the set level can now be brought into sharper focus. It is at the ER level that differing types or subsets of entities are recognized.

As with the enterprise level, the entities are in reality groups or sets of people, places, or things; however, these groups may be much smaller and much narrower in definition than those at the enterprise level.

For instance, it may be relevant to a company to differentiate between types of customers, such as between institutional and retail in the brokerage industry, between subscription and mail-order in the publishing industry, between different types of products, such as spare parts and finished items, or between elemental parts and subassemblies.

In some cases, the various entities may be differentiated by the role that they play with respect to the firm. For instance, the analysis may distinguish between executive managers, middle managers, clerical workers, professionals, and sales personnel, between full-time and part-time workers, between salaried and hourly workers, or between union and nonunion workers.

Another set of distinctions might be by function, such as between production, sales, engineering, and back office. In each of these cases, although the people in each category are all employees, they are treated differently by the firm or they play different roles with respect to the business of the firm.

As each distinct subset of each entity set is identified, it should be named. Each of the entities (and subset entities) identified at this level should be related to at least one other entity and may be related to many other entities. Each subset entity should relate to one or more subset entities of the entity sets to which its parent set is related. In addition, at this level, the specific relationships that exist between each pair of entities are identified and named.

All models below the enterprise level business model are more detailed and may use any number of distinct entity subtypes or subsets of the universal entity set in place of the universal entity set. Here, each subset is given a name corresponding to either the entity subtypes that populate it or to the role that the subset member entities play within the firm.

These names are usually something other than that of the entity name assigned to the universal set. The subsets are usually created to represent the various roles that the more global entity plays.

In some cases, the subset name is different from the role name and may represent the title by which the members, or principal members, are known within the firm. In these cases, both the role and title names by which that entity is known should be stated.

At the managerial level,

- Entities and entity subtypes are named.
- Each relationship between the pairs of entities or entity subtypes is identified and named.
- Entities and relationships may be firm wide or viewed from a variety of business unit, divisional, or other organizational perspectives. These perspectives may cross functional or business unit boundaries.

- Business rules are tactical and may apply firm wide or to a specific unit or set of units.
- Business activities may be function or process oriented.
- Business entities may be portrayed at a global or universal level or may be differentiated into more restrictive subtypes that relate to the particular business unit.

ER LEVEL MODEL

The creation of the ER level model is a two-step process. In step 1, the major entities represented at the set level on the enterprise level model are differentiated into their meaningful subsets (components, subtypes, subclasses, etc.). Here, the various types of customers are differentiated, as well as the various types of products, employees, accounts, etc. As each entity is differentiated, its subsets are named and defined. Once differentiated, each subset is treated as a complete entity from then on. In step

In step 2, each of the distinct, identifiable, relationships between each pair of entities that was determined to be related at the enterprise level is named and defined. Relationships are represented as a diamond with the relationship name within it. If an entity at the enterprise level has been differentiated into subset entities at the ER level, it is possible that not all subsets may relate to other entities or entity subsets in the same manner as the enterprise level entities.

For each pair of related entities, each distinct relationship is identified, defined, and represented on the model using a relationship symbol. The relationship symbol is connected on each side to one of the pair of entities that participates in the relationship and should contain the name of the relationship between these two entities.

The above procedure should be repeated until each distinct relationship between the pair has been named, identified, and placed on the model. It is possible to have the same named relationship for multiple pairs of subsets of each enterprise level pair.

When completed, at least one named and defined relationship should replace the line between each two related entities at the enterprise level or between some subset of each of those entities. No entities (or subsets of entities) should be related at this level that were not shown to be related at the enterprise level. Each distinct pair of related entities may have one or more named relationships between them. Except for recursive relationships (those where individual instances of the entity are related to other entities of the same type), each relationship should be between two entities of different types.

ER-ATTRIBUTE LEVEL

The analysis at the third, or ER-attribute, level builds on the work of the ER level adding attributes to both the entities and the relationships. An attribute is represented by a circle attached directly to the entity or the relationship that it describes. The circle contains the name of the attribute. Attributes might be identification information, residence information, physical description, inventory status, packaging information, hobbies, clothing sizes, etc.

The attribute names for an employee entity might be very similar to the section or item headings on an employment application, or the section or item headings on the permanent employee record form. For a customer, they might be very similar to the section headings on a new account opening form or on the customer record form.

For an entity, each attribute represents some grouping of data that is necessary, from a business perspective, to describe a physical or logical characteristic or some activity of the entity. For a relationship, each attribute represents some grouping of data that is necessary from a business perspective, to describe, qualify, or maintain the named relationship between two entities.

At the operational level,

- All attributes of each entity and entity subtype are named.
- All attributes of each relationship between each pair of entities or entity subtypes are identified and named.
- Entities, relationships, and business activities may be firm wide or viewed from the individual perspective of the operational, user, or application areas.
- Business rules are tactical and apply to a specific unit or set of units.
- Business activities may be functional, process, activity, or task oriented.
- Business entities may be portrayed at a global or universal level but are more probably portrayed as individual subtypes that relate to the specific operational unit.

The ER—attribute model is an expansion of the ER model. Until this point, the models have only identified the entities and relationships by names and context. Little is known about a given entity or relationship, other than its name, the obvious fact of its existence, and the fact that the firm is interested in it.

At the ER—attribute level, entities and relationships are described in terms of their attributes or characteristics. In other words, beyond knowing that the entity exists, we must also know what the entity looks like, how it is identified, and what it does. These descriptors or characteristics are called attributes. An attribute is thus any distinct aspect of the entity or relationship that is necessary to describe the entity or to qualify the relationship. The full description of an entity or relationship consists of the full set of attributes that describe that entity or relationship.

For an entity attribute to be significant, it must relate directly to the entity, be completely dependent on the entity for its existence and meaning, and be definable in terms of one or more data elements. It is immaterial whether there are one or more data elements in an attribute, as long as the attribute applies to all instances of the entity being represented. Seen another way, an attribute is some distinct category of mutually related data, the sum of which describes something of interest about the entity. The identifiers (unique or otherwise) of an entity are a special form of attribute.

Entity attributes represent

- A physical characteristic of that entity—size, shape, weight, or color.
- A historical attribute—date of birth or date of hire.

- A location attribute—place of residence, place of work, or place of birth.
- A nonphysical characteristic—price
- An identifier—name, title.
- An occupational characteristic—current position, skill possessed, training received, educational courses, etc.
- The intermediate or final results of some processing activities related to the entity.
- Data that relate to some current state or condition of the entity or to some past or future state or condition of the entity.
- Data that relate to some current action taken by or against the entity or to some past or future action taken by or against the entity.

For a relationship attribute to be significant, it must relate directly to the relationship, be completely dependent on the relationship for its existence and meaning, and be definable in terms of one or more data elements. It is immaterial whether there are one or more data elements in an attribute, as long as the attribute applies to all instances of the entity or relationship being represented.

A relationship attribute is some distinct category of mutually related data, the sum of which describes something of interest or some qualifier about the relationship between two entities. A relationship attribute must be dependent on the connection between both entities and should be incapable of existence in the absence of that relationship. The minimum attributes of a relationship are the necessary identifiers of each entity of the related pair.

Relationship attributes represent some descriptor or qualifier of the relationship, such as

- A historical attribute—date of marriage, sale, or storage.
- A location attribute—place of storage, work, or birth.
- A nonphysical characteristic—price or discount at time of sale or grade in course.
- Some meaningful piece of data that is not an attribute of either entity participating in the relationship, but pertains only to the relationship between them. This piece of data is sometimes called intersection data.

It is possible for the same named attribute to be used to describe many different entities and relationships. Identifier attributes in particular describe both the entities and the relationships between them.

ER—ATTRIBUTE LEVEL MODEL

The creation of an ER—attribute model is a multiple-step process. This level produces the most detailed model.

Step 1 extracts each entity from the ER model and places it at the top of a separate page. Each distinct relationship between each pair of related entities is extracted from the ER model and placed at the top of a separate page.

Step 2 identifies, names, and defines each attribute of each entity. Each attribute, represented by an attribute symbol, is drawn below the entity symbol and connected to the entity by a single line. As each attribute symbol is drawn, the attribute name should be placed within it. Although not a requirement, as each attribute is identified and named, it is helpful to annotate it with a discrete number, or n (denoting some unknown number more than 1), to indicate how many occurrences of this attribute would be necessary to describe the entity.

Step 3 identifies, names, and defines each attribute of each relationship. The attributes of a relationship are those categories of data that are necessary to qualify the relationship, describe when and under what conditions it occurs, and any other information that relates only to the connection between the entities and not to either entity independently. The relationship attributes should include all attributes necessary to clearly and completely identify any qualifications of that particular relationship between the two entities and the conditions under which the relationship exists.

As each attribute is identified and named, it is drawn below the relationship symbol and connected to the relationship by a single line. As with the attributes of entities, it is helpful to annotate the attribute with a discrete number, or n, to identify the number of occurrences of this particular attribute that are necessary to fully describe or qualify the relationship.

As the attributes of each relationship are modeled, the relevant attributes of each of the entities of the related pair that are of interest within the context of the relationship should be extracted from the attributed entity model and added to the entity symbols of the relationship model.

In data processing terms and in a very general sense, the attributes within this model can be considered to be the identification and definition of the record types (or record groupings) that will ultimately contain the data elements. It must be noted that each attribute at either the entity or relationship level represents a mutually exclusive and mutually independent category of data. However, an attribute may or may not represent an actual record type.

In the logical data structure models created at a later date from these ER−attribute models, attributes may be combined to form more general records, they may be kept separately, or in some extreme cases because of its complexity, an attribute may be split into many records. The names of the entities are the names of the logical data aggregates (or structures) of the environment.

A fourth, or data element, level may be added when the models are developed in conjunction with the data processing systems development projects. This level is most familiar to data processing specialists and consists of identifying and defining the specific data elements that are needed to describe each attribute of each entity and each relationship. *Data elements are assigned only to attributes.* In a sense, data elements are the attributes of the attributes.

ADDITIONAL RULES FOR ER MODEL CREATION

Regardless of the level being addressed, the following rules apply to the construction of an ER diagram:

1. Entities
   a. Each rectangle must represent a single entity, a homogeneous group of entities, or one subset or subtype of the entity.
   b. When developing detailed models, each identified global entity should be decomposed into its component subsets.
   c. The mode of decomposition is dependent on the characteristics of the component entities and the requirements of the firm for information about those entities.
   d. Regardless of the mode of decomposition, care should be taken to ensure that all entity subtypes can be related back to their base global entity. This may be accomplished by special notation or by including the name of the base entity within the entity subtype name.
   e. When the model includes documents, each unique type of document should be included, and the attributes for these documents should contain all data field content that must be validated, processed, and retained by the firm.
   f. When document processing requires that data be validated against preexistent reference files, code lists, spreadsheet, or other financial tables, etc., the referenced data items should be treated as if they were entities and included in the model, along with their appropriate attributes and relationships.
2. Relationships
   a. Relationship diamonds are drawn between and must be connected (by a line from each side of the diamond) to no less than one and no more than two entity rectangles.
   b. A diamond may be connected back to the same entity, in which case it represents a recursive relationship between unique occurrences of the same entity.
   c. Each diamond must represent a single relationship that is known to exist between the two connected entities *and is of interest to the firm*.
   d. For each line that connects the diamond to a rectangle, at the point where that line joins that rectangle, a notation should be made as to whether the two entities being related have a one-to-one, one-to-many, many-to-one, or many-to-many relationship.
   e. This notation should be made in the form $a:b$, where a is the entity on the left side of the diamond and b is the entity on the right side of the diamond. a and b may have any numeric value equal to or greater than 1, or n (denoting an indefinite number more than 1).
   f. If the relationship is symmetrical, i.e., entity a (the left-hand entity) has the same relationship to entity b (the right-hand entity), i.e., each a is connected to many bs, and each b is connected to only one a, the notation closest to each entity should be the same.
   g. If the relationship is asymmetrical, i.e., entity a does not have the same relationship to entity b as entity b has to entity a, i.e., each a is connected to only one b, but each b may be connected to many as, the notation closest to each entity should reflect the view from that entity to the opposite entity.
3. Attributes
   a. Circles representing attributes are connected to either rectangles or diamonds.

b. Each circle may be connected to only one rectangle or only one diamond and must represent a specific attribute of the entity or relationship to which it is connected.
c. The circles on the diagram contain a name that identifies the specific attribute, or set of attributes, being depicted.
d. The line connecting the circle to the entity or relationship should be annotated to reflect whether the named attribute may occur only once per entity (or relationship) or many times.
e. Each entity rectangle and relationship diamond must have at least one associated attribute.
f. Attributes that apply to more than one entity or to more than one relationship must be diagramed as if they were unique to each entity or relationship to which they apply. This condition will occur when a global entity has been separated into entity subsets and the members of one or more subsets share many of the same attributes. Under these conditions, each occurrence of the attribute symbol should have the same name and some notation indicating that it is identical in format to attributes that appear elsewhere.

If all attributes and all relationships connected to the entity rectangle do not have *the potential* to apply equally to each and every entity occurrence defined to it, then the definition of the entity being used must be changed and a new entity or entity set (or a new entity subset or subsets) must be created until this condition is satisfied.

Although the above discussion assumes that only one model will be created at each level, and for the firm as a whole, since most projects are for specific user areas it thus may be desirable or necessary to create different models for each user area.

Just as an entity can be viewed from many different perspectives and may seem to be different from each perspective, ER and ER—attribute models can also be different from the various perspectives of the firm. Each area of the firm defines the entities of the firm in different ways and relates to them in different ways.

All ER models need not contain every entity of the firm. The various models need only contain the entities of interest to the particular area being modeled. To illustrate,

1. A model can be built to reflect only the document entities, the entity sources for those documents, and the relationships between both types of entities.
2. A model might contain functional entities and their relationships. Here, the functional areas of the firm (managerial concepts) are treated as entities themselves and the model reflects their relationships to each other.
3. Another variation might contain only the processing entities (groups of people, machines, or workstations) and the document and/or resource entities used by them. This type of model might reflect all the processing stations through which a particular document must travel or the workstations through which a manufactured part must pass. A process entity does not reflect what processing is done or even how that processing is done but, rather, a station where processing of a particular type is done. That processing could be complex or simple.

The Entity—Relationship Approach

The various ER approach models are business models, rather than data processing models, i.e., they reflect business environments, not methods of processing. The types of entities and relationships selected to be included in each model, the definitions of those entities, and the attributes used to describe those entities and relationships all combine to describe the environment and the nature of the business itself.

IMPLEMENTING THE ER APPROACH MODEL

DBMS products are tools for structuring and managing the general business and specific application data of the firm. The variety of products on the market today offer developers the ability to produce applications using each of the three major data structure models: hierarchic, network, and relational. Some products offer more than one structural model option. However, each DBMS has a primary underlying structural model and, thus, is more effective with data whose structural characteristics correspond most closely with that specific model. Matching the right DBMS with the structural characteristics of the firm's data can impact the efficiency of the application greatly.

A data structure independent model of the applications data translated into each of the three structures can help the analyst to evaluate a model and determine which DBMS is the closest fit.

ER PERSPECTIVE OF THE DIFFERENT CATEGORIES OF BUSINESS SYSTEMS

All applications can be categorized into three types, each with differing scopes, differing levels of interaction, and differing data requirements. Generally speaking, these categories are transactional, analytical, and administrative.

Before evaluating the data model against each of the three data structure models, the analyst should have an understanding of (a) the data orientation of each of the different types of business systems and (b) the strengths and weaknesses of the various structural models upon which the DBMS products are based.

Transactional systems involve the primary record keeping of the firm. They are replacements for the paper work systems that drive the business. There are a myriad of processing systems that have been designed to support the business of the firm. They may be order processing, customer service, inventory control, statement processing, accounts payable or receivable, or sales support systems. They have in common the need to share data about the major business entities of the firm, well-defined data requirements and procedures, and highly repetitive processes. These systems are the primary data-gathering and data-generating systems of the firm.

Transactional systems tend to center around processing information about one or two entity types at a time (i.e., customers and accounts, customers and customer orders, vendors and products, etc.) and are normally key driven. Because they service the operational levels of the firm, transactional systems are vertical in nature, i.e., they support the processing and provide for the data needs of a specific user area. The operational area usually has an immediate need for data and must work with the most current information to be effective.

Because of their strong entity focus, fixed processing requirements, and limited reliance on multiple entity-to-entity relationships, transactional systems tend to work best within the hierarchic and network models.

Analytical systems also support the business of the firm but are not directly involved in transaction or record keeping. These systems are usually post facto, in that they are primarily reporting systems, using data that already exists. These data may have been generated internally or externally.

Analytical systems include sales analysis, most financial reports, marketing analysis systems, and the myriad of systems that have been called MIS, decision support, etc. Into this category, we could also place those functions that have come to be called information center or end-user computing systems.

These types of systems tend to deal with sets of entities, or selected data from multiple entity types. Because they are not usually transaction driven, they tend not to rely on occurrence keys as much as on the relationships between the various entities. Analytical systems support the managerial and strategic levels of the firm and are horizontal in nature, i.e., they cut across operational functions. As such, their need for data is more extensive, more variable, and usually less immediate than that of the operational level, and their need for data currency is usually much less.

Because of their need for data about multiple entities and their need to relate these entities in multiple ways, analytical systems will work best in the network or relational modes; however, they will perform adequately within the hierarchic model as well.

In the final category are the administrative systems of the firm. These systems service the firm as a whole and have little to do with the business of the firm. Rather, they deal with the firm as an entity.

Administrative systems include human resource, payroll, general ledger, and fixed asset control systems. They are more or less standardized from firm to firm and, for the most part, are self-contained systems. They are unrelated except tenuously with other systems, have their own data sources and files, and rarely require ongoing data from the operational files of the firm, although they may accept data from them.

Administrative systems tend to resemble both the transactional systems, in that they gather data, and analytical systems, in that they have heavy reporting requirements. They differ in that they tend to focus on one entity type at a time, (i.e., employees, accounts, offices, warehouses, etc.) rather than on groups of entity types.

Administrative systems are oriented both vertically and horizontally. They are normally firm-wide systems and provide data and support to all areas and levels of the firm.

Because of their limited focus on a single or very few entities and because of the isolated nature of those entities, administrative systems will work best in hierarchic or relational modes.

The type of system influences the type of data needed, the organizational scope of that data, and the way in which the data are accessed. Because of these differing focuses, the system type becomes a determinant in the DBMS selection.

The Entity—Relationship Approach

ER PERSPECTIVE OF HIERARCHIC, NETWORK, AND RELATIONAL MODELS

Each of the data structural models has different operational and implementation characteristics, and these differences influence the capabilities and restrictions of the data structures themselves. The natural structure of the data is one of the major factors in the determination of which DBMS is most appropriate; thus, it is important to understand how each structure looks at data and which kinds of data are most suited for each structure.

Each DBMS allows data to be fragmented, according to the same or very similar sets of rules, and in roughly the same manner. They differ in the manner each employs for connecting those fragments into larger logical data structures.

Each DBMS uses a different type of data structure diagram that depicts

- The mode of connection of the data segments within the larger data aggregates.
- The dependencies of the data segments within the larger data aggregates.
- The allowable or supported data access paths between each of the segments.
- The structure model of the *logical data record* (or entity) for that DBMS.
- How these data aggregates are defined to the DBMS itself.

The *hierarchic* diagram presents the data fragments in an inverted tree structure. This inverted tree represents the data segmentation, the segment connections, and the inherent dependencies of those segments. Each tree structure represents the collection of data about one type of entity and is also called a *logical data record*. There can only be one hierarchic structure per data base. A special implementation of the tree structure allows multiple tree structures to be combined into a larger tree, which is also called a logical data record; however, each component tree is still defined as a separate data base.

All access to the logical data record is through the base or root segment. It is this segment that contains the unique identifiers, or keys, for the entity occurrence being described. A data base contains multiple occurrences about which data are stored. Each unique entity occurrence within a given data base may have its own configuration of occurrences or non-occurrences of each segment type defined with the general entity hierarchy.

The tree structure diagram depicts each segment type only once. However, aside from the root segment of each structure, there can be multiple occurrences of any given dependent segment type within the structure. Each data segment beneath the root segment describes some aspect of the base entity. These dependent segments may be keyed or unkeyed, depending on their contents, usage, and number of occurrences. Dependent segment keys may be unique, or duplicated, both within and across occurrences.

Within the hierarchy, root level segments relate only to segments directly dependent to them. The access path to any segment beneath the root segment must include all of its immediate hierarchic predecessors, or parents, on a direct path from the root, as defined in the hierarchic structure.

Segments at the same level below the root (a) cannot relate to each other, (b) must relate as children to only one parent segment at the next higher level within the hierarchy, or to the root itself, and (c) may relate as a parent to any number of child segments, each of which must be one level lower in the hierarchy. These level-to-level, or parent-to-child, dependencies imply that the lower level segments (children) have no meaning and, indeed, cannot exist without the higher (in terms of position within the hierarchy) level segments (parents).

The hierarchic model is most effective when

1. Each hierarchic structure contains data about a single entity and each entity is relatively homogeneous, having few distinct subtypes.
2. The primary access to each hierarchy is via the identifier of the entity.
3. The entity being described is rich in descriptive attributes, and these attributes occur in multiples or not at all.
4. The entity is complete in and of itself and has few, if any, relationships between it and any other entities.
5. Entity occurrences are processed one at a time.

The *network* diagram has no implicit hierarchic relationship between the segment types and, in many cases, no implicit structure at all, with the record types seemingly placed at random. Record types are grouped in sets of two, one or both of which can, in turn, be part of another two-record type set. Within each set, one record type is the owner of the set (or parent) and the other is the member (or child). Each record type of these parent—child (or owner—member) sets may, in turn, relate to other records as either a parent or a child.

Each record within the overall diagrammatic structure must be either an owner or a member of a set within the structure. Normally, each set is accessed through the owner record type, each of which contains the identifier, or key, of a specific occurrence of the set type. Each record type may be keyed or unkeyed, and key fields may contain unique or duplicated values. Because each record type in each set can be joined to any other record type in any other set, this structure allows highly flexible access paths through the various record types for processing purposes.

Because each record can be related to one or more other records, a network diagram depicts a web of data records with their various interconnections. This composite of all records and all relationships is said to be a *schema,* and the entire schema is considered to be the data base. Firms using network-based DBMSs usually have all data defined under one master schema. A schema may have multiple entry points, one at each owner of each set.

Unlike the hierarchic model, where each tree structure is a logical data record, there are no discernible logical data records within a network diagram. Instead, each application can create its own logical data records from any combination of sets. These logical data records can then be segregated from the master schema by means of a subschema definition.

There are no levels within the network model and, thus, no level-to-level or parent-to-child dependencies beyond those of owner to member. Access to any segment may be direct or through its owner. Any given segment may own or be owned by (be related) any number of other segments, with the restriction that (a) any pair of segments thus connected must be related through a uniquely named set and (b) any given segment occurrence within a set may have only one owner.

Within the network model, hierarchic relationships may be depicted by having one segment own (through multiple sets) many other segments; each of these owned segments (members) may, in turn, own multiple other segments, again through named sets.

Within this hierarchy, however, and subject to set construction restrictions, segments types at the same level may relate to each other as either owners or members of sets, and segments at any level may relate directly to segments at any other level. Segment types may be directly related to segments at multiple other levels, either above or below the immediate level of the segments, may be related to segments outside the hierarchy through named sets, and may have multiple hierarchic parents and multiple hierarchic dependents or children.

The network model is most effective when

1. Used to contain data about multiple entities that are connected in complex interrelationships.
2. The multiple primary accesses to the data structure may be through the identifiers of the entities themselves or through their relationships with other entities.
3. There are multiple entity subsets, each with different attribute descriptors and the dependent attributes of these entities occur in multiples or not at all.
4. There are few, if any, hierarchic relationships between the entity attributes.
5. The applications need to see the universe of data entities and their relationships and process transactions that are aimed at many interrelated entities.

The *relational* diagram represents each record type in tabular form, and all records of the same type are contained in a single table.

The relational model has no implicit structure aside from the table. There are no fixed parent–child or any other relationships within a relational environment. Instead, each table may be related to any or all of the other tables in any number of ways. Any single table, or any combination of two or more tables, may be accessed by any application.

Each freestanding table is known as a relation, and each entry within each table is known as a tuple or, more commonly, a row. Whereas all data manipulation operations are "record at a time" (where each record must be accessed through its key or through its relationship with, or proximity to, another record) within the network and hierarchic models, data manipulation within the relational model is "set (or table) at a time," where the set of rows accessed may be as few as one or as many as exist in the table.

Each application can create its own logical data records from any combination, or portions, of tables as needed. These logical data records can then be accessed and manipulated by means of user views, or "projections."

Although each data table contains data assigned according to a primary key for the entries of the table, there is no explicit sequence to the entries of a table, and the table may be accessed via the contents of any field (or column) of data within it.

A table may contain any number of rows, and a row within a table may contain any number of data elements, with the restriction that all data elements must be atomic, i.e., they must be defined at their lowest possible level, they must be nonrepeating, and must be uniquely named within a table. Each table must have a column of data elements defined as a primary key, and the primary key field of each row must contain a unique value; all occurrences of a data element within a given column of a table must be identically defined and must contain a data value or a null entry.

Tables may be related, or joined, in any sequence, any table may start the sequence of joins, and a table may be joined to itself. Any number of tables may be related together, provided that each table, or each pair of tables, to be joined has a column of data that is identical in definition and is populated from an identical range of values (or domain). Any given table may be directly joined with only two other tables at any one time (A to B and B to C), and the tables must be connected in sequence (A to B, B to C, C to D, etc.), although the sequence of table joins ($ABCD$, $CDBA$, $DCBA$, etc.) is immaterial.

The relational model is most effective when

1. Each table contains data about a single entity.
2. Each entity is homogeneous with little, if any, differences between subtypes.
3. All data elements within a given table relate only to the primary key of the table.
4. The table data need to be accessed in multiple sequence or via the contents of any data element within the table.
5. There are multiple entities or entity subsets, each with different attribute descriptors and all of which are related to each other in some way.
6. The dependent attributes of each entity occur singularly or not at all.
7. There are no intervening or hierarchic relationships between the entity and its attributes.
8. The applications need to see the universe of data entities related in complex ways for retrieval purposes.
9. The applications process update transactions that can be applied to one entity table at a time and not to more than one table.

THE ER—ATTRIBUTE MODEL AS A DBMS DESIGN TOOL

Because they are DBMS data structure independent, ER models can be easily translated into any of the three logical data structure models for DBMS implementation. Given this structural independence and the ease of translation, firms with multiple DBMS products may also use the ER model to select which logical data structure, and thus which DBMS implementation, is most suited for a particular application.

The level-3 model, the ER—attribute model, is uniquely suited to use as a basis for examining the business data and comparing its inherent structure to each of the data structure models. (A fourth level of ER diagram, where data elements are added to the attributes, was also discussed. This level may be more comfortable for data processing personnel than the third; however, for the purposes of structural evaluation, there is no real difference between the two.)

The Entity—Relationship Approach 135

At this level, each entity and each relationship between each pair of entities has been segregated and attributed. Because of this and because each data structure model handles both entities and relationships differently, the preliminary translation of the ER entities and relationships to data structure model are best described independently. Once this translation is understood, it is easier to discuss which structure is best suited to the actual data.

The number of entities within the ER—attribute model, the number and complexity of the relationships between the entities, and the number and type of attributes of each entity and relationship all contribute to suiting the data to one structure or another or to multiple structures at the same time.

TRANSLATING ATTRIBUTES TO RECORDS

The ER—attribute model calls for the representation of each distinct attribute for each entity and each relationship. An attribute may be a descriptor or an identifier or it may be some physical characteristic—a record of some action taken or a status descriptor. Generally, an attribute refers to a distinct category of data or information of interest about the entity, or some category of data that describes or qualifies a relationship. An attribute should not be equated to a data element, although in some cases a single data element may suffice to describe the attribute. Generally, an attribute will require more than one data element for full definition.

Relationships usually have very few attributes, although a complex relationship may have as many as a dozen or more. Entities, on the other hand, may have several dozen attributes. The number of attributes depends on the level of interest that the firm has in the entity, the number of things the firm needs to know about the entity, the number of different kinds of actions taken by or against the entity and, more importantly, how the attributes were named and defined (the number of data elements needed to store the desired information about the attribute).

For instance, an employee entity may have a single attribute called education, it may have two different education attributes—one internal and one external—or it may have a high school attribute, a college attribute, a graduate school attribute, a vendor course attribute, and a company course attribute. Each of these three variations may contain the same information or may be represented differently, but they all describe the employee's education.

Because each attribute describes a different aspect or quality of the entity or relationship, conceptually each attribute is different. From an implementation perspective, however, it may be more practical to combine attribute types into more generalized record types.

Combining attributes only serves to reduce the number of dependent segments in a hierarchic implementation or the number of sets owned by the entity in a network implementation. Combining attributes into more generalized record types does not and should not reduce the number of data elements needed for each type of attribute. In fact, combining attributes may create the need for additional code or identifier data elements to distinguish between different attribute groupings.

There are no hard and fast rules for consolidating attributes; however, the following guidelines may assist:

1. All attributes that always occur and occur only once can be combined.
2. All attributes that may occur, and if they occur, will occur only once, may be combined.
3. Attributes that originate on the same form or are updated by data from the same form may usually be combined.
4. Attributes that look the same but represent different categories of information, such as various customer addresses (legal, primary residence, mailing addresses, etc.), may be coded and combined.
5. Attributes that are always accessed together and change or vary according to the same set of business rules may be combined.
6. Attributes that have the same access or update restrictions (security) may be combined.
7. Attributes that have the same identifier or sequence characteristics, such as attributes that record actions by date, may be combined.
8. Attributes that contain textual data, such as special shipping instructions, special handling instructions, customer service notes, or special billing instructions, may be combined.

TRANSLATING THE ER MODEL INTO HIERARCHIC DATA STRUCTURES

Within the hierarchic model, the name of the entity becomes the name of the hierarchic structure. All name or identifier attributes for the entity would be collected and aggregated into the root of a hierarchic structure. Any uniquely occurring identifier attribute can be chosen as the root key. All other attributes of the entity become, either individually or in combination, the dependent segments of the root. Because of their direct relationship to the entity, entity hierarchies normally contain only two levels, the root and the dependents.

Relationships within the hierarchic model can be implemented in a number of ways. They can be either DBMS, or programmatically maintained and can reside within the hierarchic structure of each entity of the pair or independently of either entity. The relationships between each related pair of entities must be examined one at a time.

If the relationship being examined is simple, i.e., if it has few attributes, all of which are nonrepeating, a segment type should be created for it to contain the nonkey attributes that describe and qualify the relationship. That segment is then treated as if it were an attribute of each of the entities of the pair. As such, it must also contain the key or identifier of the target entity. The target entity is the opposing entity of the related pair.

If the relationship is complex, containing multiple or multioccurring attributes, it should be maintained independently of each entity. In this case, a hierarchy is set up for the relationship as if it were an entity itself, the attributes of the relationship become dependents of the relationship, and the paired keys of each entity involved are used as the combined identifier of each occurrence of the relationship.

Selection of an entity for hierarchic implementation is appropriate if

1. The entity has attributes that occur multiple times.
2. Access to the entity is primarily through its primary key.

3. There are few relationships between the entities, and the relationships are well defined and relatively simple in that they require few attributes for description and qualification.
4. The relationships between the entity and any other entities are symmetrical, in that the same data can be used to support and qualify the relationship from either side of any given related pair.
5. Processing occurs against a single entity type or a small group of entity types, i.e., only a small number of entities (not entity occurrences) are needed by an application for reference or processing purposes at any one time.
6. Processing of the entity is either random, sequential, or both, entity at a time, and requires that all or most attributes of the entity be available at the same time.
7. The data about the entity are volatile and are changed frequently within the processing streams.
8. There are numerous entity subtypes, each with differing attribute characteristics, and the application processing dictates that the entity be processed as a set.

TRANSLATING THE ER MODEL INTO A NETWORK DATA STRUCTURE

Within the network model, each entity is set up as the owner of multiple sets, and that owner record contains any names or identifiers for the entity occurrence. Each attribute or combination of attributes becomes a member record of a set with the entity record as its owner.

Relationships within the network model can be implemented in a number of ways. They can be either DBMS or programmatically maintained and can reside as a set within the structure of each entity of the pair or independently of either entity. As with the hierarchic translation, the relationships between each related pair of entities must be examined one at a time.

If the relationship is simple, i.e., if it has few attributes, all of which are nonrepeating, a record type should be created for it to contain the nonkey attributes that describe and qualify the relationship. These records become intersection records, which are owned by each of the related entity occurrences.

If the relationship is complex and contains multiple or multioccurring attributes, it should be maintained independently of each entity. In this case, a hierarchy is set up for the relationship as if it were an entity itself, the attributes of the relationship become members of sets of the relationship entity, and the paired keys of each entity involved are used as the combined identifier of each occurrence of the relationship entity owner. That owner record is then treated as if it were an intersection record between each of the entities of the pair.

Selection of a network implementation is appropriate if

1. Some or all of the defined entities have attributes that occur multiple times.
2. Access to each of the entities is primarily through the primary key of the entity.
3. There are many relationships between the entities, and the relationships are well defined and complex, requiring multiple attributes for description and qualification.

4. Processing of the entities usually requires that most, if not all, entity types (not entity occurrences) are needed by an application for reference or processing purposes at the same time.
5. Entity processing is either random, or sequential, or both, entity at a time, and requires that all attributes of the entity be available at the same time.
6. The entities have been split into multiple subtypes, which share common attributes.
7. Entities are processed in terms of their relationships with some other entity or category.
8. The data about the entities are volatile and changed frequently within the processing streams.
9. There are numerous entity subtypes, each with differing attribute characteristics, and the application processing dictates that the entity be processed both as a complete set and by subtype.
10. Processing requires multiple paths through the entity structures, where the paths are guided by entity attribute data element values.

TRANSLATING THE ER MODEL INTO RELATIONAL DATA STRUCTURES

Within the relational model, only entities with certain characteristics, and without others, can translate into relational tables. The attributes of the entity, the number of occurrences of each attribute, the complexity of the relationships between those entities, and the number of subtypes into which each entity has been decomposed all become the determining factors.

Each distinct entity type or subtype becomes a relational table. The columns of the table include the identifiers of the entity and the data elements of its nonrepeating attributes. In cases where some of the entity attributes occur multiple times, each distinct attribute type that does so must be established as a separate table and keyed with the identifiers of the base entity.

As with the network and hierarchic models, simple and complex relationships must be handled differently. If the relationship is simple, i.e., if it has few attributes, all of which are nonrepeating, a single table can be created for it. Each row of that table implements a specific relationship occurrence between the two entities. The table should contain a pair of columns, where each column contains one of the paired keys of the related entities. These paired keys act as the identifier of each relationship occurrence. The remainder of the columns in the table contain the data elements of the attributes that describe and qualify the relationship. Each separate relationship type between each entity pair should be converted to a separate table.

Complex relationships, or those containing multiple or multioccurring attributes, should be treated as if they were entities with repeating attributes. The base table of this relationship entity should contain the data elements of all nonrepeating attributes, and a separate table must be set up for each repeating attribute type of the relationship. Each table of the relationship set must contain a set of columns, each of which contains one of the paired keys of the related entities.

The Entity—Relationship Approach

Selection of an entity for relational implementation is appropriate if

1. The entity has few, if any, attributes that occur multiple times.
2. Access to the entity may be through the primary key of the entity or through any data element defined within the table constructed from the entity's attributes.
3. There are many relationships between the entities, and the relationships are well defined or poorly defined and simple, requiring few attributes to define and qualify them.
4. The relationships between the entities may be maintained by data elements that reside wholly within each entity.
5. Processing of the entity usually occurs singly or in combination with small groups of other entity types, i.e., only a small number of entities (not entity occurrences) are needed by an application for reference or processing purposes at any one time.
6. Entity occurrence sequence is unimportant to processing.
7. Entity processing is set at a time.
8. Entity processing does not require that all attributes of the entity be available at the same time.
9. The data about the entities are stable and do not change as a result of processing.
10. The entities have been split into multiple subtypes, which do not share common attributes.
11. There are numerous entity subtypes, each with differing attribute characteristics, and the application processing does not dictate that the entity set be processed as a whole.
12. Processing does not require multiple entity types to be related to any one given entity at the same time.
13. The data about an entity are contained within one or two tables, and updating the entity data attributes of any given entity is not dependent on the data within any other entity table.
14. Updating the data within one table does not affect its relationships with any other table.

The above discussion is predicated upon the assumptions that (a) within an application and subject to the stated rules and restrictions, any given entity may be implemented using the relational, network, or hierarchic implementation, (b) each relational table or hierarchic structure contains the data about a single entity, (c) relational and hierarchic implementations can be mixed within an application, (d) the software supporting the particular DBMS products is not a factor in selecting one implementation over another, and the DBMS products chosen for implementation purposes would be compatible with each other.

EXTENSIONS AND ONGOING DEVELOPMENT OF THE ER APPROACH

The ER approach has attracted many practitioners in the decade since it was introduced. There have been annual conferences devoted to discussing and extending the definition of the ER approach. These conferences, held in various cities and various countries around the world, have attracted an international audience.

The papers presented during the conferences have been collected into proceedings (see Bibliography). A review of those papers will illustrate the variety of ways in which data modelers have used the ER approach. The models have been used to illustrate time, company processes, company organization, and a myriad of applications. Many papers discuss embellishments to the basic notation, as described above. These notation enhancements were developed to allow the modeler to add additional richness to the model.

There is a network of user groups that have been formed around the world, which draw their membership from ER practitioners in both the commercial and academic environments.

The advent of CASE (computer-aided software engineering) tools has increased the use of the ER model and added a level of complexity as well. Many of these tools have modified the notation to conform to their graphics set and thus appear to have lost some of the notational power of the original Chen proposal. As time goes on, however, it is expected that the newly formed users groups will develop a working set of notational standards for ER model development and will force a level of standardization on CASE technology as well.

BIBLIOGRAPHY

Chen, P. P., ed., *Entity-Relationship Approach to Systems Analysis and Design*, North-Holland Publishers, Amsterdam, Holland, 1979.

Chen, P. P., "The Entity-Relationship Model—Toward a Unified View of Data," *ACM Trans. Database Syst.*, 1(1), 9–36 (March 1976).

Chen, P. P., ed., *Entity-Relationship Approach to Information Modeling and Analysis*, ER Institute, Saugus, CA, 1981.

Chen, P. P., "The Entity-Relationship Approach to Logical Data Base Design," *Q.E.D. Monograph Series, Data Base Management*, No. 6, 1977.

Davis, C. G., S. Jajodia, P. A. Ng, and R. T. Yeh, eds., *Entity-Relationship Approach to Software Engineering*, North-Holland Publishers, Amsterdam, Holland, 1983.

March, S. T., ed., *Proceedings of the Sixth International Conference on Entity-Relationship Approach*, North-Holland Publishers, Amsterdam, Holland, 1988.

Martin, J. and C. McClure, *Diagramming Techniques for Analysts and Programmers*, Prentice-Hall, Englewood Cliffs, NJ, 1985.

Modell, M. E., *A Professionals Guide to Systems Analysis*, McGraw-Hill Book Company, New York, 1988.

Proceedings of the Fourth International Conference on Entity-Relationship Approach, IEEE Computer Society Press, Silver Springs, MD, 1985.

Spaccapietra, S., ed., *Entity-Relationship Approach*, North-Holland Publishers, Amsterdam, Holland, 1987.

MARTIN E. MODELL

HARDWARE DESCRIPTION LANGUAGE

1 HARDWARE DESCRIPTION LANGUAGE, DEFINITION AND PURPOSE

Hardware description language (HDL) is a language that is specially designed, or can be applied, to describe hardware. Because many designers take part in the design of large hardware, some communication methods, which are supported by computers, are inevitable to exchange design information. From the point of human readability, diagrams may be the best. However, direct handling of diagrams by computers is not so easy, and diagrams drawn by humans may have many ambiguous points. So it is necessary to express design information by some languages that are formally defined. HDLs are designed to satisfy these requirements. Some HDLs can express diagrams, whereas others can express only behavior in text form.

Like software programming languages, there are many HDLs. Currently, HDLs take the central part of computer-aided design (CAD) system in every design stage: function, logic, and implementation. The purpose of these languages may be different: some are for gate design, others are for layout design, etc. Therefore, it is important to understand the kinds of applications for which HDLs are used. To do so, we must first classify HDLs by purposes.

This article has four sections: Section 2 gives important points for classifying HDLs and shows typical HDLs of each class mainly by showing description examples. In section 3, major supporting points for HDLs—verification and synthesis—are reviewed briefly. Finally, in section 4, standardization efforts of HDLs—CONLAN and EDIF—are discussed.

2 POINTS FOR CLASSIFYING HARDWARE DESCRIPTION LANGUAGE AND EXAMPLES

There are many points to classify HDLs. They are as follows:

1. Description level.
2. Behavior description/structure description.
3. Mathematical model.
4. Text/graphic.
5. Special language/application of programming language.

In this section, we discuss the above points and show typical languages.

2.1 Description Level

Here, the hardware design flow that is widest used is reviewed briefly, and typical HDLs for each design stage are listed and briefly explained in order to make clear the objectives of HDLs.

Hardware is designed according to the flow in Figure 2.1.1. Each design stage will be explained in the following text.

Specification

First, a designer must specify what is to be made after discussing what is needed. This process is called "requirement specifications" and is one of the main themes in software engineering.

Software and hardware cannot be separated clearly in this stage. It is not easy to decide which part of specifications should be performed by hardware and which part by software. Some languages or methods suitable for expressing both hardware and software are highly suited for describing specifications. Specifications are currently described in natural language (e.g., Japanese, English, etc.) and diagrams (e.g., timing diagrams). Diagrams are used for providing additional information to the specifications in a natural language and do not give full information. Because natural languages are easy for humans to understand but difficult for computers, mechanical handling of specifications is rarely done.

Several methods using logic or algebra are proposed to formally specify systems and mechanically handle their specifications [1, 2]. Although they are applied to software and hardware as an experiment, they are not yet developed for practical use. It is difficult for a designer or a programmer to understand and use these methods because detailed descriptions in logic or algebra are required for a full specification. However, formal specification is indispensable for designing a highly complex system because it is impossible for humans alone to check specifications.

System Design

In system design, it is decided how the given specification is processed. A designer selects an algorithm and decides the division between hardware and software. The designer also describes them in a common language such as Ada, FORTRAN, Pascal, C, LISP, Occam [3], etc., and system design

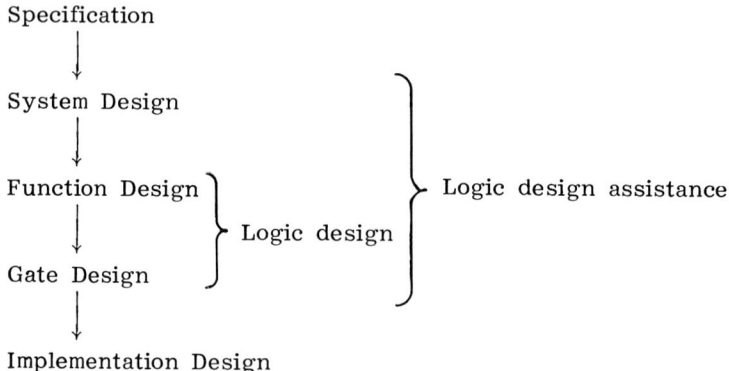

FIGURE 2.1.1 Hardware Design Flow

Hardware Description Language

is usually verified through simulations. As the parallelisms in the system to be designed must be described in this stage, sequential languages such as those mentioned, require some methods for expressing parallelisms. It is decided at this stage which part of the specification is done by hardware and which part by software. The software is transferred to software tools, and the hardware proceeds to the next design stage: logic design, as a specification for the hardware. The logic design stage accepts specifications and outputs networks of logical gates. It is divided into two stages: function design and gate design.

Function Design

As the algorithm used is decided and described as a specification in system design, in this stage a designer described the system, taking into account the hardware resources really used, i.e., the designer makes clear how the specification is processed with limited hardware. Hardware resources such as registers and memories are explicitly expressed, and data transfers among hardware resources are described, which we call register transfer level. Description languages or HDLs are common languages. There are many HDLs that can be applied to this design stage, DDL [4], CDL [5], Instruction Set Processor Specification (ISPS) [6], HSL [7], SDL [8], etc. [9], and some are explained in the following section. Although almost all the tools for verifying the descriptions are based upon simulations, several formal methods of verification are proposed. They are presented and discussed in Section 3. All the functions needed for executing the algorithm with limited hardware are examined. How each function is implemented is described in the next stage.

Gate Design

This stage decides how each function in function design is implemented with logical expressions. Function designs are expanded into Boolean expressions or state transition tables, and they are simplified and transformed into networks of logical gates. So the languages used in this stage are the same as for function design. The main works are to assign states on flip-flops and to simplify Boolean expressions. Verifications are usually done through simulations. However, some formal methods are proposed like function design. Using HDLs, some systems automatically translate function designs into logical expressions. So this stage may be skipped. In this stage, designs are technology independent, i.e., there is no need to alter designs no matter which technology is applied, e.g., TTL, CMOS, etc.

Implementation Design

Logic designs are converted to fit the technology used. Layouts and routings are also decided according to the technology. Because implementation design is directly connected to manufacturing, much effort has been expended in the area of computer supports. As a result, the CAD system for implementation of design is very practical, and a designer cannot do without CAD systems. Because the progress of device technology such as very large-scale integration (VLSI) or GaAs is dramatic, it is necessary to design very large and highly complex systems. This requires more effort to enhance the performance of CAD systems.

In recent years, systems have grown to such a scale that designers cannot handle all of them at the same time. So hierarchical structured design, which divides complex modules into several simpler ones, is indispensable for hardware logic design. The hierarchical structured design is the repetition of a basic design cycle. One basic design cycle is composed of specifying the module, dividing it into several submodules, designing them, and verifying whether or not the specification is satisfied by the submodules' designs. This procedure corresponds to the stepwise refinements of logic designs. There are HDLs that can express hierarchy explicitly [8].

Hardware is designed according to the flow described above. Currently, HDL is a central part of CAD tools.

2.2 Behavior Description/Structure Description

In the initial design stages, a designer is concerned mainly with the behavior of a system. Gradually he adds more and more structural information to the design until it can be implemented easily using physical components. HDLs are classified into two categories: behavioral description and structural description. Behavioral description shows how the hardware works. It is similar to the descriptions by software programming languages. The difference is that HDL handles hardware resources explicitly but software programming languages do not. There are many behavioral description languages such as DDL [4], CDL [5], ISPS [6], and AHPL [10] (DDL is explained in the latter part of this section.)

On the other hand, a structural description shows what composes the hardware described. For example, a structural description shows that a full adder is composed of an OR gate and two half-adders which, in turn, are composed of two inverters, two AND gates, and an OR gate. The structural description easily shows the hierarchy of systems and is particularly suited to the implementation design of VLSIs. Typical languages for structural descriptions are HSL [7], SDL [8], etc.; HSL is explained below.

Languages combining the two categories above are also proposed. SCALD [11], ALEX [12], and KARL [13] are CAD systems that are able to describe both behavior and structure of hardware and support hierarchical designs. Also, they have the graphic input utilities. In any case, behavioral and structural descriptions of hardware are the two major points of designing hardware. In the following text, a typical behavioral language (DDL) and a typical structural language (HSL) are explained with some description examples.

DDL

DDL (Digital System Design Language) is a register–transfer level HDL and has many supporting tools developed by many people [14]. It is based upon state transitions and is therefore familiar to hardware designers. Here, DDL is explained through a description example of a simple computer.

A very simple computer whose organization is shown in Figure 2.2.1 is described. The formats of internal data and instructions are shown in Figure 2.2.2. A DDL description is separated into two parts: Resource declaration and behavior description. The declaration contains information about hardware resources (registers, memories, terminals, etc.) being described.

Hardware Description Language

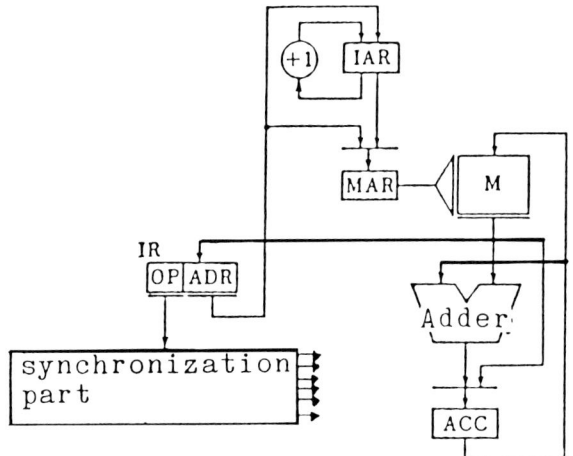

MAR : Memory Address Register
IAR : Instruction Address Register
IR : Instruction Register
ACC : Accumulator

FIGURE 2.2.1 A simple computer.

For example, the declaration of our simple computer is shown in Figure 2.2.3. <STORAGE> M(1024,16) means that M is a memory whose capacity is 1,024 words of 16 bits, and <REGISTER> ACC(16) means that ACC is a register of 16 bits. The symbol || is a concatenation operator and IR(16)= OP(6)|| ADR(10) shows IR to be a 16-bit register whose lower 6 bits are also referenced by OP(6) and whose upper 10 bits are referenced by ADR (10) (Fig. 2.2.2).

The behavior description presents information about how the computer works—in infinite repetition of the next four steps.

1. Set the address containing the next instruction: ADS.
2. Fetch the instruction: IFT.
3. Decode the instruction: DEC.
4. Execute the instructions: LDA, STA, ADD, BRA, BRP.

The repetition above is described in the state diagram shown in Figure 2.2.4. The behavioral description of our computer is then described in DDL, as in Figure 2.2.5.

Data format

| 0 | 1 | 2 | 3 | 4 | 5 | 6 | 7 | 8 | 9 | 10 | 11 | 12 | 13 | 14 | 15 |

| S | MAG |

Instruction format

| 0 | 1 | 2 | 3 | 4 | 5 | 6 | 7 | 8 | 9 | 10 | 11 | 12 | 13 | 14 | 15 |

| OP | ADR |

FIGURE 2.2.2 Format of internal data.

```
<STORAGE> M(1024, 16).
<REGISTER> ACC(16).
           IR(16)=OP(6)| | ADR(10).
           MAR(10).
           IAR(10).
```

FIGURE 2.2.3 Declaration part.

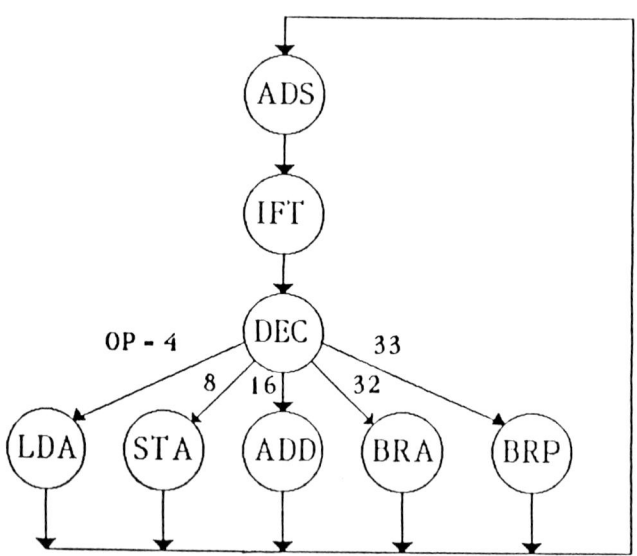

FIGURE 2.2.4 State Diagram for a simple computer.

```
<TIME>CLK<(10)>.
<AUTOMATON>CPU:CLK:
  <STATES>
    ADS:MAR<-IAR,IAR<-IAR+1,->IFT.
    IFT:IR<-M(MAR),->DEC.
    DEC:MAR<-ADR.
        ?OP  #4   ->LDA
             #8   ->STA
             #16  ->ADD
             #32  ->BRA
             #33  ->BRP
    LDA:ACC<-M(MAR),->ADS.
    STA:M(MAR)<-ACC,->ADS.
    ADD:ACC<-ACC+M(MAR),->ADS.
    BRA:IAR<-ADR,->ADS.
    BRP:| *-|ACC(0)*| IAR<-ADR.,->ADS.
  <END>.
<END>CPU
```

FIGURE 2.2.5 Behavior part description.

Hardware Description Language

Systems are described in DDL as a collection of automata. <TIME> and <AUTOMATON> show the clock and name of the automaton described below. The descriptions beginning with <STATES> and ending with <END>, show the behavior of each state in Figure 2.2.4. The statement

$$\text{state\_name : operation1, operation2} \tag{1}$$

means that in the state, state_name, operation1, and operation2 are executed in parallel, and

$$\text{register\_name} \leftarrow \text{expression} \tag{2}$$

means the register transfer to the register_name, i.e., the value of expression is transferred to register_name in the next clock. Because operations are executed in parallel, these two statements give us the same results:

$$\text{MAR} \leftarrow \text{IAR, IAR} \leftarrow \text{IAR} + 1 \tag{3}$$

and

$$\text{IAR} \leftarrow \text{IAR} + 1, \text{MAR} \leftarrow \text{IAR} \tag{4}$$

The statement

$$\rightarrow \text{state\_name} \tag{5}$$

means what is the next state after the operations of the present state have been completed. Conditional operations can be used. The statement

$$|* \text{ logical\_expression } *|\text{ operation1, operation2, ...} \tag{6}$$

means that if the condition logical_expression is satisfied, operation1, operation2, ... are executed, and if not, nothing is done. For example, | *- ACC(0)*| ... in Figure 2.2.5 shows that the lowest bit of ACC is not 1; hence, the operation IAR ← ADR is done. As for the logical operators, NOT(−), AND(&), OR(|), Exclusive OR(@) are permitted. The statement

$$? \text{ register\_name } \# \text{ value1 operation11, operation12, ...} \tag{7}$$
$$\# \text{ value2 operation21, operation22, ...}$$

is a case statement meaning that if the value of register_name is value1, operation11, operation12, ... are executed, and if the value is value2, operation21, operation22, ... are executed. The example in Figure 2.2.5 shows that if the value of OP in IR register 4, 8, 16, 32, or 33, the next state is LDA, STA, ADD, BRA, or BRP, respectively.

Behavioral descriptions of hardware are described in DDL, as mentioned above. DDL has many supporting tools, including simulators, translators (translating DDL descriptions into Boolean expressions for state transitions), automatic converter to gate circuits, etc. [14].

HSL

There are many HDLs concentrating on descriptions of structures. One such language is HSL, which is developed by NTT of Japan [7] and is almost the same as SDL [8]. The main objectives of HSL are

1. Accurate representation of structural information.
2. Useful overall levels of design stages.
3. Applicable to different purposes of a designer during a design stage.
4. Able to perform designer-controlled mapping of higher level hardware primitives into lower level ones.

Each system or subsystem is characterized by a name, as follows:

NAME: <system_name> ; (8)

Every system is connected to the outside world by external connections. This is specified as follows:

EXT: <external connector name> : <terminal name list> ; (9)

where <external connector name> refers to the name for the external connectors and <terminal name list> is a list of terminal names in the order in which they appear in the physical system. It is frequently useful to distinguish between inputs and outputs. This may be specified as follows:

INPUTS: <pin list> ; (10)
OUTPUTS: <pin list> ;

where <pin list> is a list of pin names and

<pin name> ::= <component name> . <terminal name>. (11)

A component name is either a simple identifier or a subscripted identifier. Within the context of HSL, it is necessary to explicitly declare the types of all components to be used in the descriptions:

TYPES: <type name list> ; (12)

All type names must be simple identifiers. For every type name, one has to declare all the components that are of that type:

<type name>: <component name list> ; (13)

Component names may be either simple identifiers or subscripted identifiers. Finally, one must define all the interconnections in terms of nets. The directed nets are described as follows:

<net name> = FROM (<pin list>) TO (<pin list>) ; (14)

A net name can be either a simple identifier or a subscripted identifier.

For every description, a designer must specify the possible uses of that description. Examples of usage are register–transfer level simulation, printer circuit board layout, integrated circuit mask layout, fault test generation, gate-level simulation, etc. The form of this declaration is

PURPOSE: <purpose name list> ; (15)

Besides purpose descriptions, HSL also has a declaration for a level of accuracy or detail. This level is user defined and not imposed in advance by a rigid system. A typical example would define gate level, circuit level, etc. A level is associated with a purpose, i.e., there may be more than one description of a system at the same level, depending on the purpose. The form of the declaration is

LEVEL: <level name> ; (16)

Figure 2.2.6 is an example of HSL and its circuit diagram. It is a description of a receiver of a data transfer system by handshaking sequences whose hierarchical design is shown in Figure 2.2.7. IDENT is a system identification, VERSION is a version being described, DATA is the date of coding, AUTHOR is the name of the author of the description, PROJECT is the project name of the description, and COMMENT means a comment line. The meanings of other descriptions are explained above.

Through the use of LEVEL statements, HSL can describe the hierarchy of circuit diagrams exactly. HSL is developed particularly for LSI designs. Supporting tools for HSL are translator to/from data base, simulator, automatic layout and wiring, etc.

2.3 Mathematical Model

Because hardware works intrinsically in parallel, at least in gate level, models used as a base to characterize the behavior of hardware must have some mechanisms to express parallelisms. Moreover, to formally handle designs, these mechanisms are described in a language that has well-founded mathematical backgrounds. There are several parallel formal models that can be a base of hardware description languages: temporal logic [15], CCS (calculus of communicating processes) [16], etc. [17]. Here, temporal logic, CCS, and some languages that are based on these models are briefly introduced.

Temporal Logic and Temporal Logic-Based Languages

Temporal logic is an extension of traditional logic by several temporal operators; and by using these temporal operators, various timing relationships usually shown in timing diagrams can be described easily. Temporal logic is defined on discrete time, i.e., on states, and variables may change their values through states. Temporal operators specify those changes. Here, a temporal logic, called interval temporal logic (ITL), is briefly introduced. (Please see Ref. 18 for details and see Ref. 15 for other temporal logic.)

ITL is defined on intervals, and an interval is a finite number of successive states. Meanings of variables or predicates are decided in the first state of the current interval. ITL has two temporal operators: next

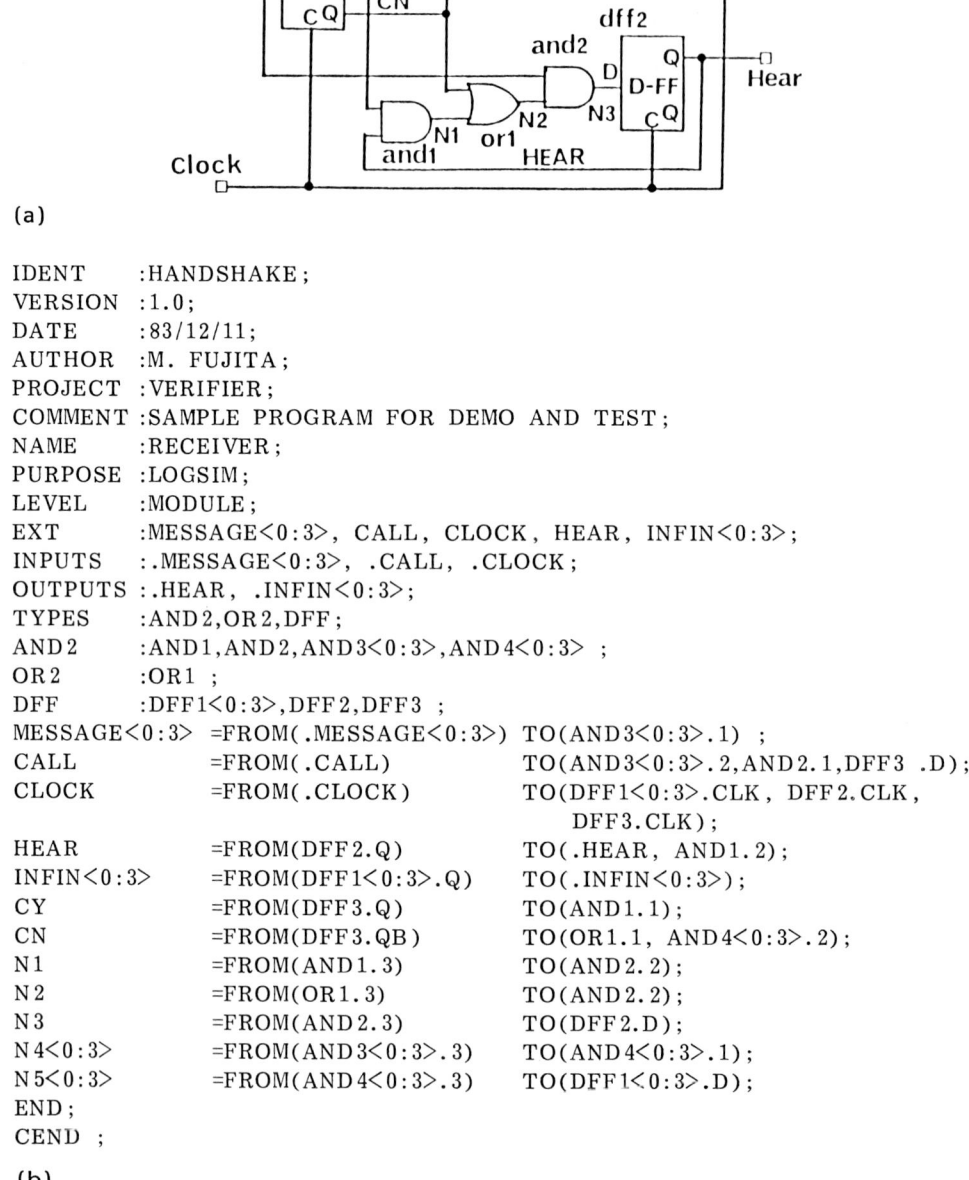

(a)

```
IDENT    :HANDSHAKE;
VERSION  :1.0;
DATE     :83/12/11;
AUTHOR   :M. FUJITA;
PROJECT  :VERIFIER;
COMMENT  :SAMPLE PROGRAM FOR DEMO AND TEST;
NAME     :RECEIVER;
PURPOSE  :LOGSIM;
LEVEL    :MODULE;
EXT      :MESSAGE<0:3>, CALL, CLOCK, HEAR, INFIN<0:3>;
INPUTS   :.MESSAGE<0:3>, .CALL, .CLOCK;
OUTPUTS  :.HEAR, .INFIN<0:3>;
TYPES    :AND2,OR2,DFF;
AND2     :AND1,AND2,AND3<0:3>,AND4<0:3> ;
OR2      :OR1 ;
DFF      :DFF1<0:3>,DFF2,DFF3 ;
MESSAGE<0:3> =FROM(.MESSAGE<0:3>) TO(AND3<0:3>.1) ;
CALL         =FROM(.CALL)         TO(AND3<0:3>.2,AND2.1,DFF3 .D);
CLOCK        =FROM(.CLOCK)        TO(DFF1<0:3>.CLK, DFF2.CLK,
                                      DFF3.CLK);
HEAR         =FROM(DFF2.Q)        TO(.HEAR, AND1.2);
INFIN<0:3>   =FROM(DFF1<0:3>.Q)   TO(.INFIN<0:3>);
CY           =FROM(DFF3.Q)        TO(AND1.1);
CN           =FROM(DFF3.QB)       TO(OR1.1, AND4<0:3>.2);
N1           =FROM(AND1.3)        TO(AND2.2);
N2           =FROM(OR1.3)         TO(AND2.2);
N3           =FROM(AND2.3)        TO(DFF2.D);
N4<0:3>      =FROM(AND3<0:3>.3)   TO(AND4<0:3>.1);
N5<0:3>      =FROM(AND4<0:3>.3)   TO(DFF1<0:3>.D);
END;
CEND ;
```

(b)

FIGURE 2.2.6 HSL description example.

Hardware Description Language   151

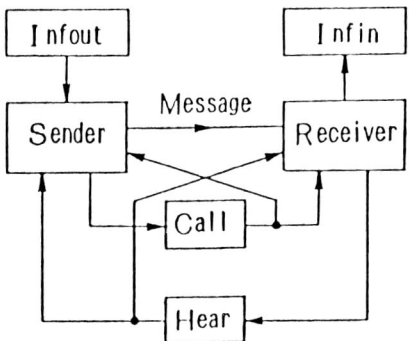

FIGURE 2.2.7 Hierarchy of data transfer system.

and chop. Next is a unary operator and chop is a binary operator. They
have the following meanings.

   P (with no temporal operators): P is true at present.
   next P: P is true in the next interval, i.e., in the next state (in
      sequential circuits, next clock).
   P chop Q: The current interval is divided into two subintervals, the
      former and the latter; P is true in the former subinterval and Q is
      true in the latter subinterval.

The relationships expressed by these operators are shown in Figure 2.3.1.
By using these two operators, several useful operators can be defined [18].

   sometime P: P is true in some state at present or in the future.
   always P: P is true in all states at present and in the future.
   P ← Q (temporal assignment): Q's value in the first state of the
      current interval is equal to P's value in the last state of the current
      interval, or the data in Q are transferred to P.
   length: Returns the length of the current interval, i.e., the number
      of states that the current interval has minus one.
   stable P; P's value does not change throughout the current interval.
   fin P: P is true in the last state of the current interval.

Through the use of these operators, complex timing relationships usually
shown in timing diagrams are easily expressed. For example, the hand-

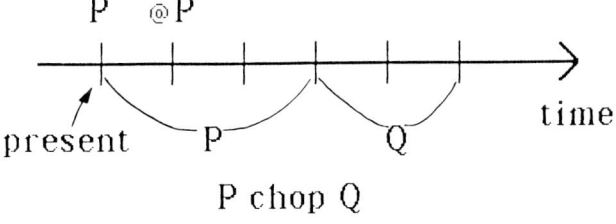

FIGURE 2.3.1 Relationships expressed by temporal logic.

shaking sequences shown in Figure 2.3.2 are described as follows:

$$\text{always}(\sim\text{Hear} \rightarrow ((\text{always } \sim\text{Call}) \text{ chop } (\text{always Call}))) \land \qquad (17)$$
$$\text{always}(\text{Call} \rightarrow ((\text{always } \sim\text{Hear}) \text{ chop } (\text{always Hear}))) \land$$
$$\text{always}(\text{Hear} \rightarrow ((\text{always Call}) \text{ chop } (\text{always } \sim\text{Call}))) \land$$
$$\text{always}(\sim\text{Call} \rightarrow ((\text{always Hear}) \text{ chop } (\text{always } \sim\text{Hear})))$$

($\land$: logical AND, $\lor$: logical OR, $\sim$: NOT, $\rightarrow$: IMPLY)

Call is a request signal from a calling module to a called module, and Hear is a response. The timing diagram says that if Hear is low, then Call rises; if Call rises, Hear rises; if Hear rises, Call falls; and if Call falls, Hear falls. The above expressions correspond to these relationships. For example,

$$\text{always}(\sim\text{Hear} \rightarrow ((\text{always } \sim\text{Call}) \text{ chop } (\text{always Call})))$$

means if Hear is low, Call will eventually rise.

Another example is a delay description. Digital circuits often require that inputs remain stable and be sampled for some minimum amount of time in order to ensure proper device operation. "The device must have m units of time to ensure that input A is sampled as an output B" is described as follows:

$$\text{always}((\text{stable}(A) \land \text{length} > m) \rightarrow \text{fin}(B=A)). \qquad (18)$$

Through the use of this kind of description for delays, various delay models, i.e., separate delays between rising and falling, setup time, fold time, etc., are easily expressed in temporal logic [18].

There are two HDLs that are based on ITL. Those are Tempura [19] and Tokio [20]. Although these two languages were originally proposed as HDLs, they can be used as software programming languages. First, Tempura is briefly introduced by showing some description examples.

Tempura and Description Examples

The device shown in Figure 2.3.3 is a simple latch composed of two cross-coupled NOR gates. When the inputs S and R are held stable long enough, the outputs Q and $\bar{Q}$ respond to them according to the table shown in Figure 2.3.4. The values of the inputs should not be held simultaneously at 1 because this can result in oscillation of the latch's outputs later.

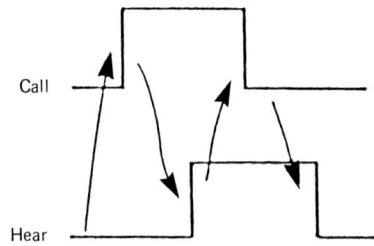

Hardware Description Language   153

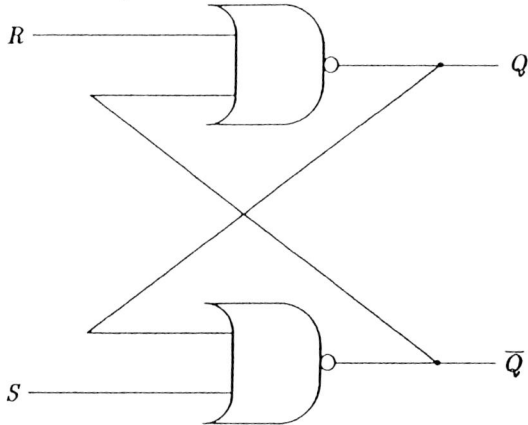

FIGURE 2.3.3 A simple latch.

The program in Figure 2.3.5 simulates the latch for values of the inputs S and R. We model each NOR gate as having unit delay. Note that the variable Q is referred to as Qbar in the program. The resulting system behavior is displayed in Figure 2.3.6. The iterative construct

for $v < e$ do w (19)

is used to sequentially assign a variable v the elements of the given list expression e and execute the statement w with each such binding.

The next example is to generate a wave form, which is shown in Figure 2.3.7. This program controls the behavior of the four variables W, X, Y, and Z. The signal W is initialized to 0 and then successively oscillates five times over 4-unit intervals by means of the following form of sequential iteration:

for 5 times do ((20)
  (length=3 $\wedge$ stable(W)) ; (skip $\wedge$ (W $\leftarrow$ ~W))
).

The semicolon (;) is used as chop in Tempura, and skip is an abbreviation of length=1.

The total length of the period is therefore 20 units. In parallel with this, the signal X is initialized to zero (0) and then receives the values of

operation	S	R	Q	$\overline{Q}$
set to 1	1	0	1	0
clear to 0	0	1	0	1
no change	0	0	old Q	old $\overline{Q}$
undefined	1	1	–	–

FIGURE 2.3.4 Function table for a latch.

$$(S = 0) \wedge (R = 0) \wedge (Q = 0) \wedge (Qbar = 0) \wedge$$
$$for\ l \in \langle\langle 1,0\rangle, \langle 0,0\rangle, \langle 0,1\rangle, \langle 1,0\rangle, \langle 0,0\rangle\rangle$$
$$do\ ($$
$$\quad len(5) \wedge (S\ gets\ l_0) \wedge (R\ gets\ l_1)$$
$$)$$
$$\wedge\ (Q\ gets\ \neg[R \vee Qbar])$$
$$\wedge\ (Qbar\ gets\ \neg[S \vee Q])$$

FIGURE 2.3.5 Tempura program for a latch.

```
State  0:  Qbar   Q     R     S
State  0:   |     |     |     |
State  1:   |     |     |     |
State  2:   |     |     |     |
State  3:   |     |     |     |
State  4:   |     |     |     |
State  5:   |     |     |     |
State  6:   |     |     |     |
State  7:   |     |     |     |
State  8:   |     |     |     |
State  9:   |     |     |     |
State 10:   |     |     |     |
State 11:   |           |     |
State 12:   |     |     |     |
State 13:         |     |     |
State 14:   |     |     |     |
State 15:   |     |     |     |
State 16:   |     |     |     |
State 17:   |     |     |     |
State 18:   |     |     |     |
State 19:   |     |     |     |
State 20:   |     |     |     |
State 21:   |     |     |     |
State 22:   |     |     |     |
State 23:   |     |     |     |
State 24:   |     |     |     |
State 25:   |     |     |     |

Done!  Computation length = 25.
```

FIGURE 2.3.6 Behaviors of latch.

$$
\begin{aligned}
&(W = 0) \wedge (X = 0) \wedge (Y = 0) \wedge \\
&\textit{for 5 times do } (\\
&\quad [len(3) \wedge (\textit{stable } W)]; \\
&\quad [\textit{skip} \wedge (W \leftarrow \neg W)] \\
&) \\
&\wedge (X \textit{ gets } W) \wedge (Y \textit{ gets } X) \\
&\wedge (Z \approx [W \wedge X \wedge Y]).
\end{aligned}
$$

FIGURE 2.3.7 Tempura programs for a wave form.

W but with unit delay. The same happens from X to Y. The value of Z is always the logical AND of W, X, and Y. In Figure 2.3.8, the behavior of the combined system in the form of a timing diagram is displayed.

The above examples are all behavior descriptions. However, structural descriptions can be expressed in logic form. Such examples are presented below.

Tokio and Description Examples

Tokio is a logic programming language based on ITL, and an extension of PROLOG to handle sequential circuits easily [20]. Here, PROLOG is briefly introduced and then Tokio is explained.

PROLOG [21] is a simple but powerful programming language founded on symbolic logic. The basic computational mechanism is a pattern-matching process (called unification or resolution), operating on general record structures ("term" of logic).

The primitive combinational gates, such as AND, OR, and NOT are described in PROLOG as facts corresponding to truth tables. For example, an AND gate is described as follows. (Only two values [0 and 1] are treated, and it is assumed that combinational circuits have no time delay.)

    and2([1,1,1]).
    and2([0,1,0]).   (21)
    and2([V,0,0]).

The last element in the list of each line above means the output value of an AND gate, and the first two elements mean the two input values. Therefore, the first line in Ex. (21) shows that if both of the input values are 1, the output value is 1, and the second line shows that if both of the input values are 0 and 1, the output value is 0. V in the arguments of the third line is a variable of PROLOG (here, any atom beginning with a capital letter is a variable), which pattern matches both 0 and 1, and means "don't care." Any combinational primitive gates are described with PROLOG in the same way.

We can ask questions about the descriptions given above. For example, if we want to know the output value, provided that both of the input values are zero (0), we only have to ask the question

    ?- and2([0,0,V]).   (22)

```
State  0: Z    Y    X    W
State  0: |    |    |    |
State  1: |    |    |    |
State  2: |    |    |    |
State  3: |    |    |    |
State  4: |    |    |    |
State  5: |    |    |    |
State  6: |    |    |    |
State  7: |    |    |    |
State  8: |    |    |    |
State  9: |    |    |    |
State 10: |    |    |    |
State 11: |    |    |    |
State 12: |    |    |    |
State 13: |    |    |    |
State 14: |    |    |    |
State 15: |    |    |    |
State 16: |    |    |    |
State 17: |    |    |    |
State 18: |    |    |    |
State 19: |    |    |    |
State 20: |    |    |    |

Done!  Computation length = 20
```

FIGURE 2.3.8 Behaviors of tempura programs for generating a wave form.

The system answers $V=0$ as the result of the pattern matching on Ex. (21). Also, input values can be obtained from an output value. For example, if we want to know the input values, provided that the output value is one (1), we ask the question

    ?- and2([I1,I2,1]).   (23)

The system answers $I1=1$ and $I2=1$.

These two questions have answers. If we ask a question that has no answers, such as

    ?- and2([1,0,1]).   (24)

the system answers "no," which means that the computation fails and there is no answer. As seen above, not only do we obtain the output value from the input values, but also the input values from the output value.

Networks are described by using the same variable on the terminals of the same net. As the results of the pattern-matching mechanism of PROLOG, the terminals of the same net have the same values. For example, the circuit (Exclusive-OR gate) of Figure 2.3.9A is described as B. eor([I1, I2,0]) is the head of the PROLOG clause, and B shows that in order to satisfy eor([I1,I2,0]), all the conditions after ":-" must be satisfied. We

Hardware Description Language

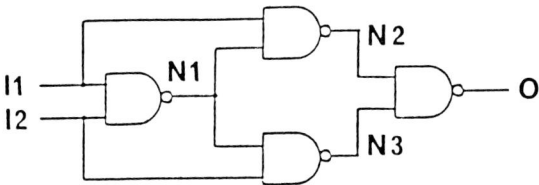

FIGURE 2.3.9 Exclusive-OR gate and Prolog description.

can ask questions to Figure 2.3.9B in the same way. For example, if we want to know the input values, provided that the output value is 1, we execute C of figure 2.3.9. However, C only obtains a single solution. If we want to know all the solutions, we execute D. In Figure 2.3.9D, "fail" is the system predicate making a failure compulsorily, and the system starts the automatic backtracking mechanism. The automatic backtracking mechanism makes it possible to examine all the selections of each predicate so as to get all the solutions. The system predicate printing its arguments is "print," so all the solutions are printed on the terminal as in Figure 2.3.9D.

So far, only combinational circuits are described. Because a variable of PROLOG can have only one value (it cannot change value, because it is a logical variable [21]), it is not possible to directly express sequential circuits in PROLOG. Thus, Tokio is proposed as an extension of PROLOG to handle sequential circuits smoothly.

As seen above, the syntax of PROLOG is like

head :- body. (25)

This is called a Horn clause, and head is implied by body or, more simply, head is a subroutine name and body if a subroutine body. The syntax of Tokio is the same as that of Prolog and is also based on the Horn clause.

Roughly speaking, the Horn clause of Tokio is a Horn clause that includes the temporal operator in its body. That is, the primitive temporal operators such as the next or chop operators may appear in the body of the Horn clause.

The execution of Tokio is a kind of resolution of temporal logic. Unification and reduction generate a model state by state. If there are no temporal operators, the reduction of Tokio is identical to that of PROLOG. A predicate with next operator or chop operator defines the following state. These predicates are queued up with the environment for the next state and are reduced later in order to realize sequential processing, which is implied by sequential circuits.

In the following text, some execution examples of Tokio are presented to understand Tokio clearly.

?-@ @write(3),@write(2),write(0),write(1) (26)

0123

yes

In Tokio, next operator is symbolized as @. Notice that the @ statement is executed after the current state.

There are many values in a variable in Tokio. These values are generated incrementally as time advances. Basic operation for accessing these values is unification. Here is a simple counter in Tokio.

  counter(X) :- #(@X=X+1).   (27)

  ?- X=0,counter(X),#write(X),length(3).

  0123

  yes

In Tokio, the operator is always symbolized as #. So, counter always increments the value of X at each state.

Hardware Description Examples in Tokio

The description of a 2-bit × 2-bit array multiplier in Tokio is discussed. The multiplier consists of six cells, as illustrated in Figure 2.3.10, and the construction of each cell is described in Figure 2.3.11. In Figure 2.3.10, X0, X1, Y0, and Y1 are input variables, and M3, M2, M1, and M0 are output variables. The multiplier executes (X1 X0) × (Y1 Y0) = (M3 M2 M1 M0).

A description for this multiplier in Tokio is shown in Figure 2.3.12. The execution is divided into three phases. In each phase, the execution of the two cells is performed in parallel, and three phases are executed sequentially. This is described in the "mul2( ):-" clause at the top of Figure 2.3.12. Comma (,) means parallelism, and chop (&&) means sequentiality. In this description, cell is realized as a single unit.

Another description for the cell in Tokio is shown in Figure 2.3.13. It is clear that one cell consists of an "and" and a "full_adder" and that a full_adder consists of "half_adder" and "or." In each cell, the execution of and is followed by the execution of full_adder. This is described in the "cell( ):-" clause in Figure 2.3.13. The execution of two half_adders and "or" in the full_adder is described in the same way. Figure 2.3.14 shows the parallelsim and sequentiality of this execution.

A data path of each cell is illustrated in Figure 2.3.15. The description in Tokio is shown in Figure 2.3.16, which describes the idea of the

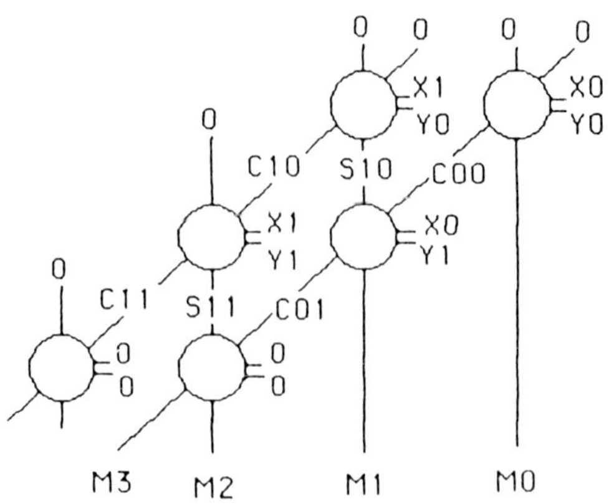

FIGURE 2.3.10 2-bit * 2-bit multiplier: mul2.

Hardware Description Language

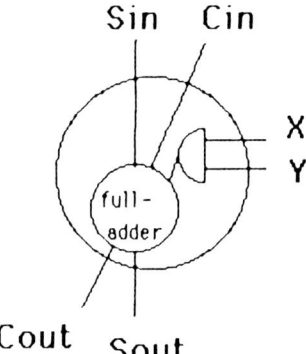

FIGURE 2.3.11 Cell in the multiplier.

data path directly. Every unit, i.e., the "delay," "and," "half_adder," and "or" is executed at every clock in the interval where the cell clause is defined and data stream sequentially. The idea of the unification of temporal variables enables us to describe the stream of data flow.

Calculus of Communicating Systems

Another parallel execution model is Calculus of Communicating Systems (CCS) [16]. The basic ideas of CCS are message passing without buffering and observation equivalence. In CCS, a behavior is defined as having a capability of communicating external behaviors. Ports are dynamically connected to other ports that have the corresponding names. For example, a port whose name is π can communicate its complementary ports, i.e., a port whose name is $-\pi$. Behaviors are defined by explicitly specifying a

```
mul2(X1, X0,Y1,Y0,M3,M2,M1,M0) :-
        cell(0,  0,  X0,Y0,M0,C00),
        cell(0,  0,  X1,Y0,S10,C10)
        &&
        cell(S10,C00,X0,Y1,M1, C01),
        cell(0 ,C10,X1,Y1,S11,C11)
        &&
        cell(S11,C01,0, 0,M2 , M3),
        cell(0,  C11,0, 0, _ , _ ).

cell(Sin,Cin,X,Y,Sout,Cout) :-
        L1 <- X /\ Y,S1 <- Sin,C1<- Cin
        &&
        Sum = L1 + S1 + C1,
        if (Sum = 0) then (Sout <- 0, Cout <- 0),
        if (Sum = 1) then (Sout <- 1, Cout <- 0),
        if (Sum = 2) then (Sout <- 0, Cout <- 1),
        if (Sum = 3) then (Sout <- 1, Cout <- 1).
```

FIGURE 2.3.12 Tokio description for mul2 and cell.

```
cell(Sin,Cin,X,Y,Sout,Cout) :-
     and(X,Y,L1),S1 <- Sin,C1<- Cin
     &&
     full_adder(S1,C1,L1,Sout,Cout).

full_adder(S1,C1,L1,Sout,Cout) :-
     half_adder(S1,C1,S2,C2),L2 <- L1
     &&
     half_adder(S2,L2,S3,C3),
     C4 <- C2
     &&
     or(C3,C4,Cout),
     Sout <- S3.

half_adder(A,B,S,C) :-
     A = 0, B = 0,
     @S = 0, @C = 0.
half_adder(A,B,S,C) :-
     A = 0, B = 1,
     @S = 1, @C = 0.
half_adder(A,B,S,C) :-
     A = 1, B = 0,
     @S = 1, @C = 0.
half_adder(A,B,S,C) :-
     A = 1, B = 1,
     @S = 0, @C = 1.

or(A,B,C) :-
     A = 0, B = 0,
     @C = 0.
or(A,B,C) :-
     A = 0, B = 1,
     @C = 1.
or(A,B,C) :-
     A = 1, B = 0,
     @C = 1.
or(A,B,C) :-
     A = 1, B = 1,
     @c = 1.
```

FIGURE 2.3.13 Another Tokio description for a cell.

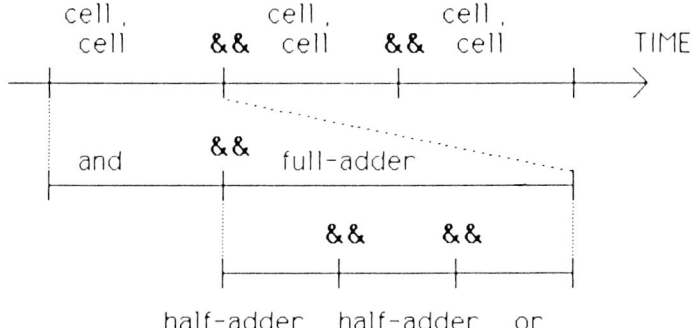

FIGURE 2.3.14 Timing relationships for Figure 2.3.13.

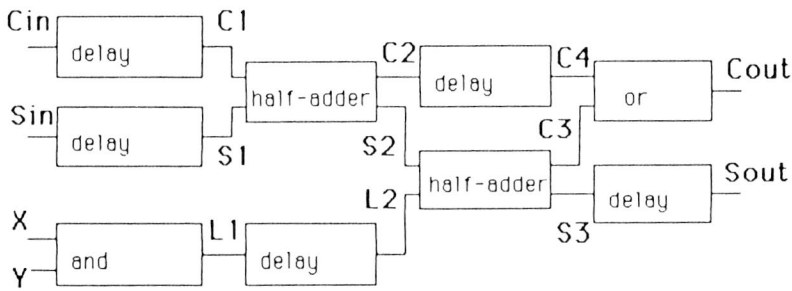

FIGURE 2.3.15 Data path for a cell.

```
cell(Sin,Cin,X,Y,Sout,Cout) :-
        #delay(Sin,S1),
        #delay(Cin,C1),
        #and(X,Y,L1),
        #delay(L1,L2),
        #delay(L1,L2),
        #half_adder(S1,C1,S2,C2),
        #delay(C2,C4),
        #half_adder(S2,L2,S3,C3),
        #delay(S3,Sout),
        #or(C3,C4,Cout).
delay(X,X1) :-
        @X1 = X.
and(A,B,C) :-
        A = 0, B = 0,
        @C = 0.
and(A,B,C) :-
        A = 0, B = 1,
        @C = 0.
and(A,B,C) :-
        A = 1, B = 0,
        @C = 0.
and(A,B,C) :-
        A = 1, B = 1,
        @C = 1.
```

FIGURE 2.3.16 Tokio description with data path.

sequence of allowed communications. Some mechanisms are shown in the following examples.

1. NIL: A behavior that does nothing.
2. $B + B'$: A behavior that does the same as the one that is non-deterministically selected from the two behaviors B and B'.
3. $\pi x1 \ldots xn.B$: A behavior that receives n values from the port π and assigns those values to $x1,\ldots,xn$ and then does the same as B.
   $\pi E1 \ldots En.B$ ($E1,\ldots,EN$ are expressions): A behavior that outputs to the port π n evaluated values from the expressions $E1,\ldots,En$ and then does the same as B.

For example, a behavior that inputs two values from the ports σ1 and σ2 and outputs the sum of those values to the port π is described as

$$\sigma1\ x.\ \sigma2\ y.\ \pi\ (x+y)\ .\ NIL + \sigma1\ y.\ \sigma2\ s.\ \pi\ (x+y)\ .\ NIL. \qquad (28)$$

Reasoning in CCS is based on the idea of "observation equivalence." The fact that p and q are observation equivalent means that all the observable sequences that can be realized by p and q are equal. CCS supplies axiomatic systems for observation equivalence. A hardware design verification system, called LCF_LSM is constructed from CCS [22].

Circal: Circal is a calculus developed from CCS [23]. Circal introduces another operator to CCS, a dot operator, so that complex devices can be modeled hierarchically with the behavior of a composite device being established from the behavior of the parts using the dot operator. The dot operator allows us to remove information and describe a device at a more abstract level.

For example, consider a hardware module composed of four submodules. Also, suppose each submodule, A, B, C, and D, has a behavior in Circal as

$$\begin{aligned} A &\leftarrow (a\ d)\ A1, \\ B &\leftarrow (a\ b)\ B1, \\ C &\leftarrow (b\ c)\ C1, \\ D &\leftarrow (c\ d)\ D1, \end{aligned} \qquad (29)$$

where a, b, c, and d are ports for communications like CCS. The first line of Ex. (29) means that A first executes communications through the ports a and d simultaneously and then behaves like $A1$. The Circal description for the whole module composed of the above four modules is constructed by using the dot operator "·."

$$A \cdot B \cdot C \cdot D \qquad (30)$$

By the properties of the dot operator [23], the above expression is reduced to the following:

$$A \cdot B \cdot C \cdot D = (a\ b\ c\ d)\ A1 \cdot B1 \cdot C1 \cdot D1. \qquad (31)$$

Example (31) means that the whole module first executes communications through ports a, b, c, and d and behaves just like $A1 \cdot B1 \cdot C1 \cdot D1$. Using the same techniques, e.g., a Circal description for an *RS* flip-flop, is easily acquired from a description for two NOR gates.

2.4 Text/Graphic

In principle, computers can handle data only in text format because of their internal representations. Therefore, HDLs are basically represented in a text style. However, it is easier to understand graphic representation of designs. Moreover, many hardware designers have used circuit diagrams for many years. So graphic representation methods of HDLs are sought by many people.

The most difficult problem for graphic representation by computers is that screens of graphic terminals do not have enough area to display large circuits. Therefore, some diagrams must be divided into several screens and many compact representations of hardware components are required to overcome this problem.

ALEX [12] is one of the systems that has graphic interface. ALEX supplies many useful tools for circuit diagram representations, some of which are shown in the following text.

A typical diagram in ALEX is shown in Figure 2.4.1. It represents the logic of a two-digit, decimal adder that is composed of simpler subcomponents: ADD1, PLUS6, SUB6, and INV [12]. In ALEX, a diagram shown in a screen is called a page. Each component on the page has a serial letter as a unique identifier in its lower boundary. The diagram shows four logic blocks (B,D,E,G) and two replication groups (C,F) interconnected by lines. The replication factors of the groups are four times and two times, respectively. Signals go through the logic on the diagram from left to right, and pages as well as components have inputs on their left boundaries and outputs on their right boundaries.

A logic block on a diagram corresponds to some component that a designer wants to define. In Figure 2.4.1, for example, block B (ADD1) represents a 1-bit, three-input binary adder, and block G (INV) represents a simple inverter.

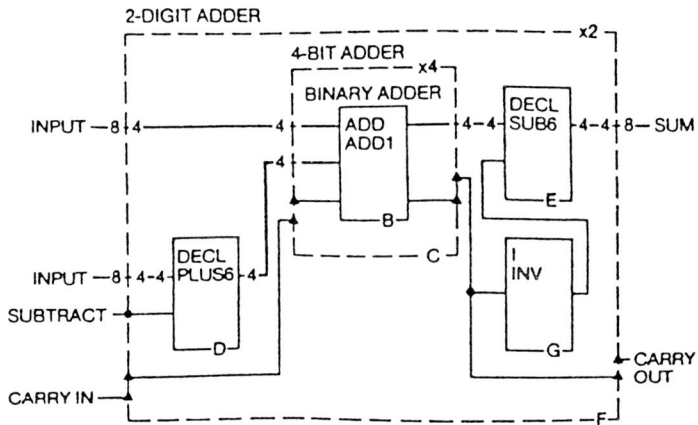

FIGURE 2.4.1 Circuit diagram in ALEX.

Some blocks such as the inverter may represent a primitive physical component. However, in general, a block will represent a macro, i.e., a collection of connected logical components that may be other macros or primitives themselves. Block B (ADD1) represents such collections. The structure of such macros are described on the page named by the second line of text within a block. Thus, block B represents a usage of the binary adder whose details are described in page ADD1.

Because each page contains logic blocks that represent the usage of other pages, it is clear that the system of pages represents a hierarchical structure.

Another powerful notation for displaying circuit diagrams is used in the diagram of Figure 2.4.2 [12], which is a part of the carry circuit of a three-input binary adder. The output is the negation of at least two inputs. The figure illustrates the usage of a graphic device that enables a signal from one replica to be used in another replica. This device is called a "warp" and is represented by a small column of deltas. The left part of Figure 2.4.2 shows three two-input AND-invert blocks whose outputs are connected to a common load. This connection of outputs, known as a DOT function, behaves as an AND gate. Each of the three inputs feeds two of the AND inverters, so that if more than one input is in the "1" state, the output is "0"; otherwise the output is "1."

The first input to each of the three AI blocks is the corresponding strand of the input bundle. The second input of each AI block is connected to the same signal as the first input of the following block, where the "following block" to the last AI is the first AI. This is represented in the right half of Figure 2.4.2, using replication with a warp. The warp is interpreted in this case as follows: The output of the warp in any replica is the same signal as the input to the warp in the following replica. The number of replicas that the signal is considered to have jumped is determined by the number of deltas in the warp, i.e., one delta per replica, including source and destination. If the warp output comes from a delta lower than the input, the signal comes from a previous replica, where the immediate predecessor to the first replica is the last. Warps may have multiple outputs, where each output corresponds to a signal from a different replica.

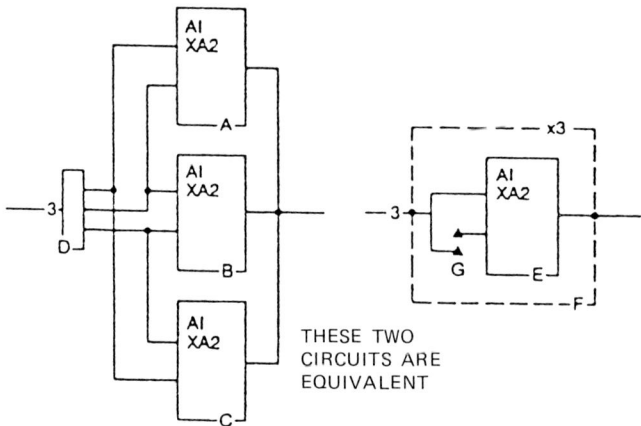

FIGURE 2.4.2 Carry circuit of a 3-input binary adder.

Hardware Description Language   165

As seen above, there are many mechanisms for displaying circuit diagrams in a compact form.

2.5 Special Language/Application of Programming Language

HDLs shown so far are all special languages designed to describe hardware. However, it is possible to apply programming languages to describe hardware. Because hardware intrinsically has parallelsims, concurrent programming languages are used. The most advantageous point for using programming languages is that a large number of accumulated programming tools, such as compiler, debugger, and structure editor, are widely and easily available. Here, hardware description in Occam is presented as an example [24].

Occam [3] is a programming language that is based on communicating sequential processes (CSP) [17]. This language can easily represent parallel processing in which each parallel processing operation communicates via a communication channel. Because each processing operation is virtually independent, the program structure is easy to understand.

Occam program is constructed by a number of processes. A process consists of a combination of primitive processes.

A pattern matcher proposed by Foster and Kung [25] is described. Figures 2.5.1 and 2.5.2 show the outline of the pattern matcher. This pattern matcher checks whether a given pattern, which is a fixed length vector of characters, is embedded in a given text string, which is an endless string of characters, as shown in Figure 2.5.1.

Let us denote the input string stream as $s0\ s1\ s2\ \ldots$, the input finite pattern stream as $p0\ p1\ p2\ \ldots\ pk$, and the output result stream as $r0\ r1\ r2\ \ldots$. Characters in the two-input streams may be compared for equality, with the wild-card character X matching any character in an input stream. The output bit ri is to be set to one (1), if the substring $si\text{-}k$ $si\text{-}k+1 \ldots si$ matches the pattern, and zero (0) otherwise. For example, in Figure 2.5.1 the pattern $A \times C$ matches the substrings $s0\ s1\ s2\ s3\ s4\ s5$, and $s4\ s5\ s6$ (ABC, AAC, and ACC, respectively).

The concurrent algorithm of the pattern matcher is described in Occam, as shown in Figures 2.5.2 and 2.5.3.

The Occam program consists of three declaration parts, (A, B, and C), and a description of parallel processes (D). The declaration parts are as follows:

> A declares channel vectors. A channel vector is a set of channels. Channels are used for communication between concurrent processes. For example, pattern[6] means that there are six channels named pattern, and they are numbered from 0 to 5, as shown in Figure 2.5.4.
>
> B declares a single comparator process. PROC gives the name comp to this process, and identifies five formal parameters, the internal channels, pin, sin, pout, sout, and dout, as shown in Figure 2.5.2. When the names process is substituted for the subsequent process (D), the formal parameters are replaced by the actual parameters. Process comp is sequential and consists of two processes. One is the initialization (B-1), and the other is an endless iterative process, WHILE TRUE. The iterative process contains a sequential process, which consists of two processes. The first

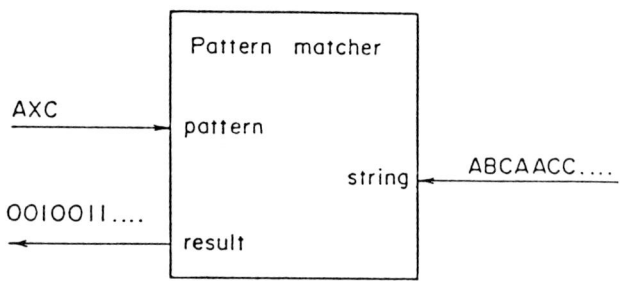

FIGURE 2.5.1 Data to and from a pattern matcher.

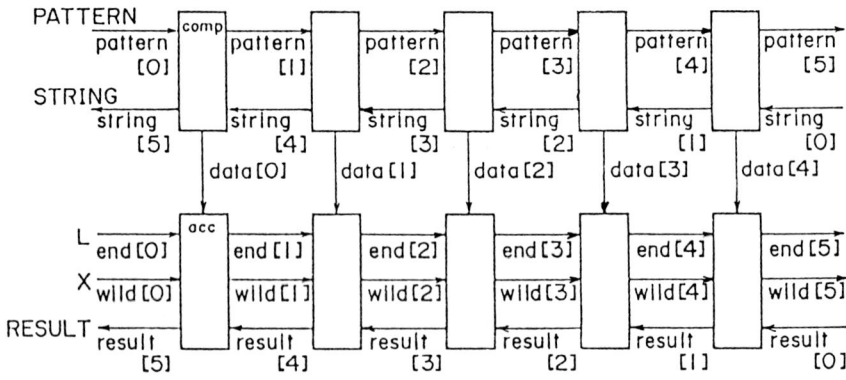

FIGURE 2.5.2 Dataflow for a pattern matcher.

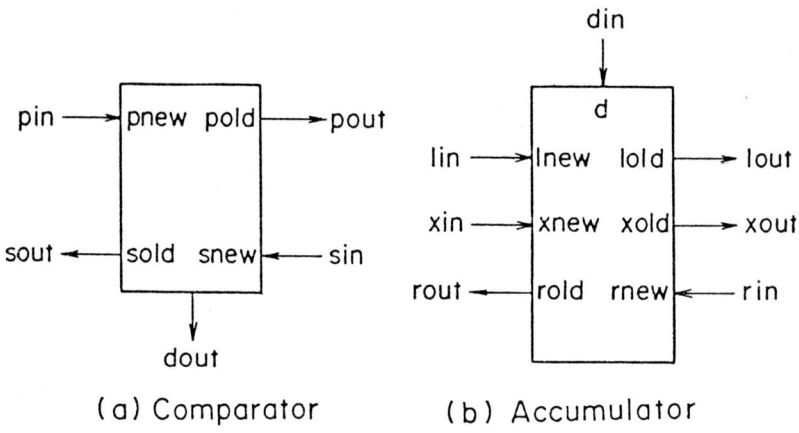

(a) Comparator   (b) Accumulator

FIGURE 2.5.3 Formal parameters and variables.

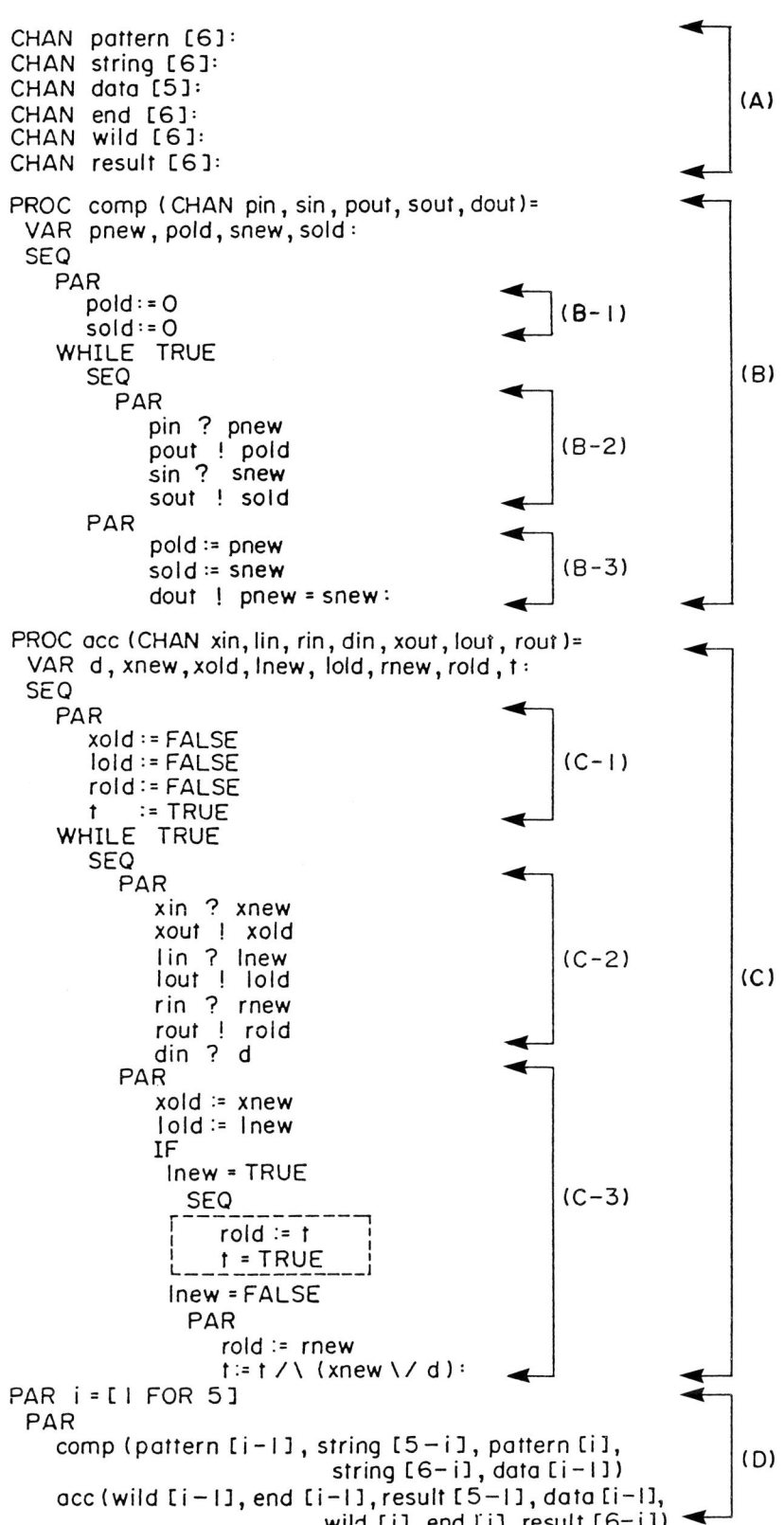

FIGURE 2.5.4 Algorithm for a pattern matcher in Occam.

two are output and input processes (B-2). The last process compares the characters in the pattern with those in the text string and outputs a Boolean value, TRUE or FALSE (B-3).

C declares a single accumulator process. The process named acc contains seven formal parameters, as shown in Figure 2.5.3. The variable d stands for the current comparison result of the comparator, xnew and xold for don't care bit, lnew and lold for end of pattern, rnew and rold for final result of matching, and t for temporary result of matching. Process acc is sequential and consists of two processes. One is the initialization of variables (C-1). The other is an iterative process, similar to process comp. The iterative process includes a sequential process, which consists of two processes. The first includes output and input processes (C-2). The second is a conditional process (C-3). When the end of the pattern is reached, an accumulator uses the value t (current temporary result) as the final result and then resets t to TRUE. Otherwise, it maintains a temporary result t, which is set by the logical expression $t := t \wedge (\text{new} \vee d)$. "$\wedge$" and "$\vee$" stand for Boolean AND and OR, respectively. Thus, if the current temporary result t is TRUE, and xnew or the current comparison result d is TRUE, then the new temporary result will be set to TRUE.

D indicates a 2 × 5 array of concurrent processes, as shown in Figure 2.5.4. The cells at the top are the comparators; the pattern flows from left to right and the string flows from right to left. The bottom cells, accumulators, receive the results of the comparison from above. They maintain partial results and shift completed results from right to left. Two bits associated with the pattern flow through the accumulators from left to right. One bit is the end of pattern, L. The other is the wild-card character, X.

As seen above, hardware can be described in concurrent programming languages, especially in design levels higher than function design. However, there is a disadvantage: No special mechanisms for expressing hardware facilities, such as registers and terminals, are supplied by the programming languages. There is enough freedom of modeling hardware facilities to confuse designers. So a clear description method by programming languages must be constructed, and some research in this area has been completed [26].

3 TOOLS FOR HDL

There are various computer-assisted tools for HDLs, e.g., verification, synthesis, graphic input. In present CAD systems, the standard approach that is taken to verify the proposed logic designs is that of simulations. Almost all the HDLs have their simulators, and some of them have tools for enhancing the man—machine interface such as graphic input/output and interactive simulations. However, it is recognized that simulations have several drawbacks. As the logic network that is to be simulated becomes more complex, the number of possible inputs to the logic structure grows exponentially, so that a complete simulation becomes infeasible. Hence,

Hardware Description Language

only a representable subset of inputs is selected for simulations. This may lead a designer to fail to notice some errors.

To avoid failing to notice some bugs, formal verification methods, which can also be considered to be the methods automatically generating all the simulation cases needed for verification, are proposed.

3.1 Verification

There are several kinds of verification techniques based on HDLs:

1. Application of software verification techniques (like inductive assertion method) [27]
2. Logic-based verification [2, 28]
3. Symbolic simulation [29]

Currently, most aggressive research is done on technique 2, which is discussed briefly here.

The first thing we can do using logic is to compare a combinational circuit with its specification, a logical expression. Figure 3.1.1 shows an implementation of AND with two NAND gates. Although this is a trivial example, it takes a number of steps of inference to prove it, as follows [30].

1. $c = \text{NAND}(\text{NAND}(a,b), \text{NAND}(a,b))$
2. $\text{NAND}(a,b) = \sim(a \wedge b)$
3. $c = \sim(\sim(a \wedge b) \wedge \sim(a \wedge b))$
4. $c = \sim(\sim(a \wedge b))$
5. $c = a \wedge b$

Steps 1 and 2 hold from the assumption. Step 3 is acquired by substituting 2 into 1. Step 4 is acquired by 3 and the law $x \wedge x = x$. Finally, step 5 is acquired by 4 and the law $\sim\sim x = x$.

As seen above, it is not so easy to verify design by logic inference. However, this approach is very promising because it may have a power for verifying large hardware by using some computer-assisted tools. Currently, this type of formal verification can be done by humans with computer-assisted systems. The system provides the mechanisms for applying various proof strategies, as well as basic theorems [31], and some types of designs can be verified automatically. Moreover, those systems make use of hierarchy of designs, so they are fairly efficient [32]. A further step is taken by other reserachers [33, 34, 41].

Although this approach is used only as a research activity at present, it can be applied to industrial use in the near future.

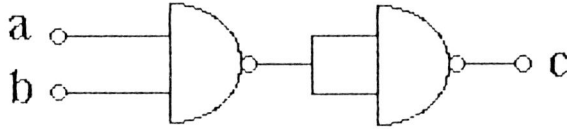

FIGURE 3.1.1 An implementation of AND gate with two NAND gates.

3.2 Synthesis

Much work has been done on hardware design synthesis in various design levels. Automatic synthesis, however, is a very hard task, and only a few studies are practical. They are mainly in gate design and implementation design levels and handle special forms of hardware such as, programmable logic array (PLA), gate array, macro modules, etc.

On the other hand, some work using artificial intelligence (AI) techniques, has been developed to increase the performance of automatically synthesized design. The main idea is to synthesize hardware as a human does with knowledge memorized in a computer.

Research on gate design synthesis can be divided into two types: data path synthesis, which synthesizes the path among hardware facilities such as memories, registers, and operators, from function design descriptions in DDL, ISPS, etc.; and control part synthesis, which synthesizes control sequences of data transfers among hardware facilities. One of the most famous works on data path synthesis is the CMU-DA system [35]. It synthesizes a data path composed of macro modules such as memories, registers, multiplexers, and arithmetic logic units (ALUs) from the ISPS description by an algorithmic or a heuristic approach. It can also explore the design cost−speed trade-offs, i.e., a user can decide the parallelism of the hardware to be synthesized and limit the amount of the hardware resources. The algorithmic approach calculates the cost−speed trade-offs, depending on the parallelism and selects the best of them by a certain algorithm. On the other hand, the heuristic approach directly synthesizes hardware based on the rules acquired from many design experts. The qualities synthesized by the two approaches above are almost the same and are almost comparable with the human designs.

Much work has been done on the control part synthesis. Usually a synthesizer accepts state transition tables and outputs networks of logic gate and flip-flops or PLA patterns. The main task for a synthesizer is to simplify logical formulas, which is not an easy one. As the number of variables in a logical formula increases, the amount of time required for the simplification of the logical formula grows drastically. Also, the state assignment to flip-flops is a hard problem, and the best method has not been found. However, if a system is designed in a hierarchical manner, the logical formula to be synthesized is not so complex and the synthesis time is not as large. Therefore, the synthesis of control part has the practical meaning because of no design errors.

In addition, recent synthesis techniques of both the data path and the control part using AI have been investigated [36]. One such work [37], synthesizes networks of TTL IC from DDL descriptions using the knowledge of design experts. The knowledge of design experts is expressed with rules, and the synthesis system takes care of design rules proper to TTL, and it can exchange rules with other ones; therefore, it can also synthesize CMOS ICs. The system is developed by applying to real hardware.

4 STANDARDIZATION OF HDL

As seen above, there are many HDLs for many design levels. Although there are basic ideas common to all HDLs, it is not necessarily easy for designers to understand descriptions in various HDLs. So a particular HDL that can be widely used and is standard is very desirable. Here, two such HDLs, CONLAN [38] and EDIF [39], are briefly explained.

4.1 CONLAN

CONLAN means consensuse language and is a language to define all HDLs. That is, CONLAN is different from other HDLs because it is not a language but provides basic mechanisms for all HDLs. CONLAN consists of two languages, which are shown in Figure 4.1.1.

CONLAN provides a fundamental language that produces HDL from register-transfer level to gate level and also provides management systems for the fundamental language. When a new HDL is produced from the fundamental language, management systems are available only if a compiler is developed from the new HDL to the fundamental language.

A brief introduction of CONLAN is shown in the following text. Many high-level HDLs have been proposed since the 1960s. However, languages that are used in industries are almost all gate-level description languages, for the following reasons:

1. One language cannot assist the design of all levels.
2. Two languages for different design levels have no concerns with each other in grammar or meanings, i.e., they are not convenient for us.
3. There are few languages that have formal grammar.
4. There are few languages for which management systems are prepared.
5. Logic designers are familiar with figures but not with languages.
6. There are no design techniques for using high-level HDLs effectively.

To solve problems 1 through 4, fundamental language pscl (primitive set of CONLAN) and bcl (base CONLAN) is produced from pscl. Those who produce HDL for common designers are requested to produce the language that is suitable for users' environment from bcl. Therefore, pscl and bcl exist as a common basic grammar, and whichever language is produced transferrability of grammar exists on bcl level.

CONLAN has REFLAN statement, which declares the names of fundamental languages. If compiler and simulator exist on bcl level, a user can use common CAD tools without development, only if the user makes a compiler from the new HDL to bcl. This leads to the advance of normalization on bcl level. Under this idea, new tools, compiler and simulator, have been developed at Darmatat University in West Germany and at IMAG in France.

The approaches of CONLAN project to language design are summarized as follows:

CONLAN ———— bcl(base conlan)
↑
pscl(primitive set of conlan)

FIGURE 4.1.1 Organization of CONLAN.

1. Self definition.
2. Extension.
3. Common grammar.

Considering these points, CONLAN has been systemized for about 10 years. The features of CONLAN are as follows:

1. Complete parallel execution of each sentence.
2. Remove GOTO sentence.
3. Step wise production as "pscl → bcl → language defined by user."

The complete parallel execution of each sentence was accepted naturally as HDL, when the suggestion of HDL design description language occurred in the 1960s. As for feature 2, some people may be against it; however, it allows easier reading of the description. Feature 3 is inherent only in CONLAN. The design levels that are supported by CONLAN are from gate level to infinite high level.

Description Example

Figure 4.1.2 is the description example of set—reset flip-flop by bcl. After this definition, rsff can be used freely as a fundamental circuit. The first statement is the declaration of definition of rsff and is a pair with END sentence. The second statement defines input and output terminals; r and s are input signals that have Boolean values and the value changes 0/1 as time passes. Also, the declaration of dimension is permitted. Output terminals are declared, as they cannot keep their values. After BODY statement, actual action is defined. Percent symbol (%) defines delay time, and %1 means unit delay, for example. Flip-flop consists of two lines of description.

CONLAN has a declaration unit called segment, and definitions are made in the segment. Language is also defined in the Language Description Segment. Within segment, key words are used with @, so that language definitions cannot be changes by users. Various supporting tools are already developed for CONLAN, which are available with license. The CONLAN project ended in 1980. It is now known as the CASCADE project [40].

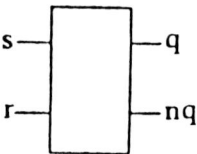

DESCRIPTIONrsff
(IN r,s : signal(bool); OUT q, nq : btm0)
BODY nq.=nor(r%1, q%1);
      q.=nor(s%1, nq%1)
ENDrsff

FIGURE 4.1.2 SR Flip-flop in CONLAN bcl.

Hardware Description Language

4.2 Electronic Design Interchange Format

With the development of VLSI, especially ASIC (Application-Specific IC), systematization by using common design data between different CAD tools advances, and the need to combine CAD system with ATE (Automatic Test Equipment) grows. It is important to standardize design data and test data. Electronic Design Interchange Format (EDIF) [39] is a typical example of this standardization.

Founders of the EDIF Committee are Motorola, Texas Instruments, National Semiconductor, Tektronix, Mentor Graphics, and Daisy Systems; University of California at Berkeley joined later. The parents of EDIF are CIDF (Common Interchange Description Format), GAIL (Gate Array Interface Language), TDF (Technology Definition File), and TIDAL (Transportable Integrated Design Automation Language) [00]. CIDF is a format developed by U. C. at Berkeley that includes schematic diagram, symbolic layout, mask pattern, and logic description. Because the syntax of CDIF is based on LISP, it is simple and easy to extend. GAIL was developed by Daisy for data interface of gate array. TDF is also a format for gate array by Motorola and Mentor. TIDAL, which Texas Instruments developed, includes a variety of data from mask pattern to test data.

EDIF is also being developed. In version 1.1, it is classified as follows:

1. Management data.
2. Connection data.
3. Input/output data for logic simulation.
4. Timing data.
5. Mask pattern data.
6. Symbolic layout data.
7. Document.

Syntax is based on LISP as CIDF is, and hierarchical description is possible. Extension is easy because of key word form. There are three levels, level0, level1, and level2, and key words that allow high-level description are added in this order.

Management Data

Figure 4.2.1 is an example of management data, and it shows that description is given by EDIF version 1.1 on level0.

Connection Data

Figure 4.2.2 shows connection data for RS latch of Figure 4.2.3. There are mask pattern and document besides connection data as a description for cell, and they are indicated by the key word "view." Key word "interface" describes input/output, and key word "instance" gives modules that are used. Connections are given by the key word "joined." A special useful statement is shown in Figure 4.2.4, which expresses that the terminal QB is intentionally unused.

Timing Data

Figure 4.2.5 is an example of description of delay. Delay time from input A, B to output Z is described, depending on state transition and fanout.

```
(EDIF LatchCircuit
  (Status (EDIFversion 1 1 0)(EDIFlevel 0)
  (written(timestamp 1985 10 26 15 22 16)))
  (Library LatchLibrary
    (Status(EDIFversion 1 1 0)(EDIFlevel 0)
      (written(timestamp 1985 10 26 15 22 16)))

(library CMOS1U
  (status
    (EDIFVersion 1 1 0)
    (EDIFLevel 0)
    (written
      (timeStamp 1985 2 16 2 22 12)
      (accounting author *Nepenthe Technology Group*))
    (written
      ( timeStamp 1985 2 17 3 44 15)
      (accounting author *N. G. Noer, Advanced Design Lab*)
      (accounting program *CIFToEDIF-2X.Y*)))
  —
  —
  (cell MUX3
    (status
      (written
        (timeStamp 1985 2 16 2 21 0)
        (accounting author)
        (accounting program)))
  —
  —
))
```

FIGURE 4.2.1 Example of Management Data.

```
(cell RSLatch
  (view Netlist RSLatch_Net
    (interface
      (define input port (multiple R S))
      (define output port (multiple Q QB))
    )
    (contents
      (define local signal (multiple Reset Set))
      (instance (qualify nMOSLibrary Nor) Nor_Net N1)
      (instance (qualify nMOSLibrary Nor) Nor_Net N2)
      (joined Reset R (qualify N1 A))
      (joined Set S (qualify N2 B))
      (joined Q (qualify N1 O)(qualify N2 A))
      (joined QB (qualify N2 O)(qualify N1 B))
    )
  )
)
```

FIGURE 4.2.2 Connection data for SR flip-flop.

Hardware Description Language

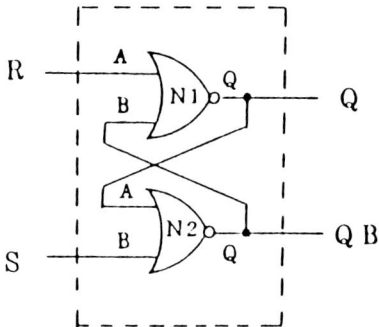

FIGURE 4.2.3 No legend.

In case of transition from L to H, delay time from A to Z is given as

5 + 2 * (fanout)

Also, in case of transition from H to L, delay time from A to Z is 2. Figure 4.2.6 is the timing condition for D flip-flop. Clock input is "phi 1" and data input is "data." This means that data must not change from 10 o'clock before the transition of "phi 1" until 5 o'clock after that transition (see Figure 4.2.7).

Document

Figure 4.2.8 is an example of a document that describes specifications of EDIF. The title is EDIF Specification and the first chapter is A TOTORIAL INTRODUCTION, which follows PREFACE. "Over the past...." is a sentence of PREFACE.

Schematic diagram, test data, functional description, layout rule, procedural layout, description of package, and PCB design are now under investigation and are not included in version 1.1. There are some problems that prevent EDIF from being allowed as a standard format. One is a competition with other formats. Another is that libraries are not opened to all users at this time. Some say that the easiness of extension of EDIF makes many kinds of local formats and that makes it difficult to decide on only one standard format.

(Unused (qualify FF1 QB))

FIGURE 4.2.4 Unuse statement.

```
(cell I
   —
   (interface
      (define input port (multiple A B C))
      (define output port Z)
      (timing a simulateValues
         (delay (transition L H 5 2)(transition H L 2 0) A Z)
         (delay (transition L H 3 1)(transition H L 1 0) B z))
```

FIGURE 4.2.5 Description of delay.

```
(stable data-10 5 phi1 L H)
```

FIGURE 4.2.6 Timing condition of D flip-flop.

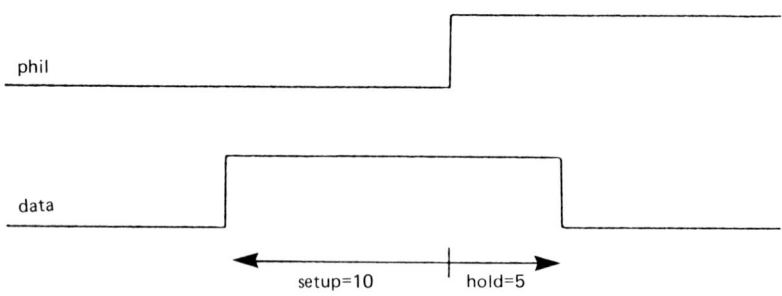

FIGURE 4.2.7 Timing diagram for Figure 4.2.6.

```
(cell DOCUMENT
   (view Document EDIFSpec
      (contents
         (section "EDIF Specification"
            (section "PREFACE"
               "Over the past few years, there has been a rapid increase..."
               "While many interchange formats and hardware description..."
               —
            )
            (section " A TUTORIAL INTRODUCTION"
               —
)))))
```

FIGURE 4.2.8 Example of Document.

REFERENCES

1. C. A. R. Hoare, "An Axiomatic Basis for Computer Programming," *Commun. ACM,* 12(10), 576–580 (October 1969).
2. T. J. Wangner, "Hardware Verification," Dept. of Computer Science, Stanford University 1977, Vol. STAN-CS-77-632.
3. Inmos Ltd., *Occam Programming Manual,* Prentice Hall International, (1984).
4. J. R. Duley and D. L. Dietmeyer, "A Digital System Design Language (DDL)," *IEEE Trans. Comput.,* C-17(9), 850–861 (September 1968).
5. Y. Chu, *Computer Organization and Microprogramming,* Prentice Hall International, 1972.
6. M. Barbacci, "Instruction Set Processor Specification (ISPS): The Notation and Its Applications," *IEEE Trans. Comput.,* C-30(1), 24–40 (1981).
7. T. Hoshino, O. Karatsu, and T. Sudo, "VLSI Hierarchical Specification Language and Design System," in *Monograph of Technical Group on Computer Architecture of Information Processing Society of Japan,* June 1982, Vol. 45-4.
8. W. M. Van Cleemput, "A Hierarchical Language for the Structural Description of Digital Systems," in *Fourteenth Design Automation Conference,* June 1977.
9. G. Shiva, "A Comparison of Hardware Description Languages: A Tutorial," *Proc. IEEE,* 1601–1605 (December 1979).
10. F. J. Hill and G. R. Peterson, "Digital Systems: Hardware Organization and Design," Wiley, New York, 1978.
11. T. M. Williams and L. C. Widdoes, "Scald, Structured Computer Aided Logic Design," in *Fifteenth Design Automation Conference,* 1978.
12. K. A. Duke, "ALEX: A Conventional Hierarchical Logic Design System," in *Seventeenth Design Automation Conference,* 1980.
13. R. W. Hartenstein and E. von Puttkamer, "KARL—A Hardware Description Language as Part of a CAD Tool for VLSI," in *IFIP Fourth Computer Hardware Description Languages and their Applications, August,* October 1979.
14. N. Kawato, T. Satito, F. Maruyama, and T. Uehara, "Design and Verification of Large-Scale Computers by Using DDL," in *Sixteenth Design Automation Conference,* June 1979.
15. Z. Manna and A. Pnueli, "Verification of Concurrent Programs, Part 1: The Temporal Framework," Dept. of Computer Science, Stanford University, June 1981, Vol. STAN-CS-81-836.
16. R. Milner, "A Calculus of Communicating Systems," in *Lecture Notes in Computer Science,* Springer-Verlag, Berlin, 1980, Vol. 92.
17. C. A. R. Hoare, "Communicating Sequential Processes," Prentice-Hall International, 1985.
18. B. Moszkowski, "A Temporal Logic for Multi-Level Reasoning about Hardware," in *IFIP Sixth Computer Hardware Description Languages and their Applications,* May 1983.
19. B. C. Moszkowski, "Executing Temporal Logic Programs," No. 55, Computer Laboratory, 1984.
20. M. Fujita, S. Kono, and H. Tanaka, "Tokio: Logic Programming Language Based on Temporal Logic and Its Compilation to Prolog," *Proc. Int. Conf. Logic Programming,* (July 1986).

21. W. F. Clocksin and C. S. Mellish, *Programming in Prolog*, Springer-Verlag, Berlin, 1981.
22. M. J. C. Gordon, "LCF-LSM: A System for Specifying and Verifying Hardware," Computer Laboratory, University of Cambridge, 1983, Vol. 41.
23. G. J. Milne, "Circal and the Representation of Communication, Concurrency, and Time," *ACM Trans. Programming Lang. Syst.*, 7(2), 270–298 (April 1985).
24. T. Mano, F. Maruyama, K. Hayashi, T. Kakuda, N. Kawato, and T. Uehara, "Occam to CMOS Experimental Logic Design Support System," in *IFIP Seventh Computer Hardware Description Languages and Their Applications, August*, August 1985.
25. M. J. Foster and H. T. Kung, "Design of Special–Purpose VLSI Chips: Example and Opinions," Dept. of Computer Science, Carnegie-Mellon University, Vol. CMU-CS-79-147 (1979).
26. M. Barbacci, S. Grout, G. Lindstron, M. P. Maloney, E. I. Organick, and D. Rudisill, "Ada as a Hardware Description Language: An Initial Report," in *IFIP Seventh Computer Hardware Description Languages and their Applications, August*, August 1985.
27. V. Pitchuman and E. P. Stabler, "A Formal Method for Computer Design Verification," in *Nineteenth Design Automation Conference*, June 1982.
28. A. S. Wojcik, "Formal Design Verification of Digital Systems," in *Twentieth Design Automation Conference*, June 1983.
29. W. C. Carter, Jr., W. H. Joyner, and D. Brand, "Symbolic Simulation for Correct Machine Design," in *Sixteenth Design Automation Conference*, June 1979.
30. A. Camilleri, M. J. C. Gordon, and T. Melham, "Hardware Verification Using Higher-Order Logic," Computer Laboratory, University of Cambridge, 1986, Vol. 91.
31. M. Gordon, R. Milner, and C. Wadsworth, "Edinburgh LCF," in *Lecture Notes in Computer Science 78*, Springer-Verlag, Berlin, 1979.
32. H. G. Barrow, "VERIFY: A Program for Proving Correctness of Digital Hardware Designs," *Artif. Intel.*, 24, 437–491 (1984).
33. B. Mishra and E. M. Clarke, "Automatic and Hierarchical Verification of Asynchronous Circuits Using Temporal Logic," Dept. of Computer Science, Carnegie–Mellon University, September 1983, Vol. CMU-CS-83-155.
34. M. J. C. Gordon, "HOL, A Machine Oriented Formulation of Higher Order Logic," Computer Laboratory, University of Cambridge, 1985, Vol. 68.
35. A. C. Parker, D. E. Thomas, D. P. Siewiorek, M. R. Barbacci, G. Leive, and J. Kim, "The CMU Design Automation System: An Example of Automated Data Path Design," in *Sixteenth DA Conference*, 1979.
36. T. J. Kowalski and D. E. Thomas, "The VLSI Design Automation Assistant: Prototype System," in *Twentieth Design Automation Conference*, June 1983.
37. T. Saito, H. Sugimoto, M. Yamazaki, and N. Kawato, "A Rule-Based Logic Circuit Synthesis System for CMOS Gate Arrays," in *Twenty-Third Design Sutomation Conference*, June 1986.
38. R. Piloty, M. Barbacci, D. Borrione, D. Dietmeyer, F. Hill, and S. Skelly, "CONLAN Report," in *Lecture Notes in Computer Science 151*, Springer-Verlag, Berlin, 1983.

39. Crawford, J. D., "EDIF, A Mechanism for the Exchange of Design Information," *IEEE Custom Integrated Circuit Conference*, (1984).
40. E. R. Marx, "EDIF, The Standard for Workstation Interconnection," *IEEE Micro* (October 1985).
41. D. Borrione and C. LeFaou, "Overview of the CASCADE Multilevel Hardware Description Language," *IFIP Seventh Computer Hardware Description Languages and their Applications, August,* August 1985.
42. M. Fujita, H. Tanaka, and T. Moto-oka, "Logic Design Assistance with temporal Logic," *IFIP 7th Computer Hardware Description Languages and their Applications, August,* (August 1985).

MASAHIRO FUJITA
TOHRU MOTO-OKA

IMAGE ENHANCEMENT

HISTORY OF IMAGING

Image enhancement is the process by which a normal image is made more interpretable to a user for a particular application. Techniques for image enhancement may be applied to any type of image or picture, including photographic, video, or digital representations of a given subject. Applications that traditionally utilize these techniques include medical imaging, remote sensing, and broadcast video processing. Although images obtained by remote sensing platforms primarily for resource analysis will be used as examples in this text, the reader should keep in mind the potential uses in other disciplines for the same, or similar, techniques.

By its very nature, image enhancement is subjective. An image that is enhanced for one person's application may be totally useless for another application.

To understand the development of image enhancement, one should be aware of the background of imaging in general. Daguerre and Niepce reported on the first photographs in 1839. After experimenting with various materials that exhibited reactions to visible light, Daguerre learned of sodium thiosulfate, which allowed a more permanent image, resistant to further changes due to light exposure. His discovery was immediately purchased by the French government, and the field of photography was initiated. In 1840, Argo, Director of the Paris Observatory suggested the use of photography in mapping topography. In 1858, a Frenchman, Gaspard Felix Tournachon, later known as "Nadar," used a balloon to obtain the first aerial photographs of Bievre, France, from an altitude of 80 meters. The "bird's eye view" provided a unique view of an urban environment distinctly showing individual houses. For such photographs to be made, an apparatus including the camera, light-sensitive material, and a development subsystem had to be taken along to develop the picture instantly after it was exposed. In 1871, Maddox developed a gelatin emulsion of silver halide that could be developed at a later time, thus freeing the photographer to embark with only a camera and emulsion surface. Processing of the emulsion for aerial photography could then occur on the ground. In 1897, with the first roll film, L. Cailetet used a balloon as platform for combining aerial photographs superimposed with readings from an aneroid barometer.

Kites began to be used for aerial photographs in 1881 with Englishman E. D. Archibald taking the first known kite observation. Kite observations continued both in Europe and in the United States, and in 1890, A. Batut published a textbook on the subject. An American, G. R. Lawrence, developed large cameras and balloon-kites for panoramic photography from heights of over 1,000 meters. By photographing the aftermath of the 1909 earthquake and fire in San Francisco from an altitude of 600 meters, Lawrence showed the capability for kite-borne aerial photography to the world. A

Image Enhancement

more mobile and unique platform for aerial photography was a carrier pigeon. In 1903, Julius Neubronner fashioned a "breast-mounted" camera system that automatically took photographs in a timed sequence as the carrier pigeon first spiraled and then headed toward its predetermined goal.

Kites, balloons, and pigeons were unsatisfactory for an organized photographic mission because they were largely unsteerable. Dirigibles could be controlled to a much greater extent than previous platforms, and they provided a platform from which aerial photography could be acquired.

An airplane (invented in 1903) was the platform for the first airborne motion pictures, when Wilber Wright flew a training flight for the Italian government. Soon after, German pilots began making training flights with cameras.

World War I saw increased use of cameras for military reconnaisance, replacing balloon observers and photography. By the end of World War I, aerial photography was considered a necessary aspect of military intelligence.

During the years between World War I and II, extensive use of aerial photography was made by newly formed aerial survey companies who photographed large areas of the United States and Canada. Government agencies began to utilize aerial photography as a means of estimating national resources over large regions. In 1934, the American Society of Photogrammetry was formed, catering to professionals involved in photogrammetry and photointerpretation.

The large majority of the photographic techniques developed during the war years for intelligence uses were focused on black-and-white imagery. The basic spectral region that was recorded was between 0.3 and 0.7 micrometers on the electromagnetic spectrum. In parallel to the strides made in the use of black-and-white (or panchromatic) photography, new developments were being made in color photography.

A film that was sensitive to the infrared portion of the electromagnetic spectrum was introduced in 1931 to try to reduce haze in aircraft photography. This and subsequent films were used during World War II for haze penetration.

Color photography was first considered seriously by Maxwell in 1855, and by 1895, a color separation process had been invented by du Hauron, using three pigments, red, yellow, and blue. A patent by Mannes and Godowsky in 1924 on a multilayer color film resulted in the introduction of Kodachrome film in 1935. Color processing reliability and repeatability questions limited the use of color film during World War II; however, it was used for estimating water depth in the Pacific basin.

In 1937, tests by the military with the newly developed Kodachrome color film resulted in the detection of disappointing haze and processing characteristics. At Kodak, work toward reducing these deficiencies resulted in the development of Kodacolor Aero Reversal film in 1942.

Color film contains three layers of dyes, each layer being sensitive to a particular wavelength band of visible light. The blue-sensitive layer contains yellow dye, the green-sensitive layer contains magenta dye, and the red-sensitive layer contains cyan dye. Reflected light from a source such as the sun would travel through a camera lens and expose each of the film layers differentially, depending on the scene imaged.

Color infrared film was developed as the result of an advisory and research effort at Harvard and MIT initiated in 1940 to evaluate factors necessary for identification of camouflage. Resultant studies indicated a large differential between healthy vegetation and camouflage in the infrared portion of the spectrum because of a strong chlorophyll reflection for natural vegetation. Cooperation between the subsequently formed National Defense Research Committee (NDRC) and Kodak led to a modification of the Kodacolor film to have layers responsive to the green, red, and infrared portions of the spectrum instead of the blue, green, and red.

Multispectral imaging was facilitated by either the use of filters, which only allow a certain wavelength range of light to pass, or beam splitters, using gratings or prisms to separate out specific spectral regions from the light entering the camera system. Each band of color may then expose a black-and-white film. Early in the 1960s, multispectral cameras were being developed for aerial terrain surveys. Multiple cameras with filters were used to portray images in different spatial locations on a single roll of film. Color additive viewers were then used to view the multispectral imagery, where selected gray-scale images were seen as red, blue, and green and optically combined to form a color image. Multispectral systems with as many as 10 ganged cameras were used extensively on the NASA Apollo missions for space photography of the earth's surface. Space photos from the Mercury, Gemini, and Apollo missions, as well as extensive experience with low altitude photographic systems, led to the formulation for many of the requirements for an Earth Resources Technology Satellite (ERTS).

During the middle 1960s, the University of Michigan's Willow Run Laboratories developed an electro-optical multispectral scanner that digitally recorded image data in multiple regions of the electromagnetic spectrum in a continuous strip image along the path of the airplane carrying the system. This system was the source of multispectral data in the Corn Blight Watch, an experiment conducted by NASA, University of Michigan, and the Purdue Laboratory for Agricultural Remote Sensing. The experiment was highly successful and showed the usefulness of multispectral digital data in accessment of the extent and growth pattern of the corn blight disease that was infesting the cropland in the central United States. A more detailed discussion on the history of imaging and remote sensing can be found in the Manual of Remote Sensing [2].

OTHER IMAGING SOURCES

Infrared Imaging

In addition to the photographic products described above, another important source of imagery that may be treated by image-enhancement techniques is an infrared scanner. An infrared scanner system is an electro-optical scanning system and has important features for civilian, as well as military, use. The term infrared used in the discussion of color infrared photography refers to the near infrared portion of the spectrum (0.9—1.2 microns wavelength). The infrared scanner systems are able to produce imagery representing spectral regions between 1.2 microns and 14 microns. Because there are no films that are responsive to the thermal infrared portion (3-12 microns) of the electromagnetic spectrum, an electro-optical control system is used to create an image that may be recorded in digital or analog form. An electro-optical scanning system may consist of a scanning mirror, a beam splitter (prism) or filter, and a detector. The mirror is designed to direct energy from a small area on the ground into the scanner system at any instant in time. As the mirror sweeps from side to side, a swath of the terrain below is imaged with a width equal to the instantaneous field of view

Image Enhancement 183

of the mirror and a length proportional to the scan angle of the sensor system. The resolution in the direction across the scan is determined by the length of time necessary to assure an appropriate response (dwell time) for a particular detector. The response time for a particular detector may be measured in the laboratory and is a function of the detectivity (D^*) of the detector material. The wavelength band of interest is selected by the choice of beamsplitter or filter through which the incident energy is passed by the mirror. After one scan of the mirror, the aircraft has moved forward along its intended path a distance determined by the aircraft velocity. Design of the scanning system and control of the aircraft are necessary to assure that a continuous strip image is obtained of the terrain. Underscan will provide gaps in coverage and overscan will image the same ground area repeatedly.

The scanner design for infrared systems has been extended to multispectral systems, such as the system at the University of Michigan, and is the basis for the design of the current multispectral scanner (MSS) and thematic mapper (TM) systems on board the U.S. Landsat earth resources satellite system.

SAR Imaging

Synthetic aperture radar (SAR) data become a digital or analog image after appropriate processing. Although the above sources of image data are passive (either measure-reflected radiation from the sun or emitted radiation from the earth's surface), SAR is an active imaging system. The system operates at radio frequency (RF), as opposed to the shorter wavelengths for visible light, near infrared and infrared. Wavelengths vary, depending on the selected RF subband from one-half centimeter to 1 meter.

Normally, SAR systems operate with a radar beam projected perpendicular to the flight path of the aircraft. Distance information perpendicular to the flight path may be determined by the amount of time it takes a radiated signal to leave the aircraft, hit the surface of the earth or manmade targets, and return to the receiver side of the radar system. Cross-range resolution for a SAR system is obtained by the use of Doppler information between multiple pulses of the radar transmitter.

SAR systems characteristically have high ground resolution capability and produce images that can normally be correllated with photographic information after processing. Because of the "look angle" of the SAR system, radar shadowing may occur, giving imagery a quality of viewing the scene optically with a very low sun angle. Shadows in SAR have nothing to do with the sun position, however, only with aircraft position. Radar shadows are extremely useful in remote sensing of earth resources, as they tend to emphasize linear features that may be related to geologic faults.

Passive Microwave Remote Sensing

Microwave remote sensing occurs in the region of the electromagnetic spectrum, with wavelengths between 1 centimeter and 1 meter. Interpretation of microwave imagery is complicated by the fact that the resultant "apparent temperature" of an object or a terrain background is a function of several variables that require additional information about the material characterisites in a scene. In the visible region of the spectrum, normally only the reflectance of the object and background and the source intensity from the sun are considered as contributors to the spectral radiance of a scene.

Atmospheric modeling is used occasionally to remove haze effects, but the correction is often done empirically, using bright areas and deep shadows within a scene. In thermal remote sensing, the major parameters have to do with the emissivity of an object or background. Emissivity is a measure of the radiance generated by an object, divided by the radiance of a perfect radiator, or "black body," for a given temperature of the object. The emitted radiation for an object is the product of the object's emissivity and its absolute temperature.

Microwave radiance is a combination of radiance from (a) the object's self-emission, (b) reflected energy, and (c) transmitted energy. The self-emission component is the emissivity of the object multiplied by its temperature. The reflected component is the reflectance coefficient of the object multiplied by the incident radiation. Finally, the transmitted component is the transmittance of the object multiplied by its incident radiation. All of these coefficients will be a function of wavelength and are not necessarily constant across large wavelength bands.

For microwave radiation, the sun is not a factor contributing to the incident radiation on an object because the radiant energy given off by the sun drops to an insignificant level at these wavelengths. Other sources of microwave radiation are the sky, clouds, stars, and subsurface features. Subsurface features may be soil or rock types that emit energy from below the object of interest. The transmissivity of the object will determine how much of the subsurface radiant energy will pass through toward the sensor system.

In the microwave region, polarization of the radiation is also important. Reflection of incident radiation from a given object is dependent on the polarization of the incident wave and the dielectric constant of the object material. The dielectric constants for many materials have been derived and archived for use in microwave interpretation.

In a given microwave image, contrast between substances within the imaged area will primarily be due to the different dielectric constants (and therefore emissivities) of the various objects and backgrounds within the scene and not their absolute temperatures. In a natural scene, a thermal equilibrium is normally established, giving a small range for the object temperatures; however, the dielectric constants of the scene's various materials may vary radically.

The difference in dielectric constants allows microwave radiometry to distinguish between sea ice and open water. Water has large dielectric effects due to its capability to act as a dipole that will tend to align itself along an electric field. When water is in the form of ice, it exhibits different characteristics from liquid water in the complex dielectric constant value.

Liquid water has a high dielectric constant, leading to a low emissivity, whereas ice has a very low dielectric constant that gives a high emissivity. Microwave radiometry is used to find the water/ice interface in ice-mapping projects.

Dry soil and rock generally have low emissivities (less than 10). Wet soil dielectric constants and therefore emissivities are directly related to the percentage of water in the sample. Using this relationship, microwave radiometry is used in aircraft to map out soil moisture variations.

Another major advantage of microwave remote sensing is that at certain wavelengths microwave sensors are able to penetrate through haze, clouds, and even rain to provide information on surface features. This gives micro-

Image Enhancement

wave sensors an all-weather capability that can be exploited in regions of constant cloud cover and bad weather.

Medical Imaging

X-ray, nuclear magnetic resonance (NMR), and thermography imaging systems are in current use in the medical field for diagnostic purposes. Although the most common form of x-ray images is film negatives, high-resolution digitization of x-ray images now allows the use of standard enhancement procedures in an interactive enhancement process. The spatial, as well as gray-scale, resolution is very important to medical doctors, and early attempts to digitize x-ray images and apply pseudocolor processing was met by significant resistance by the medical community. High-resolution digitization and less emphasis on the pseudocolor approach has led to greater acceptance of image processing of x-ray images; however, it is still not accepted without reservation.

NMR uses a strong magnetic field to induce magnetic dipole reactions within tissue of the human body. These reactions may be measured and portrayed in the form of an image for analysis. Normally, NMR systems are controlled by a computer system and thus have the ability to produce a digital picture suitable for digital enhancement.

Thermography is a passive system that measures thermal energy given off by the body. Thermography images are used for breast cancer screening and prebirth fetus examination. Thermography images may be recorded on normal video or slow-scan video. Both of these video signals can be converted to digital images for enhancement.

ANALOG ENHANCEMENT TECHNIQUES

The earliest enhancement techniques were uses in photographic processing. Special films were developed to bring out contrast in an image for particular applications. As in digital enhancement, techniques that work exceptionally well for one application do not necessarily work for all applications. High-contrast films may be totally unacceptable for uses in which a wide range of tonal changes exist in an imaged scene. High-speed film normally will be grainier than slower speed films, and high resolution films may require a long exposure time.

Many of the enhancement steps for photography occur either in film development or printing. In development, the amount of time that the film stays in the developer may be varied to bring out desired contrast. In printing, a technique called dodging may be used to bring out the contrast in some portions of an image while leaving the rest of the image with normal contrast. Dodging consists of the use of a blocking object inserted between the enlarger and the sensitive print paper. By intermittent blocking of the enlarger's beam on a particular portion of an image, that portion receives less exposure time than the rest of the image. This technique may be used to bring out contrast in shadowed regions of the original image.

INTRODUCTION TO DIGITAL PROCESSING TECHNIQUES

No matter which of the above procedures is used in forming an image, the image itself can be processed by digital image-processing techniques once it is digitized into a computer system. Digital enhancement provides the ultimate in flexibility and interactive control. Techniques developed for manual enhancement may be simulated by the computer system, and new techniques not available in analog enhancement are implemented in powerful libraries of digital enhancement functions.

Many of the current sensor systems provide multispectral data in a number of discrete channels. If three channels of multispectral data are available, they may be displayed on a color image display or used with color filters to expose color photography. Digital enhancement of the color image allows interactive contrast change on individual images as they are displayed on the red, green, and blue color guns of a cathode ray tube (CRT). Digital processing allows for techniques that allow a viewer to view images that represent the majority of the information content in a (N>3) multispectral image in three channels. With the advent of the TM and MSS systems, the thermal inertia mapping system (TIMS), and the thematic mapper scanner (TMS), multichannel data are becoming more available to the applications user. A digital processing system for enhancement must be able to handle the multichannel data in an efficient manner and present the data in such a way that the user is not overwhelmed by the source data.

HARDWARE FOR IMAGE ENHANCEMENT

Enormous breakthroughs have occurred in the past 25 years in image-processing display hardware and turnkey image-processing systems. In the early 1960s, the Jet Propulsion Laboratory developed image-processing techniques on mainframe computers to process images from manned and unmanned space missions. Digital enhancement was used on image data of the earth's moon from early Mariner missions. In the mid-1960s the University of Michigan developed their 12-channel MSS system and displays for analysis of the scanner images. The Laboratory for Agricultural Remote Sensing (LARS) used the scanner data for the corn blight experiment, using gray-scale printouts and early image displays. About the same time, Bendix Corporation developed their 24-channel MSS system and the processing system MDAS (Multipsectral Data Analysis System) located at NASA in Houston. General Electric developed their Image 100 image analysis system in the late 1960s. The Image 100 was a totally self-contained turnkey system and was the predecessor to many minicomputer-based image-processing systems in the 1970s. Image-processing systems during this early period of time cost $1 million. During the 1970s and 1980s, many different vendors began offering image displays to be attached to existing minicomputer systems. Comtal, DeAnza, Ikonix, International Imaging Systems, Grinell, and Ramtek all offered systems costing between $30,000 and $200,000 depending on system capability. In 1981, ERDAS, Inc., offered the first low-cost microcomputer turnkey image-processing and Geographic Information System at a cost between $25,000 and $50,000. During the early 1980s, many image display systems began to become available for microcomputer systems. The advent of the IBM Personal Computer as a generally accepted microcomputer system led the way for an explosion of image-processing hardware with PC compatability. Leading vendors such as Imaging Technology, Datacube, Number Nine, Matrox, and many others began offering extensive capability, including near real-time image-processing algorithms implemented in hardware.

One of the major causes for the imaging explosion was the continuous decrease in cost for memory. As more and more memory became available

Image Enhancement

on single computer boards because of 64K- and finally 256K-bit memory chips, the costs of imaging became lower and lower. Today, for several thousand dollars, one is able to acquire imaging boards for a PC with capability for an image area of 512 by 512 pixels, with a color resolution of 32 bits.

There is a significant difference between imaging systems and graphics systems. The difference highlights what operations each system is intended to perform. Graphics systems inherently have high spatial resolution, often as large as 1,024 by 1,024 to 4,096 by 4,096 pixels. The color palette used in graphics systems normally is not greater than 64 colors. A graphics system's performance is usually measured in terms of how many vectors the system can draw per second. In advanced systems, geometric transformations for three-dimensional vectors and polygon fill-shading functions are implemented in VLSI chips.

On the other hand, image processing normally has spatial resolutions of 512 pixels (now extending to 1,024) and at least 256 colors. Raster-oriented functions such as how fast the system can load a 512 by 512 image are more important in system evaluation than vector drawing capabilities. For analysis of true color and multispectral image data, an image processor will frequently have between 24 and 32 bits of 512 by 512 pixel image memory. Three of the bands (each considered a gray-scale image) of a multispectral image may be applied in any order to any of the three color guns of the color monitor.

Image processors normally have lookup tables that allow near real-time color or constant change on the color monitor. There are normally at least three lookup tables, one for each of the three primary colors of a raster color monitor. Using these lookup tables, a user may load a three-band image into the image memories 1, 2, and 3. Once the data are loaded into image memory, they must pass through the lookup tables before the image is displayed on the monitor. The lookup tables are often called function memories because the tables make the displayed image a function of the input data and the values in the table. This technique can be used extensively in contrast stretching. The lookup table or function memory has an 8-bit input and an 8-bit output. Therefore, 256 values in the image memory may be mapped into any other 256 values for display, depending on the lookup table. If the function memory is linear with a slope of one, a value in the image memory of one would correspond to a screen value of one, a two to a two, etc. If the tables were loaded with a function memory with a slope of two, an image memory value of one would be mapped to a screen value of two, a memory value of two to a screen value of four, etc. If there are image memory data values greater than 128, they will all be assigned a screen value of 256 for display. Under software control, a user may instantly change the contrast on a displayed image simply by changing the function memory lookup table.

Some of the more sophisticated (not necessarily the more expensive) image processors have additional capabilities implemented in hardware or firmware. Video processors are available that allow operations on multiple image planes in a real-time or near real-time manner. Normal functions that are available on these systems are image arithmetic (+, −, compare) and, in some systems, implementation of spatial filtering operators such as high pass filtering.

High end processors may allow multiple users to use the same image processor, may have 20 or more 8-bit 512 by 512 or 1,024 by 1,024 images, and may have special function processors for image warping, histogram calculation, and area of interest processing.

A recent trend is the implementation of image-processing workstations that may be used as stand-alone systems, external displays for host images, or networked multiuser/multiprocess systems.

IMAGE PROCESSING

Image processing (digital) involves a wider range of capabilities than enhancement. Image processing involves all the steps necessary to allow for image input, restoration, correction, enhancement, pattern recognition, and product generation.

Designers of turnkey systems for particular applications need to address all of these steps because the user of these systems' primary interest is the generation of a product that meets his needs. A system should be easy for a user to operate and, at the same time, must be comprehensive in its capabilities.

Image input into such a system defines a procedure by which a user may take an image from any source and make it suitable for processing. Typical image input functions involve the decoding of the many various image formats that are available for image data already in digital form. Landsat satellite data, in particular, are available in a number of different formats, including band interleaved by line (BIL), band sequential (BSQ), band interleaved by pixel pairs (BIP2 or X), and band interleaved by pixel (BIP). Landsat data from different receiving stations in the past have had different formats, depending on the mainframe used for processing the data (IBM and DEC have different representations for high and low order bytes). In addition, European groundstation data have a header offset for each line of the first channel of image data and no offset for the other channels.

Image input also includes video digitizing and image scanning. Many of the image processors available today have the ability to accept data from video cameras, freeze the image at a particular instant in time, and transfer the image into its image memory. Some systems also have the capability of accepting images from a video recorder. This capability is not always available because of synchronization problems between the video player and the image processor.

When a user desires a higher resolution image than is available in video, he may use an image-scanning system to raster scan a source image. Although this alternative is significantly more costly ($30,000 to $100,000) than video capture ($2,000 to $5,000), it provides a high-quality image that is suitable for further digital processing.

Image restoration involves the capability to correct for systematic and nonsystematic distortions in image geometry and gray level. When an image is captured by a camera, scanner, or pushbroom linear array, the image captured has gone through a degradation based on the characteristics of the particular optical system used. Each system has an optical transfer function (OTF) associated with it that can normally be established in system design. By knowing the OTF of a system, image-processing techniques may be applied to an image to try to recover as much information as possible. The modulation transfer function (MTF) is simply the modulus of the complex OTF. These parameters are used as merit functions for evaluation of various sensor systems.

Geometric distortions will also occur in optical systems and must be corrected for adequate analysis of spatial properties of images. For example,

Image Enhancement

a vertical image taken at a low altitude will have distortions at its edges if the optical or scanning system has a wide field of view because the area at the edge of the image is significantly farther from the optical system than the area directly beneath the aircraft. For aircraft scanning systems, aircraft motion (roll, yaw, pitch) and crabbing must be modeled to allow for correction of images to a desired scale. Scanning systems also have inherent distortions associated with the electromechanical scanning process. In the Landsat MSS system, the mirror velocity, as the mirror scanned from side to side, was not constant but was a sinusoidally varying function.

Distortions also exist in the Landsat system, which do not arise from the optical system itself, but from the fact that the scanner system takes data along the satellites' orbit heading from northeast to southwest. The amount of time necessary for the satellite to move in its path for each pseudoframe of its continuous strip image is such that earth rotation must be accounted for. Any satellite system that builds up an image by its own motion must have a correction, including the pushbroom scanner system of the French satellite SPOT.

Sensor artifacts are common in some systems such as thermal scanners. These may result from AC coupling within the system and a variety of other detector- and scanning-related phenomena. Data dropout is occasionally seen in scanner data. The dropout may involve whole lines of data or individual pixels within an image. Correction programs for whole line dropout often involve substituting an average of the line above and below the dropout line. The Landsat 3 MSS system had a line start problem that basically made the left-hand third of any image unusable.

Image enhancement, the topic of this article, accepts an image after the above restoration and corrections have been made and processes the image so that it will be more suitable for human interpretation. Spectral, spatial, and transform methods may be applied to single- or multiple-band images.

Pattern recognition is a branch of image processing that accepts an input image and produces a map or image-type output in which every pixel in the map has an associated identifier, as opposed to a gray scale associated with it. The image has been interpreted in a semiautomatic manner by the pattern-recognition algorithms. Pattern-recognition algorithms may be either parametric or nonparametric. Parametric algorithms assume a known distribution for the image data (e.g., a normal Gaussian distribution is used in a maximum likelihood classification). A nonparametric system assumes no set distribution for the image or its subregions.

Image classification algorithms may be considered as supervised or unsupervised, depending on the amount and type of interaction required of the user. In a supervised approach, the user is expected to view the image on a CRT and identify to the computer system the location of a homogeneous area of a particular category. If the project has to do with forestry productivity, e.g., the user might identify selected regions of dense pine, sparse pine, mixed, sparse hardwood, and hardwood, along with other "training samples" for the other features within the scene such as water, urban, bare ground, asphalt, etc. Once one or several samples of each type of land cover category that exist within the scene are identified, the computer will calculate statistics for each sample. For a parametric classifier such as maximum likelihood, the statistics consist of a mean value in each image channel and a covariance matrix defining the parameters of a normal distribution that are represented by the sample data. Each sample's statistics are taken as a "signature" for that particular category in the image. Next, the computer system will perform a classification of the input image data to produce the output map image. A maximum likelihood decision rule is an optimal Bayesian classifier and minimizes the probability that an image pixel might be assigned to the wrong class, given each sample's signature and an apriori probability that the pixel would be in a given class. The pixel is assigned to the class with the maximum probability by calculating a discriminant function relating the pixel to each class.

Other discriminant functions may be used that are not dependent on the sample distributions. A minimum distance classifier only uses the mean of each sample and calculates a discriminant function based on euclidean distance. A linear parallelipiped classifier only needs a minimum and maximum data value for each sample in each band.

An unsupervised approach assumes nothing about the inherent distribution of the image data. A sequential clustering algorithm uses the following approach:

1. Take the top left pixel in an image (all bands).
2. Create a cluster with a mean equal to the pixel data value.
3. Consider the next pixel to the right.
4. Calculate euclidean distance from this pixel to cluster 1.
5. If distance is less than a user input distance, assign this pixel to cluster 1. Update mean of cluster 1.
6. If distance is greater than user distance; create new cluster with mean equal to pixel 2.
7. Do steps 3 through 6 until the number of clusters is greater than user input maximum or number of pixels considered is greated than user input pixel maximum.
8. If step 7 warrants, perform merge of existing clusters.
9. Continue through all image pixels (cluster means will stabilize as more and more pixels are added).
10. Go back through image and perform minimum distance classification.

Although the output image from supervised classification will be a map of categories identified by the training sample signatures, the output of a clustering will be a map of areas that "look different from each other" to the computer, given certain user inputs. A user will have to view the output of the clustering and assign a land cover class to each cluster.

In either technique, the user has to provide "ground truth" information to the computer to achieve a map showing spatial location of various land cover categories.

The final operation for a turnkey system is product generation. The product normally consists of the enhanced imagery, the classified imagery, and summary statistics for each category (how many acres of wheat are identified within a given county). Although the statistics may usually be output on a normal line printer, the image products may be produced by a variety of means. If a user is interested in the actual data values for a small region of an image, he may print them out as characters on a line printer. Next, an image gray scale may be approximated by overstriking characters such that each character position represents an image pixel. Gray-scale printer/plotters may be used to produce geographically scaled gray-scale hard-copy images. Inexpensive ink jet printers are now available, which allow the production of a hard-copy color plot of an image using

Image Enhancement   *191*

dithering techniques to achieve a wide color range. Slides may be taken from the CRT screen for an inexpensive way to get reproducible hard copy. The high end method for output products uses a film-writing system that may use a laser scanning system to write individual pixels onto color film that will be developed and perhaps printed.

ENHANCEMENT TECHNIQUES

Enhancement techniques may be divided into three categories: spectral, spatial, and transform. Spectral enhancement allows a user to take an input digital image and process the images interactively to bring out the contrast, either of the whole image or of selected subregions within the image. Spectral enhancement may involve using the image processor's lookup tables and function memory or it may involve applying specific functions to disk file images for later display. The disadvantage of using only the image display's function memory is that the image processor is only able to show the effects of function memory processing on the part of the total image that resides in the image display memory. If an image display has a resolution of 512 by 512 pixels, it would only be able to display 1/40 of a processed Landsat MSS scene or 1/158 of a Landsat TM scene. Enhancements selected to optimize the contrast in one portion will not normally be able to extend across a whole scene. Usually, an iterative procedure of selecting the best enhancement is used with the analysis of multiple subimages within the full scene and defining a "best" overall enhancement as some function of the individual enhancements.

Spectral enhancement is inherently a process that may be applied to either single-channel images or multichannel images; however, the results of a spectral enhancement to one image do not necesarily mean that the same or similar enhancements may be applied to the other channels. In this respect, spectral enhancement of multiband images may be considered as a series of independent enhancements of single-channel data.

Spatial enhancement is a procedure that also operates independently on either single-band or multiband images; and like spectral enhancement, the selection of spatial enhancement operators for one channel does not necessarily mean that those same techniques can be applied optimally to other channels of a multiband image.

Although spectral enhancement is useful in increasing the contrast of gray-scale information for an image, spatial enhancement also brings out spatially important features within an image. Spatial information is any information within an image that gives clues to size and shape relationships that exist within an image. When a human interpreter is used to analyze information in an aerial photograph, a large part of his capability is due to the fact that not only can he identify features in the image from how bright the feature is, but also because of its relationship to other recognizable features within an image. For example, if a large airport were present in an image, a human interpreter would be able to identify multiple, long stretches of concrete inclined at angles to one another and near to large buildings with fingerlike extensions; thus, the interpreter would conclude that the area was an airport. Automatic spectral classification systems described above would not be able to make use of the proximity, connectivity, and angle information in the image and would only be able to conclude that the area had a certain percentage of concrete, grass, and asphalt. The emerging field of computer vision is addressing the spatial interactions within images, and a detailed discussion of computer vision techniques is outside the scope of this work. Spatial enhancement discussed in this article looks at the techniques in image processing that may be applied to gray-scale or multicolor images to better define the scene and object edges that may then be used in computer vision-type recognition.

Transformation enhancement is normally applied to multichannel images, as opposed to single gray-scale images. Combinations of individual channels of image data have been shown to be effective in a variety of disciplines in the analysis of multispectral data. By transforming multiple data channels into a single number that might represent vegetation vigor, an applications user can directly interpret multispectral Landsat data without extensive knowledge of computer processes. The coefficients used for combining the multiple channels into one new channel may be well defined mathematically or they may be defined through extensive experimentation using trial and error techniques.

Spectral Enhancement

Color Display of Multispectral Data

Most of the more capable image display systems have the ability to display a gray-level image in each of the primary color guns (red, green, blue). The eye of the user integrates the information from the three primaries and sees the image in color. Depending on the type and sensor ranges of various multispectral input systems, the multispectral band to color gun assignments may be different. In most cases, the most useful color assignments are those that allow the simulation of what one would see in a natural color or color infrared image. A natural color-simulated image shows trees, concrete, and bare land in the same colors that would be seen if the user were to fly over a site and look out the window. A color infrared-simulated image shows the scene as it would appear on color infrared film. Many resource analysts are familiar with direct interpretation of color infrared photography, and they will relate well to the simulated color infrared image.

Landsat MSS data have four spectral channels, including a green, red, and two near infrared channels. The normal method of presentation of MSS data is to assign the green channel (band 1) to the blue color gun, the red channel (band 2) to the green color gun, and the second near infrared channel (band 4) to the red color gun.

Landsat TM channels may be mapped to the color display color guns in the following manner:

    True color — channel 1 to the blue gun
                      channel 2 to the green gun
                      channel 3 to the red gun
    Color infrared — channel 2 to the blue gun
                           channel 3 to the green gun
                            channel 4 to the red gun

Spot multispectral data may be shown in a color infrared presentation by applying

    channel 1 to the blue color gun
    channel 2 to the green color gun
    channel 3 to the red color gun

Image Enhancement

High-resolution (10 meter) panchromatic data may be presented in a color infrared simulation by first resampling the multispectral data to a 10-meter resolution and applying

    channel 1 (MSS) to the blue gun
    panchromatic to the green gun
    channel 3 (MSS) to the red gun

Because the TM has seven channels of MSS data, there are numerous combinations of TM channels to various color guns possible. None of the other various combinations have the same appeal to a human interpreter as the true color or color infrared selections, as he has no basis for comparison to tell whether a scene "looks right."

Function Memory

Function memory processing uses the technique of lookup tables to enhance images. This processing may be implemented in hardware, as discussed above, or may be implemented in software to process larger areas of image data. In general, the technique defines a function that relates the input image to the output image:

    $y = f(x)$

where x is the input image and y is the output. The function may be linear or nonlinear or continuous or discrete, depending on the number of functions supported by a given set of software. If the input image is an 8-bit image and the output image is 8 bits, a lookup table from the input image to the output would consist of 256 values. These values are defined by the selected function. Several examples of functions are given below, and Figure 1, a through h, shows the effect of the selected functions on a Landsat TM visible image. A graph of the function is shown as graphics overlay.

(a)	linear	$y = x$
(b)	linear (scale)	$y = 2*x$
(c)	picewise linear	$y = x$ if $x < 50$
		$y = 2*x$ else
(d)	inverse linear	$y = 1/x$
(e)	logrithmic	$y = \log(x)$
(f)	discrete	if $(x = 33)$ $y = 255$
		if $(x = 55)$ $y = 100$
(g)	sinusoid	$y = 128*\sin((x/255)*pi/180) + 128$
(h)	power of 2	$y = x**2$

Any user-defined function may be used to define the lookup table for the function memory procedure. The experience gained by processing a number of single- or multiple-band images will help decide which algorithms usually have the best results.

Figure 2 shows a panchromatic representation of a MSS image over northern Georgia. The contrast available in the MSS sensor for Landsat's I, II, and III was approximately 6 bits in the visible channels and a compressed 7 bits for the near infrared channels. The function memories for this image are set to a slope of 1; $y = x$. A slope of 4 was applied to the

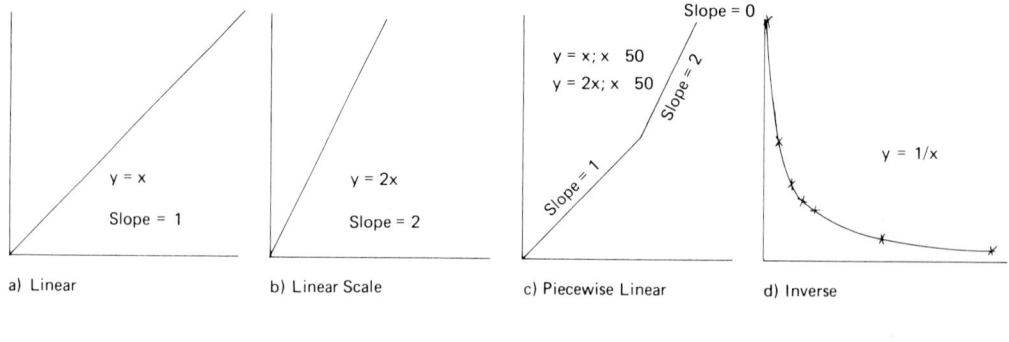

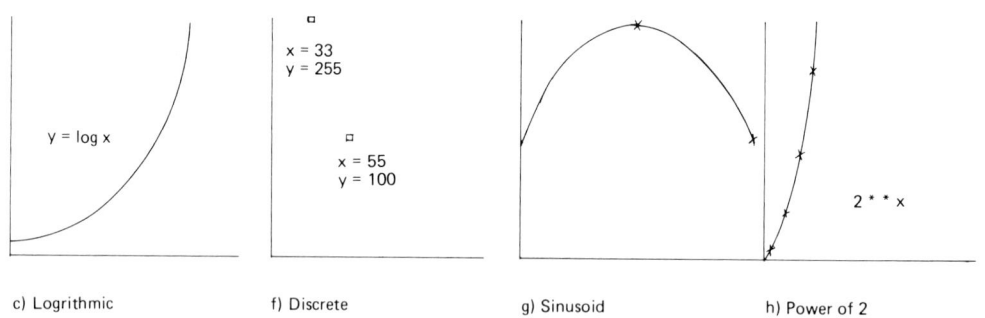

FIGURE 1. (A—H) Function memory lookup tables.

blue and green guns, and a slope of 6 was applied to the red gun to give the enhanced image of Figure 3.

It should be emphasized that a standard set of function memory slopes for automatic application would probably be erroneous. The inherent contrast of multispectral scenes may vary dramatically for different regions of the world. It would be unreasonable to expect that a set of function memory slopes determined for a low sun angle winter vegetated scene would be applicable for a summer scene totally made up of high reflecting desert. Extreme changes are normally evident, even for the same region over a years' time.

Pseudocolor

When processing a one-channel image, a common technique for enhancement is to use a pseudocolor scheme. The original image has a gray scale of 0 to 255, but it may be difficult to bring out certain features of interest in terms of gray shades on the display. The function memory discussed above can also be used to assign a color scheme to a gray-scale image. A pseudocolor image is formed when each gray-scale level is assigned a brightness level in each of the red, green, and blue colors. The levels may be assigned arbitrarily, at a user's direction, or in a particular sequence. A useful sequence for image enhancement is rainbow color scheme called ROYGBIV for

FIGURE 2. Panchromatic (B&N) image of MSS, northern Georgia.

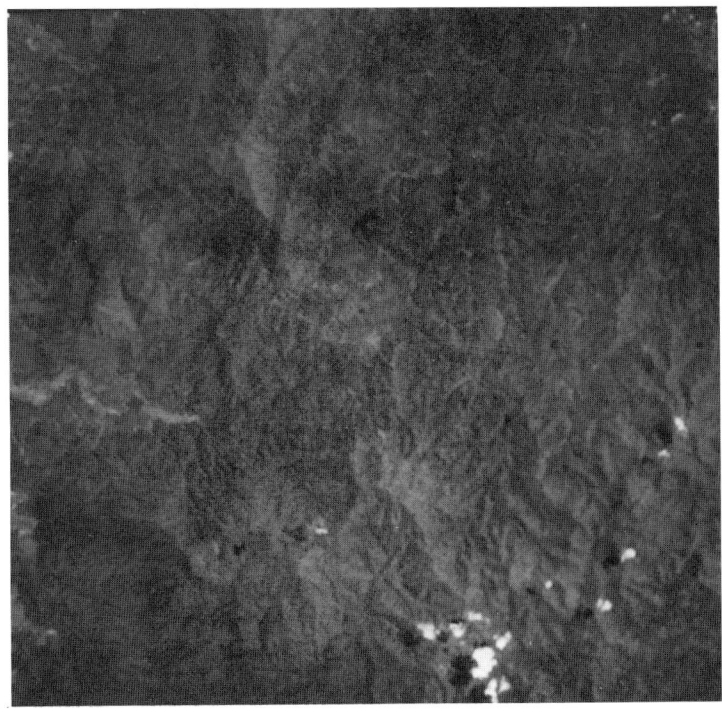

FIGURE 3. Enhanced MSS image, using function memories.

the colors red, orange, yellow, green, blue, indigo, and violet. Colors are assigned for each gray scale, so that the color range migrates smoothly between the base ROYGBIV colors.

Although it provides a brightly colored image, pseudocolor should be used with caution. In many cases, the color scheme of an image may be detrimental to image interpretation because the human eye is drawn more toward colors such as red than to blues or other colors in the image. By using a bright color scheme, the user may misinterpret spatial and gray-scale relationships within an image. In some cases, gray-scale images may be more meaningful than the "enhanced pseudocolor" image.

Histogram Equalization

One enhancement that can be used in a semiautomated manner is histogram equalization. In histogram equalization, the program reads through the selected image, automatically building a histogram of all data values for a particular scene. Figure 4 shows a 36-sample normal distribution of gray-scale values. Next, by successively summing the number of pixels for each data value and the previous data values, a cumulative histogram is built, with the horizontal axis being image gray-scale value and the vertical axis being percent of total pixels. If one also makes the y axis proportional to the number of gray scales possible in the image, a mapping may be visualized between original data values and histogram-equalized values. The horizontal arrowed lines indicate to which gray-level value each original gray-scale value is assigned. For a 36-sample image with 10 gray levels, we have the following mapping:

Gray Level	New Gray Level
1,2	1
3	2
4	4
5	6
6	7
7	9
8,9,10	10

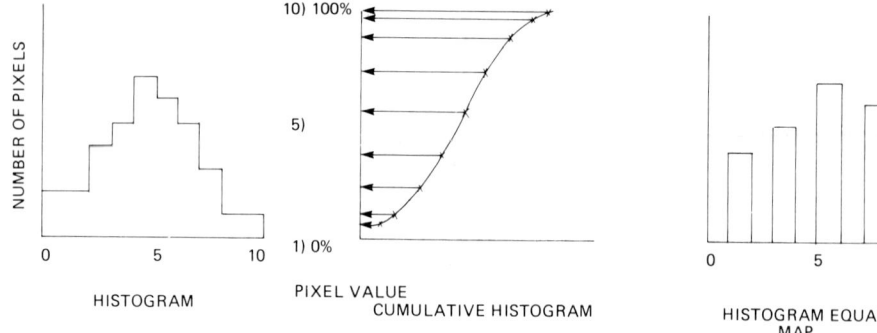

FIGURE 4. Example of normal distribution of gray scales.

Image Enhancement

From this example, we can observe several of the advantages and disadvantages of histogram equalization. An advantage is that contrast is maximized in the gray-scale region for which there are the most image pixels. This ensures that the general contrast of the image will be enhanced for almost any image. On the other hand, if the particular area of the image that is to be interpreted in detail is in the brightest or darkest gray-scale range of the original image, contrast will be lost instead of gained. If the user, e.g., is interested in analyzing a shadowed region of the original image, that user should not use histogram equalization.

Ratioing

Ratioing is a multichannel function that is used to enhance or bring certain features of interest out in multispectral imagery. Ratioing also can be used to reduce shadowing effects due to a low sun angle. In a winter TM scene, a low sun elevation angle may cause significant shading in rough terrain. By taking individual channels and dividing by the next spectral channel, the illumination effects may be reduced, as each of the images has the same source of energy, the sun. Figure 5 shows channel 4 of TM data over an area in northern Georgia. Shadows are especially evident in the long narrow valley running southwest to northeast in the image. Figure 6 shows the results of ratioing channel 2 by channel 4 of TM data and scaling the result.

The challenging part of ratioing is the scaling and interpretation of the results. Data values of greater than 1 indicate that channel 4 values are greater than channel 2 values, and ratio values of less than 1 indicate the reverse. If a simple scale factor is used to scale the ratio to the desired 0 to 255 levels, information may be lost in regions where the resultant scaling is still less than 1.

Ratio scaling sensitivities may be shown best with a simple test case. Assume an input image file has two channels of data and the dynamic range available is only 1 to 10. Further assume that there are approximately equal numbers of pixels in the input image for each gray scale value for both channels. Figure 6a shows the potential values for the raw ratio of values from image a (va) divided by the values from image b (vb). From the graph we can see that 45% of the ratio values would be less than 1. For a fixed integer dynamic range of 10, the values would be automatically clipped to 0. Similarly, 75% of the pixel ratios would be less than 2; therefore, with a scale factor of 1 for the ratio, very little of the available dynamic range would be used for 75% of the data. Scaling the ratio up by a factor of 10 would bring most of the ratio values up above 1, but original data ratios greater than 1 would be clipped at a value of 10. Linear scale factors, therefore, seem to be inadequate for representation of the ratio data potential dynamic range. Wecksung and Breedlove [2] studied different scale factors for ratios and suggested the use of an arctangent function as a scaling parameter for ratio data. For the same example shown above, a graph of the resulting ratios for 5 values of va and 10 values of vb are shown to give a more uniform use of the dynamic range of the data set. Figure 6b shows a ratio image of Landsat TM data using a simple scale factor, and Figure 7 shows the same ratio using the arctangent.

Landsat processing often involves the mapping of three individual ratios of TM bands to the three color guns of the display.

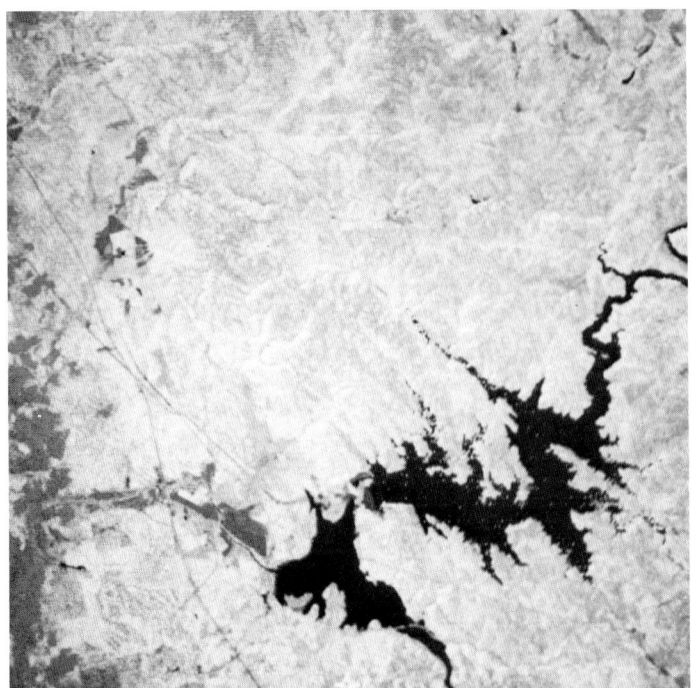

FIGURE 5. Channel 4 of the TM over northern Georgia.

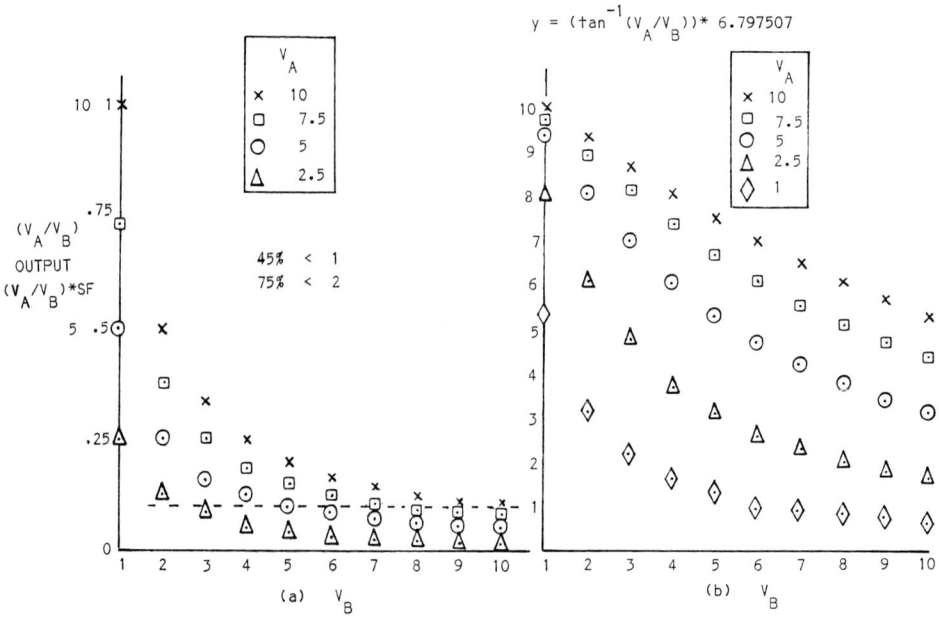

FIGURE 6a. Image ratioing.

Image Enhancement

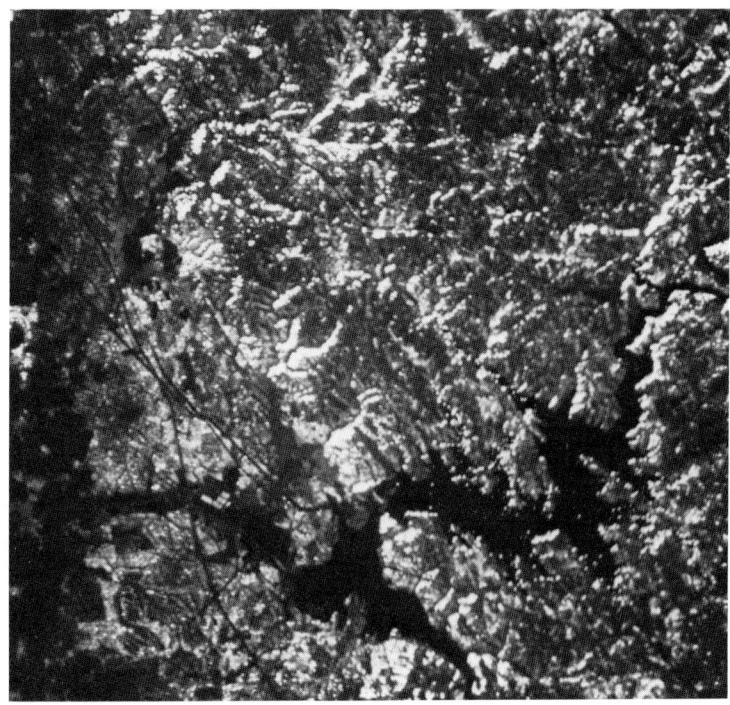

FIGURE 6b. Ratio of TM data, channel 4 divided by channel 2.

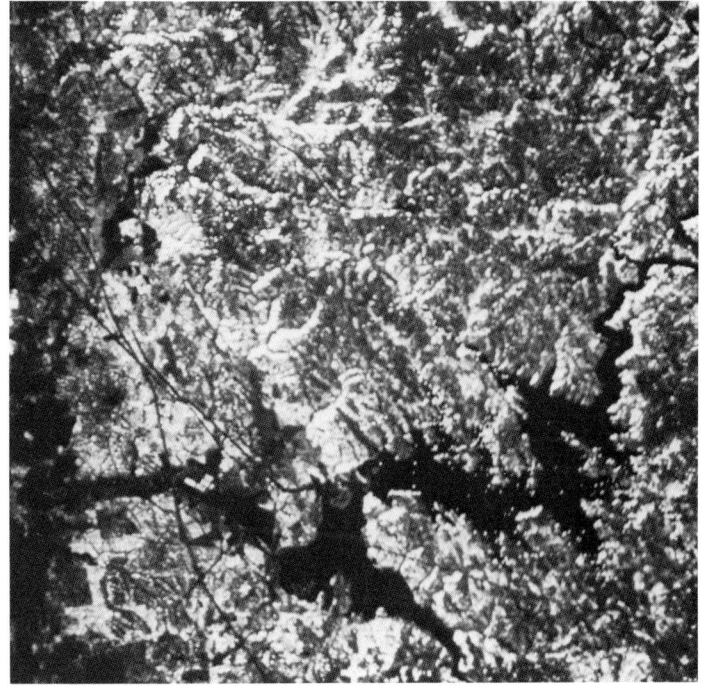

FIGURE 7. Ratio scaled by arctangent.

Linear Combinations

One of the most used enhancement techniques for multichannel files is linear combinations. Linear combinations allow the combination of some function of all the original channels in an image to be used in computing values for a single-band output image. The function may be different for each input band and may include a coefficient to be multiplied by the input data value and an exponential power to be applied to the input value. A generalized linear combination could be represented by

$$vout = a_1 v_1^{m1} + a_2 v_2^{m2} + a_3 v_3^{m3} + \;:\;:\;:\;:\; + a_n v_n^{mn}$$

where a1 is the scalar coefficient for the image data from channel 1 (v_1), and m1 is an exponent that may be applied to an input image data value. This is an extremely flexible technique for combining data. A simple case might be the addition of image data values in two channels (1 and 3) of a four-channel MSS data set and dividing by 2 for scaling. In this case, a_1 would be 0.5, a_3 would be 0.5, and a_2 and a_4 would be 0. All values for the exponents (m1 through m4) would be 1. The result would be

$$vout = 0.5 * v_1 + 0.5 * v_3$$

In practice, it is extremely difficult to arbitrarily come up with coefficients that will produce meaningful results. Several different techniques for deciding on the values for the coefficients are discussed in detail later in this article.

Spatial Enhancement

Although spectral enhancement relies on changing the gray scale representation of pixels to give an image with more contrast for interpretation, it applies the same spectral transformation to all pixels with a given gray scale in an image. Although this may allow better interpretation of an image by a user, it does not take full advantage of human recognition capabilities. When interpreting an image, a person not only uses brightness information in the image but also spatial relationships within the image to make decisions as to the identification of features in the image. Several examples will demonstrate the value of spatial characteristics in image interpretation. In a black-and-white panchromatic image, a user will recognize commercial multifamily residential or industrial buildings by the building shape and the fact that the buildings are surrounded by asphalt parking lots. The gray-scale information may tell the user that the individual pixels in the image have characteristics of concrete or asphalt, but the human ability to recognize spatial shapes will provide the capability to identify the group of pixels as a building (Figure 8). In another example, a Landsat multispectral image may provide color information that will define a specific area as being composed of concrete, grass, bare ground, and asphalt by spectral pattern recognition techniques, but the spatial relationships between groups of pixels will further allow the user to recognize the area as an airport (Figure 9). The spatial relationships will include long linear patterns associated with runways, the nearness of buildings to the runways, and the existence of grass and bare ground between the runways. The orientation of the

FIGURE 8. Landsat TM data showing buildings.

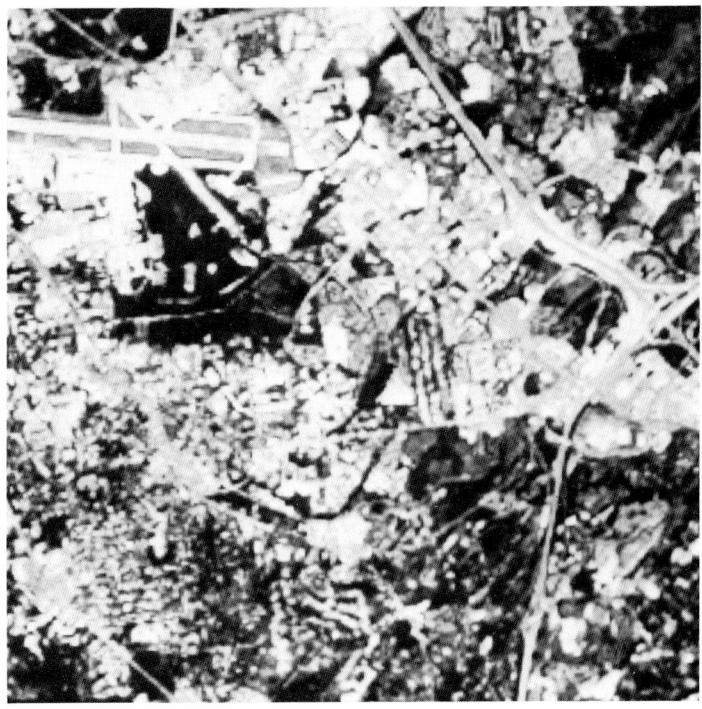

FIGURE 9. Landsat TM data showing an airport.

runways is also a spatial clue to the human interpreter. As a final example, consider a Landsat TM image that contains grassy areas, concrete, asphalt, and forest categories (Figure 10). The spatial relationships between pixels classified as concrete and asphalt will indicate to a user that the area is urban instead of rural. This information, in turn, will allow the user to decide that a large grassy area is a park or golf course within a city rather than a pasture.

The art of recognizing and using these spatial relationships in computer recognition is called image understanding. Image understanding is one of the major research areas in the relatively new field of artificial intelligence (AI). Although many breakthroughs have been made in the past few years in image understanding, much work is left to be done to totally simulate the human recognition process.

One of the major clues that allow humans to recognize and identify regions within an image is linear edges surrounding relatively homogeneous regions of pixels. Image-understanding techniques involve the search of an image for linear edges, the search for homogeneous regions, and the linking of the linear edges so that they enclose the homogeneous regions. A human interpreter would also be aided by the enhancement of an image so that edges between regions become more apparent. Spatial enhancement, then, is the mathematical processing of image pixel data to emphasize spatial relationships.

Two major methods are commonly used in spatial enhancement. Convolution involves the passing of a moving window over an image and creating a new image where each pixel in the new image is a function of the original pixel values within the moving window and the coefficients of the moving window as specified by the user. The second method of spatial enhancement involves the use of Fourier transform theory.

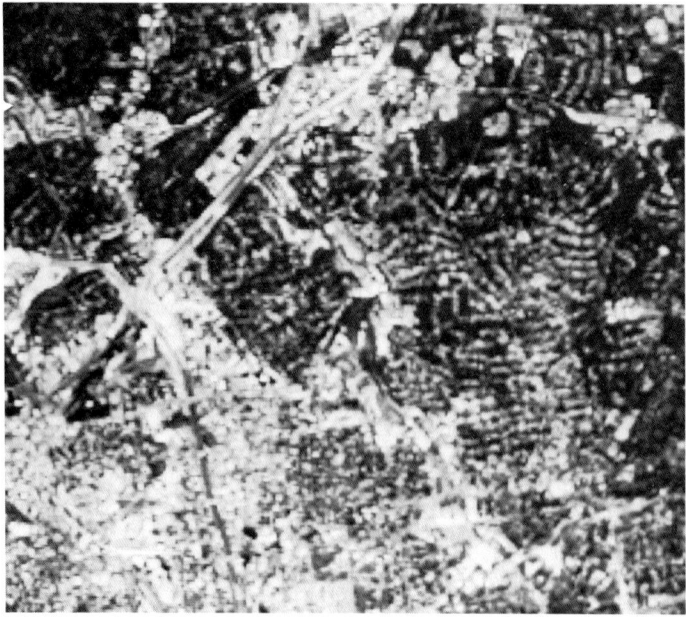

FIGURE 10. Landsat TM data, urban.

Image Enhancement

Both of the spatial enhancement techniques use the concept of spatial frequency in an image. Spatial frequency has to do with the manner in which gray-scale values change relative to their neighbors within an image. If there is a slowly varying change in gray scale in an image from one side of the image to the other, the image is said to have a low spatial frequency. If pixel values vary radically for adjacent pixels in an image, the image is said to have a high spatial frequency. An example of a low frequency digital image with gray level values of 1 through 10 is given below:

```
1 1 2 2 3 3 4 4 5 5
1 2 2 3 3 4 4 5 5 6
2 2 3 3 4 4 5 5 6 6
2 3 3 4 4 5 5 6 6 7
3 3 4 4 5 5 6 6 7 7
3 4 4 5 5 6 6 7 7 8
4 4 5 5 6 6 7 7 8 8
4 5 5 6 6 7 7 8 8 9
5 5 6 6 7 7 8 8 9 9
5 6 6 7 7 8 8 9 9 10
```

There is a slow trend of increasing intensity from top left to bottom right of the image.

An extreme example of a high spatial frequency image is a checkerboard pattern:

```
1 10  1 10  1 10  1 10  1 10
10  1 10  1 10  1 10  1 10  1
1 10  1 10  1 10  1 10  1 10
10  1 10  1 10  1 10  1 10  1
1 10  1 10  1 10  1 10  1 10
10  1 10  1 10  1 10  1 10  1
1 10  1 10  1 10  1 10  1 10
10  1 10  1 10  1 10  1 10  1
1 10  1 10  1 10  1 10  1 10
10  1 10  1 10  1 10  1 10  1
```

Here, the pixel value changes from the minimum possible value to the maximum possible value and the reverse in a distance of 1 pixel.

Normally, a given image will have many spatial frequencies represented within it. There will be slowly varying trends having to do with optical or system parameters (e.g., vignetting), high frequency features such as roads, and many spatial frequencies in between the extremes.

A low pass convolution filter is a blurring convolution kernel that emphasizes the low-frequency parts of an image and de-emphasizes the higher frequency parts of the image.

Alternately, a high pass convolution filter emphasizes the high-frequency components of an image while de-emphasizing the low frequency components.

Convolution Operators

A convolution operator may be considered as a matrix (or mask) of coefficients that are to be multiplied by image pixel values to derive a new pixel value for a resultant enhanced image. This matrix may be of any size in pixels and does not necessarily have to be square. As an example of the convolution methodology, take a 3 by 3 matrix of coefficients and see the effects on an example image subset. A set of coefficients that is used for image smoothing and noise removal is given below.

$$1/9 * \begin{vmatrix} 1 & 1 & 1 \\ 1 & 1 & 1 \\ 1 & 1 & 1 \end{vmatrix}$$

If we have a sample image, given below,

```
3  3  4  4  5  6
2  3  3  4  4  5
1  2  2  3  3  4
1  1  2  4  4  7
1  2  4 20 20 20
2  3  6 20 20 20
2  3  4 20 20 20
```

where the image normally has a low smoothly varying gray scale, except for the bottom right region, which exhibits a sharp brightness change, we can see the effects of the convolution filter on a pixel-by-pixel basis.

Because we do not wish to consider edge effects, we will start the overlay of the moving window on the x=2, y=2 pixel of the input image and end at the x=6, y=5 position of the original image.

The first p(x,y) (x=1,y=1), pixel of the output image would then be

p(1,1) = 1/9 * (3*1 + 3*1 + 4*1

  + 1*1 + 2*1 + 2*1

  + 1 *1 + 1*1 + 4*1) = 21/9 = 2.333

Because the output image, as well as the input image, is a whole number (integer) quantity,

p(1,1) = 2

Similarly,

p(1,2) = 1/9 * (3*1 + 4*1 + 4*1

  + 3*1 + 3*1 + 4*1

  + 2*1 + 2*1 + 3*1) = 28/9 = 3.111

  = 3

and

p(1,3) = 1/9 * (4*1 + 4*1 + 5*1

  + 3*1 + 4*1 + 4*1

  + 2*1 + 3*1 + 3*1) = 32/9 = 3.555

  = 3

Image Enhancement

Continued application of the same window (or filter kernel) will result in an output image given by

```
2  3   3   4
1  2   3   4
1  4   6   9
2  6  11  15
3  9  14  20
```

This should be compared to the original data values for those pixel locations of

```
3  3   4   4
2  2   3   3
1  2   4   4
2  4  20  20
3  6  20  20
```

where there is a sharp discontinuity in the image.

The moving window filter, in effect, smoothed out the sharp discontinuity in the original pixel imagery.

A sample edge detection mask might be given as

$$\begin{bmatrix} -1 & -1 & -1 \\ -1 & 8 & -1 \\ -1 & -1 & -1 \end{bmatrix}$$

and a value for p(1,1) would be

$$p(1,1) = (-1*3) + (-1*3) + (-1*4)$$
$$+ (-1*2) + (8*3) + (-1*3)$$
$$+ (-1*1) + (-1*2) + (-1*2) = 4$$

The resulting image after application of the mask is given by

```
 4   -1    4    -2
 1   -6   -2   -11
-7  -22  -26   -49
-4  -26   80    45
 0  -28   46     0
```

Assuming that only positive values are allowed in an image file, all values are offset by the absolute value of the minimum image element (in this case by +49).

The resultant image would then be

```
53  48   53  47
50  43   47  38
42  27   23   0
45  23  129  98
49  21   95  49
```

Values greater than 90 are present in the output image and represent the edge of the bright region in the original image.

Alternately, the negative values could be set to 0, giving an output image of

```
4  0   4   0
1  0   0   0
0  0   0   0
0  0  80  45
0  0  46   0
```

Again, these output images may be compared to the original pixel values:

```
3  3   4   4
2  2   3   3
1  2   4   4
2  4  20  20
3  6  20  20
```

High-Frequency Enhancement Operators: One of the most used convolution kernels for edge enhancement of images was given by Chavez [3]. The kernel is specified as

$$1/9 * \begin{vmatrix} -1 & -1 & -1 \\ -1 & 17 & -1 \\ -1 & -1 & -1 \end{vmatrix}$$

Chavez went through a description of the Modulation Transfer Function (MTF) for early ERTS digital data and also derived the above kernel for enhancement of high-frequency information in an ERTS MSS image. For a particular image pixel location and channel number, a low pass filter may be used to evaluate the average value in a 3 by 3 window. The convolution kernel would be given by

$$\text{avg} = 1/9 * \begin{vmatrix} 1 & 1 & 1 \\ 1 & 1 & 1 \\ 1 & 1 & 1 \end{vmatrix}$$

The high-frequency (HF) component in any given pixel will then be given by

$$HF = \text{pixel} - \text{avg}$$

Image Enhancement

Represented in terms of a convolution kernel, this would be

$$HF = \begin{vmatrix} 0 & 0 & 0 \\ 0 & 1 & 0 \\ 0 & 0 & 0 \end{vmatrix} - 1/9 * \begin{vmatrix} 1 & 1 & 1 \\ 1 & 1 & 1 \\ 1 & 1 & 1 \end{vmatrix}$$

which means that

$$HF = 1/9 * \begin{vmatrix} -1 & -1 & -1 \\ -1 & 8 & -1 \\ -1 & -1 & -1 \end{vmatrix}$$

By adding the high-frequency part, HF, back to the original pixel, a high-frequency enhancement will be achieved.

New value = pixel value + HF

This may be accomplished by

$$\text{New value} = \begin{vmatrix} 0 & 0 & 0 \\ 0 & 1 & 0 \\ 0 & 0 & 0 \end{vmatrix} + 1/9 * \begin{vmatrix} -1 & -1 & -1 \\ -1 & 8 & -1 \\ -1 & -1 & -1 \end{vmatrix}$$

or

$$\text{New value} = 1/9 * \begin{vmatrix} -1 & -1 & -1 \\ -1 & 17 & -1 \\ -1 & -1 & -1 \end{vmatrix}$$

Figure 11 shows one band of a Landsat TM image before enhancement, and Figure 12 shows the results of applying the above convolution kernel.

It can be seen from the above exercise that the technique may be used with larger kernels, the only difference being the evaluation of the low-frequency component within the neighborhood of the pixel to be evaluated.

For example, a high pass kernel for a 5 by 5 moving window is given by

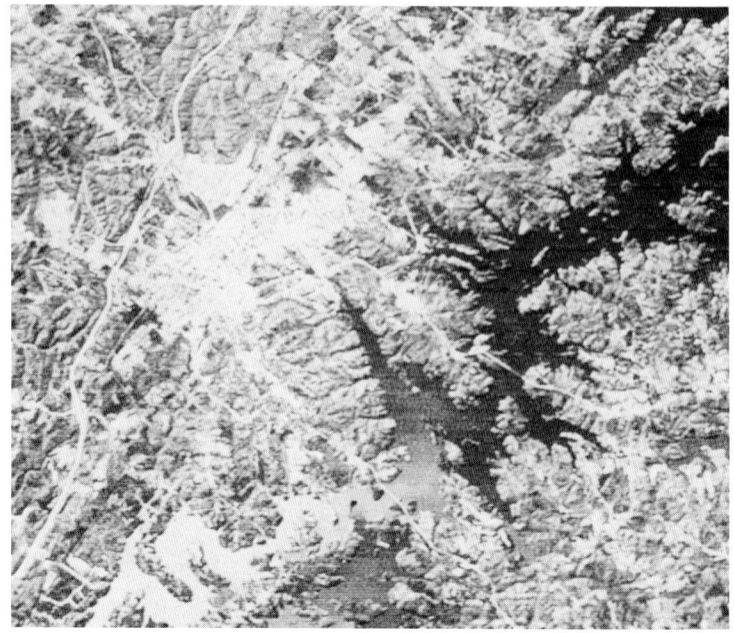

FIGURE 11. Landsat TM before spatial enhancement.

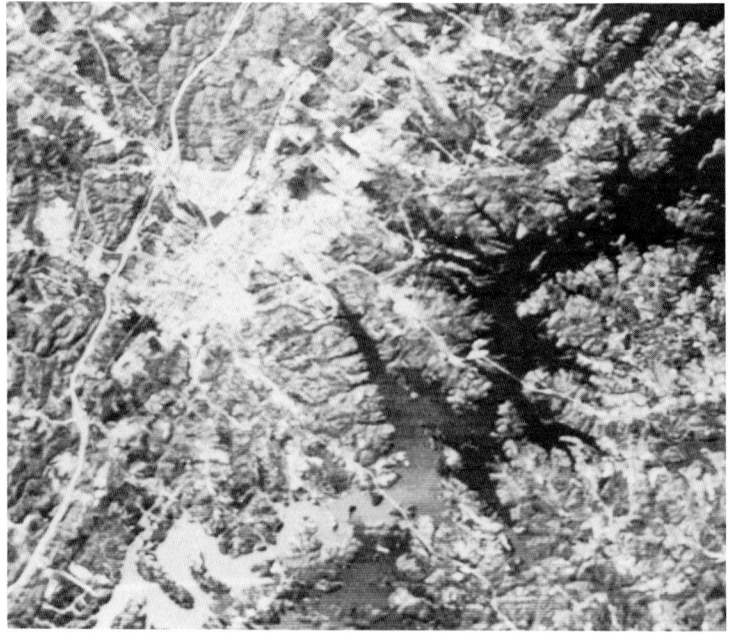

FIGURE 12. Landsat TM, high frequency enhancement.

Image Enhancement

$$HF = 1/25 * \begin{bmatrix} -1 & -1 & -1 & -1 & -1 \\ -1 & -1 & -1 & -1 & -1 \\ -1 & -1 & 49 & -1 & -1 \\ -1 & -1 & -1 & -1 & -1 \\ -1 & -1 & -1 & -1 & -1 \end{bmatrix}$$

Figure 13 shows the sample image above after the 5 by 5 convolution has been applied.

High Pass: An example of a high pass filter kernel is given above, where the center pixel weight of the convolution kernel is taken as an 8 and all other terms are -1. The above mentioned 3 by 3 HF mask is an example of a Laplacian convolution kernel. A Laplacian convolution emphasizes locally high gray-scale regions with respect to their surroundings and is a second-order technique [4]. Other forms of the Laplacian mask are

$$\begin{bmatrix} 0 & -1 & 0 \\ -1 & 4 & -1 \\ 0 & -1 & 0 \end{bmatrix} \quad \text{and} \quad \begin{bmatrix} 1 & -2 & 1 \\ -2 & 4 & -2 \\ 1 & -2 & 1 \end{bmatrix}$$

Notice that the Laplacian masks have coefficients that add up to 0. This ensures that regions of constant value in the original image will have a zero value in the output image. Thus, edges are enhanced at the expense of contrast in the original image. These filters are called zero sum filters and are used quite extensively in image processing. The Laplacian filters may be added back to the original image, as shown above, or they may be shown without the original image background (Figs. 14 and 15).

Emphasis of edges in an image in a specific direction may also be handled by zero sum filters. Several directional filter kernels are given below, and examples of their application are shown in Figures 16, 17, and 18.

Northeast   East   Southwest

$$\begin{bmatrix} 1 & 1 & 1 \\ -1 & -2 & 1 \\ -1 & -1 & 1 \end{bmatrix} \quad \begin{bmatrix} -1 & 1 & 1 \\ -1 & -2 & 1 \\ -1 & 1 & 1 \end{bmatrix} \quad \begin{bmatrix} 1 & -1 & -1 \\ 1 & -2 & -1 \\ 1 & 1 & 1 \end{bmatrix}$$

By going to larger kernels, a finer differentiation on edge direction may be achieved.

Nonlinear combinations of pixels are used in some edge-finding algorithms. Sobel operators (convolution kernels) are a gradient-finding tech-

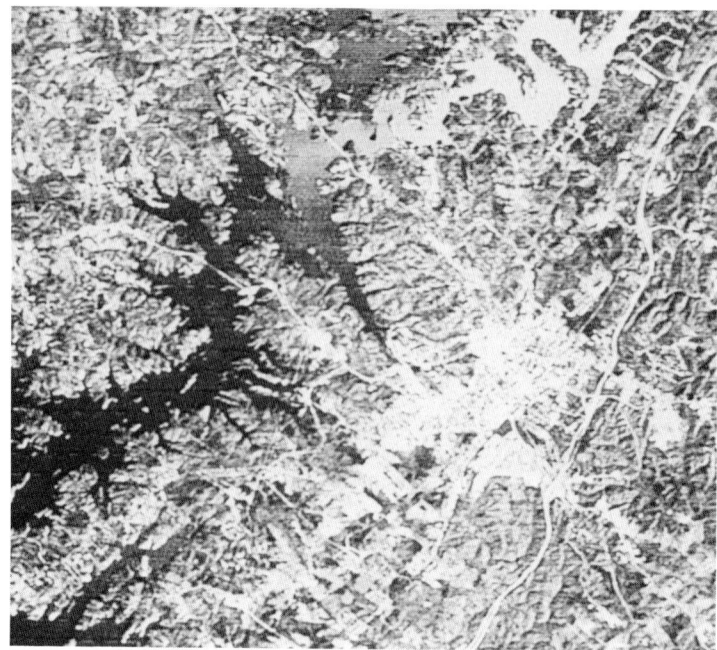

FIGURE 13. Landsat TM, 5 by 5 high frequency enhancement.

FIGURE 14. Landsat TM, Laplacian filter 1.

Image Enhancement

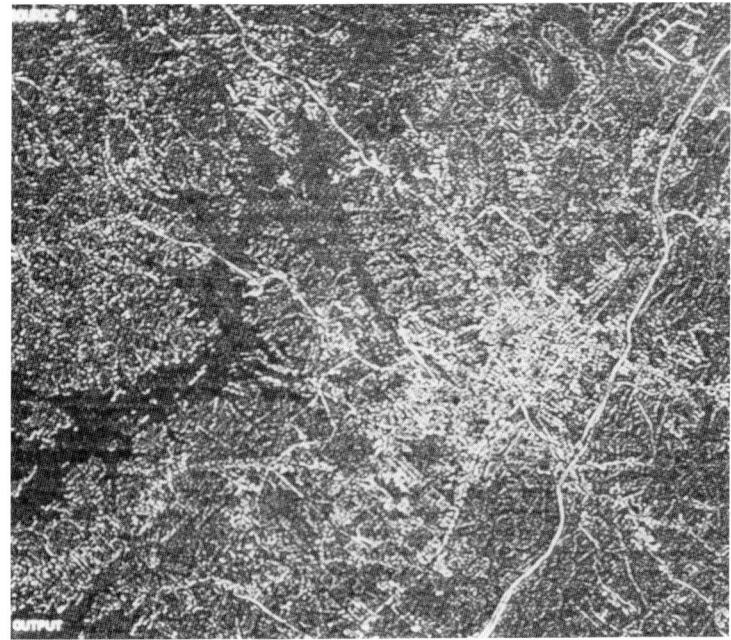

FIGURE 15. Landsat TM, Laplacian filter 2.

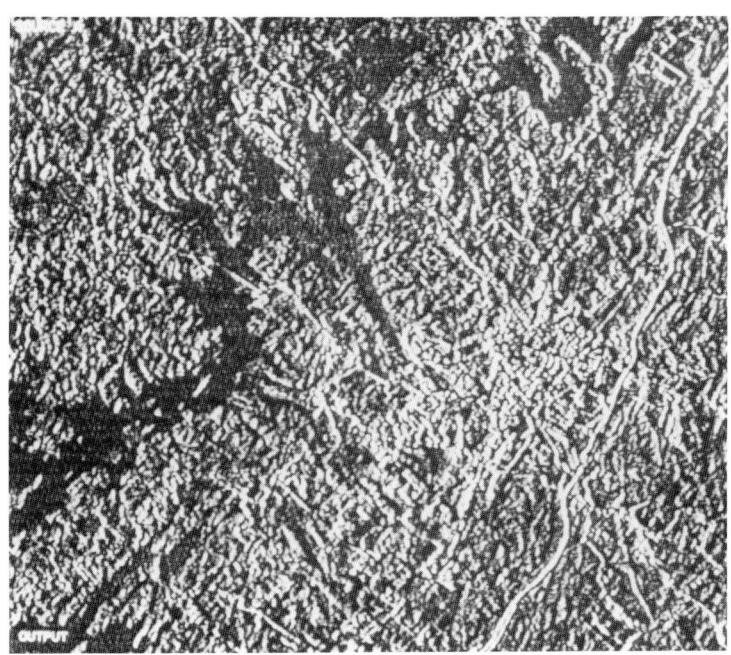

FIGURE 16. Landsat TM, northeast directional filter.

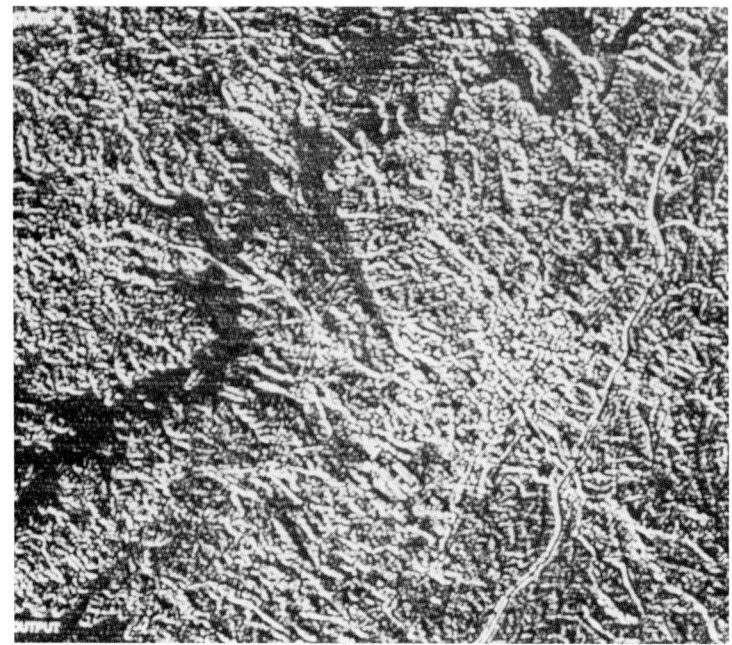

FIGURE 17. Landsat TM, east directional filter.

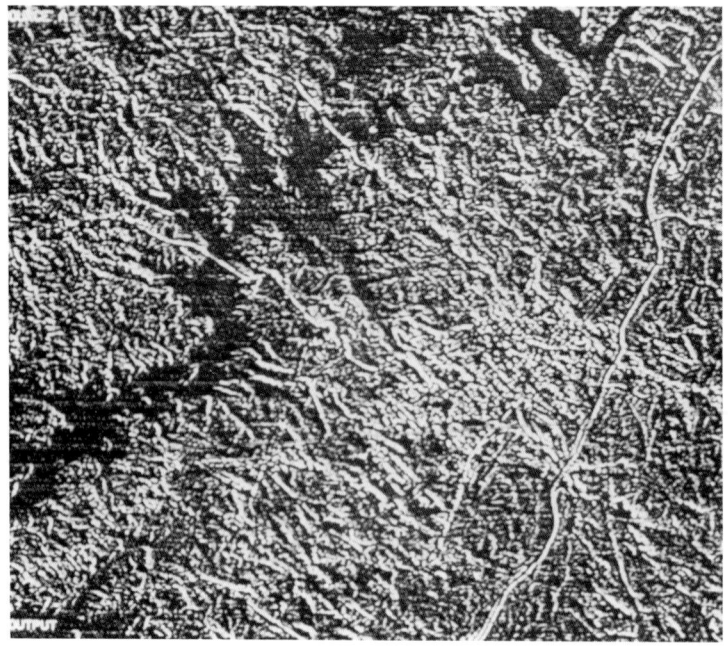

FIGURE 18. Landsat TM, southwest directional filter.

nique used to find edges in a vertical and horizontal direction for an image where the two masks are

$$\begin{vmatrix} -1 & -2 & -1 \\ 0 & 0 & 0 \\ 1 & 2 & 1 \end{vmatrix} \quad \begin{vmatrix} -1 & 0 & 1 \\ -2 & 0 & 2 \\ -1 & 0 & 1 \end{vmatrix}$$

The resulting images for each of the above convolutions may be combined in a root mean squared manner to give the final edge-detection image.

New value = sqrt(a**2 + b**2)

where a is the pixel value from the results of the first operator and b is the pixel value for the results of the second operator. Figure 19 shows the results of a Sobel filter.

A Roberts gradient uses 2 by 2 windows, given below, to estimate edge location in images:

$$\begin{vmatrix} 0 & -1 \\ 1 & 0 \end{vmatrix} \quad \begin{vmatrix} -1 & 0 \\ 0 & 1 \end{vmatrix}$$

and uses the root mean squared approach for determining the new value.

A Prewitt gradient uses the convolution masks:

$$\begin{vmatrix} 1 & 1 & 1 \\ 1 & -2 & 1 \\ -1 & -1 & -1 \end{vmatrix} \quad \begin{vmatrix} -1 & 1 & 1 \\ -1 & -2 & 1 \\ -1 & 1 & 1 \end{vmatrix}$$

Note that all of the individual gradient masks are zero sum. Figure 20 shows the Prewett gradient image.

Fourier Series

Fourier transforms are used extensively in information theory, signal processing, and image processing. This article will not dwell on the theory derivation of the Fourier transform but will try to show examples of the utility of using Fourier transforms in image enhancement. An in-depth discussion of the Fourier transform is given by Gonzales and Wintz [5].

One basic premise of Fourier transform theory is that any one-dimensional function, $f(x)$, may be fully represented by some superposition of trigonometric sine and cosine terms, $F(x)$. The estimation of the coefficients and frequencies of each term necessary for full representation of the original function is involved in the calculation of the Fourier transform.

Fourier transform theory assumes that the signal for which the transform is desired is continuous with an infinite extent. Images, on the other

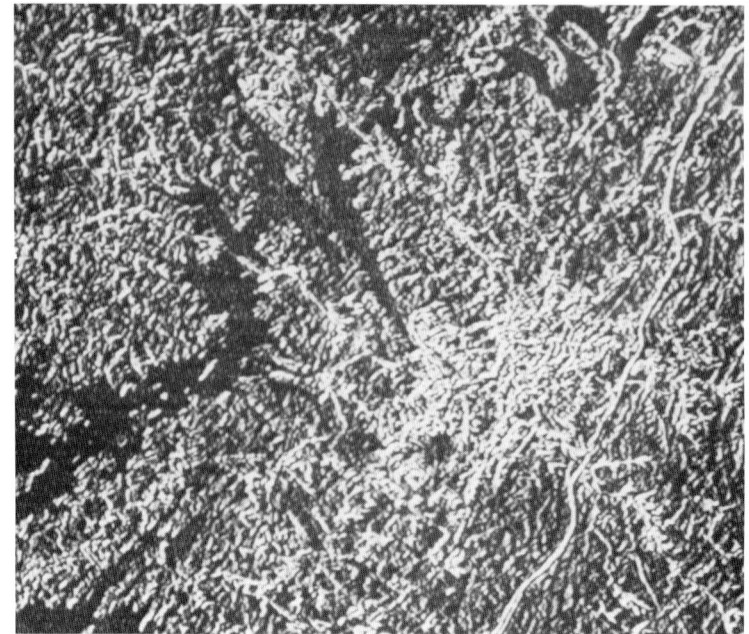

FIGURE 19. Landsat TM, Sobel filter.

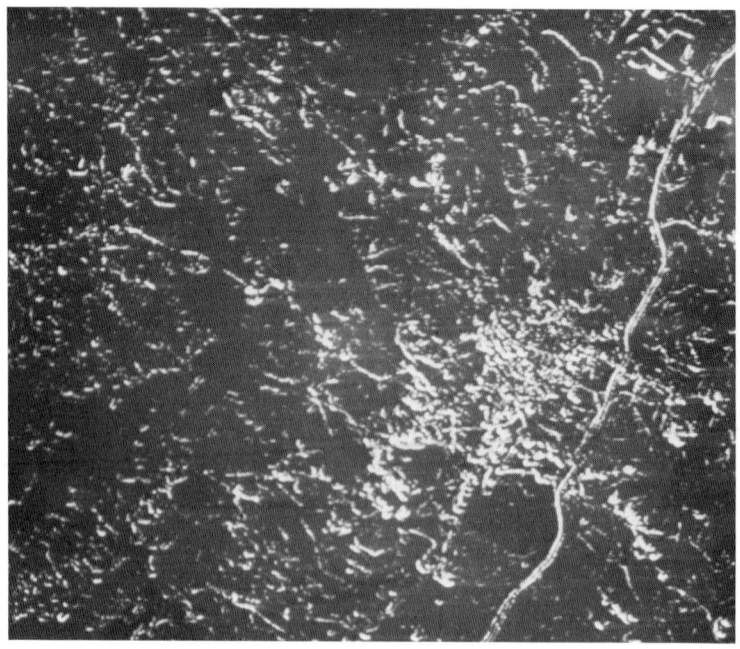

FIGURE 20. Landsat TM, Prewett filter.

Image Enhancement

hand, are often discontinuous along a line or column, and end unceremoniously at the edges of the image. To handle discrete image pixel data, a discrete version of the Fourier transform was developed. A fast implementation of a discrete Fourier transform was developed and called the fast Fourier transform (FFT). This implementation is the basis for most image-processing algorithms using Fourier transforms.

Fourier transform theory allows extension of the above characteristics into two dimensions so that we may process images, by assuring that transforms of lines of image pixels (the function f[x] above) are separable from the processing of columns of image pixels, g(x). In other words, the performing of a two-dimensional Fourier transform on an image is equivalent to independently processing each single line of image data by a one-dimensional Fourier transform and then individually processing each single column of the results of the line-oriented one-dimensional Fourier transforms through another Fourier transform. This separability is a key factor in the implementation of two-dimensional transforms.

Fourier transforms heavily utilize the theory of complex numbers and are often hard to visualize. By recalling examples at the first of the moving window convolution section, perhaps we can make the interpretation of two-dimensional Fourier transforms easier. Any image may be represented by a two-dimensional Fourier transform, which may be considered as an image with a real and a complex part. The two-dimensional FFT is a mapping of image pixel values into the image frequency space. Frequency, in this case does not refer to the time-based frequencies of electrical signals, but to spatial frequencies that may exist within an image. Earlier in this article, we discussed the existence of low- and high-frequency information in an image. By performing a two-dimensional FFT on an image, we are creating a two-dimensional map of all spatial frequencies within an image. Every output image pixel as the result of a FFT has a real and an imaginary number associated with it. The real pixels form an image that may be thought of as the magnitude of the spatial frequencies present in an image, and the imaginary pixels form an image representing the phase of the spatial frequencies. As shown above, the highest spatial frequency that can be present in an image is equivalent to every other pixel having black-and-white values. Therefore, if an x and y axis are used to represent spatial frequencies on a plot, the width of the plot will, at most, be the total width of the image divided by 2. A useful way to display the spatial frequencies within an image is by using a "star diagram" representation of the magnitude of the complex two-dimensional FFT. In such a diagram, the lowest frequency component within an image (the average value, or albedo, of the image) is shown at the center of the diagram and increasing x and y spatial frequencies increase pixel by pixel away from the center of the diagram. The brightness of the pixels at each x and y position relate to the relative occurrence of that spatial frequency in the original image. Because spatial frequencies only exist up to the Nyquist frequency in the x and y directions, the display is reflected about the center of the diagram. Thus, information in the +x and +y direction from the diagram center duplicates information in the −x and −y direction of the diagram. Figure 21 is an example of a 128 by 128 image with a smoothly varying gray scale as pixel positions increase from left to right and top to bottom. Figure 22 shows the magnitude of the two-dimensional FFT for the same image. Note that the majority of the spatial information in the two-dimensional FFT is in the lower frequencies, as indicated in the original image. As a high-frequency example, consider

FIGURE 21. Smooth varying gray-scale image.

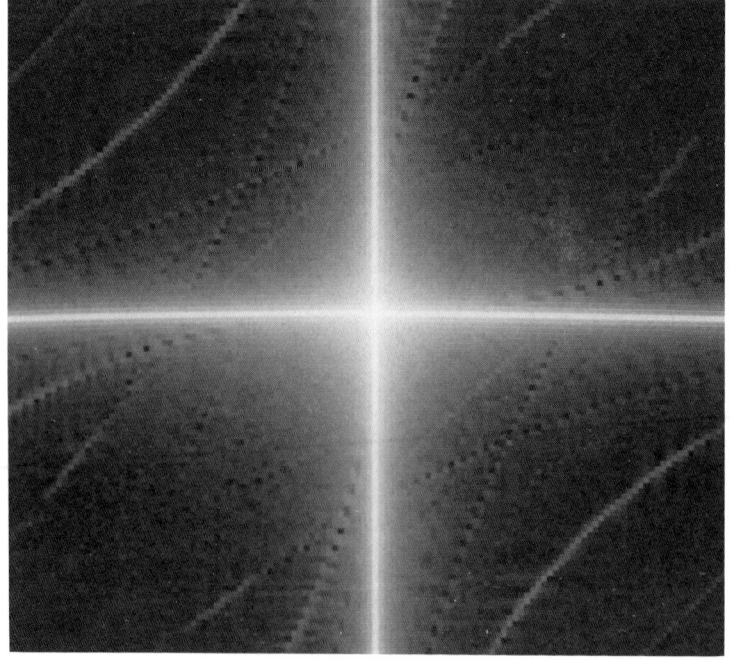

FIGURE 22. FFT magnitude for smooth gray scale.

Image Enhancement

a checkerboard black-and-white image given in Figure 23. The two-dimensional FFT of this image is shown in Figure 24. Note that there are bright spots in the resulting two-dimensional FFT image at high frequency in all directions relating to the "every other pixel" nature of the original image. There is also information at lower spatial frequencies, which are multiples of the highest frequency.

One of the more useful features of a two-dimensional FFT is the way that linear trends and edges are shown in the resulting two-dimensional FFT diagram. Figure 25 shows a sample image that has a line heading from bottom left to top right of the image and not through the center of the image. The two-dimensional FFT, Figure 26, also shows a line in it, but it is perpendicular to the original line and goes through the center of the two-dimensional FFT diagram. The sharp discontinuity in the original image introduced by a bright line against a dark background can only be represented in the spatial frequency domain by a set of functions with all possible spatial frequencies. This is similar to a square wave in signal processing, which also must be represented by all spatial one-dimensional spatial frequencies. Thus, using the two-dimensional FFT diagrams, one may quantify the existence of linear trends in the original image and ascertain their direction.

Convolution

A two-dimensional FFT image may be useful in itself in developing an understanding of individual images, but a much more powerful tool resides in Fourier transform theory. The ability to produce a two-dimensional FFT star diagram is known as the performance of a "forward FFT." In other words, we have transformed an image from the normal "time domain" to the "frequency domain." The resulting frequency domain image may be transformed back to the time domain by performing an inverse two-dimensional

FIGURE 23. High spatial frequency checkerboard image.

FIGURE 24. FFT magnitude for checkerboard.

FIGURE 25. Line image.

Image Enhancement

FIGURE 26. FFT magnitude for line image.

FFT. If no changes are made to the spatial frequency complex image, the inverse two-dimensional FFT will provide the exact same image that we began with. Fourier theory, however, tells us that we may perform certain operations, called convolutions, in the frequency domain that may enhance the image after the inverse two-dimensional FFT. A convolution in the frequency domain is a simple multiplication of an image mask that may be arbitrarily designed by a user, times the complex frequency domain image. The resultant frequency domain image is then run through the inverse two-dimensional FFT process to give a transformed image.

This process of convolution in the frequency domain is extremely valuable in the spatial enhancement of image data. We may perform the operations discussed above in the moving window analysis section in a more complete and flexible manner. In addition, there are some functions that may be done by frequency convolution that as yet have not been achieved by kernel convolution.

High-Frequency Enhancement: High-frequency enhancement may be achieved using a similar logic as determined for the kernel convolution. To create a high-frequency enhanced image, we should try to extract the high spatial frequency components of the image and add them back to the original image. This function is easily done using frequency convolution. First, a TM image (Fig. 27a) is transformed into the frequency domain (Fig. 27b). Next, a mask is developed in the frequency domain, which is 2 for all frequencies greater than an input value and 1 for all frequencies less than the specified value. The mask is multiplied by the spatial frequency complex image (Fig. 27c), and the resultant frequency image is passed through an inverse two-dimensional FFT (Fig. 27d). The resulting image shows higher contrast for edges within the image than the original image displayed.

High Pass Filters: High pass filtering uses the same technique as above, but the mask is set to 0 for all spatial frequencies less than the selected

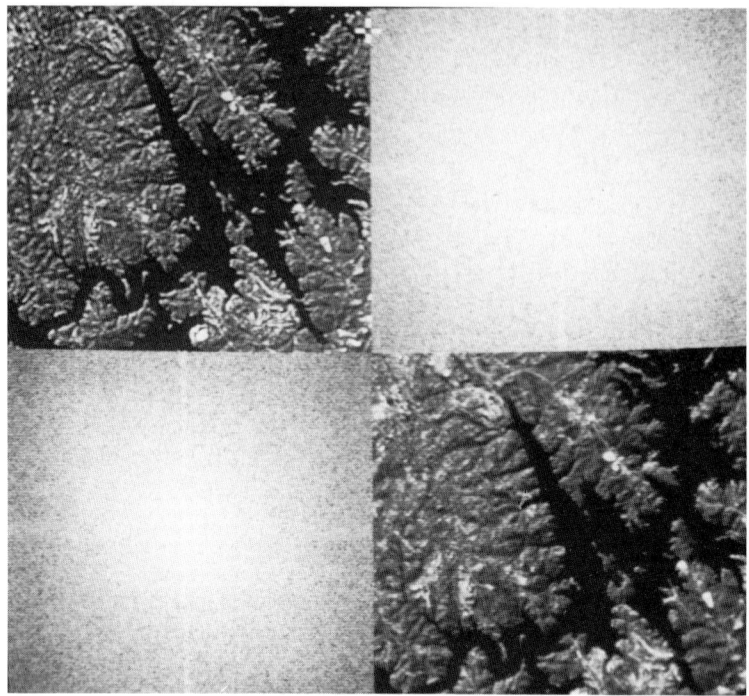

FIGURE 27. (a) TM image input; (b) FFT; (c) filter; (d) result.

value and 1 for all spatial frequencies greater than the value (Fig. 28c). Thus, only the high-frequency parts of the complex spatial frequency image are retained. When the inverse two-dimensional FFT is performed, the resultant image represents a high pass filter of the original image (Fig. 28d). It is simple to define masks to be used in the frequency domain, but one must be careful to know what types of effects to expect in the time domain.

Low Pass Filters: Low pass filters may be implemented in the same manner. After the original image has been transformed into the frequency domain, a mask is developed that is radially symmetric and has a 0 value for all spatial frequencies greater than the input value, and a 1 for all spatial frequencies less than or equal to the selected value. Figure 29a shows the low pass frequency modification of the above two-dimensional FFT. Figure 29d shows the results of the inverse two-dimensional FFT after low pass processing. This image blurring is similar to the effects of various optics on a resultant image.

Ideal filter masks that vary from 0 to 1 in a discontinuous jump also tend to introduce "ringing" effects in the image due to the sharpness of the filter. A low pass filter may be made, which varies gradually from the center of the spatial frequency plot to the cutoff frequency without introducing the discontinuity that causes the ringing effect. Several filters that provide this function are the Butterworth low pass filter and the exponential low pass filter. Similarly, sharp discontinuities in high pass and band-pass filters may be avoided by the Butterworth and exponential high pass filters.

Image Enhancement

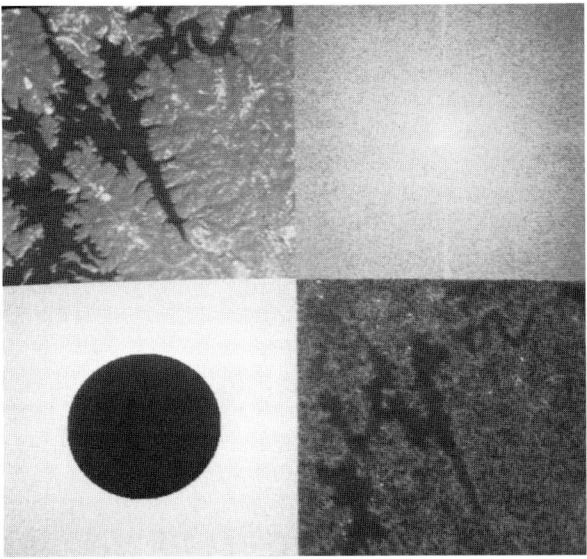

FIGURE 28. High pass filtering. (a) Original; (b) FFT; (c) filter; (d) result.

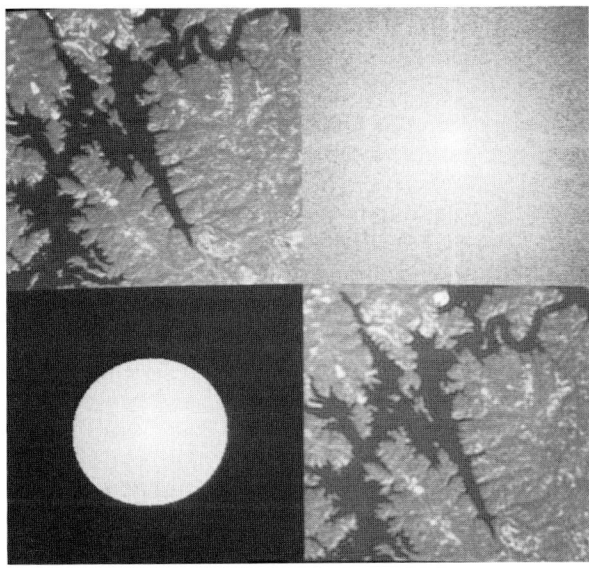

FIGURE 29. Low pass filtering. (a) Original; (b) FFT; (c) filter; (d) result.

Band-Pass Filters: For particular applications, it is desirable to have a band-pass filter operate on an image. A mask in the spatial frequency domain would then be developed that had a value of 0 for all spatial frequencies greater than a maximum frequency and 0 for all frequencies less than a minimum frequency, as defined by a user. The rest of the mask would have a value of 1 (Fig. 30c). Figure 30d shows a band-pass filtered image.

Directional Filtering: Directional filtering may be achieved by using a mask in the spatial frequency domain that is 0 everywhere, except for wedge-shaped regions in the spatial frequency image corresponding to the user-selected minimum and maximum angles. Figure 31a shows one band of a Landsat TM image of a mountainous area. Figure 31b shows the two-dimensional FFT of the area; Figure 31c shows the spatial frequency plot after it has been modified by a directional wedge filter. Figure 31d shows the results of the directional filter.

Noise Removal: Noise removal is one of the most powerful attributes of two-dimensional FFT filtering. Spacecraft sensors and ground processing often produce noise patterns in an image that are impossible to remove with normal kernel filtering. Techniques were developed for removal of early Landsat I, II, and III detector biases (banding), using a six-line sliding window, but these programs were not generic enough to handle new sensors such as the TM and SPOT MSS. Figure 32a shows early Landsat MSS data of Cairo, Egypt, which illustrates dramatically the six-line banding effects of the MSS sensor. Figure 32b is the spatial frequency domain representation of the same image. Note the bright spots on the vertical axis of the frequency plot. By creating a special mask that only zeroed out frequency data within those narrow regions of the spatial frequency plot (Fig. 32c), the striping was removed, creating a superior image (Fig. 32d).

In 1974, data from the new Landsat 4 MSS and TM sensors began to be processed in earnest. A highly variable, diagonally trending noise pattern was evident in the MSS data from Landsat 4. A mad scramble began to attempt to determine what was responsible for the noise pattern, and after a time, it was discovered to be related to the scanning mechanics of the TM sensor on the same spacecraft. By looking at the two-dimensional FFT frequency plot for that data, a notch-type filter was developed that excluded the spatial frequencies responsible for the noise patterns. Figure 33, a through d, show the results of a notched filter.

Image Restoration

Two-dimensional FFTs may also be used for image restoration. Image restoration normally involves trying to enhance an image based on a knowledge of the OTF or the MTF of the system used to form the image. By knowing these characteristics of the sensor system, a mask may be developed that will sharpen the image by compensating for effects introduced by the sensor itself.

A low pass filter may be used to reduce the effects of random noise in an image, often, however, degrading the spatial resolution of the original image.

Image Enhancement

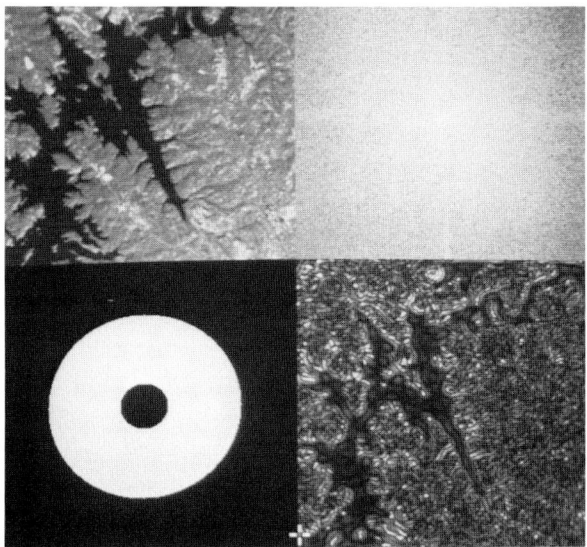

FIGURE 30. Band-pass filtering. (a) Original; (b) FFT; (c) filter; (d) result.

FIGURE 31. Directional filtering. (a) Original; (b) FFT; (c) filter; (d) result.

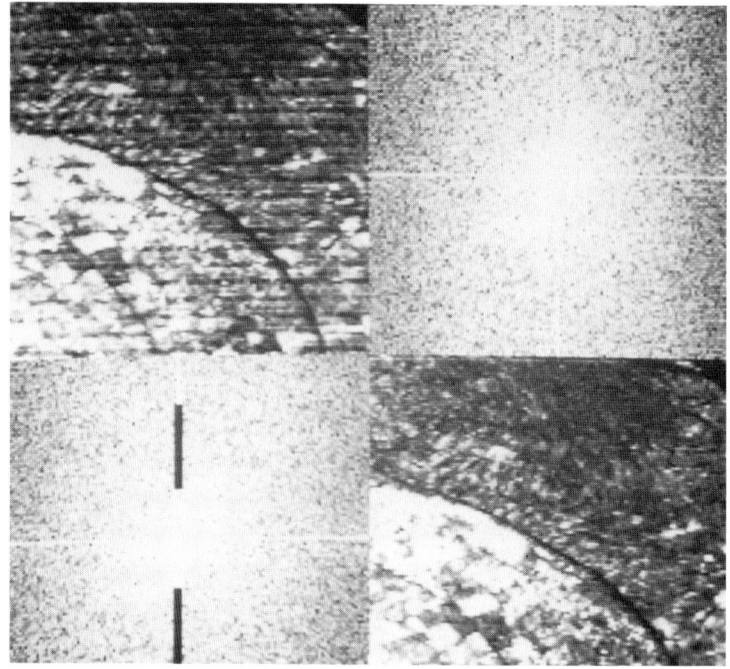

FIGURE 32. Noise removal filtering. (a) Original; (b) FFT; (c) filter; (d) result.

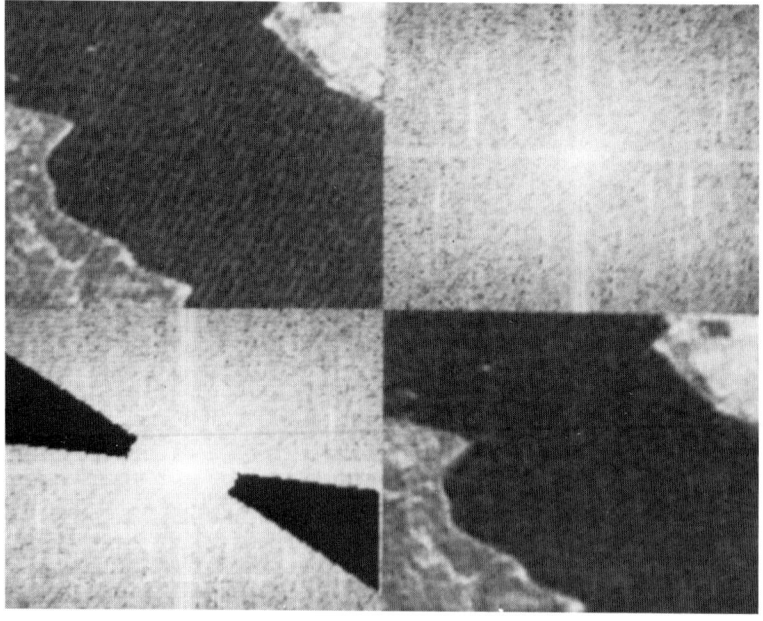

FIGURE 33. Notch filter. (a) Original; (b) FFT; (c) filter; (d) result.

Image Enhancement

Transformations

Color Space Transformations

Experience has shown that the distribution of radiance values for large area remote sensing systems such as Landsat approaches a multivariate normal distribution. Natural vegetation especially is found to be close to normal statistics. Many image-processing algorithms in enhancement and in image pattern recognition use this characterization of image statistics as an accepted fact and this are able to simplify the necessary mathematics for classification and enhancement. A univariate normal distribution may be represented as a bell-shaped curve with the mean of the distribution being x coordinate of the highest point of the curve. The distribution curve is actually a histogram plot of image data, with the ordinate being the possible data values in the image (256 for an 8-bit image), and the abcissa being the number of image pixels within the image with the data value specified by the ordinate. The width of the bell-shaped curve is related to the variance of a normal distribution. A standard deviation defines two lines on the ordinate that encompass approximately 67% of all data values for that sample (the area under the curve between the lines is equal to 67% of the total area under the curve). Figure 34 shows a histogram of natural vegetation in a Landsat image (band 2). If two channels of data over the same area were available, a dual-channel histogram could be developed as shown graphically in Figure 35. In this case, the x axis represents the spectral values in channel 1, the y axis represents potential spectral values in channel 2, and the z axis represents the number of pixels in an image that have the designated x and y values. For each two-channel combination of multispectral information, such a plot can show the relationships of the data values between the two channels. For Landsat MSS data with four channels, there are six possible combinations of two channels. A scatter diagram is simply a two-dimensional view of the dual-channel histogram plots (Fig. 36). By looking at the six scatter diagrams

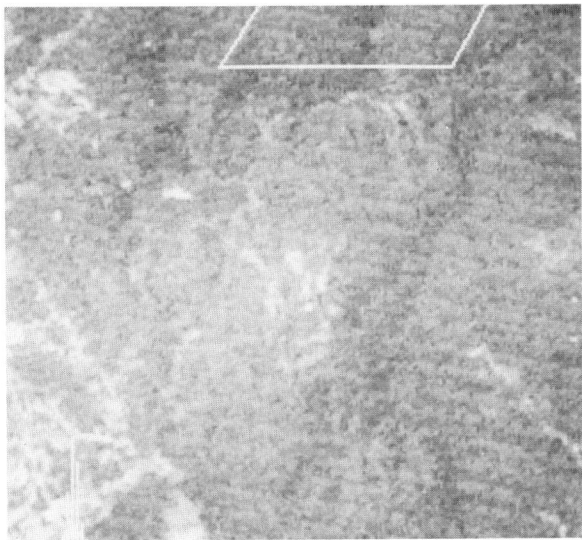

FIGURE 34. Histogram of natural vegetation.

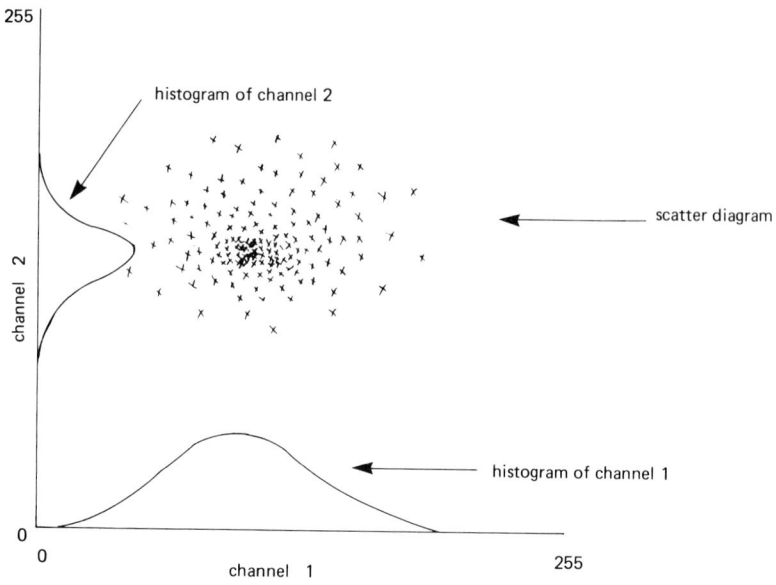

FIGURE 35. Two-channel histogram.

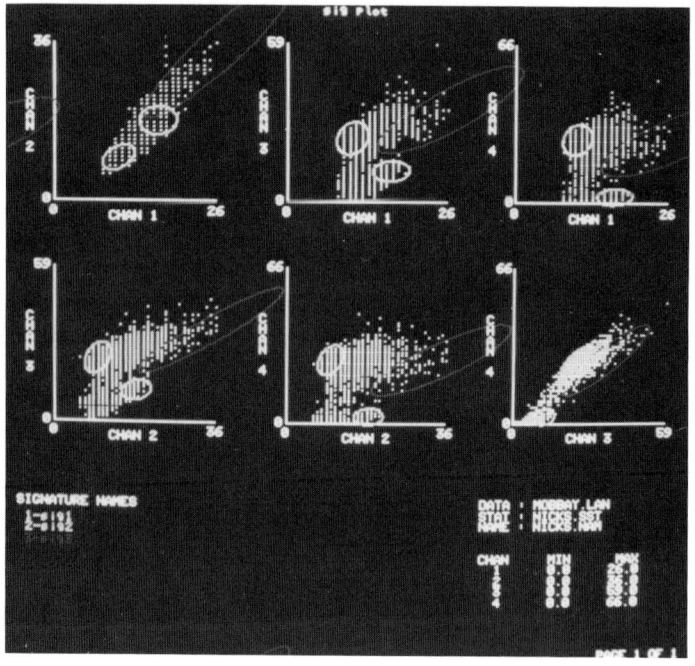

FIGURE 36. Scatter diagram of natural vegetation.

Image Enhancement

for Landsat MSS data, a high positive correlation is observed between Landsat MSS channels 1 and 2 and a high positive correlation is also observed between channels 3 and 4 of the MSS data.

A positive correlation indicates that one image may be reasonably predicted by knowing the data values in the other image. If an image looks nothing like the second image, the two images may be said to be independent of each other. The above correlation is verified by looking at the gray-scale images for all four channels of MSS. The images for channels 1 and 2 look remarkably similar, and the images for channels 3 and 4 also look similar to each other. On the other hand, it can be seen that there is little correlation between channels 2 and 4 of the MSS data; therefore, channels 2 and 4 are close to being independent of one another.

If we take the scatter diagram for channels 2 and 4 for the above example as a relatively uncorrelated set of two channels, we can visualize the methodology involved in color space transformations.

Principal Components: One of the more useful color space transformations is principal components. A principal component transformation may be applied to almost any number of channels of input data. In fact, one of the most important uses of principal components is in data volume reduction (compression). As mentioned above, there is no guarantee that spectral channels for any multispectral sensor system would be uncorrelated. If this is true, then duplicate information exists between channels, and a new set of channels in color space should be able to be found that each contain information not found in any other channel (are independent of one another). To find these new channels as a function of the original channels, an approach called factor analysis is used.

Factor analysis is not only used in remote sensing data analysis, but it is also used by psychologists to look for underlying factors that influence how a group of people might answer seemingly unrelated questions on a psychological test. The test results for a sample population would be gathered into a computer system, and a factor analysis would be run on the answers for all questions to determine the influence of poverty on crime or other basic factors that cannot be determined by direct questions. In many cases, the design of the survey might be made as a function of iterative use of factor analysis given probable responses. Questions that are found to have no bearing on the desired results of the survey may be excluded in test design. Proposed hypotheses for the underlying factors may be tested against the sample data set and accepted or rejected.

Remote sensing factor analysis has an analog with testing analysis in that the basic questions that are asked in a test would correspond to the channels of image data, the number of image pixels would be the sample population, and the data values in each channel would be the answers to the questions. The resulting underlying factors determined by factor analysis are related to a transformation of the coordinate system from the original channel space to another coordinate system. The first axis is found to be along the direction of maximum variance in n-dimensional data; the second axis is perpendicular to the first and lies along the direction of the second greatest variance in n dimensions; the third axis, similarly, is along the third-most variance and is perpendicular to both axes one and two. This continues until the number of perpendicular axes are equal to the dimension of the data set. Each of the axes are perpendicular to each other, showing independence of each axis from the others. The percent of the total variance in the original multichannel data that may be explained by projection to one of the orthogonal axes may be calculated for each axis.

The principal component transformation is also known as a Karhunen-Loeve transform and involves calculating the covariance matrix for the total multispectral image and deriving a matrix A which, when multiplied by the original covariance matrix C, gives a diagonalized matrix V (all off-diagonal terms are 0).

$$[A][C][A]^T = [V]$$

where C is the n × n covariance matrix associated with the original n channel image. V and A are also n × n matricies. T represents the transpose of a matrix. v may be shown as

$$[V] = \begin{bmatrix} v1 & 0 & 0 & 0 \\ 0 & v2 & 0 & 0 \\ 0 & 0 & v3 & 0 \\ 0 & 0 & 0 & v4 \end{bmatrix}$$

for a four-channel data set. v1 through v4 are known as eigenvalues and are representative of the variance in each of the transformed principal components channels. The total variance in the transformed channels is equal to the total variance in the original n channel image. The transform is computed such that the largest eigenvector is v1, and v1 > v2 > v3 > v4.. ..> vn. This also means that the largest amount of the original n-channel variance is found in channel 1 of the principal components transformed image. Each successive principal component image channel explains less and less of the original image variance. The last channels of an n channel principal component image often only represent noise in the original image.

The matrix A contains a set of n-column vectors known as eigenvectors. Each eigenvector is essentially a vector of coefficients that will be multiplied by the original input data vector to produce the transformed data vector. The transformation is identical to that described above in linear combinations, except that the coefficients are automatically calculated instead of being selected by the user.

The principal component transformation then is accomplished by multiplying each sample vector in the input image by the eigenvector matrix A.

The eigenvalues for a sample MSS image (Fig. 37) are given in Table 1, along with the percent of the original four-channel variance in the scene, and may be explained by each principal component image. The eigenvector matrix, A is shown below the eigenvalues.

The inherent two-dimensional nature of MSS data can be seen by the fact that the first two eigenvalues can explain over 95% of the total variance in the MSS image. By looking at the first two principal component images, one can see that the first image has high contrast and represents the basic brightness, or albedo, for the scene. Principal component image 2 is usually reversed in contrast to channel 1 for MSS data, but it also contains spectral/spatial image information. Channels 3 and 4 are represented on a small portion of the variance in an original image and often only represent noise in the MSS image. Figure 38 shows a near infrared channel of MSS data over the Nile River valley. Notice that the image has the characteristic sixth-

Image Enhancement

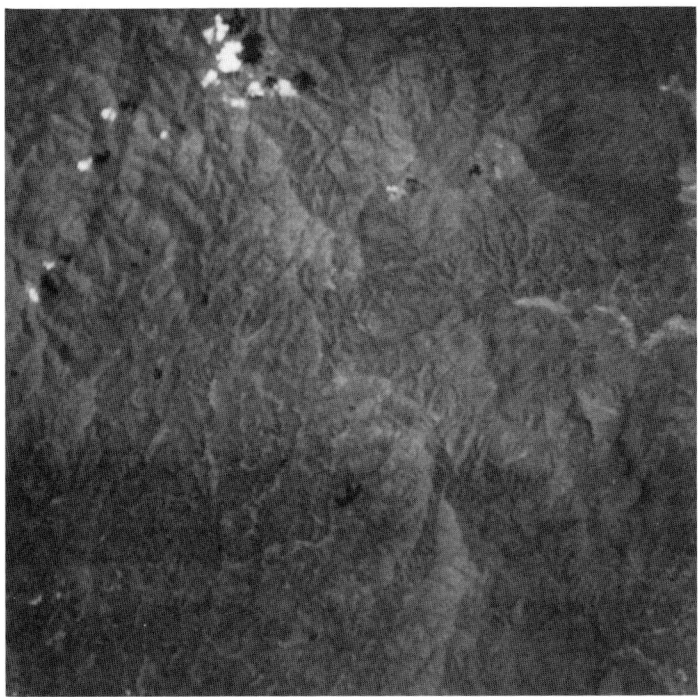

FIGURE 37. Sample MSS image for principal components.

Table 1 Principal Components Transform

```
Principal components
File : TD512TM
Covariance Matrix:
     75.172      42.679      65.151      38.826      94.922       4.636      59.430
     42.679      26.495      40.807      30.683      67.791       3.805      39.159
     65.151      40.807      68.305      61.056     129.758       7.964      69.993
     38.826      30.683      61.056     244.242     302.831      16.860     107.521
     94.922      67.791     129.758     302.831     497.900      30.404     202.215
      4.636       3.805       7.964      16.860      30.404       7.375      13.374
     59.430      39.159      69.993     107.521     202.215      13.374      95.846

Eigenvalues:   Var. %:    Total %:    Angle:      Scale:
    843.068     83.033     83.033     57.292       1.464
    125.711     12.381     95.415     77.329       3.791
     33.405      3.290     98.705     81.547       7.353
      5.768      0.568     99.273     50.435      17.696
      3.552      0.350     99.623    117.184      22.550
      3.008      0.296     99.919     98.853      24.505
      0.824      0.081    100.000     90.752      46.824

Eigenvectors:
      0.168      0.596      0.398     -0.196     -0.591       0.144     -0.225
      0.116      0.324      0.188      0.023      0.093      -0.177      0.898
      0.215      0.460      0.145      0.183      0.601      -0.430     -0.376
      0.481     -0.510      0.692      0.112      0.081       0.101     -0.015
      0.761     -0.089     -0.494     -0.243     -0.195      -0.268      0.011
      0.046     -0.003     -0.104      0.889     -0.400      -0.193     -0.003
      0.316      0.246     -0.229      0.257      0.277       0.802      0.042
```

FIGURE 38. Nile River valley MSS.

line banding effects from detector calibration problems in early Landsat data sets. Figure 39 shows all four bands of a principal component image transform. Note that bands 1 and 2 represent large contrasts present in the original image, and channel 4 shows the banding noise. Variance is related to image contrast and image information content, and two channels of the transformed image contain almost all the original information that all four original MSS channels contained. By only using the two transformed channels in classification or other time-consuming mathematical analyses, the speed of the functions may be enhanced and data volume will be reduced.

For 7-channel TM data or aircraft scanner data with 12 to 24 channels, a significant decrease in data volume may be obtained by using only several of the principal components, thus retaining the majority of the image variance information. It is often difficult with over three channels of data to decide how to display the most information on the three-color channels of a display. A color display of the principal component image shows a large amount of information; however, the colors in the image may look bizarre to a human interpreter.

It should be pointed out that the lack of variance in the last two principal components is not necessarily a reason to discard the channels. In many cases, in geological interpretation, subtle tonal variations within the image are evident in the latter principal component images but are hidden by the greater contrast of the original MSS channels.

Canonical Transformation: A canonical transformation is very similar to a principal component transformation, except that instead of aligning the the new channel axes in the directions of the majority of the n-channel variance in the original image, canonical transformations align the axis of the new coordinate system in the direction that would allow the best discrimination between two different class signatures. In place of a covariance matrix as input to the factor analysis, the canonical method uses a between class covariance matrix that is a function of the class mean and covariance for two

Image Enhancement 231

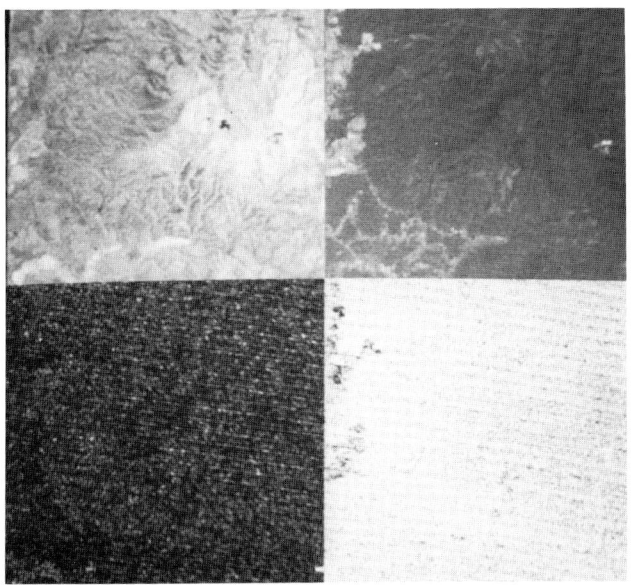

FIGURE 39. Principal components. (a) Channel 1; (b) channel 2; (c) channel 3; (d) channel 4.

signatures as obtained by training sample selection procedure used in maximum likelihood classification. The diagonalization of the resulting covariance matrix leads to eigenvectors in directions that maximize separability between the two classes.

IHS: It is often very difficult for a human interpreter to relate to a red, green, blue (RGB) color space and the changes in RGB necessary to enhance the total color of an image. Human perception of images is based on the tristimulus theory of color where the image is represented in terms of image intensity, hue, and saturation (IHS), which are the three physiological parameters commonly used to describe color. These relate to human sensations such as brightness, color, and color purity. A low intensity would indicate a dark image on a display. Hue relates to colors such as green, blue, yellow, and orange, and saturation relates to the amount of color mixing. A low saturation image would look gray, and a small amount of saturation would lead to pastel colors.

By allowing a user to change the intensity, hue, and saturation of an image instead of requiring an iterative RGB enhancement process, the color enhancement process may often be streamlined. A user's subjective perception of color balance will allow an easier incremental color enhancement process. If color is represented in a spherical color space, the IHS parameters may be defined in terms of the RGB as

$I = red^{**}2 + green^{**}2 + blue^{**}2$

$H = \arctan(-blue/red)$

$S = \arccos(green/sqrt[I])$

Haydn [6] derived an IHS transform using color theory that exists when $1 > H > 0$:

I = red + green + blue

H = (green $-$ blue)/($I - 3*$blue)

S = ($I - 3*$blue)/I

and the inverse,

red = $1/3*I*(1 + 2*S - 3*S*H)$

green = $1/3*I*(1 - S + 3*S*H)$

blue = $1/3*I*(1 - S)$

Using these formulas, a three-channel image may be transformed into an IHS image, undergo an enhancement applied in IHS, and be inverse transformed back into RGB for display on a color monitor.

Vegetative Indices: Vegetative indices have been developed for multispectral data so that a single number can be used to represent vegetation health, biomass, ground cover, or other features necessary for adequate estimation of vegetation properties. By and large, these parameters have been derived experimentally. There are large differences in the reflectance of vegetation, water, and bare ground in different regions of the electromagnetic spectrum. Healthy vegetation may be estremely bright relative to its surroundings in the near infrared portion of the spectrum but dark in the visible region. Bare land may be bright in both regions, depending on its wetness. Water may be light in the blue and green portions of the spectrum but is almost totally dark in the near infrared. Multispectral imagery captures those differences by using discrete regions of the spectrum to sample the continuous light spectrum. The spectral regions selected for the Landsat MSS system were chosen so that the combination of MSS channels would be optimum for discrimination of vegetation types.

A review paper by Perry and Lautenschlager [7] detailed the vegetative indices that have been derived using Landsat MSS data. Most vegetative indices are either ratios of linear combinations of Landsat MSS channels, with coefficients determined experimentally. The normal transformed vegetative indices TVI6 and TVI7 are given below as a function of MSS channels 5, 6, and 7:

ND6 = (MSS6 $-$ MSS5)/(MSS5 + MSS6)

ND7 = (MSS7 $-$ MSS5)/(MSS5 + MSS7)

TVI6 = [(ND6 + 0.5)/ABS(ND6 + 0.5)]*SQRT(ND6 + 0.5)

TVI7 = [(ND7 + 0.5)/ABS(ND7 + 0.5)]*SQRT(ND7 + 0.5)

where the bracketed terms are included to prevent negative results. Figure 40 shows MSS data for an agricultural region. Figure 41 shows ND6 for an agricultural region, and Figure 42 shows ND7 for the same region.

Image Enhancement

FIGURE 40. MSS data for agricultural region.

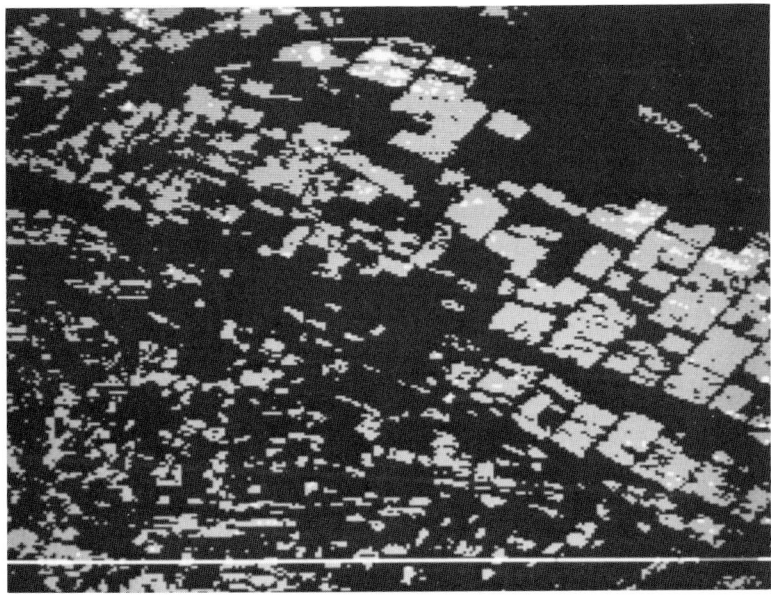

FIGURE 41. Transformed vegetation index 6.

FIGURE 42. Transformed vegetation index 7.

Two image differencing vegetative indices were developed:

DVI = 2.4 * MSS7 − MSS5

and

AVI = 2.0 * MSS7 − MSS5

Figures 43 and 44 show examples of the difference indices.

Using the Gram-Schmidt sequential orthogonalization procedure, an orthogonal set of axes was derived that represented a linear transformation of the original Landsat channel axes; it was called the "tasseled cap" transformation. By initially selecting an axis associated with soil brightness and sequentially choosing orthogonal axes, a set of linear equations was developed that defined new color axes representative of physical parameters. The new axes were defined as the soil brightness index (SBI), the greenness vegetative index (GVI), yellow stuff (YVI), and nonesuch (NSI).

A matrix equation defining the new axes is given below:

$$\begin{bmatrix} SBI \\ GVI \\ YVI \\ NSI \end{bmatrix} = \begin{bmatrix} 0.332 & 0.603 & 0.675 & 0.262 \\ -0.283 & -0.660 & 0.577 & 0.388 \\ -0.899 & 0.428 & 0.076 & -0.041 \\ -0.016 & 0.131 & -0.452 & 0.882 \end{bmatrix} \begin{bmatrix} MSS4 \\ MSS5 \\ MSS6 \\ MSS7 \end{bmatrix}$$

Image Enhancement

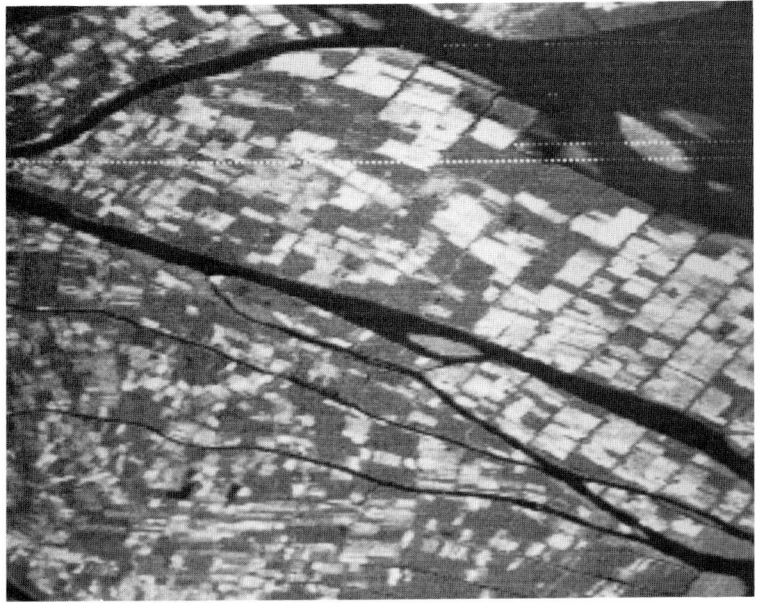

FIGURE 43. Differencing vegetation index.

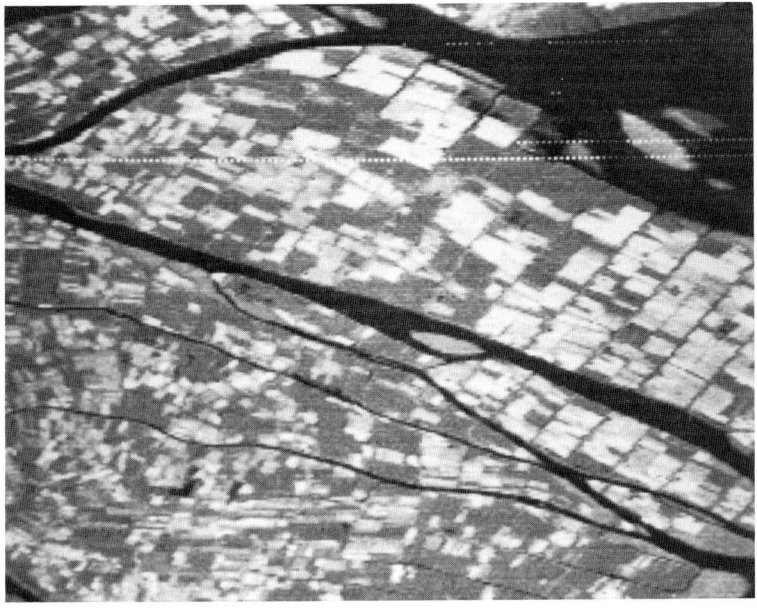

FIGURE 44. Ashburn's differencing vegetation index.

Figure 45 shows an example of each of the indices on one display.

Principal components, discussed above, were used to derive a similar set of axes:

$$\begin{bmatrix} MSBI \\ MGVI \\ MYVI \\ MNSI \end{bmatrix} = \begin{bmatrix} 0.406 & 0.600 & 0.645 & 0.243 \\ -0.386 & -0.530 & 0.535 & 0.532 \\ 0.723 & -0.597 & 0.206 & -0.278 \\ 0.404 & -0.039 & -0.505 & 0.762 \end{bmatrix} \begin{bmatrix} MSS4 \\ MSS5 \\ MSS6 \\ MSS7 \end{bmatrix}$$

An example image using these parameters is given in Figure 46.

Another transform was suggested that was based on spectral brightness and contrast. The matrix coefficients for that transform are

$$\begin{bmatrix} SSBI \\ SGVI \\ SYVI \\ SNSI \end{bmatrix} = \begin{bmatrix} 0.437 & 0.564 & 0.661 & 0.233 \\ -0.437 & -0.564 & 0.661 & 0.233 \\ -0.437 & 0.564 & -0.661 & 0.233 \\ -0.437 & 0.564 & 0.661 & -0.233 \end{bmatrix} \begin{bmatrix} MSS4 \\ MSS5 \\ MSS6 \\ MSS7 \end{bmatrix}$$

Figure 47 shows the results of the above transform elements.

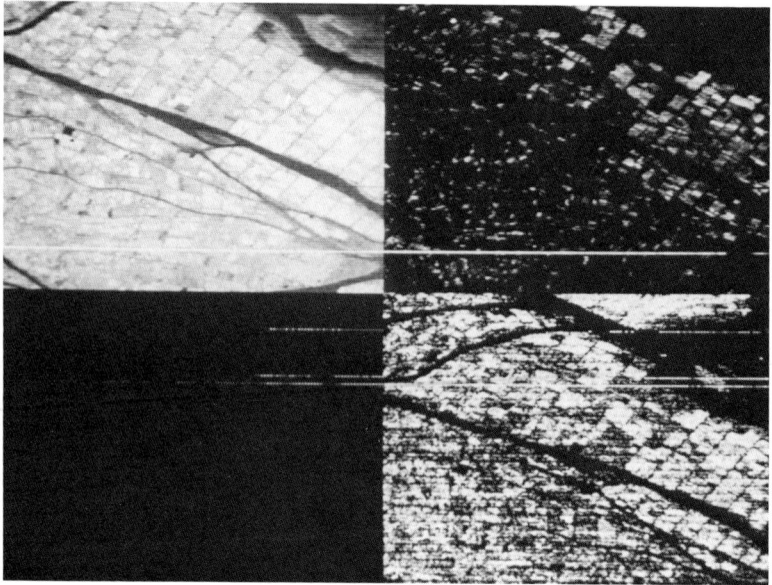

FIGURE 45. Tasseled cap. (1) SBI; (2) GVI; (3) YVI; (4) NSI.

Image Enhancement

FIGURE 46. Principal component index. (1) MSBI; (2) MGVI; (3) MYVI; (4) MNSI.

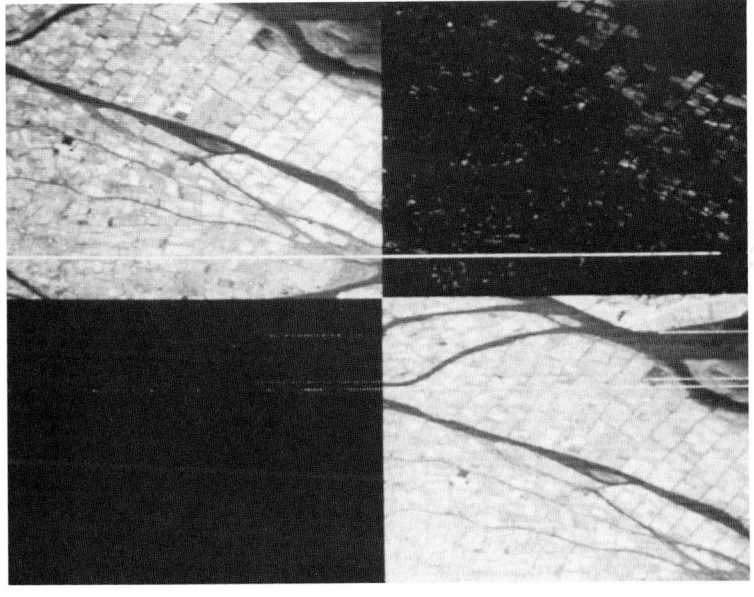

FIGURE 47. Misra index. (1) SSBI; (2) SGVI; (3) SYVI; (4) SNSI.

An index called the perpendicular vegetation index (PVI), relates vegetation to a distance from a "soil line" connecting wet and dry soil in spectral space. The PVI equations are

PVI7 = SQRT((0.355*MSS7 − 0.149*MSS5)**2
+ (0.355*MSS5 − 0.852*MSS7)**2)

and

PVI6 = SQRT((−2.507 − 0.457*MSS5 + 0.498*MSS6)**2
+ (2.734 + 0.498*MSS5 − 0.543*MSS6)**2)

with a correction suggested by Perry and Lautenschlager [7]. Figure 48 shows the PVI7 index.

A vegetation index called greenness above bare soil was developed to correct for atmospheric and sun angle effect:

GRABS = GVI − (0.09178 * SBI) + 5.58959

Regressions using wheat leaves and MSS data resulted in two indices, ELAI and CLAI:

ELAI = 2.68 − 3.69*R45 − 2.31*R46 + 2.88 * R47 + 0.43*R56
− 1.35*R57 + 3.07*(R45 − [0.5R47]*[R45])

where RNM is the ratio of MSS channels N and M, and

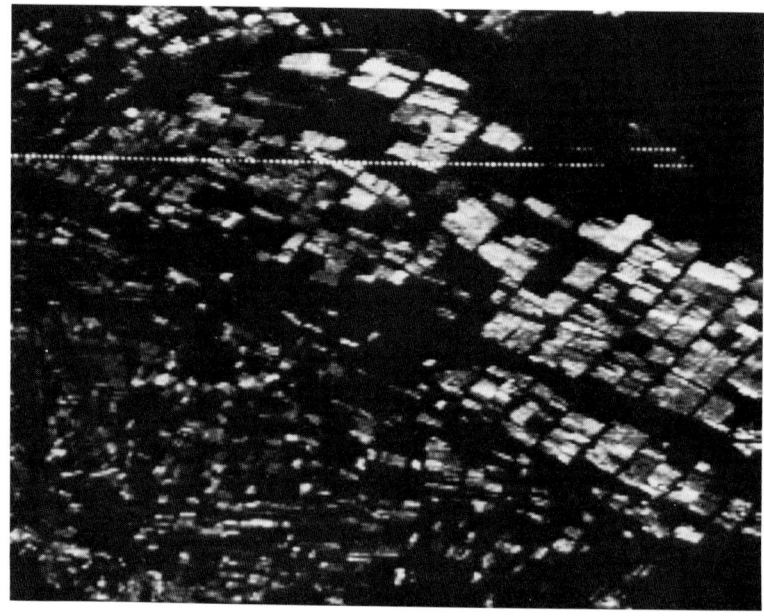

FIGURE 48. PVI 7 index.

Image Enhancement

$$\text{CLAI} = 0.366 - 2.265*R46 - 0.431*(R45 - R47)*(R45)$$
$$+ 1.745*R45 + 0.57*PVI7$$

Perry and Lautenschlager [7] took the above indices and looked at their interrelationships. They found that many of the indices were highly correlated with each other and thus contained redundant information.

Thus far, all the vegetation indices have been developed for Landsat MSS data. With the advent of Landsat TM data and multispectral data from SPOT, new indices will have to be developed that relate to the new spectral bands. A transformation of coordinate axes for Landsat TM data has been developed that has axes similar to the tasseled cap transformation. The transformation matrix is

$$\begin{bmatrix} \text{BRI} \\ \text{GRN} \\ \text{WET} \\ 4\text{th} \\ 5\text{th} \\ 6\text{th} \end{bmatrix} \begin{bmatrix} 0.2043 & 0.4158 & 0.5524 & 0.5741 & 0.3124 & 0.2303 \\ -0.1603 & -0.2819 & -0.4934 & 0.7940 & -0.0002 & -0.1446 \\ 0.0315 & 0.2021 & 0.3102 & 0.1594 & -0.6806 & -0.6109 \\ -0.2117 & -0.0284 & 0.1302 & -0.1007 & 0.6529 & -0.7078 \\ -0.8669 & -0.1835 & 0.3856 & 0.0408 & -0.1132 & 0.2272 \\ 0.3677 & -0.8200 & 0.4354 & 0.0518 & -0.0066 & -0.0104 \end{bmatrix} \begin{bmatrix} \text{TM1} \\ \text{TM2} \\ \text{TM3} \\ \text{TM4} \\ \text{TM5} \\ \text{TM7} \end{bmatrix}$$

where BRI is brightness, GRN is greenness, and WET is wetness.

Figure 49 shows the first four components of the above transform.

Combination Spectral/Spatial Enhancement

A novel technique for performing both spectral and spatial enhancement was developed called crisping. Crisping is an involved process but provides edge enhancement of multichannel images with less of the tonal changes that normally occur with simple edge enhancement.

First, the candidate multichannel image is transformed with a principal component transformation. Next, an edge-enhancement convolution filter is applied only to the first (albedo) channel of the principal component image. By inverting the principal component transformation, an enhanced image is obtained that shows little color balance effects from the filtering.

Care should be exercised during the forward and inverse transforms to allow for appropriate scaling changes. Figure 50 shows an image with three different regions. The top region is not filtered at all; the middle region has been high frequency enhanced using a convolution filter; and the bottom third shows the image after crisping.

FIGURE 49. TM version of tasseled cap.

FIGURE 50. Spatial crisping.

REFERENCES

1. *Manual of Remote Sensing*, 2nd ed., American Society of Photogrammetry and Remote Sensing, 1985.
2. G. W. Wecksung and J. R. Breedlove, Jr., "A Technique for Dynamic Range Reduction for Landsat Ratio Images," in *Proceedings of Electronics in Resources Management*, Alamogordo, NM, April, 1978.
3. P. S. Chavez, Jr., "Atmospheric, Solar, and MTF Corrections for ERTS Digital Imagery," in *Proceedings of the American Society of Photogrammetry Fall Meeting*, October 1975, p. 68.
4. John R. Jenson, *Introductory Digital Image Processing, A Remote Sensing Perspective*, Prentice-Hall, Englewood Cliffs, NJ, 1986.
5. Rafael C. Gonzalez and Paul Wintz, *Digital Image Processing*, Addison-Wesley, Reading, PA, 1977.
6. Rupert Haydn, George W. Dalke, and Jochen Henkel, "Application of the IHS Transform to the Processing of Multisensor Data and Image Enhancement," in *Proceedings of the International Symposium on Remote Sensing of Arid and Semi-Arid Lands*, Cairo, Egypt, January 1982, pp. 599–616.
7. Charles R. Perry and Lyle F. Lautenschlager, "Functional Equivalence of Spectral Vegetation Indices," *Remote Sensing of Environment*, 14, 169–182 (1984).

NICKOLAS L. FAUST

IMAGE PROCESSING

1 INTRODUCTION

1.1 Image Processing as a Form of Computer Graphics

Computer graphics is a diverse field, ranging from the simple and familiar, such as the bar and pie charts of business graphics, to the mathematical precision and complexity of synthetic geometry in CAD/CAM graphics. This article focuses on another form of computer graphics: image processing. Image processing is the part of computer graphics dealing with presentations that have some of the characteristics of photography—the ability to represent different values or characteristics at all locations in the display. Some of the techniques of image processing are directly comparable with processes in the photo darkroom, but with digital image processing, one can go much further. Color will be discussed in this article, but black and white is the main focus.

Ultimately, the purpose of computer graphics is to communicate information effectively. There are a wide range of disciplines that have adopted image processing, from medical imaging and robotics to remote sensing applications. The tools and techniques of image processing provide new capabilities, beyond those available in a photographic darkroom, to the task of effectively summarizing and presenting information to an audience.

1.2 Background

A photograph is an image; an image is not a photograph. It is important to understand the difference. A photograph is made using a camera, which has a lens and a film emulsion of some kind. An image is any complete two-dimensional representation of data—film and a lens are not necessary. A map of population density, e.g., where darker areas have higher density than lighter areas, is an image. The color-coded maps that result from a geologist's field surveys are images. The television like display of temperature of a house, used to identify where heat is leaking through inadequate insulation, is an image. And, of course, a photograph is certainly an image.

Before going any further, a small common ground of computer terms should be established. The smallest element we can work with in a digital computer is the *bit*. A bit may take the value 0 or 1, signifying off or on, false or true, like an ordinary light switch. To be able to deal with more information at once, 8 bits taken together form a *byte*. Thus, one way to display the contents of a byte is to write out its sequence of bits: 00000000 is one extreme pattern; 11111111 is the other. When displaying the bits that make up a byte, a space is sometimes put in the middle to make it easier to read, e.g., 0101 1110. The group of 4 bits is called a *nibble;* just as 8 bits make up a byte, 2 nibbles make up a byte. The left-most

Image Processing   243

nibble is sometimes called the high-order nibble; the right-most is sometimes called the low-order nibble.

There are several common ways to think about the contents of a byte. A *base-2* numbering system consists of sequences of 0 and 1, just as the base-10 numbering system we all use is made up of sequences of 0 through 9. Thus, if we have an 8-bit byte, we can count from 0 to 255. Another way to think about bytes is to code each unique sequence of 8 bits as a single character. The characters on this page are stored in my word processor as such a sequence of bits, where each 8-bit byte indicates a particular letter, number, or symbol. For example, a space is indicated by 0010 0000 (or in decimal, the value 32).

In the image-processing arena, sequences of bits ultimately code for brightness and color. Figure 1A shows a view of the California coast, based on satellite observations roughly 1,000 km above the earth's surface. In Figure 1B, an array of numbers represents the contents of a portion of Figure 1A.

1.2.1 Digital Images

The smallest area in an image whose brightness (or color) can be uniquely determined is called a *pixel*, which is an abbreviation for picture element. Some authors use *pel* as an even shorter abbreviation for the same thing. In a digital image-processing system, a sequence of bits is used to store the brightness (or color) of each pixel in the image. Bits represent tone and color, as will be seen below.

Pixels are normally organized in rectangular arrays called *rasters*. The pixels are numbered in a slightly unfamiliar order, starting in the *upper left* corner, rather than in the lower left corner, which is used as the origin of the coordinate system in most mathematical or physics problems. In many texts, the rows and columns of the pixel array are called *lines* and *samples*, respectively. In many systems designed for image operations, the pixels are square in shape; on many ordinary computer displays, the pixels are rectangular, which is an important difference.

1.2.2 Digitization

The arrays of pixels that are used to store a digital image are created in many ways. Most often, the arrays are based on some process of *remote sensing*. Remote sensing is a simple concept: recording observations from a distance. A camera pointed out the window of an airplane is perhaps the most familiar form of remote sensing. More sophisticated forms of remote sensing are medical imaging systems such as X-ray photographs and CAT scans, geophysical observations such as aeromagnetic and gravimetry surveys, as well as satellite-based observations of the Earth and other celestial bodies.

The information portrayed in Figure 1A comes from the digital data acquired by NASA's Landsat 5 satellite. The Thematic Mapper sensor on board this satellite observes the Earth through seven different spectral bands. The pixels in the resulting data are approximately 30 meters on a side, and a single image covers approximately 170 km on a side. In this portion of the entire image, which is called a *subscene*, it is easy to find the Santa Barbara Municipal Airport, the network of principal roads, the undeveloped hillsides in the upper half of the subscene, and many other features.

Note the square outlines in the lower right corner of this image. Figure 1B gives the digital numbers or DN values that make up the outlined

(A)

Image Processing

	1	2	3	4	5	6	7	8	9	10	11	12	13	14	15	16	17	18	19	20	21	22	23	24	25	26	27	28	29	30	31
1	255	255	255	255	255	255	255	255	255	255	255	255	255	255	255	255	255	255	255	255	255	255	255	255	255	255	255	255	255	255	255
2	255	105	125	125	142	164	160	145	184	179	147	151	175	241	253	243	255	189	182	194	158	159	170	154	191	207	110	255	139	255	255
3	255	100	111	111	122	134	151	154	173	196	167	141	158	213	244	241	218	201	186	173	177	214	181	182	187	138	81	86	117	151	255
4	255	105	107	107	111	118	125	146	173	192	197	146	145	174	235	231	226	203	207	193	200	239	225	185	128	84	94	103	112	134	255
5	255	117	108	108	117	126	106	122	186	203	203	146	136	213	235	224	226	204	211	213	202	222	157	107	84	95	130	114	152	136	255
6	255	122	111	111	117	114	108	111	143	181	193	194	137	149	213	237	230	211	213	209	190	237	222	119	145	156	193	205	194	217	255
7	255	118	105	105	104	102	115	118	111	157	195	195	150	138	156	226	234	212	224	204	179	155	169	210	222	232	239	205	199	189	255
8	255	120	114	114	106	104	115	125	132	115	132	200	194	137	158	205	235	212	205	149	136	169	191	170	234	245	235	237	176	149	255
9	255	119	116	116	114	114	119	123	118	115	113	194	150	189	220	234	213	169	148	129	167	187	179	170	176	175	158	150	132	127	255
10	255	132	122	122	118	112	121	120	121	123	118	226	229	157	168	205	213	138	138	129	155	187	166	132	127	137	156	136	121	156	255
11	255	119	120	120	114	116	116	121	121	129	123	201	242	222	205	144	134	132	132	131	140	159	142	123	138	130	123	119	125	195	255
12	255	137	123	123	118	116	112	118	116	114	146	202	185	147	138	143	158	134	128	132	132	134	142	131	129	125	112	127	174	179	255
13	255	129	125	125	123	116	112	118	116	116	118	125	135	137	147	178	166	143	132	129	125	131	120	120	120	128	112	171	195	153	255
14	255	131	120	120	116	114	110	116	116	118	107	121	136	154	190	138	138	149	152	129	119	131	128	120	118	120	128	171	115	119	255
15	255	131	125	125	116	118	110	118	118	116	99	110	137	190	170	138	138	142	145	129	121	124	116	118	120	114	154	182	115	135	255
16	255	118	120	120	124	118	118	122	118	116	118	116	116	125	112	118	121	110	110	122	122	111	107	118	118	140	180	150	195	206	255
17	255	118	120	120	120	118	116	120	120	118	110	112	112	116	113	118	109	110	121	122	115	107	109	106	141	161	140	135	224	214	255
18	255	112	116	116	120	122	107	124	120	120	108	108	112	114	114	118	103	110	120	120	111	105	111	129	131	138	127	198	176	156	255
19	255	105	112	112	120	122	100	121	120	122	110	112	112	114	114	116	107	116	115	111	103	112	105	128	131	178	181	208	159	222	255
20	255	105	114	114	120	121	103	120	123	123	118	112	108	110	118	112	114	109	121	103	107	124	133	159	212	250	175	241	253	255	255
21	255	118	113	113	120	123	116	124	121	116	112	116	114	110	105	112	114	112	107	96	103	111	167	248	255	255	241	255	254	243	255
22	255	113	113	113	90	82	79	78	94	112	120	118	121	114	109	118	118	92	113	132	148	212	250	255	255	255	255	240	207	172	255
23	255	96	81	81	64	81	90	83	90	90	101	107	108	118	102	90	91	115	171	180	218	255	255	255	255	242	212	177	122	76	255
24	255	81	70	70	91	133	145	117	115	98	94	76	107	85	81	92	148	204	239	241	253	255	255	240	255	168	107	68	61	63	255
25	255	111	117	117	171	204	162	189	107	101	177	152	129	124	141	152	204	246	255	255	255	255	210	191	115	61	63	65	63	67	255
26	255	143	192	192	237	248	175	210	126	167	180	219	229	129	186	175	187	204	255	255	255	236	119	65	63	71	69	65	65	70	255
27	255	183	243	243	252	235	217	243	195	92	156	194	229	220	176	196	242	255	255	242	231	193	112	67	71	73	67	65	68	65	255
28	255	235	252	252	245	245	235	235	214	109	194	202	188	176	201	253	252	199	113	73	71	70	72	76	76	65	61	65	61	59	255
29	255	235	241	241	241	228	239	235	154	154	167	165	141	168	255	255	168	83	74	73	67	72	77	72	68	65	65	65	56	61	255
30	255	176	214	214	223	223	200	150	127	127	124	141	160	247	214	235	73	74	74	70	67	68	68	69	68	59	59	59	55	63	255
31	255	166	139	139	204	217	171	106	111	127	152	160	247	255	214	125	255	255	255	255	255	255	255	255	255	255	255	255	255	255	255
	1	2	3	4	5	6	7	8	9	10	11	12	13	14	15	16	17	18	19	20	21	22	23	24	25	26	27	28	29	30	31

(B)

FIGURE 1 (A) Processed Landsat Thermatic Mapper image of Goleta, California. The box in the lower right corner frames a portion of the beach, as well as the end of a runway, at the Santa Barbara Municipal Airport. (B) Digital numbers from the area in the box.

subimage. These integer values correspond directly to the brightness of the individual pixels.

Some rasters are generated synthetically. In other words, there is no direct observation of anything but a numerical process to generate the display. Examples of synthetic images include the color-coded images of stress in a bridge section created by a civil engineer and representations of electron density in atoms and molecules based on the modeling efforts of physicists.

Many times, the original image is on a piece of paper or film, either from a photographic process or the end result of a cartographer, draftsperson, or graphic artist. There are a number of approaches to converting this analog image to a digital form. One inexpensive technique is to use a video camera, connected to a *frame grabber* and a computer. The frame grabber converts the video signal into a digital raster. Such systems have limited resolution (typically 350 to 1,000 scan lines in the image) and suffer from a number of kinds of geometric distortion.

Another inexpensive way to convert an analog image to a digital form is based on a computer printer. Several manufacturers have add-on devices that turn their printers into scanners. The print head is replaced with a light source and light detector, which is then stepped across the page by the normal print head transport mechanism. For each increment across the page on a given line, the computer records the light reflected from the page.

There are also dedicated scanning systems that have been developed for the cartographer and computer-aided design (CAD) fields. In both these disciplines, there are a tremendous number of drawings of several kinds. Automated scanning systems have been developed to digitize these images, with very high geometric accuracy. Typically, the user wraps the image around a drum in these systems. The drum then rotates at a constant speed while a photodetector and collimated light source are focused on the drum surface. The photodetector assembly is stepped along the axis of the drum while a computer records the brightness (and possibly color) of the map or drawing. In effect, the system behaves as if a regular grid has been placed on the surface of the image, and the brightness of each cell in the grid is recorded numerically.

A completely different way to convert an image to a digital form is to use a *flatbed digitizing tablet*. The image is placed on the tablet, and an analyst uses a stylus or cursor to trace the locations of important features while the computer records the stylus location. In a cartographic laboratory, the analyst might be tracing the centerline of roads and waterways. In the drafting department of an architectural firm, the analyst might be digitizing the lines on a draftsman's drawings. The computer is later used to take these records (in which lines and bounded regions are stored in a vector format) and convert them to a raster array of pixels.

More and more systems are designed to record and manipulate their data directly as digital rasters. The satellites that produce the weather maps for newspapers and television broadcasts record their images this way, rather than as a film product. Many computer graphics systems work directly with raster data. Modern medical imaging systems, such as CAT and PET scanners, create digital rasters as their output. By providing data in a reasonably standard digital form, these systems are efficiently interfaced to digital image-processing hardware.

1.2.3 Human Vision and Color

Human vision is a flexible but somewhat limited tool. We are only aware of light in a narrow range of wavelengths. When the lighting is bright, we can discern many unique colors. We can adapt to different lighting levels, given a little time, and even see in black and white when there is not enough light intensity for our color sensors to operate. Most importantly, we can apply sophisticated "processing" to the output of our visual sensors, based on previous experiences, context, and training, to make extraordinarily complex judgements about what we are seeing.

Human vision is able to distinguish something more than a dozen different levels of gray, but thousands of different colors. Thus, when presenting complex information, the intelligent use of color can better communicate information than a black-and-white (or *monochromatic*) presentation.

To discuss black-and-white images, a simple vocabulary is required. Any location on an image can be described (in a digital image, as mentioned above, one would refer to a specific *pixel*) by its brightness. The overall brightness of an image can also be discussed, as well as the contrast of an image, which is a description of the diversity of brightness. When the pixels in an image are all of similar brightness, the image is said to have little contrast. One common way to present the characteristics of the range of brightness in an image is to plot a frequency *histogram* of intensity.

It is more difficult to describe color images. One system in common usage uses the amount of the primary colors red, green, and blue to describe the color of each pixel. This is the RGB or *additive primary* color system. A few examples of this RGB system for describing color are:

Red (%)	Green (%)	Blue (%)	Resulting Color
100	100	100	White
50	50	50	Gray
0	0	0	Black
100	0	0	Bright red
20	0	0	Dark red
100	50	50	Pink
100	100	0	Bright yellow

By mixing an appropriate amount of the red, green, and blue primary colors, we can create any possible color. This system is in frequent use in the computer graphics industry, because it corresponds directly to the red, green, and blue color guns in a color video display. By storing the red, green, and blue components in the computer and then sending these components to the red, green, and blue color guns in the monitor, we have complete and direct control over the image on the display.

Another system for describing color is based on models of human color perception. In this system, colors are described by their intensity, hue, and saturation (IHS). Intensity is the brightness of a pixel—white vs. gray—and can be thought of as turning the lights up and down. Hue is the dominant color—red vs. green. Saturation describes how pure a color is. For example, the difference between red and pink is the saturation, not the hue (red in both cases) nor the intensity (which could be changed by modifying the lighting, but one would still perceive pink).

There are some *de facto* standards in the format of digital images. In a moderate-quality system, the 8 bits in a byte are all used to describe a single pixel. In a black-and-white image, this would mean there are 256 unique gray levels for each pixel. One way of describing color in an 8-bit-per-pixel system would be to use a separate *color look-up table,* so that any arbitrary set of 256 colors could be displayed. For example, a color photograph could be analyzed for the 256 dominant different colors found in it, and the image could be represented by only these 256 different colors. Another way to describe 8-bit-per-pixel color would be to use 3 of the 8 bits for the red level, 3 of the 8 for the green, and the remaining 2 for the blue level. In this way, 256 unique colors are extracted in a reasonably uniform way from all possible colors.

The highest quality color systems use three 8-bit bytes for each pixel. These systems are sometimes referred to as 24-bit deep *true-color* systems. In such systems, each byte represents the value for one of the three primary colors. Thus, there are 256 levels each of red, green, and blue, or a total of 256 × 256 × 256 = 16.8 million unique colors. This is certainly more colors than one can distinguish and more than can be uniquely displayed on an image-processing system. However, such a system gives tremendous potential dynamic range and flexibility and has become a *de facto* standard in the industry for true color display.

2 SYSTEM COMPONENTS

Some of the hardware components in an image-processing system have counterparts in a conventional computer system. Figure 2 is a block diagram, which indicates the principal elements of an image-processing system and the associated host computer system.

2.1 The Host Computer

Image-processing systems are available for the largest and smallest computers. Internal board sets are available for many desktop microcomputers; external systems for large computers may be several dozen cubic feet in volume and weigh hundreds of pounds.

An image-processing system is dependent on the computer that controls it. This controlling computer is termed the *host.* Some systems have the "host" computer physically inside the image-processing enclosure. In this case, the host is considered *embedded* in the system. In either case, the host computer is responsible for communication between the user and the image-processing system, many kinds of numerical functions, and mass storage of both image data and commands. Due to the large volume of image data, 9-track digital tape units are common in image-processing systems.

2.2 Local Processing Units

In some image-processing systems, one or more auxiliary or local processors can be found inside the image processor. These dedicated processing units can provide extremely high performance on certain operations, as they have local high-speed access to video memory. Such components may also have array-processor capabilities, improving performance for certain kinds of operations dramatically.

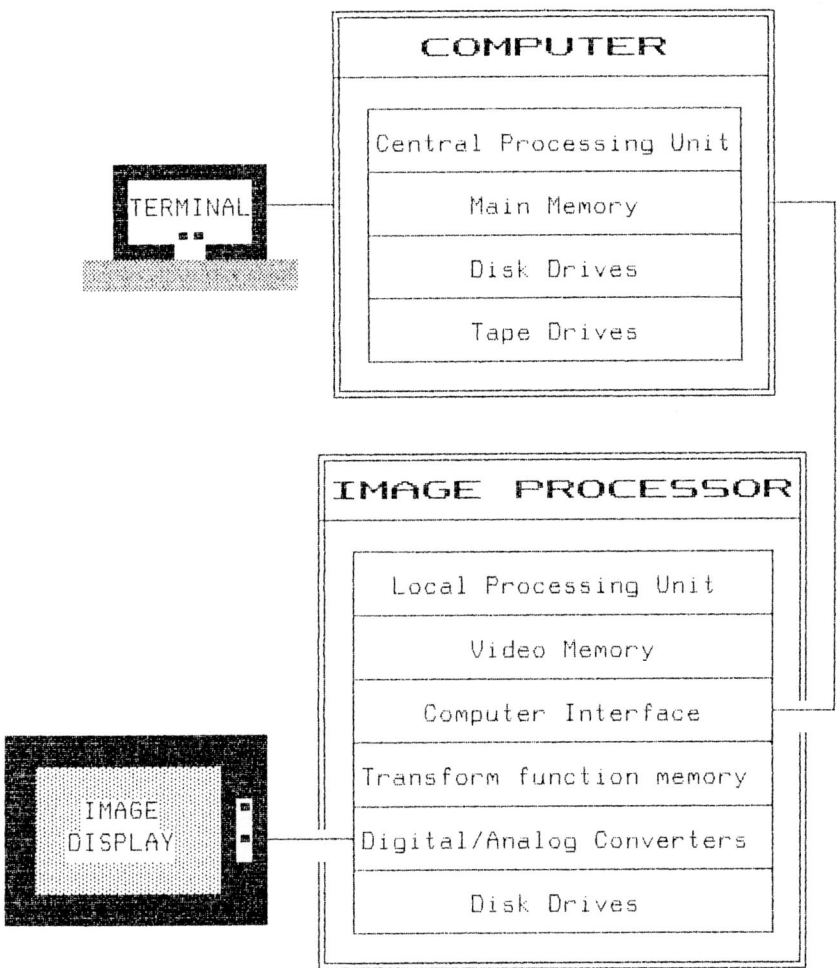

FIGURE 2 Diagram of the components in an image-processing system.

The instructions for the functions that these processors perform may often be stored in nonvolatile memory in the image processor itself or downloaded in part from the host. When a function can be performed in less than a few frame times of the video system (which is typically 1/30 of a second), the operation is considered *real time*. Of course, true real-time processing would require that the function be completed in less than one frame time.

Typical operations that are controlled by a local processor in an image-processing system include spatial filters, placing text and graphic annotation on the video display, and certain kinds of numeric functions applied to the contents of video memory.

2.3 Video Memory

Video memory in most image-processing systems is separate from the host computer's main memory. A high-performance parallel interface connects the host computer (often using direct memory access techniques) to video memory for the transfer of image data. In video memory, there is a direct correspondence between the contents of a particular memory element and the displayed value of a single pixel.

Consider the size requirements for video memory. In size, a 512-by-512 displayable 8-bit pixel video memory requires 512 × 512, or 256Kb. A top-quality 1024-by-1024 full-color system, using 1 byte each for red, green, and blue, plus 1 additional byte per pixel for graphic overlays, cursors, and annotation, would require 1024 × 1024 × 4 bytes, or 4MB, for a single image. To add to the memory requirements, often there will be storage for more than one complete image.

This memory must have sufficient speed to permit its data contents to be read in a single video frame time, plus additional data rate capability to permit access by both host and local processors. One way to minimize the conflict between host (and local processor) access versus video display requirements is to use *dual ported memory*, in which there are two independent data paths—one used exclusively for the video display components, and the other for data transfer to the host and local processors.

2.4 Function Memory

The output of video memory is normally directed through a set of *function memories*, which are also called transform function memories and look-up tables. The purpose of function memory is to store a table of values that converts the digital numbers in video memory to a different set of values. As will be seen, this is tremendously valuable.

Function memory is normally initialized with appropriate values so that data pass through the transformation unchanged. By changing elements of the function memory, intensities can be changed in the image rapidly, without reading and writing the entire image. In an 8-bit black-and-white display, a negative image could be converted easily to a positive image by changing the 256 entries of the function memory, rather than the 256Kb of image data in a 512-by-512 pixel display. In this case, if the value 0 is passed through the transformation in function memory, the output value will be 255; 1 will become 254, etc. By reversing the order of the data values with the function memory, a negative image (perhaps derived by scanning a photographic negative) changes to a positive. The same function memory contents would similarly convert a positive to a negative. The contents of the function memory are often depicted as a graph, showing the transformation between input data values (which are sometimes abbreviated DN, as mentioned above) and output data values.

One common use for function memory is to change a monochrome data set into a *pseudocolor display*. Consider a raster of 8-bit data, where we desire to convert any DN value to any arbitrary color. The function memory table would require 256 entries, one for each unique DN value. If the color display system uses 8 bits each for red, green, and blue, each entry in the function memory would require a total of 24 bits. Thus, the function memory provides the explicit translation between a brightness value in the original data set and the desired color rendition.

2.5 Digital-to-Analog Conversion

In most high-quality image-processing systems, the video displays are driven by an analog signal. This analog signal is created from the digital data

Image Processing 251

values in video and function memories by devices called digital-to-analog converters, or D/As.

In a monochrome system, a single D/A is all that is required. In a pseudocolor or true color system, where there is separate control for red, green, and blue levels, a separate D/A is used for each. The important parameters for a D/A are its speed (which indicates how many pixels can be addresses in a given time) and the number of bits of resolution that are available in the conversion process (which governs how many unique brightness levels can be reliably displayed).

2.6 Display

Home television receivers are a good starting point for a description of image-processing video displays. On a home television receiver, vertical resolution is several hundred lines. However, these lines are not displayed in sequence; all the odd-numbered lines are displayed in order, and the system then retraces the screen displaying all the even-numbered lines. This is called an *interlaced* display system and, in effect, requires two frame times to display all the information in an image.

Another characteristic of home video systems is that all of the color and brightness information is multiplexed in a single *composite* signal. In your home color television, this information is taken apart, to separate the red, green, and blue components for display.

The more sophisticated image-processing systems differ from this description in two important ways. First, they are generally noninterlaced displays, where every line in every frame is displayed in order. This provides a crisper, more flicker-free, display. Second, the red, green, and blue signals are not combined but sent through separate cables to the color guns in the display. This avoids the circuitry that puts the signal together into a composite signal, as well as that which takes it apart. Running the three color signals separately permits a greater range and purity of displayed colors.

If one sits close to a monochrome video display, one can see the individual dots of light that correspond to the pixels. In a color video display, one can see separate red, green, and blue dots (or bars on some displays). On a color display, each dot triple, composed of one dot (or bar) of each of the primary colors, is the pixel—the smallest region on the screen whose color can be controlled completely.

3 RESTORATION AND ENHANCEMENT

There are two general families of operations that are used to extract as much information as possible from the original digital image. Restoration involves removing abberations from the data. For example, a sensor's response to light might not be linear, or the optics in the system may have spectral and geometric distortions that must be removed when possible. Enhancement involves modifying the image data so that it communicates most effectively.

3.1 Radiometric Operations

Radiometric operations modify the brightness values in an image. These operations may be used both for restoring and enhancing the data in many different ways.

A frequent task is to change the contrast range in an image. Much as a photographer chooses different grades of paper, as well as the chemistry involved, to modify the contrast range in a photographic print, an image-processing system can be used to improve the presentation of image. *Linear contract stretching* is a simple precedure, where the brightest value in the image data is "stretched" (usually via the function memory) to white, and the darkest value is stretched to black. In this way, even if the original data cover only a small range of brightness values, the displayed image will use the entire dynamic range of the video display system and possibly make distinctions in the image more apparent. In a color system, the red, green, and blue bands would be stretched independently to attempt to use the widest possible range of displayed colors in a meaningful way.

Another popular contrast modification is based on the *histogram* of the image brightness values. A histogram is a graph that displays how often particular values (in this case, of brightness in an image) are found. Figure 3 is the histogram of the brightness levels in the image in Figure 1A.

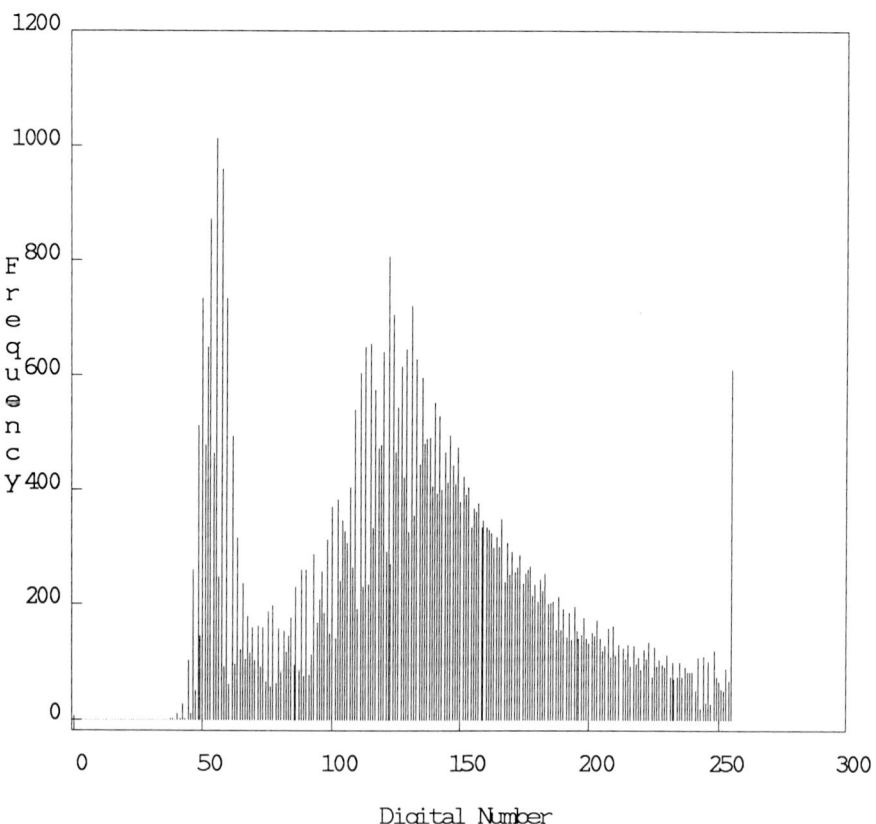

FIGURE 3 Histogram of brightness levels in the image in Figure 1A. The horizontal axis corresponds to the different DN values, and the vertical axis indicates how often a particular DN value is found in the image.

Image Processing

The histogram of many images shows that some portions of the brightness spectrum are much more common than others. In the case of Figure 3, there are two *modes* or peaks in the histogram, indicating that there are two levels of brightness that are found more commonly than others. A *histogram equalization* modifies the brightness values so that all brightness values in the displayed image are equally probable. This enhancement procedure is nonlinear and usually produces an image with more contrast than a simple linear contrast stretch. As before, in a color system, the histograms of the three color channels can be equalized independently.

There are many other radiometric operations as well. A number of these are based on *multichannel* imagery—image data where there are several information channels at once. These might arise from a multispectral sensor (ranging from the independent red/green/blue outputs of a professional television camera to an Earthward-looking multispectral sensor on a satellite), to a sequence of observations through time of the growth of a forest. In these cases, there are a variety of multiple-band operations in common use, including arithmetic operations such as band ratios and statistical procedures such as a principal components analysis. In every case, the purpose of these operations is to extract useful information from the raw data.

3.2 Geometric Operations

There are a number of kinds of geometric (or spatial) operators in common use in image processing. Some are involved in removing perturbations in the data set, which might be caused by viewing angle (i.e., the aerial photograph was not taken straight down, but from an angle), as well as distortion in the viewing optics (including typical concerns of photographers such as pincushion distortion and light intensity fall-off at the corners of the image). These are identical to those discussed in Section 4.

Other geometric operations are used specifically in the enhancement process, as will be illustrated through an example from the field of robotics. Consider the problem of providing a machine with a vision system, so that a bolt can be picked up from a box of parts, and inserted correctly into an appropriate component.

Figure 4 shows an image of a group of bolts, taken directly from a video digitizer and then histogram equalized as described above. Notice that the bolts have strong specular reflections of "hot spots" along their axes and fairly sharp boundaries at their edges. In Figure 5, a particular kind of geometric operator has been applied to the image to begin to extract useful information from the data set. The algorithm used is one kind of *texture transformation*, where for each pixel in the image, the standard deviation of the pixel values in the 3-by-3-pixel neighborhood is calculated. In this way, pixels in the middle of a homogeneous region will have very low neighborhood standard deviations (and thus, low texture according to this algorithm), pixels in neighborhoods where the brightness is slowly varying will have intermediate texture, and pixels near strong gradients will have very high texture.

Returning to Figure 5, the relatively low texture in the background and the very high texture at the edges of the bolts and the edges of the shadows and bright reflections can be distinguished easily. The next step in the sequence, Figure 6, shows the result of a boundary-finding operation applied to the texture image. In this image, an algorithm uses a binary (or yes/no) decision rule to decide where the boundaries are, based on (*a*)

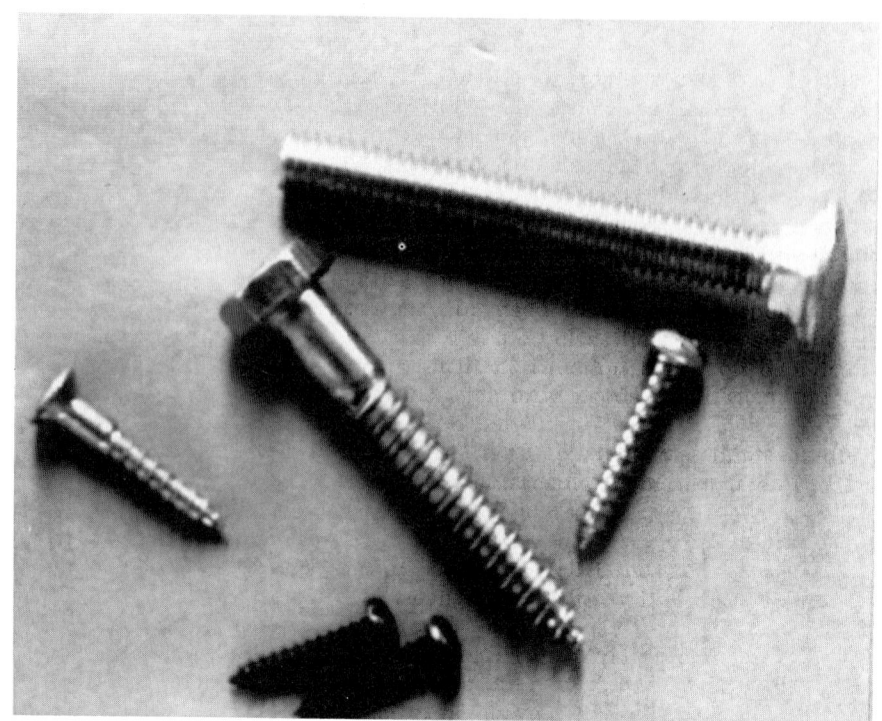

FIGURE 4 Video-scanned black-and-white image of bolts and screws.

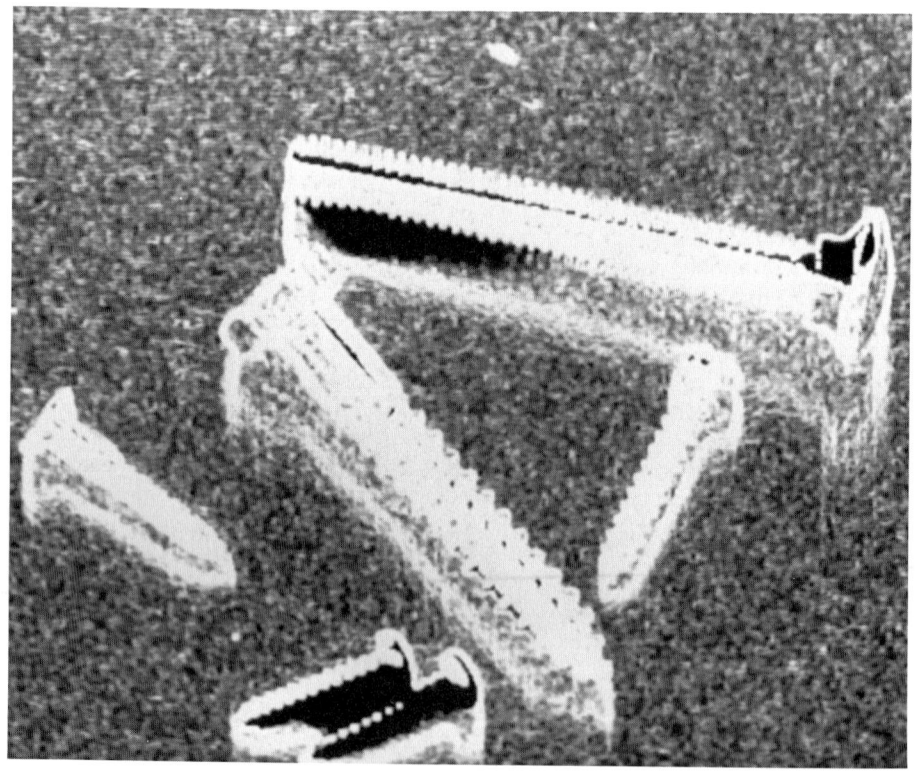

FIGURE 5 Texture enhancement of Figure 4.

Image Processing

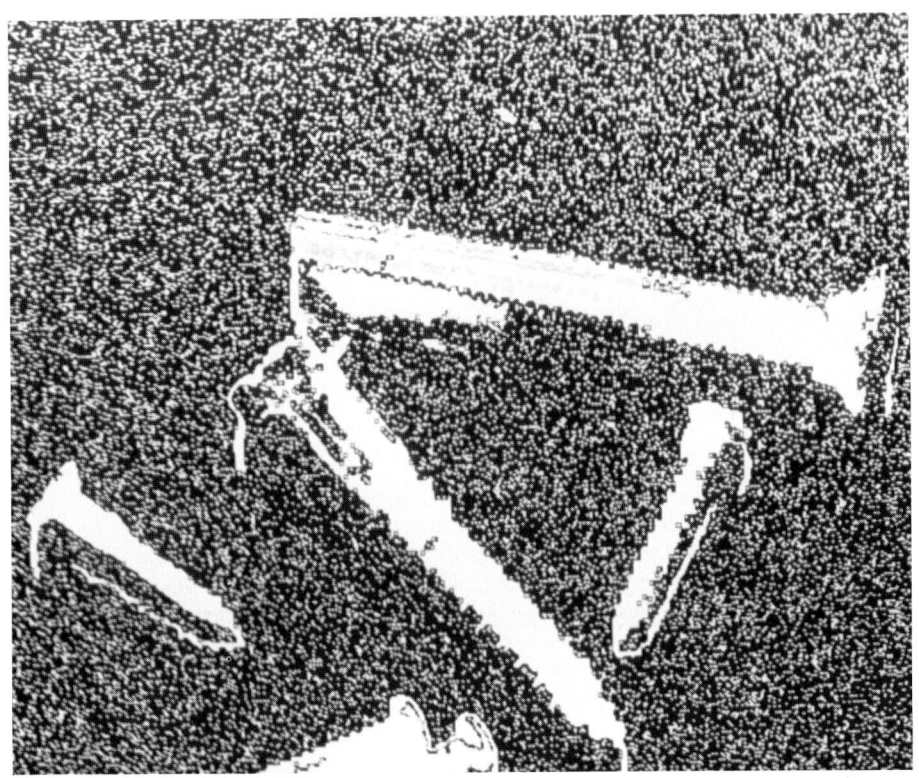

FIGURE 6 Edge enhancement of Figure 5.

high local texture, and (b) adjacency to other pixels of high texture. From this final image, it is relatively easy to identify the size of each of bolts, as well as the location of their principal axes and orientation. This is the kind of information that would be passed to the robot arm to pick up the correct bolt and insert it into an assembly.

4 RECTIFICATION

The processing functions called *rectification* (and a related set termed *registration*) are a special set of geometrical operations. Their purpose is to modify the geometric relationships in image data, without changing the contents of the actual data.

A few examples will make this family of functions clear. Consider an architectural drawing of a building elevation. A video camera and frame grabber, discussed in Section 1.2.2, are used to convert this drawing into a digital image. Unfortunately, there are some distortions in this image. The camera lens was not perfectly centered over the drawing, introducing assymetries of one kind. Further, the image plane in the sensor was not parallel to the plane of the drawing, introducing distortions of another kind. Finally, even if the camera and image had been perfectly aligned, there may be some systematic distortions within the image-forming components of the video camera. Rectification procedures are used in order to create a digital image with maximum geometric fidelity to the original data.

4.1 Exact Numerical Approach

There are situations where an exact numerical or algorithmic solution to the rectification problem exists. One common example of this is when the original image is a map of the earth, created in a particular coordinate system with a specified projection, and the desired output is another map, in another coordinate system and projection. Another example is in the field of photogrammetry, where detailed calibrations are available for the camera system. The exact numerical approaches are based on equations of three-dimensional geometry and are beyond the scope of this discussion.

4.2 Approximation Approach

More often, we do not have an exact solution to the problem of rectification. A common approach, based on statistical operations, is called a *ground control point rectification*. In this approach, specific locations on the image are compared to their "true" locations in the original data, and a statistical model is used to convert the image into a new one with the desired geometrical characteristics.

This procedure is often called a *rubber sheeting* operation, based on the following argument. Imagine taking a photograph of the ground out of the window of an airplane. This image will have many kinds of distortion, due to perspective problems, the curvature of the earth, the curvature of the glass in the window, etc. Imagine further that the film in the camera is made of a sheet of rubber, which can be stretched a great deal without tearing.

Next, place the rubber sheet over a "correct" map of the earth. Finally, identify a series of locations on the map that are easy to distinguish on the image and run pins through the location on the image, down to the corresponding locations on the map, stretching the image as required. The identified image points that have been attached to the map are the ground control points, or *tie points*.

The rectification process involves building a numerical coordinate transformation between the original image coordinates and the rectified coordinates. Frequently, these transformations are based on polynomials, whose coefficients are computed by regression on the coordinates. For example, pairs of coordinates might be used (image row, image column vs. longitude, latitude) for a dozen or more ground control points to compute

$$\text{Longitude} = a + b*row + c*column + d*row^2 + e*row*column + f*column^2$$

$$\text{Latitude} = g + h*row + i*column + j*row^2 + k*row*column + l*column^2$$

The coefficients could be generated from a statistical package and applied to the input (row, column) data to produce (longitude, latitude) data. Moik (1980), among others, goes through the details of the process.

Figure 7 demonstrates a rubber sheet procedure. The image in Figure 7A shows boundaries of forest species groupings in Canada and was generated for this article by purposely distorting the information presented in

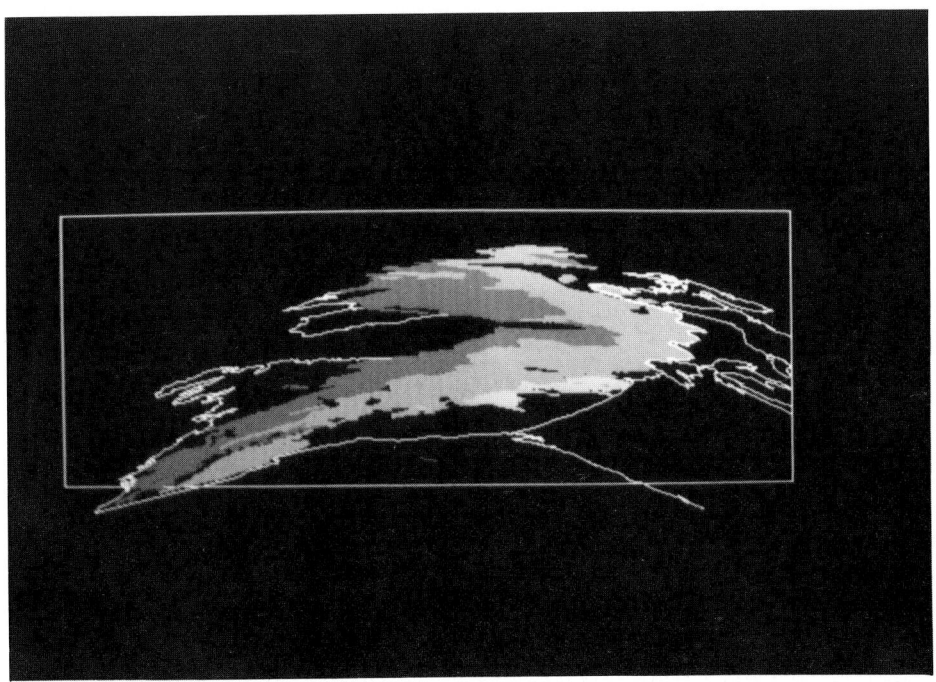

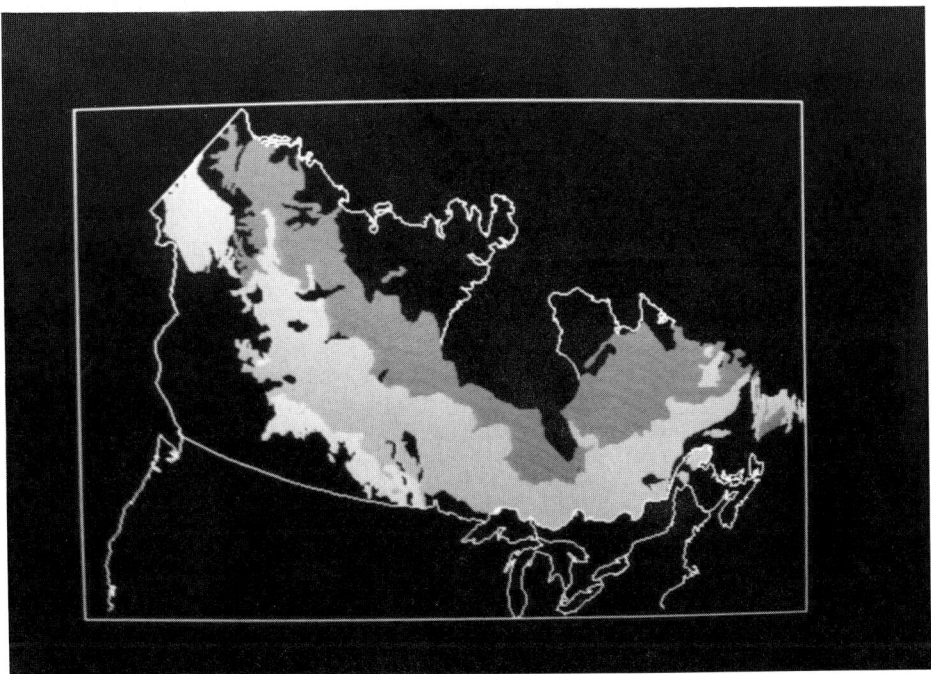

FIGURE 7 (A) Distorted view of northern North America, showing zones of vegetation in Canada, based on Rowe (1959); (B) after rectification.

Rowe (1959). The perspective of this view is most peculiar. It looks like we are in a spacecraft, orbiting over the North Pacific Ocean, looking roughly to the northeast. After the ground control point rectification, based on the latitude and longitude of a number of easy to recognize points (in this case, points on the borders of the Great Lakes, Hudson Bay, and the Canadian coastline), the view can be produced in Figure 7B, a more conventional view of the earth's surface.

5 CLASSIFICATION

Most original image data are continuous. Pixel values are in a natural and unbroken sequence, representing brightness of an original object, radar cross section, or reflectance of a drawing that has been scanned. Many uses of image-processing technology involve *classifying* this continuous data into a set of discrete categories. For example, the brightest areas in an image might be clouds, the next brightest might be bare rock, and the darkest areas might be coniferous vegetation.

Classification procedures for image data are often most effective on multichannel data. When scanning a drawing with a black-and-white system, it may not be possible to distinguish between black lines and red lines. With a color-scanning system, separating the reflected energy from the drawing into red, green, and blue components, black lines will be dark in all channels, and red lines will be dark in the green and blue channels but bright in the red. This is the same general principle behind aircraft and spacecraft multispectral sensors, which may have 200 or more distinct spectral wave bands.

5.1 Unsupervised Classification

Unsupervised classification is based on developing a phenomenological understanding of the (usually multivariate) distribution of data values. In a natural landscape, there are usually a number of distinct categories of differently colored objects. Coniferous trees, many crops, bare soil, wet soil, and water bodies (as well as the differently colored lines in a color drawing) may all have varied *spectral signatures*—different patterns of reflected energy among the available spectral bands. In unsupervised classification, statistical clustering procedures are used to try and discover a set of commonly occurring but distinct spectral signatures.

Each of the pixels in an image is assigned to a single signature class; mixes between classes are not permitted. In this way, the continuous image brightness or color information is converted to a discrete set of classes. After an unsupervised classification, the analysts msut decide which spectral classes correspond to the useful categories of objects in the image. Red lines on a map may be automatically distinguished from black; the analysts must then decide manually that the red lines are parts of the transportation network in the city, and the black lines are property boundaries.

Unsupervised classification can often successfully find boundaries between different objects in an image, particularly when the analysts have a detailed understanding of the image and goals of the task. However, in many cases, the assignment of classes to the different objects is difficult, due to differential illumination and many other effects. In coastal southern California, mustard grass provides a simple biological example that creates

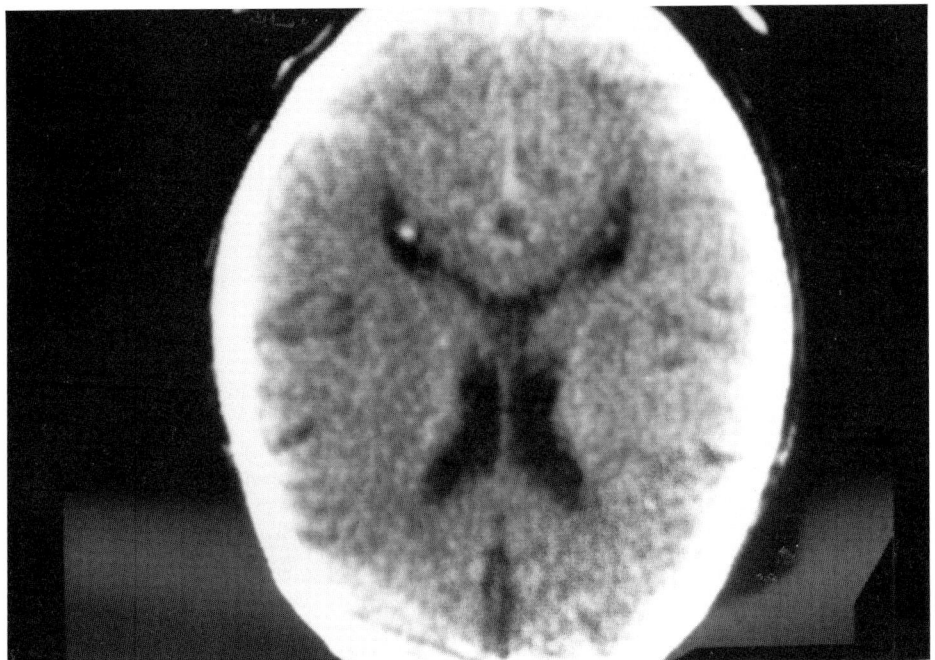

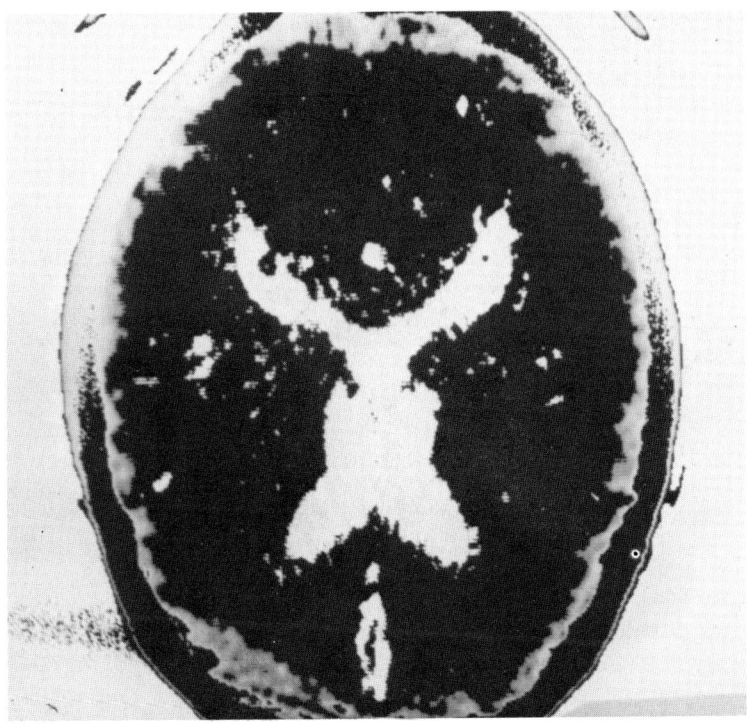

FIGURE 8 (A) CAT scan, showing the cross section of a head. (B) classified CAT scan, identifying the middle gray tones in the original image.

a complicated image-processing problem: On the south-facing sides of the hills, the mustard grass flowers and becomes bright yellow a week or more *before* it flowers on north-facing slopes. Thus, an unsupervised classification based on imagery from one date might find mustard grass on the south-facing slopes and incorrectly lump the mustard grass on the north-facing slopes with other green grasses.

5.2 Supervised Classification

In supervised classification, the analyst first identifies objects in the image that are of specific interest. In a color infrared aircraft photograph, an image analyst might identify a few deep red areas that are agricultural fields and a few blue areas that represent the central business district of the city. Using a joystick or trackball, the analyst indicates to the system where these *training fields* are located in the image. The software in the system then develops a statistical model of the pixels in the training fields and then proceeds to locate new areas in the image that seem to have similar characteristics. There are a number of different ways of building the statistical model of the pixel values in the training fields, as well as a number of different algorithms for assigning pixels to the different classes.

A simple example of supervised classification may be seen in Figure 8. In Figure 8A, we see a CAT scan—a synthesized cross section of the human head, based on the reconstruction of a series of X-ray measurements. This image was stored on a piece of film and video digitized into a 512-by-512 8-bit pixel data set in the image-processing system. A set of three training fields were selected from the image in the portions of the head that are displayed in middle gray tones. After a supervised classification procedure, the system displays a new image, which is seen in Figure 8B. In this resulting classified image, the system has marked all pixels whose DN values are close to those in the training fields by displaying them as black. By counting the number of pixels displayed in black and the total number of pixels in the head, we can develop statistics on the areal coverage of the different brightness regions in the CAT scan. The classified image also clearly presents the areal coverage of middle gray tones, which may be of use to the physician.

6 CONCLUSIONS

This article has provided an introduction to the language and tools of image processing. The accompanying references point to some of the details of the theory and applications of the field. At the college and graduate level, course work in image processing is becoming more prevalent, particularly as the costs of hardware continue to decrease. At the present time, university departments of electrical engineering, geography, and environmental sciences provide their own special insights into the field.

As the examples in this article have attempted to demonstrate, image-processing technology is at the crossroads of mathematics, engineering, computer science, photo interpretation, medical research, space science, and statistics. This creates a healthy, dynamic environment, with an ever-widening circle of applications.

ACKNOWLEDGEMENTS

I gratefully acknowledge the contributions of Professor Daniel Botkin, Mr. Larry Carver, Professor John E. Estes, Mr. Kenneth McGwire, Mr. Tad Reynales, and Dr. Diane Williams. National Aeronautics and Space Administration grant NAGW-455 provided partial support for this article.

BIBLIOGRAPHY

Ballard, D. H., and C. M. Brown, *Computer Vision*, Prentice-Hall, Englewood Cliffs, NJ, 1982.

Moik, J. G., *Digital Processing of Remotely Sensed Images*, National Aeronautics and Space Administration NASA SP;431, 1980.

Rowe, J. S., *Forest Regions of Canada*, Bulletin 123, Department of Northern Affairs and National Resources, Forestry Branch, Canada, 1959.

Tucker, C. J., and J. A. Gatlinm, "Monitoring Vegetation in the Nile Delta with NOAA-6 and NOAA-7 AVHRR Imagery," *Photogrammetric Engineering and Remote Sensing.* 50(1), 53–61 (1984).

JEFFREY L. STAR

INTEGRATED PROJECT SUPPORT ENVIRONMENTS

INTRODUCTION

During a project to develop a software and/or hardware system, the following types of engineering activities can be distinguished:

- The activities of *technical development* of the system (i.e., the software/hardware system). These activities include the definition of objectives and the problem statement, as well as the conceptual, operational, and auxiliary design, the testing of the system, and putting it into operation.
- The *project management* activities of planning, monitoring, and controlling the project.
- The *configuration control* activities for all the interim and final results during the development and, after delivery of the system, during maintenance, e.g., system requirements document, different versions of conceptual and operational design, and program code in a certain programming language.
- The *quality control* activities concerning all interim or final results mentioned above.

As indicated in Figure 1, these different types of activities are not independent of one another. Rather, there are strong mutual influences between them. As an example, Figure 2 shows the interrelation between two types of engineering activities, namely technical development and project management. The developing engineers report on current progress of their developing efforts, expenses, and trouble; they make suggestions, and they propose certain changes. The project managers, in turn, release work packages, give cost limitations, and adjust schedules and budgets.

Just as time lags and delays in a control loop can lead to poor behavior of the control variables or even to instability of the control system, the execution of a project also depends on whether the information between project management and dependent people flows accurately and without delay. Otherwise, "instabilities" concerning the success of the project involved may occur.

At present, few software/hardware development projects have the benefit of integrated support for all engineering activities. Indeed, most projects employ only a small number of loosely related tools concentrated around the programming activity. In some cases, tool systems are used to support several phases of the development process [1,2]. The support feature of another group of tool systems, the project planning and monitoring systems, has also reached a very potent and comfortable level.

The disadvantage of the use of separate tools for the different types of engineering activities results from the insufficient exchange of information between these tools. Therefore, efforts have been undertaken to build

Integrated Project Support Environments

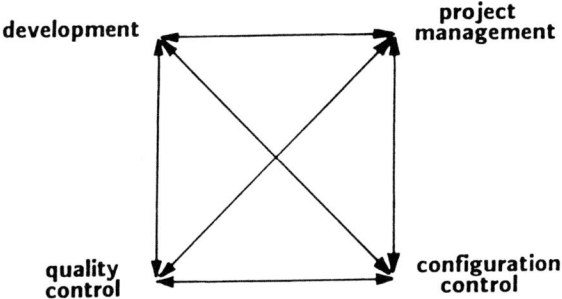

FIGURE 1. The four activity areas of a project and their mutual influences.

integrated project support environments [3,4] aiming at the following features:

1. Integrated computer support for the four types of engineering activities of a project shown in Figure 1, providing assistance for the information flow between the different types of activities (e.g., by tracing the consistency between the system requirements documents and the project work packages).
2. Consistent computer support for all phases of a project, from initial project planning and formulation of requirements, through technical conceptualization, software/hardware design, coding, and test, to system validation and continuing maintenance during operation.
3. Computer support for the teamwork that is essential between the members of a project team in order to make the project a success. This implies that the support system is suited to the various persons using it (e.g., engineers, managers, customers, etc.)

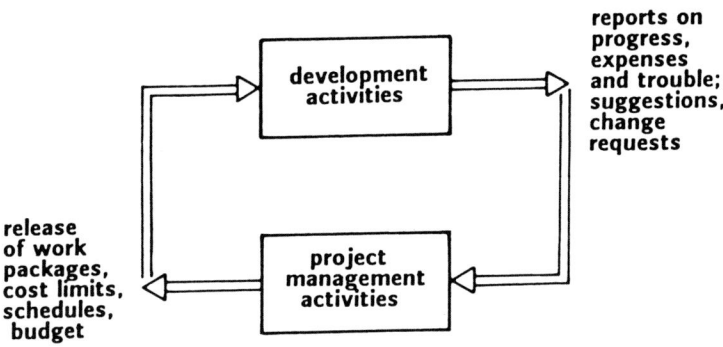

FIGURE 2. Closed loop interrelation between the engineering activities of technical development and project management.

Four necessary ingredients, each of a different nature (together called an "environment"), enable the computer to provide this support:

- A certain "view" of the different engineering activities and of their interrelation, which results in *models* representing this view.
- Ways of working based on these models, called *methods*.
- Notational means (textual or graphic *specification languages*) to express information during the engineering activities in a form that can be processed by a computer and yet can be understood easily by the project team members.
- *Software tools* evaluating the information described by the specification languages, thus enhancing the intellectual capabilities of the project team members and augmenting their power.

Figure 3 depicts these four parts that comprise an integrated project support environment.

2 MODELS AND PARADIGMS

As indicated in Figure 3, models are at the core of integrated project support environments. Therefore, the following sections discuss several types of models to be used.

2.1 Models to Describe the Engineering Activities during a Project

Figure 1 already describes a model by defining four types of activities and by assuming that there are interrelations between each of these activities. A slightly more detailed model is shown in Figure 4, where activities are represented by blocks, and information flow by arrows.

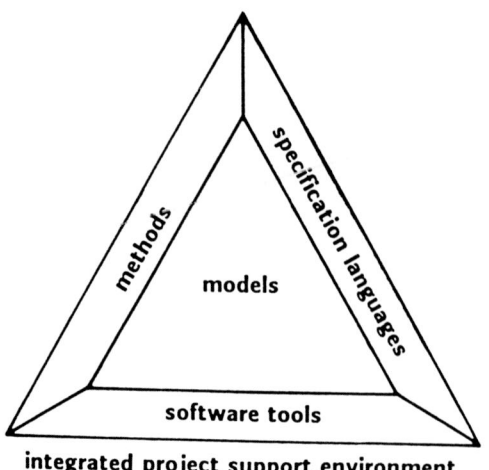

FIGURE 3. The four basic parts of an integrated project support environment.

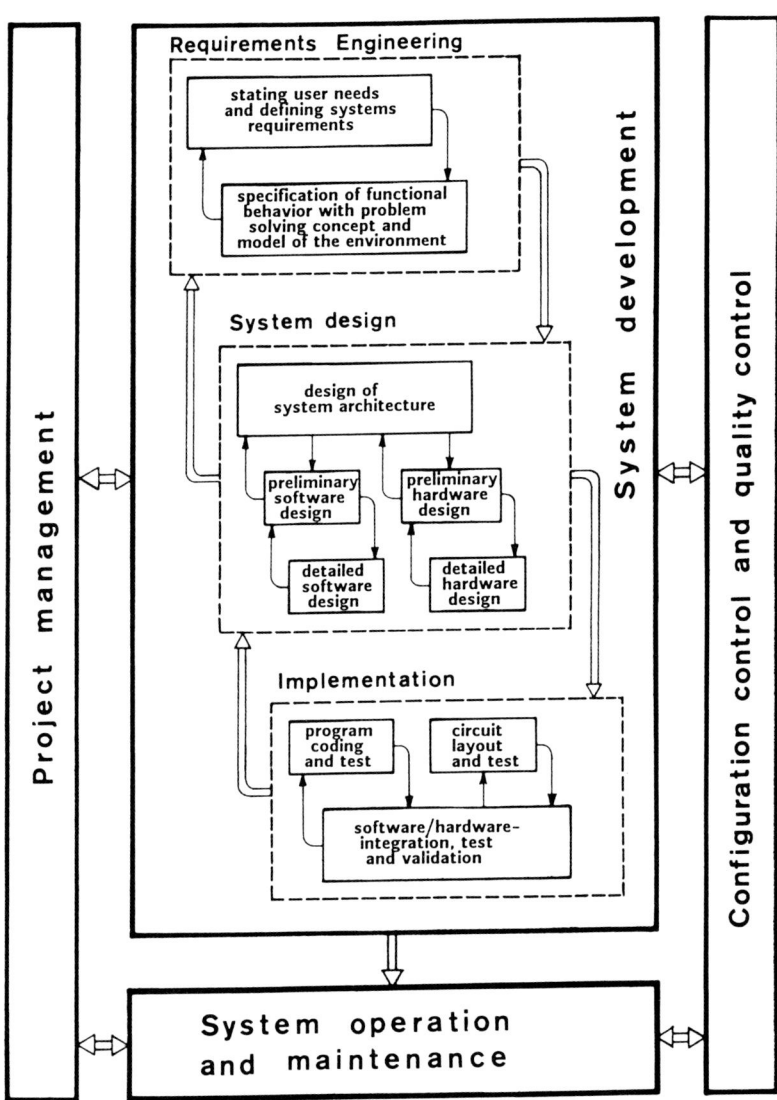

FIGURE 4. A model of the activities to be carried out during a project.

On the left side of Figure 4 are project management activities, and on the right side are the configuration and quality control activities (these two activities are combined into one block because they are dealing with the same intermediate or final results of the development). The middle part of Figure 4 contains the development process, which is further detailed into three types of developmental activities:

- Requirements engineering.
- Software/hardware system design.
- Implementation and test.

The arrows between these activities go up and down, which means that in a real project, the design activities move back and forth instead of keeping a straight top-down order [5].

The three types of developmental activities are further subdivided into subactivities in Figure 4.

Requirements engineering includes two subactivities:

- The problem statement for the system to be developed, with the definition of the user (person, customer, business) needs and the system requirements that must be met.
- The translation of the user needs into functions to be accomplished and the specification of both the functional behavior of the proposed system and the nonfunctional requirements. Usually, this implies the definition of a principal problem-solving concept and an understanding of the environment in which the software/hardware system will be used [6]. This understanding may be expressed as a model of environment (e.g., a mathematical model in the form of differential equations, an entity relationship model, a data flow model, etc.)

During system design, the specified functional behavior and the problem-solving concept are transformed into a software/hardware system. The nonfunctional requirements established within the requirements engineering activities have to be fulfilled during systems design. In Figure 4, the system design activity is subdivided into the following subactivities:

- Design of the system architecture, which contains system structuring by partitioning the total system into subsystems. At this point, it has to be determined which systems parts are to be realized in software and which in hardware.
- Preliminary software design, by defining software modules and their interfaces (and, in parallel, preliminary hardware design of those parts of the system architecture that should be realized by hardware).
- Detailed software design (and, in parallel, detailed hardware design).

The implementation activity starts by separately implementing the software and the hardware system parts. Therefore, it is subdivided into the following subactivities in Figure 4.

- Program coding and test of the software system parts (and, in parallel, implementing the hardware parts, layout, and test of the circuits).

Integrated Project Support Environments

- Integration of the software and hardware subsystems, test of the completed software/hardware system, and validation considering the system requirements.

2.2 Requirements Models

As mentioned above, the task of requirement specification has as its core the building of a requirements model (sometimes called a conceptual model), which describes in an abstract manner the environment in which the system to be developed should operate and the structural and behavioral aspects of this system. This description implicitly is based on a certain problem-solving philosophy.

Many different concepts are available to construct abstract requirements models. The best known are the following concepts:

- Dynamic system block with input, state, and output variables. Using this concept in control systems theory, the behavior of continuous output variables may be described by differential equations or (in the case of linear systems) by transfer functions. If the variables are defined only at discrete times, difference equations are used instead of differential equations, and the transfer functions are defined using the z transform (instead of the Laplace transform in continuous systems) [7]. Requirements models may be represented by networks, where different dynamic system blocks are connected via their input and output signals (block diagrams).
- Finite state machines. This concept may be used to model the behavior of the systems characterized by discrete states and transitions from one state to another at the occurrence of discrete events [8]. Requirements models may be represented by state transition diagrams (called Mealy diagrams).
- Petri nets, which may be regarded as an extension and generalization of state transition nets. The Petri net concept is suited to model the behavior of discrete event—type systems with parallel paths, especially the synchronization between these paths [9].
- Decision tables. A set of rules is used to describe the connection between input conditions and output operations.
- Entity relationship models. Using this approach, abstract entities are defined, as well as relationships between the entities [10]. The concept is well suited for building static requirements models for database systems, as well as describing static situations for information systems. It is not suited for representing time behavior.
- Structured analysis [11], which is based mainly on data flow models but uses entity relationship diagrams and state transition diagrams as well.
- Algebraic abstract data types [12]. Using this concept, domains of abstract operations are defined that manipulate abstract objects. This approach has the advantage of being strictly formal, which allows a verification of completeness and consistency of requirements.

However, we must realize that the primary purpose of a requirement specification is communication among people. In this respect, the choice of a strictly formal concept may cause problems.

A common property of all of the concepts just mentioned is that they only describe behavior based on a functional view (what the system to be developed should do). But these concepts fail to describe nonfunctional requirements, such as performance, reliability, and cost requirements. Also, many of these functional concepts assume that users possess wide-ranging knowledge about the environment in which these concepts are applied and that they use this knowledge to interpret the meaning of the requirements specification. This includes knowledge of terms, technical and scientific rules, everyday procedures and conventions, and the way various devices work, as well as common-sense knowledge [6].

Up to now, natural (English) language is used to describe the functional requirements, as well as the additional context, which is necessary to understand the functional concepts mentioned. In the future, knowledge-based representation languages may be introduced as a new means to build both functional and nonfunctional requirements models.

2.3 Design Models

To describe the activities concerned with software and/or hardware design, many different model concepts have been proposed [13]. Most of these model concepts are based on the assumption of certain types of objects, such as module, action, and data, and of interconnections between objects. A design model then consists of a network of interconnected objects (see the example in Fig. 5).

But instead of designing just one flat network of this kind, it is a generally accepted philosophy that designs should be expressible in a hierarchical manner [14]. Therefore, a design model may consist of different levels, each of them containing a network of interconnected objects.

Figure 6 shows a design model of this kind, which we call a design-level model. For the sake of readability at each level the decomposition of only one resulting system of the previous level is given (i.e., the entire hierarchy is not represented).

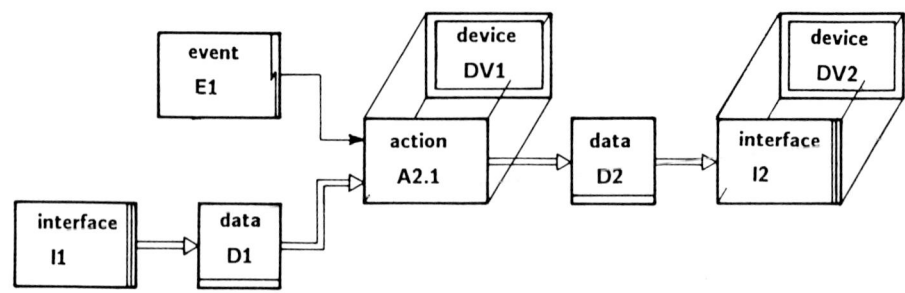

FIGURE 5. Example of a design model, consisting of a network of interconnected objects. (Different symbols are used to represent different types of objects. Single connection lines indicate control flow; double connection lines indicate data flow).

design level	engineering activity	graphical representation
-1	analysis of the level-(-1) system and definition of objectives for the level-1-system	level-(-1) system
0	analysis of the level-0-system, definition of the problem statement for the level-1 system and establishing the requirements model	level-0 system (technical plant, level-1 system)
1	design of the level-1 system and its decomposition into level-2 systems	level-1 systems
2	design of the level-2 systems and their decomposition into level-3 systems	level-2 systems
⋮	⋮	⋮
n-1	design of the level-(n-1) systems and their decomposition into level-n-systems	level-(n-1) systems
n	design of the level-n systems (terminal systems of the design process)	level-n systems

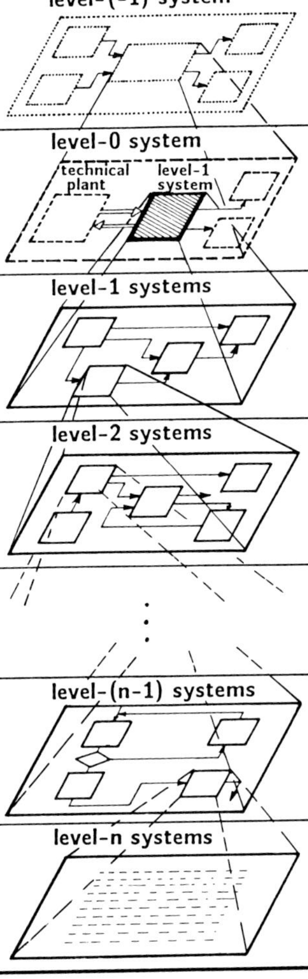

FIGURE 6. Design model, consisting of different levels. Instead of showing the hierarchy, at each level the decomposition of only one system of the previous level is shown.

Instead of using the names "total system", "subsystem", "sub-subsystem", etc., we call a partial system, which is defined at level i ($i = 1, 2, 3, \ldots, n$), a level-i system.

During the design process, a level-i system can result from refining a level-$(i-1)$ system (top-down development) or by integrating several level-$(i+1)$ systems to one level-i system (bottom-up development).

As Figure 6 shows, the definition of objectives and the problem statement can be included in the design level model by adding the design levels 0 and -1 above design level 1. The level-1 system (this is the total system to be developed) then fits into the design level structure as one of a number of subsystems of a "level-0 system" (a company or a factory are examples of level-0 systems). One of the subsystems of the level-0 system is, in the case of an automation system, the technical plant. Other subsystems could represent organizational factors.

In the same way, this level-0 system may be considered as a subsystem of a level-(-1) system; this system describes an environment of financial, sociological, ecological, or political systems on which the level-0 system is dependent. The objectives for the level-1 system to be developed usually result from this level. The problem statement, on the other hand, depends upon the relationship between the level-1 system and other subsystems of the level-0 system.

2.4 Management Models

Like the models of the design process, models of the management process (project management, product administration, and product assurance) can be based on certain types of objects and on interconnections between objects. Examples of "management objects" may be work packages, team members, change requests, etc. Management models then consist of networks of interconnected management objects. But, as is the case with design, in the case of management procedures (such as the planning of a project structure), a strategy of hierarchical decomposition is useful. Therefore, management models may consist of different levels, each consisting of interconnected management objects. Figure 6 could therefore be used as an analogy to represent a hierarchical management model, if only the blocks (which are shown in Fig. 6) are interpreted as management objects instead of design objects [3].

2.5 Software Paradigms

In the previous sections, models of project activities were discussed, because these models are the basis on which methods, specification means, and software tools for integrated project support environments are built.

In recent years, the term *paradigm* was introduced to denote a model of the basic approach that is fundamental when people produce and maintain software [15].

The current software paradigm (see Fig. 7) may be described by the following characteristics:

- Engineering activity is concentrated on coding, using a certain programming language, and on optimizing, testing, validating, and maintaining program code.

Integrated Project Support Environments

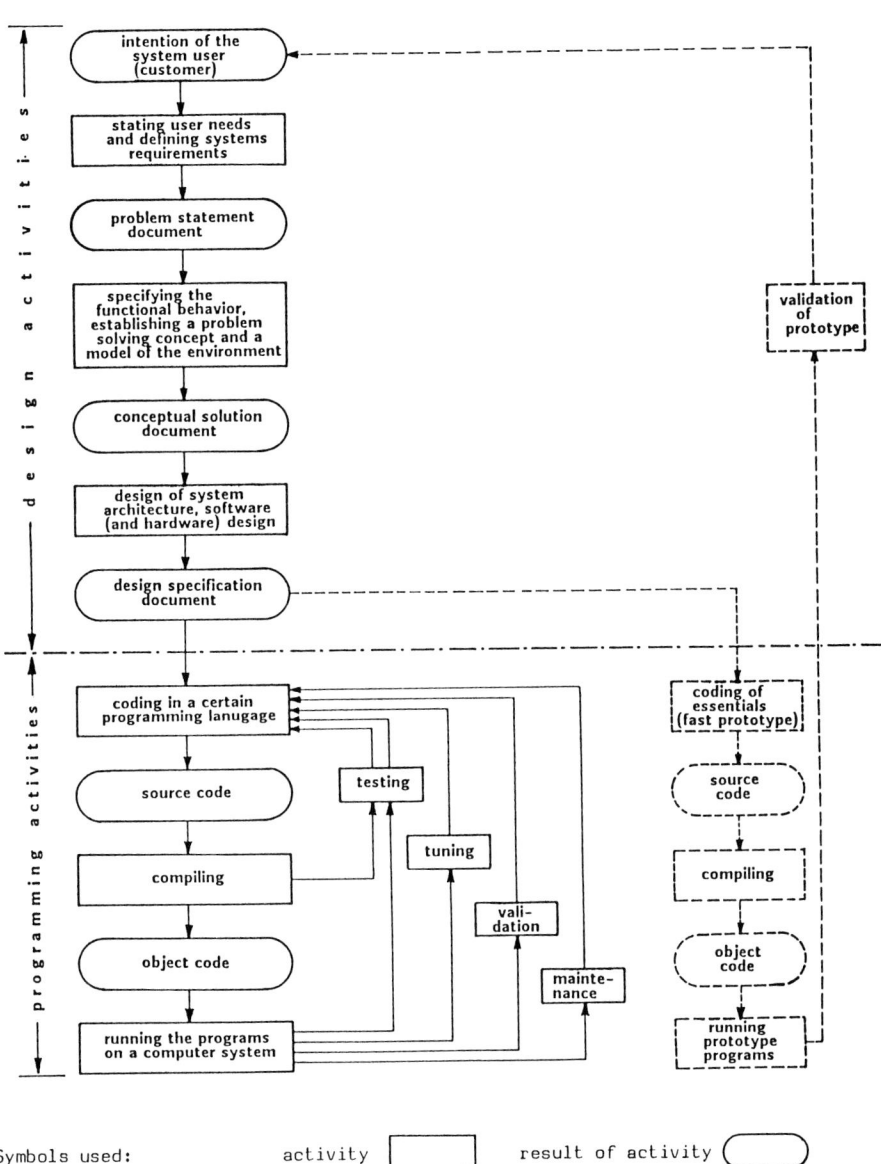

FIGURE 7. The current software paradigm (model of the basic approach taken to produce and maintain software).

- There is little or no computer support for the requirements engineering and the design process. Design specifications (if they exist) are informal.
- If fast prototyping is used to receive early feedback of the essential behavior of the software (see the dashed part in Fig. 7), the prototype program is created manually (often by using a special programming language, e.g., PROLOG), and it is discarded later on, when the real program code becomes available.

Instead of this programming-oriented paradigm, a new design-oriented paradigm was proposed [15]. This new paradigm is aimed at an automation-based approach, using formal specification means and software tools of support environments to achieve an order-of-magnitude improvement in software productivity.

As shown in Figure 8, the new paradigm may be characterized by the new characteristics:

- Engineering activity is concentrated on the development activities of requirements engineering (problem statement and conceptual solution) and of software (and hardware) design, using formal specification languages. Programming code is generated automatically. Maintenance is performed on the design specification rather than on the program code.
- There is massive computer support during requirements engineering and design, providing analysis reports on specification and design errors, as well as on the compliance of the design with the requirements, and automatically producing complete and consistently up-to-date documentation.
- Fast prototyping is substituted by animating the concept and design specification. Therefore, an early validation of the design and its compliance with the intent of the customer is a standard procedure.

Because Figure 8 stresses only the developmental aspects of a project, the managerial activities are not shown. But it is clear that the new paradigm of development must accompany a new paradigm of integrating the support of developmental and managerial activities by using an integrated project support environment.

3 CURRENT STATE OF THE ART IN THE FIELD OF INTEGRATED PROJECT SUPPORT ENVIRONMENTS

Because of the obvious and dramatic potential benefits of integrated project support environments on the reliability and cost of producing software/hardware systems, there is considerable research and development activity in universities and in the software industry. Research groups such as the MCC (Microelectronics and Computer Technology Corporation, Austin, Texas) and the federally funded Software Engineering Institute in the United States are aimed at developing future integrated support systems [16]. In Europe, the ESPRIT project (which is a large research program financed by the European Community in Brussels) is funding a number of projects in which major European corporations and universities are co-

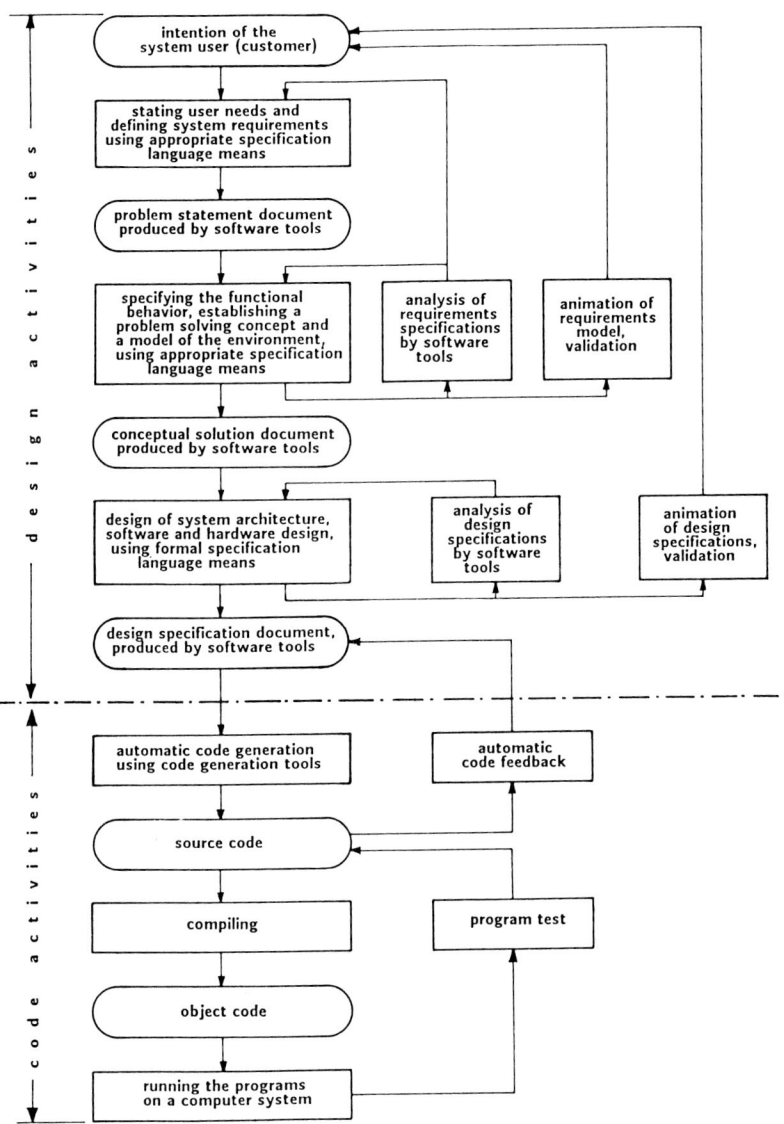

FIGURE 8. The new design and computer support—oriented software paradigm which can be realized by using an integrated project support environment.

operating in an effort to develop integrated project support environments. Similar efforts are under way in several countries, as, e.g., in Great Britain with its government-funded ALVEY program.

The present situation is characterized by many such ongoing research projects that promise results in the next 2 or 3 years. Only a small number of integrated project support environment projects are already commercially available, e.g., TAGS in the United States [17], ISTAR in Great Britain [18], and EPOS in the United States and in Germany [19].

The historical development in the area of computer support for the production of software is depicted in Figure 9. As a first step, program development systems (also called program development environments) were supplied by computer manufacturers together with their computer systems. They provide only those facilities that are essential to implement software in some chosen programming language. Thus, they would typically offer facilities for editing, compiling, linking, and debugging.

Recognizing that actual implementation in some chosen programming language is only one small part of the complete process of developing a software/hardware system, the next step was the provision of development support systems (also called software engineering or software support environments). They aimed at providing facilities to support all development activities throughout the complete life cycle, from requirements definition and initial concept formulation right through operational use and into subsequent maintenance and evolution during the operational life of the software/hardware system [2]. In some cases, this system life cycle can last for 10 years or more.

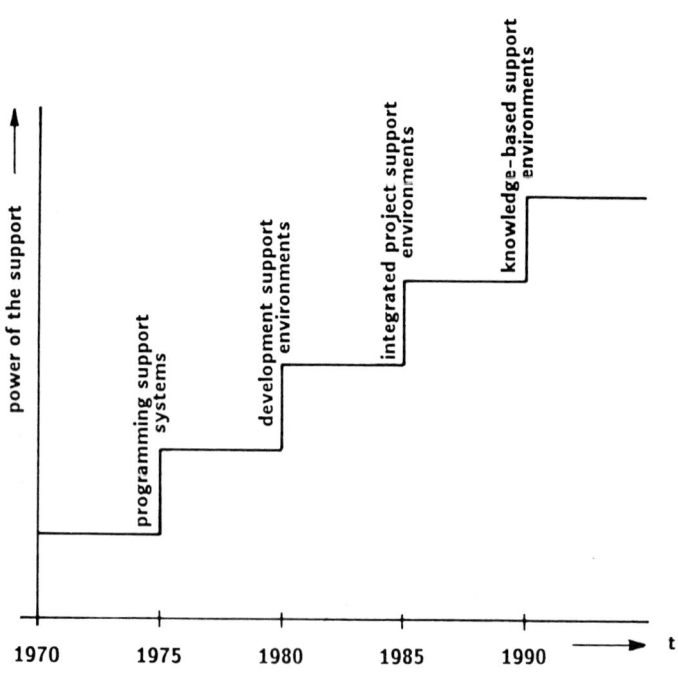

FIGURE 9. Steps of increasing power of computer support.

Because of the close relations between developmental and managerial activities (and considering the fact that good project management is one of the essentials for a successful project), the next step was to provide support to all project staff, not just to development staff. Integrated project support environments were conceived providing facilities for project management, version control and configuration management, quality assurance, document preparation, etc. Though software was the main concern, there were also efforts to provide facilities for complete system development. Thus, one would expect to see support for total system design methods, with smooth transition into individual design methods for the hardware and software elements.

The last step in Figure 9 (a development that already started but is not yet commercially available) is the additional provision of knowledge-based methods and the integration with computer-aided design systems. In Figure 10, the structure of a future support environment is indicated, containing a knowledge-based "project advisor," which provides advice in choosing the development methods and in their application, as well as in finding results of previously performed projects (concepts, cost estimates, software or hardware designs, code), which might be used or at least adapted to the project at hand [20].

It must be pointed out that Figure 9 gives an oversimplified impression of the current state of the art. In reality, this state is a fast-moving target. Table 1 is an overview of support environments that are assumed to fall into the category of integrated project support environments. The table reveals that:

- There are very few environments in wide use. Broad practical application of most of the environments has just begun or will begin in the future.
- Almost all of the environments are intended to support software projects only. The need to support total system projects has been recognized only recently.

4. EXAMPLE OF AN INTEGRATED PROJECT SUPPORT ENVIRONMENT: THE EPOS SYSTEM

4.1 General Overview

The integrated project support environment called EPOS (Engineering and Project management—Oriented Support) System has been under development at the University of Stuttgart, West Germany, since 1975. A group of about 10 computer scientists are still there working on continuing, research-oriented development and expansion of EPOS, with constant reference to user experiences.

Since 1980, the software house GPP, located near Munich, has been responsible for transforming EPOS from a university development project into an industrial product and for implementing the EPOS System on various target computers (such as DEC VAX on the operating system VMS, IBM PC-AT on MS-DOS, IBM mainframe on MVS/TSO and VM/CMS, and Intel 80286 on iRMX). The EPOS System has been marketed throughout Europe by GPP and in the United States by SPS Software Products and Services, Inc., in New York. Since 1980, EPOS systems have been installed for a

TABLE 1. Overview of Integrated Project Support Environments

Name of Integrated Project Support Environment	Reference	Date of Commercial Availability	Estimated Number of Installations (by end of 1986)	Support for	
				Software Projects Only	Total System Projects
ASPECT	4	1988	—	X	
ECLIPSE	4	1988	—	X	
EPOS	19	1980	200		X
ISTAR	18	1986	—		X
LEONARDO	16	1987	—		X
PERSPECTIVE	21	1983	50	X	
PRADOS	22	1984	30	X	
PROMOD	23	1983	100	X	
PSL/PSA	1	1977	200		X
SOFTOOL	24	1983	200	X	
TAGS	17	1984	100		X

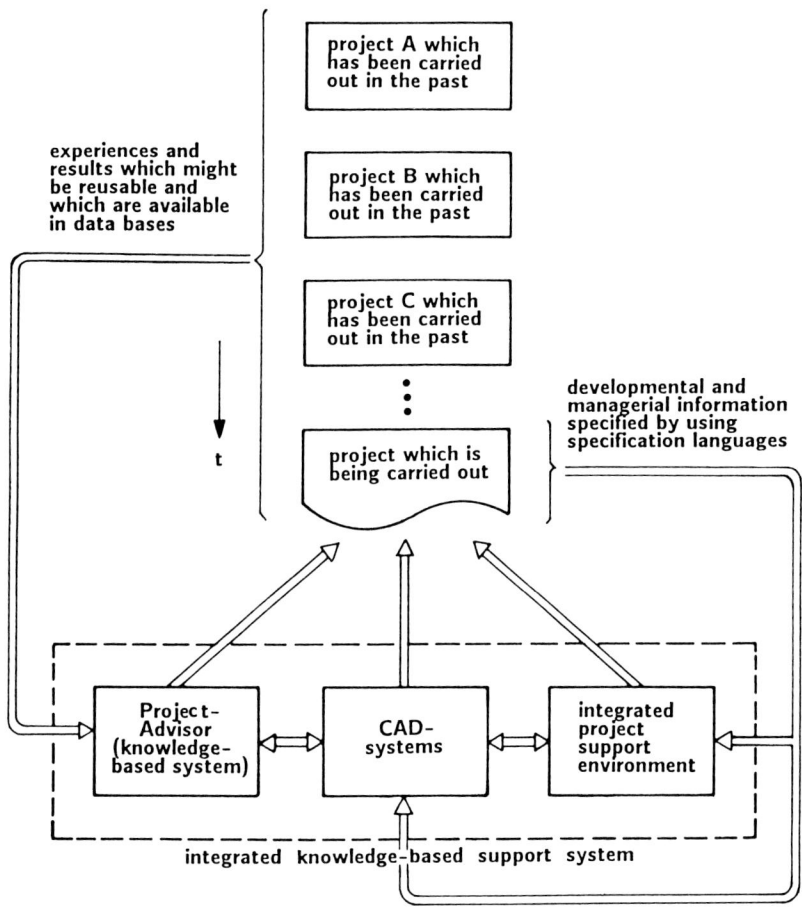

FIGURE 10. Integrated knowledge-based computer support system of the future.

growing number of users in industry, governmental agencies, research institutes, and universities. By mid-1986, more than 200 installations had been delivered worldwide.

Examples of application areas in which EPOS has been used to date are:

- Avionics and aircraft control and navigation systems.
- Motor vehicle systems.
- Local traffic control systems.
- Machine-tooling systems.
- Rescue service systems.
- X-ray-dosimeters.
- Commercial software for financial/banking houses.

To permit information exchange between EPOS users and to allow user experiences to be incorporated for further development, an EPOS User Group has been formed and holds annual meetings. In addition, the quarterly *EPOS-Info* journal gives users current reports on new EPOS applications and on the status of newly developed features.

4.2 Components of the EPOS System

The EPOS System consists of the following components (shown in Fig. 11):

- A *database* in which all project-relevant information is entered. In large projects, different members of the project team may work on a network of local EPOS workstation computers with local databases. There are mechanisms to assure consistency between these different databases.
- Three *specification languages* for different aspects of a project. The specification language EPOS-R is used to define requirements and to describe conceptual modeling during requirements engineering. The specification language EPOS-S is used to describe systems architecture, as well as software and hardware design. The specification language EPOS-P is used to describe structures and information related to project management, configuration management, and product assurance. With these specification languages, interrelated requirements, and design and management models are formulated and entered into the database after appropriate syntax checks.
- *Packages of software tools* that evaluate the contents of the data base, keeping track of data representations and transformations, documenting various aspects in a variety of textual and graphic forms, running analyses to detect specification and design errors in early phases, assisting in applying various design methods, and automatically generating code for selected programming languages.
- A *user interface program package* (not shown in Fig. 11) is provided for simplifying communication between the user and the EPOS system.

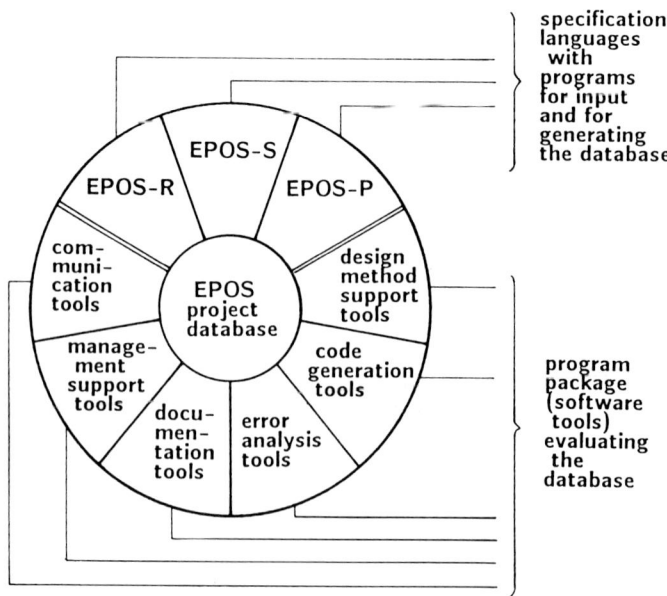

FIGURE 11. The components of the integrated project support environment EPOS.

Integrated Project Support Environments 279

The EPOS specification languages and tool systems are based on the models described above in Section 2, thus allowing us to use the design-oriented and automation-based software development paradigm shown in Figure 8.

Instead of a detailed explanation of the support features for the developmental activities (which may be found in Ref. *19*), only some examples of support for the interrelations between developmental and managerial tasks will be discussed here.

4.3 Examples of Features Providing Support for Interconnections between Developmental and Managerial Activities

Even in the very beginning of a project, there is an intertwining of technical and managerial activities. Figure 12 shows, in a simplified way, the tasks to be accomplished in project planning after the systems requirement document has been agreed upon:

- The definition of subprojects and work packages as the basis for a work breakdown structure of the project, in order to make cost estimates and plan resources.
- The planning of the project organization, i.e., the team members, departments, companies, etc., involved in the project.
- The assignment of work packages to the project team members.
- The estimation of time schedules and cash flow with the use of PERT charts.

As was shown in Figure 11, the specification language EPOS-R is used to describe the system requirements, whereas the formal specification language EPOS-P provides different types of management objects (see Table 2) for the description of project planning and control. Figure 13 shows an example of a description of a management object of type ACTIVITY. With this management object, the structure and the components of the work breakdown structure (work packages, subprojects, etc.) and of the PERT chart can be specified in detail.

It was pointed out that the technical data described using the specification language EPOS-R and the project management data described using EPOS-P are entered in a common database. The documents indicated in Figure 12 (systems requirements document, work breakdown structure chart, project organization chart, responsibility matrix, and PERT chart) have been plotted automatically by the EPOS tool systems evaluating this common database.

There are two different means available for the assessment of the project status. On the one hand, there are management objects of type PROGRESS REPORT, which may be evaluated to keep track of:

- Finished project phases.
- Milestones reached.
- Approved activities.
- Changes of the status of an activity (e.g., from the status "planned" to the status "work authorized").

On the other hand, the real development progress can be made visible by generating so-called progress charts, using the EPOS management support tools.

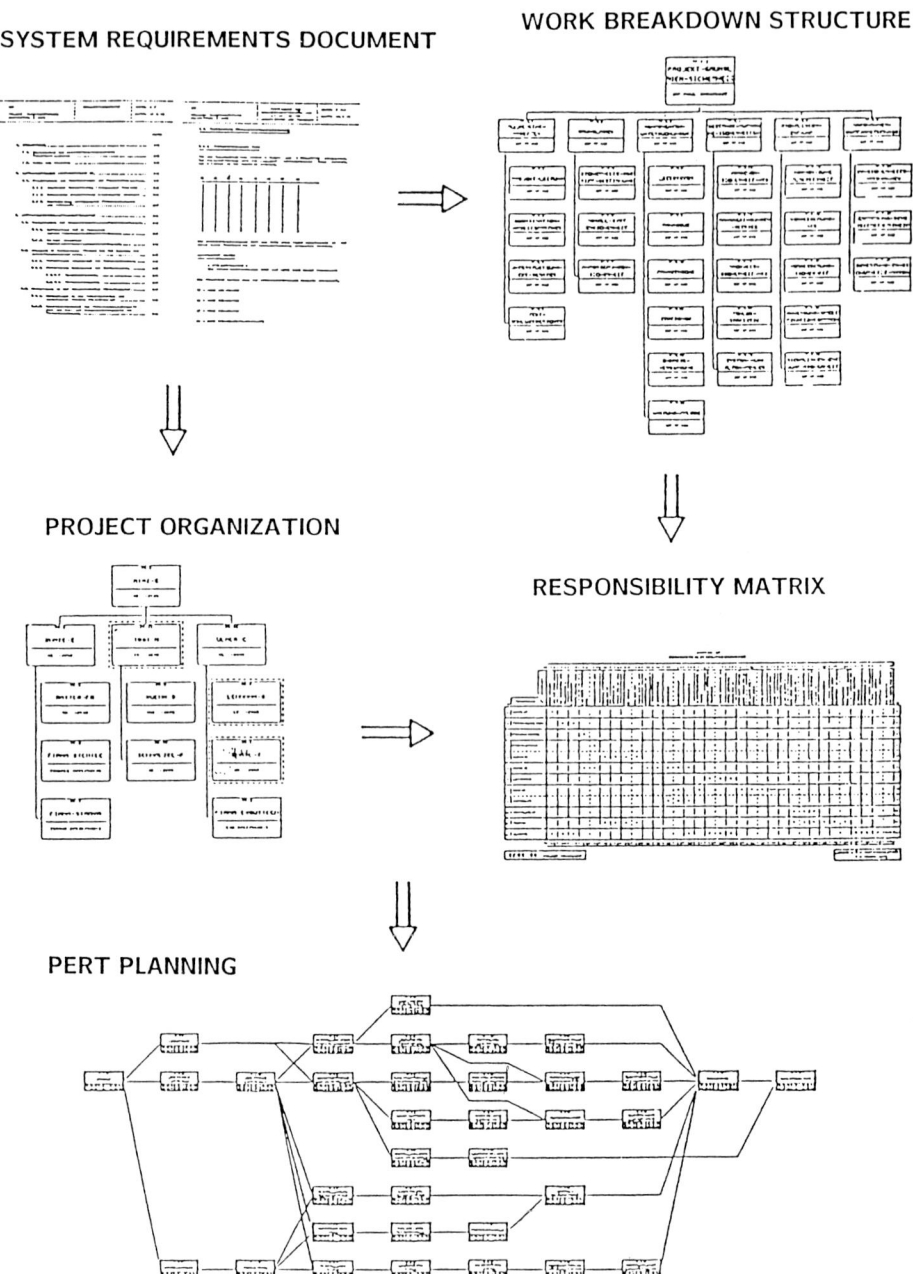

FIGURE 12. Simplified description of the intertwining of technical and managerial activities during project planning (the results of these activities are visualized by showing their rough structure only).

TABLE 2. Overview of the EPOS-P Management Object Types.

Management Object Type	Information Described
ACTIVITY	Work breakdown structure PERT planning
TEAMMEMBER	Project organization structure functions and responsibilities
RESOURCE-UNIT	Project resources and accompanying costs
PROGRESS-REPORT	Reports on progress, trouble, status changes, etc.
CHANGE-PROPOSAL	Change proposals and change evaluations
ERROR-REPORT	Reports on errors

```
ACTIVITY WP CONCEPT-DEFINITION

CATEGORY: 'review', 'concept', 'report' .

IDENTIFICATION: 'K-DB WP 122'

PROBLEM: "The general possibilities of relational data base
         structures have to be analyzed in detail in the context
         of the specific requirements stated".

DETAILS: "Especially the possibilities of system expansion and
         inclusion of additional access layers should be considered"

CONSIDERS: DOCUMENT: 'Internal report REL-DB 23/85':
           SECTION P2.2, P2.3, P2.5;
           REQUIREMENT 220(0), 224(0).

TECHNICAL-FRAMEWORK:

CONCEPT: 3 - 4 SECTIONS "Data structures, data base language,
                        administration concepts"

MANAGERIAL-FRAMEWORK:

PHASE: CONCEPT

FINISH: MILESTONE CONCEPT-DEFINED <'Top'>

DURATION: 6 WEEKS

PREDECESSORS: PRECISE-TASK-DESCRIPTION

ACTIVITYEND
```

FIGURE 13. Example of an EPOS-P management object of type ACTIVITY.

A progress chart (an example is shown in Fig. 14) is a hierarchy diagram, showing EPOS-S design objects together with a graphic indication of their state of completion. The boxes enclosed by solid lines represent design objects that were already specified before the reference date (in Fig. 14, before December 2, 1985).

Design objects entered in the database after this reference date are drawn with dotted lines, highlighting the new results. Objects that are boxed at the corners have only been referenced by name without specifying any detail. This indicates that further design work is to be carried out.

The letter "C" in the upper right corner of a box indicates that a code section has been associated with the design object, an indication of completion of the design at this point.

From the progress chart, the project manager can see which parts of the design are completed, which parts are still being worked on, and which parts still need to be designed. The tool system thus provides information on the real state of the design independent of the statements of the designers about their estimate on the percentage of completion.

4.4 Experiences Reported from Projects in Industry

An evaluation of experiences reported by EPOS users (e.g., see Refs. 25 and 26) reveals shortcomings as well as major cost savings. Shortcomings were mostly in the area of the user interface and in the poor rebustness of the early EPOS versions. The main advantages reported on were:

- The systematic and structured guidance through the whole life cycle, as well as the extensive computer support in early phases of a project, in automatic documentation, and in support for all team members led to increased productivity. But it was also mentioned that the computer support documentation generated and updated concurrently with the design phases means additional specification work in the early project phases.
- The quality of the software developed using the EPOS system was improved considerably. The high quality is a result of the structured approach and method support and also of the assistance in detecting errors already in the design stage and in the avoidance of errors by means of automatic code generation.
- Due to the integrated support for development and project management, even large, complex, multi-company projects could be kept under control.

5. PROBLEM AREAS AND FUTURE DIRECTIONS

The answer to problems in projects that encompass the development of computer software and hardware systems is to use the computer itself to solve them. Many of the difficulties that plague such projects today, e.g., high cost, late delivery, non-responsiveness to user requirements, poor maintainability and incompleteness and inconsistency of documentation, may be alleviated eventually by computer-aided engineering with integrated project support environments. But there are a number of problem areas that must be overcome to reach this goal:

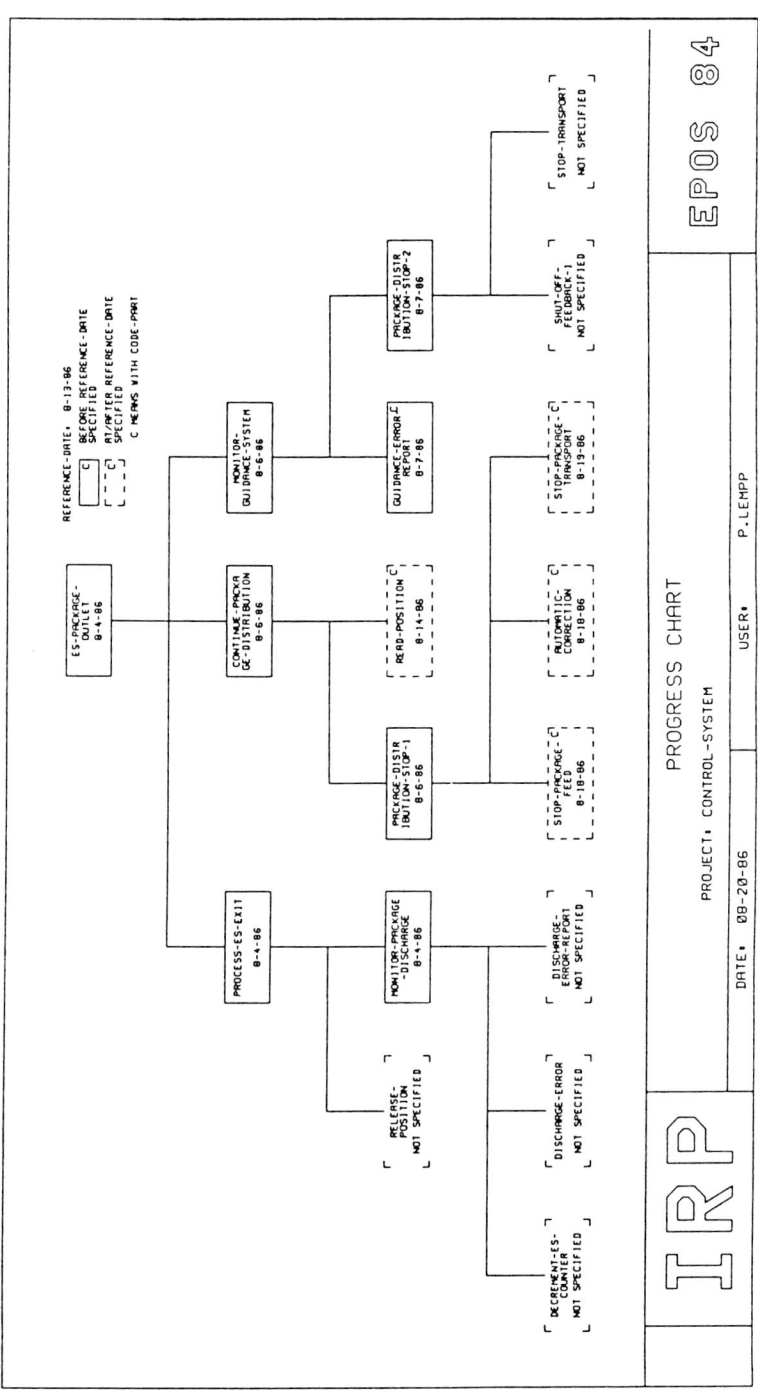

FIGURE 14. Progress chart automatically generated by the EPOS tool system providing a visual impression of the real state of the design work.

- Technical development (especially software development) and project management are still in different engineering worlds. More research is necessary on the close interrelations between these worlds (recognizing that it is really one project world with the different aspects of technical and managerial tasks).
- The approach to be taken depends critically on the size of projects in question. The techniques appropriate for a team of one or two people working for a few months are totally different from those appropriate for a team of 30 or 100 people working for 3 to 5 years. Integrated project support should be adaptable to the size of the project.
- Because of the high investment and the length of time necessary to develop an integrated project support environment (at least 100 man-years over a time span of 5 years), there is often a temptation to build a support environment around software tools that are already available, but do not fit together. Use of this approach may lead to a small short-term payoff but hardly to long-term success.
- There are two (sometimes conflicting) goals to be met by an integrated project support environment. On the one hand, it should be based on a certain paradigm (see Section 2.5 above) and on a certain philosophy of how to carry out a project. On the other hand, it should be open to new tools and new methods.
- Integrated project support must include support for the reuse of existing components, as this is certainly a most effective aid to productivity. Effective reuse, however, is hard to achieve, mainly because there is not much attention given to the aspect of reusability during development; thus, existing components may be only similar to those required. The problems of recognizing this similarity and of estimating the effort of adapting existing components still must be solved.

There are different future directions that can be taken to solve the problems. One of the most promising is the use of knowledge-based techniques (e.g., to tackle the problems of reusability). Another is the transition from the text-based approach, which has been used in most of the existing support environments and which has been inherited from the programming languages, to a new graphic-based approach. By using graphic notations for the dialogue between the members of a project team themselves and between engineers and support systems, the acceptance of these systems can be greatly improved. This, in turn, would provide a dramatic increase in productivity.

6. CONCLUSIONS

Though many separate software tools have been developed to assist engineers in performing technical tasks and managers in planning and controlling projects, there are very few integrated support systems available that take into account the close interrelations between technical and managerial activities. But the need for such integrated support has been widely recognized, and many efforts have been taken to build integrated project support systems. Therefore, it can be expected that in 3 to 5 years, the use of integrated computer support may be standard practice.

Many problems still must be solved in order to motivate engineers and managers to accept or even to request these support environments because they really make their work easier (and not only because their use has been ordered by corporate management). But eventually, integrated and knowledge-based project support environments will improve the quality of future computer-based systems and will greatly affect the way engineers and managers work and learn, although these environments will never be a substitute for creative problem solving.

REFERENCES

1. P. D. Johnson, ed., "Methodologies and Tools for Real-Time Systems," Conference and Workshop of the National Institute for Software Quality and Productivity, Washington, D.C., October 28–November 1, 1985.
2. R. Lauber, "Development Support Systems," *IEEE Comput.*, *15* (5), 36–46, (May 1982).
3. R. Lauber and P. Lempp, "Integrated Development and Project Management Support System," in *Proceedings of COMPSAC '83*, Chicago, IL, November 9–11, 1983.
4. J. McDermid, ed., *Integrated Project Support Environments*, Peter Peregrinus Ltd. on behalf of IEEE, London, 1985.
5. R. Lauber, "Impact of a Computer-aided Development Support System on Software Quality and Reliability," in *Proceedings of the Sixth International Computer Software and Applications Conference, COMPSAC '82*, Chicago, IL., November 1982. IEEE Comp. Soc. Press, Los Angeles, 1982, pp. 248–256.
6. A. Borgida, S. Greenspan, and J. Mylopoulos, "Knowledge Representation as the Basis for Requirements Specifications," *IEEE Comput.*, 82–91 (April 1985).
7. R. Isermann, *Digital Control Systems*, Springer-Verlag, New York, 1981.
8. M. W. Alford, "SREM at the Age of Eight; the Distributed Computing Design System," *IEEE Comput.*, 36–46 (April 1985).
9. J. L. Peterson, "Petri Nets," *ACM Comput. Surv.*, *9* (3) (September 1977).
10. P. P. Chen, "The Entity-Relationship Model—Toward a Unified View of Data," *ACM Trans. Databases*, *1* (1) pp. 9–36 (March 1986).
11. T. DeMarco, *Structured Analysis and System Specification*, Yourdon, Inc., New York, 1978.
12. J. V. Guttag, "The Specification and Application to Programming of Abstract Data Types," University of Toronto, Ph. D. Thesis, Report CSRG-59, 1975.
13. W. K. Giloi and B. D. Shriver, eds., *Methodologies for Computer System Design*, North-Holland, Amsterdam, New York, Oxford, 1986.
14. H. Simpson, "The Mascot Method," *Software Eng. J.*, *1* (3), 103–120, (May 1986).
15. R. Balzer, T. E. Cheatham, and C. Green, "Software Technology in the 1990's, Using a New Paradigm," *IEEE Comput.*, *1* (11), pp. 39–45, November 1983.
16. A. Wolfe, "Software Productivity Moves Upstream," *Electronics*, 80–86 (July 10, 1986).

17. G. E. Siever and T. E. Mizeli, "Specification-Based Software Engineering with TAGS," *IEEE Comput.*, 56–65 (April 1985).
18. V. Stenning, "An Introduction to ISTAR," Software Engineering Environments Conference, Lancaster, UK, April 2–4, 1986.
19. R. Lauber and P. Lempp, *EPOS Overview*, SPS Software Products and Services, Inc., New York,
20. R. Lauber, "Software Werkzeuge auf Arbeitsplatzrechnern zur Unterstuetzung des Ingenieurs bei Mikroelektronik-Projekten," *Automatisierungstechnische Praxis atp*, 27 (10), 481–488 (1985).
21. *Perspective Overview*, System Designers Ltd., London, U.K., 1983.
22. L. Hirschmann, *PRADOS—Weiterentwicklung zum objektorientierten Software-Entwicklungssystem*, SCS GmbH, Hamburg, West Germany, (1986).
23. *Promod System*, GEI Gesellschaft fuer elektronische Informationsverarbeitung mbH, Aachen, West Germany, 1986.
24. *Softool Overview*, Softool Corp., Goleta, CA., 1986.
25. A. Ghassemi and K.-P. Reinshagen, "Experiences with the industrial application of the specification and design tool EPOS for the automation of rotating printing machines," (in German) *Regelungstechnische Praxis rtp*, 25, 110–114; 156–159 (1983).
26. T. Schuler, R. S. Frank, and W. Kratschmer, "Successes and Failures using EPOS as a Software Production Tool," in *IFAC Workshop Experiences with the Management of Software Projects* (ed, P. Elzer), Heidelberg, West Germany, May 14–16, 1986 (preprints, pp. 95–100).

R. J. LAUBER

INTERVAL MATHEMATICS

1 HISTORIC AND BIBLIOGRAPHIC OUTLINE

The use of intervals in mathematics dates back at least 100 years, e.g., the definition of real numbers by means of nested intervals with rational endpoints, the use of a mean value in an interval in Taylor's formula, the interval topology (use of the closed intervals as subbase for the set of all closed subsets), Hjelmslev geometry (points, lines, planes, which are defined with a certain uncertainty), confidence intervals in statistics, etc.

In 1974, Leslie Fox proposed the word *interval mathematics*. It was meant to combine such different areas as interval arithmetic, interval analysis, interval topology, interval algebra, etc., applications of intervals in approximation theory, in numerical computation, in engineering, in psychology, etc. In a narrower sense, interval mathematics is mainly understood as the use of intervals for all kinds of error control and as a tool for representing an infinity of values. This article is only concerned with interval mathematics in the latter sense.

The work in interval mathematics began essentially with the papers of R. E. Moore, the "father" of interval mathematics and his co-workers. There are also two very early papers by W. Warmus [1] from Poland and T. Sunaga [2] from Japan, who reported on the first investigations in interval arithmetic. Up to now, three monographs introducing this subject exist: Moore's *Interval Analysis* [3], also available in German translation [58], Alefeld and Herzberger's *Einführung in die Intervallrechnung* [4], also available in English translation [16], and Moore's *Methods and Applications of Interval Analysis* [5]. Many international conferences have been held; the first was initiated by L. Fox in Oxford, England, in 1968, and the last was organized by R. E. Moore in Columbus, Ohio, in 1987. Proceedings of the symposia have been edited by E. Hansen [6], K. Nickel [7–9], J. Albrycht and H. Wisniewski [10], and R. E. Moore [82].

In 1979, the "Freiburger Intervall-Berichte" were founded by K. Nickel. Finally, a recent bibliography on interval mathematics was published by J. Garloff [11, 83]. Up to now more than 2,300 papers have been published in interval mathematics.

See Ref. 12 for more information on this topic.

2 WHY INTERVAL ARITHMETIC?

Present-day computers employ an arithmetic called fixed-length, floating-point arithmetic or short, floating-point arithmetic. In this arithmetic, real numbers are approximated by a subset of real numbers called machine-representable numbers (or short machine numbers). Because of this representation, two types of errors are generated: The first type occurs when a real valued input data item is approximated by a machine number; the second type of error is caused by intermediate results being approximated by machine numbers.

Interval arithmetic provides a tool for estimating and controlling these errors *automatically*. Instead of approximating a real value x by a machine number, the usually unknown real value x is approximated by an interval X having machine number upper and lower boundaries containing the value x. The width of this interval may be used as measure for the quality of the approximation. The calculations therefore have to be executed using intervals instead of real numbers, and the real arithmetic is replaced by interval arithmetic. The computation with the usual machine numbers $\tilde{x}$ allows no estimate of the error $|\tilde{x} - x|$. The computation *with including intervals* allows the following estimate for the absolute error:

$$|x - m(X)| \leq w(X)/2$$

where m(X) denotes the midpoint of the interval X and w(X) denotes the width of X. An estimate for the relative error is

$$\left|\frac{x - m(X)}{x}\right| \leq \frac{w(X)}{2 \min |X|} \quad \text{if } 0 \notin X$$

where $|X| = \{|x| : x \in X\}$.

Let us consider an example. The real number 1/3 cannot be represented by a machine number. It may, however, be enclosed in the machine-representable interval A = [0.33, 0.34] if we assume that the machine numbers are representable by two-digit numbers (without exponent part). If we now want to multiply 1/3 by a real number, b, which we know lies in B = [−0.01, 0.02], then we seek the smallest interval X which, (a) contains b/3; (b) depends on the intervals A and B and does not depend on 1/3 and b; (c) has machine numbers as boundaries. The realization of these requirements is accomplished by two steps: (1) Operations for intervals are defined that satisfy (a) and (b); (2) the application of certain rounding procedures to these operations yield (c). An interval arithmetic is defined by step 1, and a machine interval arithmetic is defined by step 2.

Let us consider another example and apply the mean value formula to gain a local approximation of a continuously differentiable function f: R → R (R denotes the set of reals) near a point x ∈ R,

$$f(x + h) = f(x) + f'(\xi) h. \tag{1}$$

For simplicity, we assume that h > 0. Then $\xi \in [x, x + h] =: X$. How can we represent the information given by formula (1) on a computer? How can we evaluate f(x + h) on the computer via the right side of formula (1) if x and h are given? Obviously, ξ is not assigned a numerical value, which would be necessary to have the computer run. How would formula (1) be treated for further numerical manipulation, e.g., if formula (1) is to be multiplied by a number? The answer is quite simple: Use interval arithmetic and compute F(x,h) := f(x) + f'(X)h as will be defined in the sequel. Then F(x,h) will be an interval, i.e., representable on the computer and we will know that f(x + h) ∈ F(x,h), where f(x + h) is unknown and F(x,h) is known.

Interval Mathematics

See Refs. *3, 5, 13,* and *14* for further discussion.

3 INTERVAL ARITHMETIC OPERATIONS

Let I be the set of real compact intervals (these are the ones normally considered). Operations in I satisfying the requirements (*a*) and (*b*) of Section 2 are then defined by the expression

$$A * B = \{a*b: a \in A, b \in B\} \quad \text{for } A, B \in I \tag{2}$$

where the symbol * stands for +, −, ·, and /, and where A/B is only defined if $0 \notin B$.

Definition (2) is motivated by the fact that the intervals A and B include some exact values, α and β, respectively, of the calculation. The values α and β are generally not known. The only information that is usually available consists of the including intervals A and B, i.e., $\alpha \in A$, $\beta \in B$. From definiution (2), it follows that

$$\alpha * \beta \in A * B \tag{3}$$

which is called *inclusion principle of interval arithmetic*. This means that the (generally unknown) sum, difference, product, and quotient of the two reals are contained in the sum, difference, product, and in the quotient of the including intervals, respectively. Moreover, A * B is the *smallest* set that contains the real $\alpha * \beta$. Moore [15] proved that $A * B \in I$ if $0 \notin B$.

It is emphasized that the real and the corresponding interval operations are denoted by the same symbols. So-called *point intervals*, i.e., intervals consisting of exactly one point, [a,a], are denoted by a. Expressions like aA, a + A, A/a, (−1)A, etc., for $a \in R$, $A \in I$ are therefore defined. The expression (−1)A is written as −A.

Definition (2) is useless in practical calculations. Moore [15] proved that definition (2) is equivalent to the following constructive *rules*:

$$\begin{aligned}
&[a,b] + [c,d] = [a + c, b + d], \\
&[a,b] - [c,d] = [a - d, b - c], \\
&[a,b][c,d] = [\min(ac,ad,bc,bd), \max(ac,ad,bc,bd)], \\
&[a,b]/[c,d] = [a,b][1/d, 1/c] \text{ if } 0 \notin [c,d].
\end{aligned} \tag{4}$$

These rules show that *subtraction and division in I are not the inverse operations* of addition and multiplication, respectively, as is the case in R. For example, $[0,1] - [0,1] = [-1,1]$, $[1,2]/[1,2] = [1/2,2]$. This property is one of the main differences between interval arithmetic and real arithmetic. Another main difference is given by the so-called *subdistributive law*,

$$A(B + C) \subseteq AB + AC \quad \text{for } A,B,C \in I. \tag{5}$$

Example: $[0,1][1 - 1] = 0,$
   $[0,1]1 - [0,1]1 = [-1,1].$

The *distributive law* is valid in some special cases, e.g.,

$$a(B + C) = aB + aC \quad \text{if } a \in R \text{ and } B,C \in I. \tag{6}$$

The following properties follow directly from definition (2): Let $A,B,C,D \in I$, and $*$ be any interval operation; then

$$A + B = B + A, \quad A + (B + C) = (A + B) + C,$$
$$AB = BA, \quad A(BC) = (AB)C,$$
$$A \subseteq B, \; C \subseteq D \text{ implies } A * C \subseteq B * D \text{ (if } B * D \text{ is defined)}. \tag{7}$$

The last-mentioned property is called *inclusion isotony* of the interval operations.

See Refs. *3, 5, 14,* and *16* for further discussion.

4 MACHINE INTERVAL ARITHMETIC

Let us return to the requirements (c) or 2 of Section 2, i.e., that the endpoints of our intervals must be machine numbers. This leads to a special discipline, called machine interval arithmetic. It can be considered as an approximation of interval arithmetic on computer systems.

Machine interval arithmetic is based on the inclusion isotony of the interval operations in the following manner: Let us assume again that α and β are the unknown exact values of any stage of the calculation and only including intervals are known, $\alpha \in A$, $\beta \in B$. Then A and B might not be representable on the machine. So, A and B are replaced by the *smallest machine intervals* that *contain* A and B: $A \subseteq A_M$, $B \subseteq B_M$.

The left and right endpoints of a machine interval are machine numbers. Definition (7) implies $A * B \subseteq A_M * B_M$.

The interval $A_M * B_M$ need not be a machine interval and is therefore approximated by $(A_M * B_M)_M$, which is representable on the machine. This leads to the *inclusion principle of machine interval arithmetic*:

$$\alpha \in A, \; \beta \in B \text{ implies } \alpha * \beta \in (A_M * B_M)_M. \tag{8}$$

Thus, the basic principle of interval arithmetic is kept in machine interval arithmetic, i.e., the exact unknown result is contained in the corresponding known interval, and *rounding errors are under control*.

To sum up, when a concrete problem has to be solved, our procedure is as follows: (a) The theory is done in interval arithmetic; (b) the calculation is done in machine interval arithmetic; (c) the inclusion principle (8) is kept as transition from interval arithmetic to machine interval arithmetic.

There are several software systems and software packages in which machine interval arithmetic is implemented, e.g., TRIPLEX-ALGOL-60, Pascal-SC, or ACRITH for some IBM computers, and ARITHMOS for some Siemens computers, etc.

Machine interval arithmetic is related to many interesting aspects of practical and theoretical computer science that influence each other, e.g., the algebraic structure of number spaces needed at computations; solving algebraic problems such as linear systems, matrix inversion, eigenvalue problems with high accuracy; development of an optimal computer arithmetic, that is, there is no machine number between the computed and exact result; automatic differentiation and generation of Taylor coefficients;

Interval Mathematics

ultra-arithmetic, which is a machine arithmetic for function spaces and further function operations such as composition and integration; and development of automated problem solving in function spaces (differential equations, integral equations, etc.).

See Refs. 16—22 for further discussion.

5 INCLUSION FUNCTIONS AND NATURAL INTERVAL EXTENSIONS

In this section, the inclusion principle for the interval arithmetic operations is extended to more general functions, such as programmable functions. Some notation follows:

Interval vectors $X = (X_1,\ldots,X_n) \in I^n$ are n-dimensional intervals, also called intervals (or sometimes *boxes*) for brevity.

If $D \subseteq R^n$, then $I(D)$ may denote the set of all intervals $X \in I^n$ with $X \subseteq D$. If $f: D \to R$ is any function and $Z \subseteq D$, then $\bar{f}(Z) := \{f(x) : x \in Z\}$ denotes the *range* of f over Z. An interval function $F: I(D) \to I$ is called an *inclusion function* of f if $\bar{f}(Y) \subseteq F(Y)$ for all $Y \in I(D)$.

An inclusion function F of f is called an *interval extension* of f if $F(y) = f(y)$ for $y \in D$ holds.

Let $g: D \to R$ with $D \subseteq R$ (or $D \subseteq R^m$ exceptionally) be any *function predeclared* in some programming language (like sin, cos, exp, etc.). Then define the corresponding *predeclared interval function* IG by $IG(Y) = \bar{g}(Y)$ for any $Y \in I(D)$. Because the monotonicity intervals of predeclared functions g are well known difficulties do not arise when defining $IG(Y)$. It is also easy to realize the interval functions IG on a computer. Nevertheless, the influence of rounding errors may be considered, so that $(IG(Y_M))_M$ instead of $IG(Y)$ will be computed on a machine. Clearly, IG is an inclusion function for g.

An inclusion function F is called *isotone* if $X \subseteq Y$ implies $F(X) \subseteq F(Y)$. Inclusion functions can be constructed in any programming language in which interval arithmetic is simulated or implemented via natural interval extensions, as follows: Let $f(x)$ be any function expression in the variable $x \in R^n$. So, $f(x)$ may be an explicit formula or described by an algorithm or the statements of a recursive definition. We assume that $f(x)$ is representable in a programming language. Let $Y \in I^n$ or Y be an interval variable over I^n. Then the expression that arises if each occurence of x in $f(x)$ is replaced by Y, if each occurence of a predeclared function g in $f(x)$ is replaced by IG, and if the arithmetic operations in $f(x)$ are replaced by the corresponding interval arithmetic operations is called the *natural interval extension* of $f(x)$ to Y and is denoted by $f(Y)$ [3]. Due to formula (3) and the definition of the IGs, we get the *inclusion principle* for (programmable) functions

$$a \in Y \quad \text{implies} \quad f(a) \in f(Y). \tag{9}$$

Therefore, $f(Y)$ seen as a functions in Y is an inclusion function for the function $f(x)$.

Note: Natural interval extensions could only be defined precisely via a recursion. Furthermore, one would have to distinguish between the expression $f(x)$ or $f(Y)$ and the functions defined by these expressions. However, we choose this outline for simplicity. The reader preferring a precise presentation is referred to Ref. 14.

Example: If $f(x) = x_1 \sin x_2 - x_3$ for $x \in R^3$, then $f(Y) = Y_1 \text{ ISIN } Y_2 - Y_3$ is the natural interval extension of f to $Y \in I^3$.

Important: Due to the algebraic properties of interval arithmetic, different expressions for a real function f lead to interval expressions that are different as functions.

Example: If $f_1(x) = x - x^2$ and $f_2(x) = x(1 - x)$, then $f_1(x)$ and $f_2(x)$ are different as expressions, but equal as functions. Furthermore, $f_1(Y)$ and $f_2(Y)$ are also different as functions, i.e., if $Y = [0,1]$ then $f_1(Y) = Y - Y^2 = [-1,1]$, $f_2(Y) = Y(1 - Y) = [0,1]$. For comparison, $\bar{f}(Y) = [0,1/4]$.

Problem: Find expressions of a given function that lead to natural interval extensions as good as possible i.e., $f(Y)$ shall approximate $\bar{f}(Y)$ as good as possible. A partial solution to this problem can be found in Ref. 14. It is one of the curiosities of interval mathematics that the simplest function expression does not give the best interval extension.

Example: The function $x - x^2$ can be described by the expression $f_1(x) = x - x^2$ and also be the expression $f_2(x) = -(x - 1) - (x - 1)^2$. For $Y = [0,2]$, we get the extensions $f_1(Y) = [-4,2]$ and $f_2(Y) = [-2,2]$, which is better than $f_1(Y)$. For comparison, $\bar{f}(Y) = [-2,1/4]$.

See Refs. 3, 5, 14, 16, and 23 for further discussion.

6 SOME STANDARD APPLICATIONS OF INTERVAL ARITHMETIC

Since any interval is given by two boundary points, any assertion or any theory about intervals could be reduced to a corresponding noninterval assertion or theory. Nevertheless, a language that is appropriate to speak about intervals and their properties, such as interval arithmetic, is very comfortable for theoretical as well as for practical considerations of many subjects. In this case, an interval can be seen as a complete size, and one can immediately follow relationships between intervals or operations of intervals. For example, intersection, inclusion, or elementhood, which frequently occur, can immediately be understood. This seems to be trivial but is not, as may be recognized by writing down these operations respective relations without using an interval language.

Following is a rough classification of how intervals may be applied: (a) The interval represents one value that is unknown in general; (b) the interval represents a continuum of values that may be known or unknown.

Sections 7-10 are concerned with applications of (b). In this section, the following applications of (a) are presented.

1. *Control of rounding errors*. This point was already discussed extensively. Error estimates were given in Section 2.

2. *Representation of inexact data*. This can arise by observation errors, measurement errors, data perturbations, errors of preceding computations, etc. For instance, almost all physical data are inexact, but error bounds are generally known, e.g., earth acceleration: $g = 9.807 \pm 0.027$

Interval Mathematics

m/sec^2; its interval representation: g ∈ G = [9.780, 9.834] m/sec^2. Any further numerical manipulation of g is quite uncomfortable because of the term containing ±. The interval representation is easy to process because of its compactness. The related force can then be written simple as MG, where M is the interval that contains the earth mass.

3. *Approximation and procedure errors.* In the simplest case, these errors can be truncation errors like π = 3.14159..., and we have π ∈ [3.14, 3.15]. Another simple application is the mean value formula for integrals:

$$\int_a^b f(x)dx = (b-a)f(\xi) \in (b-a)\bar{f}(A) \subseteq (b-a)F(A)$$

where f is continuous over A = [a,b], F is an inclusion function of f, and ξ ∈ A is the unknown mean value. In general, noninterval numerical analysis avoids the manipulation of the total information that is given by the mean value formula and prefers to replace the value f(ξ) by some approximate, e.g., f(a), or f(b), or f((a + b)/2), etc. Interval arithmetic takes (b − a)F(A) as an including approximation for the integral value. No information has been lost when doing so, but an error estimate has been won. It is clear that the mean value formula is only an example to demonstrate the idea. Nobody will evaluate the integral in this manner. But even when the methods are refined, the basic idea is the same. We can proceed similarly with the Taylor formula and the mean value formula of differential calculus. Let u ∨ v be the interval spanned by the points u and v. Thus u ∨ v is either [u,v] if u ≤ v or [v,u] if v ≤ u. Then, f(x) = f(c) + (x −c)f'(ξ) ∈ f(c) + (x −c)$\bar{f}$'(x ∨ c) ⊆ (x − c)F'(x ∨ c) where F' is an inclusion function of f'.

4. *Logical consistency of computer programs.* Let us look at the so-called if-statement, as an example,

if x > 0, then S else T

where S and T are any statements. At noninterval computation, it can happen and it happens that the numerical value (the one to which the errors are attached) is greater than 0 and that the exact value, which is not known, is equal to or less than 0. Then S instead of T is executed by the program, which sometimes leads to wrong results. Assume now that X is the interval that contains the exact (unknown) value x; then a correct program fragment is

if X > 0, then S (because x > 0 in this case),

if X ≤ 0, then T (because x ≤ 0 in this case).

Please note that the second statement is not the logical counterpart of the first one. It is therefore necessary to use further information to construct a sound continuation of the fragment, such as

if not X > 0 and not X ≤ 0, then U

where U is an appropriate statement. Obviously, U must be consistent with the problem.

5. *Termination criteria at iterative processes.* Let us assume that a real zero of a function $f: \mathbb{R} \to \mathbb{R}$ is to be determined and that the computer delivers a sequence of approximations x_n, $n = 0, 1, \ldots$. A widespread termination criterion is

if $|f(x_n)| < \varepsilon$, then terminate

and x_n is taken as an approximate of the zero. Now it is possible that x_n is a very good approximation, but due to rounding errors, $|f(x_n)| < \varepsilon$ is not recognized by the computer; also the converse case is possible, i.e., x_n is a poor approximation, but, numerically, $|f(x_n)| < \varepsilon$ is indicated. A logically sound criterion is the following, when $f(x_n) \in F_n$:

if $F_n \subseteq [-\varepsilon, \varepsilon]$, then terminate

and one has the guarantee that the exact value has the property $|f(x_n)| < \varepsilon$. Certainly, one has to incorporate a second criterion that stops the algorithm when $F_n \subseteq [-\varepsilon, \varepsilon]$ cannot be reached.

6. *Termination criteria at contraction methods.* In theory, the sequence of approximations, $(x_n)_{n=0}^{\infty}$, should *converge* monotonically to some fixed point x^*. Practically, the convergence is disturbed by rounding errors, and frequently it appears that the approximations dance around x^*. A sound termination criterion is offered if interval arithmetic is used: If $x^* \in X_0$ with a starting interval X_0 of the area of contraction and $x_n \in X_n \in I$, $n = 0, 1, \ldots$, then the calculation may be stopped if $w(X_n) < \varepsilon$ for some given $\varepsilon > 0$ or $X_{n+1} \supseteq X_n$.

The first condition means that an approximation is found with absolute error at most ε; the second condition indicates that the rounding errors surpass the diminishing of the contraction; and the algorithm stops at the best possible state, either if the desired accuracy is obtained or if the error interval cannot be made smaller. The assumption that $x^* \in X_0$ can be verified computationally using interval arithmetic existence tests (see, e.g., Section 7).

7 COMPUTATIONALLY VERIFIABLE TESTS FOR THE EXISTENCE AND UNIQUENESS OF SOLUTIONS TO NONLINEAR SYSTEMS

In this section, one of the most fascinating applications of interval mathematics is considered, i.e., sufficient conditions for the existence or uniqueness of zeros of systems of nonlinear equations are provided. The conditions need not be verified by a human being like a mathematician or an engineer but are verified automatically on the computer.

We are given a system of n nonlinear continuously differentiable equations in n unknowns,

$$f(x) = 0 \qquad (10)$$

with $f: D \to \mathbb{R}^n$, $D \subseteq \mathbb{R}^n$, and 0 the null vector of $\mathbb{R}^n$. Krawczyk [24] introduced an interval version of the Newton operator as follows:

$$K(X) := y - Yf(y) + \{Id - YF'(x)\}(X - y) \tag{11}$$

where $X \in I(D)$, y is any point chosen from X, Y is an arbitrary nonsingular real matrix, and Id is the identity matrix. Furthermore, $F': I(D) \to I^{n \times n}$ is an isotone interval extension of the derivative f' (which is to be understood component-wise). A fundamental theorem says that if $X \in I(D)$, then the condition

$$K(X) \subseteq X \tag{12}$$

implies the existence of a solution $x^* \in X$ of Eq. (10). This theorem is based on Schauder's fixed point theorem. Note please that the relation (12) can be verified automatically by a computer when interval arithmetic is used. The theorem mentioned, however, gives no information about the uniqueness of the solution x^* and how to determine it. For this purpose, K is used to act as iteration instruction, which shall be defined now: Let $|[a,b]| = \max(|a|,|b|)$ and $m([a,b]) = (a+b)/2$. For an interval vector, $X = (X_1,\ldots,X_n) \in I^n$ define $|X| = \max_{i=1,\ldots,n} |X_i|$, $w(X) = \max_{i=1,\ldots,n} w(X_i)$, and $m(X) = (m(X_1),\ldots,m(X_n)) \in R^n$. For an interval matrix $A \in I^{n \times n}$ with interval components A_{ij}, define $\|A\| = \max_{i=1,\ldots,n} \Sigma_{j=1}^{n} |A_{ij}|$ and $m(A)$ the real matrix with components $m(A_{ij})$. Then, given any $X^0 \in I(D)$, consider the algorithm

$$X^{k+1} := X^k \cap K(X^k) \tag{13}$$

with

$$K(X^k) = y^k - Y^k f(y^k) + \{Id - Y^k F'(X^k)\}(X^k - y^k),$$

where $y^k = m(X^k)$ and $Y^k := Y$, where Y is an approximation to $[m(F(X^k))]^{-1}$ such that

$$\|ID - YF'(X^k))\| \leq r_{k-1}$$

where $r_\nu = \|Id - Y^\nu F'(X^\nu)\|$, $\nu = 0,1\ldots$. If the approximation Y does not satisfy this inequality, then $Y^k := Y^{k-1}$.

For the starting value Y^0, it is only assumed that $K(X^0) \subseteq X^0$ holds; otherwise, the existence of a solution is not guaranteed. Now, another famous theorem says that if the (computationally verifiable) conditions

$$K(X^0) \subseteq X^0 \text{ and } r_0 < 1 \tag{14}$$

are satisfied then, there is a *unique solution* x^* of Eq. (10) in X^0; furthermore, that $(X^k)_{k=0}^{\infty}$ is a *nested sequence* of boxes converging at least linearly to the unique solution x^* [25]. Finally, the relationship $x^* \in X^k$ holds for any k and may be used for an error estimate.

Several more recent results show the trend to simplify (14). For example, if X is a box, $X = (X_1,\ldots,X_n)$ with $w(X) = w(X_i)$ for $i = 1,\ldots,n$, then (14) can be replaced by the simpler assumption

$$\|K(X^0) - m(X^0)\|_\infty < w(X^0) \tag{15}$$

with $X^0 = X$, which means that $K(X^0)$ lies in the interior of X [26]. Again, the validity of assumption (15) can be checked automatically by a computer. The assumption that X is a cube can finally be dropped if other norms are used [27].

See Refs. 25–28 for further discussion.

8 SAFE STARTING REGIONS FOR ITERATIVE METHODS

There are many good iterative methods for computing zeros or fixed points of operators or systems of equations. Nevertheless, finding starting points for these methods is an old problem.

Interval analysis presents a search procedure using "continuum" analysis. This procedure is more powerful than the common "continuation" methods [29]. The necessary means are (a) existence conditions for a region; (b) nonexistence conditions for a region; (c) convergence conditions for a region.

The conditions should be programmable such that they are verifiable by a computer. For example, let us focus again on the system of equations (10) and the operator K defined by formula (11). Appropriate candidates for the existence and convergence conditions are (12) and (14), respectively. Simple nonexistence conditions are

$$0 \notin F(X) \quad \text{or} \quad X \cap K(X) = \emptyset \tag{16}$$

where F is an inclusion function of f. Clearly, both conditions of (16) imply that f has no solution x^* in X.

Going into detail, we note that for any box $X \in I(D)$ exactly one of the following conditions will hold: (a) X satisfies the existence and convergence criteria (14), where X and X^0 of (14) are identified; (b) X satisfies one of the nonexistence criteria (16); and (c) X satisfies neither (a) nor (b). Determination of which of the above conditions holds is called analysis of X.

A search procedure consists of a recursive application of this analysis, beginning with some box $X \in I(D)$. (If a zero in the whole domain D is to be computed, then f must be extended on a box $X \supseteq D$.) At each level, the actual box, which will always be denoted by X, is analyzed. If X satisfies condition (a), we designate it a safe starting region for the solution of Eq. (10). If X satisfies condition (b), then no solution of Eq. (10) is contained in X and X is excluded from further consideration. If X satisfies condition (c) then X is bisected. One of the two resulting half-regions is chosen for analysis at the next level. The other half-region is saved for analysis in the event that the selected half-region is subsequently excluded. This ensures that no potential safe starting regions are lost during the search. Furthermore, exclusion of both half-regions resulting from the bisection of X automatically excludes X. This ensures that each half-region is analyzed at most once. If condition (c) holds and it is not possible to bisect X because of the limited resolution of computations using fixed precision computer arithmetic, there may still be a solution for Eq. (10) in X. In this case, we add X to a list of boxes too small for further analysis (without going to higher machine arithmetic precision) and continue the search as if this box had been excluded. Because D is of finite dimension and if D is compact, there can be only a finite number of such boxes obtained by bisection. Thus, the search procedure just described will, in a finite number of steps, do one of the following three things:

1. Find a safe starting box X for convergence of algorithm (13) to a solution x* of Eq. (10),
2. Discover that there are no solutions of Eq. (10) in the region under consideration;
3. Terminate with a list of small boxes that might contain solutions for Eq. (10). There are no solutions in the remaining region under consideration.

See Refs. *29—31* for further discussion.

9 AN INTERVAL NEWTON METHOD

One of the most interesting applications of the ideas discussed in the previous sections are interval Newton methods. These are superior to non-interval Newton methods with respect to regions of attractions. Under rather mild assumptions, interval Newton methods always claim to converge if they are combined with an appropriate search procedure (see, e.g., Section 8.)

We provide a simplified prototype that is similar to the concept derived in Sections 7 and 8 but is not a special case.

For simplicity, let us concentrate on the one-dimensional case, i.e., $f: X \to R$, $X \in I$. Let us further assume that f is *continuous* and that f has bounded divided differences, i.e., there is a constant c such that

$$\frac{|f(x) - f(y)|}{|x - y|} \leq c \quad \text{for } x, y, \in X, \, x \neq y.$$

We also need an inclusion function for the divided differences, F^1, i.e.,

$$\frac{f(x) - f(y)}{x - y} \in F^1(Y) \quad \text{for } x, y \in Y, \, x \neq y$$

and

$$w(F^1(Y)) \longrightarrow 0 \text{ as } w(Y) \longrightarrow 0.$$

If f is differentiable, then F^1 can be chosen, e.g., as interval extension of the derivate, f', i.e., $f'(x) \in F^1(Y)$ if $x \in Y$.

In this case, due to the mean value theorem, we have $f(y) - f(x) = (y - x)f'(\xi) \in (y - x)F^1(x \vee y)$ for $x, y \in X$, where $\xi \in x \vee y$, and $x \vee y$ is the interval, with x and y as endpoints. For example, if $f(x) = \sin x$, then $F^1(Y) = ICOS(Y)$ as defined in Section 5 is appropriate. Better inclusions may be gained if the derivative of an interval extension of f is taken [32] or if slopes of f are used [14,16,33].

If f is not differentiable, then there are no general instructions on how to get F^1. Subdifferentials can be used if available. For example, let [x] be the largest integer, which is smaller than x or equal to x, for any x ∈ R. Then define

$$f(x) = x - [x] \quad \text{if} \quad [x] \text{ is even}$$
$$= 1 - x + [x] \quad \text{if} \quad [x] \text{ is odd.}$$

An appropriate inclusion function F^1 can be defined as follows: If the interior of Y contains an integer, set $F^1(Y) = [-1,1]$. Otherwise, set $F^1(Y) = 1$ if there is an x ∈ Y such that [x] is even and if $w(Y) < 1$, and set $F^1(Y) = -1$ if there is an x ∈ Y such that [x] is odd and if $w(Y) < 1$. Finally, set $F^1([2n, 2n+1]) = 1$ and $F^1([2n-1, 2n]) = -1$ for integers n.

Let us return to the problem of finding a zero of f in X. Because f is not assumed to be continuously differentiable, we cannot use the operator K as defined by formula (11). Under the mild assumptions given above,

$$f(y_1)f(y_2) \leq 0 \quad \text{for} \quad Y = [y_1, y_2] \tag{17}$$

is an evident *existence condition* for a zero to lie in Y. As *interval Newton algorithm*, we choose

$$X^0 := Y,$$
$$X^{k+1} := X^k \cap \{[m(X^k) - f(m(X^k))]/F^1(Y)\}, \quad k \geq 0. \tag{18}$$

Algorithm (17), together with $0 \notin F^1(Y)$, gives a *convergence condition* for Y. If it is satisfied, then algorithm (18) produces a nested sequence of intervals, $(X^k)_{k=0}^\infty$, converging to x^*, where $x^* \in X^k$ for all k [16]. Clearly, $0 \notin F(Y)$ is a *nonexistence condition*.

The use of algorithm (18) is then directed by the following *global search procedure* [29]. A list T of intervals yet to be tested and a list P of intervals, which may contain a zero but are too small for further bisection, are needed.

    Step 1 (*Initialization*). Set list T to empty; set list P to empty; set Y := X, say Y = $[y_1, y_2]$.
    Step 2. Compute F(Y).
    Step 3 (*Exclusion*). If $0 \notin F(Y)$, go to step 9.
    Step 4 (*Existence*). If $f(y_1)f(y_2) \leq 0$, then go to the next step (Y contains a zero); otherwise go to step 7.
    Step 5. Compute $F^1(Y)$.
    Step 6 (*Convergence*). If $0 \notin F^1(Y)$, then terminate search procedure and apply algorithm (18) to Y as Y is a safe starting region for algorithm (18).
    Step 7. Bisect Y, say Y = $V_1 \cup V_2$. If no bisection is possible, add Y to list P and go to step 9.
    Step 8. Set Y := V_1; add V_2 to head of list T; go to step 2.

Step 9 (*Test list T*). If list T is empty, go to the next step; otherwise, delete the leading interval, say Z, from list T, set Y := Z and go to step 2.

Step 10 (*Test list P*). If list P is empty, terminate (because there is no solution in X); otherwise, print P and terminate (as a further decision is not possible without raising the machine accuracy; if a solution x* exists in X, then x* is contained in the intervals of the printed list P).

Many variants of the interval Newton method and the global search exist. The important variant of Hansen [34] concedes division through intervals containing null. This leads to an infinite interval arithmetic that could prevent one or the other user from applying this variant. This variant, however, has some methodical advantages that imply better nonexistence tests, which finally accelerates the search.

See Refs. *16, 24, 28, 29, 34, 35,* and *84* for further discussion.

10 INTERVAL TOOLS FOR GLOBAL NONLINEAR OPTIMIZATION

Solving an optimization problem generally requires the comparison of a continuum of values and the choosing of an optimum value. Because interval computation is a means of handling continua, it provides competitive methods for solving optimization problems. In order not to get too sophisticated, a simple prototype of an algorithm for unconstrained problems is discussed. It is based on ideas of Skelboe [36], Moore [5], Asaithambi et al. [37], and Hansen [38, 39].

Let $X \in I^m$ and $f: X \to R$ be the function considered. We assume that a global minimum f* of f exists in X. Let G be the set of global minimizers of f in X. Then, f* or G shall be determined.

Interval methods for solving the optimization problem consist of (*a*) the main algorithm and (*b*) accelerating devices.

The main algorithm is a *sequential deterministic* algorithm where *branch-and-bound* techniques are used. An algorithm is called sequential if the ith step of the computation depends on the former steps. A method is *deterministic* if the results are guaranteed ones, in contrast to stochastic methods where the results are established within certain percentages. Branch-and-bound techniques split up the whole domain into areas (branching) where bounds of the objective function, f, are computed (bounding). The accelerating devices will be specified later. Interval arithmetic is used for both point (*a*) and point (*b*), especially in the following:

1. To achieve the bounds needed for the branch-and-bound techniques (f need not be Lipschitz, convex, etc.).
2. To remove large parts of the domain X. (No other tools are known that can compete with interval arithmetic with respect to a sure and fast reduction of the domain.)

The main interval arithmetic tool applied to optimization problems is the concept of an inclusion function as defined in Section 5. A measure of the quality of an inclusion function F of $f: X \to R$ is the so-called *excess width*, $w(F(Y)) - w(\bar{f}(Y))$ for all $Y \in I(X)$, where $w([a,b]) = b - a$ is the width of an interval. The width of a box $Y = Y_1 \times \ldots \times Y_m \in I^m$ is defined by $w(Y) = \max\{w(Y_1),\ldots,w(Y_m)\}$. F is called of *order* $\alpha > 0$ if $w(F(Y)) - w(\bar{f}(Y)) = O(w(Y)^\alpha)$ for $Y \in I(X)$.

To obtain good computational results, it is necessary to choose inclusion functions of an order α as high as possible [14].

The prototype algorithm is appropriate to determine the global minimum f* of f in X and to localize global minimizers as described later. The algorithm has the box X, the inclusion function F of f: X → R, and some accuracy parameters that may occur in the termination criteria as input parameters. The termination criteria will depend on the actual case and will not be specified here.

Algorithm

Step 1. Calculate F(X).
Step 2. Set y := min F(X). Set Y := X.
Step 3. Initialize list L = ([Y,y]).
Step 4. Choose a coordinate direction k parallel to an edge of maximum length of $Y = Y_1 \times \ldots \times Y_m$, i.e., $k \in \{i: w(Y) = w(Y_i)\}$.
Step 5. Bisect Y in direction k getting boxes V_1, V_2 such that $Y = V_1 \cup V_2$.
Step 6. Calculate $F(V_1)$, $F(V_2)$.
Step 7. Set $v_i := \min F(V_i)$ for i = 1,2.
Step 8. Remove (Y,y) from list L.
Step 9. Enter the pairs (V_1, v_1) and (V_2, v_2) into the list such that the second members of all pairs of the list increase.
Step 10. Denote the first pair of the list by (Y,y).
Step 11. If termination criteria hold, then go to step 13.
Step 12. Go to step 4.
Step 13. END.

The algorithm initializes a list $L = L_1$ consisting of one pair (X,y) (see step 3). Then the list is modified and enlarged at each iteration (see steps 8 and 9). At the nth iteration, a list $L = L_n$ consisting of n pairs is present: $L_n = ([Z^{ni}, z^{ni}])_{i=1}^{n}$, where $z^{ni} = \min F(Z^{ni})$.

The *leading pair* of the list L_n will be denoted by $(Y^n, y^n) = (Z^{n1}, z^{n1})$.

The boxes Y^n are called the *leading boxes* of the algorithm. It is assumed that the termination criteria of step 11 are not satisfied during the whole computation such that the algorithm will not stop. In this case, an infinite sequence of lists is produced.

First of all, one can show that

$$w(Y^n) \to 0 \quad \text{as} \quad n \to \infty. \tag{19}$$

This fact seems to be self-evident but is not. For example, small modifications of the basic algorithm do not satisfy property (19), as is the case with the cyclic bisection method [5]. From the assumption

$$w(F(Y)) - w(\overline{f}(Y)) \to 0 \quad \text{as} \quad w(Y) \to 0 \; (Y \in I(X)) \tag{20}$$

it follows that

$y^n \leq f^*$ for any n,

$y^n \to f^*$ as $n \to \infty$,

$f^* - y^n \leq w(F(Y^n))$ (error estimate).

Interval Mathematics

Assumption (20) is not very restrictive. It is almost always satisfied if natural interval extensions are used. However, assumption (20) does not imply continuity, Lipschitz condition of f, etc. Let F now satisfy

$$w(F(Y)) \to 0 \quad \text{as} \quad w(Y) \to 0. \tag{21}$$

Clearly, assumption (21) implies assumption (20) and the continuity of f. Then $w(F(Y^n)) \to 0$ as $n \to \infty$, (i.e., the error estimate tends to 0 and can thus be used for termination criteria). Furthermore, *each accumulation point of the sequence* $(Y^n)_{n=1}^\infty$ *is a global minimizer*. The probability is zero that a global minimizer is not an accumulation point. The convergence order of the approach $y^n \to f^*$ is described by the following two results: Let any $\alpha > 0$ and any converging sequence be given. Then there exists an inclusion function of order α (i.e., the excess width tends to 0 as fast as desired) such that the resulting sequence (y^n) converges more slowly than the given sequence. If, on the contrary, an inclusion function F is given that is isotone and of order α, then $f^* - y^n = O(n^{-\alpha/m})$.

10.1 Modification of the Prototype Algorithm

These modifications produce sets that contain all global minimizers. Let G be the set of global minimizers. The modifications use lists reduced in the following sense: Let f_n be the lowest function value that has been calculated up to the completion of the list L_n. (If no function values are available, then $\min_{i=1...n} \max F(Y^i)$ can be taken as f_n.) All pairs (Z^{ni}, z^{ni}) of L_n are then discarded that satisfy $f_n < z^{ni}$. This gives a reduced list $\bar{L}_n$. Let

$$U_n = Z^{ni_1} \cup Z^{ni_2} \cup \ldots$$

for all Z^{ni_ν} of the reduced list. Then mainly two modifications of the previous algorithm are known:

1. Ichida-Fujii [40] use the U_n for the localization of G. One can prove that if (21) is assumed, then the sequence $(U_n)_{n=1}^\infty$ is nested and

    $$U_n \to \bigcap_{n=1}^\infty U_n \supseteq G.$$

    The probability is 0 that $\bigcap_{n=1}^\infty U_n \neq G$.

2. Hansen [38, 39] orders the lists $\bar{L}_n$ with respect to the age or the width of the boxes. Thus, if the leading box is bisected, the pairs resulting from the bisection are discarded or put to the end of the list. One can prove that if (21) is assumed, the sequence $(U_n)_{n=1}^\infty$ is nested and

    $$U_n \to \bigcap_{n=1}^\infty U_n = G.$$

10.2 Accelerating Devices

The basic algorithm and its modifications are rather slow if there are too many variables. The accelerating devices allow the calculations using a higher number of variables. Walster-Hansen-Sengupta [41] report a number 75. The two most important devices are:

1. If f is twice continuously differentiable and if an inclusion function for f" exists, then an *Interval-Newton Algorithm* is applied to f' in order to get boxes that contain all local minimizers [39, 40, 42]. The search for f* or G then only needs to be concentrated to the edge of X and to some of the boxes that contain the lowest local minimizer.
2. If f is differentiable and if an inclusion function for f' is available, then a *monotonicity test* can be applied [38, 39, 43]. It allows one to automatically recognize if f is strictly monotone in one of the variables in some subbox $Y \subseteq X$. Then Y can be discarded from the list if Y lies in the interior of X, or Y can be replaced by an edge piece of Y. That can be done as the parts removed do not contain a global minimizer.

Example: Let F_i' be an inclusion function for $\partial f/\partial x_i$ for $i = 1,\ldots m$. Then, because of the mean value theorem, $F(Y) = F(c) + (Y - c) \cdot (F_1'(Y) \cdots F_m'(Y))$ is an inclusion function for f. Here, c denotes the midpoint of Y, and the dot product is the inner product in R^m. There is now no additional effort when checking whether $0 \notin F_i'(Y)$. If this is true for some i, then f is strictly monotone in the variables x_i and Y can be discarded or replaced by an edge piece.

10.3 Unbounded Domain

It is common to consider a bounded domain X even when the unconstrained optimization problem is discussed. It is very easy to extend interval arithmetic to unbounded closed intervals [44]. Then the concept of inclusion functions and natural interval extensions can be extended to unbounded domains without difficulty. Unbounded interval function values can also be handled. So, e.g., $\exp([0,\infty)) = [1,\infty)$ such that a lower bound can be determined in this case. For branching, one has only to regulate the bisection because there is no partition in two equal parts when $[0,\infty)$ is considered. Nevertheless, the basic algorithm and its modifications can be used for unbounded domains.

10.4 Constrained Optimization

The basic branch-and-bound idea discussed in this section is also applied successfully to the constrained optimization problem [45, 46]. In this case, the higher the computational costs become, the more important it is to use all the acceleration devices available. Although the development makes good progress, the final step has not been done yet.

See Refs. 14, 23, 47, 85, and 86 for further discussion of the topics of this section.

11 CONCLUDING REMARKS

In the foregoing sections, only some areas on the very surface of interval mathematics were touched. Extended and deeper considerations would have been necessary to describe further areas or to give a characterization of them. Nevertheless, we will hint at such areas to give the reader at least a chance to go into those areas for himself. It is possible to give only a few references, the list of which can never be complete, but it helps for further reading. All the areas mentioned in the sequel are still open for further research.

First, there is the question of the *algebraic* and *topological structure* of interval arithmetic. Intervals do not form a group with respect to addition, there is no cancellation law with respect to multiplication, and there is no distributivity. Therefore, the algebraic structure is already of intrinsic interest. The structure is also important for all kinds of applications because each numerical or approximation method can only be good and effective if the algebraic and topological background is considered. This becomes more important as the discrepancy between the real and the interval structure becomes greater. For instance, compare common numerical analysis. Although an algorithm always works on the machine-representable numbers that form a very small screen of the rational numbers, the whole Hilbert space theory is—without discussion—the unavoidable backbone for being able to construct good and convergent numerical procedures. The same holds for interval analysis. See [14, 16, 19, 48–50] for further discussion of these topics.

What about the extension of real to *complex intervals*? The arising problems begin with the question of whether complex disks or complex rectangles should act as complex intervals e.g., [16, 51–53].

A theory of *interval analysis* in its literal sense, i.e., differentiation and integration of interval functions, is far from being completed. Such a theory is helpful, as is the case in noninterval analysis, for all kinds of analytic approximations [32, 54–57].

Almost all applications of interval mathematics are connected with the necessity of finding good *inclusion functions* and *interval extensions*. A very important class of interval extensions are the so-called *centered forms*, which are more interesting as it is possible to construct them with rather low computational costs [14, 16, 33, 58–62].

It is interesting that a thorough treatment of an interval analytic *approximation theory* is still missing. Some first steps in this direction are discussed by [63, 64, 65].

The advantage of using interval analysis in developing *functional analysis* is shown by [66].

Let us now focus on more specific areas of interval mathematics, where, first of all, interval techniques for solving *linear equations* and related problems are to be mentioned. They are still under intense investigation. Since [67, 68] has demonstrated that the interval version of the Gauss elimination method leads to a numerical disaster, it is one of the most challenging problems to develop appropriate methods for solving linear equations [12, 16, 69, 70].

Interval mathematics also focuses on the solving of *ordinary* or *partial differential equations*, *integral equations*, and *optimal control problems* [66, 71–73, 87].

The *processing of geometric objects* has been receiving considerable attention for its application in aircraft, ship, and automobile construction. How interval methods may be brought in is described by, e.g., [74, 75].

Applications of interval arithmetic to *electrical circuit analysis* are discussed by [76, 77]. For example, the variation of the impedance can be computed where the further elements of the circuit and their tolerances are assigned values. Or, the resistor values being given, an upper bound for the tolerance on the capacitancies are determined so that the system is stable.

Three-valued set theory features a three-valued elementhood relation within classical two-valued logic. Besides the two classical values, "a is element of A" and "a is not element of A," there is a third value that can be interpreted as "it cannot be decided whether a is element of A or not." Such cases are not exceptional but are the rule at empirical or numerical theories, such as physics, numerical analysis, astronomy, biology, psychology, etc. These are all theories based on some kind of error, like measurement error, observation error, machine errors, approximation errors, errors made by human sensory organs (e.g., let 10 persons decide which of 20 samples of wine are dry). There are fascinating relationships between interval arithmetic, three-valued set theory, and the methodology of empirical theories [45, 78, 79].

We conclude by mentioning the whole area of investigations that aim to make *scientific computation* more comfortable and easy to apply, such as *optimal automatic computation* or solving a given problem with a prescribed accuracy automatically, i.e., without further ado to the programmer, etc. See the following references for a large number of related contributions: [20, 22, 80, 81].

REFERENCES

1. M. Warmus, "Calculus of Approximations," *Bull. Acad. Pol. Sci.*, III, 4, 253–259 (1956).
2. T. Sunaga, "Theory of an Interval Algebra and Its Application to Numerical Analysis," *RAAG Memoirs*, 2, 547–564 (1958).
3. R. E. Moore, *Interval Analysis*, Prentice-Hall, Englewood Cliffs, NJ, 1966.
4. G. Alefeld and J. Herzberger, *Einführung in die Intervallrechnung*, Bibliographisches Institut, Mannheim, Germany, 1974.
5. R. E. Moore, *Methods and Applications of Interval Analysis*, SIAM Studies, Philadelphia, PA, 1979.
6. E. Hansen, ed., *Topics in Interval Analysis*, Proceedings of a symposium held in Culham, Great Britain in January 1968. Oxford University Press, London, 1969.
7. K. Nickel, *Interval Mathematics*, Proceedings of the international symposium held in Karlsruhe, May 1975. Springer-Verlag, Berlin, 1975.
8. K. Nickel, ed., *Interval Mathematics 1980*, Proceedings of the International Symposium held in Freiburg, May 1980. Academic Press, New York, 1980.
9. K. Nickel, ed., *Interval Mathematics 1985*, Proceedings of the International Symposium held in Freiburg in September 1985. Springer-Verlag, Berlin, 1986.
10. J. Albrycht and H. Wisniewski, eds., *Proc. Polish Symp. Interval and Fuzzy Mathematics*, Poznań, August 1983. Inst. Math. Technol. Univ. Poznań, Poznań, Poland, 1985.
11. J. Garloff, "Interval Mathematics—A Bibliography," *Freib. Intervall Berichte* 85/6, 1985.

12. K. Nickel, "Interval-Analysis," in *The State of the Art in Numerical Analysis* (D. Jacobs, ed.), Academic Press, New York, 1976, pp. 193–126.
13. K. Nickel, "Über die Notwendigkeit einer Fehlerschrankenarithmetik für Rechenautomaten," *Numer. Math. 9*, 69–79 (1966).
14. H. Ratschek and J. Rokne, *Computer Methods for the Range of Functions*, Horwood, Chichester, England, 1984.
15. R. E. Moore, "Interval Arithmetic and Automatic Error Analysis in Digital Computing," Ph.D. thesis, Stanford University, Stanford, CA, 1962.
16. G. Alefeld and J. Herzberger, *Introduction to Interval Computations*, Academic Press, New York, 1983. (Translation from the German original *Einführung in die Intervallrechnung*.)
17. N. Apostolatos and U. Kulisch, "Grundlagen einer Maschinenintervallarithmetik," *Computing 2*, 89–104 (1967).
18. N. Apostolatos, R. Krawczyk, U. Kulisch, B. Lortz, K. Nickel, and H. W. Wipperman, "The Algorithmic Language TRIPLEX-ALGOL-60," *Numer. Math. 11*, 175–180 (1968).
19. U. Kulisch and W. L. Miranker, *Computer Arithmetic in Theory and Practice*, Academic Press, New York, 1981.
20. U. Kulisch and W. L. Miranker, eds., *A New Approach to Scientific Computation*, Proceedings of a symposium held in New York, 1982. Academic Press, New York, 1983.
21. L. B. Rall, *Automatic Differentiation: Techniques and Applications*, Springer-Verlag, Berlin, 1981.
22. E. Kaucher and W. L. Miranker, *Self-Validating Numerics for Function Space Problems*, Academic Press, Orlando, FL, 1984.
23. H. Ratschek, "Inclusion Functions and Global Optimization," *Math. Programming 33*, 300–317 (1985).
24. R. Krawczyk, "Newton-Algorithmen zur Bestimmung von Nullstellen mit Fehlerschranken," *Computing 4*, 187–201 (1969).
25. R. E. Moore, "A Test for Existence of Solutions to Nonlinear Systems," *SIAM J. Numer. Anal. 14*, 611–615 (1977).
26. R. E. Moore, "A Computational Test for Convergence of Iterative Methods for Nonlinear Systems," *SIAM J. Numer. Anal. 15*, 1194–1196 (1978).
27. L. Qi, "A Generalization of the Krawczyk–Moore Algorithm," in Ref. 8, pp. 481–488.
28. K. Nickel, "On the Newton Method in Interval Analysis," Math. Res. Center Tech. Rep. 1136, University of Wisconsin, Madison, WI, 1971.
29. R. E. Moore and S. T. Jones, "Safe Starting Regions for Iterative Methods," *SIAM J. Numer. Anal. 14*, 1051–1065 (1977).
30. S. T. Jones, "Searching for Solutions of Finite Nonlinear Systems—An Interval Approach, Ph.D. dissertation, University of Wisconsin, Madison, WI, 1978.
31. S. T. Jones, "Locating Safe Starting Regions for Iterative Methods: A Heuristic Algorithm," in Ref. 8, pp. 377–386.
32. H. Ratschek and G. Schröder, "Über die Ableitung von intervallwertigen Funktionen," *Computing 7*, 172–187 (1971).
33. R. Krawczyk and A. Neumaier, "Interval Slopes for Rational Functions and Associated Centered Forms," *SIAM J. Numer. Anal. 22*, 604–616 (1985).
34. E. Hansen, "A Globally Convergent Interval Method for Computing and Bounding Real roots," *BIT 18*, 415–424 (1978).

35. K. Nickel, "Triplex Algol and Applications," in Ref. 6, pp. 10–24.
36. S. Skelboe, "Computation of Rational Interval Functions," *BIT*, 4, 87–95 (1974).
37. N. S. Asaithambi, Z. Shen, and R. E. Moore, "On Computing the Range of Values," *Computing* 28, 225–237 (1982).
38. E. Hansen, "Global Optimization Using Interval Analysis: The One-Dimensionsl Case," *J. Optim. Theory Appl.* 29, 331–344 (1979).
39. E. Hansen, "Global Optimization Using Interval Analysis—The Multi-dimensional Case," *Numer. Math.* 34, 247–270 (1980).
40. K. Ichida and Y. Fujii, "An Interval Arithmetic Method for Global Optimization," *Computing* 23, 85–97 (1979).
41. G. W. Walster, E. R. Hansen, and S. Sengupta, "Test Results for a Global Optimization Algorithm," in *Numerical Optimization 1984* (P. T. Boggs et al., eds.), SIAM, Philadelphia, PA, 1985, pp. 272–287.
42. Y. Fujii, K. Ichida, and M. Ozasa, "Maximization of Multivariable Functions Using Interval Analysis," in Ref. 9, pp. 17–26.
43. R. E. Moore, "On Computing the Range of a Rational Function of n variables Over a Bounded Region," *Computing* 16, 1–15 (1976).
44. W. M. Kahan, "A more complete interval arithmetic," Lecture notes at the University of Michigan, Ann Arbor, MI, 1968.
45. S. Sengupta, "Global Nonlinear Constrained Optimization," Ph.D. dissertation, Washington State University, Pullman, WA, 1981.
46. E. Hansen and S. Sengupta, *Summary and Steps of a Global Nonlinear Constrained Optimization Algorithm*. Lockheed Missiles and Space Co. Rep. No. D 889778. Sunnyvale, CA, 1983.
47. R. E. Moore and H. Ratschek, "Inclusion Functions and Global Optimization II." *Math. Programming*, 41, 341–356 (1988).
48. H. Ratschek, "Nichtnumerische Aspekte der Intervallmathematik," in Ref. 7, pp. 48–74.
49. C. Ullrich, "Über die beim numerischen Rechnen mit komplexen Zahlen und Intervallen vorliegenden mathematischen Strukturen," *Computing* 14, 51–65 (1975).
50. K. Nickel, "Verbandstheoretische Grundlagen der Intervall-Mathematik," in Ref. 7, pp. 251–261.
51. I. Gargantini and P. Henrici, "Circular Arithmetic and the Determination of Polynomial Zeros," *Numer. Math.* 18, 305–320 (1972).
52. J. Rokne and T. Wu, "The Circular Complex Centered Form," *Computing* 28, 17–30 (1982).
53. M. S. Petković, "Some Applications of Interval Arithmetic: Analysis of Linear Electrical Circuits," in *5th Conference on Applied Mathematics* (Z. Bohte, ed.), Ljubljana, Sept. 2–5, 1986, University of Ljubljana, Ljubljana, 1986.
54. R. E. Moore, W. Strother, and C. T. Yang, *Interval Integrals*, Technical Memorandum: Mathematics LMSD-703073, Lockheed Missiles and Space Division, Sunnyvale, CA, 1960.
55. S. M. Markov, "Calculus for Interval Functions of a Real Variable," *Computing* 22, 325–337 (1979).
56. O. Caprani, K. Madsen, and L. B. Rall, "Integration of Interval Functions," *SIAM J. Math. Anal.* 12, 321–341 (1981).
57. A. Marchiniak, "On Differentiation of Interval Functions," in Ref. 10, pp. 143–158.
58. R. E. Moore, *Intervallanalyse*, Oldenbourg-Verlag, München, Germany, 1969. (Translation from the English original *Interval Analysis*.)

59. R. Krawczyk and K. Nickel, "Die zentrische Form in der Intervallarithmetik, ihre quadratische Konvergenz und ihre Inklusionsisotonie," *Computing* 28, 117–137 (1982).
60. L. B. Rall, "Differentiation and Generation of Taylor Coefficients in PASCAL-SC," in Ref. 20, pp. 291–309.
61. H. Cornelius and R. Lohner, "Computing the Range of Values of Real Functions with Accuracy Higher than Second Order," *Computing* 33, 331–347 (1984).
62. J. Rokne, "A Low Complexity Explicit Rational Centered Form," *Computing* 34, 261–263 (1985).
63. H. Ratschek, "Optimal Approximations in Interval Analysis," in Ref. 8, pp. 181–202.
64. W. Witte, "Ansätze zur intervallanalytischen Approximations Theorie," Dissertation, Universität Düsseldorf, Düsseldorf, 1981.
65. H. Kolacz, "On the Optimality of Inclusion Algorithms," in Ref. 9, pp. 67–79.
66. R. E. Moore, *Computational Functional Analysis*, Horwood, Chichester, England, 1985.
67. P. Wongwises, "Experimentelle Untersuchungen zur numerischen Auflösung von linearen Gleichungssystemen mit Fehlererfassung," Dissertation, Universität Karlsruhe, Karlsruhe, 1975.
68. P. Wongwises, "Experimentelle Untersuchungen zur numerischen Auflösung von linearen Gleichungssystemen mit Fehlererfassung," in Ref. 7, pp. 316–325.
69. A. Neumaier, "New Techniques for the Analysis of Linear Interval Equations," *Linear Algebra Appl.* 58, 273–325 (1984).
70. J. Rohn, "Some Results on Interval Linear Systems," *Freib. Intervallberichte* 85/4, 93–116 (1985).
71. L. B. Rall, "A Comparison of the Existence Theorems of Kantorovich and Moore," *SIAM J. Numer. Anal.* 17, 148–161 (1980).
72. K. Nickel, *Using Interval Methods for the Numerical Solution of ODE's*, Math. Res. Center Tech. Rep. No. 2590, University of Wisconsin, Madison, WI, 1983.
73. T. Giec, "On an Interval Computational Method for Finding the Reachable Set in Time-Optimal Control Problems," in Ref. 9, pp. 57–65.
74. P. A. Koparkar and S. P. Mudur, "Subdivision Techniques for Processing Geometric Objects," in *Fundamental Algorithms for Computer Graphics*, (R. A. Earnshaw, ed.), Springer-Verlag, Berlin, 1985, pp. 751–801.
75. D. L. Toth, "On Ray Tracing Parametic Surfaces," *Computer Graphics*, 19, 171–179 (1985).
76. S. Skelboe, "True Worst-Case Analysis of Linear Electrical Circuits by Interval Arithmetic," *IEEE Trans. Circuits Syst.*, 26, 874–879 (1979).
77. M. S. Petković, Ž. M. Mitrović, and L. D. Petković, "Arithmetic of Circular Rings," in Ref. 9, pp. 133–142.
78. D. Klaua, "Partielle Mengen und Zahlen," Monatsber. Deutsch. Akad. Wiss. Berlin 11, 585–599, *1969.*
79. K. -U. Jahn, "The Importance of 3-valued Notions for Interval Mathematics," in Ref. 8, pp. 75–98 (1980).
80. S. M. Rump, "Solution of Linear and Nonlinear Algebraic Problems with Sharp, Guaranteed Bounds," *Comput. Suppl.* 5, 147–166 (1984).
81. F. Krückeberg, "Arbitrary Accuracy with Variable Precision Arithmetic," in Ref. 9, pp. 95–101.
82. R. E. Moore, ed., *Reliability in Computing: The Role of Interval Methods*

in *Scientific Computing,* Proceedings of an international workshop held in Columbus, Ohio, September 1987. Academic Press, San Diego, 1988.

83. J. Garloff, "Bibliography on Interval Mathematics, Continuation," *Freib. Intervall-Berichte 87/2,* (1987).

84. A. Neumaier, "Interval Iteration for Zeros of Systems of Equations," *BIT,* 25, 256–273 (1985).

85. H. Ratschek and J. Rokne, *New Computer Methods for Global Optimization,* Horwood, Chichester and Wiley, New York, 1988.

86. H. Ratschek and J. Rokne, "Efficiency of a Global Optimization Algorithm," *SIAM J. Numer. Analysis,* 24, 1191–1201 (1987).

87. E. Adams and W. F. Ames, "Linear or Nonlinear Hyperbolic Wave Problems with Input Sets," *J. Engineering Math.* 16, 23–45 (1982).

H. RATSCHEK

JAPANESE CHARACTERS, COMPUTER INPUT OF

INTRODUCTION

A major consideration when computer processing information in various languages is the kind of script used. If a language is one of the Romance or Germanic languages, all that is needed for computer processing are certain additional characters and diacritical marks. Languages which use non-Latin scripts must use character sets entirely different from those of Latin-alphabet languages, and hence some new approaches are necessary.

In the last three decades, people who use non-Latin languages have made enormous efforts to develop systems to process these languages in their own scripts. Why do they make such an effort to process them in their own scripts? Numerous systems using the Latin alphabet have been established and they are easy to use. Is it not sufficient to transliterate the non-Latin characters to alphabetical letters? There are various reasons for developing non-Latin systems and those reasons may be different for various languages. For the Japanese language, the answer to this question is mainly that *Kanji*, Chinese characters used for Japanese, possess visual effect. Each character signifies a certain thing, state, or act and imparts the meaning in a manner unlike that of phonetic alphabets. Besides, because of the presence of many homonyms, meanings become ambiguous without Kanji, which particularize their meanings. While it is quite possible to write Japanese only in a romanized form or in *Kana,* the Japanese counterparts of Latin alphabets, as proven by some systems already in use, it is far more efficient and precise to write Japanese in the way it is actually written and used by Japanese.

Among the many languages which use non-Latin scripts, Japanese and Chinese happen to use a great many of the same characters. Because of this, the Japanese and Chinese languages are often erroneously thought to be of the same family. However, linguistically they are entirely different. In terms of computerization, this means that a system for Japanese does not work for Chinese, and vice versa. The following are the linguistic differences between Chinese and Japanese, which affect the choice of systems.

1. Chinese uses approximately 50,000 Chinese characters, while Japanese uses about 20,000 Chinese characters, which the Japanese call *Kanji* (Han charcters). The number of characters necessary for a system is an important factor in deciding on a computer. Naturally, the fewer the characters, the easier the handling.
2. The Chinese simplified many characters on their own, and so did the Japanese. The result is that there are a great number of variants which cannot be mutually exchanged.

3. Whereas Chinese uses only Chinese characters, Japanese uses syllabaries, called *Kana,* in addition to Chinese characters. Furthermore, Kana has two styles: *Katakana,* or script style; and *Hiragana,* or cursive style. This means that a Japanese computer must have an additional capacity for Kana character sets. Similarly, it should be noted that Korean uses a phonetic alphabet called *Hankle* (or *Hangle*), thus necessitating a Hankle character set when processing Korean. One implication is that if a certain Chinese character is not included in a Japanese- or Korean-language system, a Kana or Hankle character can substitute for it. However, there are no substitutes available in Chinese.
4. The pronunciation of the characters varies according to the language. Moreover, within Japanese, characters are pronounced in several ways. Given a computer system which depended upon input by pronunciation, an enormous complexity would result when processing information in different languages.
5. With regard to reading, consideration must be made as to which romanization system to use. For Chinese, there are two widely used romanization systems, Wade–Giles and Pin-Yin. For Japanese, there are more than two: The most common are *Kun-rei* style and Hepburn style. The Library of Congress uses the so-called modified Hepburn style. These styles are similar, but Kun-rei is based on the Japanese Kana standard syllabary chart, and Hepburn is somewhat phonetically oriented.

If a system is intended to handle Chinese, Japanese, and Korean, all the preceding factors must be considered. If the system is for only one language, the requirements for a system are not as numerous as those for a multilanguage processing system. Most of the systems developed in Japan accommodate neither the Chinese language nor Korean.

JAPANESE CHARACTERS

A typical comprehensive Kanji dictionary contains approximately 50,000 characters. *Chung hua da zu dian,* a Chinese word dictionary which is scheduled to be published in 1985, will contain approximately 60,000 characters. *Han yu da zu dian,* a standard Chinese dictionary, contains a little over 48,000 characters. *Ueda's Daijiten,* considered an authoritative and standard medium-sized Kanji dictionary in Japan, includes approximately 15,000 characters. Pocket-sized dictionaries usually contain 8,000 to 10,000 characters. Though there are about 20,000 Kanji used, the survey done by the National Institute of Japanese Literature at the time of its initial planning for automation shows that the average number of Kanji used in contemporary Japanese documents is approximately 6,000. Among these, about half, or 3,000 characters, occur frequently. These figures are applicable to daily newspapers. For personal names, an additional 1,500 Kanji are necessary, and some 3,000 Kanji are necessary to cover most Japanese geographical names. In 1946 the Ministry of Education, Science, and Culture designated 1,860 Kanji as "Kanji for daily use." Those 1,860 are taught in the elementary schools and form the core of

Japanese Kanji used today. Though this number is not large, each character is read differently depending on how it is used. Depending on whether it is used initially, in the middle, or last in character compounds, whether alone or complemented by Kana, the reading of the Kanji varies. In an extreme example, one character is read in six or seven ways.

Each set of Kana includes 46 syllabaries with some additional characters such as voiced consonants, thus totaling about 170 characters for both sets, Katakana and Hiragana.

Another problem with the Japanese language is word division. When written, Japanese words are not divided as with Western languages. A whole sentence is written as a string of characters. This affects internal handling of the language and causes output problems in computer processing.

JAPANESE CHARACTER INPUT

Usually Japanese-language input devices have the capability for Latin characters, arabic numerals, some diacritical marks, and often, the Cyrillic and Greek alphabets, in addition to several thousands of Kanji and Kana in both styles. Numerous ways of inputting Japanese information into computers that are now in use can be sorted into four major types. They are (a) full keyboard type, (b) code composition type, (c) Kana-Kanji conversion type, and (d) pattern recognition type. Within each type various systems have been developed, as shown in Table 1. Of these, the first three are manual input and the last is automatic.

Full Keyboard Type

This is characterized, as the name indicates, by a full character keyboard, as opposed to a keyboard that uses codes assigned to characters. The keyboard is necessarily large. Each charcter is assigned a 2-byte code (expressed by a four-digit numeral), and when a character key is punched, the character is translated into a code and processed. Therefore, it is typical with this type that a Kanji dictionary is provided, so that when a Kanji is not found on the keyboard, the operator can search the dictionary and input the code for the Kanji listed in the dictionary. In this type there are three systems: Kanji teletypewriter system, Japanese typewriter system, and tablet-style system.

Kanji Teletypewriter System

This is the oldest system for inputting Kanji. The Kanji teletypewriter system, or multishift system, is still widely used. A certain number of Kanji are accommodated by one key, and these are arranged systematically on the keyface in a fixed pattern of columns and rows, such as three-by-five, or four-by-six. Separate function keys are arranged in a manner to indicate the position of Kanji in a Kanji key. When a Kanji key and a function key are punched, a Kanji selected by the function key is processed. A keyboard developed by the Japan National Diet Library at an early stage of its automation has 192 character keys, each having 15 characters, in

TABLE 1 Input Systems

Type	System	Method
Full keyboard	Kanji teletypewriter	
	Japanese typewriter	Character position
		Code-plate scanning
		Coded typeface
		Modified coded type-face
	Tablet style	Electromagnetic
		Electrostatic
		Photoelectric
Code composition	Component pattern input	
	Two-key-stroke input	Position correspondence
		Memory Association
	Numeric code input	Three-corner coding
		Modified three-corner coding
		Two-corner coding
Kana-Kanji conversion	Display selection	
	Word-by-word conversion (character-by-character) (clause-by-clause)	
	Context analysis	
Pattern recognition	Optical character recognition	
	Voice recognition	

three columns and five lines, as shown in Figure 1. In addition, there are 15 selection keys arranged in three columns and five rows on the lower left of the keyboard to correspond to the pattern of characters on each character key. When an operator strikes the character key B with the right hand and the selection key A with the left hand at the same time, the code for the character C is punched on the tape and processed. Included on this keyboard are

Kanji	2,006
Kana	90
Western alphabets	144
Numerals	20
Symbols and marks	210
Kanji patterns	40
Kanji components	139
Space	1
Total	2,650

Japanese Characters, Computer Input of   313

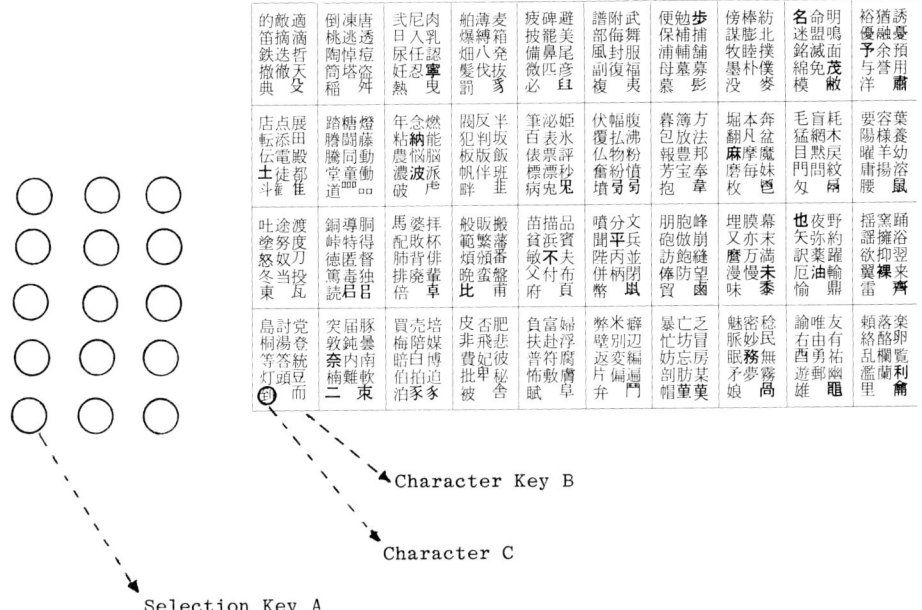

FIGURE 1 Kanji teletypewriter keyboard of the National Diet Library.

By using shift keys on the upper left of the keyboard, the operator can input Kana in both styles and alphabets, and in uppercase and lowercase. For satisfactory operation, operators must be professionally trained. One to three months are necessary for operators to be fully trained and able to input an average of 50 to 60 Kanji per minute. This is not as fast as most other methods.

Japanese Typewriter System

The second full keyboard type is the Japanese typewriter system, which uses a modified Japanese typewriter with trays filled with Kanji printing types. In this system, the operator must find a character in a tray and punch it by moving a metal handle as the type bar is punched down to print the character. This is a rather primitive operation compared to that of the English typewriter, which uses all 10 fingers in its operation. The following are four variations that have been developed on the Japanese typewriter system.

1. Character Position Method: Kanji are arranged on a keyboard by their codes. When a key is punched, the Kanji is typed on paper as if it had been typed by a regular Japanese typewriter. At the same time, the code is automatically read from the position of the key and is punched on tape and processed.
2. Code-Plate Scanning Method: Each character type bar has a plate attached on its side, and the code for the character is marked on

its plate. When a key is pressed, the Kanji is printed on paper, and the code from the plate is optically scanned at the same time for processing.
3. Coded Typeface Method: Each typeface is made with a character on the upper half and a corresponding code on the lower half. When a key is typed, both the character and code are printed. The code from the bottom half is optically scanned from the printed paper.
4. Modified Coded Typeface Method: This method prints only the characters on the front of the paper, instead of typing both characters and codes. At the same time, it prints a bar code on the back of the paper. The machine which does this is complicated. However, the size of the character on a typeface can be bigger than in the coded typeface method, and the bar code can be larger to make the scanning of the code easier and more precise.

All the Japanese typewriter systems offer the advantage of being able to monitor input at the time of keying.

The conventional Japanese typewriter has been in use for a long time in offices where a large quantity of official documents are dealt with. This means that ordinary Japanese typists can use any of these systems without much additional training. However, it should be noted that Japanese typewriters have never been as widely used as English typewriters, because of their slow speed and complexity, whereas the need for computers is felt in areas other than just those where Japanese typewriters are used. For these reasons, the use of Japanese typewriter systems is not as advantageous as their proponents claim. An obvious disadvantage is the slow speed of operation—30 to 50 characters per minute, on the average. Another disadvantage is that the number of characters on the keyboard is limited to about 3,000, and there is no way to accommodate Kanji that are not on the typefaces.

Tablet-Style System

This system, also known as the pen-touch system, was developed in the 1970s, and by the end of the decade it was the most widely used. In this system there is a key for each character, and the keys are arranged in a certain useful order on the keyboard. The position of the characters on a matrix sheet determines the 2-byte code, which consists of a two-digit numerical abscissa and a two-digit numerical ordinate. When the operator touches the key with a pen-shaped detector, the code for the character is punched on the tape. The operation is simple, requiring only the operator's light touch on the key by means of the detector. The keys are on a single flat keyboard and are color coded by sections to make it easier for the operator to locate them. Light-touch operation reduces operator fatigue and does not require special training. Again, the number of Kanji on a keyboard is limited to about 3,500. By shifting, however, twice as many characters can be handled, though not all the characters in the shift are indicated on the keyboard. The speed of input by this method is not very high—30 to 70 characters per minute. This system, already used in many libraries, has been most popular among libraries because of ease of operation. Three different technologies are in use: electromagnetic, electrostatic, and photoelectric. However, there are no differences in actual input operation among these electronically different methods.

Code Composition Type

The code composition type, like the Kana-Kanji conversion type, which is discussed later, uses a Kana keyboard. A Kana keyboard typewriter, or Japanese syllabary typewriter, is an adaptation of the conventional English typewriter keyboard and has standard Latin-alphabet keys that contain Katakana in shift. Since the number of Katakana exceeds that of Latin letters, the Katakana keys are extended to keys for numerals and punctuation marks. The arrangement of Kana on a keyboard is standardized, based on the Kana JIS (Japan Industrial Standard) standard keyboard arrangement. This means that this typewriter can be used either for Kana or for Latin letters by changing its mode. A standard-alphabet keyboard can also be used for input without Kana.

The principle of the code composition type is as follows. Each key in a keyboard is assigned a 1-byte code. When two or more keys are typed, the combination of those two or more 1-byte codes goes through a dictionary and is translated into a 2- or 3-byte code representing a particular character. There are three such systems: component pattern input system, two-key-stroke system, and numeric code input system.

Component Pattern Input System

The idea behind this approach is that most Kanji are composed of one or more basic component units, two or more of which can be put together into one Kanji, according to 1 predetermined pattern out of 40 general patterns. The inputting device has keys for these 40 patterns, along with keys for individual components on a special keyboard. To compose a Kanji, a key for an appropriate pattern is selected and typed, and components are chosen to fill each individually numbered block of the selected pattern, following the established order, as follows. Each pattern has a code, and so does each component. When a key is typed, the code is punched on a paper tape, as shown in Figure 2. There are cases where a Kanji with two components can be a component of another Kanji, as shown in the first and second examples in Figure 2. A Kanji is constructed by punching at least three codes: one for a pattern and at least two for the components. Then, a Kanji dictionary is used; this consists of several thousand master-code combinations (see Fig. 3) and is stored on a magnetic drum. The several codes used to compose a Kanji punched on paper or cassette tapes are converted through this dictionary to a 2-byte code assigned to that particular Kanji. These are then handled as other Kanji, with an individual code.

Though this system can serve as a stand-alone approach to inputting Kanji, the principle has been adopted by the Japan National Diet Library to

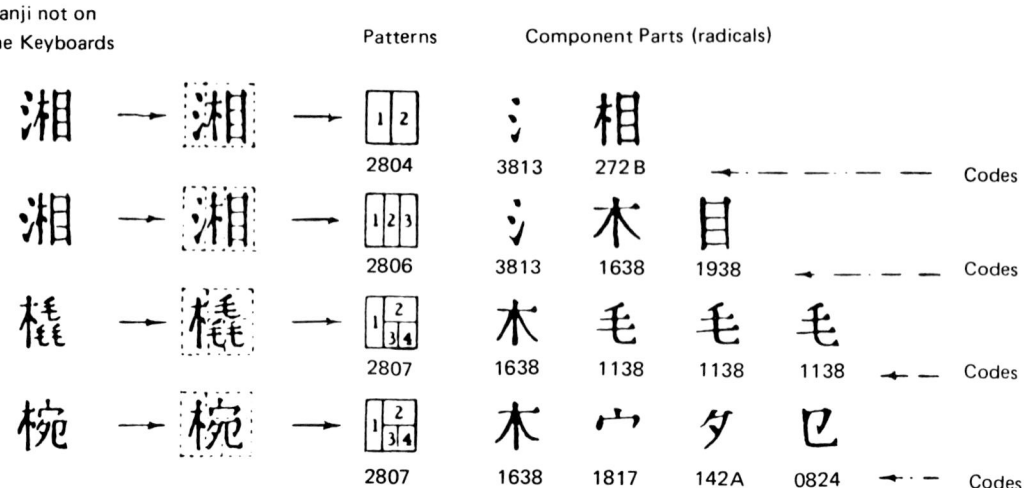

FIGURE 2 Component pattern input.

supplement the inputting of Kanji on the full keyboard Kanji teletypewriter. The Japan National Diet Library uses this system when inputting Kanji that are not included on its keyboard. Instead of using a special separate keyboard, the Kanji teletypewriter of the Japan National Diet Library integrates patterns and components as equivalents to other characters. Its keyboard includes 40 patterns and approximately 140 components.

This was begun as the most elementary basic approach to computerizing Kanji. Conceived in the early development stage of Kanji processing, it utilized one of the fundamental characteristics of Kanji, their composition from several components. In actual situations, this technique requires at least three key strokes for one Kanji, and it consumes time while the operator locates the needed component on the keyboard. Furthermore, this approach requires the complicated extra step of putting input codes through

Kanji dictionary

2804	3813	272B	0000	0000	0000	B118	→ 湘
.....	.....	.....	.....	.....	.....	.....	
2806	3813	1638	1938	0000	0000	B118	→ 湘
.....	.....	.....	.....	.....	.....	.....	
2807	1638	1138	1138	1138	0000	8117	→ 橇
2807	1638	1817	142A	0824	0000	9815	→ 椀
.....	.....	.....	.....	.....	.....	.....	

FIGURE 3 Kanji dictionary.

a Kanji dictionary to combine component codes into a code for Kanji. No library in Japan is currently using this system by itself. However, an advanced model of this type has been developed in the United States in order to handle Chinese, Japanese, and Korean. Because this system can handle a large number of characters, it seems appropriate to use it for multilanguage processing. This advanced model does not require that the pattern be input. The software recognizes the pattern if steps are taken to input the components in a certain order.

Two-Key-Stroke System

This variation of the Kana keyboard system, often referred to as the two-key-stroke system, uses Kana as codes, and not as letters. In this system, Latin letters can be used as codes, too. There are two different methods.

Position Correspondance. Keys are divided into two sections: one for the right hand and the other for the left. If two keys are to be pressed, there are four possible combinations of key strokes: (a) left hand twice, (b) left and right, (c) right and left, and (d) right twice. The keyboard is accompanied by a Kanji table in which characters are arranged in several blocks and in a certain order within each block. Each block, containing 24 Kanji in a four-by-six arrangement, is formed according to the different combinations of strokes: The first block is left and left, the second block is left and right, and so on. Within each block, the ordinate consists of keys for the first stroke; and the abscissa, for the second. A Kanji which is at the intersection of the ordinate and abscissa indicates which keys are to be typed. If Kanji C is to be typed (see Fig. 4), since it is in block A, indicating the stroke combination as left and left, the operator types key A and key W with the left hand. If Kanji D is to be typed, the operator types key A with the left hand and key P with the right, as indicated in block B. Each key has a byte code, and a combination of two key strokes makes a composite, a 2-byte code, for a Kanji. The bit may be changed by shifting, and different Kanji can be typed if another table is prepared for Kanji with different bits.

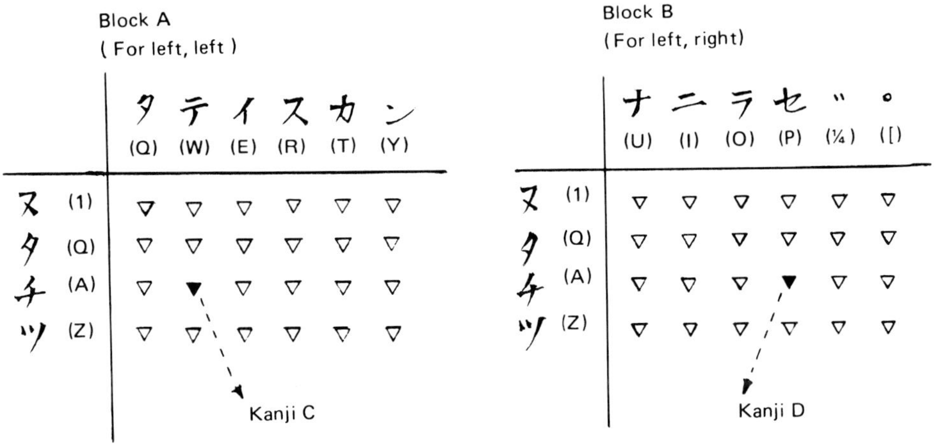

FIGURE 4 Kanji table for position correspondence.

Memory Association. In this system, each Kanji is given two Kana, which usually represent a reading of that Kanji. The operator associates a Kanji to be input with two Kana assigned to that Kanji, and types them with two strokes using the Kana keys.

Both of the two-key-stroke methods are economical as well as convenient, because of the wide availability of Kana typewriters. Mainly for this reason, both of these systems have been well accepted and are expected to become more widely used. About 4,000 characters can be processed. Since this touch method does not require the operator to look for the character on the keyboard to input, it is the fastest and is considered suitable for inputting in quantity. It is possible to input 60 to 120 characters per minute. The only drawback is that the operator must become familiar with the arrangement of Kanji in the first variation, and must memorize all the associated Kana spellings for many Kanji in the case of the second variation. In either case, the operator must be professionally trained.

The Japan Information Center for Science and Technology, which indexes many scientific publications, employs a vendor who uses the position correspondence variation of this system for inputting information.

Numeric Code Input System

Each Kanji is assigned a numeric code consisting of a string of four or six numerals. If a large number of Kanji must be accommodated, six-digit codes can be assigned. Therefore, only combinations of the numerals from 0 to 9 are used for all Kanji input. One method assigns the group of numbers like telegraphic code. The other is called the three-corner coding method.

Three-Corner Coding Method. Depending on the shape of three corners of the Kanji, each corner is translated into two-digit numerals, totaling six digits per Kanji. In order to input, the operator punches a maximum of six numeric digits using numeric keys on the keyboard. Operators must be familiar with the shape and structure of Kanji. For those who know Kanji, a few days of training is sufficient. With this method, more codes are available for a larger number of characters, since it uses a six-digit code.

Modified Three-Corner Coding Method. A variation of the three-corner coding method has become very popular in Japan lately. The keyboard of this system provides 100 keys. Each key has a basic character component which becomes one of the three corners of characters. The same key also shows a two-digit numerical code assigned for that component. The operator inputs three components which compose three corners of a character, rather than typing six numerical keys to compose three corners of the character (see Fig. 5). In other words, since each component key has a two-digit numeral, input of six-digit numerals can be done with three key strokes. The model currently available in Japan can accommodate approximately 13,000 characters.

Two-Corner Coding Method. This is another modified three-corner coding method. The number of components to be input is reduced to two: one from the upper left corner and the other from the lower right corner. However, the first sound of that character must also be input. This sys-

Japanese Characters, Computer Input of   319

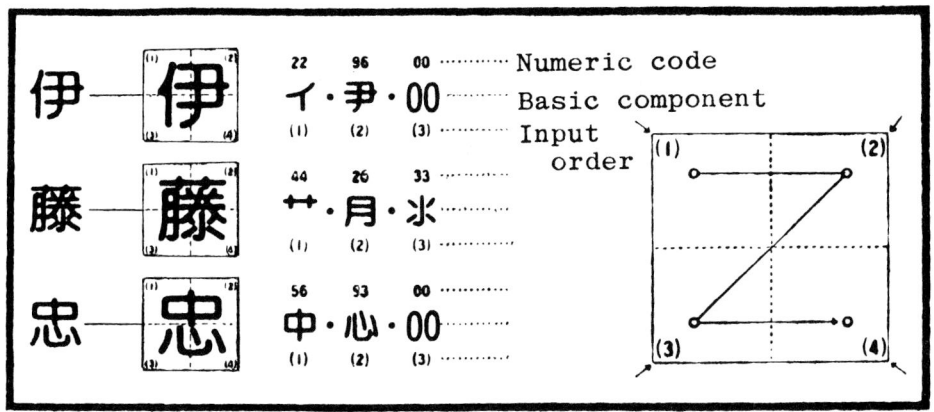

FIGURE 5 Three-corner coding.

tem can currently process about 3,000 Kanji of JIS first selection, in addition to Kana, the Latin alphabet, and symbols and marks.

Kana-Kanji Conversion Type

In contrast to the conventional approach of full keyboard inputting and code composition, an entirely new method for inputting Kanji is gaining popularity as the availability of sophisticated software increases. This type uses a Kana typewriter keyboard to input Japanese, in either syllabary or romanized form, and converts characters to Kanji by means of the software. There are various methods of conversion, the simplest being the display selection method. However, the most popular is the method which converts Kana or Latin characters into Kanji word by word. There are two similar methods: character by character and clause by clause. The most sophisticated of this type converts by means of context analysis.

Display Selection System

Like the code composition type, this system also employs a Kana typewriter facing a display screen. When a word is typed in Kana, a group of Kanji with that sound are displayed on the screen. The operator chooses the right Kanji from among the group with a light pen. This is a slow but accurate operation of 20 to 30 characters per minute. The operator does not have to be specially trained.

Word-by-Word-Conversion System

The word-by-word conversion system is widely used at present, surpassing in popularity the character-by-character and clause-by-clause conversion methods. The principle behind these different methods is the same. When a word is typed in Kana or romanized form, it is converted to the appropriate characters. When Kana-Kanji conversion is made by word or clause, a string of characters becomes more specific than when converted by character, and there are fewer problems in selecting the right Kanji from among those which have the same phonetic value.

A word processor currently available in Japan is an example of the application of a word-by-qord conversion system. Both Latin-alphabet and Kana input are available. However, since the standard English typewriter touch is easier for many, romanized input is popular. On the keyboard "the beginning of Kanji" and "the end of Kanji" keys are provided. The operator can type Japanese by Kana or romanized form and switches to and from the Kanji mode with these two keys at the beginning and end of Kanji. This system also possesses image-processing capability. The capacity of the system is 72,000 words, of which the user can register 1,000 words. It contains 2,965 JIS first selection Kanji, Kana, Latin letters, numerals, and diacritical marks, and 3,384 JIS second selection Kanji; and it can accommodate an additional 376 characters of the user's choice.

Context Analysis System

The most advanced of the Kana—Kanji conversion systems is probably the one that analyzes context. This is still in the developmental stage. However, when this system is put into operation, it will automatically select the right Kanji from among many Kanji with the same *phones,* using software which analyzes the context. This requires a sophisticated program, and there are problems to be solved. For example, if Kanji are used out of context, such as in the case of personal names, which consist of several Kanji, an appropriate contextual analysis by machine becomes impossible.

Pattern Recognition Type

Pattern recognition includes optical image pattern recognition, that is, recognition of characters or image; and sound wave pattern recognition, that is, recognition of voice.

Optical Character Recognition System

In this system the pattern of an image is optically scanned and recognized as characters or graphics. Since 1955 research has been devoted to developing a system that would recognize both printed and handwritten characters. This system can currently scan a maximum of 4,000 printed Kanji at a speed of 100 Kanji per second, or 2,200 handwritten Kanji, at 50 per second. However, the drawback is that if a Kanji is complicated and involves many strokes, it is difficult to scan precisely. One variant system connects a writing tablet to a computer so that as the operator writes Kanji on the tablet, the computer scans them in stroke order. Scanning by stroke order is considered advantageous when processing some types of Japanese documents. However, this system is still very expensive, and the number of characters that the system can recognize is still very much limited.

One of the important aspects of this system is the capability to incorporate in one document images with characters input by other systems. At present, this is used, together with the manual input of characters in today's commercial models, to integrate images or graphics with language information.

Voice Recognition System

This is an oral-visual system, in which the sound waves of the human voice are analyzed and recognized as characters by a computer. The most difficult to develop, this system is still in the experimental stage. The prototype is being demonstrated at various exhibitions, and the system obviously has great potential.

PROBLEMS PARTICULAR TO KANJI PROCESSING

Problems to be solved before processing Kanji through computers are (a) the kind of Kanji to include; (b) the number of Kanji to handle; (c) the code to assign and the arrangement of Kanji on the keyboard or table; (d) the handling of the Kanji not included on the keyboard; and (e) ease or difficulty of use.

In the early stage of Kanji computer development, different institutions made these decisions in ways best suited to their individual needs, according to the nature of the literature covered, the amount of literature processed, and the kinds of output needed. They experimented with the best capabilities available at the time. As a result, the finished systems are all independent and mutually incompatible. Yet standardization is necessary so that information can be exchanged among the systems.

In order to set the standard for selection of characters and assignment of codes, JIS (Japan Industrial Standard) C6226-1978 was compiled by the Japan Association for Development of Information Processing. This is a table of characters designed for information exchange (a portion of which is shown in Fig. 6). Each character has a 1-byte code as its abscissa and another as its ordinate. Characters are arranged so that the intersection of the abscissa and ordinate determines a Kanji whose code consists of four numerals, two from the abscissa and two from the ordinate. Included in the table are Kana in both styles; Latin, Greek, and Cyrillic alphabets in upper- and lowercase; and diacritical marks, numerals, and punctuation marks, as follows:

Special characters	108
Numerals (arabic)	10
Latin letters	52
Hiragana	83
Katakana	86
Greek letters	48
Cyrillic letters	66
Kanji	6,349
Total	6,802

In the first section of the table, numerals, letters, Kana, and special characters are grouped. In the second section, a total of 2,965 frequently used Kanji are arranged as the first priority group, and an additional 3,384 Kanji are selected as the second group in the bottom half of the table. Kanji are printed in the preferred style of printing typeface. This

							b7	0	0	0	0	0	0	0	0	0	0	0	0	0
						第2バイト	b6	1	1	1	1	1	1	1	1	1	1	1	1	1
							b5	0	0	0	0	0	0	0	0	0	0	0	0	0
							b4	0	0	0	0	0	0	0	1	1	1	1	1	1
							b3	0	0	0	1	1	1	1	0	0	0	0	1	1
							b2	0	1	1	0	0	1	1	0	0	1	1	0	0
							b1	1	0	1	0	1	0	1	0	1	0	1	0	1
第1バイト							点	1	2	3	4	5	6	7	8	9	10	11	12	13
b7	b6	b5	b4	b3	b2	b1	区													
0	1	0	0	0	0	1	1	SP	、	。	,	.	・	:	;	?	!	｢	｣	｡
0	1	0	0	0	1	0	2	◆	□	◪	△	▲	▽	▼	※	〒	→	←	↑	↓
0	1	0	0	0	1	1	3													
0	1	0	0	1	0	0	4	ぁ	あ	ぃ	い	ぅ	う	ぇ	え	ぉ	お	か	が	き
0	1	0	0	1	0	1	5	ァ	ア	ィ	イ	ゥ	ウ	ェ	エ	ォ	オ	カ	ガ	キ
0	1	0	0	1	1	0	6	A	B	Γ	Δ	E	Z	H	Θ	I	K	Λ	M	N
0	1	0	0	1	1	1	7	А	Б	В	Г	Д	Е	Ё	Ж	З	И	Й	К	Л
0	1	0	1	0	0	0	8													
0	1	0	1	0	0	1	9													
0	1	0	1	0	1	0	10													
0	1	0	1	0	1	1	11													
0	1	0	1	1	0	0	12													
0	1	0	1	1	0	1	13													
0	1	0	1	1	1	0	14													
0	1	0	1	1	1	1	15													
0	1	1	0	0	0	0	16	亞	唖	娃	阿	哀	愛	挨	姶	逢	葵	茜	穐	悪
0	1	1	0	0	0	1	17	院	陰	隠	韻	吋	右	宇	烏	羽	迂	雨	卯	鵜
0	1	1	0	0	1	0	18	押	旺	横	欧	殴	王	翁	襖	鴬	鴎	黄	岡	沖
0	1	1	0	0	1	1	19	魁	晦	械	海	灰	界	皆	絵	芥	蟹	開	階	貝
0	1	1	0	1	0	0	20	粥	刈	苅	瓦	乾	侃	冠	寒	刊	勘	勧	巻	喚
0	1	1	0	1	0	1	21	機	帰	毅	気	汽	畿	祈	季	稀	紀	徽	規	記

FIGURE 6 JIS code for information interchange.

table will resolve problems *a* through *c* mentioned at the beginning of this section. If a variant coding system is already in use, such a code can be translated into JIS code or CCCII (Chinese Character Code for Information Interchange) code for information interchange. Institutions that had arranged their own codes for Kanji, including the National Institute of

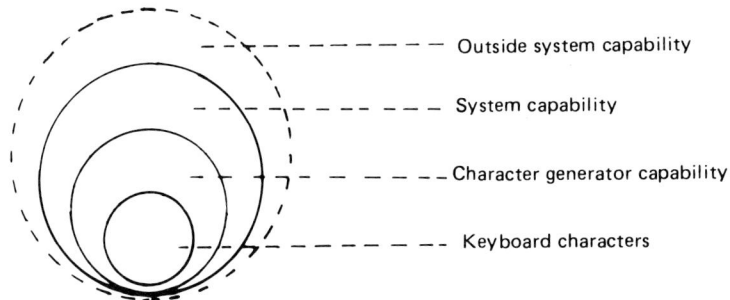

FIGURE 7 Kanji-creating capability.

Japanese Literature, are now automatically translating their own codes into JIS codes. The code was revised in 1983. For Chinese, CCCII is being established. Because of the large number of characters needed for the Chinese language, the code table is in three dimensions; that is, the tables are structured in layers. Accordingly, the code is in 3 bytes: abscissa, ordinate, and plane.

If a needed Kanji is not included on the keyboard, its handling varies. As in the Japanese typewriter system, because each Kanji is inscribed on a typeface, only the Kanji on that typeface is printed when the type bar is stroked. Therefore, only Kanji that have typefaces can be input in this system, while some other handling is possible in other systems.

While the number of characters that can be accommodated on a keyboard is limited to 2,000 to 3,500 in practical applications, depending on the type of equipment, character generators have the capability of outputting more than the number of characters on the keyboard. Figure 7 shows their relationships. Characters that are in the generator but not on the keyboard must be processed frequently, because the number of characters needed for most documents could reach 6,000 to 6,500. Using a shift key to enter another mode is a fairly common technique for inputting uncommon Kanji. The keyboard may not have a character, but if the character generator has it, the code for that character can be input by shifting. For example, if a character on the keyboard has code 0117, a bit is changed so that code 8117 can be typed by shifting and typing that key. If code 8117 is assigned to a Kanji not on the keyboard but indexed in the dictionary, it can be input. This applies for the Kanji teletypewriter system, the tablet-style system, and the two-key-stroke variations of the Kana typewriter.

In the Kanji teletypewriter system used by the National Diet Library, the keyboard accommodates 2,650 characters, while its character generator has the capability for 5,717. Operators at the National Diet Library input Kanji that are not on the keyboard by using the component pattern input method. Or, if the operator finds the Kanji code in the specially compiled dictionary in which codes for Kanji are indexed, a shift key is used to change the bit, thus creating the code for a Kanji not on the keyboard. Most other tablet systems use code dictionaries. In the two-key-stroke variations of Kana typewriters, tables of Kanji for second and third or more shifts can be built, especially when the position association method is used.

The handling of Kanji that are not in character generators is more difficult. Only the digital character generator, the kind that uses either the dot or the stroke method, can add characters fairly easily. In the flying-spot system, characters can be added, but this must be done professionally, with an additional character cylinder, and is very costly. The National Diet Library, which now uses the flying-spot system, limits the addition of Kanji to a minimum. Because its output is solely in printed book form, the National Diet Library inputs a "fill character" for Kanji, which is not in the system. When the phototypeset masters are made, the fill characters are replaced by typeset characters. The use of a fill character suffices only when the output is phototypeset, because of the additional step needed to replace fill characters with typeface. However, as long as the data base includes many fill characters on the magnetic tapes, the on-line retrieval of information or later utilization of tapes becomes unsatisfactory.

The National Institute of Japanese Literature uses a dot matrix and prints by wire-dot image. If a Kanji is not in the character generator, the institute's staff composes the Kanji in an enlarged dot matrix and creates the capability for printing in the generator. If the Kanji made in such a way is used only once, the Kanji pattern is not stored in the character generator, so that the generator does not reach its full capacity quickly. The enlarged dot composites for Kanji created by the institute are filed and indexed for future use.

Most other institutions simply do not use those less commonly used Kanji, and substitute Kana for them.

The last problem is that most of these systems require trained operators, or else their operation is very slow. Unlike the Latin-alphabet typewriter, which is fairly uniform in operation, the differences in methods of operation among Japanese character input systems are enormous. Consequently, ease or difficulty in use, depending on the type of system, becomes a deciding factor for selection.

CHARACTER OUTPUT

Pattern configuration and output devices for Japanese characters are basically the same as those for English. However, the pattern generation of Japanese characters is mechanically more complicated than that of the Latin alphabet, because Kanji have a more complicated structure then the Latin alphabet and the number of components is greater. Each Kanji is generally represented by a 2-byte code rather than 1 byte, as with the Latin alphabet. Because of this, computers which handle ASCII or EBCDIC code cannot be utilized, and the efficiency of retrieval is low. At present, hard copy and typesetting for printing of hard copy are the major output forms; on-line retrieval of information with Kanji is infrequent but is rapidly increasing in current operations.

In addition to the problems common to any character output system, such as size and number of dots, two other problems must be considered with Kanji: the space for Kanji in relation to other characters and the choice of vertical or horizontal printing of Japanese sentences.

Kanji have many strokes and, as mentioned before, are expressed by 2-byte codes. Each Kanji needs a double space when displayed on screens or printed. When Kanji are used with numerals or Kana, the Kanji appear to be correctly spaced, but the numerical portions have too much space between each numeral. Therefore, input of Kanji is done in a Kanji mode, and input of Kana, Latin characters, and numerals are in a Kana-numerical mode. Consequently, a multidigit figure looks like one whole figure, rather than a line of one-digit figures.

Some formal documents must be printed in the traditional vertical arrangement. To cope with this situation, some line printers have the capability to precompose a vertical page before printing it.

There are multicolor cathode-ray tubes on the market that can be used for the retrieval of library-related information (e.g., main entry in red, series statement in yellow).

CONCLUSION

As seen in the foregoing discussion, there are a variety of input systems. The trend in the use of Kanji in Japan is to simplify the characters themselves, and not to use complicated Kanji with many strokes. This, together with the rapid advancement of character-processing technology, has contributed significantly to the development of numerous highly sophisticated systems. The computers which handle Kanji have become very sophisticated in the last several years, and they will continue to be improved. Various systems incorporating the combined advantages of several systems are available. A variety of systems, claiming various features of high performance and simple operation, are appearing on the market. There is no indication of a few models becoming dominant. In other words, the trend today is toward diversity rather than standardization.

BIBLIOGRAPHY

Hasegawa, Jitsuo, "Kanji Shori Sōchi" [Kanji Processing Devices], *Jōhō Shori* [Information Processing], Jōhō Shori Gakkai, Tokyo, 19(4) (April 1978).

Ishiwata, Toshio, "Kanji Shori ni Motomeru Mono" [Requirements for Study on Kanji Processing], *Computopia*, Computer Age Sha, No. 9, 1977.

Japan National Diet Library, *Library Automation in the National Diet Library: 1977–83*, The Library, Tokyo, 1978–1984.

Jōhō Kanri, Journal of Information Processing and Management, Japan Information Center for Science and Technology, Tokyo, 21–27 (1978–1984).

"Jōhō Kōkan no Tame no Kanji Fugō no Hyōjunka" [Standardization of Kanji Code for Information Interchange], *Kagaku Gijitsu Bunken Sābisu* [Scientific and Technical Documents Service], Tokyo, No. 50, 1978.

Morita, Ichiko, "Japanese Character Input: Its State and Problems," *J. Libr. Automation*, 14(1) (March 1981).

National Institute of Japanese Literature, *Report*, NIJL, Tokyo, Nos. 1-6, 1978-1980.

Sugai, Kazuo, "Kanji Nyū-shutsuryoku Sōchi no Kaihatsu Dōkō" [A Trend in Development of Kanji Input-Output Devices], *Bus. Commun.*, Tokyo, 16(7) (1979).

ICHIKO T. MORITA

MANAGEMENT OF UNCERTAINTY IN KNOWLEDGE-BASED SYSTEMS

ABSTRACT

The management of uncertainty and imprecision is fundamental in knowledge-based systems, and the classical probabilistic methods are not always sufficient, because of the various types of ambiguity appearing in rules and observed facts. Fuzzy logic provides new tools to treat these problems, but a careful choice of the appropriate implication and combination law for the generalized modus ponens is necessary to avoid unacceptable conclusions.

INTRODUCTION

The knowledge base of an expert system contains (a) a series of facts observed in some experiments or characterizing the studied phenomenon and (b) the description of rules and connections between facts and conclusions, which must themselves be considered as new facts. Uncertain data are produced by imprecise measures concerning quantified criteria, by subjective factors involved in the rules obtained from a human expert, or by the impossibility of obtaining all the information about some aspect of the studied phenomenon. Unreliable rules are due to the fact that the expert is not sure of the inference expressed, the fuzziness or imprecision contained in the evidence, and/or the conclusion involved in a rule. A definitive conclusion or a diagnosis must be produced by means of a chain of inferences using a sequence of connections, and it must often be weighted with a coefficient of uncertainty.

We restrict ourselves to evidence or facts A_k described as X_k is C_k, where $k = 1, 2$, etc., and X_k is a variable (such as the size, the color, the temperature, or the nature of an object or an element) that may be expressed as $X_1(obj)$ in the framework of a first-order logic, with obj denoting the considered object or element. C_k is an attribute or a characterization of the variable X_k (high, red, very hot, rock). The rules are supposed to be expressed as "If A_1 then A_2," where A_1 and A_2 are evidence.

The concepts that are involved in the description of facts or rules such as "red," "dark," "sharp pain," "possible," "very likely," "small," "later," or "approximately," are natural in the reasoning of the expert, but they are difficult to treat automatically without losing any information.

SOME METHODS FOR TREATING UNCERTAINTIES OR IMPRECISIONS

Various techniques permit coping with all the uncertainties and imprecisions inherent in the evidence. A primary way of managing imprecise concepts would be to use the semantic meaning of the words; this needs an approach of natural language, which is an important field of research. Let us consider the following example:

(E1) "If the temperature is high, then the product will be injurious very soon."

An ambiguity stems from the meaning of "high" and "soon," which may change from one expert to another and is rather difficult to determine precisely. Another linguistic problem comes from modifiers such as "rather" or "very," which can be introduced in such a way that the fact "the temperature is rather high," will not be considered as sufficient to make the rule (E1) work directly.

Another factor of uncertainty comes from the fact that the temperature may be measured with an inaccuracy and also from the uncertainty of the expert giving the rule about its validity in any case.

A way of managing facts that are not precisely described or certain is to use non-monotonic logics in the inferences, which permit making hypotheses and inferring conclusions from incomplete information [1]. The particular case of modal logic takes into account expressions such as "it is possible that the product is injurious," leading to uncertain but plausible conclusions [2, 3]. In the particular situations where the time introduces some difficulties in the treatment of the rules, a temporal logic [4] can be a useful tool. Besides the classical connectives, it uses operators expressing that an evidence will be realized at some time or at any time after a given time t, e.g., "If the temperature is high at time t, it will be true for every time following t that the product is injurious."

A simple method of dealing with ambiguities in the knowledge base consists of splitting the information contained in the imprecise rule into several crisp rules, in order to decompose the possible cases summarized in the imprecise rule. For example, E1 can be replaced by several crisp rules, such as "If the temperature is between 20°C and 25°C, the product should be consumed within 24 hours;" "If the temperature is between 25°C and 30°C, the product should be consumed immediately;" "If the temperature is higher than 30°C, the product should be thrown away."

It is obvious that such splitting of the intervals of temperature and time is somewhat arbitrary and that the conclusion deduced at the limit points of the intervals can be discussed.

It is possible to attenuate this crisp transition by using a fuzzy logic and the description of linguistic variables. For instance, the attributes "high" and "soon" will be defined by means of continuous membership functions f_1 and f_2 taking values in the respective universes of possible temperatures and time, lying in the interval $[0,1]$, as defined in Figure 1. The modifiers ("very") applied to some attributes generate a modification of the membership functions associated with the attributes [5].

In the case of an imprecision in the observation of the evidence that corresponds to the premise of some rule, a coefficient may be associated with the fact, expressing the certainty of the observer with regard to this evidence. Weighting parameters may also be linked with the rule itself,

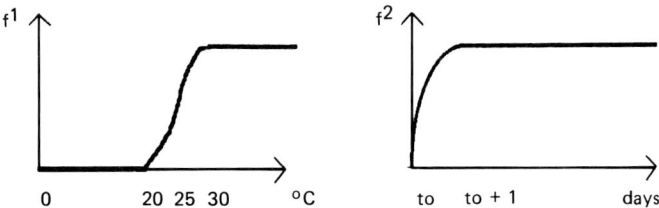

FIGURE 1 Membership functions f_1 of attribute "high" for the variable "temperature" and f_2 of attribute "son" for the variable "time".

corresponding to the confidence of the expert in the conclusion or to the strength of his rejection of the conclusion. Several studies have been devoted to these methods, and expert systems have been constructed by using particular management of these parameters or coefficients [6, 7].

The next section introduces the main methods for managing uncertainties and imprecision in a logical way, but this domain is very rich and research is intensive [8].

FUZZY LOGIC

Fuzzy Inferences

Let us consider a rule such as "If A_1 then A_2," where A_k, $k = 1,2$, are facts defined as "X_k is C_k," for a variable X_k defined on a universe U_k and a characterization C_k of X_k represented by a membership function f_k defined on U_k and lying in $[0,1]$. In Boolean logic, propositions A_1 and A_2 would be considered as true or false, depending on the value zero or one associated with them, and the implication expressed in the rule would take the value corresponding to A_1 or A_2. In the case of a fuzzy logic, A_1 and A_2 are considered satisfied with a degree $f_k(x)$, $k = 1,2$, in every point x of U_k. They are not satisfied if the value is zero, completely satisfied if it equals one, and intermediate values of satisfaction are possible. The implication is defined, in the case of fuzzy logic, in several ways that lead to various definitions of the value $r_{12}(x,y)$, representing the strength of the inference that involves the facts A_1 and A_2 as premise and conclusion of the rule, for any pair (x,y) of elements of the universes U_1 and U_2.

Even if it is important to know the strength of the deduction rule, this value is principally useful in determining the fact that will be obtained as a conclusion of such a rule when the observation that enables us to use it is somewhat different from the premise of the rule. For instance, rule E1 supposes that the temperature corresponds to the characterization "high" to be used directly. In the case of classical logic, an observation of the temperature expressed as "The temperature is 22°C" (F_1) or "The temperature is rather high" (F_2), would not allow us to obtain a deduction from this rule, because the inference process is generally based on a modus ponens working in such a way that "If X_1 is C_1 than X_2 is C_2" and "X_1 is C_1" holds, implies that "X_2 is C_2" holds. In the case of fuzzy logic, a generalized modus ponens has been introduced [9] and takes into account the rule "If X_1 is C_1 then X_2 is C_2" and an evidence "X_1 is C'_1," where

C'_1 is identical or not to C_1, yielding a conclusion "X_2 is C'_2" for a characterization C'_2, which can be different from C_2. The observation is described by means of a membership function g_1 defined on U_1 and lying in [0,1]. The conclusion obtained is given through a membership function g_2 defined on U_2 and also lying in [0,1]. In the above-mentioned example, the observations (F_1) and (F_2) are described in Figure 2.

Obviously, if C'_1 is too different from C_1, the given rule cannot provide any interesting result and the conclusion C'_2, which is deduced, is weighted with a coefficient of uncertainty, which equals one when the doubt is absolute and the obtained result of the inference cannot be used any more to match the premise of any other rule, even in a generalized modus ponens process.

Classical Fuzzy Implications

We present here the most classical forms of *fuzzy inferences* [10–12], and we give the value $r_{12}(x,y)$, $\forall x \in U_1$, $\forall y \in U_2$, of the implication involving premise A_1 and conclusion A_2:

$$r^1_{12}(x,y) = 1 - f_1(x) + f_1(x)f_2(y)$$

$$r^2_{12}(x,y) = \max(1 - f_1(x), \min(f_1(x), f_2(y)))$$

$$r^3_{12}(x,y) = \min(f_1(x), f_2(y))$$

$$r^4_{12}(x,y) = 1 \text{ if } f_1(x) \leq f_2(y), \text{ and } 0 \text{ otherwise,}$$

$$r^5_{12}(x,y) = \max(1 - f_1(x), f_2(y))$$

$$r^6_{12}(x,y) = 1 \text{ if } f_1(x) \leq f_2(y) \text{ and } f_2(y) \text{ otherwise,}$$

$$r^7_{12}(x,y) = \min(f_2(y)/f_1(x), 1) \text{ if } f_1(x) \neq 0 \text{ and } 1 \text{ otherwise,}$$

$$r^8_{12}(x,y) = \min(1 - f_1(x) + f_2(y), 1),$$

$$r^N_{12}(x,y) = \max(N(f_1(x)), f_2(y)),$$

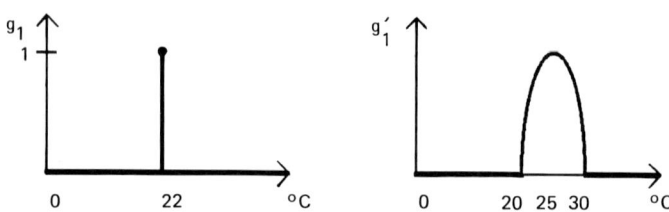

FIGURE 2 Membership functions g_1 of attribute "22°C" of temperature and g'_1 of attribute "rather high" of temperature.

for a strong negation N defined by $N(u) = f^{(-1)}(f(0) - f(u))$, where f is the additive generator of a triangular norm [12–14], which can be written

$$F(u,v) = f^{(-1)}(f(u) + f(v)), \quad u \in [0,1], \quad v \in [0,1]$$

with regard to the continuous, strictly decreasing function f defined on [0,1] and lying on R^+, such that $f(1) = 0$ and $f(0) < +\infty$, with $f^{(-1)}(u)$ equal to $f^{-1}(u)$, if $0 \leq u \leq f(0)$, to 0 if $u \geq f(0)$ and to 1 if $u \leq 0$. It admits $r^5{}_{12}(x,y)$ as a *particular case*, with $N(u) = 1$, $f(u) = 1 - u$.

$$r^F{}_{12}(x,y) = f(f_1(x), f_2(y))$$

where f is the quasi-inverse of a t-norm F, defined by

$$f(u,v) = \max[w \in [0,1], F(u,w) \leq v]$$

It admits as *particular cases* $r^6{}_{12}(x,y)$, with $F(u,v) = \min(u,v)$, $r^7{}_{12}(x,y)$ with $F(u,v) = uv$, $f(u) = -\log u$, $r^8{}_{12}(x,y)$ with $F(u,v) = \max(u+v-1,0)$, $f(u) = 1 - u$.

With the object of a comparison of fuzzy implications with the Boolean one, we write the latter as

$$r^B{}_{12}(x,y) = 1 \text{ if } f_1(x) = 0 \text{ or } f_2(y) = 1, \text{ and } 0 \text{ if } f_1(x) = 1 \text{ and } f_2(y) = 0,$$

with $U_1 = \{x\}$ AND $U_2 = \{y\}$ and f_1 and f_2 ranging in $\{0,1\}$ in this case.

Comparison of the Implications

The choice of the fuzzy implication used to represent the inference considered in a rule depends on the specialist constructing the knowledge base. The definitions give more or less equivalent results, but some differences appear when we consider particular situations [15–17].

The first interesting case corresponds to a *nonambiguous* (or *crisp*) conclusion A_2, obtained by considering a membership function f_2, which equals one at one point y_0 of U_2 and zero elsewhere. Such a situation corresponds, e.g., to the following rule E2, with a very precise conclusion:

(E2) "If the temperature is high, the product should not be consumed."

Then the strength $r^k{}_{12}(x,y)$ of the rule equals 1 for $y = y_0$, whatever k may be, except $k = 2,3$, which yield values equal to $\max(f_1(x), 1 - f_1(x))$ and $f_1(x)$, respectively, and, thus, depend on the premise A_1. We note that this would not be the case in Boolean logic. For $k = 4,6,7$, we obtain, in any y different from y_0, $r^k{}_{12}(x,y)$ equal to zero for any x in U_1 such that $f_1(x) \neq 0$ and to 1 otherwise. The value of $r^k{}_{12}(x,y)$ is a function of $f_1(x)$ otherwise, which is $1 - f_1(x)$, for $k = 1,2,5,8$, and $N(f_1(x))$ if $k = N$ or F, for implications r^F and r^N defined, e.g., through the same generator f. The only exception concerns $k = 3$, which is zero in any point of U_1 different from y_0.

The second interesting case is dual of the first one and it corresponds to a *nonambiguous premise* A_1, characterized by a membership function f_1 equal to 1 at some point x_0 of U_1 and zero elsewhere. We can consider the following example E3:

(E3) "If the temperature is 22°C, then the product will be injurious very soon."

Differences appear once more in the results given by the fuzzy implications, but the classes of similar behavior are easier to study in this case. It can be noted that the value of $r^k{}_{12}(x,y)$ is $f_2(y)$, for $x = x_0$, in every case, except $k = 4$, when $f_2(y) \neq 0$, which produces a zero value. If x is different from x_0, this value is generally equal to one, and the only exception concerns the case $k = 3$, yielding zero.

An interesting point concerns the conditions equivalent to a *value of the fuzzy implication equal to zero or one*, which is important when we combine this value characterizing the given rule, with a description of the observation concerning X_1 as it will be explained in the next section.

We observe that $r^k{}_{12}(x,y)$ is zero if and only if $f_1(x) = 1$ and $f_2(y) = 0$, in most cases ($k = 1,2,5,8,N$), or, less strictly, if and only if $f_1(x) > f_2(y)$ for $k = 4$, or $f_1(x) \neq 0$ and $f_2(y) = 0$ for $k = 6,7,N$. An exception occurs when $k = 3$, corresponding to situations for which $f_1(x) = f_2(y) = 0$.

The value of $r^k{}_{12}(x,y)$ is one if and only if $f_1(x) = 0$ or $f_2(y) = 1$, for $k = 1,2,5,N$ or, less strictly as for the previous case, if and only if $f_1(x) \leq f_2(y)$, for $k = 4,6,7,8,F$. The only exception concerns the case $k = 3$ (once again), which corresponds to the situation $f_1(x) = f_2(y) = 1$.

The characteristics of the indicated fuzzy implications are given in Table 1.

The specialist must adopt a definitive position on this matter: Either he chooses fuzzy logic, which has the same behavior as Boolean logic with regard to the criteria we have presented above, e.g., $k = 1,5,N$, or he prefers fuzzy implication, which generalizes the Boolean properties. This seems understandable because the fuzzy logic involves less strict data than the classical logic, e.g., $k = 4,6,7,8,F$, and otherwise he prefers a strength of the fuzzy implication monotonous with regard to the value of f_1 and consequently equal to 1 if and only if $f_1(x) = f_2(y) = 1$. This is the case for $k = 3$ (the more possible A_1, the stronger the rule) [16]. Various other criteria may be considered to compare the qualities of the fuzzy implications, which are useful in choosing the most interesting one for a given knowledge-bases system [12,17].

Generalized Modus Ponens

In the case where an observation (e.g., F_1 or F_2) is more or less different from the premise of the rule to be used (say E1), a combination law must be introduced to associate the membership function describing this observation (g_1) with the value of the fuzzy implication expressing the rule (r_{12}) to give the membership function (g_2) representing the conclusion inferred from the data. Once more, several possibilities exist, defined in a general way as follows, for a given operation G defined and ranging on [0,1]:

$$g_2(y) = \max_{x \in U_1} (G(g_1(x), r^k_{12}(x,y))), \text{ for any } y \in U_2, x \in U_1$$

TABLE 1 Values $r^k_{12}(x,y)$ of the fuzzy implications in any $x \in U_1$, $y \in U_2$

k	A_2 crisp		A_1 crisp		Value = 0	Value = 1
	$y = y_0$	$y \neq y_0$	$x = x_0$	$x \neq x_0$	(if and only if)	
B,1,5	1	$1 - f_1(x)$	$f_2(y)$	1	$f_1(x) = 1$ AND $f_2(y) = 0$	$f_1(x) = 0$ OR $f_2(y) = 1$
2	$\max(f_1(x), 1 - f_1(x))$					$f_1(x) = 0$ OR $f_1(x) = f_2(y) = 1$
4	1	1 if $f_1(x) = 0$; 0 otherwise	1 if $f_2(y) = 1$; 0 otherwise		$f_1(x) > f_2(y)$	$f_1(x) \leq f_2(y)$
6,7		$N(f_1(x))$	$f_2(y)$		$f_1(x) \neq 0$ AND $f_2(y) = 0$	
F		$1 - f_1(x)$				
8		$N(f_1(x))$			$f_1(x) = 1$ AND $f_2(y) = 0$	
N						$f_1(x) = 0$ OR $f_2(y) = 1$
3	$f_1(x)$	0		0	$f_1(x) = 0$ OR $f_2(y) = 0$	$f_1(x) = f_2(y) = 1$

An important property (P) to require from this combination law is that it preserves the conclusion of the rule when the observation coincides with the premise of the rule. It can be proved [15] that the choice, for G, of the t-norm F associated with the definition of the fuzzy implication (r^N or r^F, e.g., and consequently $r^k{}_{12}$, for $5 \leq k \leq 8$) ensures that this requirement (P) is satisfied. Obviously, the choice of G is not uniquely determined, and further studies [16, 18] give several reasons to prefer one combination law according to the characterization of the conclusion when the observation (e.g., F_1 or F_2) is not ambiguous or less precise than the premise of the rule. A list of possible combination operators providing a generalized modus ponens satisfying (P) is given in Table 2.

The conclusion "X_2 is C'_2" depends on the compatibility of the premise "X_1 is C_1" and the observation "X_1 is C'_1." The lowest value of the membership function g_2 should be almost equal to one if the uncertainty is important, which means that C'_1 is very different from C_1. On the contrary, g_2 must be almost identical with f_2 if C'_1 and C_1 are very similar.

The following properties hold with the t-norms G satisfying requirement (P), listed in Table 2:

- If C'_1 is more specific than C_1, which means that $g_1(x) \leq f_1(x)$ $\forall x \in U_1$, then C'_2 is also more specific than C_2: $g_2(y) \leq f_2$, $\forall y \in U_2$ if we choose $r^k{}_{12}$ with $k = 4$, but we generally get C'_2 identical with C_2 when $k \neq 4$. *Expansive modifiers*, such as "very," "strongly," and "really," which reinforce the attribute can be represented by such transformations of the membership functions describing the attribute they modify. For instance, if C_1 is "high" in the rule and C'_1 is "really high" for the observation, the conclusion would generally (k = N or F) be "very soon" as indicated by E1, but could be more specific ($g_2 \leq f_2$) for $k = 4$.
- If C'_1 is less specific than C_1, i.e., $g_1(x) \geq f_1(x)$ $\forall x \in U_1$, then C'_2 is also less specific than C_2: $g_2(y) \geq f_2(y)$, $\forall y \in U_2$ in all the cases $r^k{}_{12}$, except $k = 3$, which gives C_2 itself as a conclusion. *Restrictive modifiers*, such as "not," "very," "moderately," or "somewhat," can be represented by such transformations of the membership function describing the attribute they modify. For instance, if C_1 is "high" and C'_1 is "not very high," we deduce a conclusion from (E1) telling that C'_2 is "pretty soon" if we choose $r^k{}_{12}$ with $k \neq 3$, and C'_2 is C_2 ("very soon") otherwise.
- If C'_1 is not ambiguous (example F_1), its membership function g_1 is zero in every point of the universe U_1 different from a given one, say x_1, where its value is one. Then any t-norm G gives a conclusion defined by $g_2(y) = r^k{}_{12}(x_1, y)$.

If the premise of the rule itself is crisp with $f_1(x_0) = 1$ (example E3), then two possibilities may occur: *either* $x_0 = x_1$ and, according to Table 1, the deduced evidence coincides with the conclusion of the rule in all cases r^k, except $k = 4$; *or* $x_0 \neq x_1$, the fact is incompatible with the rule, and the value of $g_2(y)$ is generally 1 (except for $k = 3$), $\forall y \in U_1$, for any fuzzy inference, expressing that the indetermination is maximum, and every element of U_2 is possible. The choice of $k = 3$ entails that no element of U_2 can be taken into account in a further utilization of the conclusion of the rule, because $f_2(y) = 0$, $\forall y \in U_2$.

TABLE 2 Combination Operators G Defining a Generalized Modus Ponens Compatible with the Modus Ponens for Every Fuzzy Inference r^k

k	G	$g_1 \leq f_1$	$g_1 \geq f_1$	C_1 crisp $\neq C_1'$	C_1' crisp, C_1 fuzzy
1,2,5,8	$G(a,b) = \max(a+b-1,0)$	$g_2 = f_2$	$g_2 \geq f_2$	$g_2(y) = 1 \; \forall y$	$H = 1 - f_1(x_1)$
6	$G(a,b) = \max(a+b-1,0)$ $G(a,b) = \min(a,b)$ $G(a,b) = ab$				$H = 1$ if $f_1(x_1) = 0$ 0 otherwise
7	$G(a,b) = \max(a+b-1,0)$ $G(a,b) = ab$		$g_2 = f_2$	$g_2(y) = 0 \; \forall y$	$H = 0$
3	$G(a,b) = \max(a+b-1,0)$ $G(a,b) = \min(a,b)$ $G(a,b) = ab$		$g_2 \geq f_2$	$g_2(y) = 1 \; \forall y$	$H = N(f_1(x_1))$
N,F	The associated t-norm F				

If the premise of the rule is fuzzy (example E1), in the case where $f_1(x_1) = 0$, the fact is incompatible with the rule and the previous remarks are still valid. In the case where $f_1(x_1) \neq 0$, we can observe that any point y of U_2 with a zero membership function $f_2(y)$ (which means that there is no possibility of y to be concerned in the conclusion of the rule) corresponds to an *indetermination* H when the observed fact is crisp for most implications. The value of $g_2(y)$ is then equal to $1 - f_1(x_1)$ (for k = 1,2,5,8) or to $N(f_1x_1)$) if k = N or F. It corresponds to the lowest possibility of an element y of U_2 to be involved in the conclusion of the inference. It could be equal to zero for some N or F, such as for k = 6,7, and also for k = 3,4, implying that the possibility of $y \in U_2$ is zero in the conclusion of generalized modus ponens as soon as it is zero in the conclusion of the rule.

More generally, an indetermination H appears when the following facts occur at the same time: Some elements y of U_2 are not possible with regard to the characterization of X_2 expressed in the conclusion of the rule ($f_2(y) = 0$), and the observed evidence is not perfectly identical with the premise of the rule ($g_1 \neq f_1$). Then the graph of g_2 may admit a bottom different from zero and its height indicates the least possibility of an element of U_2 to be involved in the deduced evidence. The value of this indetermination is zero for the fuzzy inferences r^k_{12}, with k = 3, it is

$$\max_{\{x \in U_1 / f_1(x) = 0\}} g_1(x) \text{ for } k = 4,6,7$$

It is $\max_{\{x \in U_1\}} G(g_1(x), 1 - f_1(x))$ for k = 1,2,5,8, and

$$\max_{\{x \in U_1\}} F(g_1(x), N(f_1(x))), \text{ for } k = N \text{ or } F.$$

Once more, a position must be adopted by the specialist. Either he chooses a combination law and a fuzzy implication such that an indetermination appears (expressed by the minimum value of g_2), which entails that the fact deduced from the inference can be used in a further rule if it matches its premise in a generalized modus ponens process. Of he prefers a solution such that an element of the universe U_2 is not possible in the deduced evidence if it was not possible in the conclusion of the rule.

REFERENCES

1. D. McDermott and J. Doyle, "Non-monotonic logic," *Artif. Intell.*, 13, 41–72 (1980).
2. L. Farinas Del Cerro, "Resolution Modal Logic," *Logique et analyse*, 110–111; 153–172 (1985).
3. D. McDermott, "Nonmonotonic II. Nonmonotonic Modal Theories," *J. ACM*, 29, 33–57 (1982).
4. P. Wolper, "The Tableau Method for Temporal Logic: An Overview," *Logique et Analyse*, 110–111; 119–136 (1985).
5. L. A. Zadeh, "The Concept of Linguistic Variable and Its Application

to Approximate Reasoning," *Inf. Sci.* 8 (part I), 199–249; (part II), 301–357 (1975).
6. R. Duda, J. Gaschnig, and P. Hart, "Model Design in the PROSPECTOR Consultant System for Mineral Exploration," in *Expert Systems in the Micro-electronic Age* (D. Michie, ed.), Edinburgh University Press, Scotland, 1979.
7. E. H. Shortlife, "Computer-based Medical Consultations, MYCIN," Elsevier, New York, 1976.
8. *Proceedings of the International Conference on Information Processing and Management of Uncertainty in Knowledge-based Systems*, International Conference IPMU, Paris, (1986).
9. L. A. Zadeh, "The Role of Fuzzy Logic in the Management of Uncertainty in Expert Systems," *Fuzzy Sets and Syst.*, 11, 199–227 (1983).
10. B. Bouchon, "Fuzzy Inferences and Conditional Possibility Distributions," *Fuzzy Sets and Systems*, 23, 33–41 (1987).
11. E. Trillas and L. Valverde, "On Indistinguishability and Implication," Memorandum 82/04, Universitat Politecnica de Barcelona, 1982.
12. S. Weber, "A general concept of fuzzy connectives, negations, and implications based on t-norms and t-conorms," *Fuzzy Sets and Syst.*, 11, 115–134 (1983).
13. E. P. Klement, "Operations on Fuzzy Sets and Fuzzy Numbers Related to Triangular Norms," in *Eleventh International Symposium on Multiple-Valued Logic*, IEEE, Oklahoma, 1981.
14. L. Valverde, "On the Structure of F-Indistinguishability Operators," *Fuzzy Sets and Syst.*, 17(3), 313–328 (1985).
15. B. Bouchon, "On the Forms of Reasoning in Expert Systems," in *Approximate Reasoning in Expert Systems* (M. M. Gupta et al., eds.), North Holland, Amsterdam, 1985.
16. B. Bouchon and S. Désprès, "Propagation of Uncertainties and Inaccuracies in an Expert System," in *Uncertainty in Knowledge-Based Systems* (B. Bouchon and R. R. Yager, eds.), Lecture Notes in Computer Science 286, Springer-Verlag (1987).
17. T. Whalen and B. Schott, "Issues in Fuzzy Production Systems," *Int. J. Man-Mach. Stud.*, 19, 57–71 (1983).
18. S. Desprès, "Un apport à la conception de systèmes à base de connaissances: les opérations de déduction floues," Thèse de l'Université Paris 6 (1988).

BERNADETTE BOUCHON

MOTOROLA, INC.

INTRODUCTION TO THE COMPANY'S EARLY BEGINNING

The high technology Motorola, Inc., of today, founded by Paul Galvin in 1928, was originally named The Galvin Manufacturing Corporation. A strong believer in the dignity of the individual, Paul's integrity and energy later earned him a place of honor in the Business Hall of Fame. The enterprising Galvin started his venture in a rented building in Chicago located at 847 Harrison Street, with $565, five employees, and a dream. Nevertheless, Paul Galvin went forward with the idea of getting the world ready to accept the concept of having sound on wheels.

CRASHING STOCK MARKET

Following the stock market crash of 1929, numerous small businesses, similar to that of the Galvin operation, found it difficult to survive the current economic conditions. Even in the times when other businesses were folding on a daily basis, young Galvin was determined to make a success of his company. He wanted to improve on the existing procedures of the manufacturing process of his main product—home radio receivers.

MASS PRODUCTION CONCEPT

During a trip to New York, Galvin discovered that automobiles were being equipped with high dollar car radios that had to be custom built for proper installation. Unfortunately, this new and innovative approach to putting sound on wheels was too costly for the average person.

Galvin found that the most efficient method of high quantity production was being demonstrated in Detroit's industrial district, the relatively new automobile industry. The car business in Detroit was surviving well. Galvin's new plan was to mass produce high quality yet low cost car radios. If nearly every new car manufactured came equipped with an economical car radio, Galvin felt sure his company would survive the depression era.

With the enthusiastic assistance of his employees, Galvin performed some very successful experiments with radio-equipped cars. The basic elements of the system, the bulky batteries, receiver set, and speaker, fitted snuggly into Galvin's car. The result was a radio that worked in a car, either while stopped or in motion.

THE BIRTH OF MOTOROLA—1930s

At a very popular convention held during this period, the Radio Manufacturer's Convention, all types of early radio receivers and the latest breakthroughs

MOTOROLA, INC.

were displayed. It was at this convention in 1930 that the company's name was changed from The Galvin Manufacturing Company to Motorola. Authorized Motorola car radio installation stations were established, adding to their popularity.

The quality of radio products continued to improve with the increase in new and interesting features. By the mid- to late 1930s, the Motorola, Inc., trademark also appeared on newly introduced models of home radios, pacing the way for future electronic products under the newly named company.

During the 1930s era, such "people programs" as the Service Club and the Engineering Club began at the company. These morale-type programs proved very favorable to the Motorola work force.

TWO-WAY COMMUNICATIONS—1940s

In 1941, Motorola introduced a significant new product, the first FM two-way mobile system. This new concept of two-way communication really revolutionized police dispatching for emergency calls. In a short period of time, two-way communication expanded to other areas of safety such as fire departments and emergency ambulance vehicles.

With the coming of World War II new opportunities arose for Motorola to demonstrate its innovative expertise in communication. The rules of ground warfare were partially rewritten by Motorola thanks to the development of the Handie-Talkie, a two-way crystal-controlled portable radio that was smaller than a cracker box. It came complete with a microphone, head antenna, and self-contained batteries. About 40,000 Handie-Talkies were produced to support the war effort. Motorola developed and produced about 50,000 of the Walkie-Talkie, SCR-300, an FM portable two-way communication system for the Signal Corps. It was very popular because of its ability to communicate through interfering ignition noise of vehicles and its ability to withstand tropical temperature and humidity. It gained the reputation as the most significant piece of communications equipment used during the war. These products played a major role in the coordination and success of mass amphibious landings in Europe, as well as in the South Pacific.

During the 1940s, the company established the employee profit-sharing fund to enable employees to build income to be used for retirement. Because of increased product demands, the employee population grew rapidly.

PEACETIME BREAKTHROUGHS—1950s

With the war behind them, research and development laboratories concentrated their efforts more in the direction of consumer-type products rather than military and defense-support items. With peace, television offered Americans a new form of entertainment and an alternative to radio. Television was immediately accepted by the public. Motorola was the first manufacturer of televisions to offer a black-and-white set for under the very low price of $200. Named the VT-11, this was quite a step from the first radio receivers used for sound reception to a cathode ray tube in a television used for displaying moving pictures.

Up until this time, vaccum tubes were used as switching devices and amplification units in electrical equipment. The birth of the transistor changed the electronics industry forever. In 1954, Motorola selected Phoenix, Arizona, for their research and development laboratory, the Semiconductor Development Group. This facility soon evolved into the largest semiconductor manufacturing plant.

The Semiconductor Development Group created a 3-amp power transistor. This milestone proved that these devices could be used in a variety of high power applications. Other transistors were produced, capable of switching between on and off at high speeds.

Upon Paul Galvin's death, leadership of the company went to Robert (Bob) Galvin in 1959. Bob became the new board chairman and chief executive officer of Motorola, Inc.

UNIVERSAL EXPANSION—1960s

Motorola, Inc., expanded its operation on a global basis to the United Kingdom, Japan, Switzerland, France, Mexico, Canada, Hong Kong, Korea, and Israel. A major advancement in television production came with the introduction of the first rectangular color picture tube. Since the Explorer I flight in 1958, almost all manned and unmanned space flights have used Motorola technology and communications expertise. The voice of Neil Armstrong was transmitted from the moon via a Motorola S-band transponder. The Lunar Rover, the first car on the moon, came equipped with a distributorless ignition system designed by Motorola.

ADVANCEMENTS IN INTEGRATED CIRCUITS—1970s

As sophistication increased, the early transistor designers discovered that their designs required more transistor sites than a single printed circuit board could readily offer. The next logical step was to increase the number of transistors on a small piece of silicon resulting in integrated circuit technology. From the integrated circuit developments in the early 1970s, the microprocessor (MPU) evolved. An MPU basically consists of a central processor, an arithmetic logic unit, and a few registers used for temporary storage.

The MPU is the brain power of many of the computer systems of today. With its introduction came an increased awareness of the need for more and more power (faster with greater efficiency) at the chip level. The first MPUs had about the equivalent to several tens of thousands of transistors on a single chip. The speed at which these devices operate is amazing. The manner in which they function can be compared to that of a minature brain.

Motorola, Phoenix, soon became saturated with manufacturing facilities. Integrated circuit development needed a new location to continue its research and production. Austin, Texas, was selected for the new MOS integrated circuits plant in 1973. Several individual product groups and divisions currently exist at this plant site.

The first Motorola MPU was the MC6800, which is an 8-bit machine made up of a few thousand transistors. The 16-bit MC68000 MPU was introduced shortly thereafter. Portable cellular phones made mobile telephone usage a reality. Codex modem equipment made high-speed data communications possible over an existing phone line.

In 1976, Motorola products were on board the flight to Mars. There is a good chance that the sophisticated design scaling that made this event possible will result in an MPU integrated with as many as 1,000,000 transistors. The size of this chip would be no more than 1.4-inch square. The MPU is basic to the future success of many functions in our daily lives, such as personal computers, automobile electronic technology, entertainment equipment, appliance control, factory automation, and communications support, just to name a few.

In addition to the basic MPU that came about during the 1970s, other integrated circuits are designed and fabricated at Motorola facilities. One of these, the memory device, is an essential part of every computer system. It is in memory that coded data are stored for representing programs used in calculations and other reference information. Many types of memory chips are manufactured in the modern semiconductor house, including static random access memory (SRAM), dynamic random access memory (DRAM), read-only memory (ROM), electrically programmable ROM (EPROM), and electrically erasable programmable ROM (EEPROM). The 256K bit DRAM is used as main memory in numerous computer systems.

The three basic logic symbols, AND, OR, and NOT are functions of integrated circuit logic devices manufactured by Motorola. They can be configured in such a manner that they mathematically solve problems arising from interfacing between the MPU and memory, as well as providing communication to the outside world.

MOTOROLA AT WORK—1980s

Motorola offers thousands of different types of semiconductor devices, computer systems, and communication equipment that are used in both the public and private sectors. In addition, every nation in the world is touched in one way or another by the microelectronics of Motorola.

Some of the areas served by Motorola products are the many agencies of the police and fire protection departments, along with emergency service vehicles and the United States Coast Guard.

Motorola electronic communications assists in the search for oil at offshore installations. Motorola provides government communications equipment for U.S. naval vessels and provides constant worldwide reception for these same ships via satellite.

The very first photos of the red planet were sent back to earth thanks to a Motorola communication system. Motorola is preparing for future flights to Saturn and beyond. Four-Phase Systems, Inc., was acquired by Motorola to allow further expansion in the office computer system business. Alphanumeric display pagers were introduced, along with the first commercially available 32-bit MPU, the MC68020.

MOTOROLA STRUCTURE TODAY

Today's Motorola, Inc., consists of two sectors and four major groups: Communications Sector (CS), Semiconductor Products Sector (SPS), Information Systems Group (ISG), Government Electronics Group (GEG), General Systems Group (GSG), and the Automotive and Industrial Electronics Group (AIEG).

COMMUNICATIONS SECTOR

The CS had net sales in excess of $2 billion for the year of 1986, up 11% from the previous year. In addition, the FCC added an additional 26 megahertz to the 900-megahertz spectrum. This significantly enhanced the available space for mobile radio transmission and the use of cellular telephones. Alphanumeric paging networks are now operating in France. In Singapore, a Motorola paging system is interconnected with the standard telephone network. Mobile data terminals for taxi dispatching applications and the Personal Message Receiver alphanumeric pager, offering twice the memory of previously introduced products, are also available.

SEMICONDUCTOR PRODUCTS SECTOR

Motorola and Toshiba established a cooperative agreement in which Motorola receives advanced DRAM and SRAM designs and process technologies. In return, Toshiba purchases 8-, 16- and, finally, 32-bit microprocessors.

Leadership continues for high performance microprocessors and single-chip 8-bit microcomputers, as well as memories like the fast SRAMs, analog and logic chips supporting integrated services digital network (ISDN) markets and general interface chips, and discrete components such as the MOSFET transistors. Application-specific integrated circuit (ASIC) libraries have also been introduced and expanded.

INFORMATION SYSTEMS GROUP

Both Codex and Universal Data Systems of Motorola introduced major products that included high-speed modems with speeds of up to 14,400 bits per second for the dial line market and a multiplexer with a built-in digital service unit operating at speeds of up to 56,000 bits per second.

To increase efficiency and improve quality and productivity, Motorola implemented the use of customized robots.

GOVERNMENT ELECTRONICS GROUP

The GEG acquired major follow-on funding from the U.S. Navy and Air Force despite the increased amount of aggressive competition. Several new contracts were awarded for target-detection devices, electronic maintenance components, a joint service radar-based surveillance system, a future secure voice system, and the definition of an RF receiver system.

The historic nonstop nonrefuel around-the-world flight of the Voyager aircraft used a 7.5-pound advanced Motorola military radio, the LST-5B UHF satellite transceiver, to communicate with the ground mission control crew and track the weather conditions.

GENERAL SYSTEMS GROUP

The Cellular Group and Motorola Computer Systems make up the GSG. Currently 125 markets, including major metropolitan areas, have been

MOTOROLA, INC.

awarded to Motorola to supply cellular telephone systems. On an international basis, the Cellnet system in England continues to grow. In addition, the group received new system awards from Thailand, Gabon, the Dominican Republic, and Shanghai in the People's Republic of China. New products recently introduced include the Mini T.A.C., Digital Micro Transceiver and a new transportable, the Tough Talker.

Motorola Computer Systems introduced high performance microcomputers including the VISION/32 and the System 8000 family. Key features of these are the use of the MC68020 32-bit microprocessor as the controller, VMEbus architecture, and the UNIX V/68 operating system. (UNIX is a trademark of AT&T.)

AUTOMOTIVE AND INDUSTRIAL ELECTRONICS GROUP

The AIEG uses Motorola's MC68HC11 microcomputer in an advanced instrument cluster. It offers programmability, reliability, and ease of installation. The group also developed control modules for an early warning food care system for monitoring the temperature of a freezer and refrigerator. Other products offered include electronic cruise control modules, electronic appliance control units, LCD instrument displays, engine controllers, and monochrome monitors.

THE MOTOROLA SUMMARY

Motorola provides systems and components to both the United States and international markets. Cellular telephones, pocket pagers, and two-way radios are a few of the products manufactured by Motorola to serve these markets.

Motorola is committed to creating high technology products, one of the primary reasons for the company's success. The company that originally started with one man, a handful of employees, and $565 has grown to approximately 100,000 workers, speaking as many as 25 different languages. The annual net sales are well over $5 billion. An early car radio manufacturer evolved into a company creating some of the most sophisticated design technologies yet conceived.

Motorola is an active semiconductor manufacturer involved in the development of single-chip microcomputers like the MC68HC11, the first such device with on-chip EEPROM. In addition, products to support the General Motor's manufacturing automation protocol (MAP) are part of their product offering, as well as the ISDN supporting simultaneous voice/data communication.

Research in the area of converting natural resources into usable energy is ongoing at Motorola. The most practical of these is solar energy. The sun will be burning for billions of years, making it an obvious choice of resources for development. Motorola's advances technology is looking to the sky and pioneering the way for the creation of solar-powered systems of the future.

BIBLIOGRAPHY

Motorola Inc., "The First Fifty Years" (video), 1985.
Motorola Inc., *Annual Report*, 1986.
Motorola Inc., *Leadership Brochure*, 1986.

LAURA R. TOLPEN
ROBERT A. KING

OPEN SYSTEMS-INTERCONNECTION

INTRODUCTION

Until recent years computer-to-computer communication was limited largely to communication between similar computers. Economic and technological barriers limited the capability for communication between computers of different make, model, size, and age. As a result, the potential for information resource sharing by computer networking was seriously inhibited.

As concern for this problem began to intensify, the International Organization for Standardization (ISO) created a subcommittee in 1978 named Open Systems Interconnection (OSI); its task was to specify a framework for the continuing development of standards for computer-to-computer communication. The efforts of this group produced the OSI Reference Model [1]. The model provides a framework to coordinate the development of standards for the interconnection of computer systems and to allow existing standards to be placed into perspective within the model.

The term *open systems interconnection*, according to the OSI model, "qualifies standards for the exchange of information among systems that are 'open' to one another for this purpose, by virtue of their mutual use of applicable standards." A system is a set of one or more computers, associated software, peripherals, terminals, human operators, procedures, and communication capability, which forms an autonomous whole, capable of information processing and/or information transfer. The term *systems interconnection* refers to the cooperation between systems to achieve a common, distributed task.

Communication Functions

Computer communication poses a variety of technical issues. To transmit information from one computer to another, the two computers must agree to employ common solutions to various communication functions. For example,

- Two communicating computers must agree how to distinguish a "zero" bit from a "one," how to distinguish between successive bits, and how to recognize the start and the end of a message.
- Messages tend to pick up errors during transmission, so error-detection information is often included in messages so that the receiving computer can recognize error conditions, acknowledge messages received correctly, and request retransmission of those in error. Sometimes successive messages are routed on different transmission paths and, consequently, arrive out of order; sometimes messages are lost in transmission. Message sequence numbers

are therefore often included in messages so that the receiving computer can properly sequence arriving messages and detect lost messages.
- A computer might transmit data faster than the receiving computer can process it, and a mechanism is required for the receiving computer to throttle the flow of data, e.g., by interrupting transmission with a message saying "do not send more data until further notice" and, subsequently, "ready for more data."

These are just a few examples of the numerous problems involved in computer communication. For two computers to communicate, they must agree to common solutions to these problems.

Protocol

Meaningful computer communication requires that data be exchanged according to mutually agreed upon procedures and formats. When a message is transmitted from one computer to another, more information is transmitted than just the contents of the message. Control information, such as sequence number and error-detection information accompanies the actual data. Some transmitted messages (e.g., data acknowledgment messages) do not even contain data. Furthermore, information such as "ready for more data" must be encoded in a format recognized by both computers. Messages comprising data and control information must be exchanged according to a *protocol*: a set of formats and procedures governing the exchange of information.

Networking Models

There are many operational computer networks in the world, utilizing various network models, or communication protocols. Some of these models are manufacturer specific. Most manufacturers of large and mid-size computers have developed products to allow networking of their own computers. For example, two IBM computers can communicate using IBM protocol, and two Honeywell computers can communicate using Honeywell protocol. Unfortunately, however, these products are mutually incompatible: An IBM and a Honeywell computer cannot communicate if each uses its own native protocol. In fact, there has been very little effort to make these native protocols compatible to allow communication between computers from different manufacturers.

One reason for the proliferation of native protocols was that manufacturers recognized the need for their own computers to communicate with one another before there was emphasis on the need for communication between dissimilar computers; consequently, the need to coordinate the development of protocols was not foreseen. Typically, a manufacturer provides to its customers a protocol to allow its own computers to communicate and, additionally, one or more software packages that emulate the protocols of the "more important" computers. Theoretically, full interconnection of all computers is possible by this so-called "protocol emulation." In practice, however, protocol emulation is a very poor solution for several reasons. One reason is development cost. It might cost a manufacturer several hundred thousand dollars to develop for its computer protocol emulation of another computer. Another reason is operational cost. A computer might need to communicate with several other computers of various types; the complexity and overhead of operating multiple protocols can be prohibitive. In addition to these two economic factors associated with protocol emulation, there is also a political factor: The lack of standard communication protocols tends to perpetuate the market advantage of the larger manufacturers.

The most prominent of the manufacturer-provided network models is IBM's System Network Architecture (SNA). Although SNA is a proprietary IBM product, not all computers in an SNA network are IBM systems; many vendors market SNA-compatible products. In fact, SNA is considered by some people to be a de facto standard. However, a non-IBM member of an SNA network is at a distinct disadvantage for three reasons: (a) SNA was developed specifically for IBM hardware; (b) only IBM can best provide customer support for SNA, and IBM supports only IBM customers; (c) without prior notice IBM can unilaterally change the SNA specifications; this leaves non-IBM users of SNA rather vulnerable.

Another prominent network architecture is the Defense Department's TCP (Transmission Control Protocol). Unlike SNA, TCP is not the proprietary product of a particular manufacturer but, instead, evolved to meet the unique functional and operational requirements of military networks, e.g., to survive after part of the network has been destroyed. There are many operational TCP networks, civilian as well as military and, like SNA, some consider TCP to be a de facto standard.

Although SNA and TCP each are considered de facto standards by some, SNA-based computer systems can communicate only with other SNA systems, and TCP systems can communicate only with other TCP systems. Neither SNA nor TCP can ever be universally accepted as a network model; no model will ever be commonly accepted if it is developed specifically for any particular hardware or type of application.

Any ultimate solution to computer networking must involve multiple vendors implementing products based on common communication protocols. The best chance that any particular network model has of gaining general acceptance is if it is based on standards. The process of standardization of communication protocols affords the opportunity of participation to all of the computer manufacturers and special interest and consumer groups. This assures that no single manufacturer's hardware is favored. The only network model that is based on a formal standardization effort is that of OSI.

LEVELS OF PROTOCOL

OSI is based on a principle known as "layering," a formalization of the concept of "protocol levels," which evolved to facilitate the description and understanding of computer protocol. There are many diverse communication functions, but there is also a hierarchy to these functions; some functions are prerequisite to others. The following discussion illustrates this hierarchy.

The most fundamental communication function is the transmission of a bit. Before bits can be transmitted reliably, the sender and receiver must synchronize; thus, before any actual data bits are transmitted, the sender transmits a stream of "synchronization" bits. As successive bits are transmitted, there is a gradual loss of synchronization, and eventually another stream of synchronization bits must be transmitted by the sender to allow the receiver to resynchronize. For this and other reasons, there is a maximum number of data bits that can be included in a single physical transmission. Messages longer than that size must be segmented by the sender and reassembled by the receiver. A string of bits comprising a single physical transmission, not including synchronization bits, is called a frame. A typical frame size might be 1,024 bits. Included in a frame, along with the actual data, might be error-detection bits and message sequence number.

Thus, the capability to transmit a *bit* is required in order to transmit a *frame*. The capability to transmit a frame is required in order to transmit a *message,* consisting of several frames.

The issues involved in transmitting a bit, such as voltage level, are distinct from issues involved in transmitting a frame, such as error detection and data acknowledgment. These are, in turn, distinct from issues involved in dividing a long message into multiple segments (individually transmitted) and correctly reassembling the message at its destination. Thus, three hierarchical levels of protocol can be defined:

1. Level 1—For transmission of bits.
2. Level 2—For transmission of frames.
3. Level 3—For segmentation and subsequent reassembly of messages.

Level 3 passes a message segment to level 2, which creates a frame from the message segment and relies on level one to transmit the actual bits. Level-3 protocol is simplified because it assumes that the actual transmission of a frame is a level-2 responsibility. The level-2 protocol provides for the correct transmission of frames by including error-detection information, sequence numbers, and frame acknowledgment. However, the level-2 protocol does not address the issues involved in the transmission of the individual bits of the frame, such as voltage level and synchronization; the level-1 protocol handles these issues.

Actually, level 3 is responsible for more than just segmenting and reassembly. Often the transmission path between two computers is several physical circuits, separated by intermediate network nodes. Data must be routed from one end system to another, across the intermediate nodes. This is the second responsibility of level 3.

Thus, the two responsibilities of level 3 are (*a*) segmentation and reassembly of messages and (*b*) routing of data from source system to destination, across any intermediate nodes.

Note that this second level-3 responsibility introduces another hierarchical relationship: Transmitting a frame between two adjacent systems (level 2) is a prerequisite to routing a message segment between end systems (level 3).

LAYERING

The OSI Reference Model has formalized the concept of levels of protocol into the principle called "layering," which says divide the communication functions into a hierarchy of layers and develop individual protocols for each layer. Similar functions are placed in the same layer, and generally, if one function is a prerequisite for a second function, the first function is in a lower layer than the second.

The OSI model defines seven layers. The three protocol levels described above correspond to OSI layers 1, 2, and 3.

Each layer can be visualized as two programs, residing on different computers, communicating according to the protocol for that layer. In OSI terminology, the two programs are called "peer entities."

Conceptually, two peer entities perform the functions of their layer by exchanging messages with one another. Actually, each message sent across a layer is passed down through all of the layers below it. For example, if the layer-seven entity on one system wishes to send a message to its peer on the other system, it passes the message down to the layer-6 entity on the same system. The layer-6 entity adds information meaningful to its peer layer-6 entity and passes the message to the layer-5 entity, which adds information meaningful to its peer layer-5 entity, etc. The message continues down through the entities of the sending system, across the telecommunications medium, and up through the layers of the receiving system. Each entity on the receiving system acts upon that information within the message provided by its peer but strips off that information before passing the message up to the entity above. Ultimately, the message from the sending layer-7 entity arrives intact at the receiving layer-7 entity.

In the layering example shown in Figure 1, layer 2 is responsible for error detection. The sending layer-2 entity appends error-detection bits, and the receiving layer-2 entity performs error checking and strips off the error-detection bits before passing the message up to the layer-3 entity. In this example, layer 3 is responsible for lost messages, so the sending layer-3 entity has appended a sequence number to the message.

NOTE: Although the example in Figure 1 shows a sending and a receiving system, communication between computers involves two-way exchange of messages; thus, each system assumes the role of both sending and receiving system.

A message passed between two entities of a layer contains both control information meaningful to that layer, and data to be passed up to the next layer. The control information meaningful to layer 3 (sequence number) has no meaning to layer two and is part of the data that are passed transparently up by layer 2 to layer 3.

The layering example in Figure 1 is somewhat oversimplified. An entity does not always simply add information to a message and pass it along. For example, a layer might be responsible for encrypting sensitive data; in that case, the sending entity will convert the data according to an agreed upon encryption algorithm, and the receiving entity will decrypt the data to their original form. As another example, if a layer is responsible for segmenting and reassembling long messages, a single message from the layer above results in multiple messages at that layer.

To summarize the layering principle, each layer performs a specified set of functions via communication between its peer entities, according to a protocol for that layer. From the viewpoint of a given layer, communication between its entities is performed by the layer below. A layer is aware only of the layers immediately above and below; it provides service to the layer above and requests service from the layer below.

FIGURE 1: LAYERING EXAMPLE

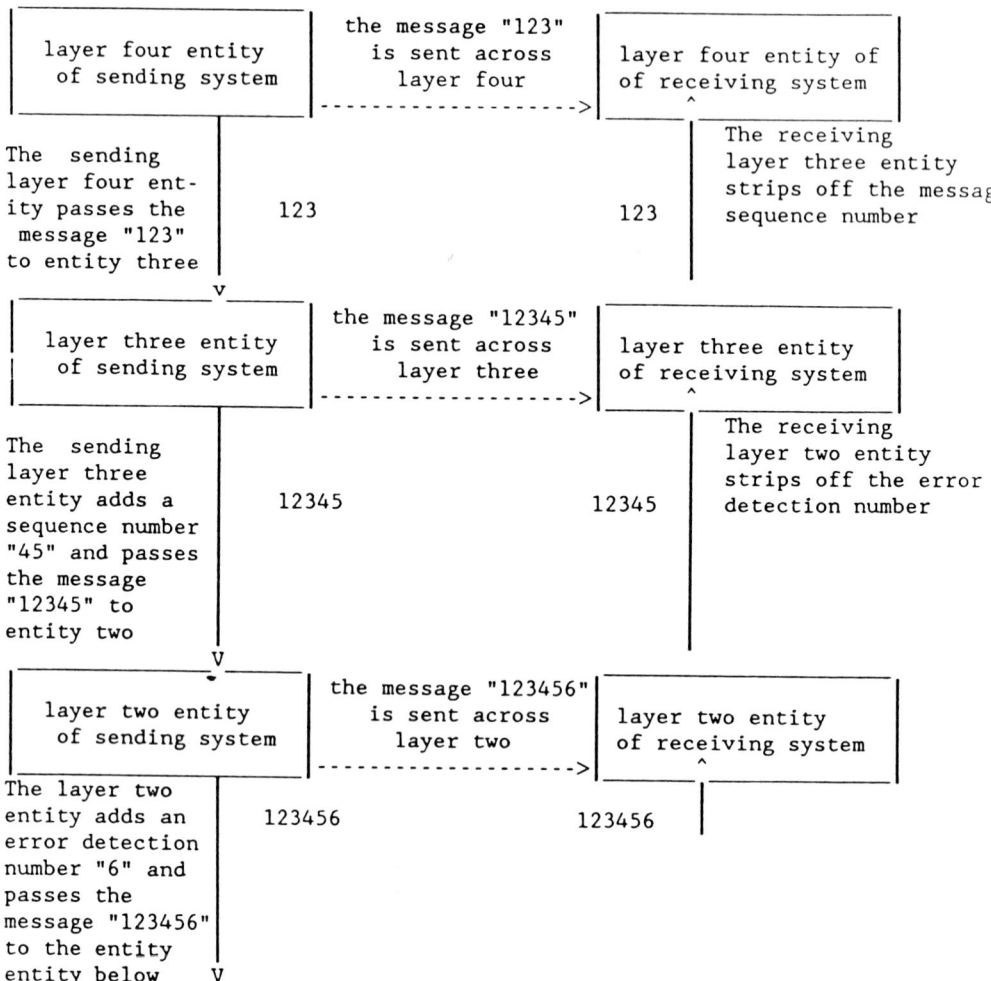

The sending layer four entity wishes to send the message "123" to its peer. For the purpose of this example, the function of layer four is not defined, layer three detects lost messages, and layer two detects corrupted data. The layer four entity at the sending system passes the message to the layer three entity on the same system, which appends the message sequence number "45" and passed the message "12345" to the layer two entity on the same system, which appends an error detection number "6". Layer one is not shown, but it might also append information at the sending end and strip it off at the receiving end. In any case, the message "123456" is communicated across layer two. At the receiving system, the layer two entity strips off the error detection information after performing an error check, and passes the message "12345" up to the layer three entity. Thus the communication of the message "12345" across layer three is accomplished. The layer three entity performs a sequence check, then strips off the message sequence number and passes the message "123" up to the layer four entity. Thus the communication of the message "123" across layer four is accomplished.

FIGURE 1 Layering example.

Open Systems Interconnection

THE OSI LAYERS

The OSI model defines seven layers, shown in Figure 2. Their composite function is to provide meaningful and reliable communication between two computers. The upper three layers provide for the meaningful exchange of information, whereas the lower four layers provide for the reliable transmission of data.

The upper three layers (layers 7, 6, and 5) are named the Application, Presentation, and Session layers. The lower four layers (layers 4, 3, 2, and 1) are named the Transport, Network, Data Link, and Physical layers.

The discussion below of the OSI layers describes the upper three layers as top down and the lower four layers as bottom up. First, the concept of the end user is developed.

The End User: The Application

Each of the lower six layers provides service to a layer above. The Application layer is the highest, but it is useful to conceptualize an "end user," or "application," above the Application layer, to which the Application layer provides service. The end user might be a program or a user at a terminal, or both. The distinction between the end user and the Application entity is conceptual; both might be incorporated into a single program, and there might not be any defined distinction within a given implementation.

Application Layer	(7)
Presentation Layer	(6)
Session Layer	(5)
Transport Layer	(4)
Network Layer	(3)
Data Link Layer	(2)
Physical Layer	(1)

FIGURE 2 The seven layers of the OSI Reference Model.

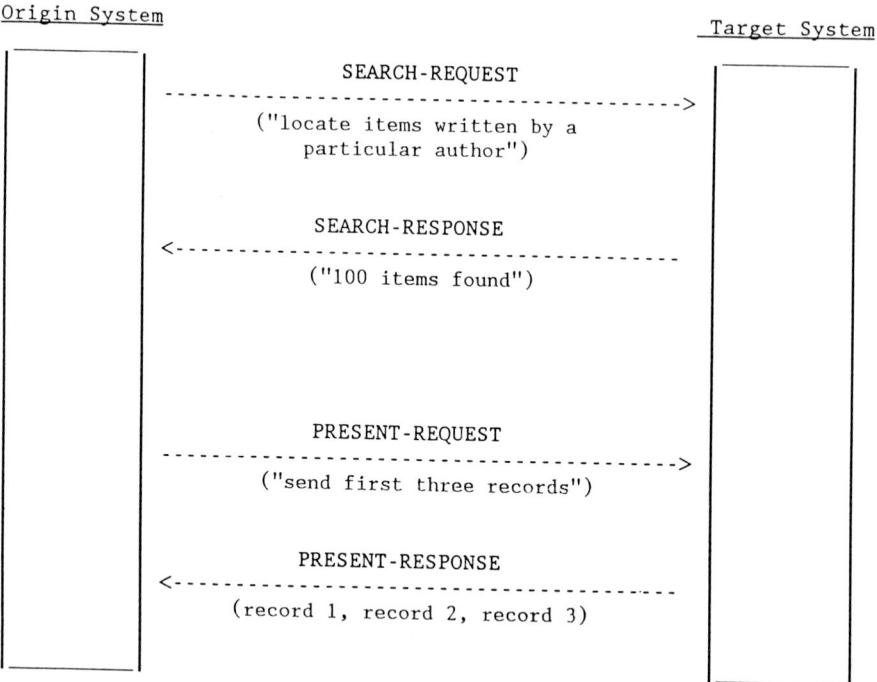

The origin system uses the Information Retrieval protocol to access a bibliographic database which resides on the target system. The origin requests the target to identify all items written by a particular author and to respond with a count of the items identified. The origin application entity transmits a SEARCH-REQUEST protocol message, which identifies the database and includes the search terms, operators, attributes, etc., in the agreed-upon intersystem format, to the target application entity. At the target, the search is processed and a SEARCH-RESPONSE protocol message is sent from the target application entity to the origin application entity. The target responds that 100 items have been identified. Just as SEARCH and SEARCH-RESPONSE protocol messages are used for a search transaction, another pair of messages, PRESENT and PRESENT-RESPONSE, are used in the same manner subsequent to a search transaction, to allow the origin to retrieve records identified by the search. In this example, the origin requests that the first three items to be transmitted.

FIGURE 3 Information retrieval protocol.

Open Systems Interconnection

The conceptual distinction is between those elements of processing that involve communication between systems and those that do not. The end user is said to be outside of the OSI environment.

Consider a terminal operator, inputting search queries to an information retrieval program residing on the local computer (the computer to which the terminal is connected), accessing the local bibliographic data base (Fig. 3). The user requests the system to identify all items written by a particular author and to respond with a count of the items identified. The system responds that 100 items have been identified. The user then requests that the first three items be displayed, then the next three, etc.

Next, consider an intersystem search; assume that the same interactions occur between the user and the local system, but the data base is on a remote system. The user and the query program together are the end user. The program, recognizing that the requested information is not local, but resides on the data base of a remote computer, passes the query down to the Application layer. The local Application entity sends the query to its peer Application entity at the remote computer (via the lower layers, of course), which passes it up to a query program, the peer end user. The remote query program accesses its data base and returns the query results to its Application entity. The query results are then sent across the Application layer (again via the lower layers) to the local Application entity, up to the local query program, and to the user's terminal.

In effect, the user has a direct connection to the remote query program. Of course, the user could instead dial in directly to the remote system, but then the query would have to be formulated according to the conventions of that system; in fact, a different terminal might be required. (It must be emphasized that it is not the objective of OSI to standardize interactions between user and computer; this applies to the dialogue between the user and the query program, the formulation of the query, and also to the protocol used by the terminal.) More importantly, by transferring the records from computer to computer rather than from computer to terminal, the user now has access to the records in machine-readable form, so they can be modified and added to the local database.

LAYER 7: THE APPLICATION LAYER

The Application layer provides direct support to the application. In general, different applications employ different Application layer protocols. The application described above, in which the local system invokes a search at the remote system and, subsequently, retrieves records identified by the search, is supported by an Application layer protocol known as Information Retrieval, briefly described below. The Information Retrieval protocol is currently being proposed as an American National Standard by the National Information Standards Organization, NISO (Z39) [2] (Fig. 3).

The local and remote systems are referred to as the origin and target, respectively. The origin application entity transmits a SEARCH-REQUEST protocol message, which identifies the database and includes the search terms, operators, attributes, etc., in the agreed-upon intersystem format, to the target application entity. At the target, the search is processed, and a SEARCH-RESPONSE protocol message is sent from the target application entity to the origin application entity. Just as SEARCH and SEARCH-RESPONSE protocol messages are used for a search transaction, another pair of messages, PRESENT and PRESENT-RESPONSE, are used in the same manner subsequent to a search transaction to allow the origin to retrieve records identified by the search.

The Information Retrieval protocol consists of the four messages shown in Figure 3. It also specifies the procedures governing the exchange of these messages, e.g., what action to take upon receipt of a SEARCH-REQUEST. The protocol also specifies a common syntax for representing a search query and also a common format for representing response records (e.g., if bibliographic records are transferred, the protocol specifies that the USMARC format is to be used).

LAYER 6: THE PRESENTATION LAYER

The Presentation layer exists to ensure that the information content of the Application layer messages is preserved during transit between Application entities.

One particular Application layer protocol rule states that "a SEARCH-REQUEST is identified by the number 22." But Application protocol does not prescribe how that value is to be conveyed, i.e., the configuration of bits that represent the number 22. It could be a binary integer, ASCII digits, or any of several other representation.

Semantics, Abstract Syntax, and Concrete Syntax

The Application layer is responsible for the semantics of transmitted information (its meaning), and the Presentation layer is responsible for syntax (its representation).

The distinction between semantics and syntax is facilitated by a further distinction, between abstract syntax and transfer syntax. Application layer protocol specifies, e.g., what action a target system is to take upon receiving a SEARCH-REQUEST. This is part of the semantics of the protocol. The Presentation layer enforces rules such as "request type is represented as a binary integer." This is a rule of the transfer syntax. However, the rule that states "SEARCH-REQUEST is represented by the number 22" is neither semantics nor transfer syntax. Rather, it is considered to be abstract syntax.

Another example further illustrates the relationship among semantics, abstract syntax, and transfer syntax. In the Information Retrieval protocol, in the PRESENT-RESPONSE message, there is a field called "present-status," whose possible values are 1, 2, and 3. The rule stating that this particular field must occur in this message and assume one of these values is part of the abstract syntax. It does not convey any semantic information, nor does it prescribe a concrete representation. The semantic interpretation of the field might be expressed as follows:

> One (1) means that the request was processed normally, and all of the requested items are included in this response message. Two (2) means that the request has been processed, but some of the requested information could not be retrieved. Three (3) means that the request could not be processed.

The concrete representation might be "the value of 'search status' (i.e., 1, 2, or 3) is to be represented by a single ASCII digit."

Context

Application layer protocol specifies semantics and abstract syntax. The Presentation layer entities are responsible for selecting a mutually acceptable transfer syntax that preserves the information content of the Application entities message during transit. Thus, the presentation protocol includes a "Presentation context": an association of an abstract syntax with a compatible transfer syntax (compatible in the sense that it is capable of expressing all of the information transfer requirements of the abstract syntax). Associated with a given communication session is an "active context set," which is a set of Presentation contexts that have been actively agreed to by the two Presentation entities.

Potentially then, the Presentation layer provides for dynamic context definition and context switching to meet the needs of complex data representation requirements. However, the Presentation layer protocol also provides the mechanism to agree to use a static, predefined syntax. For example, if text information is being exchanged, the two Presentation entities might agree that all data will be transmitted in the ASCII character code.

To summarize, the Presentation layer is responsible for the syntactic representation of data and might perform transformations, including character code conversion, data compression, data encryption, and representation of graphic information such as videotext. In many cases, however, the Presentation layer responsibility will be to gain explicit agreement that a predefined syntax will be used.

LAYER 5: THE SESSION LAYER

OSI layer 5, the Session layer, provides the means for organized and synchronized exchange of data between applications. During session establishment, two peer applications agree to certain rules governing their dialogue. This agreement, as well as the enforcement of these rules during the session, is accomplished by the Session layer protocol.

There are various potential Session layer services that may or may not be required by a given application. The Session layer protocol defines several "functional units," which are logical groupings of related services. During the establishment of a session, both entities propose a set of functional units to be employed during the session, and those that are in both sets (the intersection) are in force during the session.

Full or Half-Duplex

Duplex and half-duplex are two functional units; one and only one must be in force during a session. In duplex mode, both entities can transmit data at the same time. In half-duplex mode, only one entity can transmit data at any given time; protocol messages are exchanged to pass a "token" back and forth to designate which entity has the "right" to transmit data.

Half-duplex imposes additional overhead and complexity and would not normally be selected unless the application requires explicit dialog control. The Information Retrieval protocol described above is implicitly half-duplex (i.e., the procedures of the Application protocol preclude both sides from transmitting at the same time) and, thus, the Information Retrieval application would not select the Session layer half-duplex functional unit. However, consider an (hypothetical) application with a protocol somewhat less structured. Suppose each system can search the other's database, provided there is only one outstanding request at a time. The application could then use the Session layer half-duplex feature to ensure that both systems do not transmit requests simultaneously.

Resynchronization

The Session layer allows an application to establish synchronization points ("synch points") within the dialogue. In the event of errors, the two peer applications may return to a previous state in the current session by resuming the dialogue from an agreed upon synch point.

An application may insert synch points, identified by serial numbers, into the data it transmits. There are "major" and "minor" synch points. Major synch points delineate "dialogue units," and there may be more than one minor synch point within a dialogue unit. An application may resynchronize the dialogue to any defined minor synch point within the current dialogue unit; in other words, it can go back as far as the most recent major synch point. Thus, the characteristic of a dialogue unit is that all communication within it is completely isolated from all communication before and after it.

Activities

The Session layer provides for the recovery of a session in the event of network failure, so that two communicating applications can resume their dialogue at (or close to) the point of interruption, when the network is recovered. Thus, e.g., a file transfer need not be restarted from the beginning if the network fails.

An application can distinguish between different logical pieces of work, called "activities." An activity can be interrupted and later resumed during the same or a subsequent session.

Quality of Service

An application conveys to the Session layer (via the Application and Presentation layers) certain "quality-of-service" requirements, e.g.,

1. Connection delay—The maximum acceptable time to set up the connection.
2. Connection priority—The priority of the connection, relative to other connections, in terms of
   a. The order in which connections are to have their quality of service degraded, if necessary.
   b. The order in which connections are to be broken to recover resources, if necessary.
3. Protection—The extent to which data are to be protected from unauthorized monitoring or modification.
4. Resilience—The average (or expected) time before premature session termination due to network failure.
5. Throughput—Bits per second (e.g., 2,400, 9,600, 56,000).
6. Transit (propagation) delay—The delay between the time a message starts transmitting until receipt of the message begins at the destination.

Open Systems Interconnection 357

  7. Error rate—The percentage of messages lost, duplicated, out of order, or in error.
  8. Transfer failure probability—The percentage of messages in which the performance is below the minimum acceptable level in terms of throughput, transit delay, or error rate.

It is the responsibility of the application to decide the values of these parameters; in general, they depend upon the nature of the application and the data. For long messages, throughput is more important than transit delay, and vice versa for short messages. For a connection with a short lifetime, such as a single interactive transaction, connection delay is important, but resilience is not, and vice versa for a connection whose lifetime is long, such as file transfer. For banking applications, security and error rate are important.

The two peer Session entities communicate with one another during connection set up to establish some of these quality-of-service parameters as those in force during the connection. Other parameters are passed down to the layer below, Transport.

OVERVIEW OF THE LOWER FOUR OSI LAYERS

The most important delineation between OSI layers is at the layer-4/5 boundary: the upper three layers are connected with application-related matters and the lower four with telecommunications.

However (see Fig. 4), another important delineation occurs at the layer 3/4 boundary. Layers 1 through 4 of the OSI model are collectively responsible for end-to-end, cost-effective, and reliable transmission of data between computers; Layers 1 through 3 are responsible for data transmission; layer 4 "adds value" to the lower three layers, so that collectively, layers 1 through 4 meet the specific communication needs of the upper three layers.

It was noted earlier that the transmission path between two end systems might include intermediate network nodes. These are also computer systems. OSI not only addresses the end-to-end communication; OSI layers 1 through 3 address communication between adjacent network nodes. Moreover, the protocols of the first three layers operate only between adjacent nodes of a network. Separate instances of all three protocols are required between each pair of adjacent nodes, including end-system and intermediate nodes. Layer 4, the Transport layer, is distinguished from layers 1 through 3 below by the end-to-end nature of its communication: Peer Transport entities, in the end systems, exchange protocol messages. Transport entities exist only at the end systems and not at intermediate nodes, and this end-to-end significance is also a property of the layers above Transport. This is another reason why the layer 3/4 boundary marks an important delineation in the seven layers: layers 3 and below provide network access to the layers above.

LAYERS 1 AND 2: THE PHYSICAL AND DATA LINK LAYERS

The Physical layer is responsible for the transmission of bits. More formally, it provides the mechanical, electrical, functional, and procedural means to activate, maintain, and deactivate physical connections for bit transmission.

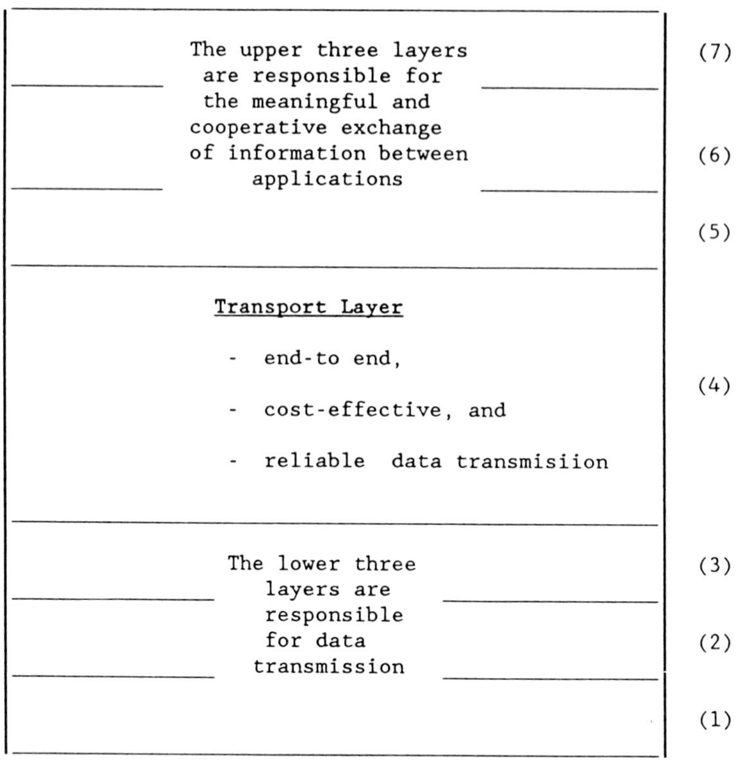

```
┌─────────────────────────────────────────────────┬──────┐
│                                                 │      │
│            The upper three layers               │ (7)  │
│   _____  are responsible for       _____    │      │
│            the meaningful and                   │      │
│            cooperative exchange                 │ (6)  │
│            of information between               │      │
│   _____  applications              _____    │      │
│                                                 │ (5)  │
├─────────────────────────────────────────────────┼──────┤
│                                                 │      │
│              Transport Layer                    │      │
│                                                 │      │
│              - end-to end,                      │ (4)  │
│                                                 │      │
│              - cost-effective, and              │      │
│                                                 │      │
│              - reliable data transmisiion       │      │
│                                                 │      │
├─────────────────────────────────────────────────┼──────┤
│                                                 │      │
│            The lower three                      │ (3)  │
│   _____  layers are                _____    │      │
│            responsible                          │      │
│            for data                             │ (2)  │
│   _____  transmission              _____    │      │
│                                                 │      │
│                                                 │ (1)  │
│                                                 │      │
└─────────────────────────────────────────────────┴──────┘
```

The Transport layer "adds value" to the lower three layers, so that collectively, layers one through four meet the specific communication needs of the upper three layers. In other words, the lower three layers are responsible for *data transmission*, the lower *four* layers are responsible for *end-to-end, cost-effective, and reliable* data transmission.

FIGURE 4 Transport: the "middle" layer.

Mechanical aspects cover items such as connectors and arrangement of pins. Electrical aspects specify, e.g., how many volts represent a zero (or a one) bit. Functional characteristics pertain to timing and synchronization. Physical layer procedures specify under what conditions various subcircuits of the physical channel should transmit control and timing information. (For example, a procedure might specify that a system will signal that it is not ready to accept data bits by transmitting a continuous stream of alternate zero and one bits on a particular subcircuit.)

The Physical layer provides for the transparent transmission of bit streams between the two entities of the Data Link layer. A primary responsibility of the Data Link layer is to delimit the beginning and end of a unit of transmitted information (a frame). The Data Link layer also provides an addressing mechanism to identify the sender and receiver of data, among several who might be using the same circuit. It might also perform functions such as error detection (and possibly recovery) and flow control.

However, these functions might alternatively be performed at a higher layer, and they are discussed in detail later.

LAYER 3: THE NETWORK LAYER

The transmission path between two computer systems might be a single physical circuit (Fig. 5A) or several circuits separated by intermediate network nodes (Fig. 5B). These are examples of network topologies. A topology is a description of the communication environment in the terms of the types of transmission facilities and equipment.

Protocols for layers 1 and 2 govern communication between two systems connected by a single circuit. Thus, they apply to topology 1, and also to each pair of adjacent systems (end systems and intermediate nodes) in topology 2. However, topology 2 introduces a requirement not applicable to topology 1. Data must be routed from one end system to another. Layer 3, the Network layer, has two primary responsibilities: (a) routing messages from source system to destination, across any intermediate nodes and (b) segmentation of messages by the sending end system and their subsequent reassembly at the receiving end system.

The protocols used for the lower three layers depend on the particular topology used for communication. The following is an example of a specific topology.

CCITT Recommendation X.25

A special case of topology 2 is topology 3 (Fig. 5C), in which the two end systems communicate over a public data network such as Telenet or Tymnet.

In the early 1970s a technology called "packet switching" evolved, whereby data messages are broken into smaller units (typically 1,024 bits), which are individually transmitted, and the message is reassembled at the destination system. Each unit is called a packet. Usually, in a packet-switched network, the communication path, or logical connection between two users consist of several physical circuits, or channels. The important feature of packet switching is that each channel is dedicated to a logical connection only during transmission of a packet, after which the channel is available for use by packets being transmitted over other logical connections. Any channel along the transmission path between two users may be part of a path between other users at the same time, although the illusion is created that the two users have a dedicated connection, as in a telephone call.

In 1976, with packet switching coming of age, to prevent the proliferation of incompatible protocols, the International Consultative Committee for Telephony and Telegraphy (CCITT, who along with ISO are the two most prominent international standards bodies) proposed a standard called Recommendation X.25 [3]. It defines three levels of protocol for communication between a computer and the local network nodes on a packet-switched network. Level 1 defines the protocol to maintain a physical connection and to transmit bits over that connection. Level 2 defines the protocol for error-free transmission of frames over the connection. Level 3 defines the formats of packets and the procedures for establishing and maintaining a logical connection.

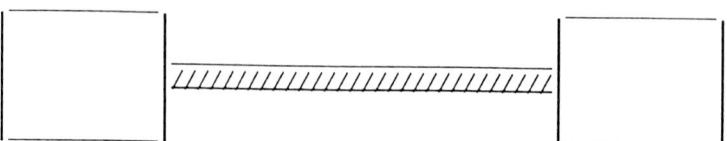

Topology one. End-systems connected by a single circuit.

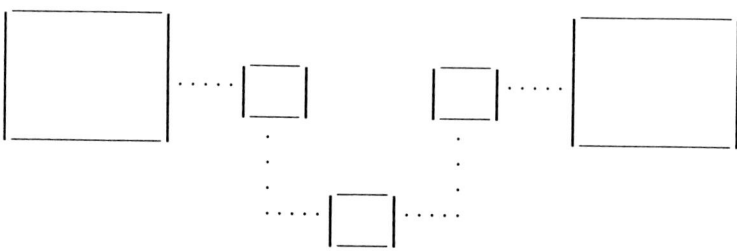

Topology two. End-systems connected via intermediate nodes.

Topology three. End-systems Connected to a Public Data Network.

A topology is a description of the communication environment in terms of the types of transmission facilities and equipment. The transmission path between two end-systems might be (1) a single circuit, or (2) several circuits separated by intermediate nodes. A special case of (2) is (3) in which both systems are connected to a common Public Data Network.

FIGURE 5 Network topologies.

Open Systems Interconnection 361

Today, the use of X.25 is widespread; it is used by virtually all of the packet-switched, public data networks. X.25 preceded OSI, but the three protocols of X.25 have retrospectively been accepted as OSI protocols for layers 1, 2, and 3 for use in a packet-switched network. X.25 products (i.e., the combination of hardware and software that implements the X.25 protocol) have been available for many types of computer systems for several years.

LAYER 4: THE TRANSPORT LAYER

The role of layer 4, the Transport layer, is to provide cost-effective, reliable data transfer between end systems and to relieve the layers above from concern about the details of how the supporting communication media are utilized to achieve this data transfer.

The OSI model envisions that a computer system has at its disposal a variety of communication facilities and can choose among several options for a specific instance of communication. It is the responsibility of the Session layer to specify to Transport a desired quality of service in terms of various parameters. The Transport layer selects, among the communication facilities, one that provides the required quality of service at the lowest cost.

In reality, a system might have only one facility for communication, or perhaps none of the available facilities can provide the requested quality of service. In that case, the Transport layer must "make up the difference" between the requested quality of service and that provided by the network. Quality of service is provided by various communication functions. Although it is the ultimate responsibility of the Transport layer to ensure quality of service, Transport itself does not necessarily perform all of the functions. It must be aware which of the required functions are performed by the underlying network and perform those that are not.

For example, X.25 networks guarantee a high degree of error-free transmission, and so a Transport layer operating over an X.25 network would, in most cases, not perform error detection. On the other hand, the lower three protocol layers used for local area networks (LANs) do not usually guarantee error-free transmission to the same degree as X.25 networks, so the Transport layer operating over a LAN is more likely to perform error detection. In both cases, of course, it depends on the quality of service required.

In some networks, data units might be routed along different paths and possibly arrive out of order. In these cases, Transport protocol messages will include message sequence numbers. When Transport then detects messages out of order, it might attempt to resequence them properly or might terminate the connection abruptly, declaring a network failure. The choice depends upon the expected rate of out-of-sequence messages and the resilience required by the application; sequence recovery need not be built into the Transport layer—it can simply abort the connection whenever a message arrives out of order—as long as the resulting resilience does not fall below an acceptable level.

If the throughput requirement of an application exceeds the capability (bandwidth) of any available channel, Transport performs the function known as "splitting." Suppose, e.g., an application requires throughput of 9,600 bps, and no such channel is available, but many channels of lower throughput are. Transport might then split the data for that application over two 4,800-bps channels or four 2,400-bps channels.

Multiplexing is the opposite of splitting, and it illustrates the Transport layer's role of providing cost-effective data transfer. Suppose several concurrent communication sessions require throughput of only 300 bps and all available channels are 2400 bps. In this case, transport might assign up to eight such sessions to a single channel.

Transport Layer Protocol Classes

Different environments might have quite different Transport layers, because there are various potential telecommunication requirements that might be imposed by an application, and there are various types of networks. However, for a specific instance of communication, for any given potential Transport layer function, either both Transport entities must perform the function, or both must not. Otherwise, the two entities will be employing different protocols and will not be able to communicate.

Thus, the Transport protocol must resolve conflicting objectives: compatibility and efficiency. The latter refers to the objective that a given Transport entity not be required to employ a capability that it does not need. On the one hand, universal compatibility can be guaranteed only if all systems implement all of the required functions. On the other hand, maximum incompatibility results if each system chooses the set of functions it wishes to implement.

A compromise between these objectives is achieved by defining a set of five Transport "protocol classes." Two Transport entities must communicate according to a specific class, and within a given class there is a good chance of compatibility (however, even within a given class there are some selectable options, so compatibility is not assured). Generally, two Transport entities choose the simplest class that provides all of the functions applicable to their communication environment. Of course, the selected class might specify functions that are unnecessary or redundant, because they are either not required or they are provided by the network.

The selection of a Transport protocol class is one of the more important choices that an OSI implementor must make. In general, the choice is not straightforward. Before describing the Transport classes in detail, it is necessary to first consider the Transport layer's view of errors and flow control.

Network Errors: The Transport Layer's View

Errors in the network (layers 1 through 3) can occur, e.g., in the form of lost messages, corrupted bits, or messages out of order. Some errors are detected, and some are not. Of those that are detected, some can be corrected (e.g., by requesting retransmission), and some cannot. If an error that occurs in the network is detected and corrected in the network, the error never occurred as far as the Transport layer is concerned. Thus, the Transport layer is concerned with two types of errors: (a) those detected, but not corrected, within the network and (b) those not detected by the network. The first type is called "signaled" errors (because the Network layer signals the Transport layer of their occurrence), and the second type is called "residual" errors. Depending on the Transport protocol class, the Transport layer might be able to recover from signaled errors (those from which the network could not recover). Recovery is possible because a Transport entity may retain a message after transmission until acknowledgment has been received for the message from the peer system; if a message is lost, retransmission can be requested. Again, depending on the protocol class, the Transport layer might be able to detect and possibly recover from residual errors (those that the network could not detect). Therefore, selection of a transport protocol class is based, in part, on the rate of signaled errors and the rate of residual errors produced by the network.

X.25 networks have an extremely low rate of residual errors; the rate is acceptably low for most applications. In an environment where the residual error rate of the network is acceptably low, the only errors of concern to the Transport layer are signaled errors—the rate of signaled errors is either acceptable or it is not. This defines two environments, referred to as Type A and Type B. A third environment, Type C, is defined for those environments in which the network cannot provide a residual error rate low enough for the application. These three environments are defined to facilitate the definition (see below) of the Transport classes.

Flow Control

Flow control is the mechanism used by a receiving system to regulate the flow of data from the sender, so that data will not arrive faster than the receiver can process it.

In an X.25 network, layers 1 through 3 govern communication between an end system and the network node to which it is connected. In X.25 parlance, an end system is referred to as DTE (data terminal equipment), and the local network node as DCE (data circuit terminating equipment). Between DTE and the DCE, flow control is relatively simple. The DCE can send a message to the DTE (or vice versa) saying "stop sending data until further notice" and, subsequently, "ready for more data." But consider the problem of flow control between end systems communicating over a path of intermediate nodes. If data are arriving too fast at an end system, it may be because the peer end system is sending data too fast. In that case, throttling the flow from the DCE will only result in congestion within the network, and eventually a message will be lost, resulting in a signaled error to the Transport layer. Therefore, the rate of signaled errors can be reduced by end-to-end flow control, applied at the Transport layer, by a Transport protocol mechanism allowing two peer entities to communicate directly to regulate the flow of data. End-to-end flow control is a feature of the Transport layer that may or may not be applied, depending on the Transport class chosen.

The Five Transport Classes

Recall first that there are three types of network environments defined:

1. Type A—Acceptable rate of residual errors; acceptable rate of signaled errors.
2. Type B—Acceptable rate of residual errors; unacceptable rate of signaled errors.
3. Type C—Unacceptable rate of residual errors.

The five Transport layer protocol classes are as follows:

1. Class 0—For use by type-A environments; provides the absolute minimal Transport service.
2. Class 1—For use by type-B environments; attempts to recover from signaled errors.
3. Class 2—For use by type-A environments; provides the services of class 0 and, additionally, flow control and multiplexing.
4. Class 3—For use by type-B environments; provides the services of class 1 plus those of class 2.
5. Class 4—For use in a type-C environment; provides the services of class 3 and, additionally, detection of residual errors and attempted recovery. Class 4 has additional features that provide resilience from signaled errors and increased throughput.

NOTE: The detection and recovery of residual errors in class 4 is far more complex than recovery of signaled errors in classes 1 and 3.

The Choice of a Transport Protocol Class

The choice of a Transport protocol class for a given communication environment is based, in part, on technical and economic factors, but often these considerations are overshadowed by issues of compatibility. There are those who propose that Class 4 be employed universally to ensure maximum compatibility. There are also strong advocates of class 0 (class 4 is very complex and expensive to implement; class 0 is relatively simple and inexpensive). The following (brief) discussion considers only the technical and economic aspects.

In choosing a Transport protocol class, it is often easy to determine whether or not class 4 is required. For example, if residual error detection is needed, class 4 is required. If none of the functions available only in class 4 is needed, class 4 would not be used.

If class 4 is eliminated from consideration, the choice often becomes complicated. Consider the remaining four classes, with respect to (signaled) error recovery and flow control:

1. Class 1 provides error recovery but not flow control.
2. Class 2 provides flow control but not error recovery.
3. Class 3 provides both.
4. Class 0 provides neither.

Any of these four might be appropriate for a given environment. The choice depends largely upon whether error recovery and/or flow control is required. The requirement for error recovery depends upon whether the signaled-error rate of the network is acceptable. The requirement for flow control depends upon several factors, including the relative throughput characteristics of the two-peer systems and the ability of the network to cope with congestion. However, sometimes error recovery can compensate for lack of flow control, and vice versa. This often makes a choice between classes 1 and 2 difficult.

To further complicate matters, classes 2 and 3 prescribe multiplexing: assigning several logical communication sessions to the same communication channel to better utilize available bandwidth, thereby reducing telecommunication costs. Thus, if one must implement class 2 because of a requirement for flow control, multiplexing must be implemented whether it is needed or not.

OSI PROTOCOLS AND STANDARDS

The following is a brief summary of the protocols used for the various OSI layers and the status of their standardization. For packet-switched networks, CCITT Recommendation X.25 is accepted as the standard for the protocols of the first three layers for communication over a packet-switched network. In general, protocols for OSI layers 1 through 3 are developed for specific topologies, such as LANs and concatenated networks.

ISO has standardized protocols for the Transport layer [4] and Session layer [5] and has developed a draft standard for tne Presentation layer. At the Application layer, protocols will, in general, be developed by various industry groups. ISO will standardize some of the "utility" Application layer protocols, including file transfer and virtual terminal protocols.

MODELING OSI

A system that complies with applicable OSI standards is termed an "open system." The fact that a system is open does not imply any particular means of implementing such standards. Only the external behavior of systems (the information communicated between systems) is pertinent to OSI. But to specify external behavior, some abstract modeling is required. The OSI model states

> To specify the external behavior of...open systems, only the interconnection aspects...would strictly need to be defined. However, to accomplish this, it is necessary to describe both the internal and external behavior...only the external behavior is retained as the standard of behavior...the description of the internal behavior of open systems is provided...only to support the definition of interconnection aspects....

Internal characteristics of implementation, including hardware configuration, design of software, programming language, and operating system, are not pertinent to OSI. However, a more subtle but equally important aspect of the distinction between internal and external behavior applies to layering. The purpose of layering is to allow individual groups of experts, developing protocols, to concentrate on well-defined subsets of the range of communication functions. However, OSI does not prescribe that the internal implementation of a system reflect layering. The layering examples discussed earlier show a layer entity passing a message to the layer entity below, etc. In reality, these interactions need not take place. Several or all layer entities can be combined into a single software program or a single hardware chip. These implementation details are transparent to the peer system.

Some of the criticism leveled at OSI reflects a misunderstanding of this point. It has been said that "layering is elegant but too expensive." This refers to a mistaken interpretation of the OSI model, that individual layer entities must be constructed, and that the resulting system is overburdened by all of the interactions between layer entities. In fact, these distinctions and interactions between layers are conceptual only.

OSI Products

The objective of OSI is to define a set of standards to enable open systems to cooperate. This is not the objective of the OSI model. The OSI model is a reality; OSI, however, has not yet been achieved. It will become a reality only when OSI protocols are supported by manufacturers, i.e., they must be available as software or hardware products at reasonable prices from a variety of vendors.

Some of the OSI protocols are still open to interpretation in certain areas. They also require the selection of parameters and options and, generally, two conforming implementations might not be capable of communicating successfully. In fact, two implementations of the Transport protocol might not be compatible, even though they implement the same protocol class. To add another dimension to the problem, it is often difficult to make purely technical decisions concerning one layer, independent of other layers. For example, one particular OSI product implements the ISO Transport and Session layer protocols. The product implements Transport class 2 and the half-duplex feature of the Session layer. Because it is an integrated package, a customer cannot buy only the Transport part or only the Session part of the product. The Transport layer features of the product might meet the requirements of a particular customer fully, whereas the Session layer requirements of the customer preclude the use of half-duplex. In that case, the product will not be suitable for the customer. Presentation layer issues add yet another level of complexity.

It is reasonable to expect that the "marketplace" will resolve these types of problems. The theoretical goal of the OSI effort is that one day, for every type of system there will be one or more OSI products available, and they will all work with one another. This will not happen solely as a result of standardization but also be various so-called "harmonization" efforts. Several computer manufacturers who are developing OSI products for their computers are involved, along with various agencies and consumer groups, in a number of collaborative efforts. These efforts are aimed at ensuring that these different OSI products are compatible, developing testing procedures, developing implementation strategies for converting operational networks to OSI and, in general, for bringing OSI products to market quickly.

REFERENCES

1. International Standard ISO 7498, *Information Processing Systems—Open Systems Interconnection—Basic Reference Model*, first ed. 1984-10-15, Ref. No ISO 7498-1985(E), American National Standards Institute, New York, 1984.
2. *American National Standard for Information Retrieval: Application Service Definition and Protocol Specification for Open Systems Interconnection (Basic Kernel)*, Z39.50, August 1986, WORKING DRAFT, ISSN: 0276-0762 (August 1986).

3. CCITT Recommendation X.25, *Interface Between Data Terminal Equipment (DTE) and Data Circuit-Terminating Equipment (DCE) for Terminals Operating in the Packet Mode and Connected to Public Data Networks by Dedicated Circuits.*
4. International Standard ISO 8072, *Information Processing Systems—Open Systems Interconnection—Transport Service Definition;* International Standard ISO 8073, *Information Processing Systems—Open Systems Interconnection—Connection Oriented Transport Protocol Specification.*
5. International Standard ISO 8326, *Information Processing Systems—Open Systems Interconnection—Basic Connection Oriented Session Service Definition;* International Standard ISO 8027, *Information Processing System—Open Systems Interconnection—Basic Connection Oriented Session Protocol Specification.*

SELECT BIBLIOGRAPHY

Avram, Henriette D., "The Linked Systems Project: Its Implications for Resource Sharing," *Libr. Resources and Tech. Serv.*, 30(1), 36–46 (January/March 1986).

Deasington, R. J., *X.25 Explained: Protocols for Packet Switching Networks,* Halsted Press, New York (Ellis Horwood series in computers and their applications), 1985.

Denenberg, Ray, "Open Systems Interconnection," *Libr. Hi-Tech* (9), 15–26 (1985).

Denenberg, Ray, and Sally H. McCallum, "RLG/WLN/LC Computers Ready to 'Talk'," *Am. Libr.*, 400–403 (June 1984).

Denenberg, Ray, Bob Rader, and Tonia Metka, "The LSP/SNI Test Facility," *Libr. Hi-Tech* (13), 41–49 (1986).

Denenberg, Ray, Bob Rader, Thomas P. Brown, Wayne Davison, and Fred Lauber, "Implementation of the Linked Systems Project: A Technical Report," *Libr. Hi-Tech* (11), 87–107 (1985).

Martin, James, *Computer Networks and Distributed Processing: Software, Techniques, Architecture,* Prentice-Hall, Inc., Englewood Cliffs, NJ, 1981.

McCallum, Sally H., "Linked Systems Project, Part 1: Authorities Implementation"; Denenberg, Ray, "Linked Systems Project, Part 2: Standard Network Interconnection," *Libr. Hi-Tech* (10), 61–79 (1985).

Network Architectures, State of the Art Reports—1982 Series, Series 10, Number 1.

Open Systems Data Communication (published monthly) and *Open Systems Data Transfer* published bimonthly), Omnicom, Inc., Vienna, VA, ISSN 0741-286X.

"Protocols and Standards," special issue of *J. Telecommun. Networks* (Fall 1984).

Rutledge, James H., "OSI and SNA: A Perspective," *J. Telecommun. Networks,* 13–27 (Spring 1982).

Stallings, William, *Local Networks,* Macmillan Publishing Company, New York, 1984.

Tanenbaum, Andrew S., *Computer Networks,* Prentice-Hall, Inc., Englewood Cliffs, NJ, 1981 (Prentice-Hall Software Series).

RAY DENENBERG

PARALLEL PROCESSING

INTRODUCTION

A typical uniprocessor system consists of four interrelated functional units: the main memory, the control unit (CU), the arithmetic-logic unit (ALU), and input–output subsystems (I/O). Usually the CU and ALU are combined and known as the central processing unit (CPU). Central to such organization is the concept of the stored program — the principle that instructions and data are to be stored intermixed in a single and uniform storage medium. A uniprocessor system, based on the concept of the stored program, is known as the von Neumann machine. During the past four decades, the von Neumann concept has proven its practical applications. However, it has been shown in practice that many real-time applications demand a computational power beyond the extended computational capability of the von Neumann design (extended due to the advances in technology). Such a computation gap has motivated the concept of parallelism and parallel processing as a generic term to cope with the ever-increasing demands for faster operations and higher performance. The major theme of this article centers around the concept of parallelism and its contribution in reducing the computation gap. However, for the sake of clarity, before any further discussion, the following terms should be defined:

- Parallelism: A generic term to define the ability of the simultaneous execution of many actions at any instant.
- Parallel processing: An efficient form of information processing that emphasizes the exploitation of concurrent events in the computing process. Concurrency implies parallelism, simultaneity, and pipelining. Parallel events may occur in multiple resources during the same time interval, simultaneous events may occur at the same time instant, and pipelined events may occur in overlapped time spans. Parallel processing demands concurrent execution of many programs in the computer, in contrast to sequential processing. It is a cost-effective means to improve system performance through concurrent activities in the computer [1].
- Parallel processors: The systems that emphasizes parallel processing.

This article is divided into three parts. The first part discusses Parallel computers, which are based on the von Neumann principle. The second section addresses the architectures, which are based on the data flow concept. The third section overviews some special-purpose architectures proposed in the literature.

1 PARALLEL COMPUTERS

1.1 Classifications

In the early processors, the ALU was designed to perform operations only on a bit or a bit pair (serial ALU). Therefore, an operation on an M-bit operand or operand pair must be repeated bit serially M times. To speed up the processing, a parallel ALU is usually used, so that all bits of an operand or operand pair can be operated on simultaneously. This discussion can be extended to the cases in which either (a) all the ith bits of n operands or operand pairs (i.e., bit slice-Bis) may be operated on simultaneously or (b) the operation is performed on n M-bit operands or operand pairs. Points A—D in Figure 1 illustrate these four approaches respectively.

This discussion represents Feng's classification [2], where the concurrent space is identified as a two-dimensional space based on the bit and word multiplicities. Figure 1 shows the allocation of some of the systems in Feng's concurrent space.

Flynn [3] has classified the concurrent space according to the multiplicity of instruction and data streams, where, computer systems are partitioned into four groups:

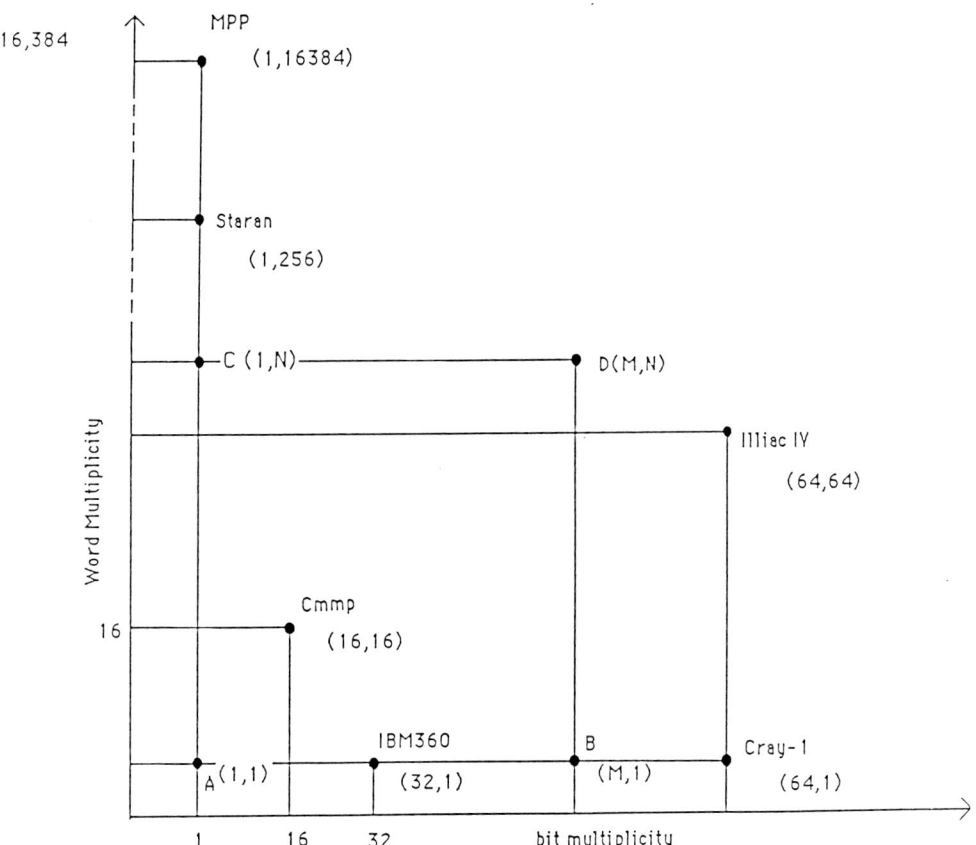

FIGURE 1   Feng's classification.

1. SISD (single instruction stream—single data stream): The classical von Neumann architecture (with serial or parallel ALU).
2. SIMD (single instruction stream—multiple data stream): The multiple ALU-type architectures (e.g., array processor).
3. MISD (multiple instruction stream—single data stream): Not as practical as the other classes. A data base machine—search processor [4] represents a model in this class.
4. MIMD (multiple instruction stream—multiple data stream): The multiprocessor system (loosely or tightly coupled).

As a general rule, one could make the conclusion that SISD and SIMD machines are single CU systems, whereas MIMD machines are multiple CU systems. Flynn's classification does not address the interactions among the processing modules and the methods in which processing modules in a concurrent system are controlled. As a result, one can classify a pipeline computer and a uniprocessor computer as SISD machines, because both instructions and data are provided sequentially.

Händler [5] has extended Feng's concurrent space by a third dimension, namely the number of control units. Händler's space is defined as $t = (k, d, w,)$, in which k is the number of CUs interpreting a program, d is the number of ALUs controlled by a CU, and w is the word length or number of bits handled in one of the ALUs. According to this classification, a von Neumann machine with serial/parallel ALUs is represented as (1, 1, 1), (1, 1, M), respectively. Figure 2 depicts the position of some of the computer systems in the Händler space. To represent pipelining at different levels (e.g., macropipeline, instruction pipeline, and arithmetic pipeline) and illustrate the diversity, sequentiality, and flexibility/adaptability of an organization, the above triplet has been extended by three variables (e.g., k', d', w',) and three operators (e.g., +, *, v), where k' represents the marcopipline—the number of CUs interpreting tasks of a program, where the data flow through them is sequential; d' represents instruction pipeline—the number of functional units managed by one CU and working on one data stream; w' represents arithmetic pipe—the number of stages; + represents diversity—existence of more than one structure; * represents sequentiality—for sequentially ordered structures; and v represents flexibility/adaptability—for reconfigurable organization. According to this extension to Händler's notation, CDC 7600 [1] and DAP [6, 7] are represented as (15*1, 1*1, 12*1)*(1*1, 1*9, 60*1) and (1*1, 1*1, 32*1)*[(1*1, 128*1, 32*1) v (1*1, 4096*1, 1*1)], respectively.

These classifications suffer from the fact that either they do not uniquely identify a specific organization or, they cannot thoroughly determine the interrelationships among different modules in an organization. In the following, we classify the conventional parallel systems into three groups: (a) parallel SIMD, (b) pipeline, and (c) multiprocessors.

Our distinction is according to the exploitation of concurrency and the interrelationships among the CU, processing elements (PEs), and memory modules in each of the aforementioned groups. First, for the sake of clarity, some parameters, which will be referenced throughout this article, are discussed. Second, the definition, major characteristics, and general organization of each group are discussed. Finally, we address the shortcomings of the conventional parallel systems in order to motivate our discussion in Section 2.

Parallel Processing

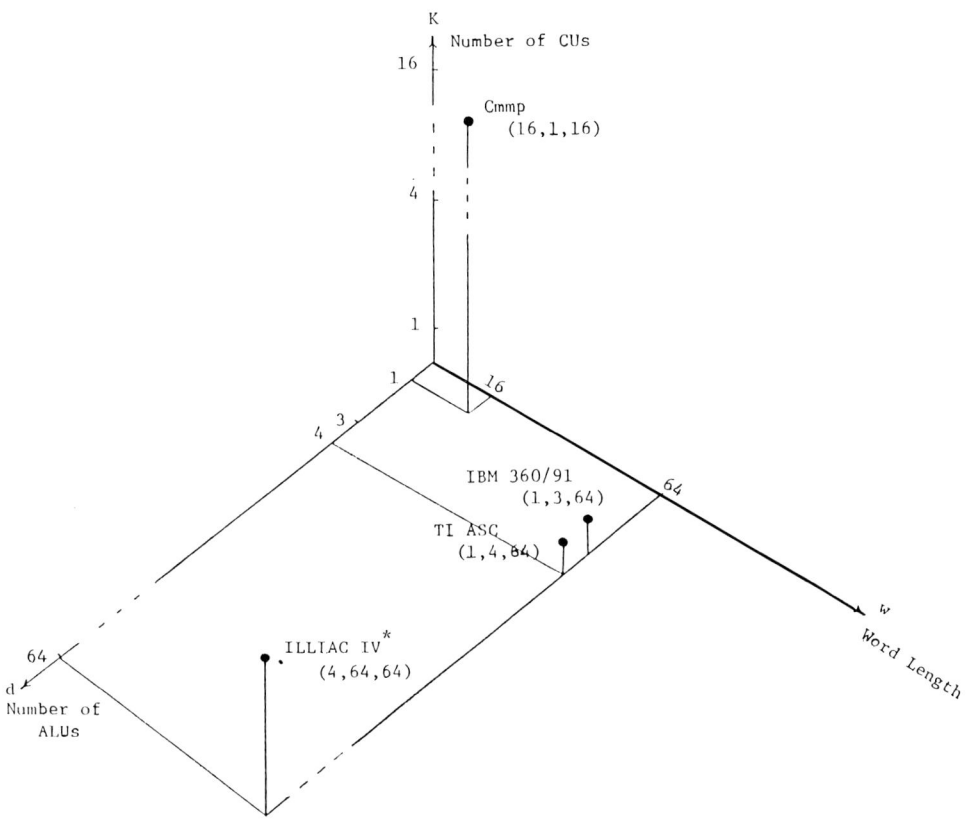

FIGURE 2 Händler's space.

1.2 System Utilization

As discussed previously, for any computer there is a maximum number of bits or bit pairs that can be processed concurrently whether it is under single-instruction or multiple-instruction control [2]. This maximum degree of concurrency, or maximum concurrency (C_m), is an indication of the computer-processing capability. The actual utilization of this capability is indicated by the average concurrency defined to be

$$C_a = \frac{\sum c_i \Delta t_i}{\sum \Delta t_i} \tag{1}$$

where C_i is the concurrency at Δt_i. If Δt_i is set to one time unit, then the average concurrency over a period of T time units is

$$C_a = \frac{\sum_{i=1}^{T} C_i}{T} \qquad (2)$$

The average hardware utilization is then

$$\mu = \frac{C_a}{C_m} = \frac{\sum_{i=1}^{T} C_i}{TC_m} = \frac{1}{T} \sum_{i=1}^{T} \sigma_i \qquad (3)$$

where σ_i is the hardware utilization at time i. Whereas C_m is determined by the hardware design, C_a or μ is highly dependent on the software and applications. A general-purpose computer should achieve a high μ for as many applications as possible, whereas a special-purpose computer would yield a high μ for at least the intended applications. In either case, maximizing the value of μ for a computer design is important. Equation (3) can also be used to evaluate the relative effectiveness of machine designs.

For a parallel processor, the degree of concurrency is called the degree of parallelism. A similar discussion can be used to define the average hardware utilization of a parallel processor. The maximum parallelism is then P_m, and the average parallelism is

$$P_a = \frac{\sum P_i \Delta t_i}{\sum \Delta t_i} \qquad (4)$$

or

$$P_a = \frac{\sum_{i=1}^{T} P_i}{T} \qquad (5)$$

for T time units. The average hardware utilization becomes

$$\nu = \frac{P_a}{P_m} = \frac{\sum_{i=1}^{T} P_i}{TP_m} = \frac{1}{T} \sum_{i=1}^{T} \rho_i \qquad (6)$$

where ρ_i is the hardware utilization for parallel processors at time i. With appropriate instrumentation, the average hardware utilization of a system can be determined.

In practice, however, it is not always true that every bit or bit pair that is being processed would be productive. Some of the bits produce only repetitious (superfluous) or even meaningless results. This happens more often and more severely in a parallel processor than in a word sequential processor. Consider, e.g., performing a maximum search operation in a mesh-connected parallel processor (such as ILLIAC IV). For N operands it takes $N/2 \log_2 N$ comparisons ($N/2$ comparisons for each $\log_2 N$ iterations) instead of the usual $N-1$ comparisons in word sequential machines. Thus, in effect there are

$$(\frac{N}{2} \log_2 N) - (N - 1) = \frac{N}{2} (\log_2 N - 2) + 1$$

comparisons that are nonproductive. If we let $\hat{P}_a$ be the effective parallelism over a period of T time units, and $\hat{\upsilon}$, $\hat{P}$, and $\hat{\rho}_i$ be the corresponding effective values, the effective hardware utilization is then

$$\hat{\upsilon} = \frac{\hat{P}_a}{P_m} = \frac{\sum_{i=1}^{T} \hat{P}_i}{TP_m} = \frac{1}{T} \sum_{i=1}^{T} \hat{\rho}_i \qquad (7)$$

A successful parallel processor design should yield a high $\hat{\upsilon}$, as well as the required throughput for, at least, the intended applications. This not only involves a proper hardware and software design but also the development of efficient parallel algorithms for these applications.

Suppose T_u is the execution time of an application program using a conventional von Neumann machine, and T_c is the execution time of the same program using a concurrent system; the speedup ratio is then defined as

$$S = \frac{T_u}{T_c} \qquad (8)$$

Naturally, for a specific parallel organization, the speedup ratio determines how well an application program can utilize the hardware resources. Supporting softwares have a direct effect on the speedup ratio.

1.3 Parallel SIMD Systems

Parallel SIMD systems are the natural extension of parallel ALU systems. Point D in Feng's concurrent space represents parallel SIMD systems, where concurrency is exploited through the replication of the processing modules under the management of a unique control unit. As a result, arithmetic and logic operations can be performed on a collection of operands (operand pairs) simultaneously. In this study we distinguish three groups of parallel SIMD systems: (a) ensemble processors, (b) array processors, and (c) associative processors.

Ensemble Processors

An ensemble system is an extension of the conventional uniprocessor systems. It is a collection of N PEs (a PE consists of an ALU, a set of local registers, and very limited local control capability) and N memories, under the control of a single CU. Such a simple organization does not provide any direct communication paths among PEs. Moreover, it does not allow flexible interconnections between PEs and memories. Such communications are done through the CU. As a result, the system is able to execute up to N identical jobs simultaneously. However, due to the lack of direct interprocessor communications, this organization has very limited applications.

Array Processors

The schematic diagram of an array processor is shown in Figure 3. The system is composed of n identical PEs under the control of a single CU and a number of memory units [6-11]. The PEs and memory units communicate with each other through an interconnection network (the simplest interconnection network is a unibus). This network usually provides a uniform interconnection among PEs on the one hand and PEs and memory modules on the other hand. In ILLIAC IV [11], the complexity of the interconnection networks among the memory modules and PEs has been reduced by distribution of memory modules among the PEs. As a result, the system is a collection of n identical PEs with their own local memory modules. Different array processor organizations might use different interconnection networks among the processing elements. ILLIAC IV uses a mesh-structured network, whereas the Burroughs Scientific Processor (BSP) [12] uses a crossbar network.

The CU is usually a computer with its own high-speed registers, local memory, and arithmetic unit. As in conventional machines, the instructions are stored in a main memory, together with data. However, in ILLIAC IV design, programs are distributed among the local memories of the PEs. Hence, the instructions are fetched from the processors' memory modules into an instruction buffer in the CU. Each instruction is either a local type instruction, where it is executed entirely within the CU, or it is a vector instruction and is executed in the processing array. The primary function of the CU is to examine each instruction as it is to be executed and to determine where the execution should take place.

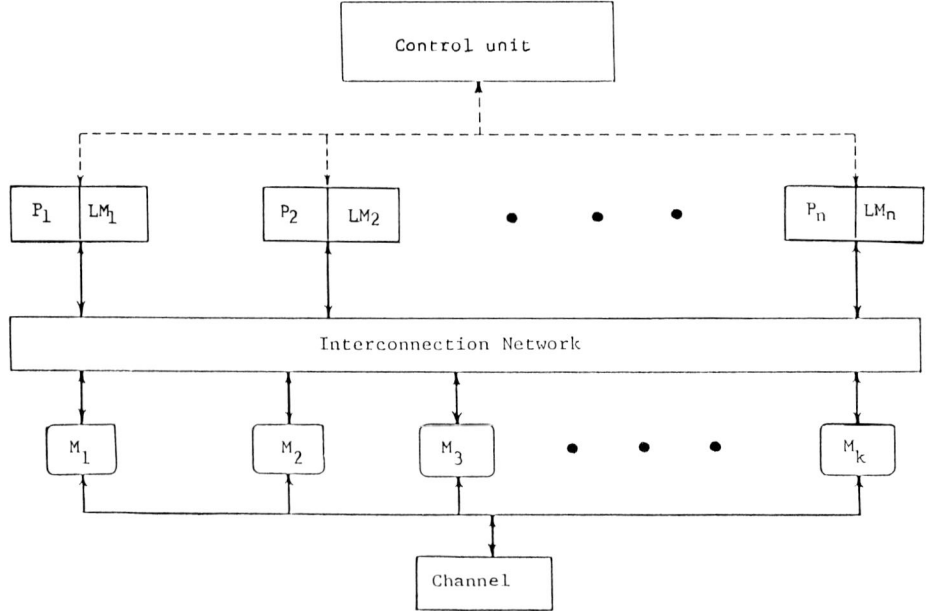

FIGURE 3 Array processor system; (P) Processor; (LM) local memory; (M) memory module.

Parallel Processing

An array processor is a synchronous parallel computer. PEs are synchronized to perform in parallel the same function at the same time. The problem of data structuring and detecting parallelism in a program is a major bottleneck, although the design of the CU is simple and is almost like the one in sequential systems. In array processors an operation such as

$$x(i) = A(i) * B(i) \qquad i = 1, 2, \ldots, N$$

could be executed in one step, if the elements of A and B arrays are distributed properly among the N processors; as a result, the ith processor is assigned the task of computing x(i). However, if we have to compute

$$y = \sum_{i=1}^{T} A(i) * B(i)$$

while the product terms are generated in one step as discussed before, the summations will be performed in $\log_2 N$ steps, assuming that the intermediate operands are properly aligned and only a subset of processors that handle these operands become active at successive steps. Thus, the speedup ratio becomes

$$S = \frac{2N - 1}{1 + \log_2 N} \approx 0 \left(\frac{N}{\log_2 N} \right) \tag{9}$$

It should be noted that in an algorithm as discussed above, such a speedup factor is at the expense of a poor resource utilization.

Associative Processor

Associative memories have been generally defined as a collection or assemblage of data storage elements that are accessed in parallel on the basis of data content rather than by specific address or location [13–17]. As a result, each associative cell should have hardware capability to store and search its contents against the data that are broadcast by the CU. With such a definition in mind one could conclude that although read and write are the basic operations in the conventional random access memory (RAM), search as well as the read and write are the basic operations for associative memory. The typical components of an associative memory are depicted in Figure 4: Memory array provides storage space for the data; comparand register holds the data to be compared against the contents of the memory array. However, by proper setting of the bit pattern in the mask register one can mask off portions of the data words from comparison and other operations; a response bit indicates the success or failure of a search against the content of the corresponding associative word; and, finally, multiple match resolver is used to narrow the result of a search to a specific word in case of multiple responses (e.g., matches). An associative processor is defined as an associative memory capable of performing arithmetic and logic operations. Usually, in such an organization, arithmetic and logic operations are performed in bit-slice fashion. This implies the extension of each associative word by a serial ALU. An associative computer then is defined as a system that uses an associative processor as an essential component for storage and processing. An obvious advantage of asso-

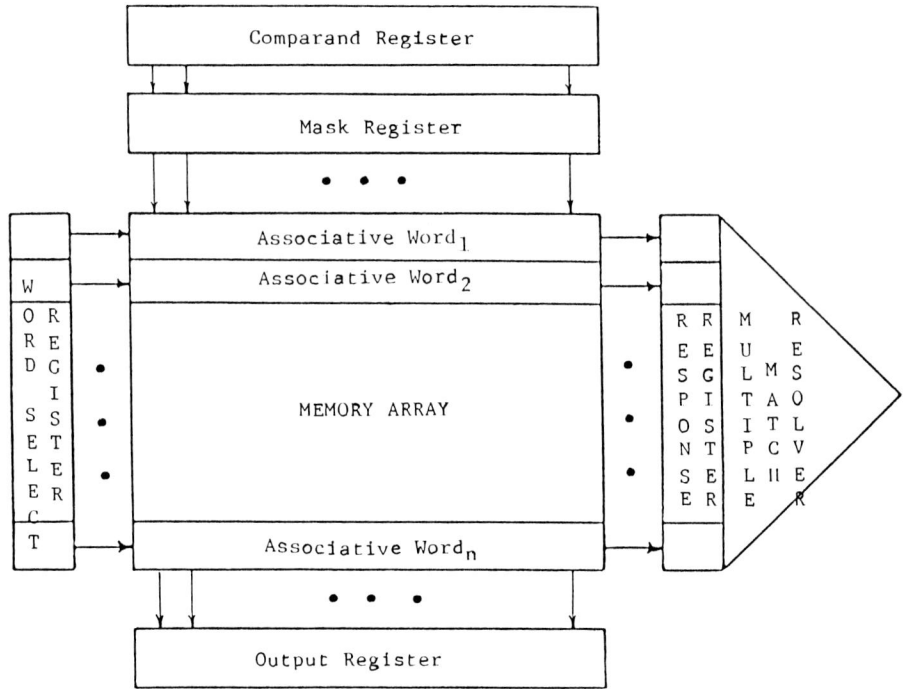

FIGURE 4   A word parallel associative memory.

ciative processing can be found in its application in nonnumeric processing, radar signal tracking and processing, image processing, and arithmetic and logic operations on large sets of data. The main motivation for the study of the associative systems centers around its capability in (a) reducing the semantic gap (i.e., a measure of the difference between the concepts in high-level languages and the concepts in the underlying computer architectures [18]) in the conventional systems, and (b) increasing the performance due to the parallel operations at the storage level and elimination of address computation.

The concept of electronic associative memory was first introduced by Slade and McMahon [13], who described the design of a cryogenic memory system. Since then, associative memories have been implemented using techniques such as tunnel diodes, evaporated organic diode arrays, magnetic cores, plated wires, semiconductors, bubble memory, integrated circuits [16] and, recently, optical technology. Moreover, literature has addressed several modifications to the basic associative operations (e.g., hybrid associative memory, read-only associative memory [17]). However, up to the last decade, a widespread application of associative memory had not been fully explored. This was due to the hardware complexity of associative cells in comparison with RAM cells, conservatism, and lack of suitable associative algorithms. However, since the mid-1970s there is growing evidence that the above trend has changed. This is due to the advances in technology and its effect on cost and size of the hardware components, and the strong applications of associative processing in nonnumeric operations, image processing, and pattern recognition.

Associative memories have been classified into four categories: fully parallel, bit serial, word serial, and block oriented [13, 16]. This classification is in accordance with the basic unit of data to which the search operation is applied and reflects the trade-off between speed and cost.

Fully Parallel: In a fully parallel organization, the search capability is associated with the basic unit of information (e.g., bit level). Therefore, the associative operation can be performed along two dimensions simultaneously. Such a direction implies larger cell size and more expensive modules, in comparison with a bit in the RAM. Point D in Figure 1 represents a fully parallel associative memory. In practice, fully parallel associative memories have been realized as two- or one-dimensional memory arrays. In the two-dimensional organization (word organized), memory is composed of fixed-length entities called words. In a one-dimensional organization (distributed logic) [19, 20], memory is arranged as a string of search character cells, where each cell communicates with its neighbor and the control unit. Naturally fixed-length record size is an obvious shortcoming of a word-organized model. This will limit/complicate the implementation of the variable-length word applications. However, one should remember that associative operations in a word-organized memory are handled easier than the ones in a distributed logic organization.

Bit Serial: This organization represents point C in Feng's concurrent space (Fig. 1). Memory is organized as a collection of circular shift registers in which search capability is associated with a designated bit within each word (e.g., bit slice). To achieve efficiency at a reasonable cost, a variation of this organization (i.e., byte serial associative memory) has also been proposed in the literature. In a byte-serial model, byte search capability is associated with each associative word.

Word Serial: In this class, search capability is associated with a word. This will represent point B in Figure 1. As can be seen, this class of associative memory is very similar to the parallel ALU systems. However, one should recognize that the hardware realization of word serial organization is totally different than the one in the parallel ALU systems. This organization represents a hardware realization of a simple program loop in linear search.

Block-Oriented System: In this class, associative capability is provided at the mass storage level (e.g., secondary storage). This concept is an extension of fixed-head rotating secondary storage technology. However, the fixed read/write heads are extended as a small processor (i.e., logic per track). As the data pass under the read/write heads, they will be investigated and marked for the later accesses. During the 1970s, the concept of logic per track, originally proposed by Slotnick [21], was used as a guideline in the design of many data base machines.

1.4 Multiprocessor Systems

The multiprocessor organization (Fig. 5) is the practical extension of the array processing [1, 22—26]. Originally, multiprocessors were designed as a model to improve the fault-tolerance capability of the conventional systems. The attribute that characterizes a multiprocessing system is the sharing of a global memory by the processors that make up the system. The argument that justifies such an approach is the existence of a large class of problems,

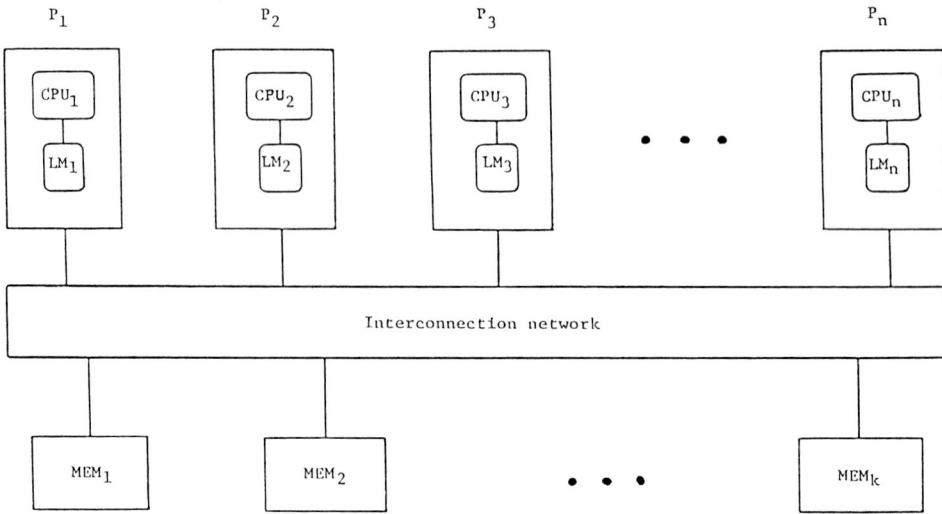

FIGURE 5 Multiprocessor system. (P) processor; (MEM) memory module; (CPU) central processing unit; (LM) local memory.

which can be split up into a number of tasks. Each task can be simultaneously run on a different processor in a multiprocessor system. This will reduce the execution time and, hence, will increase the system's throughput. Reliability is a major advantage of multiprocessor systems, because failure in any of the redundant components can be tolerated due to the reconfigurability of the system. However, in multiprocess systems, one has to find practical solutions for problems such as task partitioning, processors coordination and communication, and resource allocation and contention; otherwise, lack of such sophisticated algorithms will drastically degrade the performance and resource utilization. These problems have enforced a limitation on the number of processors, as will be discussed later.

In general, a multiprocessor system can be defined as follows:

- There are two or more CPUs. The processors could be homogeneous or nonhomogeneous. However, they should be general enough to be able to perform general-purpose operations.
- Main memory is shared among the processors. However, we do not rule out the possibility of private memory for each processor. As a matter of fact, recently there has been a surge to study the so-called coherence problem in a multiprocessor environment with private memory [27–29].
- The resources are sharable among the processors.
- The whole system is under control of a single integrated operating system.
- There should be a means of interaction at different levels (i.e., hardware/software) among the system's modules.

By a close observation one can realize the natural trend in the evolution of the multiprocessor systems. Practically, multiprocessing like parallel

Parallel Processing 379

processing, achieves concurrency as the result of hardware replication
(e.g., redundancy). However, in a multiprocessor system, the degree of
freedom associated with the processors is much higher than the one in the
parallel systems. Therefore, processors are more independent with respect
to each other and the central CU. This independence and resource-sharing
capability of the multiprocessor systems will introduce a degree of complexity
on the dynamic communication capability among the processors and among the
processors and the global memory. In addition, in contrast to the parallel
systems, the CU and software supports should be much more complex in
order to map application programs into the hardware features. Multiprocessor systems are further subdivided into loosely coupled and tightly coupled
systems. This distinction is based on the degree of the communication
among the system's modules. Though it is not within the scope of this
article, the aforementioned freedom can be traced in the evolution of distributed systems.

The performance of a multiprocessor system depends on a mix of jobs.
With n processors, the throughput is certainly less than the sum of the
throughput of n independent processors. For n=2, and n=4, typical values
of throughput are 1.5 and 2.5, respectively. It should be noted that in
practice, the number of the PEs in an array processor can be relatively
much larger than the number of processors in a multiprocessor system.
For example, the design of MPP was based on 16,384 PEs, whereas Cmmp
utilized 16 processors in its organization. This difference is due to the
overall complexity of MIMD organizations in comparison to SIMD organizations.

1.5 Pipeline Systems

The idea of a pipeline system is similar to an automobile assembly line. The
term pipelining refers to the design techniques that introduce concurrency
into a computer system by taking some basic functions to be involved repeatedly in the system and partitioning them into several subfunctions with
the following properties [1, 26, 30–32]:

- Evaluation of the basic function is equivalent to some sequential evaluation of the subfunctions.
- Other than the exchange of inputs and outputs, there are no inter-relationships between subfunctions.
- Hardware may be developed to execute each subfunction.
- The time required for these hardware units to perform their individual evaluations is usually approximately equal.

Therefore, in a pipeline system a process is decomposed into a series of
sequential subprocesses. Each subprocess is executed on a dedicated
module called segment, stage, or station. In addition, because the logic
that actually performs the subprocesses at each stage is without memory,
the presentation of data to each stage usually demands some kind of buffer
to be included at either the beginning or end of each stage. This will help
to synchronize the overall flow of data throughout the pipe. The concept
of pipelining has been implemented in systems such as Amdahl 470 V/8,
[33], CRAY [34–35], TI-ASC [36], CDC STAR-100 [37], CDC 7600-6600
[38], and IBM 360-91 [39–40].

Figure 6 dipicts a schematic diagram of a pipeline processor where k
different sections correspond to the distinct hardware steps. Thus, several

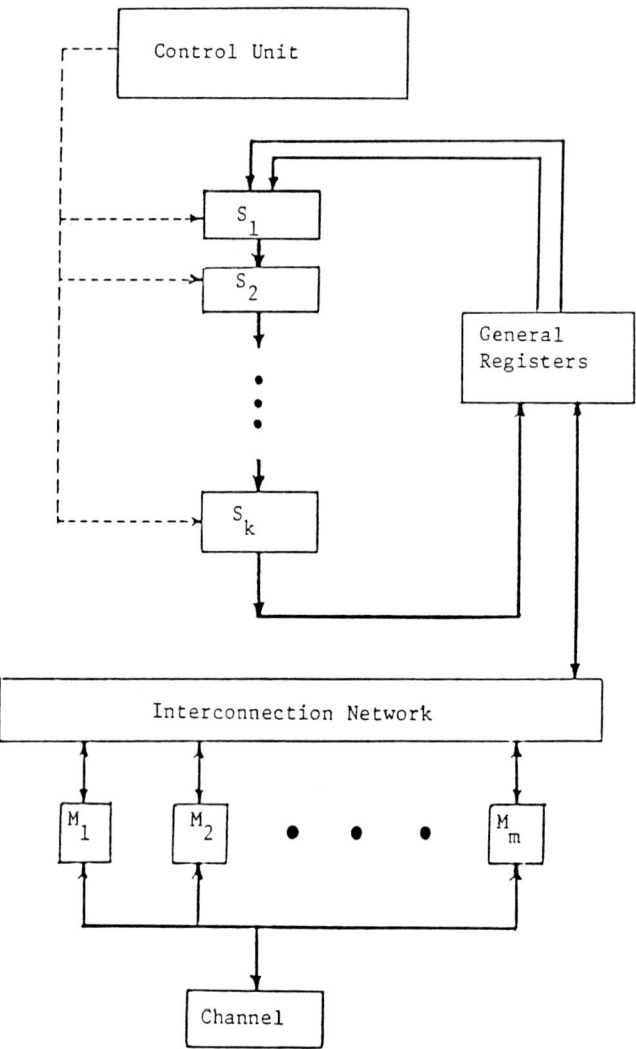

FIGURE 6   Pipeline processor system. (M) Memory module; (S) segment.

partial operations can be in progress concurrently within a pipeline, which will result in an increase in throughput.

Suppose we want to compute the elements x(i) defined as

$$x(i) = A(i)*B(i) \qquad i=1, 2, \ldots, N$$

Assuming that the multiplier unit is a pipeline of five stages, the overall execution time will be $([N-1] + 5)\Delta t$ (Δt is the delay time due to operation in a stage) provided that a constant flow of data is always available to the pipeline and the system can store x(i) as fast as it is generated. Now, suppose one has to calculate

$$y = \sum_{i=1}^{T} x(i)$$

using the same pipe for addition. The formation of products will take (N+ 4) stage delays. Then the pipeline is drained out and set for addition operations. Due to the data dependence, additions are performed in several passes. After the first pass, the pipeline yield N/2 results; in the second pass, it yields approximately N/4 results, etc. Hence, the total execution time would be

$$5 + (\frac{N}{2} - 1) + 5 + (\frac{N}{4} - 1) + \ldots + 5 + (1 - 1) = 4 \log_2 N + \frac{N}{2} + \frac{N}{4} + \ldots$$
$$\leq 4 \log_2 N + N$$

stage delays. Hence, the total execution time is $\leq 2N + 4 \log_2 N + 4$ stage delays. A serial process would have taken $5(2N - 1) = 10N - 5$ stage delays. As a result, the speedup ratio is equal to

$$S = \frac{10N - 5}{2N + 4 \log_2 N + 4} \tag{10}$$

However, experiences on CRAY have shown that vector operations for small vectors demonstrate a performance degradation over scalar operations [34]. This is due to the fact that performance of the pipeline operations is heavily dependent on the number of operands and uniformity of operations. Pipelines can be classified according to their capabilities. A *unifunction* pipeline is capable of only one basic kind of operation. On the other hand, a *Multifunction* pipeline is capable of handling several different kinds of functional evaluation. A multifunctional pipeline can be further grouped into *statically configured* and *dynamically configured* pipelines. This classification is based on the frequency of changes in the functions they perform. A concept known as *hazard* is a major concern in a pipeline architecture. A hazard prevents the pipeline from accepting data at the maximum rate that the staging clock might support. Hazard is the result of the structural and data dependence. A structural hazard is the one where two different pieces of data attempt to use the same stage at the same time (e.g., collisions). Data-dependent hazards occur when a pass through a stage is a function of the data value. For statically configured pipelines, the designers can predict precisely when a structural hazard might occur and, hence, can schedule the pipeline so that the collisions do not occur. The data-dependent hazards are clearly system and usage dependent and not as amenable to analytical study as are structural hazards.

1.6 Pipelining vs. Parallelism

The theme of Sections 1.6 and 1.7 is twofold: First, the general characteristics of parallel SIMD and pipeline systems are compared. Our comparison is intended to clarify the existing ambiguity between pipeline and parallel SIMD systems. However, one can extend such a general discussion for other classes of parallel systems. Second, the shortcomings of the conventional concurrent systems are addressed to motivate our discussion in the second part of this article.

Based on the discussion in Sections 1.3 and 1.5, both techniques attempt to increase the performance of some functions by increasing the number of simultaneously operating hardware modules. For a conventionally designed module to perform some generic function, either technique can be used to derive a new design running up to N times faster. However, parallelism is achieved through the replication of the basic hardware unit N times, with all replicated units running simultaneously, whereas pipelining is the result of staging the hardware unit into a sequence of k subunits. Because a pipeline cannot be broken up into an arbitrary number of stages, one can conclude that parallel systems are more expandable than pipeline systems. The difference between pipelining and parallelism also shows up in memory organization and bandwidth, internal interconnection of modules, and control. For example, in a pipeline system, memory organization should support a constant and smooth flow of data to the pipeline. On the other hand, in a parallel system, accesses to the memory system are not smooth, and each processor could initiate an access to any memory module. This implies a complex and dynamic interconnection network between processing modules and memory modules [41–42]. Such a network should provide simultaneous accesses to the memory modules, where one access does not block other accesses to the memory modules. Reliability is another feature that separates these two techniques. In general, parallelism offers a more reliable system. This is due to the fact that the task of any faulty module can be distributed among other replicated modules in a parallel system, whereas this cannot be achieved in a pipeline system.

Architectural analysis of the so-called supercomputers [43–45] reveals a new trend in the design of the parallel systems, which can be classified as parallel pipelined systems [34–36].

1.7 Shortcomings of the Conventional Parallel Systems

The class of the parallel system and its successor have shown their effectiveness in many real-time applications. By their very nature, these computers are more complex than their predecessor architectures. This complexity is mainly due to the simultaneous competition/cooperation of several modules over common resources, which leads to more complexity and sophsi-tication at the (a) control structure, in order to manage the flow of data and operations within the system's modules; (b) interconnection network, to allow simultaneous interactions among the system's modules.

Although the growth in complexity could result in higher cost, lower resource utilization, and performance degradation, the major disadvantage of these systems is associated with two interrelated factors, namely *specialization* and *semantic gap*.

In contrast to the conventional von Neumann architectures, parallel systems are specialized architectures. For example, parallel systems are superior in handling computation-bound applications; however, they offer low performance in I/O-bound applications such as data base systems. In addition, these machines demand specific domain(s) to guarantee the performance improvement. Studies on ILLIAC IV-type architecture have shown that the allocation of data within the memory modules has a drastic effect on the performance [46]. Experiences on CRAY have shown that vector operations for small vectors demonstrate a performance degradation over scalar operations [34]. These examples reflect the fact that the conventional concurrent systems require specialized and sometimes different programming skills for efficient resource utilization. As a result, in a multifunctional unit system (i.e., an extension of the conventional systems consists of a single CU and a processor unit composed of several independent functional units), a mixed sequence of instructions increases the performance, whereas in a pipeline system a uniform sequence of instructions increases the performance. Therefore, we can conclude that conventional parallel systems introduce a wider semantic gap than the conventional systems in handling general-purpose applications. Therefore, they require an extensive software support to express and determine the inherent parallelism in an application program.

The performance improvement of parallel systems is greatly dependent on the proper utilization of the hardware resources. However, it has been shown in practice that in many applications, such goals are usually not achieved. This problem is attributed to (a) the inherent sequential nature of many algorithms; (b) overhead time required for data alignment, process coordination, etc., in a parallel system; (c) lack of suitable parallel algorithms for various application areas; (d) lack of suitable parallel high-level language, which enables the programmer to express the inherent parallelism explicity in the problem being encoded; and (e) lack of suitable compilation techniques to detect embedded parallelism in a sequential program.

High-level languages rooted in the 1950s have been developed as programming tools to increase the machine's independence and productivity. Naturally, these languages reflect the structure of the conventional uniprocessor systems, i.e., the existence of a primitive set of arithmetic operations, which are carried out sequentially on data stored in some form of memory device. However, for a parallel system there is a need to express the parallelism in an algorithm for parallel execution. This goal can be achieved either through the definition of new parallel languages or the addition of parallel constructs in the definition of the conventional sequential high-level languages.

Since the introduction of parallelism and parallel computers, there has been a surge to design and develop parallel languages to facilitate the utilization and performance of parallel systems [47–50]. The so-called Parallel Fortran (P-FOR) proposed for PEPE architecture [47], TRANQUIL for ILLIAC IV [48], and APPLE for STARAN [49] are among the pioneer efforts in this area.

Generation of parallelism from sequential constructs (e.g., vectorization) requires an extensive analysis of the sequential programs. This analysis must check that the ordering is, in fact, arbitrary and that there are no sequential dependencies in the process. This approach is a means of increasing the adaptability of the parallel systems and protecting the previous investments of the users. Naturally, this direction requires the development of sophisticated compilers (e.g., vectorizing compilers) to generate parallel machine instructions from sequences of operations without violating the program semantics. This means more sophisticated compilation techniques, more complex operating systems, and more advanced program development tools. The growth of the software overhead and its by-products in the parallel systems is the source of our discussion in the next section.

2 DATA FLOW COMPUTERS

As discussed in Section 1, the challenge of closing the computation gap has motivated the introduction of some alternative architectures to the von Neumann machines. These alternatives offer more computational power than their conventional von Neumann counterparts through the concurrent execution of more than one operation at a time. However, it has been shown in practice that the pipelined and parallel architectures cannot achieve the computational power demanded by real-time applications [51]. Such a deficiency is due to (a) the practical limitation of the physical laws, (b) the sequential nature of the von Neumann architecture, and (c) the software/hardware complexities introduced by the traditional concurrent systems.

These deficiencies are the basis for the design and implementation of machines that are inherently parallel and conceptually far from the von Neumann philosophy (e.g., control flow architecture). These new architectures are based on the concept of data flow computation in which the operations are executed in an order determined by the data interdependencies and the availability of the resources. Therefore, in contrast to the conventional control flow program, the ordering of operations is not specified by the programmer in a data flow program, but is that implied by the data interdependencies. Two variations of data flow computation can be distinguished, namely data-driven computations and demand-driven computations. In the data-driven computations, operations are executed in an order determined by the availability of the input data, whereas in the demand-driven computations, operations are executed in an order determined by the requirements for data. Figure 7 shows a data flow graph (i.e., directed graph whose nodes correspond to operators and arcs are pointers for forwarding data tokens), to find the roots of a quadratic equation.

2.1 Data-Driven Architectures

The computation gap, coupled with the inherent sequential nature of the von Neumann architectures, has motivated the design and implementation of a special class of decentralized concurrent system that supports concurrency as its basic architecture. Data-driven architecture is an example of such an organization. In data-driven computation, the availability of the data for an operation will initiate the execution of that instruction. Thus, by eliminating the control dependency among the basic instructions, one can achieve ultimate parallelism within a data-driven architecture. In this environment, a program is represented as an acyclic directed graph in which the nodes are the operations to be performed and the arcs direct the data among the nodes. Such a radical departure from the sequential von Neumann-type organizations has eliminated familiar concepts such as program counter, addressing schemes, and central memory, with an eye toward increasing the degree of parallelism.

Since the mid-1970s a number of data-driven architectures have been proposed, and recently we have witnessed the design of some prototype data-driven computers. The concept of "asynchrony" embedded in the definition of a data-driven architecture provides grounds for a high degree of implicit parallelism. In addition, the data-driven organization eliminates the need for an updatable storage, use of identifiers, and all of their associated by-products such as global side effects and aliasing.

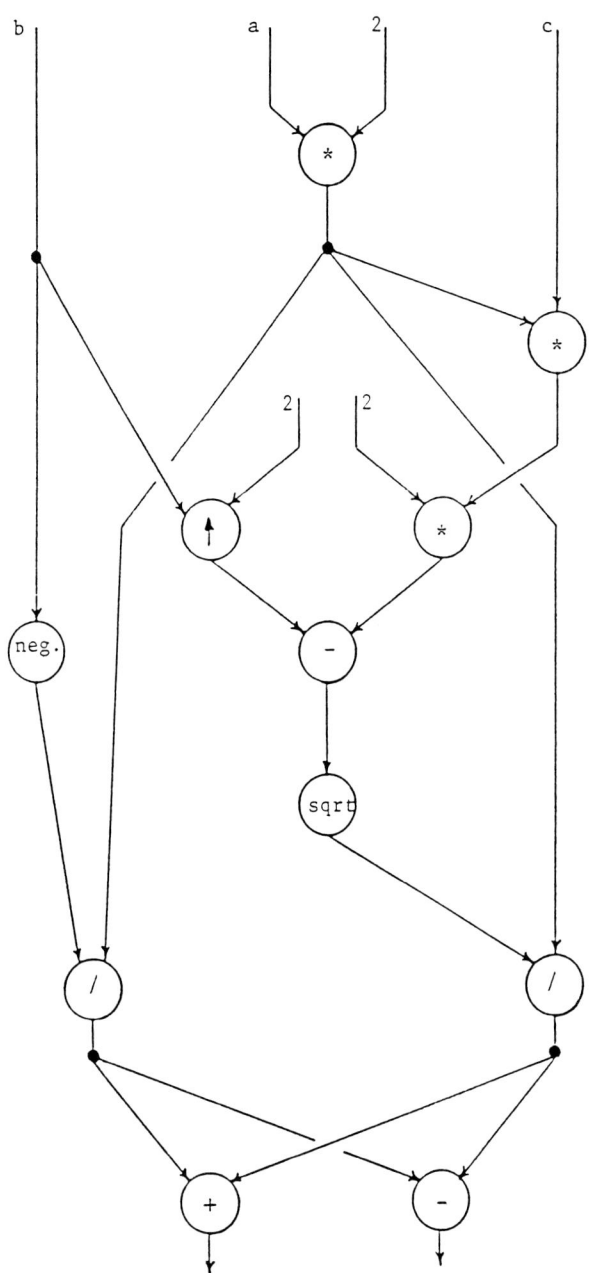

FIGURE 7   Data flow graph of quadratic equation.

Due to the nature of the data-driven computations, all the data-driven computers can be classified as MIMD processors. Hwang and Briggs [1] have categorized data-driven computers into *static* and *dynamic* organizations. Such a classification is based on the firing rule and the number of data tokens that could be available on a single arc. In a static data-driven system, there must not be more than one token on any arc at any given instance. Therefore, the static firing condition consists of the presence of tokens on each of the input arcs of an operation and the absence of any token on its output arcs. These machines often use an acknowledge signal system to implement the firing rule. The MIT machine [52] is an example of a machine in the static category.

A dynamic data-driven system simultaneously allows multiple tokens on a single arc. These systems use a token labeling mechanism to represent different activations of a program block. Therefore, the firing rule is defined as the existence of the tokens with the same label on each of the input arcs and no token with the same label on the output arcs. The machines in this category utilize a queuing system to temporarily store the multiple tokens for each activation. The Irvine machine [53] and the Manchester machine [54] are two examples in this class.

Another classification can be derived based on the relationship and communication among the data memory, the instruction memory, and the PEs. According to this classification, data-driven architectures are grouped into three classes. In class I, the instruction memory and the data memory are combined. Therefore, during the instruction cycle, the memory is accessed in three phases due to the following operations: (*a*) the available operand(s) of an instruction cause the instruction to be fired; (*b*) the operation packets (opcode, operands, and destination addresses) are sent to the processing unit; and (*c*) the result packet(s) is routed to the data memory. The machines in this class include the Irvine machine [53], the Manchester machine [54], and the data flow multiprocessor [55].

In class II, as opposed to the organization of class I, the data memory is eliminated and the operands are contained in the instructions. During the instruction cycle, the fired instructions are routed to the processing unit and the result tokens produced by the processing unit are sent to the destination instructions. Some examples of the machines in this class include the MIT machine [52], the distributed data processor [56], and DDM1 [57].

To reduce the existing memory access overhead and additional interconnection networks among the system's major units, class III machines have been proposed. In this class, the processing power is distributed among the memory cells. As a result, the collection of PEs and memory cells construct the basic building blocks for the whole system. The organization of block-driven data flow machines [53] at a higher level can be included in this class.

The parallel nature of the data-driven computations, coupled with the freedom from side effects, implies a strain on the interconnection network of these systems. This leads to the increased cost and complexity of the network, as well as erecting a potential bottleneck due to delays of the network for token transmission. In addition, the lack of updatable storage and asynchrony in the operations requires special procedures and mechanisms for the handling of the data structures. Finally, the elimination of the global variables and addressing mechanisms enforces the tokens (instruction and data) to carry large volumes of information in order to utilize the processing power efficiently. This violates the pin limitation constraint imposed

Parallel Processing 387

by current technology. A number of recently designed data-driven machines, which are suitable for current technology, have attempted to overcome these problems by (a) reducing the interconnection paths and (b) developing new algorithms for handling data structures and I/O operations.

The increasing demand for higher performance, coupled with the advances in technology; has motivated much research since the early days of electronic computing devices. Two general approaches [58], one based on the von Neumann philosophy and the other with a distinct deviation from it, have been addressed. Both directions carry their own merits and subjects to further research and study. Naturally, current advances in technology and development of new application areas will determine the merit of each direction and their evolutions in the future.

2.2 Demand-Driven Architectures

As mentioned before, demand-driven computation denotes a computation organization where instructions are only activated when the value they produce is needed by another already activated instruction. As a result, an instruction is executed only when its result is demanded. From this discussion, we can conclude that data-driven computation functions by checking the status of the instructions based on a fixed firing rule. If an instruction does not satisfy the firing conditions, no action is taken to force its execution. The data flow firing rule requires that all arguments be available before an instruction becomes active. The advantage of this computation is that instructions are executed as soon as their arguments are available, giving a high degree of implicit parallelism. The disadvantage is that instructions may waste time waiting for unneeded arguments. For example an IF-THEN-ELSE statement, which uses only two of its three arguments, will always be forced to wait for all three arguments before being fired.

In demand-driven computations, instruction sequencing is driven by the need to produce a result, rather than to insist on following a set pattern. Therefore, only instructions whose result is needed are executed. As a result, an IF-THEN-ELSE statement does not require the availability of all three arguments. This improves the performance and offers a higher resource utilization. However, in demand-driven computations, first the demand should be propagated and then operations will be started. In arithmetic operations where all the arguments are necessary for execution, this overhead degrades the performance.

3 SPECIAL-PURPOSE ARCHITECTURES

In this section, three classes of special-purpose architectures, influenced by application areas and advances in technology, will be described. Though these architectures utilize the concept of parallelism as discussed in Section 1, they are not based on the von Neumann philosophy conceptually.

3.1 Data Base Machines

Since the early 1970s, the complexity of the conventional data base management systems has been gradually increased by (a) the number and size of data bases, (b) the number and type of application programs, and (c) the number and type of on-line users. For example, among the estimated 20,000

U.S. government data bases, the Patent Office has a data base of 65 billion characters and a query retrieval of one item every 24 seconds. As another example, the Ballistic Missile Defense Systems require a distributed and dynamic data base that can maintain and upgrade itself in a complex and rapidly evolving battleground. The system should be able to perform about 60–120 million operations per second to verify, track, classify, and eliminate a threat. It is projected that by 1995, the Defense Mapping Agency will have a data base of 10^{19} bits supporting 1,000 on-line users needing 10^{14} bits each.

Conventional systems using typical software approaches fail to meet the requirements of the aformentioned applications. A software implementation of direct search on an IBM 370/158 can process approximately 100,000 characters per second. But even if this speed could be increased 10-fold, it would take 18 hours to search the 65 billion characters in the U.S. Patent Office's data file system.

To avoid the need for an exhaustive search, most existing software systems are based on an indexing mechanism. An indexed system improves performance by means of a sophisticated software system and additional redundancy of data. Nevertheless, this has created some additional problems. The indexed structures require extra space for the indices. It has been estimated that in a fully inverted file, the space needed to store the index ranges from 50% to 300% of the size of the data base itself [59]. In addition, the use of a directory creates complexity in the search, update, and delete algorithms. In fact, indexing merely shifts the processing burden, and so it offers only a partial solution in terms of the efficiency of data base operations.

The inefficiency of conventional systems in handling large data bases can be associated with the existing semantic gap, computation gap, and size gap. These gaps stem from the fact that (a) conventional systems, by their very nature, are sequential machines, (b) a conventional ALU is structured for numeric computations (e.g., the CRAY-1 is able to perform 250 million floating-point operations per second, although it cannot handle more than 15 million characters per second) and, finally, (c) the memory hierarchy has a passive role in the organization; hence, there is a massive amount of data movement between processing elements and storage units. Therefore, there is a great need to design and develop new architectures specialized to the demand of a data base environment.

Since the mid-1970s, a great deal of effort has been directed toward the design of special-purpose architectures for efficient handling of large data base systems [60–70]. In addition, recent advances in technology have forced drastic changes in the architectural aspects of these machines.

A viable data base machine suitable for current and future data base environments should satisfy

1. The constraints imposed by technology that will be available in the foreseeable future.
2. The throughput and functionality that are demanded by the data base environment.
3. The reliability, fault tolerance, reconfigurability, and survivability demanded by the data base environment.
4. Issues related to integrity, recovery, security, and privacy in a multiple-user environment.

Parallel Processing

Conditions 1—3 could be satisfied through the design of an inherently parallel special-purpose data base machine that satisfies the constraints imposed by the technology. Conditions 3 and 4 will be fulfilled by consideration of the aforementioned issues during the design phase. The next section overviews different classifications of the data base machines, as proposed in the literature. In addition, a set of criteria will be discussed for evaluation of the data base machines.

Classification of Data Base Machines

Data bases fall into two general categories, namely *formatted* and *unformatted* structures. Formatted data bases are mainly time-variant entities and are subject to extensive alteration as well as search operations. Unformatted data bases (bibliographic or full text) are archival in nature and are processed by searching for a pattern or a combination of patterns. As a result, operations on the formatted data bases are based on the contents of the attribute values of the records, whereas the patterns are unpredictable combinations of terms and words in the unformatted data bases. The discussion in this section is centered around formatted data bases. Unformatted data base systems are the subject of the next section. Several classifications of data base machines have been addressed in the literature [60—63, 66—69]. In the following, we concentrate on three classifications. Table 1 is a summary of different classifications and their comparisons to the Bray and Freeman classification.

Bray and Freeman [63] have classified data base machines into five categories: *single processor indirect search* (SPIS), *single processor direct search* (SPDS), *multiple processor direct search* (MPDS), *multiple processor indirect search* (MPIS), *multiple processor combined search* (MPCS). Direct search processing implies the ability to search a data base at the secondary storage level, whereas indirect search represents the fact that data need to be transferred to an intermediate storage media before the search can be conducted.

SPIS represents the conventional von Neumann-type architecture with no degree of parallelism. Naturally, such an architecture bears all the aforementioned deficiencies in handling large data bases. SPDS represents a conventional system enhanced by searching capability at the secondary storage. As a result, only the desired records or their specified parts are sent to the host. MPDS/MPIS machines represent parallel versions of SPDS/SPIS organizations. MPCS is a combination of the MPDS and MPIS organizations, where the search is performed on the data loaded into intermediate storage, whereas multiple processing units are assigned to the blocks of intermediate storages.

Song [68] has defined data base machines as computer systems enhanced by special-purpose logic for handling data base operations. With such a view, he has classified these machines according to three parameters:

1. The place where hardware logic is applied. This could be either at (close to) secondary storage or primary memory.
2. Allocation of logic to the storage unit. This could be static or dynamic. Naturally, a dynamic allocation offers better resource utilization.
3. Degree of logic distribution, which defines the number of storage elements associated with each processing unit. This parameter

TABLE 1 Relationships among Different Classifications of Data Base Machines

Bray and Freeman [63]	Rosenthal [60]	Berra [61]	Champine [62]	Sue et. al. [66]	Hsiao [67]	Song [68]	Qadah [69]
SPDS	Smart peripheral system		Intelligent peripheral CU			Logic at secondary storage with static allocation (sequential operation)	SOSD with relation indexing on the disk search
SPIS	Large back-end	Back-end system	Back-end processor			Logic at primary storage with static allocation (sequential operation)	SOSD with relation or page indexing off disk search
MPDS	Smart peripheral system	Logic in memory	Intelligent peripheral CU	Cellular logic	Cellular logic	Logic at secondary storage with static/dynamic allocation (parallel operation)	MOMD/SOMD with relation indexing on disk search

MPIS	Large back-end processor	Back-end system/ large associative processor	Back-end processor	High-speed associative system/ back-end system	Associative array	Logic at primary memory with static/ dynamic allocation (parallel operations)	MOMD/SOMD with relation or page in- dexing off disk search
MPCS	Distributed network data node		Network node	Integrated data base machine	Functionally specialized system	Logic at primary/ secondary memory with static/ dynamic allocation; medium to high level of parallelism	MOMD/SOMD with relation or page indexing on off/hybrid search

represents the degree of parallelism, and hence, directly affects the performance.

Qadah [69] has extended Bray and Freeman's data base space by a third dimension, namely the indexing level. The coordinates of this data base space are indexing level, query processing place, and processing multiplicity. The indexing coordinate represents the smallest addressable unit of data. Along this coordinate, data base machines can be grouped into data base indexing level, relation indexing level, and page indexing level. The query-processing place determines the location where data are searched. This could be away from the secondary stroage, on the secondary storage, or a hybrid of both. The third coordinate represents the degree of parallelism. Along this coordinate we can group data base machines into single operation stream—single data stream (SOSD), single operation stream—multiple data stream (SOMD), and multiple operation stream—multiple data stream (MOMD).

A New Classification

Similar to Flynn's classification of concurrent systems [3], some of the proposed classifications suffer from the fact that there is some overlap between the categories. For example, there is no clear way of determining when a smart peripheral system becomes a back-end computer as functions are moved from the host to the peripheral system. In addition, these classifications do not address the effect of the advances in technology on the architecture and adaptability of a specific architecture for the current and foreseeable technology. We believe such a parameter should be used as a coordinate of the data base space. Recent developments in technology have influenced the architecture of these systems in two directions:

1. Reconfiguration and re-evaluation of the previously designed data base architectures according to the constraints imposed by the technology. (The evolution of RAP [71] demonstrates the validity of this discussion.)
2. The design of new architectures based on the constraints imposed by the technology [72–74].

Qadah's data base space can be extended by a fourth dimension, namely technology adaptability. Therefore, one can define a data base space of four coordinates: Technology adaptability, degree of parallelism, query processing place, and indexing level. According to these parameters one can characterize an architecture based on its ability to handle (a) computational gap, (b) semantic gap, (c) size gap, (d) data communication problem, and (e) name-mapping resolution.

The indexing level determines the smallest accessible unit of data. Such a coordinate determines name-mapping resolution and the proper protocol that one should take to enforce the security and guarantee the system's integrity. Along the technology adaptability coordinate, data base architectures are characterized as fully, semi- or low adaptable designs. The query-processing coordinate characterizes four classes: searching at the secondary storage, close to the secondary storage, indirect, or a combination of different approaches.

3.2 Text-Retrieval Machines

The utility of free-text search and retrieval has been recognized widely for some time. Text data bases now commonly store a variety of information, such as legal decision, patent documentation, government memoranda, research papers, etc. Though the theory of retrieving information from unformatted text data bases is the same as that from formatted data bases, they differ substantially from each other in practice:

1. Besides the lack of formatting, text data bases are orders of magnitude larger than formatted data bases, because information is not encoded and a wealth of language may be used to describe a single concept. For example, although a 5 million byte formatted data base would be considered reasonably large, it would only hold one volume of the National Computer Conference Proceedings.
2. User capabilities in text retrieval are usually limited to searching and reading, whereas in formatted data bases users are permitted to alter or update the data bases.
3. Query languages for formatted data bases are often restrictive in the operations that a user may express; on the other hand, a query language for a text data base offers powerful direct expression by the user of many string-matching operations, including the specification that certain characters are to be ignored during a search procedure.
4. Although the single queries are generally the rule in formatted data base systems, users of text data bases may require complex series of queries to successively refine the subsets of the data base being searched.

Due to the characteristics of conventional digital computers and the text retrieval environment, there is a great need to design and develop a new architecture specialized to meet the demand of the text retrieval operations. A viable text retrieval machine must be able to search simultaneously for the occurrence of a number of different terms or phrases, allow the specifications of "don't care" characters, and be able to determine whether a query consisting of a complex expression has been satisfied. In addition, to eliminate the potential bottlenecks, its processing unit must be distributed away from the CPU. In most of the proposals that have been advanced for such a machine, the critical engineering problem is within the "term comparator," which must examine input data for matches against query terms at a speed equal to the delivery rate of characters.

Three principle techniques have been advanced for a term comparator implementation: the use of a number of discrete comparators or an associative memory, a cellular structure, where a special element matches a single character and propagates an enabling signal to its neighbor, and the application of a finite state automaton to hardware.

Discrete Parallel Comparators/Associative Memory

The most direct, but also the most limited, approach to the term comparator was proposed by Stellhorn [75]. In this design, serial data are shifted into a data window buffer, whose length represents the maximum number of contiguous characters that can be examined. Parallel outputs of this buffer are bused to N identical fixed-length comparators, each holding a different term in a query. As data are brought into the window buffer, the comparators attempt to match the data one character at a time against their stored query terms in unison. Later on, a "query resolver" examines the outputs of the comparators (result of the searches) to determine whether the proper terms occurred in the text just searched.

The fixed number of fixed-length comparators places a severe restriction upon both query terms and textual terms. In addition, the design cannot handle embedded variable-length don't cares of either fixed or variable length efficiently. Finally, the query resolver lacks sufficient input to perform certain text operations, such as matching on word proximity or multiple context searches.

A closely related alternative to the parallel discrete comparators of Stellhorn is the associative array approach taken by Bird et al. [76]. Again, parallelism is exploited to speed up comparisons, but here an associative memory is the comparison device rather than replicated parallel comparators. As the Bird machine (associative file processor [AFP]) encounters a word in the input data, it uses the word as the argument to an associative parallel search of query terms loaded into an associative memory. The result of a match between the input data and a stored query term will be sent to and analyzed by the query resolver. The system could hold up to 70 complex queries for simultaneous processing. No structuring, indexing, editing, or preprocessing of text data is required. Queries may be of an unrestricted natural English or Boolean vocabulary, with single quotes placed around the search terms. The machine can handle initial, intermediate, or terminal fixed-length don't cares, and has the capability to perform numeric ranging and proximity searching.

On the negative side, the AFP cannot handle embedded variable-length don't cares. Moreover, fixed length don't cares must be clearly enumerated. In addition, only a single input comparand may be matched against the query term memory at one time, and the fixed length of this comparand limits the use of elaborate matching patterns to only a part of a pattern at one time. This, in turn, means that for each part of a complex pattern, the entire data base will have to be passed through the comparand register, and so multiple searches of the data base seem likely in cases with a complex search pattern.

Cellular Logic

Suggested independently by Copeland [77] and Mukhopadhyay [78], the cellular logic approach is based upon a single cell capable of matching a single character. Cell operation begins with the loading of a single match character into a register of the cell. Then characters from the input text stream are each applied to the cell and compared against the match character held within. If a match occurs and the enable to the cell is set, then a match output signal is generated from the cell.

Individual cells are connected in cascades to match multicharacter strings, where each successive cell is programmed to match a successive character of the string. The input character stream is applied in parallel to each cell, and the enable for the first cell is set in either the anchored or unanchored mode. When an enabled cell matches an input character, its match output signal is applied to the next cell in the cascade as an enable to that cell for possible matching of the next input character.

Obviously, this scheme can handle fixed-length don't cares, and there is no need for any special action for initial or terminal variable-length don't cares. In the case of embedded variable-length don't cares, a cell may be introduced whose output is set for the remaining operations, once its input enable is set. Cascades of cells may be configured to match against long character strings, patterns with alternate possible substring matches, and a variety of other conditions, as long as the proper network connections are provided [78]. The principal criticism of the cellular logic approach is with the requirement that individual cells and their related support logic and registers be connected based on the form of a query. This implies the need for a sophisticated switching network to realize all possible selections of the architectural components. In a large cellular structure, however, the complexity of such a network could probably make the approach more expensive. Finally, the complexity of the logic associated with each cell should be high for cells to realize the majority of operations considered by Mukhopadhyay.

Finite State Automaton

This approach to the design of a term comparator is based upon the theoretical concept of a finite state machine. In its application to text retrieval, each state attempts to match one character of the input data steam. A match at one state generates a transition signal to cause the next input character to be handled by a specific next state. In its simplest form, transitions among states are deterministic, so only one distinct state is entered after a match at the previous state.

In such a system, implementation of fixed and variable-length don't care is simple: By specifying proper transitions among states, finite state automata (FSA) can be made to recognize substrings embedded within other strings. In addition, the well-developed theory of the finite state model could be employed for a better and more efficient design. The actions of an FSA system have been emulated on a conventional system [79]. Roberts [80] and Hollaar [81] have proposed specialized back-end architectures to employ the FSA mechanisms. In their approach, states are single character comparators. However, the memory requirements for each state are excessive for any transition table indicating all possible cases. It is possible to reduce the memory requirement by condensing the transition table. However, this means substantially higher processing time per character. As an alternative solution, Bird et al. [76] have suggested an indexing mechanism to organize the entries in the transition table for improved processing time. The Roberts [80] back-end comparator uses Bird's indexing mechanism in its architecture. The system is able to handle all types of don't cares, as well as operations such as numeric merging and limitation of search to a specific context. However, the approach requires an excessive number of accesses to memory, and incorporation of Bird's arrangement creates overhead due to additional processing of the index vectors.

In response to the inefficiencies inherent in an FSA implementation, Haskin and Hollaar [82] proposed a system using nondeterministic FSA, whose state table is partitioned into a smaller number of incompatible state tables that are then assigned to separate FSAs. The major question of this approach is directed at the overhead involved in the partitioning of the state tables. However, it has been reported [82] that real-time computation of the state table partitions can be achieved using special heuristics.

Of the approaches presented here, it appears that the partitioned FSA design of Haskin and Hollaar holds the most promise. Their approach has the possibility of handling all types of don't care characters, and although the approach is reasonably subject to questions of overhead and efficiency, there is evidence to suggest that such questions may be unfounded. As reported in Ref. 82, a viable text retrieval machines well suited to the idiosyncracies of textual data has been fabricated using this approach.

In some respects, this conclusion should not be surprising. It seems clear that given the nature of text retrieval problems, some degree of nondeterminism must be introduced to the term comparator for it to handle all varieties of input text against the desirable query operations. Parallelism must be employed to allow the term comparator to follow multiple paths in attempting to match input characters to any given sequence of characters in query terms. In pursuit of the best term comparator design, it seems advantageous to exploit such a well-grounded and well-suited concept as that of the FSA. The development of a parallel, nondeterministic class of FSA appears to offer a research direction that could have most significant results for the evolution of text retrieval architecture [83].

3.3 Systolic Organizations

Recent advances in technology have made it economically possible to implant systems with gate complexity of the order of 10^5 on a single chip. Nevertheless, with the exception of memory organization, the great potential of such a development has not yet been exploited fully. Such a gap between theory and practice is partially due to the lack of suitable architectures for hardware implementation. A suitable architecture should bear a set of constraints in order to be suitable for hardware implementation. A suitable architecture should reduce communications as well as computation, based on the replication of a few basic building blocks in space or time. This simply implies modularity, regularity and simplicity.

The systolic architecture [84, 85], orginally proposed for VLSI implementation of some matrix operations, is a general methodology for mapping high-level computations into hardware structure with respect to the technological constraints. Systolic organization is a collection of few basic blocks (e.g., processing elements) replicated in a one- or two-dimensional space, with simple and regular communication paths among the processing elements. Moreover, the flow of data from memory to the PEs is rhythmic, and each set of data passes through many PEs before it returns back to the memory, much as blood circulates in the human body. This allows multiple computations for each memory access in a compute bound operation without increasing I/O requirements. Figure 8 shows a systolic model proposed for text retrieval operation, as reported in Ref. 86. Each cell (e.g., PE) performs two separate functions; hence, the cell is composed of two separate basic cells, namely comparator and accumulator. The operations within the comparator and accumulator cells are defined as

$$P_{out} \leftarrow P_{in}$$
$$S_{out} \leftarrow S_{in}$$
$$d_{out} \leftarrow d_{in} \wedge (P_{in} = S_{in})$$

$$\lambda_{out} \leftarrow \lambda_{in}$$
$$x_{out} \leftarrow x_{in}$$
$$\text{if } \lambda_{in}$$
$$\text{then } r_{out} \leftarrow t : t \leftarrow \text{True}$$
$$\text{else } r_{out} \leftarrow r_{in} : t \leftarrow t \wedge (x_{in} \text{ or } d_{in})$$

Parallel Processing

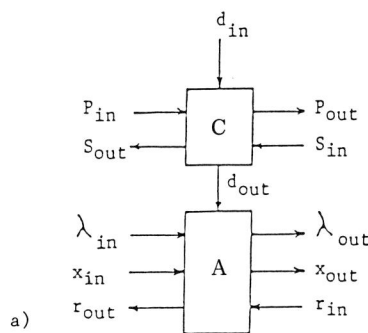

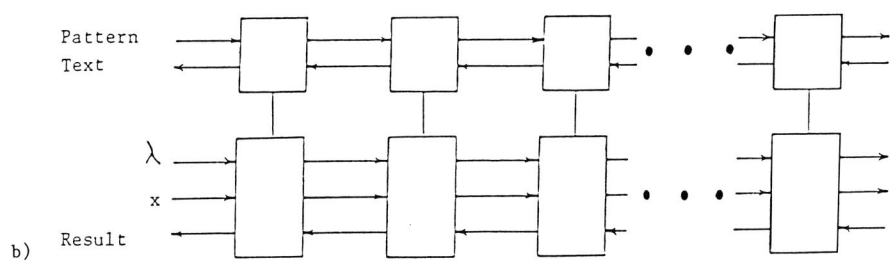

FIGURE 8   A systolic model for pattern matching operation. (A) Structure of a cell; (B) systolic array

λ and x are the end of pattern and don't care markers, respectively. According to this discussion, systolic organization is similar to the pipelining discussed in Section 1.5. However, one should remember that the pipeline systems are linear organization, whereas systolic systems can be organized in a two-dimensional space. Moreover, the basic elements can be rectangular, triangular, or hexagonal [84] to achieve a higher degree of parallelism in the operations. In addition, data flow in a systolic organization can be at multiple speeds in multiple direction, i.e., both inputs and partial results, whereas in classical pipelined organizations only partial results are flowing among stages in one direction.

The basic philosophy of the systolic model has been used as a model to design many special-purpose units to enhance the performance of the conventional, as well as unconventional, parallel systems [73, 86, 87]. The ability to use each input data item in a number of computations, modular expandability, simple and uniform interconnection and communication paths among the PEs and, finally, fast response time represents the many advantages of systolic model.

REFERENCES

1. K. Hwang, and F. A. Briggs, *Computer Architecture and Parallel Processing*, McGraw Hill Book Company, New York, 1984.
2. T. Y. Feng, "Some Considerations in Multiprocessor Architecture," in *Multiprocessor Systems*, (C. H. White, ed.), Infotech International Ltd., Nicholson House, Maindenhead, England, 1976, pp. 277–286.
3. M. J. Flynn, "Very High Speed Computing Systems," *Proc. IEEE*, 54 (12), 1901–1909 (December 1966).
4. H. O. Leilich, G. Stiege, and H. C. Zeidler, "A Search Processor for Database Management Systems" (Technical reports) University of Braunschweig, Braunschweig, Germany, 1978.
5. W. Händler, "Innovative Computer Architecture — How to Increase Parallelism but Not Complexity," in *Parallel Processing Systems*, (D. J. Evans, ed.) Cambridge University Press, London, 1982, pp. 1–41.
6. S. F. Reddaway, "DAP—A Districuted Array Processor," in *Proceedings of First Symposium on Computer Architecture*, University of Florida, Gainesville, December 1973, pp. 61–65.
7. T. Fountain, *Processor Arrays: Architectures and Applications*, Academic Press, London, 1987.
8. K. J. Thurber, *Large Scale Computer Architecture*, Hayden Book Company, Rochelle Park, NJ, 1976.
9. "Array Processor Architecture," *Computer* (Special issue on array processor), 14(9), (September 1981).
10. K. Hwang, S. P. Su, and L. M. Ni, "Vector Computer Architecture and Processing Techniques," *Adv. Comput.*, 20, 115–197 (1981).
11. R. M. Hold, *The ILLIAC IV*, Computer Science Press, Rockville, MD, 1982.
12. D. J. Kuck and R. A. Stokes, "The Borroughs Scientific Processor (BSP)," *IEEE Trans. Comput.*, C-31(5), 363–376 (May 1982).
13. B. Parhami, "Associative Memories and Processors: An Overview and Selected Bibliography," *Proc. IEEE*, 61(6), 722–730 (1973).
14. T. Y. Feng, "Search Algorithms for Associative Memories," in *Proceedings of Fourth Annual Princeton Conference on Information Science and Systems*, Princeton University, Princeton, NJ, 1970, pp. 442–446.
15. C. R. Petrie and A. R. Hurson, "A VLSI Join Module," *VLSI System Design*, 9(10), 48–58 (1988).
16. S. S. Yau, and H. S. Fung, "Associative Processor Architecture—A Survey," *ACM Comput. Surv.* 9(1), pp. 3–28 (1977).
17. T. Kohonen, *Content Addressable Memories*, Springer-Verlag, Berlin, 1980.
18. G. J. Myers, *Advances in Computer Architecture*, 2nd ed., John Wiley and Sons, New York, 1982.
19. C. Y. Lee and M. C. Paull, "A Content Addressable Distrubuted Logic Memory with Applications to Information Retrieval," *Proc. IEEE*, 51(7), 924–932 (1963).
20. R. S. Gaines and C. Y. Lee, "An Improved Cell Memory," *IEEE Trans. Electron Comput.*, 14(2) 72–75 (1965).
21. D. L. Slotnick, "Logic Per Track Devices," in *Adv. Comput.* 10, 291–296 (1970).
22. P. H. Enslow, Jr., "Multiprocessor Organization—A Survey," *ACM Comput. Surv.*, 9(1), 103–129 (1977).

23. M. Satyanarayan, *Multiprocessors—A Comparative Study*, Prentice-Hall, Englewood Cliffs, NJ, 1980.
24. M. Satyanarayan, "Multiprocessing: An Annotated Bibliography," *Computer*, 5, 101–116 (May 1980).
25. W. A. Wulf, R. Levin, and S. P. Harbison, *HYDRA/C mmp: An Experimental Computer System*, McGraw-Hill Company, New York, 1981.
26. H. S. Stone, *High-Performance Computer Architecture*, Addison Wesley Company, Reading, MA, 1987.
27. M. Dubois, and F. A. Briggs, "Effects of Cache Coherency in Multiprocessors," *IEEE Trans. Comput.* C-31(11), 1083–1099 (November 1982).
28. F. A. Briggs and M. Dubois, "Effectiveness of Private Caches in Multiprocessor Systems with Parallel Pipelined Memories," *IEEE Trans. Comput.* C-32(1), 48–59 (January 1983).
29. M. S. Papamarcos and J. H. Patel, "A Low-Overhead Coherence Solution for Multiprocessors with Private Cache Memories," in *International Symposium on Computer Architecture*, IEEE Computer Society Press, Silver Spring, MD, 1984, pp. 1–7.
30. C. V. Ramamoorthy and H. F. Li, "Pipeline Architecture," *ACM Comput. Surv.*, 9(1), 61–102 (March 1977).
31. P. M. Kogge, *The Architecture of Pipelined Computers*, McGraw-Hill Company, New York, 1981.
32. R. W. Hockney and C. R. Jesshope, *Parallel Computers*, Adam Hilger Ltd., Bristol, England, 1981.
33. R. W. Doran, "The Amdahl 470V/8 and the IBM 3033: A Comparison of Processor Designs," *Computer*, 15(4), 28–36 (April 1982).
34. R. M. Russell, "The CRAY-1 Computer System," *Comm. ACM*, 21(2), 63–72 (January 1978).
35. J. S. Koladzey, "CRAY-1 Computer Technology," *IEEE Trans. Components Hybrids Manufacturing Technol.*, CHMT-4(2), 181–186 (1981).
36. W. J. Watson, "The TI ASC—A Highly Modular and Flexible Super Computer Architecture," *AFIPS*, 41, 221–228 (1972).
37. R. G. Hintz and D. P. Tate, "Control Data STAR-100 Processor Design," in *Proceedings of ComCon 72*, IEEE Computer Society Press, Silver Spring, MD, 1972, pp. 1–4.
38. J. E. Thornton, *Design of a Computer, The Control Data 6600*, Scott, Foresman, and Company, New York, 1970.
39. R. M. Tomasulo, "An Efficient Algorithm for Exploiting Multiple Arithmetic Unit," *IBM J.*, 11, 25–33 (January 1967).
40. S. F. Anderson, J. G. Earle, R. E. Goldschmidt, and D. M. Powers, "The IBM System/360 Model 91: Floating Point Execution Unit," *IBM J.*, 11, 34–53 (January 1967).
41. H. J. Siegel, "A Model of SIMD Machines and a Comparison of Various Interconnection Networkd," *IEEE Trans. Comput.* C-28(12), 907–917 (December 1979).
42. T. Y. Feng, "A Survey of Interconnection Networks," *Computers*, 14(12), 12–27 (December 1981).
43. H. H. Love, Jr., "The Highly Parallel Super Computers: Definitions, Applications and Predictions," *AFIPS*, 49, 181–190 (1980).
44. *Computer* (Special issue on super systems), 13(11) (November 1980).
45. E. E. Swartzlander, Jr., and B. K. Gilbert, "Super Systems: Technology and Architecture," *IEEE Trans. Comput.*, C-31(5), 399–409 (May 1982).

46. D. J. Kuck, "A Survey of Parallel Machine Organization and Programming," *Comput. Surv.*, *9*(1), 29–59 (March 1977).
47. R. O. Berg, G. H. Schmitz, and S. J. Nuspl, "PEPE—An Overview of Architecture, Operations, and Implementation," in *Proceedings of the National Electronics Conference*, Chicago, Ill., 1972, pp. 312–317.
48. D. J. Kuck, "ILLIAC IV Software and Application Programming," *IEEE Trans. Comput.*, *C-17*(8), 758–770 (August, 1968).
49. E. W. Davis, "STARAN/RADCAP System Software," in *Proceedings of 1973 Sagamore Computer Conference on Parallel Processing*, University of Syracuse, Syracuse, 1973, pp. 153–159.
50. *Computer* (Special issue on paralle programming languages), *19*(8) (August 1986).
51. P. C. Treleaven and J. G. Lima, "Japan's Fifth-Generation Computer Systems," *Computer*, *15*(8), 79–88 (August 1982).
52. *Computer* (Special issue on data flow architecture), *15*(2) (1982).
53. D. C. Treleaven, D. R. Brownbridge, and R. P. Hopkins, "Data-Driven and Demand-Driven Computer Architecture, "*ACM Comput. Surv.* *14*(1), 93–143 (March 1982).
54. J. R. Gurd, C. C. Kirkham, and I. Watson, "The Manchester Prototype Dataflow Computer," *Comm. ACM*, *28*(1), 34–52 (January 1985).
55. J. E. Rumbaugh, "A Dataflow Multiprocessor," *IEEE Trans. Comput.* *C-26*(2), 138–146 (February 1977).
56. M. Cornish, "The TI Dataflow Architecture—The Power of Concurrency for Avionics," in *Proceedings of Third Conference on Digital Avionics Systems*, IEEE, New York, 1979, pp. 9–26.
57. A. L. Davis, "The Architecture and System method of DDMI: A Recursively Structured Data Driven Machine," in *Proceedings of Fifth Annual Symposium on Computer Architecture*, IEEE Computer Society Press, Silver Spring, MD, 1978, pp. 210–215.
58. J. A. Sharp, *Data Flow Computing*, Ellis Horwood, New York, 1985.
59. R. Haskin, "Hardware for Searching Very Large Text Databases," in *Proceedings of Fifth Workshop on Computer Architecture for Non-Numeric Processing*, Association for Computing Machinery, New York, 1979, pp. 49–56.
60. R. S. Rosenthal, "The Data Management Machine, A Classification," in *Third Computer Architecture for Non-Numeric Processing*, Association for Computing Machinery, New York, 1977, pp. 35–39.
61. B. P. Berra, "Database Machines," *ACM SIGIR Forum*, *13*(3), 4–23 (1977).
62. G. A. Champine, "Four Approaches to a Data Base Computer," *Datamation*, 101–106 (December 1978).
63. H. O. Bray and H. A. Freeman, *Database Computers*, Lexington Books, Lexington, MA, 1979.
64. Won Kim, "Relational Database Systems," *ACM Comput. Surv.*, *11*, 185–211 (1979).
65. F. J. Maryanski, "Backend Database Systems," *ACM Comput. Surv.*, *12*, 3–26 (1980).
66. S. Y. W. Su, *Database Computers: Principles, Architectures and Techniques*, McGraw-Hill Book, New York, 1988.
67. D. K. Hsiao, "Data Base Computers," in *Advances in Computers*, Academic Press, New York, 1980, pp. 1–64.

68. S. W. Song, "A Survey and Taxonomy of Database Machines," *Database Eng.*, *1*, 5–15 (1983).
69. G. Z. Qadah, "Database Machines: A Survey," *AFIPS*, *54*, 211–223 (1985).
70. E. Ozkarahan, *Database Machines and Database Management*, Prentice-Hall, Englewood Cliffs, NJ, 1986.
71. K. Oflazer, "A Reconfigurable VLSI Architecture for a Database Processor," *AFIPS*, *52*, 271–281 (1983).
72. S. W. Song, "A Highly Concurent Tree Machine for Database Applications," in *Proceedings of the International Conference on Parallel Processing*, 1980, pp. 259–268.
73. P. L. Lehman, "A Systolic (VLSI) Array for Processing Simple Relational Querie," in *VLSI Systems and Computations*, (Kung et. al., ed.), Computer Sciences Press, Rockville, MD, 1981, pp. 285–295.
74. A. R. Hurson, "VLSI Time/Space Complexities of an Associative Join Module," in *Proceedings of International Conference on Parallel Processing*, IEEE Computer Society Press, Silver Spring, MD, 1986, pp. 379–386.
75. W. H. Stellhorn, "A Processor for Direct Scanning of Text," presented at First Workshop on Computer Architecture for Non-Numeric Processing, Dallas, Association for Computing Machinery, New York, 1974.
76. R. M. Bird, J. C. Tu, and R. M. Worthy, "Associative/Parallel Processors for Searching Very Large Textual Databases," in *Third Workshop on Computer Architecture for Non-Numeric Processing*, Association for Computing Machinery, New York, 1978, pp. 42–50.
77. G. P. Copeland, "String Storage and Searching for Database Applications: Implementation of the INDY Backend Kernel," in *Fourth Workshop on Computer Architecture for Non-Numeric Processing*, Association for Computing Machinery, New York, 1979, pp. 8–17.
78. A. Mukhopadhyay, "Hardware Algorithms for Non-Numeric Computation," *IEEE Trans. Comput.*, *C-28*(6), 384–394 (June 1979).
79. R. J. Bullen, Jr., and J. K. Millen, "Microtext—the design of a Microprogrammed Finite State Search Machine for Full Text Retrieval," *AFIPS*, *41*, 479–488 (1972).
80. D. C. Roberts, "A Specialized Computer Architecture for Text Retrieval," in *Fourth Workshop on Computer Architecture for Non-Numeric Processing*, Association for Computing Machinery, New York, 1978, pp. 51–59.
81. L. A. Hollaar, "Text Retrieval Computers," *Computer*, *12*(3), 40–50 (March 1979).
82. L. Hollaar, "The Utah Text Search Engine: Implementation Experiences and Future Plans," *Database Machines 4th International Workshop*, Springer-Verlag, New York, 1985, pp. 367–376.
83. A. R. Hurson, "A VLSI Design for the Parallel Finite State Automaton and its Performance Evaluation as a Hardware Scanner," *J. Comput. Inf. Sci.*, *13*(6), 491–508 (1984).
84. H. T. Kung, "The Structure of Parallel Algorithms," *Adv. Comp.*, *19*, 65–112 (1980).
85. H. T. Kung, "Why Systolic Architectures?" *Computer*, *15*(1), 37–46 (1982).
86. M. J. Foster, and H. T. Kung, "The Design of Special Purpose VLSI Chips," *Computer*, *13*(1), 26–40 (1980).

87. A. R. Hurson, and B. Shirazi, "A Systolic Multiplier Unit and its VLSI Design," in *Proceedings of the 12th Annual International Symposium on Computer Architecture,* IEEE Computer Society Press, Silver Spring, MD, 1985, pp. 302–309.

TSE-YUN FENG
A. R. HURSON